The Young Ones

The Young Ones

American Airmen of WW II

Erik Dyreborg

iUniverse, Inc.
New York Lincoln Shanghai

The Young Ones
American Airmen of WW II

iUniverse, Inc.

For information address:
iUniverse, Inc.
2021 Pine Lake Road, Suite 100
Lincoln, NE 68512
www.iuniverse.com

ISBN: 0-595-28237-7

Printed in the United States of America

Contents

Foreword

By Margaret Cawood

To some of us, liberation came almost too late to have any meaning. Through jagged barbed wire, empty eyes stared unbelieving...afraid to look...yet even more afraid not to look.

To our would-be conqueror...to the pompous, arrogant superman...the master...it meant the cold, hard realization of final punishment...the proof that right can still win over might.

But...to most of us...liberation is the chance for a better tomorrow when wounds are reasonably healed...and the factories, which turn out artificial limbs, are back on one shift daily.

Submitted by Ernest W. White, Sr. (Ernest W. White, Sr. passed away on 19 August 1993) Reprinted with permission from "A Time of Great Rewarding" by Joseph P. O'Donnell)

History, as most of us know it, is based on facts. Oral history is a different kind of history; it is history passed on by word of mouth.

In oral history, we do not depend on written documentation to tell the whole story, we rely on oral transmission. On occasion, documentary material will appear within or accompany an oral history, but we usually rely on the observations, experiences, and memory of the narrator.

You'll find the stories of and about thirty-three historical witnesses in this book. In most cases, they are the memories of events, which occurred almost sixty years ago. In all cases, the people involved have given the facts as honestly as they can, but it must be recognized that there may have been memory lapses or cases where attempts to avoid hurting others have been made.

An important influence on the understanding of a history is the standards of the society in which one lives. Without belaboring the point, it must be noted that the standards of today's society are not the same as those, which existed during World War II.

In 1988, I became an interviewer for the Commemorative Air Force (CAF) Oral History Program. At that time, the group was known as the Confederate Air Force, a group that maintained and flew World War II aircraft. The Information Officer was Herschel Whittington, who asked me if I'd like to become involved in the Oral History Program he was attempting to develop.

Since then, I have conducted many interviews with men, primarily, who were members of the United States Air Force during World War II or were closely associated with that group, as well as with men who served with the Navy and Marine Corps. (The United States Air Force did not exist at that time; the Air Groups were a part of the Army).

During the course of these interviews, I've had the privilege of meeting many air-crew members who were shot down and parachuted into enemy territory or who crash-landed when their damaged airplanes would no longer fly. Some of these men evaded their would-be captors and were able to return to England, some were able to evade for a few days, then were captured and sent to prison camps, and some were captured immediately upon landing.

In Germany, if the military captured the men, they usually received bearable treatment, but if civilians captured them, they were beaten to insensibility or even killed by angry citizens.

Why was I interested in the Oral History Program?

When I was sixteen, I spent the summer with one of my aunts. Her oldest son had been in the Air Corps during World War II. He was known to our family as "Carmie". He had served with the 8th Air Force, 95th Bomb Group, 534th Bomb Squadron, which was stationed at Horham, England. He was the radio/gunner aboard a B-17 shot down on 25 August 1944 while on a mission to bomb the oil refinery at Politz, Germany. At 13:05 hours, flak hit the #3 and #4 engines; they caught fire. Two chutes were seen to leave the aircraft before it exploded. Both chutes were set afire by the explosion. (MACR, Missing Air Crew Report, 8279)

Fortunately, the explosion was not as deadly as it had at first appeared. Seven of the ten crewmen survived and Carmie was one of them. Within two weeks, all were German Prisoners of War (POWs).

Carmie evaded capture for ten days. He ended up in Stalag Luft IV, Barracks 4, Room 3, C Lager. Stalag Luft IV was located near Grosstychow, Pomerania, Germany.

One day my aunt showed me a rusty tin cup, a cheaply made metal spoon, and a list of German towns and villages printed on the inside of cigarette pack wrappers. These were the only reminders Carmie had retained from his eight months as a Prisoner of War and the Death March, the name the prisoners gave the march of 487.8 miles from Grosstychow, Germany, which began February 6, 1945 and ended in Halle on April 26, 1945.

At the time, I did not fully appreciate the importance of these three items. Should a POW lose his cup and spoon, he had no way to receive and eat the meager rations doled out to him. The towns were those through which Carmie and his comrades had been marched during the almost unendurable conditions of the Death March.

This incident marked the beginning of my interest in the stories of men who had been POWs or who had been able to evade capture and, occasionally, escape and return to England. It also brings me to the contents of this book.

You'll find Carmie's story, titled, "So We Walked And Walked And Walked Some More," in this book. In many ways, it is typical of the misery, illness, cold, discomfort, and mind set of the men who were in the German POW camps, and who were forced to march for weeks in the bitter cold of that German winter. Most lacked proper clothing, food, water, and just about everything else necessary for such a venture. They did, however, have the determination to stay the course and survive. I do not know how many POWs were in the Death Marches that winter. I've heard the number put at about 20,000, for there were several groups of them. The amazing thing, to me, is that almost all of the men survived the ordeal

Friendship was an important part of surviving the POW and Death March experience. Men broke up into groups, usually from three to five in each group. These "combines," so called because the prisoners combined their resources such as food, shelter, blankets, etc., became the basis for the strength the men needed. Joe O'Donnell's story, "Joe, We Only Got A Little Way To Go…" typifies the value of this friendship.

One day on the March, Joe felt he could walk no farther. But his friends came up to him, helped him to his feet, and told him that they had only a little way to go to the barn where they would spend the night. These friends ministered to him the best they could, both emotionally and physically. And today, you can read Joe's story.

Not all the victims in war are military people. Gerhard Ruhlow, a young German boy when World War II ended, writes of his trek from Pomerania to the west, the same time period during which the prisoners were engaged in the Death Marches. The hardships these civilians endured were not much different from those of the POWs. You'll find Gerhard's story, "From A Different Point Of View" in this book, too.

Some of the tales you'll read are stories of courage almost beyond belief. Warren Christianson's story, "The Hell I Crashed...I'm Shot Up Like Hell," typifies this kind of courage. Where does such courage come from? Warren got his badly shot up B-17 back to his base after he'd ordered his crew to bail out over Yugoslavia. You can call it luck or amazing talent or whatever you wish, but like the popular song of World War II, it was pretty much by A Wing and A Prayer. Exciting—no doubt about that.

Some men who were sent overseas saw no combat. They fought the war of loneliness and separation from family, but at the same time, when they could get away from the base, they visited the land in which they were living, took photographs, etc. James T. Kay, Jr., was an airplane engine mechanic. He spent time in England and Germany, but he was never in the line of fire. His material reads almost like a tour booklet.

There were the men who were hidden and protected by the underground, who were sometimes caught and killed. Claude Murray, was aided in his evasion by Dutch citizens. His story, "Jan Pieter Smit, A Dutch Deaf And Dumb Salesman", is included in this collection of adventures.

And make no mistake, the emotional toll war took on all the men, but especially those taken prisoner or subjected to long periods of combat, was very real. Hap Halloran's story, "Thirty-nine Years of Nightmares" chronicles this problem, and just as importantly, tells of his victory over it. You'll admire this man and the way he has lived his life after his terrible experiences stemming from his time as a Prisoner of War in Tokyo, Japan. Today, Hap talks to young people all over the world about his experiences and patriotism. He's a supreme motivational speaker.

It's impractical to mention all of the book's contents in this Foreword, but they are all a wonderful insight into the human condition under wartime stress and in ultimate victory.

I'm grateful to Erik Dyreborg, for undertaking the difficult task of putting this book together, just as I'm grateful to the men and women who contributed their stories. There have been rocks in Erik's path, but he, too, persevered and stayed the course. These stories deserve to be brought out into the open where people can read them. These men are the heroes of our past, some of the men who kept our Freedoms for us, the reason I stand when the flag passes or when the National Anthem is played, and why I get tears in my eyes whenever I hear Taps. This wonderful country owes them so much.

Introduction

By Erik Dyreborg

The heavy bombers

A friend of mine, Karen Cline, gave me a free ride, her ride, on the Collings Foundation's B-17. Karen was handling the Collings Foundation's event at Dinwiddie, Virginia, in October 2002, where the B-17 and the B-24 were displayed for a few days. The Collings Foundation operates these planes, and they tour America every year from January to November. The planes can be viewed inside and out, and they have been modified to carry passengers and can give a 30-minute ride for 350 Dollars.

My ride aboard the B-17 was scheduled from Lynchburg, Virginia to Dinwiddie, Virginia, on Thursday October 24, sometime in the afternoon. I was to fly with my good friend, Nelson Liddle. Nelson served as a ball turret gunner in the 8th Air Force, 401st Bomb Group 615th Bomb Squadron during the war. He was shot down on his second mission, May 24, 1944, a mission to Berlin, or Big-B as it was called by the Air Groups. The plane crash-landed on the Danish Island of Bornholm in the Baltic Sea. Nelson and the rest of the crew managed to escape to Sweden.

I was filled with excitement and anticipation over the prospect of this ride. For three years I'd been writing books about these planes and their crews, and now it was my turn to ride in one of them. It was something I wanted to do for a long time.

The great day came. We arrived at Lynchburg about 11 in the morning and checked in. Everything had been arranged. We were ready to go.

It would be several hours before the planes were ready to fly, so Nelson and I went aboard the B-17 and the B-24. We quickly discovered that the men who'd been aboard the planes in wartime must have been smaller and slimmer. You don't walk around in a B-17 or a B-24, you crawl. Nelson said that the B-17 had definitely shrunk since he'd last flown aboard one in 1945.

Pictured above, me, crawling around in the B-17.

Well, we did a lot of crawling, which was good exercise. To me, passing along the catwalk sounded like corks being pulled from champagne bottles. I hate to imagine moving around in one of those planes in combat wearing heavy flight gear.

Finally, it was time for us to board the B-17. I entered through the door in the right side at the rear of the plane. There was a little staircase there, so I just walked in. When it was time for Nelson to get in, the little staircase had been removed, so Nelson just swung in as they did in the old days. Mind you, Nelson turned 80 in January 2003.

We were advised to take our seats. Nelson and I went up to the radio compartment, but there were no seats. We were then told that our seats were right there on the floor. Nelson was on the right side, and I was on the left. We sat face to face. Not very comfortable, but this was our "mission," and we really wanted to go. From our positions on the floor, we couldn't see a damn thing. Nelson told me he was sure this was going to be a milk run.

So we were just sitting there, waiting for those big, beautiful engines to start, which they finally did. When they were wound up, I was immediately transported to Cloud 9. I stayed there for the entire trip.

Nelson wore his A-2 leather jacket and his AFEES (Air Forces Evasion & Escape Society) cap. I had on my MA-1 nylon jacket and my 401st BG cap. Oh yes, we were some good-looking dudes.

They started up the engines, one at a time. It absolutely makes you feel alive.

Mind you, these are real engines. They have their own special sound. You feel the vibration all over the plane. During take off, you hear the roar of those engines; you feel the tremendous power of the B-17. And before you know it, your ship is airborne. Our "mission" had started.

The B-24 took off just a couple of minutes later. The weather was sunny and warm, the visibility excellent. We moved around in the plane from the nose to the tail. We were flying at 1,200 feet, no oxygen needed (just kidding), and it wasn't even cold.

The B-24 came closer and closer; we were flying in formation. My guess is that the distance between the two planes was less than 100 feet. I thought that was pretty close and told Nelson I thought they were flying too close. Suddenly, the B-24 disappeared. Our crew and passengers were all shouting, running and crawling around, looking for the B-24. We couldn't see it anywhere.

Then it came up from below and was on our right wing and very close. It had been "hiding" below us and not one of us had noticed. Then, it flew above us. I hurried into the top turret. Boy, was he close, very close. I would say less than 50 feet. And would you believe it, this sucker, me, ran out of film. But I **did** see it, and for as long as I live, I'll never forget this beautiful experience.

I've always been nuts about the B-17, but that day, I think I got myself a new "sweetheart". The B-24 is beautiful in flight.

The B-17, shot from the gunner's window of the B-24 is pictured above.

Our pilot, a young fellow in his late twenties, who back in the WW II days must have been one of those they called Pops, made a perfect landing at Dinwiddie. But when taxiing to our hardstand, he took his right turn too sharp and the plane's right wheel went off the tarmac. We were stuck in the mud.

We were ordered off the plane and started walking. In a couple of minutes, a WW II Jeep with a big white star on the hood and all, picked Nelson and me up and took us to the hard stand of the B-24.

It took a tow company, using two heavy trucks, more than two hours to get the B-17 out of the mud. After that, the tow company changed their slogan to, "We tow B-17s and other stuff."

The day before Nelson and I flew aboard the B-17, the ordered copies of my first book in English, *The Lucky Ones* had arrived. The book had just been published in the States. We had brought a couple of copies with us to Dinwiddie.

Several of the airmen, whose stories were in *The Lucky Ones* had arrived, and we had a great get together that same day.

The new book

Sometime before the October trip to the States, I had decided to write another book, also about the Army Air Corps in World War II.

I was looking for stories narrated by the airmen themselves. In the early going, everything moved quite slowly, but by the end of 2002, things began to accelerate. Stories began to pour in. In less than five months, I was up to my eyeballs in stories, good stories.

Since I had a full time job, I had to work on the book almost every evening and on most weekends. I must admit that I have a very understanding wife, Vivian, and fortunately, I still have her. Writing books is, in fact, a full time job, at least these kinds of books.

During the writing of this book, I came in contact with some very helpful people like Carol Auslander of the Army Air Forces Historical Association and Margaret Cawood, Sylvia Hill, Don Norton, and Stan Spurgeon of The Oral History Archive of the American Airpower Heritage Museum.

These people, who are working on a voluntary basis, have interviewed hundreds and hundreds of veterans on audio tapes, transcribed the tapes, proofed the stories, made copies of the tapes, and handled the coordination of this huge operation.

Many hours of work had been done on the Oral Histories before I got some of them for this book. Within a short time, I was put in contact with the narrators of those stories, the airmen themselves.

Later, I asked Margaret Cawood to write the foreword, and she accepted. It was important to me that the writer of the foreword has the right background and a special interest in World War II Airmen. I'm personally very pleased with the way it turned out.

One of the most difficult tasks an author has is obtaining loyal people to proof every page for you. I've been very lucky to have Pat and Arden Houser proof my work and help in the battle against typos. Does a book without typos exist? Pat and Arden have proofed all the material in this book three times. Each has read and proofed more than 2,000 pages for this project.

The cover

The pictures on the front cover are almost all related to the stories in this book. The front cover picture has been designed and produced by Ed Markham of www.markhamstudios.com in Great Barrington, MA.

Top row L to R:	Frank Mastronardi, back in the States in 1945.
	The Jug, "Paula," in France with Ken Glemby in the cockpit, and his ground crew on either side.
	Wayne Eveland, after his return from his three month long escape through France and Spain.
2nd row L to R:	John Balog (he did 36 missions) and his crew.
	A ground crew in UK. James T. Kay, Jr.,
	Joe Peterburs, The Strafing Kid.
3rd row L to R:	Walter Rusch as POW.
	A crash landed B-17G. The plane went down on "my" island, Bornholm, Denmark in the Baltic Sea, April 11, 1944, after a mission to Stettin, Poland. The name of this plane was "BIG STOOP". I'm sure several readers will recognize the name, however in quite another relation.
	Frank Mastronardi as POW.
Bottom:	A B-17G, 401st Bomb Group, 613th Bomb Squadron. I got this photo from Bob Harrington, and here is his story about the photo:
	"The photo is a scan of a Kodachrome slide taken through a normal 50 mm lens by my father, Capt. Charles W. Harrington, from the pilot's seat of his C-47 'Skytrain'. I'm not certain of the photograph's date,

but it was from the time he 'drove C-47s for the Army' (his words) from a little before D-Day through the end of the war. I think it may be from late in that time frame, and even possibly a little after VE Day, but alas my father is no longer here to ask...It was taken 'over Europe'. He said that on this day, they had met a lone B-17 returning to England, so they tagged along."

The airmen

This book differs from my last book, *The Lucky Ones*, in that this book contains a wider mix of stories, i.e. stories of airmen, who were not only bomber crews, but also fighter pilots, Carpetbaggers and even ground crews. This book is also different from the first in that it is about airmen who served in the 8th, 9th, 13th, 15th and 20th Air Forces. So this book covers stories of not only the U. S. Army Air Forces, stationed in England, but also those Air Forces in Italy, France, and the Pacific.

Some of the stories in this book are about airmen, who are no longer with us. Their wives, daughters, sons, relatives took over and wrote their stories. Even a young Slovakian, Peter Kassak, contributed with stories about American airmen downed in Slovakia during the war.

The best thing to do, when writing this kind of book, would be to visit every single one of the airmen and the narrators. I'm sure this would add a more personal aspect to their stories.

In spite of not being able to do so, I feel that the airmen, their families and many other people involved, have all been extremely interested, trusting, and willing to step forward to tell these stories in a published book.

I've had a great deal of correspondence with all the narrators involved as well as a good number of telephone calls. The e-mails, letters, and talks have inspired me and encouraged me en route.

The stories of the men in this book are about young Americans, who went overseas. These young men went into harms way, because it was the right thing to do. It was the only thing to do. Thousands of them gave their lives for you and for me, but fortunately, thousands more made it back to their homes and families.

Some were wounded in action and lost all or part of their mobility. Some were forever emotionally marked due to imprisonment and the treatment they were given at the hands of their captors.

The airmen mentioned in this book are but a fraction of the ones who came back. It is their stories, which have made the publication of this book possible.

Before you start reading, please remember one thing. This book is not fiction. The contents and the stories are **all true** and have been experienced—and narrated by real people.

Those are the stories of *The Young Ones—American Airmen of WW II.*

Previous published books by Erik Dyreborg:

Title:	"Flugten fra Bornholm 1944"
	("The Escape from Bornholm 1944")
Language:	Danish
Published:	May 2001
ISBN:	87-7799-090-0
Publisher:	Bornholms Tidendes Forlag, Bornholm, Denmark
Title:	"The Lucky Ones—Airmen of the Mighty Eighth"
Language:	English
Published:	October 2002
ISBN:	0-595-24990-6
Publisher:	iUniverse, Inc., Lincoln, NE, United States of America

"The Hell I Crashed…I'm Shot Up Like Hell"

Narrated by Warren Christianson, B-17 pilot
15th Air Force, 99th Bomb Group, 347th Bomb Squadron
Edited by Erik Dyreborg

Beginning and enlisting

Although my mother and father lived in Hinkley, Minnesota, about eighty miles from Minneapolis, I was born in Minneapolis on October 24, 1920. I lived in Minnesota until I went to Alaska in 1949.

I attended the University of Minnesota, where I took one year of law. At that time, there was a two-year undergraduate program, then four years of law school. The war was coming, and I wanted to get a degree before it got here. I knew I'd be going into the military sooner or later, so I went into the business school my last year, took some electives, and graduated from the University of Minnesota in early June, 1942, as a graduate accountant.

I was supposed to go into the service in March or April 1942, but since I was so close to graduation, the draft board gave me a deferment. I was editor of the year-book at the University of Minnesota my senior year, which might have helped in getting my deferment, but I don't really think it made much difference.

I wanted to be a pilot, but I had never flown in my life. I went to the Navy office and tried to get in. I had played football in high school, had a bad accident, and ended up with a rather bad scar on my neck. So the Navy rejected me.

I hitchhiked up into Canada and tried to join the Royal Canadian Air Force in early June 1942. I almost got into the RCAF, but because of my neck, I was again rejected.

So that left the Army Air Force (Corps). I was asked what happened to my neck. "I was in an automobile accident. I don't know what the hell happened, but there's a scar there." The muscles had all torn from the spine—that's what had happened to my neck. I'd had a very serious operation when I was seventeen.

Training and going overseas

I went into the Air Corps. I went through pre-flight at Nashville, was put into an accelerated group and sent to Arcadia, Florida, for primary. Next, I went to Cochran Field in Macon, Georgia, then to advanced training at Moody Field at Valdosta, Georgia. Transition took place at Siebring, Florida, and phase training at Avon Park Florida.

From Avon Park, I went overseas. I guess it was late April 1944 when we started. We went to Gander, Newfoundland; the Azores; Marrakesh, where we stayed for a little while; Tunis; then to Italy. Several months earlier, the 99th had gone from Tunis over to Foggia, Italy. I was assigned to the 99th Bomb Group, 347th Squadron at Sand Fly Tower, outside of Foggia.

One of my disappointments was the Group flew a mission to Poltava, Russia, and I didn't get to go because I didn't have a crew and was a green combat pilot.

The first missions

I flew co-pilot for the first one or two missions. Men destined to become first pilots flew co-pilot for the first one or two missions with an experienced pilot. Lt. John Hammond was my pilot on that first mission. We've maintained contact ever since.

I remember that first mission rather vividly; it was a raid on Munich. I was flying—Lt. Hammond was flying wing on the Group leader, so we were right up in the very front part of the 99th Bomb Group. One of the fellows I'd known in training—I found this out later—was in the lower Squadron of the Group ahead of us. An 88 mm shell hit his ship and the plane caught fire. Chutes came out. We counted them. This one chute, the guy got in a panic and pulled the cord right away, which was a mistake, and when the ship exploded, burning gas fall on the chute. Of course, the guy fell to the ground, and we saw it. I also saw three fighters going down at the same time. I couldn't tell whether they were ours or Germans. That was my initiation to combat.

One other thing I remember, when we got down to briefing, I said, "Well, flak was light and inaccurate." Hammond said, "Hell, Christianson, it was heavy and accurate."

I said, "It didn't knock any of us down, it just put holes in our ships."

The Christianson crew with Warren circled, is pictured above.

The worst mission, 23 July 1944

We were bombing Vienna. I had five missions over Vienna and four over Ploesti. I never once got out of Vienna without some holes in my ship somewhere from somehow. On this particular trip, we got pretty badly shot up. I was flying at the time. It was pretty bad.

Flak had knocked out one engine completely, and then knocked the supercharger out of the second. In those days, that meant you were limited to atmospheric pressure, i.e. 29.92 at sea level, but at 25,000 feet, effectively no power. As soon as we were hit, we had to abort and lost altitude fast. So 29.92 was the check-off manifold pressure in a B-17; you were not supposed to fly that for more than five minutes. Then another engine got a shot through either the propeller head or the engine, and was leaking oil very, very badly. The ball turret gunner kept calling and saying, "Warren, we're losing a lot of oil."

We were over the target; there were fighters in the area. I had to make a decision whether I would feather or continue to use some power until we got away from the fighters. The decision was not to feather—which was what caused all the trouble.

After awhile, I tried to feather and couldn't. The engine had gotten real hot, and then caught fire. Things were getting kind of tight. The plane started to vibrate very badly; I knew the propeller was going to come off. There were no fighters around then. We were just about at the border of Austria and Yugoslavia, the northern border of Yugoslavia. I ordered the bombardier, navigator and the top turret gunner back. I figured there was about a twenty percent chance that when the propeller came off, and it was obvious it was going to, and maybe part of the engine, would go through the cockpit. I figured that if it didn't go through the cockpit, we'd still have one and one-half engines, and maybe we could get home.

We were doing about 135 air miles an hour, just above stalling speed, not too much, but enough, but the vibration of the ship was such that it destroyed the airfoil characteristics of the plane. It stalled out, went into a spin, and fell. I got on the intercom and told everybody to get out. I found out later they'd already gone. I was going to bail out, too.

I figured the thing was on fire and going to explode. The configuration of the B-17 is such that the pilot is supposed to go out the navigators escape hatch. I pulled the emergency release and the door fell off. I looked up. We were spinning down, and hell, part of the engine had fallen off and the fire with it.

I thought, "Well, blazes, man, I can pull this thing out."

I went back to the cockpit. There was a loose parachute bouncing around in my seat, so I got in the co-pilot's seat. I was pretty excited. I kind of overdid it. I dumped the stick too far. Okay, now what am I supposed to do? Okay, the plane was in a semi-inverted position, so from this semi-inverted position, about ten or fifteen degrees off vertical, the plane was going straight down like hell. I pulled the power off as gingerly as possible. I knew everything was shot up. I started pulling out.

I didn't want to pull the plane out too fast and pull a wing off or something. The speedometer on a B-17 has a red line of 305 miles an hour. I didn't even notice what the air speed was until I was already in pull out and going up. I watched the air speed as the speed started going down—420, 410—something like that.

Those B-17s were really put together. At the bottom of my dive, I was about 1,000 feet above the ground.

Later on, after I'd landed, I counted eighty-eight holes in the ship. One of the crew chiefs said later, "You didn't count them all."

"No, I just counted the big ones." There were 424 holes in that ship. I pulled the ship out, and once I got to where the airspeed was down around 300 or so, I put full power on—what power was available to me. I was on the wrong side of the Alps. I wanted to get as much altitude as I possibly could while I still had all this speed.

I got up to about 7,000 feet, something like that. The Alps are higher than that. Well, there are passes. The navigator had taken his maps with him, and I didn't know if anyone was back the ship or not.

I got the ship squared and was pulling 46 inches (take off power) on this one good engine, and as much as I could on the others. I had about 60 inches all together. Fifteen inches per engine is considered as good as nothing, so at the altitude I was flying, I had, essentially, a little more than one engine. When I got lower, I had a bit more power.

I thought, "Well, I might as well take her home."

I trimmed the ship up as much as I could. I tried to put in the autopilot, but it didn't work very well. The bombardier has to push it in. I trimmed the ship with the trim tabs and made just a quick dash to the after section to see if anybody was back there. Nobody was. I trimmed the ship up again when I got back to the cockpit, because it was in a slight dive by that time. It was lop-sided.

I was lucky. It was the inboard number two (engine) that was good. It was the inboard number three (engine) that had the supercharger shot off. At least it wasn't one of the engines over on the end of the wing that was good. (Both out-boards were gone.) I dashed very quickly down into the navigator's compart-ment. "Where the hell am I?"

I knew, generally speaking, where I was. We had been given an escape kit that had a map of Europe from south Sweden down to North Africa, something the size of this (indicates a sheet of paper). It helped some. I decided to try to go down the Yugoslav coast east of the Doheric Alps; they were a helluva lot lower. I tried to go right across to the coast. I was east of the highest Alps. I thought I'd watch my altitude, and if I saw a pass, I'd cut through it.

I started losing altitude, so I thought I'd experiment. I put a little bit of flap in and flew between 110 to 115 miles an hour, just barely above stalling speed with-out full flaps. I wanted to get the most possible lift and lose the least possible alti-tude.

I thought maybe I should go faster and get farther, but it looked like I was doing the best thing. I kept on going. I found I was getting a bit low; I was down to 5500. I thought, "Boy, I know things aren't all that bad, but something is going to happen here pretty soon."

There was a big valley, and I could see a good-sized river coming out of it. I thought, "That river has to be coming from a pass. I'm going to take a chance and go up that valley. If I have to and can't make it, I'll turn around and crash land." I figured I'd probably crash land.

I went into the valley. It looked pretty good. I could see clouds, small cumulus clouds, right in the middle of the pass. (Cumulus are fair weather clouds.) I thought, "Well, I think that goes all the way through. Jeemeny Christmas, I am going to go through the middle of that. I'll take a chance. I hope I don't end up in the middle of a mountain."

I wanted to go through the middle of the pass, because I'd have the least chance of hitting a mountain, you know, one side jumping out, an abutment coming out. So I went through, scared stiff that I was going to see ground coming up at me.

Then I could see the pass. I saw it was going to be close. I could see that I'd prob-ably make it. I thought, "Well, maybe if I have to lift it up a little bit—don't stretch your glide, Christianson." So again, I just did the best I could to get the most altitude. As I got closer, I could see I was going to make it. As I got close to the pass, I found I was about 150 feet above the ground. I wasn't just at treetops.

There was a woman, a house, a Yugoslav mountain house on the right side of the pass about 150 feet above the pass, and I just sort of thundered in front of the lady's front porch. She came out and waved a towel or something at me, wishing me good luck. I was crying with relief and at her warmth.

Once I got over the pass, it was all right. I gradually continued to lose altitude. I got down to the Adriatic, and was able to hold my altitude at 400 feet. The air was thicker. I had a full thirty inches on the one engine and was still pulling forty-six on the other one.

About that time, I got on the air and called Big Fence, the rescue homing type deal. I explained who I was, and said I wanted a bearing, because I didn't know exactly where I was. I had a pretty good idea, but I wanted a bearing to my field.

I took the heading Big Fence gave me. I gradually lost a little more altitude until just before I hit the Italian coast. I couldn't see—I didn't have very god visibility ahead at my altitude. I knew the ground fairly well, but usually from much higher up. I came in. I stayed on the same heading.

I saw a field, a fighter field. I almost thought, "To hell with it, I'll land on that field. Nope, I'm going back home."

I'd lost about another 100 feet of altitude, but then it held. I was over a fairly low plain.

I kept going on in. I got close and called the tower. They said, "Who are you? You're supposed to be dead. You crashed."

I said, "The hell I crashed. Give me landing instructions. I'm shot up like hell. Don't give me any crap."

So the tower called Colonel Shaffer, our CO at that time. I made my landing and dragged it in. I didn't realize it, but my tires were shot up and the ball turret guy had left his guns down when he bailed out. Clankety, clank, clank. I ripped up some steel mat runway. I came to a pretty quick stop. I was sure glad to get back.

The new crew

The Colonel was in the tower. He hadn't flown that day. As it happened, only my co-pilot and I out of my crew were in the ship. We were not supposed to fly, but someone got sick or something, and we were put into this crew. Norse Domain was another guy who was also put in.

There was a reaction, all right. I got out of the plane. The rest of my crew was there, and we went back and had a number of drinks. That was about it.

The plane was sure as hell shot up. Among other things, we'd had the oxygen system shot out—that's four systems.

I got a Distinguished Service Cross out of it. That's next to the Congressional. Afterwards, the guys said they liked to fly behind me, that I should lead if we had a rough mission.

A few days later, I was sitting in the tent and someone said, "This is a big day." I was feeling kind of down. Where in the hell was the crew? What should I have done? Maybe I should have done this or that. Self-searching. A sergeant came in and said, "The Colonel sends his compliments, Lt. Christianson. There's a ship ready for you if you want to pick up your crew at Bari."

Wow! I tore out of that tent and went down and grabbed somebody for engineer, the three of us went down to Bari. We reported to headquarters and were told the crew was down in the mess hall.

We went on down to the mess hall. It was this big mess hall. There were about 300 guys there—ex-POWs, guys rescued from various places. Bare walls and seats and tables—you know how mess halls look. Way down in front a guy was standing. I recognized my co-pilot. I said, "Andy."

"Chris, you're dead."

We went down and just threw our arms around each other and kissed each other on the lips, and man, I'll tell you....

The aftermath was that about that time, the crew came up to me—this was after we got lunch. "Lt. Christianson, we want to ask you a favor."

"You guys can about have anything. What do you want?"

"Don't ask any questions. We are going to be gone for two hours. Just don't ask any questions."

"All right."

So the guys I'd flown down with and Andy and I sat down to wait. The men had been gone just a little less than two hours when they came driving up in a 6 x 6 (six wheels, six cylinders).

What they had done, they had taken their escape money, about eighty bucks apiece, and bought a truckload of Italian Champagne. A truckload! They loaded it all on the ship. We flew back and threw a party for the Squadron that night—officers, enlisted men, everybody.

I wasn't drinking anything that night. I was boss, trying to keep the thing on low key as much as I could. I felt I was responsible. I was afraid some of those guys were going to get bombed and get in trouble. The radio operator was a small Tennessee guy who kept downing drinks. I was getting kind of worried.

Four or five of my crew said, "Lt., you're not doing enough drinking. We're going to settle that." They grabbed me, one under each arm, filled a water bucket with champagne, and ducked my head in it. "Drink, you son-of-a-bitch, drink." They'd let me up for air, the dunk my head again. "Drink, you son-of-a-bitch."

I drank as little as I could, two or three glasses, something like that.

I carried my radio operator back to his tent in my arms.

Other memories and thoughts

The next day, the Colonel put out an order saying, "Henceforth, there will be no familiarization between enlisted men and officers." The funny part of it is—not the funny part, but the curious part is that in Seattle, in 1985 at the 99th Bomb Group Reunion, the first one I attended, I came on in to where the guys were sitting around a little pool-like thing, having drinks, and this guy was saying, "You know, when I was commander of the 347th, the damndest thing that ever happened when I was commander was over Vienna. All the planes were accounted for. One had been shot down. About three hours after everyone else had landed, the tower called me and said, "This guy is coming, part of the 99th. He's all beat up. You'd better get down here"

"Everybody is accounted for," I said.

"Well, I don't know what the deal is, but he says he's from the 347th." I went down to the field.

This guy is telling this story to the guys around this pool

I'd gotten there just he started the story. I stood there and said nothing, just listened. The Colonel continued, "I don't know if that guy is here or not. I haven't seen him. I don't remember exactly what his name was, Chrisman or something like that. He was from Minnesota."

I said, "Well, Colonel Shafer, here's your man. My name's Christianson."

That was the roughest mission I had. We had a bunch of other funny stories.

On my 51st mission, also coming back after having had an engine shot up—we had three good engines, no problem. I aborted the lead; I didn't want to lead on three engines. We were on the coast coming the Adriatic when the bombardier called up. He said, "Bombardier to pilot. I've got an anoxia victim here."

Jesus Christ. I didn't think our oxygen system was shot out. It must be Kerwin, our navigator. "Andy (the co-pilot) take over." So I rushed down to the navigator's station. The guys had a little mouse in a shoe-box. I didn't say anything.

My crew had bailed out right over a little skirmish between the Germans and the Yugoslav partisans. When they bailed out, the guys had seen part of our engine fall off; they figured I was a goner. One of those guys had had a piece of flak go through his chute, so he came down fast. The other guys—the wind was blowing toward the partisan lines—drifted into the partisan lines. But the guy with the hole in his chute looked like he was going to land in no-man's land between the two groups. The partisans were going to make a charge and rescue him, but although he landed in no-man's land, he was close to the partisan lines, and they rescued him. He broke his leg, and the partisans immediately picked them up. There was no question as to who the men were.

The partisans sneaked them through the back roads. They had a mule pulling a little cart, and they put the fellow with the broken leg on the cart since he couldn't walk. The crew was no match for the physical condition of these partisans up and down the mountains. One guy was allowed to sit on the back of the cart. The men would change off on that.

It was late evening, and one of the partisan girls sat up alongside the fellow with the broken leg. He said this was about the third or fourth day, and those girls were getting better looking every day. Andy Anderson, my co-pilot, who was sitting on the cart and in OK condition said, "Well, I put my arm around here, and she didn't seem to object. She kind of snuggled up, then I snuggled up a little more and put my arm around her a little more. And you know what? My hand hit a hand grenade on her belt. That cooled me off."

Then the boys said, "Jeez, Chris, you should have been with us. We had a fine time." They said they lived in a hut and ate fish and had a fine time. When they got to this secret airfield, the British came over and took them back to Bari.

A lot of other light stuff, but most of the time in combat, I had enough engines left. Most, about three-fourths, of the missions were really milk runs; they weren't all that dangerous.

The German Air Force had definitely diminished its effectiveness toward the summer and latter part of 1944. There were fewer planes, and the quality of their pilots was poorer.

After I left in November 1944, some of the guys, the man who had taken over as Squadron lead, for example, said that in the very last part of his missions, the Germans took the ace pilots who had been instructors, and threw them into the battle. Those guys were good. We lost quite a few planes at the very end. Proportionately, considering the number of American planes, the percentage wasn't good. It was felt we lost far too many.

The book, "The First and the Last," by Galland, the German ace—I don't know how many American kills he had, but a helluva lot. Over one hundred, way high. He was one of those instructors. He never ran up against us.

Also, toward the end of the war, we had ground rockets shot at us. The bad thing about the ground rockets was you couldn't see just where they were going to hit. At the very last minute, you could maneuver away from one if it looked like it was going to hit you. They didn't shoot at us too many times.

Actually, I remember only once did I even try to maneuver away from a rocket. And as I was doing it, I realized it wasn't necessary. They were highly inaccurate.

Those rockets looked like they were coming right at you when you were flying at about 25,000 feet—five miles up—and they'd miss you by 100 yards. When they're first coming at you, though, you'd swear they are going to hit you.

The point is, you had to wait and see if the rocket was going to hit you. You had to estimate its speed, because it was going a helluva lot faster than you were.

My feeling is, and it was in Galland's book, too, that had Hitler followed better advice, the enemy air force would have done a lot better.

Printed with permission of Thor Christianson and The Oral History Archive of The American Airpower Heritage Museum.

Thirty-nine Years Of Nightmares

Narrated by Raymond "HAP" Halloran, B-29 Navigator
20th Air Force, 499th Bomb Group, 878th Bomb Squadron
Edited by Erik Dyreborg

Introduction

I was born in Cincinnati, Ohio, February 4, 1922. I was nick-named Hap during my service days, and am best known that way. I enlisted in the Air Force at Wright Patterson Field, Dayton, Ohio, in mid 1942. I was not called into the service until January 19, 1943. I completed basic training at Wichita Falls, Texas, Sheppard Field. I went through Texas A&M College Air Crew Training School of some sort—they were really waiting for places to put us for actual training.

From there I went through navigation school at Hondo, Texas, completing that, then was asked to volunteer for a new plane, which I hadn't heard of yet. It was going to be long range and they really needed dual rated navigator/bombardiers. So I volunteered for bombardier training at Roswell, New Mexico. Upon completion of that, I was assigned to training at Salina, Kansas.

There were no B-29s available, so we did our early training in B-17s.

The B-29 and our crew

One morning as we came out of the barracks and walked to the field, there on the ramp was a beautiful, silver B-29—the very first I had ever seen. It was 100 feet long with a 141-foot wingspan; beautiful.

Some of the unique features about it; it was a pressurized plane. It also had central fire control, and it was designed for long range bombing missions. We were never told, at that time, our specific destination, but we did complete our training. And we were ready to go into combat.

We had a great crew. Our crew was named the Rover Boys Express. It was sort of Americana personified. There were people from New Jersey, Michigan, Missouri, Oregon, California, Illinois, Oklahoma, North Carolina, Ohio, and Montana. It was a great crew. The average age was 22. The gunners were about 19; Captain Smith was 25 and he had had combat in the African Theater.

The crew with Raymond Halloran circled is pictured above.

Having completed training, we went to Herington, Kansas, where we received a brand new B-29. We flew it to Mather Field, California. In December 1944, we took off from Mather. I'll never forget. Our orders were given to us to proceed to Hawaii. We knew we were going west, but at the time, we didn't know how far west.

Flight to Hawaii

As we left San Francisco that night, we climbed to about 20,000 feet. I'll never forget looking out the side window from my seat and looking at the lights of San

Francisco. It was a brilliant, clear night. Then we went out over the ocean, I took one final look. Those were the lights. That was a transition period of moving from peace in the United States to combat in the Pacific.

Over the Pacific, it was dark. We were on our own, and you felt the pressure of navigating for the first time for the crew and for the plane and for the purpose of our mission. We came right in on target; we lined up on Diamond Head. I didn't want to use any of that radio which was available to us in a peaceful atmosphere, because later on, it wouldn't be permissible, it wouldn't be possible.

Saipan

We spent a couple of days in Hawaii, and then received our next orders. Kwajelein, a very small flat island in the Pacific. I'd never heard of it before, and I've never been back since. But it served an admirable purpose then. We came in landed, refueled, rested, and were then given our ultimate destination, Saipan. I had heard of it before, but I thought it was a vacation territory.

We did proceed promptly to Saipan and landed at Isely. In most of the history books it's spelled incorrectly as Isely, but that's beside the point. It is Isley field, named after a flyer was shot down on a strafing run during the invasion—a Navy flyer.

It wasn't too long after we had rolled in there, about six hours, before, the air raid sirens sounded.

From the north, the island of Iwo Jima about 600 miles north, we'd been told about the Japanese planes, bombers and strafers which would come down, and there we were, six hours into Saipan.

I didn't really know what was coming off. I thought it might have been a practice raid like back home, but it wasn't. They were over and got about four B-29s that night—burned them up on the runway. Only B-29s were at Saipan then. We did not have Tinian or Guam, the two other bases, which were eventually used.

You saw these fighters coming in; you saw Black Widows going up. You saw the searchlights. If you were ever in doubt about whether you were ever in combat or back at some officers club in Salina, Kansas, you knew it right then. It wasn't frightening; it was just, I think, the thing we needed to do this transformation.

Shortly after that, we did fly a mission to Iwo Jima. The Japanese,obviously, still held it at that time. Our purpose was to bomb the runway and make it inoperable for the raids against Saipan and/or ships at sea.

The missions

On the first mission, we were going west to east, which was the prevailing wind. And we were not lined up; it was at low altitude for a 29—about 20.000 feet. We had a bad bomb run and said let's go out and do it again; we'll come in the other way so we'll get a good run. It was Christmas Eve afternoon, and I thought of Christmas at home in Cincinnati, Ohio, 8000 miles east of where I was. We were by ourselves. As we came back into the wind, we slowed down appreciably. After they (Japanese) had our altitude and everything, the flak opened up on us. I don't think we ever ran backwards over the target again. So that was part of the learning process.

We did have quite a bit of damage to the plane. We came back and said, "Wow!" And that was further transformation into what was really going to happen over the mainland.

If you have any questions, you just go right ahead. I'm just kind of rolling as it comes to me.

Then we started going on some of the longer raids/missions.

A typical mission up there Saipan or, say, Nagoya, or Tokyo, was about a 1500-mile trip, one way, over water, no intermediate auxiliary bases or anything. No fighter escort. It would take us anywhere from—the very shortest would be 14 1/2 hours—and 16 hours on one mission we flew, and 15 1/2 on the other. We went up in loose formation, 1000 feet off the water. About an hour and a half out, we would pull in a little tighter and climb to altitude. When we hit the coastline, we wanted to be at bombing altitude. In those days, we had never heard of the jet stream.

Tonight I see it on television every night, and the jet stream is coming through here and here and here. But I can tell you one thing, when we got over Japan at that altitude and you tried to make that right turn to get lined up with the target, that wind was so strong that crabbing wasn't going to do it. You'd have about an 80 ° crab trying to hold a true course.

At any event, we went up to Nagoya and had a good mission there.

The first mission on Iwo Jima was Christmas Eve afternoon. There was no Christmas tree, but it was a great mission, in 1944.

I believe it was January 3rd; we went up north to Nagoya and bombed an aircraft factory very successfully. When we went up to a little town west of Osaka, on about January 17 or 19, 1945—and again, we were bombing at an altitude of 32,000 feet in those days. That mission was 60 % good, I would say. We got about 90 planes over the target. There was only one B-29 wing in the whole Pacific then—that was the one we were in on Saipan.

Later on, I think there were four or five other wings on Tinian and on Guam.

As I said before, we had no fighter escort. We were on our own.

On a typical mission, returning home, because the island of Saipan was only four miles by ten miles, because the radio was jammed, because we really could not home on it because Iwo Jima was so close, and because we'd be attacked on the way home, low on fuel, the decision was made that each plane, on leaving the target area, would go home independently. So if there were a navigational error by the lead navigator, we wouldn't end up right of the small island and fly into oblivion or we wouldn't end up left and run out of fuel. So it was up to each of us. We concentrated. At the time you were most tired, at the end of about thirteen hours or so, the last three hours was the time that required the greatest concentration. We did celestial navigation over the Pacific. We'd get up in the dome and shoot the stars, then plot them, to advance them for the time lapse, then replot the whole group and form an island. The crew really stuck with you. "Do you need anything, Hap? Do you need this, do you need that?" We were all sweating it out. I'm sure there were a few Hail Mary's and Glory be's said.

We'd come back in total blackness. Even the lights on the base would be kept down as long as they could, until somebody was coming in. There would be planes coming in with emergency landings, an engine out or two engines out. I would say the average fuel left in any plane coming back from one of those missions—and some were lost at sea, and some of them flew by the base, right or left of it—was probably never more than twenty minutes, max. We'd come in, and hit that runway, and God, it sure felt good.

We'd go for debriefing; tell them what we saw. I remember we were allowed an ounce of liquor by a chaplain. You'd drink that down. I was never a drinker before, but after sixteen hours up there, I found myself taking it. It served sort of as a medication, I think. So we did that.

I'll focus on our fourth mission. We did go north to Tokyo one time, but about three hours out, we lost two engines. The engines were not too reliable in those days—they overheated. We had to turn back. And that's a terrible feeling, to leave your guys go ahead and you're struggling to get back. So, really, that was not a mission.

The fourth mission

On our fourth actual mission, the target that day—we'd get up in the morning about three thirty. I say get up out of bed, because you never slept. Anxiety prevailed during the night; we were in a bunker building, we had rough beds. Everybody was very anxious, but nobody wanted to show any fear. As long as any of the people in the squadron didn't show it, or in the crew or whatever it was, everything was pretty solid. But everyone, I think, was holding it inside. So when I say got up, I got up out of bed. Maybe it was about 3:30 they came around to call us—mission time. We got dressed and went up and had breakfast. Then we went over to briefing. If anyone wanted to go to the chaplain, you could to that.

Then we'd go up on the hard stand and go by our plane. The Japanese had burnt the plane we had taken over about two weeks before. So we had to take any plane that was available. So we ended up with V (Victor) Square 27. That was the designation for the 878th Squadron, 499th Group, 73rd Wing. We used that so in flight, as we were assembling, we could see who was who in the air. And there were other alphabetical identifications. Those were later changed. So we had V Square 27. It belonged to a good friend of ours, another crew. They were in the barracks, and they came up to see us off.

We got in taxi position; flares would go off—OK to taxi. We'd go on down the roadway and line up on the runway. Early in the game, we would take off at about 45 second intervals on parallel runways. Later they had that down to half a minute on each runway. We would lose some planes on take off.

The flares would go and the chaplain would be down at the end of the runway. I used to look back at him and do that sign of the cross as long as I could.

But on this day, January 27, 1945, target 357 Musashino Aircraft Factory, on the west edge of Tokyo. It was really a Nakajima engine plant, but our groups had had trouble over there before and had not gotten any good hits. There was tremendous fighter opposition and, generally, pretty heavy flak. Even through the rest of the war, until the night raids, the crews all hated to take on 357. We finally wiped it out, but that was long after I was not flying.

It was the same routine; going up low over the water, climbing.

We went over a city called Hamamatsu, down on the very tip, probably 100 or so miles west of Tokyo. Again, that was to counteract those strong winds. As we moved north from Hamamatsu, and made the right turn, we had enough time to make the turn, line up on Mount Fuji—which is probably about 50 or 60 miles southwest of Tokyo—which was a good aiming point, a good navigational point, and we were set up do to either visual bombing and/or radar bombing.

FLAK and enemy fighters

After we made the turn, it wasn't very long until there was heavy flak, extremely heavy flak. This is where they shoot shells in the air and they explode. God. The sky had these bursting shells all around. We could just hear the puff, puff. Then it stopped. And we knew that wasn't a good sign, because there were going to be fighters.

On that particular day, as recorded in the Air Force history books, or Air Corps history books, there were more Japanese fighters up that day in more attacks on our wing than at any time during the rest of the war in all of Japan.

That was their maximum effort. A lot of that was related to the fact that we had hit them so successfully over Nagoya not too long before, and they had to protect this plant. They needed it.

I had never, ever seen so many fighters in my life, coming in.

Our briefing that morning said the flak would be light—this is no accusation, it is just a statement of fact. So we were doing the very best we could, our intelligence. The flak will be extremely light and there will be no fighters at your altitude. And that was mostly true on the fighters, because most of them were up on top of us, coming in.

The Japanese had some good two-engine fighters in those days. We called them Nicks, they called them Toryus. They came in. They were very aggressive. There were two of them coming in at one o'clock high. This would be slightly to the right of center. He was probably five or six miles out, above us. We were at 32,000 feet, approximately, he was probably at 34,000 looking at his angle of attack. With central fire control, there were a lot of commands being given—fighters at three o'clock high, nine o'clock high. There was nothing at six o'clock. We had nobody behind us.

Going down

But these two Nicks came in a pair, twin engine. We did get one, credited with one. It exploded out in front of us, but the other one did get in and blew off a segment of our nose. He came in high, and then dove underneath the ship. We had pretty much of a greenhouse effect in a B-29, up front. In any event, he destroyed most of that. We had a situation there, we lost all of our electrical controls and lost all controls in the plane. The temperature inside the plane, being pressurized—which was great, being contrasted with a B-17—was normally about 70 degrees.

When the nose section was blown off, the temperature went to 58 degrees below zero in about 10 or 15 seconds.

Without oxygen, now we did have portable, and we were grabbing that, trying to suck, but you're also trying to figure out what was going on, what we were going to do. We couldn't believe that the plane was fatally wounded. You just couldn't believe it.

You said it could happen to somebody else, but not to us. As I was primary navigator, I also had a scope set up for a bomb run on radar, but I had written down, on my hand, the coordinates of the nearest submarine off the east side of Japan. I told Smitty, the pilot, "We're going to head for this, so let's take a course of 130 °", I think it was. He said, "Hell, Hap, I have no controls. I can't do anything at all."

So then, we recognized we were in deep trouble. I think our radioman was one of the bravest men I've ever seen. We had a tunnel connecting the front part of the B-29 to the rear part; it was built over the bomb bay and was pressurized. The bomb bays were not. This fellow, Guy Knobel from Broadview, Montana, took off his parachute, crawled all the way to the back, because we had no radio communications within the plane, to tell our six people in the back that it was bail out time over Tokyo.

This fellow, I can still see him going back, leaving his chute there—he had a chest chute. We were on fire, we had two engines out, we had one run away. The inside of the plane was filling with smoke. We had no controls. And he went back there and advised them all to bail out.

When he got to the tail gunner, Cecil Laird, from Portland, Oregon-Cecil had been attacked, probably by one of the Tojos that had set up a pattern—these are single engine planes—after we had reduced altitude, maybe to 28 or 29 thousand, they had swooped in—I saw twelve of them coming in, all of them firing at us. The plane would just vibrate and shake. We were being torn apart in the air. I think one of those—I'm not certain—must have hit Laird, and he was dead over the tail position.

Bailing out

Later we did parachute out up front. Our normal escape hatch—a B-29 is a three wheel, with a nose wheel out front that folds back up into the plane. Where the nose wheel folds up into the plane (is an opening about four feet by four feet. When the nose wheel isn't in there, you have a perfect escape hatch to drop through and parachute. The wheel was up, as I said, we lost all electrical controls before that, so we had no way to get out (because we could not drop that front gear).

Our alternate, and by then we were smoking badly and our engines were out and vibrating. The magic thing was, and it had to be a miracle, we kept in sort of a slow glide forward, which shouldn't have happened. We still had the bombs in. The bomb bay doors were about 80 per cent of the way open, which means that instead of being all the way out with a clear drop, they were partially closed. The bombs never did drop. We couldn't get them out. We tried to release them manually—we had procedures for everything. As I put my hand against the manual release knob for the bombs, because the aluminium there was 58 degrees below zero, your hand would stick to it and the skin—we never could release the bombs. We gave up and said, "We've gotta go."

We decided to go through the bomb bay, even though it was jammed. We had to get between the bombs and the side of the plane. Looking down below, you could see Tokyo, probably 27,000 feet or so below.

It was extremely cold. You took a grab of oxygen on the way out. Bobby Grace, the navigator from Oakland, California, a great guy, and I put our arms around each other and said, "See ya on the ground." I don't think we really believed that at that time. It was a loving gesture, because we did love each other.

Then the engineer from New Jersey went next. The co-pilot from North Carolina, Jimmy Edwards—and I talked to him just recently—went next. Then there was Captain E. G. Smith and Hap Halloran in the plane. I knew we were in trouble. I think it could have been lack of guts, or it could have been not realizing the critical situation, but Smith said, "I'm going to be the last one to leave the plane, that's what the Captain is supposed to do." I said, "Well, give me a minute." We always carried food with us. You could order what you wanted. On the way up (to the target) the anxiety was so great that you never ate food, even though you were eight and one-half hours before you got to the target. So I said, "I'm going up." I had ordered turkey sandwiches on white bread with the crust cut off and mayonnaise on for my lunch that day, and chocolate pudding.

So while we're on fire, I went up there and sat down on where the escape hatch was and ate a turkey sandwich. I stuffed them down rather rapidly, and took two chocolate puddings and sucked those down. Snuffy Smith said, "Let's get the Hell out of here, Hap."

Floating down

So at that point I did work my way down the side of the bombs, and pushed myself out. When you're about half way out, hanging in the air, the speed of the plane at the time we were hit, I had taken a wind speed and knew it was about 170 miles an hour from the rear, I knew we were actually doing about 460 miles an hour ground speed in a propeller plane over the target. That is pretty good speed. Now we had lost some speed with the loss of power; we obviously had lost speed. But we were still moving pretty well. When you were hanging there, suspended in the air, and took one more push, then the wind sucked you out into the air.

I had made up my mind, for several reasons, at that altitude you wouldn't last very long. And as it was, I lost (the use of) my hands and the nails were frozen. Later on, on the ground, I lost all my fingernails. My face was frozen. I decided I would not open my chute high, because lack of oxygen, because of extreme cold, and the fighter planes were shooting at us at high altitude in parachutes in those days. So I decided I'd free fall down to somewhere between four and six thousand feet off the ground.

I rolled over slowly all the way down. It's amazing, while I had never jumped before, it seems somebody gives you supernatural powers to take care of things at that time. You roll over and say, "The next time I'd better pull it." Then you saw you had a lot of clearance yet, so I held it.

When I did open the chute about three or four thousand feet above Tokyo, I saw I was on the northeast side of the city. God, it was so quiet. I was just hanging there, suspended, and looking down. And the shock of seeing Tokyo and knowing it wouldn't be long, and in your mind you kind of reach out for something to hold onto and you couldn't. And then I saw three Zeros. They were not good for high altitude. They fluttered out at about 22 thousand feet. But they were down below. As I was hanging in my chute, my hands were frozen; I couldn't do anything with the cords. And I'm not sure I would have known what to do anyhow, but they made a pass. You just kind of tighten up and think, "Well, here it comes."

You think you're going to be shot in your chute. They went by the first time; they were very close. The prop wash of the planes set me in a tremendous pendulum, maybe thirty or forty feet. I was really out of control, totally. I couldn't do anything with my hands.

Then the planes came by again, and I think there's maybe a kind of comradeship between flyers. I held my hands up and just kind of waved to them. They circled off. They are short winged planes. I'll bet they weren't any farther out than fifty feet. You could see the pilots in the planes. The three of them came by in loose string formation.

Then the Zeros came by again and the pilots smiled and waved and left. I thought that was a pretty good indication.

We had been hit about 3:15 p.m. Tokyo time.

The hard landing, the brutal treatment and the humiliation

I came on down. I could see the civilians down below, thousands of them. As my chute was blowing in the wind and the pendulum effect was still taking place because of the prop wash, I hit backwards in sort of a residential, small industrial neighborhood, which was common for Japan. It wasn't right in the city, it was up on the northeast side of Tokyo. I hit backwards on the back of one of these arcs and God, it was a terrible hit. So I was in shock.

It was like in any mob rule, I think. The people in the front were close to me were pushing back, away from me. They probably thought I was armed or had a grenade, or something. The people in the back were pushing forward; I could see them trying to overrun.

I was lying on the ground. I was probably fifty to sixty percent conscious, at the most. I was conscious, but I really wasn't as alert as I would have liked to have been. Maybe that was a blessing. I had left my .45, my gun, in the plane, not brilliantly, but as it turned out, it was a great thing to do. The people on the ground had no knives, no guns, but they did have rakes and clubs and sticks and stones.

I think that, before we judge those people, we must ask what we'd do in a similar situation. If your city was being burned and bombed and the soldiers were being killed and planes shot down.

At that time, I wasn't really that munificent in my judgement, but I really think that now, looking back, and I had to do some reconciliation so that I could live my own life. So on the ground there, in very bad shape, and beaten severely by the civilians, I don't think I had very much longer to live. But I did hear some noise and some screaming.

All of a sudden the crowd was separated. I don't know why, but I thought of the Red Sea as I looked up, but coming through there were three or four soldiers in uniform. They had what I would call a Luger, they called them something else, in their hands. They came up. My parachute was on the ground. The first one came up and put his Luger on the right side of my head and was pressing it. It was cold, but I was so cold that it didn't make a lot of difference. I was hurting so bad that I thought that might be a blessing.

I hadn't made a determination to live yet. Until you do that, anything can happen.

When the other soldiers gathered around, a couple of them, I guess they thought they were really brave; they put their gun one at one side of my head and one at the other, and they pulled the triggers. But they had no bullets at that time, at least in that chamber, and that went on. I never knew when they would. That went on twenty or thirty times. I guess they were showing the muscle men they were.

Then they took my parachute and cut it up and stuffed it in my mouth.

So I was tied and bound, and they beat me across the ground and threw me on a truck, it would be like a coal truck over here—that's what I used to call them when I was growing up—a metal truck that had sides on it about four feet high. They threw me up there like a log.

The soldiers were trying to throw me up on the truck. They finally did get me on there, and we went, obviously and as I now know, we headed for downtown Tokyo. On the way, maybe after three or four miles, they stopped the truck in what I would call a shopping center over here. They unbound all the ties on my hands and feet, and made me stand up in the truck.

The purpose of this, I think, of this drill, was to show the people who gathered around, there were always thousands of them, and they made me bow. It was to show that this was a big, major coup—this was a B-29 person. See, they are not super beings, look at him bowing to you.

I had made a mistake the night before. I had painted my GI shoes. I took the dye you put in the water if you're ever forced down. I cracked one of those open, it's pure gold. I made my shoes shiny gold. You can imagine. You could fall out in those shoes in San Francisco and nobody would pay any attention, but in Tokyo, to have gold shoes, they thought I was something special, having to do with religion. I had to explain those things fifty times.

But I would bow to the civilians. I had a high school ring on my left finger. It belonged to some gal. When my hand was hanging over the back (of the truck), some of the people with scissors were trying to cut the ring off for souvenirs.

Then I was tied up again and we went on towards Tokyo. And the same thing happened again.

The prison, the interrogation and the beating

As I now know, it was dark by then and I ended up in Kempei Tai, a federal military torture prison, which is in Tokyo, just adjoining the northern moat of the emperor's palace. They never anticipated any Americans being taken prisoner, because that was contrary to their creed. They certainly believed that never would there be any Americans coming over Japan or into Japan. So they had no place to put any prisoners of war.

The first B-29 people who were shot down, I'd say 90 per cent of those, were killed on the ground. There was no desire to save them, because there wasn't. But apparently, as we became a more serious threat, in January, whoever was running things over there said, "Let's get some of these B-29 people and bring them in for interrogation."

So that's why I was saved from the civilians by these people who ended up being based at Kempei Tai. And there we were. They just pushed me out on the ground. I was still tied together. Then I was untied and taken into this building.

I have since been back to this building on several occasions. But it was a four-story building, maybe more than that. At that time, I couldn't take in all the details around me. Fear is a powerful thing. It occupies so much of your mental process.

I was taken inside and lined up in an interrogation room, just like you'd see in the newscast of old. There was a light hanging in the center of the room, it was pivoting and swinging. There was a chair and I was tied to that. There were other chairs and there was a table. Behind that were about ten guards with their bayonets.

The guards always had bayonets on. I think it was to give them stature. To look at that sight with the light coming across you, you can imagine the interrogation. There were constant beatings, generally a rifle butt in the stomach that would knock you over in the chair. Then you'd be set up again. That went on for maybe three or four hours.

I ended up being put in a temporary cell in that building. In that cell, which was about four feet by five feet, there were two Japanese people, civilians I guess, would be the best way to describe them. I'll never know why they were there. I can tell you what they told me. One had invented a secret bomber with six engines that that very week was going to be bombing New York, and the other was a religious conscientious objector.

But they, too, were beaten. So the three of us had something in common. But I never really felt at ease in there. I felt that they were plants, and that as soon as I fell asleep that they would kill me. I tried to stay awake so I'd be safe.

Finally, at the end of a couple of days, I may have dozed off or something. Then I re-established a relationship that we were really all three of us in trouble, and I think there was empathy. But how do you express that to the enemy? He was, after all, Japanese, rather they were.

Finally, one day, they showed me the dead lice and fleas and dead bugs, that within a week, infested us terribly. So they showed me how they went up and down the seams in their pants to try and help me do this. So they were trying to help me in a situation, in which we were all (involved).

I was in very bad shape. I was moaning and hurting. I couldn't walk. I could hardly talk, but I could get water down. I knew that was imperative. Without that, you die. I couldn't get food down, because as I now know and our co-pilot ended up telling me about that, I didn't even know it then.

One day, the Japanese came into my cell. There was a Japanese officer. It was unusual that they came in. And there was a doctor. The doctor spoke excellent English. He said to me that the Japanese prisoners were complaining about me my screaming and what I was doing, they said that I was being disruptive.

So the Japanese lieutenant and the Japanese doctor did come in.

The basis of their visit was that the other prisoners in those close by cells were complaining about the American prisoner because of his screaming and pain. They had a long green tube. It probably held about a half a pint of liquid. The doctor was explaining to me, in very good English, that he sympathized with my pain. He told me about the other prisoners. They thought it best if they give me a sedative, a painkiller. I knew what it was; I had heard of these things.

I begged of him, I said, "Please give me one week. I will get myself under control as best I can. At the end of a week, if I'm still disturbing the other people, then you go ahead and proceed. But if you won't do it for me, at least do it for my mother and father and four brothers who are expecting me to come home."

The doctor went into a long discussion, in Japanese, with the Japanese first lieutenant. You anxiously await if he's going to be successful in carrying that message. The doctor came to me. They called me Hop, they couldn't say Hap. He said, "Hop, I wish you good luck." And the two Japanese left.

I was probably very close to death. That was the way they injected quite a few of the B-29 people over there.

The quarters of the Doolittle crew

Shortly, I was taken out and put in a horse stall that was part of that Kempei Tai torture chamber. The horses were gone by now, and there was wood on the floor. There was no heat, no toilet facilities, no water. It was January and February and March, and extremely cold over there. It was dark. Every now and then, they'd turn on what was about a 15-watt light to make certain we hadn't committed suicide. The Japanese were always concerned that I was going to commit suicide, that I couldn't take the pain. Later on, I did tell them that I had made up my mind that I was going to live. That was a transition period for me.

You are always wondering what's going on. I did see some names in the cell when they turned the light on. The wooden cell on the side of me there was Chase Neilson, Red Barr. I recognized those names from the Doolittle crew. The date was April 17 or 18, 1942. They had scratched their names on the sides of this horse stall. So I knew, or could assume, they had been there before me.

I had lost most of the nails on my hands. I had a little bit to scratch with, and I thought I would start keeping time. The other men (Chase and Red) had scratched nineteen days there. I always thought something was going to happen. The chances of escape were absolutely zero if you were a Caucasian in Japan, and were not able to walk. So I spent time there.

Then a flyer who had been shot down in February was brought in, a Navy flyer off a carrier. I can fill these things in now. I knew he was an American and he was severely burned. He moaned for three days and died next to me.

By this time, I could see through the cell when the light was turned on. You heard an American and you couldn't help him.

And there was an intelligence Colonel down in the third cell. And I will use no names, now, because of the families. But he lost his mental balance, and you could hear him going beyond the periphery of life. He died. There were others.

It's pretty hard to keep going when those about you are dying. I did pray a lot. I didn't do the formal prayers that the good nuns taught me. I did the short version—Dear God, I'm in trouble. I really need some help, give me strength to get through this morning. I never did try to plan a whole day in advance—about two or three hours, and if you really wanted a break point, I hope that if we're going to raid Tokyo today, I hope it won't be before lunch, because then we wouldn't get anything to eat. That was the Japanese retaliation (for a raid).

So I'd always hope the carriers would come in after lunch or something, and later on, the 29s.

A typical meal would be—and this was just a dark cell. The front was bamboo very close together. There were little cracks in it of maybe a half inch. Occasionally you could see the guard out in front. There was a door about four feet by four feet that was always locked except when I went out for interrogation. Within that four foot door was a little door that was always open. They would roll a ball of rice in there, a ball of rice about as big as a golf ball. It's amazing. You get animal instincts after a while. I could hear the ball in the dark and could almost see it in the dark. You would get it, because that was your meal. You'd eat that. Occasionally, we'd get some black sea weed. I go in restaurants now and order black seaweed. I don't eat it all, but I want to have all of it I can. I eat a lot of rice now. I don't eat as much as I order, but I never want to be hungry again, so I do those things now.

I eat a lot of Japanese food now.

More interrogation and more beating

I spent 69 days in the small cell and in the large cell. For interrogation, I was taken over—when I couldn't walk, I'd be dragged over. The Japanese would drag me over by my feet, through the snow, and through a large courtyard. I'd be taken in and they'd sit me up in a chair. Then, they'd drag me back. This went on day after day, sometimes then not for three or four days.

Then one day, after they'd asked me millions of questions, and most of them were really irrelevant, they pulled aside a drape, and there was a full blueprint sketch of a B-29 from nose to tail—all the architectural, the engineer drawings. They had all that stuff all the while. I told them there was a lot I didn't know, and I really didn't know. What's the horsepower and stuff like that? I really didn't know.

They asked a lot of questions. There never was a right answer. Such as, "Did you see any Japanese on Saipan?" As well as the beatings and slapping.

"No sir, not to my knowledge." Then they beat me and said, "You killed them all. You killed all of our men down there."

Two days later, they'd say, "Did you see any Japanese prisoners?"
I'd say, "I'm really not so sure, because I saw some natives, but I couldn't tell the Japanese from the Chimorrans." Then they beat me because they said there was a great difference, and that I should know that.
Then I said there were prisoners, and they beat me for that, saying there was no way.

And did I vote for Roosevelt? I said, "No." and they beat me. Or if I said yes, they beat me. That was just life over there. You learned to live a different way. I'll get off that kick, off the interrogations.

I did learn one thing one day I think I learned a lesson from. I used it in business. A little guard would come by my cell, even when I was with those other two Japanese. These were in the early days when I could hardly talk. Maybe it was the eighth day. He came by and said, "Ohio." Immediately, and because he was the enemy, I said, "I'm from Cincinnati, Ohio." He was trying to make me homesick by saying Ohio. The next day, he said, "Ohio." And I thought, that little no good son-of-a-gun, he's trying to make me homesick.

On the third day, when he came by—there comes a time in life when you cannot be totally passive, I'd made the decision I was going to live and I was going to work for it. So when he came by the next morning and said, Ohio," I said, "Yeah, you son-of-a-gun you, Cincinnati, Ohio,—I really didn't say son-of-a-gun, I said something very strong—I'll get back there someday and you never will. I felt good inside.

The next day, they took me for interrogation and said, "You're with us Hop, and some words you might as well learn. I even learned how to count in Japanese. Another word you'll hear used quite often is "Ohio." That means good morning. I had a guilt complex like you wouldn't believe. To be blaming that little guy. He was probably the only friend I had in all of Tokyo. So I tried to apologize as best I could. Then I was taken to the other horse stall and never did see him again. But in business, when I personally negotiated with Jimmy Hoffa and the Teamsters, I would also say to myself, when he was putting the muscle on, "Ohio. Do I really understand what he is talking about?"

So it has been a little code word for me through business. I maybe used it two or three hundred times. So sometimes, even in adversity, you can learn some things that might put you in good stead.

The Zoo

On the 69th day, when I was taken out (of the cell) and thought I was going to be interrogated. This time I was told to put on my shoes, which were always outside the door, the gold shoes. Most of the time, for interrogation, even when I could walk, I wasn't allowed to wear my shoes, because they were gold. I'd be going barefoot through the snow in the wintertime. This day I was told to put on my shoes.

Those tear you apart, and then you scratch. When you're on the floor at night, you could see the bed bugs hopping out of the cracks in the wood and coming at you. I had not had any water to wash with in 69 days, and I had not shaved. I had no medical treatment or anything. I had a long beard by this time, and this was where the lice and fleas and bed bugs would go—and through your legs. So you would tear them apart when you rolled over in your sleep. I had one blanket, so my scabs would stick to it. So I was just constantly running sores.

I was put on a truck for the first time since I'd come in there. I wondered where I was going now. It couldn't be any worse. I always had the thought they were going to take me out and kill me or do something.

It ended up that they took me to a zoo. I now know these things; I didn't know it then. I knew it was a zoo, because I had to be in what was a lions cage. It's the Veno Zoo on the north edge of Tokyo. I have been back there, also, in the last five years—several times. I've been back to the very cage where I spent two days.

The purpose of my being there was to put me on display. All my clothes were taken. I was filthy dirty—hair hanging down, a beard. I was made to stand in front of the cage, and civilians would be paraded through. See, here is a B-29 person, nothing to fear. For two days that went on, then I was put on another truck and taken down through Tokyo. I was always blindfolded.

I'd try to hold my head up and see where I was. I could see the streets, and I could see that most of Tokyo was leveled from the fire raids that started on March 10; that was the first big fire raid.

The big fire

On that particular night, I was in the cell across from the emperor's palace, and I heard these planes, multi engine. I wondered, "Where did the Japanese get them?"

Then the bombs started to fall and the fires started. Then I realized what it was. I didn't know we had changed our strategy to come in at low level and bomb from five to seven or eight thousand feet.

This fire developed. I just had this one little window with a black cloth over it, but I could see the reflection of the flames through there. Then part of the end of our building flew off, but I must say that the fire was put out with sand. I was tied, my hands and feet, and blindfolded.

The fire burned. It started at 0100 in the morning. Some guards would tell you the time, and you could tell by guard shifts. The bombing went on for about four hours. God, it was terrible. All around you were the flames and the anti aircraft. There must have been a 90 millimeter right outside. My cell was bouncing the whole time.

There were the fires. Then I heard people screaming. The mothers and fathers and children were running past my stable to get into the moat to keep cool. My guard, one of them, came in the next morning two hours late—a pretty decent guy, a Christian. He said, "Hop, I fear for your safety. I just attended a meeting.

We are going to kill the B-29 prisoners today in retaliation for the bombing." He put his hand in that little door and shook hands and said, "Good luck."

So here, again, you see this adversarial thing, you do have people who have a concern and a love for other people. To live with that in your mind, that you were going to be killed that day, the anxiety and fear were rampant.

There were more people killed that night in that fire raid on Tokyo on March 10, 1945, than were killed in either one of the atomic blasts.

The visitor

One day after that, I was briefed by a guard, a sergeant, English speaking, who told me that I was in the first cell. I had a lot of visitors coming in so close to the emperors' palace and so close to downtown. They wanted to see a B-29 person, alive or half alive. I'd have to stand up and the light would be turned on, the 15-watt light, and they'd all say, "I have seen a B-29 person."

Then the guard told me that the emperor was going to come and visit me. This was after the big fire raid. It was sort of like after a flood or a hurricane; the president jumps on a plane and goes down and says, "I am concerned." It's one of those token things.

So the guard said the emperor was coming over. That was a very, very, very special occasion. He briefed me about how sacred that was and that there would be people to clear the way. He had me practice for four days what I should do. He came in the cell with me. I had to lie down on the floor with my feet right up at the end in that little door, facing the other way. I had to put a blanket over my head, totally. I practiced that for four days about twice a day.

Then came the great day. I never saw the emperor; I was covered with the blanket. I heard very soft talk; I heard Kiotskis (attention) ; I heard somebody describing something B-Nejucu (B-29) and American. All I know is that I was told by a guard, and I have every reason to believe, that the emperor did come in, stay about three minutes, and did leave. That was prior to my going to the zoo. Which is where I will now pick up.

"Omori" POW camp

I was taken out of the zoo after two days. God, it was cold there. I could look out, I could actually see outside. I could see a monkey island, and sitting up in one of two trees that had a runway for the monkeys between. All the animals were killed by fire or they were shot so they wouldn't escape running through the city or were killed to eat. But sitting up in that tree was the biggest, blackest vulture I've ever seen in my life. It was almost like he was waiting for me. I think I said something stupid to him like, "Don't wait for me."

But I was taken out, handcuffed, and taken down through Tokyo. I could see some of the sights if I lifted my head at an angle. I now ended up in what I now know was a Prisoner of War camp called Omori, on the south edge of Tokyo. There were probably eight or ten barracks in there, sort of like butler buildings—a little better than that.

We were taken out of the truck and untied. We stood at parade rest. There was, as I now know, a group of people there; they looked like they could have been Americans, but I wasn't sure. Then I saw some flight clothes. Most of them were so dirty. In my own case, my flight clothes were caked with black blood, and I was so dirty and with a beard. But with the 32 of us standing there, the Japanese did call roll call after half an hour.

They called Smith, E. G. Here on my right side; I was touching him all the time, was our Aircraft Commander, Snuffy Smith. We didn't even recognize each other.

I had lost maybe eighty or ninety pounds by then. He had lost also. And dirty filthy. A little bit later down the line, Edwards, James. He was the copilot. As it ended up, another one in that line that day was an American by the name of Greg Boyington, better known as Pappy Boyington. God, when I heard that name. He was a hero to me long before that prison camp. He had been shot down off Rabaul on January 3, 1944. We ended up in the same camp. As it turned out, we became life long friends. I did his eulogy in 1988; I wrote it and delivered it in Arlington National Cemetery.

So there we were standing there, thirty-two of us. We were put into one barracks.

The very first night I was shot down, we had to sign a three-page statement in Japanese. What it was, "I am guilty of indiscriminately bombing, and therefore killing civilians, and I understand I am on trial for my life and charged with murder. Geneva Conference Rules do not apply." I know all of these things now; I didn't know that night. But it made no difference. When I had two guns touching my head, I would have signed any pages they had.

So there we were in a special Prisoner of War category, all on trial for our lives. But we did have a few people other than B-29 people. We were the nucleus in there. We had Colonel Carmichael, shot down over Yahata, flying out of India; Colonel King and others.

After we got together, we all wanted to talk at one time. There were other prisoners in camp, they were from Corregidor and Bataan. They had far more freedom than we did. They could go into town and work in the railroad yards. They stripped the railroad cars of canned goods, etc. Very candidly, they had worked something out with the guards that they could share the food in the railroad yards. So they all looked very, very healthy. If any of you ever saw a liberation picture, you could look and see the flyers and submarine men as distinguished from the Corregidor and Bataan guys, who had a terrible time down south and on the prison ships coming north. But we had no contact with them. We couldn't. We were always under guard, day and night. We couldn't even go outside to the bathroom without going up to the guard, bowing in the darkness or in the daylight, saying "Benjo, yoroshi desca—kudasai?"—may I go to the bathroom, please?"

At night, when you couldn't see, you'd go up to him. I was thirteen steps from the guard, and I never wanted to touch the bayonet, because he could always say that I had attacked him in the dark. We all feared that, being stabbed to death right there. But we'd get to pass most of the time. We'd go out and come back in. But we never got to mix with the other prisoners.

Finally we were allowed to go out to work, always under guard, in Omori. Our job was to clean up the homes that were burned down by the B-29s, the F4Us, and F6Fs. They strafed through there regularly.

We'd be out in the garden and ZOOM, down through the railroad tracks down below would come our planes. A little later on, TBFs and Avengers would dive bomb below us. We'd see B-29s shot down and explode in the sky and a few chutes. The strange thing was that if those chutes had landed in our neighborhood, the civilians would have killed the men, even though, while we were working there. We were accepted. We'd be cleaning out their toilets in the neighborhood, and the neighbors would even give us a few beans out of their meager diet.

One little lady working in an aircraft factory close by, would give us maybe a quarter of a sweet potato. We'd take a pole and put it over our shoulders, Colonel Goldsworthy out of Rosalia, Washington, and I would always work together. We'd go out and scoop these toilets out; the Japanese had no sewage system, and we'd put it in buckets and bring it back and fertilize the garden. But we were never allowed to eat anything we grew.

We'd work along the railroad tracks. It was really terrible. But it was good to be out where you could see the sun once in a while and see our planes coming over.

It ended up that I was made an air raid warden. The guard, Horseface, would take some of the squash down and socialize with the local ladies. I'd be on top of the burned out homes with a Japanese rifle. If you think life doesn't take strange turns! If we saw Japanese planes, they were friendly, and the P-51s were the enemy.

The ending of the war and the liberation

But we obviously did survive. Before August 15, the Japanese wanted volunteers to dig holes in the sides of the hills. That was after the atomic bomb. We didn't know what that was; we had no knowledge of that. But we were in the garden that day, and some of the guards, who were fairly cool and didn't beat you as much as the other ones, came out and told us to go back to camp immediately.

We knew something was up. The very people who befriended us as we worked out there among them, became very hostile. We made a decision that we would fight. None of us could really do anything; we had little hoes that we'd made ourselves from damaged homes, but we decided to fight.

Obviously, that had been the people's response to the atomic bombs down south, at least the first one. We stayed in the barracks under constant guard then.

Finally, the Japanese Colonel came into the camp and said there was a temporary truce and the War for Prosperity of Greater Asia or something. He gave us a lot of talk. We did get to meet with the other prisoners at that time and talk with them.

On August 29, two weeks after the war was over—in the intermediate period, one of the first things we had to do, was to identify ourselves. Some paint was dropped to us and we had to put POW CAMP on the roof and how many men were there. That was done so they could identify us. Otherwise, they were strafing us during the war. So that was up on top. And we put "Pappy Boyington here." We figured that would get a little quicker action.

We were the first camp liberated on the mainland, up on the north end. What a sight to see the landing craft coming in. A few days before that, B-29s had flown over at maybe 800 feet, opened the bomb bay doors and dropped food to us in 55-gallon drums. A lot of the chutes didn't open. For the first time, we were allowed to get into an air raid shelter. Before, that had always been denied us.

Some people were injured by the drums and some chutes didn't open on some drums also.

Liberation of POWs. Raymond Halloran circled is pictured above.

We could see our ships out in Tokyo Bay. A landing craft came in and took us out. We were all too weak to climb the ladder to the ship, so they dropped nets. We climbed into the nets and were lifted onto the deck.

Because we were all infested with bugs, all our clothes were taken away.

To get into a shower—I think I stood there a minimum of two hours. It took three weeks to get the dirt off of us, though. The joy of getting into a clean bed with clean sheets; to be aboard the hospital ship Benevolence; to have food.

I went down to the ships store and got a Hershey bars and Milky Way candy bars. Then all night long I was quietly opening them so I wouldn't disturb anyone. I ate those things all night, and everyone else was doing the same thing. So we all confessed and kept eating and eating and eating.

We were fairly close to the Missouri for the signing of the armistice on September 2. We went out on the deck and saw the ship. Then coming down Tokyo Bay, up from the south, were Navy and Army aircraft, all types—fighters, bombers. Just everything you can imagine, a sheer display of power coming over at maybe 800 to 1000 feet, wave after wave of them. Then at the very end, a minimum of 500 B-29s came over at low altitude. You really break down and cry when you see your guys coming back. And to see them that close to you and that low—you really knew we had won the war.

That was probably the greatest emotional feeling I think I've had in my life—to see our planes, and more specifically, the P-51s. I loved the sound of the engines. I loved all those planes, the 6s, the 4Us. But those 29s were something special. I knew a lot of those guys up there were my friends.

I was later flown to the hospital at Guam, then Hawaii for a week in the hospital, and then to Letterman General Hospital in San Francisco. Then I spent six months in the hospital in West Virginia, recuperating physically. There was no concern about the mind at that time; we didn't know anything about that. Everyone did a perfect job for us. Maybe the treatment wasn't total, but the object was to go back to the job you were doing before and assume a normal life. I did that.

The nightmares

I was a clerical person in a railroad office. I could never adjust. I couldn't stand being inside again, and I couldn't stand confining hours. I couldn't stand any of those things. I was not doing a very good job.

I was moved to another position outside, and I felt better. But for 39 years, at intervals, I had nightmares. The nightmares sometimes three times a week, sometimes twice, and sometimes once in ten days.

The dreams were only of three types; falling through space, trying to get something to hold on to, which, obviously had to be the parachute jump, screaming; and the other was fire. I'm fearful of fire. Even matches today make me nervous. The fires in Tokyo were the fires where we were. The third one was the beatings. I would jump out of bed and go in a corner or under the bed. Sometimes, I'd try to tear the door down.

If we were in a hotel during those times, sometimes the desk would call, because I would be screaming and the people next door would report it, I guess. They'd want to know if someone was being attacked. They wanted to know if I was all right. And security would come up and check. I'm sure a lot of people had those things.

This is just a build up to what I finally had to do.

When I went to Detroit, I had to tell the neighbors on either side and in the back, that if they heard screaming that it was all right. You sort of figure that that is just a part of your life.

Returning to Japan

After all of those years, I finally decided I had to cure that thing, the nightmares, it couldn't go on forever. I thought that if I went back to the place where it all happened that maybe it could be worked out, with God's help.

I wrote long letters to Ambassador Mike Mansfield in Tokyo and said, this is what I would like to do, this is why I think it might help, and these are the things that I think you could help me with.

The former guard I had kept in touch with and had seen in the interim period, and other things. I wanted to go to the schools, I wanted to see Tokyo as it was today, and see the land when it wasn't afire, and when I would be free and be in charge. So I did go back, and Ambassador Mansfield assigned about four people to me who made all the contacts with the people, so I could meet them. They met me at the airport.

I spent two weeks over there. I gave talks at air bases and some of the schools and museums—in English. That's compulsory over there now. I went in the shrines and visited with the people. Because of the TV and newspaper coverage, a lot of the people knew who this fellow was. And I did have a chance to visit with all of them.

Then, at the end, I asked Ambassador Mansfield, before I went to Hiroshima, if he'd grant me one final request. "Saburo Sakai is one of the Japanese Aces; I read his book. I think, maybe, if I could visit with him, maybe he could help me on something I'd like to do beyond this." What I really had in mind was that maybe he could help me meet the pilot who shot us down. It was a clearly distinguishable event, short of the target. I had pictures in my briefcase and drawings by a plane alongside of us.

Mansfield said that the pilot probably wouldn't want to meet me. I said, "Well, let's give it a try." So he did.

When I came back from Hiroshima, I was picked up at the hotel, the Palace Hotel, right across from the emperor's palace. The reason I wanted to stay there, I wanted to be very close to where I was before, but I wanted to be up where I could look down on the palace ground and be in charge.

I tried to go to bed that night, and I couldn't. I got up and got dressed. The very first night there, I walked around maybe three or four miles, all around the palace grounds and the wall. The guards were there without bayonets. These were young kids who didn't know who I was and could care less. I'd greet them and walk around. I went back to bed and went to sleep. I think that was really a key turning point in this healing process. I did now feel that I was really OK and I was in charge.

At the end of the trip, I did ask if I could meet Saburo Sakai. It was arranged, and when my driver picked me up at the Palace Hotel, he told me that Sakai was on the way to Yakoda Air Base at that time, that he was taking me out there now, and that there would be an interpreter there. I was also told that I'd be speaking to the field grade officers at noon at the Officers Club.

I went out and spent about two hours with him. He's a fine person. I spent about a half hour with his daughter and his two grandchildren. She ended up marrying an American soldier. They're based at Fort Knox now.

But he did meet me, he is a genuine person. After two hours with an interpreter I said, "I think we're friendly enough now that maybe I could ask you a question. Would you help me in identifying the pilot who shot us down? He was flying a Toryu, a Nick. I have the photos taken of our plane by the planes behind us going over.

I have a sketch done by an artist, who happened to be in the plane behind us in the next squadron, very detailed. I have the location. We were hit this side of the target." I showed him the pictures I had.

I could tell right away that he had a pretty good idea of who the pilot was. These people still meet today and talk about what happened on this date and that date and who did what. It's like catching a forty-pound trout. The end result was Sakai said yes, that the man was a friend of his. His name is Isimu Kashiide. He lives up at Kashiwazaka Niigata.

From that, there was a long process of working with the embassy and my writing to Isamu Kashiide personally. It frightened him after all these years. "What are they going to do? Take me out of the closet and terrorize me?" Finally, working through Saburo Sakai as an emissary and a third party and a friend of mine, the meeting did take place a year later in Tokyo, at the embassy.

We spent a couple of days together.

Finally cured

Since the 1984 trip, I haven't had one nightmare. I can consider people in Japan friends—I know quite a few of them. I've been back. I went back last year and flew the final mission, which was when I was shot down over Tokyo. I'd never gone back to Saipan.

In Tokyo, I was invited to a reunion for some of the fighter pilots and others. They took me to their lair, where they meet today in a private place, where they meet and talk about how it used to be. I sat there with them in a back room. The fellow who owns the place now, and that's probably why they go there, was being taught to fly by Saburo Sakai, was being trained as a young fellow of 16 to be a Kamikaze pilot. Had the war lasted another two weeks, he wouldn't have been in the place we were. God, had made a special Saki for us. We sat there and toasted each other. It was a kind of occasion that most people will never experience in their lives. It was one of friendship and reconciliation and understanding, so that worked. I came home.

Saipan

I did go back this last year. I wanted to fly from Tokyo to Saipan. Arrangements were made, and I did fly down in a DC 10 with Captain Jim Rennell, of Continental. We flew by Saipan or Iwo Jima going south. When we were about 100 miles north of Saipan (Isley Field was still there, 68 degrees W. runway), the Captain called me in and I rode up front. The NBC show "Today" was with us for four days, we covered Tokyo, and then they asked if they could fly south with us. They wanted to cover my going home again. This was January 27, 1989.

I left that island on January 27, 1945. So forty-four years later, precisely to the same day, I came back. The Captain had permission to circle the island at low altitude. That's a great Japanese tourist island now. In the back of the plane there were probably 190 to 220 Japanese young people, all flying to Saipan to enjoy the beach, ride the Skidoos there and all of that. I was up front, and they all wondered, "Who was this American?"

The Captain did tell them as we circled at low altitude with permission from the tower. We banked all around the island, one and a half times, then came in and landed. I had to leave the cockpit for the landing. But I could see. We touched down on the same runway that had been surfaced now, versus what we had. We had coral top. But there it was, the same one, 8500 feet long. We landed on that and went back in. That was a long time between take off and landing.

I spent a lot of time there. It was a good occasion.

That's pretty much it. I think I've learned a lot. The adversity was severe. There are just three of the Rover Boys that was our crew name, alive today. Some of the crew were killed by the civilians when they hit the ground. One was killed in the plane. Five survived camp. Three died at intervals after that. So I thank God for my being able to get back and have a family. I probably enjoy life as much as anybody I know.

Epilogue

In the morning, I go out on the deck at home and say, thank God for another great day, a bonus day. I've tried to make the best I could out of what was there.

Someday, if young Americans read this story, I'd just like to have them know that this is a great country. Everything I went through was worth it because of America.

If in some way this made their life just a little bit better, that's good. I just want them to live up to the code of integrity and loving America and do a good job. If they do that, all what we did was worthwhile.

I say thanks to all of you, and treasure your freedom.

Printed with permission of Raymond "HAP" Halloran and The Oral History Archive of The American Airpower Heritage Museum.

On The Run For Three Months

Narrated by Ivan Wayne Eveland, Squadron Commander
8th Air Force, 401st Bomb Group, 614th Bomb Squadron
Edited by Erik Dyreborg

July 21, 1942, to December 30, 1943

Marriage to Dawn

My assignment at Salt Lake City was short. I was happy to find that my friend, Don Stoeger, had also reported in. Each of us was ordered to report to the 34th Bomb Group, Gieger Field, Spokane, Washington.

Enroute, I telephoned ahead and made a date with Dawn Farrar in Butte, Montana. Dawn had been in my high school art class when I was a senior and she was a sophomore. When I first saw her, I had been captivated.

She was sweet like the "girl next door", only prettier. To myself I thought, when she grows up she's going to be really <u>some-thing</u>! I was so taken with her that I <u>avoided</u> her! If a guy were to get to know a girl like this and she were half as wonderful as she looked, he might be tempted to throw away all college ambition…just to be near her. So, I continued to stay out of her way and did not even make conversation with her. However, I did continue to watch her out of the corner of my eye, when I thought she wouldn't notice.

Two years later, while a sophomore at Montana School of Mines, my friend, Dan Kelly, happened to mention that he had been at a party and Dawn Farrer had been there. In fact, he had known her for some time. I confided in Dan that there was a girl I had been purposely avoiding and intended to continue avoiding. Staying in college was a full time obsession and I couldn't stand any diversions. No way!! School and job were all I could handle.

45

A month or so later, as I was locking up the service station about 9:00 P.M. (I worked four hours per day, Monday through Friday, and eight hours on Saturdays and Sundays. These hours were while attending Montana School of Mines and the pay was 25 cents an hour).

In the summer I managed to get in 48 or more hours a week. Dan Kelly drove up and said he would give me a ride home.

When I got to the car, there was Dawn Farrar in the front passenger seat. She was about five feet tall, a very pretty and quiet girl, and just under 100 pounds of pure charm. She had dark auburn hair and sort of gray-green eyes. I can't really describe her smile, but it just did things to me!

That same summer I managed to take her to a couple of movies. She was always dated up far in advance so I had to ask early and wait long. I remember once I had a date for a Saturday night movie and by the time Saturday arrived I was a case of nerves. Of course, I had to work that day as a shipping clerk at the Firestone Store. Amongst the dozens of orders I prepared that day was an order for two massive tractor tires to Wolf Creek, Montana. On Monday following, it was discovered that I had shipped the tires to Wolf Point, Montana—due, no doubt to my temporary insanity in anticipation of the date with Dawn! I darn near lost my job!

The following school term, Dawn enrolled at Montana School of Mines (in Butte) and I transferred to the University of Montana at Missoula. I saw her now and then, but very seldom. I kept close track of her, however, through mutual friends. When I was a senior, she also transferred to U of M as a sophomore. I believe I was able to get one movie date. Then she got caught up in the social whirl. She pledged Delta Gamma sorority and was an immediate success with the students, especially male students.

She loved to dance and was really good at it. I think she attended practically all the formal balls on campus (how the lads could afford to rent tuxedos was a mystery to me), and all the other social events. I did telephone her once again for a date but, as usual, I was too late. I also had a feeling that I had lost many points on her priority list. So I tried to put her out of my mind. I was not able to do this too successfully. I merely kept in touch by a movie or dinner once or twice per year for the next few years.

My feelings remained much the same. I was totally charmed! But I never told her. I remained in debt, my career was unsettled, etc., so I didn't think I should say anything. When she (and Dan Kelly and Jack Carver) accompanied me to the Butte Airport in November 1941 as I left for Africa, I wanted to tell her. But to tell her my feelings then would be much like asking her to wait for me, and I knew I had no right to do that.

Remember, I left Missoula in August 1939. As I said, I had seen very little of Dawn in the previous few years. And we exchanged only a few letters. But I did have her picture with me throughout my various stations in the USA, Africa, India, etc.

Many of my military classmates were married immediately on receiving their commissions as Second Lieutenants in May 1940. The chapel at Randolph Field was fully scheduled. Many sent for the hometown sweethearts, and many other married San Antonio girls. It was not uncommon for officers stationed in the San Antonio area (which had a large complex of Army bases) to send for their kid sisters, nieces, etc., and see that they were introduced to the Randolph and Kelly Field cadets who would soon be Air Corps officers—and high on the matrimonial eligibility scale, at least for those depression years. Further, most cadets were so darn lonesome and turned off by barracks life that many were "easy pickins" for a little feminine sweetness! In fact, San Antonio for years had been known as the "the mother-in-law of the Army Air Corps"!

During the years 1939 to 1942, I had been ready for marriage. In fact, after receiving my commission and especially the silver wings that went with it, and experiencing the great ease of dating (for the first time in my life), I almost felt like a "traitor to the Corps" because I really wanted to spoil it all by getting married! For example, there had been a special southern girl whom I dated considerably and with whom I exchanged frequent letters when away. I was extremely fond of her.

Until I got to Butte in July of 1942, I never did understand why I had not asked her to marry me. But when I got to Butte, and saw Dawn again, I finally knew why! Heaven had reserved Dawn for me. This was to be my destiny! And that solved the mystery as to why I had not proposed to that little southern girl.

When we got to Butte this time, I took her to dinner. I was amazed that she could still be single! In my head, lights went on for me. At last—now I could tell her how I felt about her. So I did tell her. I also told her that maybe someday she would wear diamonds and sable, and maybe not—but I did feel that at least <u>some day</u> I could make her a "Colonel's Lady." Pretty brash statement for a Second Lieutenant, but I did say it!

We were married at the little White Base Chapel at Geiger Field, Spokane, Washington, on September 10, 1942. The only guests were her parents, her Aunt Gladys, my mother, my sister Ellen and her husband Paul Schilling, my sister Jeannette and her husband Al Johnson. Don and Dottie Stoeger had married a week or two before and also became a part of the wedding party.

I proudly withdrew $1,200 from my New Savings Account and sent it to Harry Urton, a Missoula real estate agent. That became a down payment on a little two-bedroom house on Plymouth Ave. The total purchase price was only $4,800—but remember—a buck in those days was as big as a wagon wheel today! I had a wife! And a home! Now I had roots! A big empty space in my life was filled.

Getting married caused a temporary set-back to my career. Not that there was anything wrong with Dawn. She was the greatest thing that ever happened to me. It was just that my marriage triggered some other little happenings that I had not counted on.

For one thing, I have already mentioned that my July orders had been addressed to "Second Lieutenant" and my ego and morale were damaged considerably. Next, on arrival at Geiger Field, I found that officers in training were not being treated as officers, but more like Flying Cadets; e.g., marched in ranks, confined to Base, etc. The pre-war Army that I had known had been entirely different. Officers had been Officers. Their word was never questioned—nor did it need to be! Status, pride, and prestige were important.

Training

Also, since I had more flying time than other lieutenants present, someone decided I should not be checked out and prepared for a combat assignment but should be retained for assignment as an instructor. The pilots due for early combat were top priority to fly the limited number of B-24s available. This meant that, although I received some four-engine instruction, most of my 12-hour work shifts were spent reading B-24 Tech Orders.

A week or two of such duty—from midnight 'till noon (or vice versa)—and an eager pilot is apt to go looking for a dog to bite! Further, I was unable to secure even weekend leave to get married because all official leaves were cancelled. I was in a box! The refusal to grant my leave to get married, when the Air Force had no relevant duty for me to perform, was aggravating. In fact, keeping me on Base, when they had nothing for me to do, I considered absolutely stupid and asinine! My anger festered.

The pre-war Army had an unofficial and seldom used category called "Basket Leave." In an emergency situation when official leave was prohibited, sometimes an officer could fill out his leave application and the commander would "freeze" it in his "IN" basket. No action would be taken on it, but the officer would go on "basket leave" for 48 hours or so. He could be called back to Base if needed and it must be clear as to how he could be reached on short notice.

Well, I decided I would see the Group Adjutant and arrange basket leave for the weekend. The Adjutant turned out to be a young Captain, with pink cheeks and NO pre-war service. He denied my request and admitted he had never heard of basket leave. I explained it to him again. No Dice. Absolutely NO!

My morale was rotten and my fuse was short. I lost my temper! Instead of remaining at "Attention" in front of his desk, I grabbed a chair, pulled it up alongside his chair, flopped into it, pulled out the bottom drawer of his desk, put my feet up on it and spouted off! I told him I was certain the Group Commander (a Lieutenant Colonel) was an old Army man who knew a lot about "basket leave" and if he (the Captain) did not grant my request, I would walk right into the Colonels office and inform him of the ignorance of his Adjutant. (I am not sure, but I think I even called him "son".)

The Captain got mad as a hornet but finally assented. (Because of his inexperience and the fact that I was a "combat returnee," I think he was confused and afraid to "lower the boom" on me for insubordination. Had he been more experienced I might have received a serious reprimand, or worse).

But I had made an enemy—and no wonder. It was a stupid way to go about it. Temper can be a bad thing!

After the marriage, including two days at Priest Lake, I came back to duty, which began in the pilots' locker room on the flight line. There must have been 50 or 60 lieutenants, most newly assigned, in the room. The Flight Commander, a First

Lieutenant and West Point graduate, was taking roll call. My name was not called, so I pointed out the omission. As soon as he heard my name he shouted at me—saying I had been reassigned to another unit and been AWOL the past few days; that was a bad example to these new officers, etc., etc.

Again, I flipped! I told him I had been flying Army airplanes, as a commissioned officer, when he had been a student carrying text books under his arm at the "Trade School on the Hudson!"

Also, it was obvious that he had slept through many lectures or he would not attempt to discipline or degrade and officer in the presence of others! If necessary, it would be done privately! The other young new lieutenants must have been shocked. Again, I made an enemy and a bad name for myself.

Dawn and I had a room at the Davenport Hotel for a week or so and then moved to the Spokane Hotel. (I was now out of debt and had some savings on deposit—a new feeling of well being.)

Meanwhile, I had been transferred to B-17s and had been assigned my first B-17 crew:

The co-pilot was 2nd Lt. Toy Bane Husband, a tall, skinny California kid who just loved to fly.
The navigator was 2nd Lt. Andy Bycott from West "By God" Virginia.
The Bombardier was Edwardo Maria Montoya from New Mexico.

The enlisted men were:

Francis Kilbride, Engineer.
William J. Skahan, Radio Operator.
Donald T. McCann, Tail Gunner.
Paul Mardis, Ball Turret.
Darwin E. Neff, Waist Gunner.

I cannot find the name of the remaining waist gunner, but I hope to do so at a future date.

They were a good gang the officer crewmembers became life-long friends. Unfortunately, our good friend Andy Bycott was a cancer victim at a tragically young age.

The three of us still living, get together every few years in Colorado, California, or Montana, and in the future we may schedule reunions God-only-knows-where! If we can locate any of the gunners, perhaps they can join with us.

It was obvious I would no longer be held back as an instructor. With the assignment of my full crew it was apparent that we would all undergo B-17 combat training together. We were assigned to the 399th Bomb Squadron of the 88th Bombardment Group. We received plenty of flying time thereafter.

Dawn did not drive, so whenever I had a chance I put her behind the wheel of my Chevy and had her practice—mostly on country roads between Spokane and Coeur d-Alene, Idaho. One day, long before Dawn was competent as a driver, I received orders to proceed to Walla Walla, Washington, for assignment.

My whole crew was transferred and we were to fly our B-17 there, meaning Dawn would have to drive the Chevy (and our few belongings) to Walla Walla solo. It was not a really long drive, but I got a map and explained that it might be best if she left Spokane before 5:30 AM so as to avoid the early morning traffic, etc. Also, my mother (who could not drive either) offered to go with her as moral support and on arrival at Walla Walla, Mother would take a bus on to Yakima to visit friends.

My advice was well intended but proved to be poor advice. I had not counted on the fact nearly all the truckers were on the highway before 5:00 AM. The highway was narrow and two lanes only. Thus, the traffic was much worse than if she had left at noon. When she finally got to Walla Walla, she found the Marcus Whitman Hotel and left the Chevy for the bell captain to take care of parking it. She was a nervous wreck.

Our crew navigator, "Andy" Bycott, was engaged to marry Patricia McCoy. Before leaving Spokane, Patty had arrived but I was unable to get Andy a day off for the wedding. So now at Walla Walla, I continued to try as hard as I could and as fast as I could to get a day or two off for Andy and for my crew, also. I ran into a stone wall. Each day poor Patty would say, "But, Andy, I've been here four days now! What will my parents think?" Later she was saying, "I've been here a week now," then "Andy, I've been here two weeks, etc., etc. You must get a day off."

Meanwhile, Dawn, Patty and other young lieutenant's wife kept shopping for an apartment or house, or whatever. I left the Chevy with them in town so they could house-shop full time. Andy's older brother had purchased the engagement and wedding rings. He gave them to Patty back in West Virginia when she got on the airplane to fly to Spokane. Of course, she had no intention of wearing the wedding band until married to Andy. But, while apartment shopping, she thought it best to put on the wedding ring—so she did. By the way, Patty was a sweet girl only 19 years old.

Finally, the girls found a house and paid a month's rent. They couldn't understand why the rent was so reasonable in view of the scarcity of units. After they moved in, some winter storms came early. The bedrooms and living rooms were impossible to heat properly. They spent most of their time in the kitchen, in their fur coats, stuffing wood into the kitchen stove! Also, it seemed very odd that passers-by always stared at them whenever they went out, and even stared at the house itself. Cars would slow up while the male occupants stared. Finally, they learned that the house location was in the wrong part of town! No wonder they got stares wherever they went! Andy and I knew nothing of this until later. We were confined to Base for our training.

Part of our schedule was known as "compulsory recreation." Depending on ground school hours and calisthenics and flying schedules (usually six to eight hours per flight), "compulsory recreation" might fall at 4 PM to 6PM, or just as likely, from 2AM to 4AM. Training went on 24 hours per day, utilizing three shifts per day. So, if we had "recreation" at 2 AM, that is when Andy and I could expect Patty and Dawn to drive out to the Base and join us. Often we danced to the jukebox or just talked. The hours were precious just to be together. Young lovers prized privacy, as everyone knows. My Chevy was a convertible and because of the canvas top the door locks were meaningless. Frequently, our married friends (likewise looking for privacy) competed for the relative privacy of our Chevy!

The day came when I could get the crew a day off. I persuaded the operations officer at about 4 AM, when we returned from a long flight. We had already been up for about 24 hours. In the next few hours we arranged for a church, a minister, a wedding cake, a hotel room for a small reception, champagne, and the whole "ball of wax", as they say. Also, we crew members managed to shop fast and secure small wedding gifts.

It was a nice little church wedding and the bride was radiant. The groom, handsome, but already beginning to look worn out. (In the early evening, the gunners had finally located and purchased a wedding present, so they took it to Any and

Patty's room. Patty answered the door in her nightie and robe; they asked were Andy was. She told them Andy was sound asleep, and had been since the reception!)

Within a few weeks we were ordered to Rapid City, South Dakota. Again, our crew was to fly our B-17F, so Dawn would have to drive the Chevy. This time Patty would accompany her. After arriving at Rapid City, they found a motel where they could rent a unit with one bathroom off the one bedroom and sitting room with a hide-a-bed settee.

The schedule of flying, ground school classes, calisthenics, and "compulsory recreation" were similar to the Walla Walla schedule. One big improvement, however, was that presumably we would get one day and night off weekly and could go to town.

So, most of my visiting with Dawn was at the Air Base for two hours at mid-day or midnight, or whenever. On our rare "days off," Andy I flipped to see which couple got the bedroom and which got the sitting room with the make-up bed.

Later, we got lucky and were able to rent the residence of the Episcopal minister, complete with nice furniture, piano and all. However, within a couple of weeks of that great event, we were transferred again—this time to Pierre, S. D., the state capitol city. Dawn and I got a room in the major hotel, but were soon told we must vacate because the State Legislature was due to commence and the rooms were needed by the legislators. Somehow, combined with several other lieutenants, I was able to rent a large old home—sort of an 1885 mansion, you might call it. With a married lieutenant in each bedroom we could share the rent payments. Although it had plumbing and electricity it was also piped for gaslights. But, once again, I was able to keep Dawn with me for a while longer.

Meanwhile, I had been appointed Squadron Operations Officer and was now engaged in drawing up the training schedules for flying, ground school, gunnery, etc., and we were training other new B-17 crews for combat.

I was even able to get a few days leave to return to Montana for Christmas and see my family and Dawn's family. Since Pierre, S. D., did not have train service, we drove north to intercept the east-west Milwaukee line, where we left the Chevy and boarded. We got a lower berth (chummy)! Surely enjoyed my first Christmas at home in almost four long, eventful years.

Almost immediately after our return to Pierre Air Base, I was summoned to fly up to Headquarters, 383rd Bomb Group, in Rapid City, to report to the commanding officer. The C.O. was Major Vandevanter. He was a West Point graduate and he had been in my underclass at Randolph and Kelly Fields (though I had not known him at that time). He told me that when he had taken over as C.O. of the 383rd, he had been told there were two officers he should keep his eyes on, as they might be "bad apples." I was one of them.

Hence, he had been watching me and getting reports on me ever since. He said he didn't know where or how I got my bad reputation and that, he said, was my own business. However, it seemed to him that there was no reason for the negatives he had heard about me. He liked my work. Now he was about to name a new commanding officer for the 540th Bombardment Squadron located at Ainsworth, Nebraska. He congratulated me as his selection to be the new commander! My rank was only 1st Lieutenant!

On January 2, 1943, Dawn and I arrived in Ainsworth (after driving all night) and I took over my first squadron command.

On the outskirts of Ainsworth was a road sign, "Population 1,280." I'm sure that score was before the manpower draft. The people were very friendly. We were able to get in the hotel and secured a room with a bath. (The only private bath in the hotel, I was told.)

However, the toilet was centered along one wall on a platform about 6-8 inches high (to hide the remodeled plumbing, I'm sure) without so much as a curtain for privacy! There were two tiny restaurants in town, so Dawn could have her choice. The Air Base was some miles out of town. There were no houses or apartments for rent. The hotel had a limit of how many days guests could stay. It looked like I would have to send Dawn back to her folks in Butte.

On Sunday, after going to church, Dawn and I drove around town looking for homes large enough to possibly have an extra bedroom or two. My plan was to merely go to the door, introduce myself as the Commander of the 540th Squadron out at the Air Base, introduce Dawn as my lovely wife. I was counting on her unbelievably irresistible smile as my secret weapon and would ask if they had an extra room—and would they consider renting it to us? Or, if they did not have such a room themselves, surely they would know of a friend in town who might? Otherwise, I would have to send my bride back to Montana! I believe that at the second house where we stopped the lady invited us in. She did not have a room, but after a cup of tea, and I told her I had returned not long ago from Africa and China, she said, "By golly," she would get on that telephone and get her friends to join our search team!! Soon she arranged for us to go see her friend, Mrs. Shrimpton, a very nice lady who accepted us into her home. Once again I had lucked out and could keep Dawn with me for a while longer.

The job at the Air Base was a real challenge. B-17 combat crews were there to receive their final month of flight training here before being sent overseas. These crews had previously received training elsewhere, with frequent change of station and personnel records, pay records, medical records, etc., nearly always messed up and incomplete. Many of the aircraft gunners (mostly corporals and sergeants) had not been paid in three months or in some cases had been paid only as privates, instead of receiving pay according to proper rank. In the month these crews were at Ainsworth we had to find proper orders on each of the men, individually, and send them on with pay records straightened out, as well as all other administrative items completed (all of this in addition to the flight training, of course).

I don't think my administrative people like me much. I worked them on shift, 24 hours a day—the same as the flying crews. These flight crews were also worked hard because so much had to be done and there was so little time to do it. As soon as one group of crews finished training (and were sent to combat) another group arrived and we repeated the same hectic program.

January, February, and March were unusually cold. We had several real blizzards. Such details complicated the flight schedules. For example: If the weather was bad in the Dakotas we would try to schedule our aircraft training missions toward Colorado, Minnesota, or Utah. As the storms moved we radioed changes in their flight plans. We also had to coordinate ground school with flight school, gunnery, bombing, instrument checks, medical shots, etc. Actually, there were about a hundred things going on, around the clock, and I doubt if I ever worked as hard in all my life; but, looking back at it, I think it was a hell of a great job! I seldom got to town except for a few short hours to take Dawn to dinner or maybe breakfast. When lucky, I stayed in town two or three nights per week. The other nights I slept on a cot in my office because I usually could only sleep two to four hours at a time. For one thing, the weather was changeable and we had B-17s all over the country.

Once I was called up to Rapid City Headquarters for a two or three day conference. I left my operations officer, Lt. James Foster, in charge. When I returned to Base, I walked into my office and there was Lt. Foster with a two-day's growth of beard, rumpled uniform, hair unruly, red-eyed, and an absolute mess. He asked me if we could talk "man-to-man" without this military "B.S.". I had him sit down and told him to spout off..whatever it was, get it off his chest. I wasn't prepared for what happened then. He really blasted and began by calling me a son-of-a-bitch! He ranted away, and I let him do it! His big theme was—I had selected him to be operations officer and second in command. That was why I was a S.O.B. He was trying to coordinate ground school, flying school, weather, bombing, high altitude training, formation flying, etc., for about 400 men—24 hours a day—and keeping training charts on each and every man, as well as each crew, etc.! He was up to his neck in this mess because of me! And he was only 22 years old and should be on a college campus instead of trying to do a man's job!

I realized that poor Jim probably had not seen a bed in all the time I had been gone. (Operations Officers and Unit Commanders and others sometimes find that is part of the job.) I told him to go to bed—I could run the store for the next 24 hours while he got some rest.

What is important about this incident is not the above personal story of Jim Foster. It was the principle of the thing. All over America, youngsters who should still be in school were holding down tough jobs made for mature men—and succeeding at it. That's how we eventually won the War! I have reflected on this many times since the War. I also have a belief that many of these youngsters had been toughened by the fact they had grown up during the painful years of the Great Depression. Many of them had experienced previous hardship before they found themselves in the military.

The 401st Bomb Group

One day, toward the end of April 1943, I received TWX orders to report to the C.O. of the 401st Bombardment Group at Ephrata, Washington. I was to leave immediately. I phoned Dawn and had her get our belongings together (don't forget things at the laundry and dry cleaners), load them in the Chevy, etc., and we left Ainsworth behind us. I left Dawn and the Chevy at Butte and reported in at Ephrata.

The 401st Bomb Group (H) was newly formed as a unit. We had only a few B-17s and only a bare cadre of staff personnel. Col. Neil B. Harding was the Commander. I was assigned as Commander of the 614th Squadron. Within days of arrival at Ephrata most of the flight echelon were ordered to the School of Applied Tactics at Orlando, Florida. While we were flying practice missions around the Florida area, studying tactics, attending lectures, etc., the administrative sections back at Ephrata were receiving personnel to flesh out the group complement of mechanics, radio repairmen, armorers, cooks, clerks, etc.

Col. Neil Harding proved to be a most popular C.O. He was an old-timer and seemed to know his business. He also had a good sense of humor and in that month or six weeks with us we all became fond of him. When you are expecting to go to war, it helps to believe your C.O. is a real professional and a good guy to boot!

Soon after we left Florida we learned Col. Harding was to be taken away from us to be sent to England to take over a bomb group already in combat. (It proved to be the 100th Bomb Group)....our morale dropped about 99 points. Next we heard a colonel from Headquarters, Washington, D. C. (a staff officer and desk pilot) had been selected to take over the 401st. Our morale dropped some more. Whoever heard of drawing two good commanding colonels in succession, especially when the second was reputed to be a paper-pushing specialist?

The new C.O. was Col. Harold Bowman. He won each of us over, and in short order. I think he used about the same technique on all his squadron commanders and staff.

He took me to lunch, privately. He explained that he knew he had some big shoes to fill. He also knew we all felt badly about losing Col. Harding. He also volunteered he had gone from Captain to Colonel as a staff officer largely in public relations work. His only command, years ago, was a Flight Commander. On the other hand, he thought his young squadron commanders had been well trained and had a lot of the field experience, which he had not received in Staff. He said he needed lots of help. He would rely on me—and others—to assist him wherever his experience was short. He promised to learn as fast as he could and with luck, in a month or two, he would have mastered enough detail knowledge to *help me and the other commanders with our problems.*

Remember, this guy was a full Colonel and I was only a very junior Captain. He talked in a frank, modest, and sincere manner. And he *asked me* for suggestions—and *help*! It caught me completely by surprise! This guy was not just another headquarters colonel. His modesty and sincerity was really special. I knew I could work for this guy. In fact, if this man's actions measured up to his words, I knew I'd work my butt off for him! And I did! I now believe his "downplaying" his experience was exaggerated, to say the least, but combined with modesty and a man-to-man appeal for help—that's *salesmanship*—and—plenty smart!

After several weeks of additional training, again at Geiger Field, Spokane, we moved to the "East Base" at Great Falls, Montana. (It is now known as Malmstrom AFB.) New crews, new personnel kept arriving. Air training, ground school, gunnery, bombing, etc., began again in earnest. But by now I was experienced on this sort of thing. And I as able to bring some of my previous staff with me, and this helped smooth out some of the rough places. I drafted Jim Foster (again) as my Operations Officer, Gordon Closway as Intelligence Officer, M/ Sgt. Earl K. Williams as Line Chief, and a few other key people.

Dawn brought our few possessions and the Chevy to Great Falls. She rented a room at the Johnson Hotel and later rented us a cabin at a tourist court located at the east end of the bridge between the city and the fairgrounds. It was bit on the dilapidated side (holes in the screen doors, and worse items elsewhere) and the Missouri River sent us a lot of mosquitoes. Many of the staff stayed at the same tourist court, not because of the accommodations but because of the lack of better accommodations. Again, I found it frequently necessary to sleep on a cot in my office instead of being with Dawn. But I came to town just as often as possible. She was now about six months pregnant. Her face was full, good color, and prettier than ever! I hated the thought of leaving her, although I knew this had to happen sooner or later.

It was not long until the 401st Group split into four locations, with Group Headquarters and the 612th (under Capt. Martin) remaining at Great Falls, the 613th Squadron (with 614th Squadron (mine) moving to Glasgow, and the 615th (with Capt. Bill Seawell) moving to Lewistown. I managed to drive Dawn to Butte where she would stay with her parents and could receive the best of medical care.

At Glasgow we went into our final phase of training before becoming eligible for overseas assignment. In addition to receiving the last of our needed people, we also received new airplanes—the latest B-17 G's. Major Albert E. Barrs, whom I had chosen as my Executive Officer prior to coming to Great Falls, and my Adjutant, Dick Mettlen, did a great job with the administrative crew. In engineering we had Lt. Mc Alexander as head honcho, and backed up by, in my opinion, one of the best Master Sergeant line chiefs in the business, Earl K. Williams. In fact, I remember talking to Sgt. Williams about trying to get him a direct commission, probably as a 1st lieutenant, but possibly even a captain.

At the moment there was a movement in higher headquarters to find and commission outstanding, experienced noncommissioned officers with engineering backgrounds. I told him I as not certain, but would try if he okayed it. Williams turned me down, saying he would rather stay with the 614th as line chief than accept a commission and be transferred elsewhere. I thought he was making a poor decision, but I was glad because I really didn't want to lose him.

The rest of the squadron staff should be likewise praised. I had good people throughout and they all worked hard. I have always been very proud of them. Due to their performances, I could look good and I received my major's leaves. Also, of course, we had many inspections from HQ 401st Group, Wing HQ, and 2nd Air Force inspectors, etc. I left standing orders at the control tower that whenever a "foreign aircraft" (not belonging to the 614th) entered the traffic pattern, the tower should find out the name of the senior officer aboard and, if possible, what command he represented. And I was to be notified immediately, day or night. One of the inspectors proved to be "1st Lt. X", the West Pointer with whom I had quarreled in the locker room at Geiger Field. Only now, he was a Lt. Colonel and he still ranked me. I expected the fur to fly...my fur!! However, after a quick perusal of the crew training charts, he congratulated me and got into his B-17 and took off. This was too good to be true, so for a week or two I kept wondering if maybe a curt "Reply By Endorsement" report might wrap itself around my neck. I need not have worried.

While at Glasgow AFB, we suffered a sudden increase in the number of aircraft engine failures. Preliminary investigation indicated some iron filings in the engine oil supply. I placed an armed guard at the storage facility and I notified HQ in Great Falls, of course. Soon after, at the apartment in town, I received a telephone call from a person who stated he was working on the problem within my squadron engineering section. If I should receive a call from a Corporal John Wright (or whatever), day or night, I was to do as he said. Also, I was to tell my wife that if a Corporal John Wright called, she was to take any message and inter-cept me immediately.

A week or two later, I received a call from Corporal Wright. He said he knew my blue Chevy convertible—and at certain hour he would be hitchhiking westward from Glasgow, and I was to pick him up, which I did. His only report was that he had been unable to definitely pin down the source of the problem. However, he had some theories that would be checked out by his successor, as the time had come for him to be replaced by another investigator. He did not know whether his replacement would identify himself to me or not. However, if I should find a number of my men had been transferred out of my squadron just before overseas assignment, I was *not* to fight it (as would be my normal inclination). As it worked out, I did receive some transfers at the last minute. Perhaps the culprit was amongst the outgoing transfer—and perhaps not. In any event, we no longer had an abnormal number of engine failures.

Birth of Nicole

I received letters from Dawn almost daily and talked with her frequently on the phone. She kept insisting there was no need of her staying in Butte as she was in good health and Glasgow had a little hospital and a doctor. I kept trying to per-suade her to stay with her folks—so I would not worry about her and the baby. One day she phoned me and *"notified"* me that she was coming, so I had only a few days to locate a place for her to stay! Actually, I had anticipated that she would do this so I finally admitted that the previous week I had rented a small apartment! It was pretty awful but would have to do until she could find some-thing better. After her arrival she was able to rent a better apartment above the local mortuary. Our landlords were Mr. and Mrs. Holland (the local mortician) and they were very good to us.

Then came the time to take Dawn to the hospital. It was early evening. Once at the hospital, everything slowed down for Dawn. However, by midnight there were three mothers-to-be in labor, only one nurse on duty, and no doctor present. I called Betty Foster (Jim's wife) who was a nurse. She came and helped. At the last we were giving Dawn bits of ether to hold her back until the doctor could get there. There is not much a husband can do—but at least I could hold Dawn's hand. I felt every contraction and pain. (Later, Dawn mentioned she didn't think having a baby was so bad. I replied that she just couldn't remember—but I sure as hell could!! It isn't easy at all, and I recommend that husbands be present for most, if not all, the procedure.)

Our wonderful baby girl arrived about 8 AM, on the 10th of September—our first wedding anniversary. She had ten fingers, ten toes, and the doctor said mother and daughter were just fine. I thought it wonderful to be the father of a baby girl, but the most fantastic thrill was to be the father of *Dawn Farrar's* child. A great honor—believe me! Dawn's mother came for a few days to lend a hand, and later my mother did likewise. We named the baby Nicole and, like all fathers (I suppose), I thought she was really extra special. Unfortunately, she bore some resemblance to me but I told Dawn not to worry or be discouraged as I was sure she would grow out of it. (And she did, thanks be!)

Preparing for combat

At Glasgow, I knew our next assignment would be combat. I took my job very seriously. Days, even hours, were precious to complete the best training possible. The crews were worked hard and often very long hours. On day my squadron surgeon reminded me that all personnel had to have a final round of required vaccinations and *when* did I plan to run the combat crews through his dispensary? I told him I did not plan to the combat crews through his dispensary at all (as would be the ground personnel). Instead, his dispensary medical staff would be at the operation office on the flight line as each flight crew landed. He would have between five and ten minutes per crew for the inoculations before the crews proceeded on to ground school. He protested because his medical detachment would have to go without sleep, or change to a three shift per day basis, to meet the planes. I told him my decision was final but I was certain he could handle it! And he did! But I'm sure his professional ego was disturbed by my imperious decision—and, remember, I had no graduate school degrees, let alone ever having attended medical school!

On another occasion, I decided to practice the coordination of the ambulance crews and the landing of aircraft with simulated combat wounded aboard. This required the copilot of an aircraft with wounded aboard to fire a red flare as he approached the field. The control tower would give the aircraft as much precedence as possible in the landing sequence, and the ambulance (with doctor aboard) would race down the runway, pell-mell, to meet the aircraft as it came to a stop. Inasmuch as a landing B-17 is still traveling about 95 miles per hours, the medical crew on the ambulance are going to get one hell of a ride! (If possible, we sometimes positioned ambulances at the end of the runway in use, but this was not always feasible.)

On the first simulated wounded aircrew interception, my flight surgeon elected to ride on the running board of the ambulance. In my jeep, I arrived at least at least two minutes before the ambulance arrived. I told him he would have to do better—much better! He turned white as a sheet, and mumbled something like, "My God, I could get *killed!*" "That's right," I told him, "not just the air crews were expendable—*we all are expendable, even doctors!*"

This young doctor was about 37-38 years old, about 10 years my senior. I knew he had just recently been married, for the first time, and was having some adjustment problems. He was kind of a likeable guy—from Brooklyn, I believe—with a great sense of humor. Or so I thought. Anyway, within a few days of the last ambulance incident, two medical officers came from Great Falls and took him away for medical treatment. He had suffered some sort of breakdown. Perhaps all he needed was rest. Or perhaps a tough commanding officer, plus a new bride, was too much to cope with simultaneously. I only hope I did not add unreasonable burdens to his problems! Captain Hardesty became his replacement and went to England with us, and did a great job.

We continued flying training missions as individual aircraft, formations of aircraft as a squadron, and several missions as a group, collecting all four squadrons at rendezvous points and proceeding on simulated bombing missions.

The time for overseas assignment was getting near. We knew orders would come through most any day. Major Barrs and I thought a parade for the people of Glasgow and the morale of the men might be good. So, on October 12th, we marched from the Air Base (near town in those days), through the main streets of Glasgow, with the high school band providing the music. Then, for humor, we "decorated" each man with a fake service ribbon as a survivor of the Battle of Glasgow.

A few days later the ground echelon boarded a troop train and headed east. Eventually they would cross the Atlantic, safely, on the Queen Mary. Then our air echelon boarded our aircraft and joined the other squadron air echelons in Great Falls before proceeding to Scott Field (St. Louis, Missouri).

At Scott Field each crewmember's qualifications were rechecked. (Example: the pilots had to re-pass their instrument flight exams, etc.) There were repeated inspections on all matters, both administrative and flight. We were there for several very busy days. One day before leaving Scott Field, I as walking toward the Officers' Mess when a staff car pulled over to the curb and the driver called me to the car. Inside was Caleb V. Haynes, whom I had last seen in India a year and a half before. He was now wearing the two stars of a Major General.

With him was his aide, Lt. Col. Neil Van Sickle, whom I had known at Manchester AFB before leaving for Africa and PAA Africa. We chatted for a few minutes, and then Gen. Haynes asked why I was not wearing the Silver Star ribbon on my tunic. Of course, I told him I had never received any such decoration. He told me the orders had been published back in India long ago. He also told me to get in touch with his Aide, Lt. Col. Van Sickle, who would solve the problem. In the remaining day or two at Scott Field, I made repeated efforts to locate Co. Van Sickle but none were successful, so I proceeded on to England.

(It appears the General was in error. A 1987 requested search of 10th Air Force General Orders failed to verify the existence of such orders. The only citations to be received were to be later, in England, and would consist of the Bronze Star Medal with "V", Purple Heart and Air Medal. Until January 1994, when Leo Viens and I were awarded the DFC in recognition of our overloaded mercy flights in Burma—52 years before)!

To war

Before the end of November, all was in readiness and our planes took off for England, individually, and by different routes—the route being determined by the weather on the day (or night) of takeoff.

Some flew to Gander Army Air Base in Newfoundland and on to Prestwick, Scotland. Others, including myself, flew by way of Goose Bay (Labrador), then to Meeks Field (Iceland) and on to Prestwick. Col. Bowman assigned me the job of making certain all planes and personnel preceded me to England. I, as the "follow-up" man to handle any problems with planes or personnel.

In those days early winter North Atlantic flights were not exactly a routine matter—but would soon be. Remember, most of the pilots had only a few hundred hours of experience. However, all the 401st crews arrived safely in Scotland and proceeded to our proper English bases.

The 401st Bomb Group took over Station 128 at Deenethorpe (in the Midlands, about 80 miles north of London). Before we got into combat operations, eight of the seventeen 614th combat crews were transferred to the 351st Bomb Group at Polebrook, a few miles away. These were the crews of Clay, Meyers, Logan, Bartzocas, McLawhorn, Lewis, Cavanaugh, and Newburg. The nine crews remaining were those of Peck, Chapman, Stimson, Holland, Camack, Kirkhuff, Kaufman, Wilson, and Dawes.

The 401st flew its first combat mission on November 26, 1943, to Breman, Germany. The early winter weather was not too cooperative. If flyable in England, our targets over the continent were usually obscured, and vice versa. Often our assemblies were through 10,000 to 20,000 feet of solid overcast. For the benefit of the non-flying reader, perhaps I should explain a little.

Picture England as a rectangular polka dot map. Each dot is an English Fighter Base or an English Bomber Base, each *closely* adjacent to the other. And each base has dozens and dozens of aircraft to assemble on top of a dense layer of cloud cover. While within this cloud layer, each pilot flies on instruments only, keeping his assigned compass heading and keeping his assigned rate-of-climb. He also prays that each and every of the other hundreds (or thousands) of pilots do likewise.

The clouds are full of aircraft headed in many different directions, at all altitudes, and *none can see the other*. Eventually, they break out on top of the overcast and the individual planes assemble into their proper unit formations.

Many pilots thought an assembly through heavy overcast was as hazardous as the enemy who waited for us over the continent. While on the ground, I personally observed the collision of two B-17s on such an assembly. The pale white faces of the dead crewmen will live with me forever.

December 31, 1943—March, 1944

The final mission, the last day of the year.

It was the morning of December 31, 1943. We were aroused from our cots about 3 AM. We dressed and shaved hurriedly, had breakfast in the mess hall and arrived at the briefing room.

My job was as Commanding Officer of the 614th Bombardment Squadron, which was one of four squadrons comprising the 401st Bomb Group. We were equipped with the latest of the B-17 aircraft, known as the "G" model.

On this particular day, Capt. James Foster (who had grown up in Mullan, Idaho) was to lead my squadron and I was to remain at Base. The rule at the time was that commanders and certain air-staff officers were only to fly with their units on approximately one out of five missions. This was not a popular rule because most were anxious to fly as often as possible so that they could complete their assigned 25 combat missions rapidly—and either secure reassignment in the States or accept a brief statewide leave of absence and a return assignment for an additional 25 missions.

The knowledge that if we succeeded in completing 25 missions we could go home was a great morale builder. We also knew, on the other hand that the average crew survival rate was only 10 or 12 missions before being shot down. In spite of this, a few who completed their full 25 missions actually volunteered for 30 days leave in the States and a return to England for an additional 25 missions! Incredible! The rule of one out of five was predicated on the heavy combat losses of the more experienced commanders in the summer and spring preceding.

The name of the game was to fly often and get back home soon. My feelings were no different than the others.

Before the briefing took place, I spotted Col. Harold Bowman, the Group Commander, and presented a verbal request that I be permitted to fly with a newly assigned crew to give them their first mission "check-off." This would also permit Capt. Foster to gain experience in the squadron "lead" position.
Col. Bowman finally assented, in spite of the general one out of five rule. (I must have been quite persuasive, if I do say so myself.)

The mission for the day would be to bomb the airfield at Bordeaux, France. An alternate target would be the airfield at Cognac. The route to target would take us over the sea to the west of the French coast (Brittany peninsula), continue south at sea, thence east to enter France proper, south of Bordeaux (somewhere near Arcachon), and strike the Bordeaux target on a northerly heading.

Of the several newly arrived crews available, one was the crew of 2nd LT. Homer McDanal. Accordingly, his copilot was informed he could not fly because I would replace him. Thus, I flew as McDanal's copilot, and from this position would also observe Foster in the lead position and the general squadron formation.

The Plane and the crew

B-17 #42-37770. Nick name: FLAK RAT

Pilot, LT	H. E. McDanal	Evaded
Co-pilot, Major	I. W. Eveland	Evaded
Navigator, LT	L. H. Sprinkler	POW
Bombardier, LT	D.H. Goetsch	Evaded
Radio Operator S/Sgt.	J. L. Kirkner	Evaded
Engr./Top Turret S/Sgt.	D. L. Jerue	KIA
Ball Turret S/Sgt.	H. J. Reasoner	POW
Tail Gunner Gun. Sgt.	M. Arinsberg	POW
Left Waist Gunner Sgt.	F. G. Kelly	POW
Right Waist Gunner Sgt.	H. W. Sanders	KIA

Nothing went as planned. We took the number four slot in the low echelon, better known as "Tail-Ass-Charlie" position. The assembly was a little sloppy on our part because of a deficient supercharger, but after some time it seemed to behave better and we proceeded out to sea in formation. Later, when it seemed too late to abort, the supercharger again gave us difficulty, and again it was virtually impossible to hold tight formation.

Shot down

Soon after we made landfall near Arcachon we experienced light flak and further damage in one engine. By this time, we were under attack by German fighters. Since we were now a "cripple" and could not hold tight formation, we were singled out for special attention and we were "worked over" thoroughly from the front and rear. Our 50-calibers made quite a chatter as they responded to each attack. We could also feel the 20-miillimeteres as they hit—and something went through the cockpit above the din. Our gunners were busy—but not for long.

Suddenly the steering column leaped back in our laps and the aircraft's nose went up. McDanal and I together managed to get enough downward pressure to bring the nose down. But there was now no doubt about it—something was wrong—our flight controls did not function. We were out of control!

There was only one thing to do, so I gave the "Bail-Out" order on the intercom. Simultaneously, McDanal hit the bailout switch on the panel in front of him. This rang a "bail-out" bell at each crew position. We received intercom acknowledgement from the nose, but not from the rear gunners. Later, I realized the intercom was out completely at all stations, including pilot to copilot. And the aircraft was alternately heading nose up and nose down, in spite of all we could do. The fighters continued to attack.

I had a hard time getting McDanal to bail out. He seemed to delay too long (in his efforts to assist me with the controls) and I was mad! With no intercom he could not understand. Finally, he disengaged his seat belt, oxygen, etc., and headed to the compartment below where he would go out the bottom hatch.

I had great difficulty disengaging radio set, oxygen, seat belt, etc., because each time I took a hand from the steering column the nose of the plane would tend to climb for the blue sky *up* position! I feared a fatal spin! After what seemed a lifetime (and what almost was), I also made it out the bottom hatch. The plane was then almost inverted and it required all the strength I had to pull myself up through the hatch and free of the aircraft.

The parachute that I was wearing was the backpack type. The pilot chute, which pulls out of the main chute, was located slightly lower than between the shoulder blades. I wondered if the pilot chute would pull out the main chute when I decided to pull the ripcord. I kept thinking that if it malfunctioned I would need time to reach back and pull the pilot chute out with my fingers. I decided I should not wait until the last minute. I pulled the ripcord, The chute worked beautifully—in fact it worked with a "thud" and I found myself gently floating toward the earth. What a beautiful feeling!

Now I had a new problem. One of the German fighters in the vicinity spotted my chute. He circled and came at me head on. From my view it seemed he had turned on some flashing Christmas tree lights. There was no noise from the guns, but I knew what he was doing—he was shooting at me. I started pulling the chute shrouds in hopes I could slip. I made a terribly fervent but profane prayer,

"Dear God, don't let that son-of-a-bitch kill me!" The Lord must have been listening because after several passes at me the fighter left and I continue my swinging fall toward earth.

The landing

Now I had time to look at the ground. I was over a wooded area with large evergreens. The trees seemed to be closely spaced. As I landed, the tree branches lifted one corner of my chute, emptying the canopy of air and dropping me many feet to the ground. When I ht the ground it was a shattering thud. I remembered the Intelligence briefings regarding parachuting into enemy territory: "Hide the chute and get away from the place of impact, because doubtless the enemy in the vicinity would spot the place of ground contact, which would assist them in their capture."

My mind locked in on "get away from the spot." I ran—and found myself thudded back to the ground again. I got up, tried once more, and again I was jerked back to the ground. Each time I tried to run I would come to the end of my shrouds and of course they would yank me back onto my fanny. I finally sat down, cleared my head a little bit from my hard landing, and realized that I should disengage myself from my parachute harness. I did, and then started to hide the parachute when I heard shouting and dogs barking. There must be dogs and Germans approaching me.

I quit trying to hide the parachute. Every instinct told me to head south, which was the course for Spain. However, I decided it would be much safer to run north. The shouting and the barking continued. I spotted a small stream. I ran northward in that stream in the event the dogs had been brought to track me. The stream petered out very soon but the noise was not quite as close.

I was out of breath and I decided I must rest. I picked a bramble bush that was very thick and very thorny. I crawled into the center of it in the hope that no searching soldier would discover me. I lay there scarcely breathing. There were soldiers who came near, but none entered my thorny sanctuary. Apparently there were no dogs with them. I waiting for several hours and proceeded north again for about a mile. I then found cover again and waited until dark before heading eastward and then south to begin the long walk to Spain.

In taking stock of myself, I still had my bad cold; I also was in a certain state of shock from the parachute incident and the realization that I was behind enemy lines. Further, I had a flesh wound on one hand and one ankle from bits of shrapnel that had gone through the cockpit.

The escape procedures that I had listened to in Intelligence briefings all stated that an escapee should travel to the nearest neutral country. That meant Spain for me. They further stated the best procedure was to travel at night, avoiding contacts with other people, staying in the woods, and so forth. We were all provided with an "escape kit" consisting of maps, compass, currency, and halizone tablets for purifying water.

I tried walking at night but it was cloud-covered and black as the inside of a coal bin. I had a compass (with a luminous dial) about the size of a button, from which I could pick up the heading of south. I followed all roads or paths in that general direction. However, I kept running into trees and bushes, falling off the path, or rolling down the grade. The squadron intelligence officer's procedure on this point was yielding mighty few kilometers southward and many, many bruises. Further, many farm houses seemed to have dogs.

My crashing around in the blackness alerted the dogs and set up a considerable din. This caused me a great deal of anxiety. I clearly remember cussing the intelligence officer, who was my friend, Gordon Clausway. I wished that the smart bastard was with me to take over on procedure! I decided that so long as the nights were overcast I had best change the procedure to day travel, sticking as close as I could to the woods, hedgerows, and places of cover, but always with a southern objective.

Cover was not always available, of course, and this brought up the question of whether or not to remain in my flight uniform or attempt to secure civilian clothing so that perhaps I could walk more freely on roads. That option, I knew, had certain inherent risks because, according to the Rules of Warfare, if captured out of uniform behind enemy lines I could be shot as a spy. In truth I knew that the Germans seldom did this, but it was my understanding that they did have the legalistic justification for it. Even so, I decided that at the first opportunity I would attempt to steal civilian clothing.

My other problems were shelter, food, and water. It was now January and the nights were cold; also, there was a light rain. I was unable to keep warm. I cut some pine branches, put about three layers under me and another layer or two over me, but even so it was a miserable night. In the morning, the little puddles had a thin film of ice on them.

I was terribly thirsty and had a very high fever. In my escape kit, I had started out with some Halizone tablets to purify bad water. The directions on the box said to put two tablets in a pint of water and wait 20 minutes before drinking. I opened the packet and discovered the tablets were no longer tablets at all, but now were merely pulverized powder. I also found an old bottle along the pathway and eventually I found a little stream. I filled the bottle and put into it what I estimated to be two tablets of powder. After drinking the water I was vomiting and suffering diarrhea.

Meeting the French

After several days of no food, high fever, and fatigue, I realized I had to do something. I had spotted a peasant's home and I watched from the shrubbery for several hours, trying to be certain that no men were present. Finally, I approached the house and knocked. The housewife came to the door. She was wide-eyed because my clothing was not recognizable, and worse when she found I could not speak French.

She did understand my pantomime of airplane and parachute. At this point her eyes got very wide indeed and she slammed the door in my face! This happened several times in later efforts to get food and drink. (I learned later that the Gestapo had previously gone through this part of the countryside impersonating American airmen who were shot down. Those who had befriended them were in serious trouble indeed. In fact, I was told some had been executed.)

Eventually I remembered two key words of French. They were the words for German soldier—"Alleman Soldat." On one or two later attempts to secure food and drink at farmhouses, I had better results. When the farm wife would come to the door and shoot a torrent of French questions at me, I would merely shrug my shoulders and explain all with the key words. "Alleman Soldat."

This had a less terrifying effect. Then I would pantomime eating and drinking. My questions were brief and forceful, as if I expected her to bring something at once! It worked, at least for wine, if not for food! And the wine had its usual effect, not only to slake my thirst but also to enhance my sense of well being and general confidence for the moment. Often I became somewhat intoxicated.

Once a lady brought me some wine and also a small jar of lard that contained a few small pieces of pork. I put the jar in my pocket but drank the wine. Then I gave her the truth—my pantomime of airplane and parachute routine. I also indicated I needed different clothing. She then brought me a beret and an overcoat. I left my flying suit and sheep-lined boots with her, pantomiming with all the effort I could muster that she must burn them. I retained my gabardine trousers and shirt, which were partially hid by the overcoat, and also my British shoes. The beret and overcoat were quite disreputable and matched my unkept beard.

The German soldier

I remember my first close encounter with a uniformed German soldier.

A small river, or canal, stopped my southern progress because it ran east and west. A path turned east along the northern bank and I followed it. It was nightfall. The path joined a road, headed south over a bridge. The bridge was arched, high in the center, as if designed for small boats to go under it. A dense fog had descended. As I walked up the slope to the center of the bridge and started to descend the other side of the bridge, in the fog, I realized that at the bottom of the bridge slope was an indistinct figure, but that figure was a German Soldier!

He was only 20 feet away, maybe less, but his back was toward me. His rifle was at his side, slung over his shoulder. I was startled! I thought he must be stationed there to monitor traffic over the bridge. I stopped—and walked backwards and upwards to the center of the bridge—and then turned and hurried into the fog, turning east along the north bank of the canal. Apparently the soldier never knew of my presence, but I was not certain. Thanks be for the fog!

There were residences along the north shore of the stream. I had trouble avoiding them but eventually I found a tiny rowboat at a dock. I stole it, and crossed the stream about ¼ mile eastward. I realized that I should knock a hole in the boat and sink it so that no one could pick up my trail on the southern bank. But the French boat owner had helped me (unknowingly) and I hated to destroy his property. Finally, I tried to hide it with branches, etc., instead of destroying it! So I continued trying to make my way southward.

Rescued

My fever progressed and fatigue likewise. Some days later, I recall vaguely several incidents where I was surprised to find myself lying on the ground and the sun had moved. I knew then I was probably having short intervals of unconsciousness.

Eventually a French peasant found me asleep in his field. He brought me to his home and put me to bed and I slept for 24 hours. This was the first of many hospitable shelters I would receive. This particular peasant had a son, probably 18-20 years of age, and he traded a pair of oxfords with me for my British army shoes. This particular peasant not only gave me rest and nourishment—he also gave me key information that proved the turning point for receiving help thereafter.

I had inquired of him as to the name of any local Frenchman nearby who might be able to give me assistance, especially someone who could speak English. All of this was done with his understanding no English and me understanding no French. Thanks to gestures and patience, he told me there was a French Count in a nearby village that he referred to as "Monsieur DeLaron." He gave me an idea as to the location of this man's residence and his appearance, age, and general physical characteristics.

As I recall, the village was five to ten kilometers away. It was named Benquet. As I entered the village I found the streets practically deserted. As I watched from a doorway I saw a man crossing the street closely resembling the description of Monsieur DeLaron. I overtook him until I was two or three paces behind him and I studied him closely. He seemed to meet the description very well. I then called him by name. He stopped dead in his tracks. In English, I told him who I was. He told me he could not be seen talking to me and to please follow him at the distance of about half a block. I did so and he led me to his home. On arrival there, he arranged for a bath for me and gave me the best hot soup I have ever tasted. It was cabbage soup, which I have always detested, but then I really enjoyed it!

I met his wife and his mother, and I learned that their home was under surveillance by the Germans. In fact, a brother had already been apprehended by the Germans; they had not heard from him in some time, and they were greatly concerned with is whereabouts and safety. Needless to say, my presence in their home represented a great hazard.

Nevertheless, Monsieur DeLaron made arrangements for me to stay in a room up above the barn and also made arrangements for a servant to come twice a day with something to eat and drink. A signal was arranged for the servant as he went up the stairway so that I would know it was a friend that approached. (He was to go up two or three steps, then knock or kick the sidewall.) If the proper signal were not given, I could then anticipate trouble.

On one occasion the servant forgot to give the signal. When he opened the door of my room, I came very close to bashing his head in. I had a chair in my hand, and I stood behind the door as he opened it. I recognized him just barely in time. I stayed in the barn possibly three days, my only companion being a mouse which roamed my room and which I remember fondly.

New hiding place

My host finally arranged a new hiding place for me some miles away. He drove his little French automobile into the barn and had me lie down behind the driver's seat. He covered me over with a blanket and delivered me to Pierre Lemee, who was then the mayor of the town of Bretagne De Marsan. Pierre Lemee's home was in the country some distance from the town.

Apparently Mr. Lemee was a farmer and as such he had a few hired hands. One proved to be a man who had escaped out of Algeria and was hiding there. Another was a young lady about 18 years of age whose home was in either Alsace or Lorraine. Now I was hiding there, too. Possibly there were others.

Pierre was delighted to play host to an American Major. He was very exuberant. He asked all kinds of questions that I was unable to answer because of the language barrier. The first evening there, he arranged a party in my honor. He killed a fatted goose from the barnyard and invited, among others, a doctor to treat my hand and feet, and a French nurse who spoke English. The party was very festive, with lots of wine and Cognac.

I was greatly concerned for fear the presence of so many people might provide a leak as to my presence in the house, with resultant damage, not only to me, but also to this marvelous host and his friends. (Apparently my fears were not unfounded because after the war, Pierre reported that soon after I had left his home the Germans arrived in force and molested his family. He fled and spent the rest of the war with the Maquis. The Germans did apprehend the doctor. He did not respond to their interrogation. They shot him and continued the interrogation for several days, during his suffering, before they finally killed him.)

Moving again

After several days of recuperation in Pierre's house, where I had good food, a clean bed, a good companionship, he arranged for the next leg of my journey. Travel, of course, was very hazardous, so considerable planning took place in Pierre's home. Somehow, Pierre got me from his home to Mont de Marsan and to my new host, named Dupeyron. I do not recall whether by train, by foot, or by auto.

Monsieur Dupeyron was an auto mechanic and operated his own garage. His living quarters were over the garage. He and his wife received me warmly and then looked after me for some days. They had a daughter who was of high school age and she studied English, but being extremely shy, was most reluctant to try to talk to me. It seems to me there was a son, also. As always, we had a language barrier.

However, I recall one time they told me that Madame Dupeyron also flew airplanes. As I understood it, she had participated in a race from Paris to Baghdad during the depression years of the 1930s. It so happens I remember this race. The lady entrant, a French lady, was lost in the desert for several days and this fact hit the headlines of the United States' newspapers. Being a budding aviation enthusiast at the time, I recalled there was such an incident.

It seems that my hostess, Madame Dupeyron, was this same French aviatrix. As a school lad I always visualized this lady to be a French socialite who flew airplanes for the adventure and thrill of it. Instead, I now found that Madame Dupeyron was no socialite whatsoever, and further, that the airplane that she had flown on this race had been one built by her auto mechanic husband.

The garage of my host had been taken over by the Germans and his primary duty was to repair German vehicles. Consequently, there were many officers and drivers popping up at all times of the day and evening, both in the garage below and also at the kitchen door, which was at the head of the stairs leading from the garage below.

My host seemed to dearly love aiding an American officer within his home and shielding him from the Germans. Often the Germans would bring him some beer, cigarettes, or cigars as tokens of their friendship. He would share the loot with me and laugh heartily, gesturing. "I am like an Arab. I shake their hand and stab them in the back while doing so," he would say.

Each time steps were heard on the staircase leading to the little apartment, I hurried off to the side bedroom, which was over a pub. When the visitor would leave, I could then return to the kitchen or living room to visit with my hosts. The room over the pub proved to be interesting, but nerve-racking. Many German soldiers patronized the pub.

In the evening there would be laughter and the usual barroom activities, but I was listening mostly to the German language. The floor was made of simple boards, and I did not turn on the light at any time because of this. At times I could see movement below and hear the German soldiers underneath me. They were much too near for comfort.

On another occasion, the French brought me information as to the exact location of the officer's barracks, the fuel dumps, and other pertinent data to the airbase at Mont de Marsan.

For example, one of the messages they wished me to carry back was to tell the British or the Yanks to bomb the hospital near the airbase because the Germans had long ago moved all patients out and were using the hospital as an officers' barracks.

In order to pass away the time, I spent hour after hour redrawing this map so that I could draw all runways, fuel dumps, barracks, shops, and so forth, by memory, with the proper distances and compass of free time and boredom while hiding out.

Trip to Bordeaux

It was in this place above the garage and in the near vicinity of the German soldiers that the Dupeyrons, in conjunction with Pierre Lemee, arranged the next leg of my journey—the train trip to Bordeaux.

Pierre Lemee got me a "Carte Identite" (identification card). On it was my name (false), occupation, signature, and description. Another card stated, in essence, that I was a German collaborator and gave other details of my occupation and job assignment, and included my fingerprints. Since I had not given them my fingerprints, I inquired as to whose fingerprints were used. I was informed that they were Pierre's. It seems that as Mayor of the village, he had access to police procedures and other information.

His plan was that they would deposit me in the railroad station with the proper identification so that I could ride a German troop train to the city of Bordeaux, where other hosts would receive me. Pierre was delighted with the theory of the escape plan because, as he reasoned, who would ever expect to find an American Major on a German troop train? It fascinated him—and it scared the hell out of me!

There were to be at least two railroad cars that would have German troops and at least one car that would have civilian passengers, all of whom were certified as "faithful Frenchmen working for the Germans." I was to be one of these and that is why the special card had been prepared for me. Needless to say, the detailing to me of this information required someone who spoke English, and though I cannot remember clearly, I believe it was the nurse, whose name was Miss Nicod. She also bandaged my hand and ankle. She had performed duty with French forces in Algeria, but had avoided capture there when the Germans took over that region and had returned to France.

Since it would be too hazardous for any Frenchman to sit with me on this journey, I was briefed as to precisely which railroad car I was to enter so as to avoid contact with the German soldiers.

I proceeded at the station as briefed and entered the proper car, showing my special card to the German soldier as I entered. I entered the car thinking, "All's well, so far." But later, German soldiers entered the same car. I had not counted on this. I hastily decided it was better for me to get off this car, past the guard, and get on the car behind.

As I got off the car, the German guard said something to me. I don't remember whether he spoke to me in German or French. I ran into the crowd on the platform, being very fortunate that a throng was there. As I am short in stature, I also pulled off my French tam and managed to wriggle out of my tattered overcoat and put it over my arm. It seems that the first guard who yelled as I ran away had excited the guards on the following car, but I was able to get on the second car with no problem.

The train departure, however, seemed to be delayed by some excitement amongst the throng of people on the platform. It was obvious the Germans were looking for someone. Conceitedly, I thought I knew who they were looking for! Perhaps only minutes later, but it seemed much longer, the train moved out. Each moment I expected Germans to enter the car, reviewing the special passes and interrogating all aboard. Fortunately, this did not happen. We arrived at the next railroad station with no further incidents and with no damage except to my frayed nerves.

Gustave, my new host

My recollection of arrival at the station in Bordeaux is hazy. I do remember that I met someone; I remember following him through concourses of people and light motor traffic. I presume that Gustave Souillac, who became my host in Bordeaux, met me there. He and his wife lived at 54 Avenue Hugo, LeBouscat, Bordeaux.

He, and his wife, and their family were charming people. They had two children—the boy, Christian, and daughter (cannot remember her name). Mrs. Souillac's mother, who had been raised in Peru, was also a member of the household. They had a housekeeper-maid by the name of Maria, and her husband served as the gardener, chauffeur, and handyman. The Souillacs were dedicated French patriots.

Gustave and his brother owned a shoe factory near his residence. The Germans had taken over the factory and were producing items for the German Army. The Souillacs were permitted limited production of shoes, but having no leather, they were constructed of wood, with grooves in the soles to give a little bit of flexibility.

A German officer supervised activity within the factory every day. Gustave and the officer had desks facing one another, as Gustave described it to me.

Formerly, Gustave and his family had resided in a large mansion in Bordeaux. Gustave was active in an intelligence unit of the French underground (Maquis) and for this reason did not wish to have any German officers billeted to him.

Therefore, Gustave had elected to take over this very small home and his brother had taken over the large home.

On the other hand, Gustave's brother was a collaborator with the Germans. The brother and his wife believed that the Germans were in France permanently and the best adjustment was to get along with them. Gustave and his brother disagreed on this point.

As time passed, I became very nervous about my presence in Gustave's household. The Gestapo headquarters were close by in the neighborhood. At times we heard gunfire nearby, which Gustave would say was "target practice." (But his gestures were sinister.) Gustave and his family spoke Spanish as well as French, but did not speak English. We carried on a bit of conversation using gestures and bits of the three languages.

While in Bordeaux, I rode a streetcar several times. There had been a meeting, with cognac, and farewells with more cognac. The combination was in sufficient quantity to cloud my judgment and over stimulate my courage. The streetcar was extremely crowded and I was on the rear platform, crowded elbow-to-elbow with other standing riders. The rider on my right elbow happened to be about 6'2" and was a very young, handsome German officer dressed in his snappy uniform, including a great coat. He was really a fine sight to behold.

Contrary wise, I had a dingy, dirty tam on my head and most dingy, ragged old overcoat, probably a day or two of beard, but in any sense, I must have looked like a rag-picker. The ride was rough and every time the trolley bumped, I would jostle into this officer. Each time we stopped or started there was a similar automatic jostling. It startled me a little bit, and I tried to avoid any physical contact with the German officer.

Then all of a sudden my mood changed completely. The cognac had taken its effect! I thought it was very funny indeed—and I gave him several intentional bumps, coordinated with the antics of the trolley! It was shameful lack of judgment but the situation amused me tremendously and gave me great satisfaction.

Gustave had several interesting visitors, one of whom we called "the young man." This man's job in the Underground was to set up radio communication in Paris for several days, communicating with London and then setting up communication again with London from Bordeaux for a few days. There was also a third point of communication. Though this young man didn't speak English, we did manage to communicate. One time he showed me an American hand grenade and some other explosives, thinking I would know how these explosives should be used. Unfortunately, my knowledge was most limited.

One time the "young man" arrived at Gustave's home rather breathless, with his suitcase in hand. The suitcase contained his radio equipment. It seems that on his trip from Paris the train was stopped mid-point between towns. He suspected something amiss and as the train slowed down he was able to jump off.

The Germans had received information that there might be a wireless operator or underground member aboard the train and they interrogated every passenger. But our "young man" was no longer aboard. On arrival at Gustave's home he was exuberant over his escape triumph.

Another visitor was known as "Le Bard," which I think means the beard. This full-bearded man headed a resistance group someplace in the south of France and he came to the house once or twice working on plans to get me safely out of Bordeaux.

Another visitor that I enjoyed very much was a Catholic priest who came to see me several times and each time he brought me a gift. Usually, believe it or not, it was a pack of Lucky Strike cigarettes or a bottle of wine, and once a bottle of Irish whiskey. The priest spoke English and sometimes brought me something English to read. I looked forward to his visits.

Gustave knew I was very lonesome due to the language barrier and my confinement within the house. He deplored the fact that there was so little opportunity for me to visit with anyone who spoke my own language. His collaborator brother had an English-speaking wife. She had been married to an American Colonel during WWI and had been deserted by him. Gustave therefore invited her to dinner in spite of her and her husband's political views.

She spoke English very well indeed. She said Communists dominated all resistance movements in France. Having seen so many of those individual patriotic Frenchmen, I didn't like that Axiom. She also said much of the American bombing in France was terrorist bombing. She claimed there was a good deal of intentional bombing of non-industrial targets.

I put her straight, in as restrained a manner as I could, that when the industrial target within France was cloud-covered, the American planes flew their bombs back to England and landed with bombs aboard. We sure as hell did not take such precautions on bombing missions over Germany! In no way did we wish to harm the French people. I was greatly distressed that Gustave's well-meaning gesture had worked out so poorly.

After his sister-in-law's departure that evening, I worried considerably that I would bring about a rift between Gustave, the Patriot, and his brother, the Collaborator, and this all might tumble somehow into chaos for this family.

Gustave tried to console me. He explained that in spite of the bitterness of the war and the differences between family members, the family would protect one another. For this reason, the sister-in-law would not report me to the Germans nor say anything to cause trouble.

On another occasion, another of Gustave's brothers who lived near Mont Blanc came one evening. In this instance, I was guided to an open window where I could step outside into the courtyard without being seen. Gustave explained to me that it was best that this brother not know of my presence in his home.

I was at Gustave's home for about four weeks, I believe. The nights were cold and thin ice formed on the puddles.

Soon after my arrival Gustave told me about one of his employees who had to pass a railroad spur enroute to work each day. This railroad spur had several cattle cars lined up. They were filled with Jewish people. This employee gave Gustave periodic reports as the cars remained unmoved on the spur for several weeks. Obviously, there were no latrine provisions, he said, and the stench increased day by day. Gustave compared the smell with that of swine enroute to market. I had driven through Iowa on a hot summer day and I could clearly remember the acrid stench of pigs in a rail car. The image in my mind cannot be forgotten. The suffering of such inhumanity must be beyond description.

The escape

Daily I became more anxious to leave and requested that they give me wine and bread and let me proceed southward on my own before my presence caused disaster. Gustave would become furious, saying that under no circumstances would he let me leave until he had engineered a plan to get me over the Pyrenees into

Spain. Eventually a plan was developed, at least another phase in the plan was developed.

The idea was to wait until a friend had an opportunity to steal a wine truck from his employer. This would be done the first day the employer was not to be at work. Meanwhile, Gustave had heard through his underground intelligence group that there were a least three Americans in Bordeaux who were likewise awaiting a plan to get out of the city. The truck would answer the purpose for all four of us.

One morning before daylight the truck arrived in the back yard (February 10, 1944). We had been expecting it. My host embraced me with tears in his eyes, gave me a bottle of wine, and bid me adieu.

In France they deliver wine in trucks much similar to the trucks that carry gasoline to service stations in the U. S., except the wine trucks are smaller. In essence, they consist of a large steel horizontal cylinder, with an opening at the center top, and a hatch that bolts over the opening. The horizontal cylinder is divided into three compartments by means of vertical baffle palates. The baffles have a small opening at the bottom to let the wine run freely at the bottom only. If you were to open the center top hatch and peer down with a flashlight you would never believe that the opening at the bottom of each baffle plate was large enough for a man to crawl from the center compartment into either end compartment. But the opening was barely large enough for a man to crawl through on his stomach.

I was told there were two other men in the front compartment. I was to crawl into the rear compartment. There would be an American lieutenant in the darkness of that compartment. So there was. They bolted down the center top hatch and we left for the first German highway checkpoint.

At this point, as anticipated, the German guard climbed up on the wine truck, opened the hatch, peered down, saw the tank appeared empty, bolted the hatch back down, and took the driver into his post to fill out the necessary clearance papers. This was done at each sentry point. Between checkpoints the driver opened the top hatch to help refresh the air and then would close and lock the hatch before the next checkpoint.

At one particular sentry point the guard must have given the driver a bad time. Sitting there in the darkness of the rear compartment and suffering claustrophobia, it seemed that half a lifetime elapsed. Knowing the truck had been stolen did not add to our comfort. With the hatch battened down, the air within the tank was getting bad.

It seemed an eternity that we waited for the driver. All kinds of unpleasant thoughts went through my mind, such as suffocation. Or, as an alternative, we could holler or beat on the tank to attract attention, which could mean capture or probable death for the driver, and possible death or imprisonment for all of us also.

Eventually the driver returned and continued on. But in the intervening 45 to 60 minutes (or whatever) I probably aged at least ten years. Finally we reached the outskirts of the city of Perigueux.

The driver pulled up near some trees and bushes and told us to run to a nearby farmhouse, staying in the trees. This we did. Here we made our first contact with the actual Maquis. Up until now I'd been hosted by patriotic Frenchmen, who knew little about escape routes and procedures but only wished to help and shelter the likes of me. It had taken approximately six weeks to get this far.

Later the same day my three wine truck companions and I were in the city of Perigueux, making our way to a previously designated barroom. We entered the barroom individually. There were several people present in the bar and one, a lady, spoke to me in English. I pretended I did not understand, because I feared a trap. I tried to walk away from her but eventually she led me into a little room and laughed and said, "You are safe. You are safe."

It was in this little room off the barroom that I met the young Frenchman who the lady told me was the head of the local Maquis organization. He told me that he knew what to do with evading Americans because his group assisted with moving them to Spain. Glad tidings! I do not recall just how I separated from the other members of the wine truck, but either the same day or the following day I was in an automobile alone with this young Maquis leader and he gave me a most memorable ride.

He drove like a madman. I thought he was likely to draw unwanted attention to our vehicle. He raced down back roads to avoid sentry posts. I had the feeling he knew every foot of the way. He indicated to me that in front of me, in the glove compartment, was a loaded revolver. I was to familiarize myself with it by checking it over. I did. He indicated by gesture that if anyone attempted to stop us, he would slow the car down and I was to put the gun out of the window and shoot them, aiming at the forehead, while he did the driving. (I felt like Humphrey Bogart in an old movie!) Fortunately, this did not prove to be necessary.

Someplace I was reassembled with my three wine truck companions. I do not recall precisely where or how long I was with the Maquis leader. I do recall that he used me as a "show piece" article, probably to enhance his prestige within his organization.

I remember being in his company in various homes, apartments, and locations with various hosts at each. In good French fashion they always brought out the wine and cognac, or both, at introductions, during conversation, and at departing! I left each location a bit inebriated.

Eventually he informed me that he had made contact with another Maquis leader who would take us on the next leg of our journey and soon we would be over the mountains to Spain.

The rendezvous point selected to meet our new contact was in a cemetery near Perigueux. In the very early morning, just at dawn, we Americans and several Maquis walked singly and in two's among the graves. One of the Maquis indicated that I was to walk into a small mausoleum-type structure.

Inside the large entry a man who spoke the King's English greeted way me. This Englishman told us that as soon as he took our name, rank, and serial number he would see that the information was transmitted to London so that our families would know that we were not dead, but were proceeding on a successful escape route.

We were greatly elated! I understood very well the anxiety that my family was suffering until such a message could be received. I fully realized that a "Missing In Action" notice had been sent soon after I was shot down. (His message to London may have been sent, but it was not relayed to our families.)

The Englishman paired off Lt. Plytinsky and myself and told us what route to follow to exit from the cemetery and to follow a certain man. We were not to talk to him, merely follow him and enter the residence where he entered.

We found the man and followed him through several streets in Perigueux. When he entered a small residential building we followed him inside. Inside we were warmly greeted. We knew him as Renee Lamy, (I discovered after the war, that his real name was Claude Lamy.)

Renee had a terrific escape story. He had been captured as a French soldier in the early part of the war and sent to a German prison camp. From the prison, he was reassigned to a German farmer to assist with the farm work. He finally arranged a successful escape through Germany and into Switzerland where he almost died in a blizzard. He later made his way back to France and rejoined his family and became a policeman. Part of his duty as a policeman was to trace down American and British airmen who were trying to escape through the vicinity of Perigueux. Instead, he helped them escape. Prior to receiving us into his home, he had sheltered several British airmen.

He had a wife, Marie, and three children—Marilou, Annick and Claude. His only resource, financially, was his police salary. His quarters were very modest, consisting of a kitchen, living room, and one bedroom. I never did learn where they all slept, because Stanley Plytinsky and I were ordered into the only bedroom they possessed. There was no bathroom within the house, but an outhouse in the back yard. The food was meager and they shared with us in a most generous manner, always trying to get us to take the largest helpings so as to build up our strength for the trip over the Pyrenees Mountains that was yet to follow. Stanley and I ate lightly, saying our stomachs had "shrunk" and that we couldn't possibly eat any more. I do not recall how many days Stanley and I stayed with Renee and his family. The details of the departure are likewise unclear.

After the war I heard from Madame Lamy. After our departure they continued to harbor and assist escapees and evades. At one time, Renee knew of several people in the Paris vicinity who were awaiting an escape connection. He decided to take a train through Paris to collect these people and assist them. He was in the marshalling yard aboard a French passenger train when P-51's strafed the marshalling yards. An American fighter killed him! They were a heroic family.

Madame continued her work with the French underground throughout the balance of the war. I have been told that the Stars and Stripes, at the end of the war, published an article about this heroic couple and their contribution to the war effort. I do not know the date or the issue number of that publication.

As I moved from family to family, and place to place, I was requested to convey certain messages to London, if I should succeed in getting there. This brings up the matter of the map—which, if nothing else, proved my lack of knowledge of intelligence gathering. Several of my hosts put me in touch with individuals who were in close touch with various groups of French underground units. This was both before and after I arrived at Perigueaux.

Since I did not speak French I found it very difficult to remember the names and locations of these underground units. Three or four had fed me information as to their needs in hopes that I might succeed in my escape back to England so that I could convey specific messages for them to London. Several suggested suitable places for parachute drops and my job was to try and memorize these locations. Also, I had to memorize certain coordinated radio messages that would be broadcast from London radio to notify the French if I had arrived safely in England and delivered their messages.

These French people listened at certain hours of the day and night. As the messages grew in number, I became afraid of being confused. Therefore, I had one of the Frenchmen bring me a map and I very carefully took a pin and punched through the point on the map where the parachute drop was supposed to occur, or where the Maquis leadership was located, etc. It was my belief that should my memory "fuss up" I would be able to look at the map, hold it to the light, and at least find the pinpoints and then I'd be able to restudy and get the message straight—have it all come back to me clearly.

Toward the latter part of my escape route out of France and before arriving at the Pyrenees Mountains, I had an interesting visit to a Maquis encampment in the woods. I had been told to stay a considerable distance behind a Frenchman who walked ahead of me, taking various paths through this wooded area. I tried to stay as far back as possible without losing sight of him. Sometimes I did lose sight of him as the path curved here and there through trees and the bush. At one point this happened, but I was not greatly concerned because I knew I was among friendly people.

All of a sudden there was a rifle muzzle touching my stomach! Behind the rifle was a man in camouflage clothing! He had moved so quickly he had caught me by surprise. He looked very stern—and all business! For a moment I thought something had gone amiss. He motioned for me to walk ahead and fell in behind me. Now I had a guide in front and a guard behind.

I was quite amazed when I arrived at the camp. There were about 100 men going about various duties. I was led to a hut in a thicket where I met the Commander. Several others were present, each of whom knew a little English, and with their help the Commander and I were able to converse reasonably well.

He showed me most interesting things. In one area, under the trees, he showed me three German vehicles, including a truck. He explained that the Germans no longer sent troops, vehicles or supplies through this area unless they did so in battalion strength. The reason for this was because this Maquis unit would ambush them along the roads. If the Germans entered the area in strength, of course, the Maquis just let them pass through, or tried to pick off a straggler. He also explained that his Maquis unit controlled a rather wide area of the countryside. I no longer remember the size of the area but I was amazed to think that the Maquis in occupied France could be of sufficient strength to do this during WWII. (Again, my recollection could be in error.)

The Frenchmen in the unit did not wear uniforms as such. However, they proudly showed me that most of clothing that they had were dyed German uniforms. They laughed and bragged a bit and let me know how wonderful it was to kill the "Bosche" (as they called them) and at the same time get their side arms, rifles and also clothing. These items of clothing were then dyed and not easily recognizable as German uniforms.

The Maquis unit also liked to get the clothing from the young Frenchmen who had been drafted into work battalions at age 18 or 19. The Germans, of course, clothed them and directed them in roadwork and other assignments in various areas of France. The Maquis would find a group of eight or ten of these boys with one or two German guards whom they could quickly "dispatch." Then they would disrobe them on the spot and take their clothing back to their unit where it was quite badly needed. They knew that the Germans would have to give them (the boys) new clothing.

The Commander had a considerable list of needs that he wished for me to convey to London, should I be fortunate enough to get there. I memorized the items and the quantities that he was requesting. In addition, he had something of a formal inspection. He assembled the troops and, as a visiting Major, I went down the line inspecting their clothing, their shoes, equipment, guns, and, of course, relayed this information to London on my debriefing there. The Commander also gave me some parachute airdrop information as well as some radio codes to be broadcast if I succeeded in getting back to London. I presume this was all done after my debriefing.

I stayed with a couple of other families for short periods in the vicinity of Perigueaux. I believe it was from Perigueaux that I took the train to Carcasonne. The plan was for a small group of evadees, including Plytinsky and my self, to ride in a railroad coach and to watch a young couple and be sure that we got off the train when they did. The young couple either was in love or were good actors as they were most ardent in their attentions to one another. It was a long ride. We disembarked when the young couple disembarked at Carcasonne. It was midnight.

We met our appointed guides at the station and we started a long march into the countryside to an assembling point in the mountains, somewhere on the French side of the Pyrenees. It proved to be extremely difficult. We walked at least the first night and possibly a second. We arrived at what I believe had been a logging camp deep in the mountains. The Basque guides had trouble keeping our group of Americans, French and English on their feet due to our terrific exhaustion.

While recuperating at the camp, our French hosts continued their resistance projects. One of these involved the execution of a Frenchman who was collaborating with the Germans. For some reason they thought it important that I accompany the execution squad and personally report the affair to the Allies in England when I arrived there.

I was not at all anxious to participate, but if they thought it important, so be it. I was their guest and available. However, they changed their plans and deleted me from the execution group at the last minute because of my inability to understand the French language, and if any procedural changes were needed, none of the Maquis party could communicate these changes to me. I felt relieved.

However, before the departure of the execution squad, we went to a large farm barn where a barn dance was in progress with a fiddle or two and an accordion. At the end they played and sang the "Marseillaise" (French national anthem) that was strictly forbidden during the German occupation. It was a fantastically emotional experience! At the end there was not a dry eye present, including my own!

In the previous many weeks since being shot down, and especially while in Bordeaux and some of the other places where I had been in hiding, I had slept lightly—very lightly—in direct contrast to my normal youthful deep sleep. If a dog barked, perhaps even a city block or more away, I was immediately awake.

If an auto or truck passed the house at night, I heard it, and listened to determine if it stopped or passed on. Week by week my nerves became more frayed. (After the war I read an article written by a retired Scotland Yard Officer, who stated that after years of searching out and apprehending fugitives, he could watch the people—for example, at a railway station—and he could pick out the individuals who were fugitives. He could tell they were on the run, but of course he did not know why they were on the run. But he could detect the tension they carried on their faces and in their eyes—something special possessed only by people on the run! I believe him! Definitely!)

In my case my nerves became so taut that I could feel the eyes of individuals behind me while they studied me! It sounds ridiculous, I know. But on several occasions (twice on trains) it was proven true as far as I was concerned. I was developing a sixth sense, I'm sure.

Another personality change born of the stress of the situation was happening to me. Since I was frequently on the move, house-to-house and place-to-place. I developed a habit of noting all entrances and exits to each room I entered, as well as observing each and every window and how far it was to the ground below. This room inventory became instinctive. I always had ideas of how to exit—fast, if need be! Actually, as a civilian even 40 years later, I have caught myself relapsing into this previously automatic procedure. Today it is perhaps amusing, but in those days it certainly was not! I guess the psychologists call it ESP (Extra Sensory Perception.

Also, I had an obsession to communicate with my family, especially Dawn. I wanted so fervently to let them know I was not dead. And I wanted them to relax! It is not possible to clearly relate the power of this compelling thought. Many nights I spent alone would project the message to Dawn that I was still alive—our baby daughter had a living father!

Further, I wanted them to believe, as I did, that eventually the Good Lord would reunite us! Perhaps the reader of these notes may think it sounds as if I were coming apart mentally. Maybe yes—maybe no. But I think it interesting that as the crew KIA and POW notices arrived back in the States, and no change in my MIA status arrived, Dawn continued to hope, and believe, that I was alive. Some of the others counted the odds and reluctantly accepted them. Not Dawn. She did, however, have many nightmares. A recurrent theme of these nightmares was that

I was alive, but cold—freezing, in fact. From this she deducted that perhaps I was making my way through Switzerland and maybe somehow I would make it.

We stayed at the assembly point for some days, recuperating and waiting for a good full moon. While I was there one group started over the mountains but I did not accompany them because I had a bad leg muscle and realized that I could not make the trip. I left with the next group.

There were about 19 of us, possibly more, which included English, French, and Americans, at least one New Zealander and four or five Poles. We took off just before dark. We thought by nightfall of the next day we would be safe in Spain. Instead, it took us three days, probably the most perilous days of my life.

At this point I would like to digress somewhat and relate a story on the lighter side. It has something to do with the B-17, Col. Harold Bowman and also my own predicament while trying to escape from France.

As you know, the B-17 was designed for long missions and deep penetration of enemy territory. The designers did a great job. But the men who fly them are designed with certain limitations. Among these is the necessity to urinate at reasonable intervals. Also, the necessity for frequent urination increases as anxiety and fear increases!

The B-17 was designed with a "relief tube" located at each crew station. It consisted of a funnel attached to a rubber hose, which drained the contents outside the fuselage. Excellent at low altitude. But at high altitude where the B-17 missions were usually flown those temperatures were usually 30 to 50 degrees (F) below zero. Any fluid in the tube froze immediately and it became inoperable! The result was that many crewmen were hospitalized for frostbite, not only of the hands and feet, but other vital areas as well. Many crewmen used their "tin hats" as receptacles. It was definitely a problem.

Our Group Commander, Col. Hal Bowman is credited with the most popular solution. Why not issue every crewman on each mission six to ten rubber condoms to stuff in his pockets until the need for them arises? As he said "overzealous planners had supplied us with enough rubber condoms to last through World War Ten!"

So, Col. Bowman phones and got Major Julius Pickoff out of bed and appointed him "Group Pee Officer" and told him that before the next mornings bombing mission he wanted 2,000 condoms delivered! Bowman had trouble convincing Pickoff he was serious. Once that was done, Pickoff had to phone the Supply officer. The sleepy Supply Officer didn't believe it and just said "That dirty old man", hung up, and went back to sleep. Pickoff had to pull him out of bed to get the condoms to the flight crews by briefing time!

Incidentally, once a condom was used for relief it could be set on the floor and in minutes would be frozen solid and over Germany the crewmen sometimes threw them overboard as frozen "Bombs"!

While escaping from France, in addition to my other problems, I also worried about those dam condoms! You see I knew my belongings would be packed up by my adjutant and friend, Dick Mettlen, and be sent to the quartermasters warehouse for forwarding to Dawn as my next of kin.

I knew he would be careful to remove any condoms found in my pockets—because I was sure he would realize what a nasty shock such items would be to her! After all, she knew nothing at all about condoms being associated with bomber missions and could not be blamed for thinking otherwise. Also, there were ten of us on this one crew. That made Mettlen a busy man. And maybe there were other crews who failed to return from this mission. Maybe Mettlen had to delegate this duty—or maybe he was off duty, or in the infirmary—or whatever! Anyway, I did worry! Needlessly, I'm pleased to say.

Back to the escape....

One of the Englishmen had a pair of shoes that were much too large for him. He tried on my shoes and wanted to trade with me. I explained that large shoes, in freezing climates, were definitely preferable to tight shoes, or even properly fitted shoes. He continued to insist that I trade. Finally I did. His shoes were so large for me that I found some burlap and I wrapped strips of it loosely around my feet before putting on the shoes. In spite of this, I still suffered frostbite—but not as severely as the Englishman. I was told later that the Englishman eventually had to have his feet amputated. Had I refused to trade, it is most probable I would have lost my feet!

Toward evening we started south, headed over the remaining mountains to Spain. It began to snow and before long we were in the middle of a full-fledged blizzard. We had to cross small streams where the ice would not hold us, so we ended up with wet feet. The mountains ran mostly east and west, and our heading was south, crossing ridge after ridge. There were no paths or roadways, or if there were, we did not dare use them.

We would climb each steep and slippery slope, then make our way down the other side—only to find another mountain ahead of us.

Soon we were all exhausted. We took rest periods of up to five minutes each and found it difficult to keep one another awake. We knew if anyone slept it was not likely we could wake him and he would die. Practically all had some measure of frostbite but several became badly frozen. Our food ran out.

The blizzard continued. We carried one another as best we could. I clearly recall one of the few flat areas. It was covered with snow, two or three feet deep. "Thank God! This will be easier," I thought. But the snow was crusted over—but the crust was not strong enough to keep our feet from breaking through. As a result it was really tough trying to walk through drifts with the snow clear up to our hips. It was almost impossible to carry an exhausted or freezing companion due to the crust—but we found that in a prone position the crust would usually hold, so it was easier to drag a companion.

One of our evadees pleaded to be left to die. He had come to the end of the line. I was the senior officer of the escapee party. I told him no one had the right to die! We would all live and no one was permitted to quit! In fact, I "chewed him out!" So we continued to carry or drag him, and others. One man went delirious from exhaustion and snow blindness. As we descended to the bottom of each mountain we could look up and see another ahead. The Basque guides would say in Spanish and French and by gestures, "Only one more mountain to go! This is the last, then Espana!"

We knew they lied but it helped us to keep going! We passed a deserted cabin where one of the Basque guides, also badly frozen, and the snow blind and frozen American were left. Someone would return for them later.

At some point I pulled a muscle in my left upper leg. Each step was agony and I could not keep up. I fell behind. A guide came back to hurry me along. He put the muzzle of his rifle at the base of my skull and nudged me forward. I marched—pain or no pain! Near the end of the ordeal I lost consciousness and had to be carried. Thank Heaven the precedent had already been set! No one could be left to die. My companions got me across!

In Spain, in the village of Alp, we were quartered in a sheep barn and twice a day our Basque guides would bring us mashed potatoes, wine, and sometimes a piece of bread. Since the blizzard continued, we were most fortunate to have shelter, even if we shared it with the sheep. There was straw in the barn and we kept from freezing.

After many days of watching our comrades' feet and hands turn blacker, we finally persuaded our Basque guides to get some medical assistance. A doctor came once, but I cannot recall what he prescribed (several later required amputation of their feet).

The Basque guides insisted that no member of the group leave, because if one did and was captured, probably we all would be captured. The Basque guides risked prison. The reason the escapees did not want to be apprehended by the Spanish police was because Franco had a "neutral" nation—but it was "neutral" in favor of Hitler and Mussolini; consequently, escapees and evadees frequently ended up in Spanish jails and would stay there for the duration of the war. The Spanish jails were full of lice and maltreatment, or at least so we had been indoctrinated in England.

Anyway, to prevent escape, the Basques threatened to shoot anyone who attempted to leave. These guides had been armed with rifles and shotguns as they had guided us over the mountains and were still armed, although their arms were no longer as visible.

As mentioned before, I was the senior officer of the group. I was being badgered by my fellow evadees to plan and engineer an escape as gangrene had set in on some of our companions. But the Basques seemed to be our only available resource for medical attention and food until the blizzard abated. Also, the Basques deeply resented my refusal to sign a statement to the British consulate that, in effect, was a room and board charge. Or maybe the word for it should be ransom. To add emphasis to their arguments, they batted me about the head to let me know they were dead serious. That only served to raise my personal obstinacy.

They finally accepted my compromise. I would sign a statement to the effect that so many allied people had been kept so many days in the sheep barn and these Basques had been our guides in the walk over the Pyrenees. This seemed to solve the problem at the moment. I had, however, refused to sign for any dollar value for the escape and the so-called room and board. I felt that this was much better determined by the British representative at the consulate in Barcelona, whoever or wherever he might be.

As we continued living in the sheep barn, I was gravely concerned that my reliance on the Basques was not well founded. We therefore began to formulate an escape plan, which might get some of us through to the British Consul in Barcelona. Then the balance of our group who could not leave might be rescued.

Before we could complete the plan, however, we were notified one night that we would be moved to Puigcerda, a small town nearby where we would be met by a Spanish captain with a lorry. He would drive us to Barcelona where all of us, and especially the sick and frozen, would be placed in the hands of the British Consul.

I remember the walk to Puigcerda. I think it was not long, but considering the physical condition of the others, and myself it was almost like the Pyrenees again, only not quite as bad and definitely not as long. Those who could not walk we carried and as I recall, we had two donkeys to help. We met the Spanish captain who had the truck and a driver.

On the way to Barcelona we went through a couple of checkpoints. Having a Spanish captain in front with the driver kept the lorry from being searched. I don't know what the driver told the sentries or guard-posts, but he told them the right things because they did not come to the rear of the lorry to inspect the contraband. Eventually we were delivered inside a garage in Barcelona.

Although I spoke no French, as mentioned before, I did recall a small portion of my college Spanish. This served me well at the garage in Barcelona. I was talking with a Spaniard, owner or mechanic I do not know, but in conversing with him he asked me if I knew an American who had flown with the Loyalist forces during the Spanish War by the name of Baumer. It so happened that I did know this chap. He had been one of the flight instructors at Kelly Field when I was there and although he was not my instructor, I did know him and I remembered talking with him several times at Kelly. As it turns out, this American by the name of Baumer was a great hero in this region of Spain and the fact that I knew him personally was most impressive to the Spaniard.

The British Consulate

We now had one last important leg of our journey and that was to present ourselves at the British Consulate there in Barcelona where we understood they knew how to get us to Gibraltar and back to England. The contact, however, still had to be established.

I was to go to a certain building where the British consul was on one of the upper floors, now forgotten—say the fifth. I was told that there would be a guard at the ground floor where one entered the elevator. I was told to enter the elevator and tell the operator, "fifth floor." They corrected my Spanish so that it would sound right. They briefed me on what to do if the guard at the elevator spoke to me, but I cannot recall what my instructions were.

We walked in one by one to this building and made our way to the fifth floor. I do not recall how those unable to walk were provided for, but we were assured that they had separate plans to get them there. On getting off the elevator, I had been told to walk right into a waiting room and say nothing, which I did. After some waiting I was escorted into another room where a very nice looking young blond said, "You must be Major Eveland?" How pleasant it was to hear my native tongue and to be in such surroundings. She then told me that she had arranged for a bath, food, haircut and shave, new clothes, and some money and a good clean bed. She damn near got kissed!

She arranged all of these things for me. I learned that one of the new requirements would be that I must have police papers. Everyone in Spain carried an identification card, including a picture, and this was essential as you could not purchase food in a restaurant nor go into a hotel without such a card. All hotels or pensions had a concierge on duty day and night. The young lady and her assistant knew all the answers and how to do it.

Each man was sent to the police station with a fabricated story as to his identity. I presume that certain people within the police department must have been paid off in order to accept some of the ridiculous stories that were concocted and memorized by persons such as myself. The story given to me to relate was a wild one.

At the police station an underling interrogated me in broken English. I told him that I was 19 years of age, I had lived in France with the English father and my

French mother. My father returned to England. My mother had to hide me in the woods with French peasants. I had spent several years chopping wood. I lived with another English boy of like circumstance. The French peasants merely brought food into the woods where we retrieved it.

Thus, my English companion and I spoke only English and neither of us had had an opportunity to learn French. The subordinate officer refused to believe this story and he passed me on to the Captain. The Captain either was sincere or he had to go through a pretty good act to convince his staff that he was not being paid off. I do recall that when I made some of my absurd statements, he would shout, "I do not believe it" (in Spanish, of course). I would then say most humbly, and with my palms upright as a gesture of futility and frustration, "Es la Verdad, senor." Whereupon he would shout, scream, and pound the table, but eventually he gave me the papers.

If this man were on the payroll of the British or the Americans, I must say they hired an excellent actor. I hope his pay, if any, was considerable, because surely we were taxing his dramatic talents and the credibility of his staff. I hope Franco never hung him up by the thumbs.

Arrangements were made for me and others to be quartered at a small hotel or pension. It was complete with concierge, to whom one showed an identity card, coming and going. On one floor was a small restaurant. At some tables only German was spoken, and at other tables only French. Other tables mixed languages, not all of which I could identify.

At our table there was practically no speaking. We had been briefed to transfer food to our mouths, keeping the fork in our left hand at all times in the Continental manner. Also, of course, to say as little as possible to one another. Several times after the restaurant and bar had closed, the owner of the establishment came to my room and took me and one or two others down to the bar. He had been a supporter of the defeated government forces during the Revolution in Spain and his sentiments were definitely anti-Franco. It was his greatest hope that once the present war was completed in Europe that the Americans would help free his country from Franco. He spoke nearly all European languages.

To Madrid, Gibraltar, and finally back to England

In due time arrangements were completed for us to proceed to Madrid and to Gibraltar for the flight back to England. Prior to leaving on the Madrid leg I was quartered in a Spanish home with a Spanish family for two or three days. I remember it was the first time I ever saw the operation of a charcoal brazier, which is placed under the table and the tablecloth draped over the table, thus retaining some of the heat while you ate.

I had borrowed some consulate money through assistance of the blonde officer and, since I could not leave the house, I arranged for the maid of my hosts to purchase some chocolate for me. She was absolutely aghast that I would spend the great sum required on the black market. I had an insatiable desire for chocolate, which I had always liked—and almond nuts, which previously I had never cared for. (I suppose my system craved protein, fats, and sugar.)

Later I made the trip to Madrid by train and witnessed a bullfight there, at the conclusion of which we Yanks in the stands joined in the Falangist salute to Franco so as not to attract attention to ourselves (by not doing so).

Also by train we eventually arrived at Gibraltar. Even though dressed properly and having the luxury of good food and lodging for a short interval, we were a sorry, emaciated lot.

My nerves were as tight as a violin string. I was nicely greeted by the British. I recall seeing the British flag at Gibraltar. Other than Old Glory, I could not remember seeing anything quite so beautiful! To me it meant safety, dignity, decency, humanity and friends! Thank God!

From April, 1944 till the return to the States

England

After arriving in London, I was anxious to convey the messages I had collected in France. Intelligence officers, both British and American, were anxious to hear. I do not know what actions, if any, was taken as a result of my clumsy efforts.

Wayne Eveland, after his return to England, is pictured above.

For example, I mentioned that I had spent hours, even days, memorizing the data about the Mont-de-Marsan airfield. A British intelligence officer quizzed me about this and I drew my map for him, by memory, and once again I was very pleased with myself. However, the following day at interrogation he said, "It was most informative, Major. However, I checked it out and I'm afraid it shall be of very little value to us—inasmuch as we already had prior information—and we blew the place up many weeks ago!"

I do not know just which of my many radio messaged were beamed to France. One was to be very simple: "Too-Too learned English," if sent, would notify Gustave Soulliac and his friends in the Bordeau area that I had arrived back in England. Another radio message had several variations. If an air drop to one Maquis unit was approved, Radio London would send the message, "Hortense had twins," meaning the drop would be made two nights after the date of the broadcast; or if "Hortense had triplets," it would mean three nights hence. The place of drop was part of my memorized data, etc. There were many messages on my mind, but few can be remembered at this late date. But I do remember a few items that were acutely disappointing.

Perhaps the greatest disappointment concerned the map with the pin-prinks to help jog my memory. I was downright embarrassed! This map had been taken from me at Gibraltar and preceded me to London. A British intelligence officer brought up the subject—by telling me what a <u>fool</u> I was!

He said that had I been caught with that map it could easily have cost me my life. "Any German intelligence idiot would know enough to hold it to the light and discover the pinpoints. He would also realize that you were carrying intelligence information—and that <u>somehow</u> they would get that information out of you! They would then deal with you as a spy, or not, as they pleased, but likely with fatal results for you."

Since then I have been told that although the Luftwaffe seldom shot such persons, the Gestapo and the SS Troops very frequently did so. Although I was not brilliant, it seems I was extremely lucky!

It was a happy day when I arrived back in London in late March 1944, after a flight from Gibraltar.

We were taken to a "Safe House" at #63 Brooks Street, near Grosvener Square (sometimes then known as Eisenhower Plaza because of the many American Offices in the area.) All Air Force evadees and escapees were quartered in this building and none could leave until fully identified. This meant that someone from my previous unit of assignment who knew me personally had to come to London and verify that I was in truth the Major Eveland that I said I was.

So it was with each of us evadees. Major "Pop" Frye and Tech/Sgt. Joseph L. Kirkner came to London and made my identification. Finally, I was permitted to send a telegram to Dawn, stating that I was alive and back in England at last. She and all my family could now relax. Three months of anxiety is a horribly long time!

Now I could come and go as I pleased, except for the innumerable appointments with both English and American intelligence officers. They interrogated me for several hours daily, for about a week or so. They wanted to know who had helped me, in what towns, what I had seen or heard, what was the weather, etc., etc.

Back to the base

My first objective, naturally, was to get off that telegram to Dawn. My next objective was to get to Deenthorpe and see all my good friends of the Squadron and Group. I managed to get a car and driver assigned. I had every intention of calling on Colonel Bowman first, as a matter of courtesy, then returning to my Squadron area to visit with the lads of my own outfit.

However, I made a strategic mistake. The route to Col. Bowman's quarters led past the 614th area. I lost my resolve, and had the driver turn in! In no time at all I was clinking glasses with my friends and I found it necessary to phone Col. Bowman.

I apologized for making this impulsive stop at the 614th, and after the alcoholic greeting I received, I thought it best to delay my visit to his quarters until the next evening. He laughed, understood, and agreed!

Unofficial intelligence sources had once reported me *probably* Killed-in-Action, due to a military class ring with a red garnet stone setting. This later proved to belong to another officer, KIA, near where my aircraft crashed.

Before I had been shot down, there had been a corporal in the parachute department who kept asking me to get him assigned to gunnery training so that he could become a B-17 gunner and assigned to the combat crew. He wanted a greater commitment to the war effort. At my request, he had ordered a special "back-pack" type of parachute for me and he had carefully fitted it to me the morning of my last mission. He made certain all straps were just right so that if I had to use it, it worked just fine.

Naturally, on return to my squadron, I had to look him up and tell him that as far as I was concerned, he was just about the most <u>important</u> man on the Base! I hope that, thereafter, he was happier about his parachute job.

My new job

Before leaving London to visit Deenthorpe, I had already been told I would not be allowed to resume command of my squadron. In fact, I would no longer fly combat—because I knew too much about the "underground" and if shot down again and captured, too many others would be at risk.

I could be reassigned to the States, if I so desired. And I did so desire, with every fiber of my being! But Colonel Bowman made a sage comment—if I returned to the States I would probably be reassigned to combat in the Pacific and surely that would be rough on Dawn—especially after three months of torment while I was "MIA." Would a short reunion be worth it?

On the other hand, B/Gen. J.K. Lacey, C.O. of the 94th Combat Wing (of which the 401st, 351st, and 457th Groups were the components), needed an Assistant Wing Operations Officer. The job called for a Lt. Colonel, the same rank level as Squadron Commander. I would have a chance at the promotion, would not be in combat, but would have to forego a reunion with Dawn, Nicole, and the family. However, Col. Bowman arranged for General Lacey to agree I could go home if I didn't like the job after a trail period. He recommended that I accept—and I did.

Almost immediately after I had settled into the job, the Operations Officer (my direct boss) Colonel Cobb, was shot down over France (later he was reported Killed-in-Action), so for the next many weeks I as not only Assistant Operations Officer but also Acting Operations Officer. I slept damn little. Many shifts were 48 hours or more with no sleep at all.

The 94th Combat Wing Headquarters consisted of perhaps a dozen officers and about the same number of clerks and technicians. We coordinated the activities of the three Bombardment Groups. Most of the time was devoted to supervision of the radio aircraft control room, especially when bombing missions were in progress, preparing the supplement to each Mission Field Order, specifying bomb loads according to target information, and performing such odd jobs as the C.O. assigned.

Our living quarters were in a separate area at Pole Brook Air Base, where the 351st Bomb Group was stationed. Our Wing Headquarters was within easy walking distance of our quarters. We had our own kitchen staff, one of which was most unusual but enterprising corporal. He often supplied all of us with fresh eggs—a tremendous achievement in those days and a welcome relief from the normal powered eggs.

This corporal would borrow the General's staff car and call on each of the English farmers for miles around. He put on a high-pressure sales talk about his boss, an American General, who loved eggs but had not had any in many weeks! Could they sell him two or three, perhaps? It would be appreciated so much! Often he received a whole dozen! And then he was off to the next farm and repeated the act again. Once, however, as he opened the door to deposit the sack of eggs, another sack of eggs fell off the seat and smashed—and all this in the presence of the kindly English farmer and his wife! The corporal had to make substantial geographical changes in his "egg route" thereafter.

Trips to London

I managed two or three overnight trips to London. Once I stayed at the Savoy Hotel that was quite famous and fancy. The waiters in the dining room dressed very formally with their morning coats (tails and all). Included on the menu was egg omelet. I visualized real fresh eggs, thinking the Savoy could do anything. I ordered it with enthusiasm. When it came, the waiter stood over me and seemed to really enjoy my disappointment. He stood very tall and very straight and seemed to look down his very British nose at me and he said, "Yes, sir, I know. Powdered eggs, sir. Lend-lease, you know, sir!" And he walked away, chuckling.

Once, in London, I had a room in a small hotel taken over by the Red Cross. I was on about the third floor and my roommate was a young first lieutenant. The air raid siren was just outside our window and the bedlam created was terrific. Kinda turned one's blood to ice water.

I told the lieutenant this was my first experience; were we supposed to go to the basement, or what? He said, "Major, you do anything you want—but me, I've got my 25 missions completed and I'm getting as far underground as I can—'cause I'm on my way <u>HOME</u>!" His logic sounded excellent and I followed him down the stairs, two at a time!

On another occasion, one of the "V-1" rockets demolished the building adjacent to my hotel. Early the next morning I went over to take a look. A group of Englishmen were sorting through the wreckage as calm and collected as if it were an everyday occurrence. Which it was, unfortunately! But I wondered if my countrymen could withstand such a pounding in an equally courageous manner! And I was very thankful America had not had to suffer such a test.

Back to work

When we had a bombing mission scheduled for the next morning, I as usually in my 94th Combat Wing office by 1:00 or 2:00 A.M., or so (if I got to bed at all).

As mentioned earlier in this report, part of my job was to put out the Field Order specifying required bomb loads and other details of the mission.

Also, I used the "scramble phone" and called each of our three Bomb Groups, in turn, giving them a few extra minutes to prepare for the mission requirements while the printed Field Order was being transmitted by TWX machine.

One morning, after all aircraft were airborne and headed over the Channel, Brig. Gen. Julius K. Lacey (my top boss) and I were in Operations where we had a cup of coffee as I monitored the radio transmissions.

This particular mission specified Munich as the primary target. The bomb load was 500# bombs, then the next bomber formation would drop incendiaries, and the following formation would drop another layer of 500-pounders, etc. Blow it up, start fires, and stir the fire with more bombs. Very effective! But it so happened that this was the third consecutive daily mission against Munich with this same horribly effective bomb load. Further, if there was cloud cover over Munich, and our lead bombardiers could not see our specific strategic targets, they would bomb by radar.

That meant that not just the specific targets would be hit, but the whole damn area would burn. Anyway, I foolishly told General Lacey that, although I knew it was necessary, I could not help but feel sorry for the civilians of Munich on this particular day! I recognized the necessity of such missions, but it made me half sick. I guess my imagination was getting out of hand. Gen. Lacey gave me a "dressing down" I will never forget.

To quote: My personal feelings were unprofessional. Remember, the damn Krauts had started the war; Hitler was a savage, responsible for the death of millions—we were there to end this savagery—and we would end it, for sure, even if civilians, including women and children, had to be sacrificed. If they didn't kill Hitler, we would do it any way we could.

I know he was right, but I have thought about this scolding many times. Perhaps Gen. Lacey believed I needed a "dressing down." Maybe he really thought I had gone soft. On the other hand, I have another theory that presents the possibility that Gen. Lacey was as sick of radar bombing and civilian casualties as I was—and he gave me hell partly to reinforce his own resolve that what was being done HAD TO BE DONE! As a combat wing commander, he could not let himself question the facts that be, nor show any compassion for the enemy.

When shot down, I weighted about 135 pounds. On my return, I had lost at least 20 pounds. But my control of nerves, and emotions, was the greatest loss. I should have been sent to the "flak-shack" for a few weeks—although now I realize that, at the time, it never entered my mind, nor the minds of my superiors, as far as I know.

D-Day

Of course all of us knew "D-Day" was coming but none of us knew when. But you could feel the build-up. In my office, several times I briefed colonels and generals of ground forces as to how we operated and why. You could see their unmentioned excitement about the coming invasion. For one thing, several commented on how calm our Air Force people seemed to be.

Naturally, we looked calm. Our people were in combat every time they flew a mission. Combat had been part of their life pattern for months. Yes, the Air Force knew when D-Day came it would be one of the greatest events in history—but their concentration was riveted on completion of their personal assigned missions—so they could go home!

The ground forces were focused on the magnitude of the historical event about to happen, and excited about their first entry into combat and their subsequent performance.

One day we were told to wear our .45 side arms at all times. For some time, nearly all missions had been "maximum effort" missions. The build-up was obvious and imminent. Then some of us were told that tomorrow was it!

The excitement was electric! 1944—regardless of how the invasion turned out—would rank in history—along with 1066, 1776, 1914, and all other top historical events! June 6, 1944 was here!

Long before daylight, the transports (DC-3 types) were heard overhead, some towing gliders behind. I put out the 94th Combat Wing supplement to the Field Order. And then the big bombers took off for their missions. I tried to borrow an aircraft to see the show from above. I was outranked everywhere. So, on this historic date, all I can say is, "I flew a desk!"

Even so, it was an exciting day. Our bombers made several missions per day to soften up the enemy near the beach areas and on transportation centers.

Some days after the successful Normandy landing the weather turned bad and the Air Force could not support the ground forces as we had hoped to do. If the weather permitted assembly in England, clouds obscured the group targets on the continent.

I kept the "drop release" map in our War Room. It was obvious our ground forces were held up and needed air assistance, which we could not provide. For some days all we could give was our prayers. We all felt much better when we were able to fly and help those poor guys on the ground.

While assigned to Wing Headquarters I did very little flying. In fact, the ground job was so intense that I could hardly find time for sleep, let alone the pleasant luxury of flying. Assigned to our Wing HQ as administrative aircraft was a P-51 (I think the General was the only one permitted to fly it) an A-20 (which I enjoyed) and a little fabric covered twin-engine craft that the English called an Oxford.

More hard work and conflicts

Col. Bowman was right. My assignment as Assistant Operations Officer was a good opportunity to continue to serve the combat needs of the Air Force, without a repeat of personal combat risk, and even a possible promotion to the Lt. Colonelcy I had lost by being shot down. However, after Colonel Cobb was shot down, my duties escalated. I functioned as both Assistant Wing Operations Officer and Acting Operations Officer. Also, I found that although B/Gen. Lacey was undoubtedly a brilliant officer, he did not have a happy staff.

Practically all were at least one rank less than the Table of Organization and had been held there for a year or more, with the sole exception of Col Harris E. Rogner (formerly Deputy Commander of the 401st Bomb Group).

General Lacey had promoted Rogner to full colonel soon after his assignment to 94th Wing Headquarters as Executive Officer. I believe Col. Rogner was probably happy in his staff job and that was in contrast to most of the other officers on the staff. In addition, Col. Rogner (a West Point and All-American football player) was a very competent officer. I liked him. However, he had an incredible ability to bring out the very worst in me—and in the absence of Colonel Cobb (shot down), Col. Rogner became my immediate superior.

Before I was shot down, I had my first conflict with Col. Rogner. He had led the 401ˢᵗ Bomb Group on a mission to Paris and I had led my squadron in the "high" position on his right. (We did not drop our bombs because of cloud cover over the target so we carried them back home to Base and landed with them intact.)

On the return to the English coast there was 100% low cloud cover in the London area. The radio signals confirmed that the British had sent up their barrage balloons, with explosives on the cables tethering them, to prevent the Germans from attacking <u>below</u> the overcast.

Colonel Rogner decided to ignore the balloon barrage and have the Group formation descend below the overcast. To me, this was a totally unjustified risk. I refused—and ordered my squadron to stay on my wing—and I proceeded to Base <u>above</u> the overcast. We made our letdown through broken clouds near Base. No problem. No risk, either.

Lt. Col. Rogner was furious, perhaps rightly so. I had defied a direct order. Graciously, he said he would accept a simple apology! But I as furious, also! I refused, but offered to accept <u>his</u> apology! We were stalemated, except—he was then a Lt. Colonel, in command, and I was a Major, not in command.

Now, in the absence of Col. Cobb, Col. Rogner was my immediate boss at the 94ᵗʰ Combat Wing. I still say he was a good guy, but we never analyzed the same problem in the same manner, and I almost always ended up in disagreement.

A written record was made, daily, of all radio transmissions (in or out) on our Wing radio. One day, as our bombers were returning from a mission, I had a call from a pilot saying he had wounded aboard; also, antiaircraft had knocked out a window and his weather code was lost. He wanted weather information—<u>in the clear</u>—because he was on top of a low overcast and needed to know where he could safely let down beneath the overcast, and fast, because of his wounded.

A cardinal operating rule precluded any transmission of weather conditions in the clear. But his radio code (such as "Red Dog," etc.) identified the pilot's unit to me so I knew what Base he had taken off from to begin his mission. A quick check and I found a different airbase reporting the base of the overcast to be about 900 feet. So instead of giving him this information in the clear, I told him he could descend to a Base about 40 miles southwest of the Base he had taken off from that morning. It was most unlikely that the enemy could correctly identify the area designated, but the pilot could do so easily.

The next morning Col. Rogner read the typed transcript of the above and accosted me with a serious violation of the rules, as well as judgment. He said he would have to take it up with the General. He said I should have known better than to risk career by such action. I replied that I disagreed. The reason a Field Grade Officer had to be on radio duty, instead of a Lieutenant, was because of just this type of incident. It was a judgment call. If any superiors disagreed, they could fire the Field Grade Officer—who had something to lose. That's why a Field Grade Officer is there instead of a Lieutenant.

Once again we disagreed on the "judgment" issue. I sort of held my breath for a few days. I really wanted to go home, but I had never been fired and I didn't wish to start now. Col. Rogner never mentioned the incident again. Neither did Gen. Lacey. I think I was cleared of any misdeeds.

Going home

After some months on the job, I decided to remind the General of my option to go home. Looking back, perhaps I was a bit spoiled.

When in the 401st working for Colonel Bowman, things seemed to go smoothly, and he had a happy and hard-working staff. As I mentioned before, the staff of the 94th Combat Wing, although hard working, was not happy at all. And I still was unable to throw off the tension that had built up during my three months trying to get out of France and back to England. I needed to see my family again! And, luckily, I had the option!

After another month or so, he finally found a replacement that he thought would be acceptable. He proved to be a (West Point) Lt. Colonel, and Gen. Lacey had me train him for several weeks before my relief orders came through. Thanks be, my orders to the U.S. were travel by air. I sure didn't want to go by ship! Too slow!

From New York City westward, however, I had to travel by train. I kept reasonably calm until the train got into Minnesota where we passed through many small towns and forests with beautiful blue lakes, all of which reminded me of home. My anticipation kept rising to a crescendo. I couldn't read or sit more than a few minutes. I mostly walked the aisles until we arrived at Great Falls, Montana.

Dawn met me at the station. God, it was wonderful! She had left Nicole in Butte with her parents and the next day we were in Butte. Nikki was just under a year old. She had grown since the last snapshot Dawn had sent me. And, fortunately, she no longer looked so much like her Daddy. She had golden curly hair, a hint of her Mother's smile, and I thought she was one cute kid! (Dawn was thin, weighing only in the low nineties, which was better than the middle eighties while I had been missing in action!) I was ecstatic to be with her again!

Printed with permission of Lois Eveland.

The First and Only Mission

Narrated by Homer McDanal, B-17 pilot
8th Air Force, 401st Bomb Group, 614th Bomb Squadron
Edited by Erik Dyreborg

Introduction

It was the last day of the year 1943, Friday December 31.

Twenty-one B-17s from the 401st Bomb Group started their engines at 06:55. Take off was at 07:25, and the estimated time of return of the bombers was 16:23, thus nine hours airborne.

The primary target (Bordeaux) was obscured by a cloud so the Wing Leader (Major Seawell) ordered the formation to proceed to the secondary target, a Luftwaffe Airbase at Cognac, which was bombed with excellent results.

The Group lost four planes that day:

The wreckage of the B-17 "Hey Lou" (42-31064), piloted by Lt. D. H. Lawry, was found off the coast of southern England. The cause of the loss was not determined, and only one **body** was recovered.

Two other aircraft ran out of fuel and were abandoned by the crews.

The entire crew of "Flak Rat" (42-37770), were shot down by FLAK and fighters. Major I. Wayne Eveland, 614th Squadron Commander, flying with LT H.E. McDanal.

The crew:

Homer McDanal, front row to the left

Pilot,	LT H. E. McDanal	EVD
Navigator,	LT L. H. Sprinkler	POW
Bombardier,	LT D.H. Goetsch	EVD
Radio Operator	S/Sgt. J. L. Kirkner	EVD
Engr./Top Turret	S/Sgt. D. L. Jerue	KIA
Ball Turret	S/Sgt. H. J. Reasoner	POW
Tail Gunner Gun.	Sgt. M. Arinsberg	POW
Left Waist Gunner	Sgt. F. G. Kelly	POW
Right Waist Gunner	Sgt.H. W. Sanders	KIA

The plane arrived from the States at Deenethorpe, England on November 19, 1943. It was to become the one and only mission for both crew and plane.

Homer McDanal begins his story after FLAK and enemy fighters hit the plane, and after he bailed out.

The landing and meeting the French

As I descended in my parachute, I noticed a small village below me. I was afraid I was going to fall into the village, but I was fortunate enough to fall just on the outskirts into a pine forest. I hit the ground pretty hard and was momentarily stunned. When I came to, I felt a pain in my neck and felt blood oozing from a wound I apparently received when we were hit by FLAK just before the FW-190 blew off our tail and set us on fire.

I covered my parachute with pine bows and started running through the woods, heading south toward Spain. The sound of motorcycles on the road near me led me to believe that the Germans had seen me come down and were trying to find me.

The rest of the afternoon was spent moving as fast as possible through the woods and staying as close to the road as possible without being seen. I figured this road would eventually take me to the Pyrenees Mountains and Spain. When it started to get dark I looked for a farmhouse that I thought would keep me for the night. I found one and watched it for a while, making sure that there were no Germans around. Eventually a farmer and his son came out and went into the barn. I approached them, and when they saw me they became very excited and motioned for me to follow them into the house. Not being able to converse in English and I not knowing French, we understood each other by sign language. Some of the words that we used were bombardier, parachute, and American. In all of the time that I was in France I never met anyone who could speak English.

This farmer didn't want me to stay with him, so took me to two other houses, and each time people would talk excitedly but didn't want me to stay with them. Finally at the third house, where an elderly couple lived, they took me in for the night. This is the way I spent the last day of 1943. I was completely exhausted and went right to sleep on a feather bed in a spare room. I don't think I have ever found a bed so wonderful.

Before sunrise I was awakened and with a breakfast of bread and eggs I was taken outside where the old man pointed to the south and said, "Espana." I started out with new energy and optimism. I figured I could keep doing this until I reached Spain.

New Year's day was a beautiful day. I kept following the highway by walking in the woods and making sure I was not seen by anyone. I checked my escape kit and the waterproof maps that we carried for that particular part of France. I filled my rubber water bottle with water from small creeks along the way and used the halazone tablets from the escape kit to keep the water as pure as possible.

Jean Laborde

Late in the afternoon I came to an area where there were few trees and by accident ran into a farmer who was chopping wood. He became very excited, and we used the same words again, Bombardier, parachute, American, etc. He motioned for me to follow him, which I did, and after walking through a plowed field we came to his house.

This farmer and patriot, I learned, was Jean Laborde. His wife was Odette and they had a three-year-old baby girl, Janine. Jean's mother and brother also lived there. The brother, I could tell, didn't like to have me there. However, I was to stay there for eight days. At meal times the table was always set for five, never six. They didn't want any of the neighbors to know that I was there.

The first night there was knock at the door and I was hurried into a bedroom and under the bed. In a few minutes a man with a gun in uniform looked under the bed and motioned for me to come out. He questioned me for a time in French and finally decided I really was an American. I learned that this man was a policeman from the local village and a member of the French Underground. Jean had ridden his bicycle into the village that afternoon and contacted this man.

The second night that I was there, two-men came, and as far as I could understand they had a plan to get me back to England. This plan was to take me by car to a lake near Bordeaux. There, at some time in the night, a plane with pontoons from England would land on the lake and take me back to England. After thinking this over, I vetoed the plan. It looked too risky for me. I would rather take my chances on climbing over the Pyrenees into Spain.

This house where I was staying was on the highway leading into Spain. Several times a day, German patrols would go by and each time Jean would shake his fist at them. However, most of the time he and Odette were in the fields preparing for spring planting.

My stay with the Laborde's was not too exciting as I was not to go out of the house for fear of being seen by neighbors. I ate only the vegetables and one of the meats they served. The meat didn't look good to me and I was afraid of getting sick. I had no water to drink, "only" wine, for more than a week. The family used very little water and did not bathe very often.

This is where I gave up my flying suit and GI shoes to Jean. This was a bad mistake because the shoes he gave me were very cheap and too small (my feet were covered with blisters when we got to Spain). Jean gave me an old shirt and suit that I later found out were inadequate for the cold weather of the Pyrenees. I still kept my "dog tags" around my neck just in case I was caught and had to prove that I was an escapee and not a spy.

I left parts of my escape kit with Odette and the 1,000 Francs. (When my wife and I visited in 1985 she still had the 1,000 Francs.)

Moving on

On the morning of the eighth day I was awakened very early with a quick cup of coffee and a kiss from the family, and I was put into the back end of a pick-up type of truck. This truck was fueled by charcoal gas generated by a huge furnace type tank on the back. The gas from this was piped to the engine. Needless to say the engine did not have much power.

After a ride for about a half hour, the truck suddenly stopped and I was told to follow the driver. We walked through a cemetery and on the other side I was taken to a farmhouse where I met James Evans who had been a gunner on a B-17, who had been shot down some time before I was. His forehead had been slightly burned when his B-17 exploded and blew him out of his airplane.

Now I had someone to talk to, and it was a pleasant experience. We were placed in a building away from the house and told not to go out at any time. Members of the family brought food to us, and we ate all of our meals in our building.

We were quite close to a German airfield and could see biplane type airplanes with the swastika on the side. This family was definitely more prosperous than the Laborde family. The food was much better, and the house itself was very modern.

On Monday morning we were awakened very early and with a light breakfast, we bid this family goodbye with the usual kisses on each cheek. The same truck I had been in before took us. The bed of the truck was lined with charcoal bags with a canvas over the whole thing so we couldn't be seen. We traveled for perhaps an hour and while it was still dark, we entered a town and stopped in front of a house.

We were rushed inside and there were two more American boys, Bill Olson, a navigator, and Nick Carusone, a gunner, on the same B-17 that was shot down several weeks before, north of Paris. Their tale of being moved through Paris by the Underground is an exciting story in itself. They rode trains down to the town of Dax where we met them.

We were introduced to a man by the name of Robert. He was head of the Paris Underground and a most unusual man. He had been wounded in 1940 and was using two artificial legs. We were there only a few minutes and a member of the underground made me an identification card from pictures I had with me in my escape kit. My name was Henri Laborde.

We left this house with the driver, a member of the underground, and Robert. The four of us Americans were hidden in the back of the truck. Sometime during the morning we came to a hill on the highway that was too steep for the truck and we all had to get out and help push it until we were over the top. We had just gotten back in the truck when a German patrol came by. They went on by and didn't even stop. We all gave a sigh of relief. I have thought about this many times since. It was just like something out of a movie spy thriller.

The rest of the way was uneventful, and we finally were put in a barn. We were told then that we were very close to the Pyrenees in Spain. We shook hands with the three Frenchmen, and they wished us good luck. They told us to stay where we were until darkness when someone would come to start our journey through the mountains. We gave these men our name, rank, and serial number. Every guide we had from then did the same thing. Our government paid all of these people who helped us. We still hadn't had much to eat since the day before.

The Pyrenees

After dark we heard a whistle, and when we came out of the barn there were two men who were to guide us for a while. We later learned that they were Basques and knew all of the best ways through the mountains.

For the first part of the night we walked through flat lands. About midnight we started up the mountains. The night was very clear, but cold. The guides kept us at a fast walk with only an occasional stop to rest. About an hour before sunrise we reached a barn on a mountainside. We slept there in the hay until the sun was high. We walked outside and could see a small village far below us. The warm sun felt good. There were a number of snow-fed streams that we crossed, so we had plenty of water to drink but were still short of food.

The second night was pretty much the same as the first. We finally reached another barn high in the mountains and were told that it would take one more night of tough climbing to reach Spain. The third night our guide brought us some bread and sausages. They certainly tasted good. We were able to understand the Basques pretty well because they spoke Spanish and Nick, who spoke Italian, could converse with them.

Finally Spain

When we got high in the Pyrenees we knew we were near Spain. We came close to a cabin and our guide told us that German patrols were in there and for us to be quiet and hurry on by. About 1:00 am we crossed a bridge over a rushing stream and we reached the far side, our guide told us that we were in Spain. This was January 14, 1944. Our guide shook hands with all of us and turned around and left. We were now on our own.

In a few minutes we came to a hotel with lights on. We hadn't seen outside lights for a long time. The hotelkeeper wouldn't give us any food, but said we could sleep in the barn. After just a few minutes we knew we couldn't stay there. It was too cold, so we decided to follow the dirt road down the mountain. Some time in the afternoon we came to a village. As we approached the village, several men in uniform surrounded us with machine guns pointed at us and motioned for us to follow them. They took us to a police station and we were told that on Monday morning we would be taken by bus and then train to Pamplona where we would be interned for the rest of the war.

We begged for food from small merchants, but were not very successful. The police put us in a loft over a barn that was fairly warm and where they were cooking slop for pigs. We ate a lot of that and it tasted pretty good.

Monday morning the police came and put us on a bus for the railroad station. They guarded us at the time with their guns pointed at us. We rode the train into Pamplona and were taken to a hotel where Bill and I, being the only officers, stayed for a couple of weeks. Jim and Nick had to stay in a military camp.

There is a great difference between officers and enlisted in Spain. The manager of the hotel took Bill and me to a men's clothing store where we were completely outfitted with new clothes—suits, shirts, ties, underwear, socks, shoes and top coat. This all was authorized by a telephone conversation with our military attache in Bilbao, Spain.

We were also told not to tell anyone of our escape, as there were several German spies in Pamplona. It was great to finally shave and take a hot bath. It had been more than two weeks and we had walked a lot. I figured we had walked almost 60 miles in the three nights.

I learned that our bombardier, Danny Goetsch, had been there and already left, so I knew he was still alive. One night a group of escapees were brought to the hotel and among them was Sgt. Joseph Kirkner, our engineer and top turret gunner. I knew then that at least three of our crew was safe.

Bill and I enjoyed our stay in Pamplona and met an American girl and her family who treated us royally. She was from San Francisco and had married a Spanish doctor. She was glad to have someone from America to talk to. We stayed in Pamplona ten days, then the Spanish military moved us by train to Saragoza and finally to the resort town of Allama de Aragon. By then there were 33 Americans interned in this beautiful resort hotel.

Back to England

We were there only a few days when several private cars came from the American Military Consulate in Madrid and took us all to Madrid where we then boarded a train for Gibraltar. On the Rock of Gibraltar we exchanged our civilian clothes for British uniforms with American insignias.

After a week on Gibraltar British military passenger planes flew us at night back to England. I landed in London, March 2, 1944. I was stationed in London at the Red Cross Reindeer Club. In the meantime, I returned to the 401st Bomb Group at Deenethorpe, reporting to Col. Hal Bowman and Maj. Frye and telling them my story of escape. Maj. Frye said he would keep me in England until orders for my promotion to 1st LT came through. I also was able to see my regular co-pilot, Robert Timberlake, who had had the sad task of packing up the belongings of our crew. These were all shipped to Liverpool, England for eventual shipment back to the U.S.

Maj. Frye asked me about Maj. Wayne Eveland and I told him I was afraid he went down with our plane. Before I left England I was told the goods news that Wayne was still alive and in Spain. I also learned that our navigator, Luke Sprinker, had been captured and was in a German prison camp. That accounted for five of our crew who were alive. The other five were reported to have been killed the day we were shot down.

I stayed in London for about a month and during that time experienced about a dozen bombing raids on the city. They were very exciting to watch. We always went outside instead of going down in the bomb shelters. The subways were lined with bunk beds and thousands of Londonites went down there every night.

Going home

One day in April I was told to go down to Eisenhower's headquarters to get my promotion orders and "return home" orders. I was under secret orders and carried a document that proved my identification.

I was ordered to proceed immediately to Glasgow, Scotland by train. When I got there I found out that I would be returning to the U.S. aboard the Queen Mary. The staterooms were equipped with bunk beds and had brought about 20,000 troops over. They were getting ready for the invasion of Europe, which were only a few weeks away.

After a rather pleasant ocean voyage, I landed in New York City about the 1st of May and was still under secret orders. I was told not to say anything about my escape for fear of identifying the French people who had helped me.

I was given a two-week leave to visit my family in Denver and then I proceeded to Santa Monica, California.

Lois Eveland, widow of Wayne Eveland, gave her permission to print Wayne's copy of Homer's experience. She felt Homer would have been honored to have been included in this book.

Any Time You Went Down, You Were Beaten

Narrated by Edwin Hays, B-17 Tail Gunner
8ᵗʰ Air Force, 95ᵗʰ Bomb Group, 335ᵗʰ Bomb Squadron
Edited by Erik Dyreborg

Enlisting and basic training

In October 1942, I enlisted in the Air Force, because I wanted to fly. I didn't want to be fighting on the ground. My friends and I were all in high school. I was seventeen years old and 1942 was my senior year. We were very anxious to get out and enlist before the war was over. Little did we realize it would go on another three years. Some of my classmates left immediately after Pearl Harbor to enlist. Of course, my parents wouldn't let me do that. I had to wait until I graduated.

I was sent to Atlantic City, New Jersey, for Basic Training, which consisted of marching up and down the Boardwalk. We were looking for bathing beauties. My impression was not one to remember, really. I wasn't there very long, only a couple of weeks. I was very fortunate. I didn't have to go through any Basic Training to speak of. I signed up for Gunnery School, and I couldn't wait to get out of Atlantic City.

We went right from New Jersey to Fort Myers, Florida, to Gunnery School, which is about a seven or eight week course. Then we went to Armorers School at Lowry Field in Denver, Colorado, to learn all about turrets and guns.

After that, we were assigned to an Operational Group in Redmond, Oregon, for Operational Flight Training. They called it O T U. We went through three or four months of that training, and then went through it a second time. That's when the crews were formed and all ten guys came together. And together, we went all through our Advanced Flight Training: night flying, daytime flying, navigational trips, bombardier training missions, gunnery missions, and so forth.

The Tailgunner, Ed Hays, 1943, is pictured above.

I had two leaves during Operational Training. You go through a certain Phase of training and you get a leave. I mainly spent my time with my family and my high school sweetheart, Joan, who later became my wife.

England and combat missions

Next we went to Ephrata, Washington. That was a large, very popular base. After we trained there, we were ready for overseas. Instead of flying overseas, they took our plane away from us, and we went over on the *Queen Mary*. Our journey took four days and eleven hours, which at that time, was a record crossing.

We landed in Scotland, got on a train and went right down to our base at Horham, England. The 95th Bomb Group. The 95th flew with the 390th and the 100th Bomb Groups. The 100th was a famous Bomb Group, because they had a lot of bad luck during the war. They were known as the *Bloody 100th*. The Germans used to pick on them and shoot them up pretty badly.

Those three Groups formed the 13th Combat Wing, which was part of the Third Air Division. There were three Air Divisions—the First and the Third were B-17s, the second was a B-24 outfit.

It was several weeks before we went into combat. We spent those first weeks getting acclimated to the Group. We had practice missions, and we practiced formation flying, which we didn't do much of in the States. Most of the guys that came over were just raw pilots with no real formation flying experience. We landed in November of '43 and I flew my first mission on December 30, 1943.

In all, I flew twelve and a half missions, which was about average for crews at that time. They'd get about half way through their required twenty-five. We thought we were going to make it, everybody did, but we flew several really rough missions. On our mission to Brunswick on February 20th we lost seven ships out of our Group of twenty-one planes. Some raids were easy and some were hard. Just the luck of the draw sometimes.

Combat was completely different from the training program. It didn't even compare to training. Training was just taking a plane up and flying around—navigation flights or gunnery flights. It was tame stuff compared to flying in close formation with twenty other planes. It was really a frightening experience for a while. The fact that you had nine other guys in the same position helped. We muddled through together until the day we were shot down.

The day we were shot down, we were the only plane to be lost out of the Group of twenty-one. At this time in the war, the usual number of planes that went out from Group was twenty-one. Later on, as they got more replacement planes, they were able to put up two separate Groups, in other words, forty-two to forty-five planes.

When I first started flying, we didn't even have escorts. We had Spitfires, but they flew at a much lower altitude and we never saw them. It was frightening to go into a target with no escort. Really a terrible feeling. You could tell the difference later on, when we got P-51s. They were able to escort us all the way into a target and back. There was a difference in your attitude and your feelings. You felt you had all of America with you. So I flew with and without escort. I flew on the first 1,000-plane raid. It doesn't mean much, but it was a tremendous effort by the Air Force at that time.

We didn't start missions at a certain time. Some missions started very early in the morning. We had to get up out of bed at four or five o'clock, have breakfast, go to briefing. It might be five or 5:30 before you got into your plane. Then you assembled out on the runways ready for take off.

Briefings were just an educational lecture telling you where you were going to go, what kind of bombs you'd drop, what altitude you'd be at, and the flak and fighter resistance to expect. They were very strenuous affairs, because nobody knew where we were going to go. We found out when they pulled back the curtain to reveal the map. When they pulled the curtain, there would usually be a gasp, two hundred guys groaning, "Oh, No!"

At Briefings, we were just told what to do. It was cut and dried. There was a lot of excitement because of the uncertainty before they pulled that curtain. There'd be a lot of rumors such as, "We're going to Berlin today!" I was very fortunate. I never got to go to Berlin, but my Group, the 95th Bomb Group was the first Group to bomb Berlin on March 4, 1944, just a little over a week after I was shot down. This was a very proud moment in our Group, to be the first Bomb Group to drop their bombs on Berlin.

The 95th was also the only Group in the Eighth Air Force to receive three Presidential Citations. One was for that Berlin Raid, one was for Regensburg, and one was for Munster.

The citation for Berlin was quite an honor for the Group; they're still crowing about it. All the other Groups turned back that day over Berlin, all the Divisions. That's a lot of planes. And I think my Group got the recall order, but they ignored it. They plowed on and they took some bad losses, but they got the bombs on the target. It was a great honor for them.

The night before, we knew there would be a raid on, because they would put a flag up over the headquarters. A red flag meant that a mission was scheduled. A blue flag meant that the Group was "stood down."

If there wasn't a mission at Horham, we either had practice missions or we were at some sort of school. We had idle time, but for the most part, we practiced formation flying, because the biggest drawback to the Eighth Air Force was our inexperience in formation flying. Close formation flying had the greatest impact on German fighters, but it was very difficult to do. You had to be very skillful to hold those formations under all kinds of weather conditions, never mind inclement weather. So for that reason, we flew almost all the time when the weather permitted.

The time I was there, November, December, and January, was the worst weather in months in England. In those three months, I only got thirteen missions in. As the weather got better in the summer months, they were flying every day. No, they kept us busy. We didn't have much leisure time.

Other than the mission during which we were shot down, the Brunswick mission stands out in my mind. On that mission, we lost seven planes. It was the biggest air battle I had been in. It was over in a matter of maybe a minute or two. I'm not talking about the flak, now, I'm just talking about the fighters as they came screaming through our formation, went around and came through again.

They were (Messerschmitt) ME 109s, (Fockewulf) FW 190s, and (Junkers) JU 88s. The Germans were skillful pilots. In the beginning, when I first started flying, they were mainly attacking from the tail position. Then they found out that too many of their planes were being shot down, and they changed their tactics. They began to attack from 12 o'clock, the nose position, because we only had two hand held guns in the nose plus the top turret, which could shoot at them.

We were never hit by flak. We did have some damage to our plane, which was caused by one of our own gunners. A hand held gun put a few holes in, but very minor. We were very fortunate. We didn't have anybody wounded or hit until the day we were shot down.

Our plane was called *Just Elmer's Tune*. It was named after a Glenn Miller hit of the time, and my pilot was named Elmer Costales. Our crew got together, without his knowledge, and had this name painted on the plane. Then we took him down there and surprised him. He's still talking about it. He thought that was great. He was a great guy.

The food was adequate. We got better food, such as fresh eggs, on the mornings when we were going on a mission. Otherwise, it was typical Army hash. Much better than being in the front lines.

One of my main duties as a Tail Gunner was on Take offs and Assembly. We used to take off in the dark, in foggy, overcast conditions, and were up as high as ten, twelve, fifteen thousand feet before we broke out of the clouds. One of my duties was to stay in that tail and blink an Aldus Lamp, which is just a glorified flash light. But it gave out a signal so that a plane approaching from the rear wouldn't run into you. I used to do that, sometimes, for maybe an hour, until my fingers were sore from squeezing that trigger. But let me tell you, that light kept blinking. One of the greatest feelings in the world was to break out of that fog and come up into the sunlight. It was a very risky and hair raising experience to assemble in bad weather.

Then of course, the main duty of a Tail Gunner was to keep a sharp lookout for enemy planes, to report the positions of other planes in our formation or the location of damaged planes. You had to be a lookout; you had to be on the ball watching for anything that moved.

We had an intercom so the crewmembers on the plane could stay in contact with each other. It was very simple—just report in and say, "Tail Gunner to Pilot." Usually the co-pilot was the guy that contacted everybody else. You reported in to him.

As for medals, the Air Medal is given as a matter of course. When you complete five combat missions, they award you the Air Medal. So it isn't awarded for any specific or individual heroic event. It isn't necessarily a prestigious award. You could get an Air Medal and five clusters, and all it meant was that you had completed so many missions.

I have the Air Medal with one oak leaf cluster, the Purple Heart, which is for being wounded, the POW Medal, and the New Jersey Distinguished Service Medal, which is awarded to veterans who were inducted into the service from New Jersey and who are eligible by having received either the Bronze Star or the Air Medal or an award of higher merit.

I recall my first mission for the simple reason that I saw a B-17 break in half and the Ball Turret drop out of it. That stuck in my mind. You could see planes go down and explode, but to see this plane crack in half and the Ball Turret drop down on the first mission really stuck with me. The hit was caused by flak. That was on December 30, 1943, to Ludwigshafen. I'll never forget that one.

After you complete that first mission, you think you're a hero and you've got it licked and you're gonna make it. But it's only the beginning.

I think the support and the camaraderie of having the nine other fellows with you is what brings you through. You don't want to look like a jerk in front of nine guys. It was kind of a mutual admiration society. Of course my crew had been together quite a while. We'd flown for seven or eight months together in England and in the States, and that helped tremendously.

The members of my crew were :

Pilot: Elmer "Costy" Cosatles. He's still alive and lives in Fresno, California

Co-pilot: Steve Kish. He died in 1988 and was buried in Arlington Cemetery.

Navigator: Cliff Sahner: He died in the plane. He was badly wounded and couldn't get out before it blew up.

Bombardier: Lars Skoug. Died about twenty years ago.

Top Turret Gunner: George Pechacek. He was killed when he hit the ground, because he bailed out too low and his parachute didn't have time to open fully.

Radio Operator: Lester W. Seelig. Has since died.

Waist Gunner: Norman Carnie. He's still alive.

Waist Gunner: Leamon McCulloch. He's since died.

Ball Turret Gunner: Bob Joyce. Still alive and living in San Antonio, Texas.

I, myself, live in Paramus, New Jersey.

The B-17 was the only plane we flew in. We thought they were the best. The B-24 was the other heavy bomber. We ridiculed that every chance we got. But both planes did their job. Our plane had a sort of glamorous reputation in the Air Force.

The cities in the Ruhr Valley were exceptionally difficult targets. They were very well defended. Schweinfurt was a big one, Regensburg, and Berlin. Almost all of the targets in early 1943 were well defended, and we didn't have fighter escort. The Air Force took tremendous losses on those missions. But any target that's shooting at you with heavy flak was a tough mission. Heavy flak is worse than fighters, because you can't do anything to evade it.

As I said before, I don't think our training reflected combat situations at all. Outside of being familiar with my particular crew position and the knowledge of how the machine guns operated, it didn't compare to what we experienced in combat.

In combat, your guns could freeze up, all kinds of things could happen, emergency situations that we weren't trained for. I think our training in the States was mainly for the purpose of getting a crew together, have them fly together for a while, and then get them overseas. It wasn't really preparation for actual combat situations.

There is no training to prepare you for combat, but you can be made ready for it. We had a close supportive group. You take other branches of service, I think they probably had the same close camaraderie in the Navy and the Infantry. Togetherness is what will hold you through combat. The reason the experience of being a Prisoner Of War is really lonesome and terrifying is because you didn't have the same guys with you. They were all a bunch of strangers. It took a long time for our prison group to get together.

German equipment was excellent. From my experience in combat, the Germans were fearsome and to be feared. But as the Allies got stronger and our fighter escorts, the P-51s and the P-47s with their drop tanks were able to escort us farther into enemy territory, the Germans were no match for our fighters.

Our equipment was excellent. We had heated flying suits. We flew at anywhere between 40 and 60 degrees below zero on a lot of those missions, and you needed to be protected from that cold. You could get frostbite or your guns could freeze up. Our equipment was good.

To stay informed, we read YANK Magazine and the English newspapers, and we knew about the raids. But we were over there, in combat for a very short time, November to February, and at that time, we were mostly caught up in what our crew was doing. We didn't really pay a lot of attention to world affairs.

I don't think the scuttlebutt was very accurate. I had worse scuttlebutt as a prisoner, and none of it was accurate. In the camps, we got news from the BBC every day over hidden radios. The news was sent to each barracks by a courier, and we had lookouts so German guards wouldn't surprise the couriers. After D-Day, we knew a lot about how the war was progressing.

The English people were highly respected by the Americans, especially the 8th Air Force, and we got along fine. I think later on there were some problems. The longer the Americans stayed, the more problems there were. In Denmark, the people were wonderful to us.

Shot down

Some missions were started later in the morning. If the mission was to bomb France, near the coastline, you didn't have to start that early. But the raid I was shot down on was a long raid—over Denmark, down into Poland, and then back to England. We had bombed the target and were on the way back. We were very fortunate that we were shot down over Denmark, because a few minutes more and we would have been in the North Sea, and I'd be history. It was also only a few minutes flying time from Sweden, but we weren't able to make that, because the plane was shot up so badly.

I had a few items that I always carried with me, but when I got shot down, the first thing that came into my mind was to get rid of that stuff. I had a picture of my girl friend, Joan, and a cigarette lighter and a couple of little trinkets. I dug a hole and buried everything immediately. I thought I was in Germany, I didn't know I was in Denmark. In face, Johannes, the Danish boy who found and helped me, was trying to persuade me that I was in Denmark. He took coins out of his pocket and was showing me pictures of the King and Queen of Denmark on the coins, trying to convince me that I was in Denmark. He finally did convince me.

Although I was wounded, I think I was more scared than anything else. When you're in shock, you don't feel the pain so much. I was really bewildered. It's a kind of a lonesome feeling to be knocked out of the sky and not knew where you are and wondering what's going to happen in the next half hour.

My most terrifying moment would be when we were shot down and those attacking airplanes were following me.

The parachuting itself—it was something I had to do immediately. I thought I was going to be killed. So I jumped out. I was the first one out and the plane was on fire and there was a lot of confusion and bedlam. We just went out. Our communication system was out and the bell system for bailing out was out. Everything was out. So we had to make our minds up ourselves to go, and we went. Norman Carnie and I went first and then as the plane came down gradually and was being attacked, other guys were coming out.

It was a very peaceful moment when the chute opened. It's hard to describe. There's no feeling of emotion. You're just sort of suspended. Of course, as you get nearer the ground, you know something is going to happen. That's a little scary. But it's a very peaceful moment to be up there in a chute. I'd like to experience it again someday, but I haven't had the guts to do it.

I recall most of my last mission very vividly. Not all of it. I still have some blank spots, even after going back to Denmark and going into those fields and seeing where we were shot down and talking to eyewitnesses. They told me I was in two hospitals. One hospital I remember vividly, but the other hospital they told me I was in, I don't remember at all. I think that was due to my head injury. So there are some blank spots.

We were on a mission to a target in Poland, Posen. We were not able to bomb except visually in occupied countries, so we went on to a secondary target, a port called Rostock in Germany. We were able to get our bombs off, and we continued on our way home and got hit over Denmark. Just four days earlier, we had flown the exact route and mission with no trouble. That was on February 20th.

There are twenty-one planes in a Group. The formation is comprised of three squadrons, a high, a low, and a lead squadron of seven planes each. We were flying in the "tail end Charlie" position in the high squadron when we got hit. That's the most vulnerable position to fly.

We got hit very badly; in fact all four officers in the front of the plane were hit. The German fighter just raked the entire length of our plane. That first pass did all the main damage. He came back and did some more shooting, so did two other fighters, but the first pass was the one that caused us to crash. We didn't have any fighter escort at that time.

Usually, if you got hit badly enough, you had to drop out of formation, then the German fighters picked on you. That's what they did in our case. There were four FW190 Fighters involved in this attack on our plane over a period of about ten minutes. Our gunners were able to shoot down three of them.

All I knew was that I was that I was shot down, survived, was a prisoner and came home. If course, I knew some details, but most of this information has come to me in the past twelve months, thanks to Johannes and Fritz, Johannes' son, and the eyewitnesses.

One moment we were flying along fairly peacefully, and the next moment it sounded like a clap of thunder over my head. That resulted in a hole blown through the tail that you could have driven a Volkswagen through. That was the first pass the fighter made when he did his major damage. That started the panic. In a matter of a minute, I was out of that plane.

I was the first one out of the plane, and the others soon followed. In a period of probably only two minutes, everybody left the plane, except the ones who had to crash land; because they were so badly wounded they couldn't parachute out. Due to his injuries, Elmer kept losing consciousness, so it was Steve who brought the plane down for the crash landing. Elmer says that Steve could have bailed out, but stayed to help the others and bring the plane in. And of course, that saved Elmer's life. Lars was the only officer who bailed out. He didn't want to go, and Bob Joyce had to push him out.

Elmer made Steve Kish get out of the plane. Steve had been shot through both legs, but he got out of the plane. Elmer then went down into the nose section to assist my navigator, Cliff Sahner, who was dying. Cliff handed him his pistol and said, "I want you to shoot me."

Elmer said, "I can't do that. Don't worry, I'll get you out."

Cliff's body was lying across the door of the nose hatch. There was no way to get the door open, because Cliff was lying on the handle. Elmer couldn't move him; he had no strength, because he was so badly wounded. So he said, "I'll go out through the opening in the waist and come around to the front and open the door from the outside." As he walked back through the plane and got into the bomb bay area, the plane blew up and he was badly burned. All he could do was roll out of the plane in agony and into a ditch. In addition to his chest wounds, his face was burned and he lost the tips of his ears and his eyelashes. Steve was later found, conscious, lying out in the field.

So my navigator, Cliff Sahner, died in the plane and it's very questionable whether he could have gotten out anyway. But the pilot has had to live with that all these years. He promised Cliff he would come in and help him. So he rolled out of the plane into a ditch, and the next thing he knew, people were attending him.

But the ammunition was flying all over the place. Elmer just recently finished writing his story. He lives in Fresno, California. His story is just unbelievable.

George Pachacek, our Top Turret Gunner, was also killed. He bailed out too low. His parachute did partially open, but there just wasn't enough time to break his fall. Bob Joyce went out just before him and he said, "As soon as my chute popped, my feet hit the ground." George went out right behind Bob, and just that couple of seconds was enough to make the difference.

When I hit the ground, I was injured, and the next thing I knew, this young boy, Johannes, (I didn't know his name or anything about him then.) picked me up, put me on his bicycle and wheeled me to the farmhouse at Anton Lund's farm. Norman Carnie, who had bailed out right after me, landed unhurt and walked along side Johannes and me.

It was the middle of the day, 3:30 in the afternoon. We sat down for coffee and cake, because it happened to be Mrs. Lund's fortieth birthday. Shortly thereafter, Dr. Jens Hein arrived. He was a Danish doctor who was called to the house to treat our wounds. He said, "We can't get you out to Sweden, because the Germans know you're here. We're going to have to take you to the hospital and get you fixed up. Then the Germans will take over." Which is what happened.

I was in the hospital for two days with a German guard outside the door. The Danish nurses and other hospital personnel would come into the room and smuggle food to us—oranges and bananas, whatever they had there. They were very friendly and very helpful. They also wrote letters to my family, which were smuggled out through the Underground at great risk. On one letter, the signature of the writer had been cut off by the censor and was replaced with the words, "Somebody Dane." Then the Germans took us away from the hospital, and we were on our way to Germany.

I had a fractured skull and a broken ankle and spent only two days in the hospital. The Germans were determined to get us out of Denmark. The only person they let stay was my pilot, who was shot through the chest, right through the lungs, and he spent four months in Denmark in the hospital and five months in Germany in the hospital, and then he ended up at Barth, the last camp I was in. He was seriously wounded.

I had some problems. For four or five months, I couldn't really walk. Now, I'm okay. My ankle did heal up. The Danish doctors fought to keep us there those two days. You could never determine what the Germans were going to do. The Germans wanted to take Elmer, too, but Dr. Hein wouldn't let them. He convinced them that the pilot would have died. It was an incredible experience for us to go back there and talk to people who were eyewitnesses to this whole thing.

On the way to the hospital from the farm in Dr. Hein's car, he told us to duck down in the back seat and said, "I don't want anybody to see you." So I didn't get to see anybody until I got to the hospital.

Captured

The first Germans I saw were just ordinary German guards. It was a fairly frightening experience to see the people you were supposed to be fighting, but it didn't take us long to get used to that. We came in close contact the Germans from that time on.

Before we left Denmark, some German official questioned me. While he was talking to me, a German airman came into the room, and I was introduced to him. He said he was the pilot who shot me down.

We were then transported from Denmark to Frankfurt in the southern part of Germany, which is where all prisoners went. They were all processed through Dulag Luft, the main base in Frankfurt. Some stayed short periods of time, some maybe a couple of weeks. I was there about three days and I spent one day in solitary, which was standard procedure.

When they finished processing us, they put 50 or 60 Americans in a boxcar and shipped us almost all the way back to where we had been. It was very crowded in the boxcar. We were in there for six days, until we got to a camp up in an area of the country called Pomerania, near Estonia. It was very cold up there.

Stalag VI, Heydekrug

The camp we were put into was Stalag VI. It was near the small town of Heydekrug.

Stalag VI was not a camp just for Americans. Each nationality had its own compound. All the RAF guys were in one compound. There were four compounds to the camp. At one time, we were all mixed up—Australians, New Zealanders, Canadians, and Russians. But the Germans got smart and separated us.

There were about 10,000 men at Heydekrug. We stayed there from February until June or July of 1944. We were evacuated from the camp because the Russians were approaching.

They shipped us, by boxcar, to the port of Memel, up on the Baltic. It was west of the camp we had been in.

They took us and put about 2500 of us in the hold of a ship. It was a ship called the Masuren—I'll never forget that name. We were in the hold of the ship for two days. Then we sailed to Stettin and our fear was that we'd be bombed by our own fighters or bombers. It was a miserable trip. We didn't see daylight. We just stayed in the hold of that ship.

I don't think the ship had any kind of marking on it to show it was a POW ship. As far as I know, they flew only their own Nazi flag.

It was a famous ship because of that evacuation incident.

It was a bad experience being in the dark down in the hold of that ship. We were very crowded; we couldn't even stretch our legs.

They would lower buckets down to us. The same buckets were used for drinking water and for "obvious reasons." However, we got out of there safely.

When we got off the ship, we were taken, by boxcar, to another railroad station. On that boxcar trip, they handcuffed us together. Two men would be handcuffed together. I don't know why the Germans did that, because they had never done it before.

The Heydekrug Run

When we arrived at the railroad depot, they got us out of the boxcars, but they wouldn't take our handcuffs off.

We then went on a two-mile run from that station to this new camp. That two-mile run was later classified as a war crimes event. And it was an event all right!

My right arm was handcuffed to my buddy's left arm so that we were able, with the other hand, to carry whatever we had. They were trying to provoke us to make some sort of escape. They had guards with dogs and bayonets, and off on the side of the road, about thirty or forty yards into the woods, they had machine gun emplacements all along this two-mile stretch.

So they were trying to provoke us to make a break. We were stumbling along with out belongings, and any time you went down, you were beaten. It was a nightmare.

Unfortunately, I was handcuffed to Bob Richards, (who was from Chicago), one of my best friends in the camp. He still had an open wound in his leg and was limping and only had one eye. He had lost an eye when he was shot down, which was sometime prior to my being shot down. They'd fitted him with a glass eye. In any event, here he was in not very good physical shape, and I was handcuffed to him. This was in July of 1944.

We learned after the war that this run had been classified as a war crime. They had rounded up all the Germans who were responsible, but those guys got off. Believe it or not, they weren't able to get enough proof that this happened.

We had one death and many guys who were badly bayoneted, badly beaten. My buddy and I were badly beaten. We went down twice; we stumbled. And as soon as you hit the ground, they were on you.

When we arrived in the camp, about 2500 of us, they put us out in the field and they just left us in that field until they were damn good and ready to put us in the camp. It was a new camp that had just been opened.

The Luftwaffe was partially responsible for troop movement. When we got to that railroad depot and got out of the train to make that two-mile run, it was a completely different contingent of troops. They were Wehrmacht and the headman was a *Hauptman*, a captain, by the name of Walther Pickardt. He was a Nazi and the troops that ran alongside us with their dogs and bayonets, were young naval cadets. They were youngsters, fifteen, sixteen, and seventeen year olds. Their job was just to prod us and do whatever they could to provoke us. They were definitely trying to get us to make a break so they could shoot us. Nobody was shot.

I have all this on a video put out by the 8th Air Force Historical Society, called "Behind the Wire." It's a marvelous video. It shows the whole POW experience, including this event, which is called the Heydekrug Run. There were a lot of guys involved in this run, about 2500, so there were many eyewitnesses. Unfortunately, by the time the war was over, it was too difficult for many of them to make the trip back to Germany to the war crimes trial. They just wanted to be home and to get on with their lives, which is very understandable.

But our American prisoners, at the end of the war, were able to take out retribution on one German guard, who was particularly cruel. We called him *Big Stoop*. His real name was Schmidt. He used to beat up prisoners just for the heck of it. Well, they got him after the war. He's history and he was part of that whole event.

The trip to Stalag Luft I

The name of the camp we went into was Stalag IV. It was in Keiefheide.
It was one of the big Air Force camps in Germany. We stayed in that camp until the following January (of 1945). The Russians were again approaching, so we had to evacuate. I was fortunate enough to go with a small contingent, again, about 2500 men. We were transported, by boxcar, to a camp at Barth, Germany, Stalag 1, up on the Baltic. It was a well-established camp for Officers and had been there for years.

The rest of the prisoners, the other 8,000, went on the road and marched from that point until the end of the war. They marched from January until May. They just kept moving. I was very fortunate to get on that train to the Baltic.

Why did the Germans take the time to move us away from the Russians?

Word came down that the American prisoners were valuable to the Germans to be used as a possible bargaining chip at the end of the war for surrender terms. Of course, you talk about rumors and scuttlebutt. We had rumors where they were going to shoot everybody, which wasn't the case. We were valuable to them, or they wouldn't have bothered to move us.

The American Officer in charge at Stalag I at Barth was Colonel Hubert Zemke, the famous fighter pilot. He was the highest-ranking officer in our camp, one of the Aces of the 56th Fighter Group, a well-known personality. He had had a lot of experience in dealing with the Russians. The Russians actually liberated us from Barth and wanted to take us all back into Russia. Zemke wouldn't let them. He said, "You're not taking one man out of this camp."

So he held them off and it worked out to our advantage, because it was helter skelter there for about a week with no Americans in command, just the Russians who liberated us. There was a lot of confusion, people running into town and around the countryside and getting into trouble.

Eventually, Zemke got everybody back into camp and under control.

Apparently, before the war, in 1940, he had been assigned to Russia as a liaison officer, so he knew their mentality and how to handle them.

After the camp was liberated, I went into town once. We ran into a Russian who was quite drunk and was attempting to have his way with a girl who lived in the town. We tried to persuade him to leave her alone. We traded items that we had with him. I traded my watch for his, and I still have that Russian watch today. That was the only time I went into town. We decided it was better to stay in the camp.

All of our camps were run by the Luftwaffe, which was fortunate, because they had some feelings of respect for fellow airmen.

Every couple of months, the Gestapo would come in. They'd come in with their long leather coats and their boots and the skull insignia on their caps, and everybody was terrified of them, including the Luftwaffe.

Our guards could be mean, but they still gave us better treatment than you would get at other camps. However, beatings were a common occurrence, and we had three or four fellows who were shot.

They were shot because they weren't obeying the rules. For instance, we had certain hours when you could leave your barracks. You couldn't leave before six a.m. or after eight p.m. You had to be inside your barracks with the shutters closed. If you were out at any other time, you could be beaten or shot. We had someone shot who was standing in the doorway of the barracks, another had gone outside to go to the latrine. One guy was shot sitting on the windowsill. If you had a belligerent attitude, you could be shot at the slightest provocation.

We had lots of guys who attempted to escape. They would get out and be brought back and thrown into solitary. But our camps were generally well run. They didn't usually shoot men for trying to escape, but they punished them. They'd get three weeks in the cooler (solitary) or something like that.

I never tried to escape, but I had friends who were involved in the digging of a tunnel. They couldn't have everyone involved in the escape plan, because, for one thing, they needed secrecy. You know, "too many cooks spoil the broth." I did have a close friend who was involved in the digging, but we never had a successful escape from any camp I was in. The British did. We weren't really any place long enough to get anything organized. We'd just get started on something, and we'd be moved out.

We tried to keep busy with all kinds of hobbies, whatever you could do. We played sports, we played cards. While I was at Stalag VI, we received Red Cross packages fairly frequently, but after the Invasion (Normandy), that slowed down.

At the end of the war, when I was at Barth, I lost a lot of weight. The last few months of the war, we didn't have much of anything to eat, and I lost about forty pounds. It doesn't take long to lose weight if you don't have anything to eat. You lose the weight fast.

Prison camp food consisted of German bread, soup and potatoes, which were supplemented by Red Cross parcels, when we could get them. Sometimes there were two to four men to a parcel, depending on how many parcels came into the camp. But we had enough calories to survive on until the last three months of the war.

I received about fifty letters and a couple of packages from home while I was in the prison camp. I heard from Joan, who later became my wife, and my parents and friends. Interestingly enough, the guys in my barracks back at Horham sent all of my things home to my parents. They didn't divide up my stuff between them, which is what often happened.

We had two doctors at Camp IV. They were also prisoners. One was American, the other was British. One of the barracks was used as an infirmary. I tried to get some medical treatment when I was beaten up on the Heydekrug Run, but so many were hurt that I was unable to get any treatment.

I wasn't on the Shoe Leather Express (the forced march). The Shoe Leather Express was the group of 8,000 guys from our camp that went on the march instead of being transported by boxcar. The Germans wanted to take 2,000 men that were sick or wounded by train from Stalag IV to Barth. Well, there weren't quite enough to fill that contingent, so the Germans told us to hand pick the additional men. We drew cards. I drew a high card, so I got to go on that train ride instead of the Shoe Leather Express. That was just a stroke of luck.

Liberation and post war

We knew the Shoe leather Express was on the road, but we didn't have any details until after the war. When we got back to Camp Lucky Strike in France, which was where everybody was processed to go home, we got to talk to all the guys that had been on the Shoe Leather Express. They were all over Germany living in barns and fields, scrounging food, whatever they could do. I missed all that, which was very fortunate for me.

Of the three surviving officers on my crew, Steve and Lars were sent to Sagan, Stalag III, an officer's camp. Elmer was sent to another officer's camp, then to Barth, Camp I, where I eventually met up with him.

All the rest of us enlisted men were in Heydekrug. Carnie, Bob and I were in the same compound at Heydekrug and McCullock and Seelig in another. Carnie and I were in the same barracks room. We were also all in Stalag IV, but not in the same compound, and after that we were split up as the Russians were advancing. We were moved out to different camps.

For many years, I did not keep in touch with any of the fellows I was in prison camp with. But now, since I've joined this Prisoners of War organization here in New Jersey, I'm in close contact about a hundred guys, whom I see every Tuesday. We meet at Lyons Veterans Hospital, down below Bedminster, at Liberty Corners. We help each other out on filing claims for benefits.

Ex-prisoners of war have special benefits that are not available to other veterans. It doesn't seem fair, but that's the way it is. We didn't set it up, the Veteran's Administration died. There are about twenty different presumptives that an ex-prisoner of war can apply for. They presume that these ailments happened while you were a prisoner, however, you have to prove it. But the benefit is available. So we take fellows in and we guide them through this process, which could take two or three years to get to 100 percent.

We help each other. I have three or four men that I'm working with right now who have just come into the group and didn't even know about these benefits. I met a guy at Teterboro, at the air show, by the name of Bernie Levine. He was standing behind me in line, and we got to talking.

He was in the same Camp I was in Barth. He was a Bombardier. Now I've got him in the program. So I'm in contact with a lot of the ex-prisoners, guys in the Air Force especially.

The name of the group is the American Ex-Prisoners of War. It's a national organization with about 30,000 members. Our New Jersey chapter is very active. We meet every week. Other chapters throughout the country may only meet once every three months. But we do more for our members than any other group. We have more 100 percenters, men on 100 percent disability. The rest of the chapters look on our group as the model for filing claims. We have a very good rapport with the Veterans Administration in Newark and East Orange and at Lyons. So we're doing a lot of good for our fellow ex-prisoners.

I got started in the group when Karnig Thomasian saw my license plates, beeped his horn and pulled me over, and told me about it.

We flew out of Barth in May of 1945. They brought a bunch of B-17s up to an airfield close by the camp and flew us out over a period of two or three days. They took us to France, to Camp Lucky Strike. Lucky Strike was a RAMP (Recovered Allied Military Personnel) camp. From Lucky Strike, we were processed and then sent home by ship, an old Liberty Ship. It took five or six days clunking along, but we were very happy to be on the way.

It felt marvelous just to be liberated. You can't explain the feeling. Just to know that you're free. It's a wonderful feeling.

I came back to Camp Patrick Henry in Virginia, where we were re-processed. But first, we were given a sixty-day furlough. At that time, they had a point system, and you needed to have a certain number of points to get discharged from the service. You got so many points for being overseas, so many points for each decoration awarded, and so forth. At that time, you had to have sixty points to be discharged.

I didn't have sixty points, so they reassigned me to an outfit in Rome, New York, for another thirty days, after which time they lowered the point system. It was the middle of August when I had to go back to get reassigned after my sixty-day furlough. You were supposed to be assigned as close to home as possible, but Rome, New York, was about 300 miles away from my home. I got out in October of '45.

I used the GI Bill for college. I went to the New Bedford Textile

Institute in Bedford, Massachusetts. My family has been involved in the textile business for three generations.

How did it come about that I was able to revisit the place in Denmark where I was shot down?

Call from Denmark

On February 24, 1995, the phone rang, and I wasn't home. My wife answered, and this voice said, "My name is Johannes Ulrich. I'm the man who put your husband on a bicycle and took him in to the farm." She couldn't believe it. I came home about half an hour later. She had his phone number, and I called him right back.

Johannes has tracked me down through Gary, the son of Bob Joyce, my ball turret gunner. Gary had written the mayor of Tonder, Denmark, the town where I was in the hospital, saying, "I'm the son of Bob Joyce who was shot down near Tonder during World War Two. I'm trying to get some information about the crash. Can you help me out? We'd even like to come over there and visit the place where my father was shot down." Well, that letter got pigeonholed.

Somehow or other, Johannes found out about the letter. He seems to know everybody in Denmark. When he found out, he called up the mayor and said, "Listen, you can't let that letter just sit there, you've got to do something about it." So that's how Johannes found out about Bob Joyce. He knew that Bob was part of our crew; his name is on the memorial stone in the park at Oster Hojst. So he called Gary and eventually got my phone number through Gary.

Visiting the Danes and vice versa

February 24th was the anniversary of the day we were shot down. Johannes called Bob, Gary, and me. I thought I'd have to go to Denmark by myself, I didn't know that Bob and Gary wanted to go too. So I called the Danish Consulate in New York City to ask them what kind of VE Day celebration they were going to have. I said I was interested in going over there. Then I wrote them a letter telling of my circumstances. They wrote me back thanking me for my nice letter. They were taken by this letter and the story. That started the ball rolling.

Then, of course, I got hold of Bob and Gary, and we all decided to go to Denmark. Johannes made out the itinerary for us and the town of Logumkloster, which is the town near where we were shot down, arranged the trip. The committee from that town, the mayor and all the councilmen, the farmers, and eyewitnesses got together, pooled their money, and they put the trip together.

We paid for the flight over and a day and a half in Copenhagen, the rest of it was on them. We didn't spend a nickel! They had a special dinner for us and honored us at a commemorative ceremony. Each day got better.

We were in Denmark from May 1st to May 7th, and stayed in the town of Logumkloster, in a place called the Refugium. It's like a retreat. There's a huge church there built in the 1500s. That was our headquarters. Johannes would pick us up there every morning.

The Royal Danish Air Force was kind enough to take us up in a helicopter to tour the site of our crash landing and the places where the seven of us had parachuted out. Johannes had previously marked the location of the crash with a white cloth so that it was visible from the air.

At the final dinner, which was on the 5th of May, the committee presented each of the three of us with a leather bound photo album containing pictures of the plane crash taken fifty-one years before, as well as a copy of the speeches from the ceremonies and other memorabilia. They went to a great deal of expense.

One of the men on the committee, a local high school teacher, is also the town historian. He had researched the crash from top to bottom. His name is Frede Gutthardson, and he has a museum set up in the Town Hall in Oster Hojst. In it, he has hung pictures of the crash.

At the commemoration ceremony, the townspeople of Oster Hojst honored us with a full military ceremony. In the park, a large stone monument was erected in honor of the crew of "Just Elmer's Tune." This particular ceremony was for us, but the other event was the Danish people's way of honoring America and commemorating the 50th anniversary of the liberation of Denmark from the Nazis. The Danes are very appreciative of what the Allies did to help liberate them in World War Two.

The stone was erected in 1950 by a Danish Underground military contingent, called DSK. This organization dated back to World War I. They raised the money to buy and engrave this stone, and they put it up in the park at Logumkloster. Every May 5th since the stone was erected, they have held a ceremony there to commemorate the Danish Liberation. Gary, Bob, and I wanted to donate some money to them in appreciation, but found that the organization is no longer in existence.

The stone was dedicated in 1950. In 1970, my co-pilot and his wife traveled to Denmark and visited it. I have a newspaper article here concerning it. Anee and Steve Kish didn't run into the special ceremonies that we did, but still, it was very emotional for them. Steve and his wife sent me a snapshot of the stone.

But this affair in 1995 was really the Cat's Meow. The celebration was in conjunction with the 50th Anniversary of the Danish liberation. The local people just went overboard in honoring us Americans, my crew in particular. They were tickled to death that we came all the way to Denmark

We got Johannes to come to the States for the 95th Bomb Group reunion in October 1995. We went over in May and he came here in October. Now my wife and I are going back next May. All this has just happened this year.

Going back to the crash site in 1995 and going through the field where the plane had crashed and then exploded and burned was incredible. At the time, all our ammunition fired off. So ammunition and pieces of the melted aluminum are still there. All they did at the time was drag the carcass of the plane away. So when we went back, fifty-one years later, we picked up souvenir projectile points from the .50 caliber ammunition.

A German farmer owns the place now. There are quite a few Germans living up there. He saw us going back to the field where the plane had crashed. The field had been freshly plowed and it was furrowed. We had a long ways to walk to get to the actual spot where the plane crashed, maybe 300 yards. When the farmer saw that we were having a little problem walking in the uneven terrain, he got this huge combine-tractor with fourteen-inch tires, and he just ran back and forth and made a road for us to walk on.

I think he knew we were coming; the word was out. But it was very nice of him to do that. After he did that, he just continued plowing his field. We walked all through the area and picked up these pieces of aluminum and the .50 caliber ammunition. I even have a piece of the FW 190 that shot me down.

I now keep in touch with other members of my crew and the Bomb Group, but we went for many, many years just exchanging Christmas cards. We did this until our 95th Bomb Group reunion this last October in San Antonio. Now, we pick up the phone, and we call each other. From our crew, six were represented at the reunion: Elmer Costales; my wife and I; my co-pilot's widow, Anee; Bob Joyce's son, Gary; and Johannes. Norman Carnie didn't make it because of ill health.

Bob didn't come. He had a previous commitment. It was his 50th Wedding Anniversary. Incidentally, I went to his wedding, so I hadn't seen him in fifty-one years. He went to Lake Tahoe for the 50th celebration with his wife. I don't think he dared break it.

But Johannes came over from Denmark and stayed with Gary, Bob's son, for a few days. Gary took him to visit various universities to see their agricultural programs for raising pigs. Gary told me that Johannes knew more about raising pigs than all those farmers in Texas.

There were approximately 1,000 people at the 95th Bomb Group celebration. There were about 300 people at our POW breakfast. Johannes got up and gave his story. The man who was videotaping the reunion for the Group said, "You know, that story is so marvelous. I want you, Johannes, and Elmer to get together after this, pick a time, and we'll make a separate tape of it." So Johannes, Elmer, myself, Gary, and Annee sat at a round table for about an hour and a half taping. We just went through this whole story.

Johannes speaks English every well. And let me say this about the Danish people. In the one week I was there, I only met one person who couldn't speak English. And I'm talking now of everyone from young school children to people in their 70s and 80s. They teach English in the schools. So we got along just great in Denmark.

There was a Danish-American celebration that honored us at the New York Yacht Club. I got invited because of that contact I had made with the Danish Consulate. They remembered me, and they knew they were going to have this affair in New York. Just let me show you this, because I'm so proud of it. This is the invitation. It is captioned: "*Thanks to America.'* The Event of the Year." May 12, 1995 at the New York Yacht Club. It was a very posh affair.

It was attended by the Danish-American Society and The Danish-American Chamber of Commerce. His Royal Highness Prince Joachim of Denmark was the main guest of honor. Werner Valeur-Jensen, who was in the Danish Underground during the war, was the Emcee. There were three honored guests: Victor Borge; Jeffrey Montgomery Jones, who was with the OSS; and myself.

When we were in Denmark, Johannes had driven us around in his car past the homes where Prince Joachim and his mother, Queen Margrethe lived. We went to her castle, more like a parliament building. The flag was flying, which meant that she was in residence. So a month later, when I got to meet the Prince at the New York Yacht Club, I shook his hand and said, "Oh, by the way, I saw your mother last month. I drove by your house." Of course, he knew I was pulling his leg. He got a kick out of it. I said, "Your mother's a very beautiful woman. You should be very proud of her."

That night in Copenhagen, we stayed up until midnight, until Queen Margrethe came out of the Opera House. When she came out, they had candlelight and torches, and she stayed on the steps about fifteen minutes listening to the group singing. She was smiling. She's a wonderful woman. It was a beautiful celebration.

Then at the New York Yacht Club, they turned all the lights out, and we each had a little candle and we sang. So the torch and the lamps are a symbol of their liberation. The significance is that on May 4,1945, the German's left Denmark.

Then on May 5th, it came over the BBC that the Germans had officially surrendered, and the whole country lit up. Everybody in Denmark put a candle in their window.

Movies

There were several good Air Force movies that captured the experience of World War II as I knew it. *Twelve O'clock High* was an exceptionally well-made film. You can watch that film and pick out the spots that really hit the mark. That one stands out. I think anybody that flew in the 8th Air Force, or any Air Force, would get the same lump in the throat when they saw that film.

Stalag 17 was hammed up here and there, but I found it to be typical of POW life and one of the best and most accurate movies of prison life.

Ex POW

I've had some problems from all that I endured and saw, most of which I just have to live with. I would say, overall, that I got along as well as most prisoners. I had some bad moments as a POW, some really bad ones. But, hey, I was fortunate. Most of the other guys in our crew were badly wounded, and they took most of the suffering.

But I will say this; the Veteran's Administration is treating me very nicely and helping me with 100 percent disability benefits. The nice thing about going to these EX-POW meetings is that we can talk to each other. It's comforting.

Printed with permission of Ed Hays and the Army Air Forces Historical Association

It Finally Happened To Me, Too...

Narrated by Jack Ilfrey, Squadron Commander
8th Air Force, 20th Fighter Group, 79th Fighter Squadron
Edited by Erik Dyreborg

Introduction

by Erik Dyreborg

This story is from the book: "Happy Jack's Go Buggy—A Fighter Pilot's Story" by Jack Ilfrey. He became the first P-38 Ace in the 12th Air Force on March 3rd 1943.

Jack Ilfrey flew with the 8th and 12th Air Force, and amassed a total of 142 combat missions and 508 combat hours.

In May 2003, Don Hayes put a note in his newsletter for me, "The B17 Flying Fortress Association." I was looking for stories of American airmen of WW II for my next book, and Jack Ilfrey responded, and even mailed his book to me, which is based on the manuscript he finished in 1946.

I called Jack Ilfrey and thanked him for sending the book, and furthermore, he gave me permission to use any chapter and photo in his book for my next book (this book).

Of all the chapters in Jack Ilfrey's book, I have chosen this story, which by the way is Jack Ilfrey's own favorite.

Hit by flak

All of us fighter pilots had said it couldn't happen to us. "I'm too damn good to get shot down", but deep down in our minds I think we all had a plan as to what we would do if it ever did happen.

It was ironic, just before takeoff late that afternoon, the way I had briefed my squadron. I had told the boys it was my opinion from now on that if anyone was shot down in France, the best thing to do would be to lie low and try to find a hiding place with some French family until the allied moved into their section or to possibly work up toward the front lines.

Since the afternoon and evening of June 5th the 20th Group had been covering the invasion in our easily recognizable P-38 Lightnings. At Zero hour, 0756 June 6th we had a ringside "command performance" view of the invasion. A sight we will never forget.

By June 11th, Hitler's vaunted Atlantic Wall had been cracked wide open and a great allied army was firmly established on the Normandy coast. The 20th was taken off patrol and assigned dive-bombing and strafing mission targets behind the lines.

Our mission this day was to dive bomb the railroad bridge over the Loire River at LaPossiniere not far from the city of Angers.

Our P-38s were loaded with two 1000-pounders and I led 16 ships of the 79th Squadron. We took off at 18:48 and arrived in the target area at 2030. We came in out of the west with the sun on our backs and successfully dive-bombed the bridge. Several direct hits severed the tracks and inflicted serious damage on the bridge structure. We were then to strafe rail and motor traffic and any other targets of opportunity from the Loire, north into Normandy.

We had just reassembled at about 8,000 feet when I spied a locomotive with steam up in the village of LeLion just north of Angers. The Germans had become pretty wise to our attacks on trains and usually had several flak cars on the trains, especially one behind the engine; therefore, in order to do a complete job of knocking out the locomotives, we planned coordinated attacks on them. The leader, as a rule, went after the engine while his wingman went in after the guns on the flak car, and the others in the squadron provided cover.

Bail out Jack...

I dived down towards the engine, and while taking aim at it, caught a glimpse, out of the corner of my eye, at some tracer bullets coming up at me from the flak car behind the engine. Just after I opened up on the locomotive I saw the boiler explode and pulled up, my whole right engine burst into flame and smoke and some body yelled over the radio. "Bail out Jack; you're on fire." My cockpit immediately filled with smoke, blinding and choking me. I jettisoned my canopy and the smoke cleared momentarily, and I could tell I certainly wasn't very high above the ground. However, without any hesitation, I released my safety belt and shoulder harness and went over the left side, opening the parachute immediately. I had just looked up and yelled, "that S.O.B. works", when I hit the corner of a farmhouse and bounced off into the yard.

Jesse Carpenter, a pilot who was with me that day described it years later, "a horrible scene when the flak got you the day you strafed the train and your right engine torched—and your chute popped—oscillated once before you hit the corner of that French building—too damned close, Jack".

Art Heiden, another pilot on that mission, said there were some camouflaged 88's, field artillery guns in a field right next to the village and as I flew over this field, going in for the kill of the locomotive, they were just snapping at my ass.

He looked around for a field to land in so he could pick me up, but too many trees and glider barriers were erected in cleared spots. Now this is total camaraderie—a bond that existed between combat fighter pilots that few people can attain in a lifetime.

On the ground

So there I was—one minute, the sound of guns, the roar of engines, the smell of smoke, the touch of fire and rush of air as my body hurtled through it. Then the jolt of stopping in mid air, complete silence and laying flat on the ground in enemy occupied territory.

We pilots used to joke with each other about a "Pucker Factor" scale of from one to ten. I had just hit the ultimate—Number ten.

In a matter of seconds I was up on my feet and determined that physically I was still in one piece…threw off my parachute harness and dinghy and saw that the parachute canopy had fallen across the roof of the house—so not wanting it to be a beacon for the Germans I pulled it off and wadded into a pile—and threw off my helmet, oxygen mask and goggles, Mae West and heavy flying boots. Meanwhile, during all this a man with a pitchfork in his hand came out of a barn across the yard and three children appeared. They all stood watching me. Without thinking about it I asked the direction north and the man pointed. By this time I could see the smoke from my crashed and burning P-38 and hear the ammunition exploding. I wanted to make tracks out of the vicinity. I ran through trees, over, under, and through hedgerows until exhausted and fell into some tall grass.

I now had to urinate in the worst way but could not, as I was still registering too high on the Pucker Factor Scale.

I got out my rubberised waterproof map and determined my position to be about ten miles northwest of Angers, deep inside German territory.

Thinking of what I had told my squadron several hours before. I decided to get farther away from where I was shot down and try to find a place to hide.

I dismissed entirely the idea of heading south and across the Pyrenees Mountains into Spain, which had been the accustomed route of airmen who made their escape before the allied invasion.

I took off my flying suit, insignia and tie. That left me dressed in a gray sweater, shirt with open neck, no insignia, a pair of green O.D. trousers, and G.I. shoes. I put all items from my escape and first-aid kits in my pockets and tried to relax in the grass. In a short while it became dusk, at which time I got out on a small country road and started walking north.

The café

In a few minutes two boys on bicycles approached me from the rear and one of them rode right up to me and asked in very broken English if I was the American "aviateur" who had jumped out of a Lightning earlier. Sensing he was friendly and having nothing to lose one way or another, because of the way I was dressed and knowing very little French, I told him I was.

He smiled and said that he and his friend had just come from the wreckage of my P-38 and that the Germans were in the neighborhood looking for me.

He asked me to come with them to their village and he would see about hiding me. He pumped me on the bicycle and after a little while I let him ride while I pumped the bicycle.

It was after dark when we got to the village of Andigne and he asked me to hide on the side of the road while he and his friend Raymond went to see what might be arranged. My young friend was named Jean, 17 years old. Raymond was 19 and lived with his sister Odette and father, who ran a café and bar in the village. Jean and his family lived next door to the café.

After a short while they came back and took me to the café, which had living quarters upstairs. I met everyone and we sat down over wine, bread and a hastily prepared dish for me.

Jean was the only one who spoke any English, but as they talked about my staying there I could gather that the father seemed somewhat against it because of a few German soldiers who came into the café from time to time. But Odette pointed out there were no Germans stationed in the area and the chances of my being discovered were very remote.

After a long discussion and much hesitation the family agreed that, even at great risk to themselves, I could stay with them until liberated by the allies in the north which we all knew would take place sooner or later through the father had heard the Germans say they were "*driving them back into the sea*". We all lifted our glasses and said "*A Votre Sante*" and went to bed. I shared the one with Raymond.

It had been a hectic day for me and I had the feeling that God had been holding my hand.

When I went down to the kitchen next morning, it was quite a surprise to see these people seemed to have plenty of foods, chicken, eggs, mild, butter, and some fresh fruit. We very seldom saw these in England. However, they lacked such things as coffee, salt, and sugar. The kitchen with its big table in the middle, served as the family living and dining area and the rest of the downstairs was given over to the café. Just off to one side of the kitchen was the cellar that was well stocked with the wines they had made. There was no running water and all water had to be carried from the well in the village square a half a block away.

The whole family made every effort to please me and was eager to talk. The limited French I had picked up in North Africa seemed to be of no use to me, but when Jean was there we were able to understand one another, and when he was away at school the English-French dictionary that he found for me was a great help in trying to talk with the girls. There was another girl who came and helped out in the café during the day. It didn't take much doing to pick up a little kitchen lingo. Whenever Odette wanted wood for the stove she would just point to the stove. If she wanted the floor swept she'd point to the broom. Then with the dictionary we could make conversation out of one-word sentences.

My first paralysing fear of the Germans was partly overcome by watching them through the window when they passed on the road in front of the café and while I was never allowed in the café when customers were present, once I happened to be sweeping up the floor when some young German soldiers came in for a drink of cool wine. I immediately started sweeping toward the back and right into the kitchen and hoped the Germans hadn't noticed my casual but none-the-less hurried retreat.

The Jerries laughed a great deal and looked more like Boy Scouts than soldiers. Whenever the Germans came in I got a signal from Odette and dashed for the cellar. She said the enemy had never tried to take anything away from them and that they always paid for their drinks.

She kept me busy, chopping wood, washing dishes, sweeping floors, even tried my hand at cooking, however, more wine was served in the café than food.

The electricity came on two or three times for five or ten minutes each day and whenever it did I'd make a mad dash for the radio to tune in on the BBC in hope of catching the English news. At other times they would listen to the French news, broadcast by the Germans.

After supper we'd gather around the big table in the kitchen, drink wine and play records on an ancient victrola. The well-used needles scratched out "Flatfoot Floogie," "Tuxedo Junction" and assorted French tunes. Scratching or no scratching the music was good to hear and we would have done a little dancing if there would have been room in the kitchen.

These evenings brought on a bombardment of questions about America. Example, when I told them my father was a banker and that I had an automobile back home they wanted to know if I, too, were rich like the Americans they had seen in movies. They did not full understand when I explained that I was not rich; that when I was commissioned a 2nd Lt. In 1941, my base pay was $125.00 per month plus $75.00 for flight pay and that it was very easy to trade in my 1937 LaSalle, which I had just finished paying for, for a new 1941 Mercury and come out the $27.50 per month payments. No problem, those car dealers and finance companies were glad to see us.

The villagers would come into the café at night to talk over the war situation with the family, and I met a number of the trustworthy ones.

Jacques Robert & "Tour de France"

After a few days however, the family became worried over the fact that word had spread around that they were hiding me, an American aviateur. At that time I did not fully realize the extent these wonderful French people were putting themselves in jeopardy with their German captors.

In any event I had been piecing together the news broadcasts that I was able to hear and had come to the conclusion that the allies were bogged down on the Normandy front and it looked like they were going to stay put for a while. Plus, the fact the family was telling me the French news, which of course was put out by the Germans, were claiming to be driving the allies back into the sea.

So I made up my mind that I'd better try to get the hell up there before it became another Dunkirk.

I approached the family with my ideas. Could they give me one of their bicycles and some French clothing, as I wanted to try to make the journey up to and possibly across the front lines. At first they balked, but then after talking it over thoroughly it was decided that Jean could get me a French identity card from the town hall, as all Frenchmen were registered with the Germans. I had several pictures of myself taken in civilian clothing in my escape kit that worked fine on the identity card. Jean took my first name and Robert's and called me Jacques Robert (Jack Roberts), cultivateur (farmer); my age height and weight were given and under remarks he put that I had been injured due to bombings in Angers and was deaf.

Odette obligingly said I could have her bicycle.

In discussing the route I should take we decided it best for me to take the main road north, N162, to Caen that at the time was being besieged by the British.

I sat down and completely memorized my set of maps and some French maps that Jean provided me. The roads I was to take, towns I was to pass through and distances interpolated into kilometers. The father and the boys gave me many hints and pointers. I was now able to say many phrases in French, ask for food and water, directions, greet people, etc.

I gave them all the money in my escape kit, which included American dollars and gold coins, English pounds, Belgian and French francs, German marks, Dutch guilders and Spanish pesetas.

They laughed at my crisp new looking franc notes saying they had not seen any of these in several years and in turn provided me with a few worn franc notes and some bread coupons to help me on my journey.

Odette composed a note in French that read something like this: To Whom It May Concern: This boy, Jacques Robert, from Angers, is trying to get to Bayeux (which was in American hands) to see his parents. He has been injured in a bombing raid and is deaf and cannot speak. Please let him pass. Dr. R. Armand.

We all got up early the morning I left and Odette fixed me a good breakfast and prepared some chicken, bread and butter in a small canvas bag to tie to the bicycle, including the inevitable bottle of wine.

I was dressed in Robert's black beret, pants and coat. Odette's green shirt and a pair of Jean's old shoes. I had nothing on me that would identify me as an American or British in the event I was searched. Not even my dog tags, which I later caught hell about from American intelligence in London. Jean gave me a pocket-knife and a few matches. I felt confident I would make the trip.

As I pedaled away from the village in the cool, crisp morning, it was good to be out-of-doors again and I fairly lapped up the fresh air and longed for a cup of coffee and a cigarette.

After going about five kilometers I reached the main road, N162, that was to take me north, and up to this time I had not seen anyone on the road. I looked up and down the road and a short distance to the south, towards Angers, I saw three parked German trucks and some soldiers and was relieved I didn't have to go that way. This observation was soon to be of use because after a few more kilometers I came upon a lone-parked German truck.

Literally shaking in my boots I managed to pedal on, but just as I came along side the truck a German soldier jumped out of the truck and started yelling at me in German. I thought sure as hell this was it and was ready to surrender. But it didn't prove to be that serious. I had enough presence of mind to realize he wanted to know if I had seen two or three trucks back down the road. I answered "Oui, Monsieur." He got back into the truck and I continued on with renewed confidence. Here was the first German I had seen at close range. He had spoken to me and I hadn't died yet.

The French countryside looked very peaceful in the early morning. Some of the farms along the road were beginning to wake up. The men and boys seemed to have no modesty when it came to relieving themselves in the front yard, against the houses or trees. The women would come to the door with the slop jar and just toss it out.

I passed through several small villages, not seeing much of anything along the road and around mid-morning came to a Chateau Gonier, my first large town. I was first impressed with the friendliness of the people, walking or bicycling in the streets. Everyone had a "Bon jour, Monsieur" to say and I would mostly just nod back, hoping this wasn't too American. I did notice some damage along the railroad tracks that I presumed were leading towards the railway station. Men were working on the tracks and I did see one shot up boxcar. The rest of my passing through the town was uneventful and I hit the countryside again. About noon I picked out a nice spot off the road and sat down to eat my chicken. While I was eating I saw some German trucks loaded with soldiers go by. The trucks were highly camouflaged with tree limbs and branches.

After resting and drinking my wine, which did not quench my thirst, I started out again and knew I was going to have to find some water to drink very soon.

I spied a farmhouse off the road with a woman working in the front yard. I rode up and asked her in my best French for a drink of water, but she, evidently seeing I was a traveler insisted on my having wine, but I insisted on H^2O and she pointed to a well and I went and got myself a drink, hoping my typhoid shots would take care of me.

I saw many Germans and much equipment off and on the road that afternoon. The Jerries didn't seem to bother the French and the French stayed away from the Germans. There were refugees on the road on bicycles and in carts and I looked just like one of them, even though most of them were going south but I was going north.

I was still in fairly flat country and the going was easy—easier than the next few days proved to be. Even with frequent rests, this first day was getting rugged.

I was making very good time down a small grade into the town of Laval when I suddenly noticed that the main road I was on was going to pass through the outer perimeter of an airdrome and before I knew it I was right upon a sentry gate and a German soldier had stepped out to stop me. I decided it was too late and would look suspicious to turn around, so gathering all my wits I rode straight up to the sentry and stopped. He spoke to me in French and wanted to know where I was going and wanted to see my identification.

I had to play my deaf act here because it would have been a dead give-away if I had tried to speak French to him. I put over that I was deaf, "sound," with hand motions and showed him my identity card, that I hoped didn't look too new. He shook his head and said "nein," stepped into his booth and punched a buzzer. I knew for sure the game was up now. A German officer appeared from a building next to the road and the two were talking in German as they came up to me. I handed the officer my note from the doctor. He read it and it seemed to satisfy him and he passed it back to me with a wave-on signal. However, the other sentry was still holding my identity care and being afraid to speak, I politely reached out and took it out of his hand, putting both documents in my jacket pocket. Trying not to faint I was able to get back on my bicycle quickly and shoved off.

I rode right through the airdrome and saw what was left of the installations. Most of the building and hangars were on the ground and I took pride in the fact that I had dive-bombed this airdrome and had contributed to some of the wreckage. I saw two wrecked P-38's and wondered what had happened to the pilots, and there were also several of our external belly tanks lying around.

In a very camouflaged revetment under some trees, not over 100 feet off my road, were several Messerschmitt 109s being warmed up as if preparing for a flight. I pedaled slowly, looking, and it brought to my mind the time in North Africa, over a year and half ago, that I had flown one of these at Biskra that had been left behind by the Germans when we took over the airfield there. One of our Sgt., crew chief mechanics, who knew German, had carefully turned it back to good flying condition and over all the instruments and flying controls had written in English on adhesive tape the proper names of each, gas, R.P.M., air speed, etc. It was on a dare that I took it up, however, came time to land, I quite suddenly discovered that neither the Sgt. nor I had ever mentioned or adhesive marked the flaps control. I had one hell of a time getting that mean little s.o.b. back on the ground.

With these thoughts in mind there was a fleeting moment that—maybe I could do it again? But these "illusions of grandeur" left as quickly as they had come up, and I pedaled on.

The Germans had quite a contingent of French laborers working on the field, but I continued right through, past the sentry box on the other end without being molested and then on in to Laval.

And here I saw my first big damage from American bombers. The railroad station and yards and surrounding blocks of houses were destroyed. There were a lot of Germans in town, including women who were the equivalent of our WACS.

It was almost dark when I got through the town and knowing the Germans had a curfew on the French from sunrise to daybreak, and also being tired, hungry and thirsty I started looking for a place to spend the night. I saw a barn way off to itself in the corner of a field and went over to it.

Inside the barn was a nice sandy dirt floor, which felt pretty good when I fell down on it. I ate the rest of my food and drank what little wine was left, but I had to go without water. Sleep was not to be far off but it started to get real cool. There was a two-wheel dray in the barn with a canvas top on it, so with my little Boy Scout knife that Jean had given me. I cut out the canvas top and covered up with it. Poor Frenchman…at least he had donated to the allied cause.

I slept soundly and awoke with the chickens. My legs felt stiff and sore but otherwise I was greatly refreshed. When I pushed my bicycle out to the road I discovered I had a flat tire on the front wheel. I sat down feeling disgusted and at a loss as to what to do. It wasn't long, however, until a priest, dressed in his black robe and funny hat, came by on a bicycle and stopped, asking if he could be of assistance. I felt safe in telling him I was an American trying to make my way up through the lines. He was amazed at first and then in good English told me to follow him to his parish about three miles up the road and that he would fix my tie and give me something to eat. He got off his bicycle and we both pushed our wheels and talked all the way to his church.

His fellow priest prepared a very good meal for me that I ate heartily and after some tea and cognac I felt invigorated. I had never been an agnostic nor had I ever been a Catholic but these young fellows in this, what turned out to be a seminary, treated me like royalty. I spent the rest of the day and that night with them. Most of them spoke, at least, some English and continually asked me all kinds of questions about the U.S., how the war was going, and couldn't get over the fact that I was an ace (killer, one said) fighter pilot. Although I didn't feel like a killer, I suppose you could say we fighter pilots had a license to kill. My only thought was to get that s.o.b. before he got me.

In any event a good time was had by all. They had been hoarding things since before the war and for the occasion brought out Early Times, Lucky Strikes, (before the green went to war), German chocolate yet, and Green River. If memory serves me, that was what we used to buy in high school, shortly after prohibition for 99 cents a fifth, or was it a pint. I hazily remember them throwing me into a feather mattress bed like I had never experienced in South Texas, that folded up around me and I went off into blissful dreams, oblivious to the war around me.

Next morning, back to reality, hangover and all, hearty breakfast, tire repaired on the bicycle, I'm somewhat thinking I might like to stay here in this Utopia until the glorious allies come through the area.

But a priest came pedaling up the driveway and the others told me he's very Anti-American and I should get going right away. It seemed the Americans had bombed him out of his church and killed many of his parishioners and friends in Laval. So with my canvas bag filled with more food and water this time, I took off.

I pedaled on north for a while without much difficulty and until I came to a blockade in the road. A German sentry asked for my identity card, looked at my knapsack and me over thoroughly and let me through. I had been told that I would probably run across these blockades and that they were nothing to be afraid of.

In the early afternoon I reached the town of Mayenne and went through it without incident, seeing very little damage. The road I was on followed a pretty little river and at a secluded spot off the road I decided to take a much needed overall bath, as I hadn't had one since before leaving England that afternoon of my uncompleted mission, although at the moment I was working hard to complete it.

I was living from minute to minute, knowing only the events that were behind me, and being unable to foretell what was ahead. I stripped to my birthday suit and plunged into the cool water. It felt wonderful. While I was using some of the sand as a substitute for soap, I looked up and saw two French boys on the bank where my bicycle and clothes were, staring at me. Both of them appeared to be in their late teens or early twenties and one spoke to me but I didn't understand what he said. When I started swimming toward them, the boy spoke to me but I didn't understand what he said. When I started swimming toward them, the boy spoke again and when I did not reply he got angry and talked louder. Having no clothes on I stayed down in the water, sorta sweating out what was going to come next. Then finally I got the idea they wanted to know what I was doing there and it came to the point where I had to talk, or do something. So with gestures and a few words in French I told them I was deaf. I climbed out and brushed the water off me as I was going to put my clothes on over a wet body. The boy who had been doing a lot of the talking threw me a rag he had and gave me a friendly smile.

I felt relieved and reached into my bag and pulled out the food and the few remaining cigarettes the priests had given me and offered them some. They both immediately took a cigarette and while I was putting on my clothes tried to engage in conversation through gestures. I was now convinced that they were good boys so I told them in my best French I was an American aviator on my way to join the allies. This brought on exclamations of surprise and the one who had done all the previous talking burst out in almost perfect English, "Why didn't you tell us? You had us fooled. We thought you might just be up to no good and we were only interested in seeing that you didn't get too far on our property and steal something from us."

They invited me to their home and upon our arrival there, immediately opened a bottle of Calvados. We later named this, American Anti-Freeze. The two boys were brothers and the older one who spoke fair English had been in Canada and the U.S. before the war visiting relatives and friends. We seemed to have a lot in common and talked about everything.

They thought my plan was a good one but wanted me to stay with them for a while. I gratefully accepted their offer of food and a bed for the night. We arose early the next morning and even though I had a calvados headache my confidence and morale were way up.

I bade farewell to my friends on the little farm by the river near Ambrieres.

Now I began to hit the hilly rolling countryside of Normandy and, oh, how I did cuss those hills if I pushed that bicycle up a hill once, I did it a thousand times, each time falling on it and coasting swiftly to the bottom, only to start all over again. All of my previous thoughts of a bicycle trip through Europe were now leaving my head. But I'd be thankful that I had this bicycle.

All in all I did pretty well that day. During mid-morning I had sort of been playing tag with a convoy of six trucks fell of Nazi youths. None of them appeared to be over seventeen or eighteen years old. The trucks were moving slowly and would stop very often. Once, after passing each other three or four times, the soldiers motioned for me to hang on if I wanted to, and as tired as I was, I did. The Germans said nothing to me but they were all laughing and talking just like any group of teenagers anywhere.

We had covered a few more miles when a flight of six P-38's appeared and, brother; did those Germans stop and get out of the trucks in a hurry. I pedaled on for all I was worth. The Lightnings spotted the trucks, in spite of the fact that the vehicles were highly camouflaged with leaves and branches, and echeloned for attack.

I got up to the top of the next hill and watched the fighters ground stafe the hell out of the trucks. It was a very exhilarating experience for me and I felt like jumping up and down, clapping and screaming approval. They set all of them on fire. But it did mean I was without a lift.

It was a beautiful country in this part of France. The road was still following a river and there were only occasional Germans and equipment to mar the beauty of the scene.

At one point in the river several soldiers, the priests, my swimming companions, and others had said one of my greatest dangers would be that the Germans would probably take my bicycle away from me.

As I neared Domfront a lone German soldier walking in the opposite direction stopped me and demanded my bicycle. I put a determined fight to keep it by telling him my "mama" and my "papa" lived down the road quite apiece and I had to get there.

My getting home didn't make a difference to the Nazi and I was just going to get off the bicycle when a truck came down the road going his way. I pointed to it and he flagged it down and got in. What saved me again, I don't know?

I went on through Domfront, that had been pretty badly damaged by the allied bombers, and when I got on the other side of the town a truckload of Germans stopped and asked me for directions to someplace I didn't know and I just pointed and they tore off. Lucky again.

Toward late afternoon I approached the town of Flers, which appeared to be a very beautiful placed, sitting upon a hill. Everything was pretty and green and large open valleys were all around. I heard a large group of bombers in the distance and knew by the sound that they were B-17's.

I sat down to rest and watch the show. I had not waited long until the bombers, escorted by P-38's, most likely some from my own Fighter Group, came right to the town of Flers and bombed the railroad yards. Flers was an important railroad junction, and while I had been working my way out of occupied France, our American 8th Air Force fighters and bombers out of England had been bombing and strafing every military target they could find to allow the allied ground forces to advance.

It was a beautiful sight to me, not to the French, I'm sure, to watch the B-17's roll in and drop their bombs. I was several miles out of the city on a hill looking down on the spectacle. As far away as I was the ground trembled from the impact of the bombs.

After the planes left the whole center of the town was a maze of dust, fire, and smoke, which rose several thousand feet above the city. I could have taken some wonderfully revealing pictures of what a bombing means if I had only had a camera. French civilians had not seen cameras or film for several years.

There was no doubt on this raid that bombers were supposed to bomb only the railroad yards, but it was impossible to concentrate on so small a target from such a high altitude that that bombers had to fly, and I was soon to see, at very first-hand view, that even though the bombs had hit the railroad yards, many bombs had hit long and short and crashed into the buildings surrounding the yards, causing destruction and fires. The streets were full of rubble, lots of it from previous bombings.

After having pushed my bicycle over piles of rubble I was able to get back to the main road on the other side of Flers and it was time for me to start thinking again about looking for a place to stay. For several days now I had been doing this and felt like an old hand at it. I was beginning to hear the guns on the front and a new sort of feeling came over me. Was I to complete this mission at last? And even though I still had thirty or so miles to go, hearing the guns made it seem closer.

I saw two old ladies in a farmyard and I went up and asked them for food and drink. When they hesitated, I pulled out a few of my French francs and offered to pay. I suddenly realized that in almost 200 miles of travel I had not spent a franc. The old ladies still hesitated so I pulled out a few of the bread ration coupons I had never used and that turned the trick.

They took me into the dirt floor kitchen where chickens were roaming around at will and cooked up some eggs, potatoes, and meat. I couldn't tell what kind of meat but I ate it along with the wine offered me and it was good. One of the ladies indicated I could sleep in the barn and I didn't know whether to trust them or not, however, being a light sleeper I figured I could hear if anything out of the ordinary took place. Hell, I slept like a log on the hay and even the bugs in it didn't bother me until the first crow, which was practically in my ear.

When I was washing my face and drinking some cool well water one of the old gals came to the back door and said she had something to eat for me. It turned out to be more eggs and some sort of hot chocolate drink that was rather tasty. It helped out, did the trick, and all I had to use was a well-worn franc note. I thanked the old ladies in my best French, gave them a few of those franc notes, the chickens were now devouring the one I had used, and departed to the north. I was always traveling towards the north. My memory was beginning to fail somewhat but I finally remembered the Condè was the next largest town up from Flers. I was seeing more refugees heading south, German trucks and equipment moving north. I didn't bother anyone and no one bothered me. I reached Condé at an estimated noontime. I knew I was getting closer and closer to the front, but didn't have any idea what I would do once I did get there. I could only imagine, that this time it wouldn't be or look anything like "All Quiet on the Western Front."

It took me a couple of hours to get through Condé, or I should say over Condé, as most of it was one big mass of rubble. The bombers had really done a job here. Instead of streets, there were just lanes several feet deep in toppled buildings, and now and then there was a gaping hole where a bomb had spread the rubble.

A river ran through the town and for a moment I didn't know how I was going to get across as there were no bridges left standing. I saw dead cows and other live-stock floating in the river and a couple of bloated human bodies and wondered what had happened to the rest of the people. No one was stirring and it was ghostly quiet. A few small fires and smoke were coming from some of the rubble around me. I finally found a pieced of the under structure of a bridge that still stretched erratically across the river and I inched my way over to the other side.

It was hard to decide which way to go but my fighter pilot training or combat fly-ing had instilled a sixth sense, of sorts, as to directions and I instinctually knew which way to go north towards Caen. I had to carry my bicycle over long blocks of knocked out building and strewn rubble. I gradually worked out toward the residential section, which was not so badly damaged, and the streets were pass-able. I pedaled on in to open country and was able to make better time.

There were many more Germans now and a lot of equipment. Communications men were busy stringing wires. I noticed there were yellow, red, and blue wires. I pedaled and pedaled and was feeling somewhat oblivious to the war going on around me and middle to late afternoon I approached Thury-Harcourt.

I was beginning to see large guns, the infamous 88's in position in the fields, all expertly camouflaged. At this point I became undecided as to whether to try going on to Caen or not. It was not too very far off and I didn't know who held it, British Americans or German, so I turned northwest toward Bayeax relying on my note from the doctor and the fact that it had, at least earlier, been in Ameri-can hands.

In a round about way, again relying on my directions instinct, I pedaled into the village of Erecy. Dead cows and horses were lying around and I could hear the whiz and explosions of shells from the long-range allied guns. I still didn't know whether I was in front of American or British troops.

While I was at the village well in the square, drinking and filling my bottle with water, a young boy came up and asked me a question I didn't understand. He repeated the question and I caught something about my being a stranger and where was I going. I replied "Bayeux." He started shaking his head no, and again I caught the words "Yanks and Tommys".

It was easy to see this village was in German hands because of all the feverish activity that was taking place. Several Frenchmen stood around looking unconcerned and the kid seemed just as detached as the others. But I took a chance with him and told him I was hungry. He asked me to follow hi to his house on the outskirts of the village. His mother and sister made me welcome and the first thing they did was show me an American and British flag.

I gathered from what I could make out from the conversation they were preparing for the liberation by the allies and were very much enthused. When I told them I was an American "aviateur" there was much embracing and kissing, in the good old French manner.

It developed the mother had lived in Maryland, right out of Baltimore, for several years before the war and she spoke fair to good English. The daughter brought out wine and in addition to the usual eggs, she fixed some cabbage and something that resembled sweet potatoes, and some goat meat. We had a celebration that night, although we had to keep quiet, as we didn't want to arouse the suspicions of the Germans. Friends came in, mostly young people around the age of the girl and myself and it was interesting to talk with them, mostly through the mother. I learned how the occupation had been the shortages of everything, what they thought of the Germans, however, I'm sure the mother didn't translate all the cuss words.

We could hear the whine of the shells before they hit and the noise didn't seem to bother those Frenchmen; but it sure bothered the hell out of me. One man reported that he had learned Caen had been under a terrific siege, very bad destruction, but should be in British hands by now. He also thought the Americans held Bayeux and that the only thing holding up the allied advance was the Jerry's big guns. They seemed to think that if I just went on up the road I was on I should eventually make contact with the British or possibly the Americans.

Good for them, I thought, but the mother didn't translate any percentages to me of my making it.

Around dusk, after 10 p.m. they prepared to retire. The mother said I could sleep with the boy but that we should all leave our clothes and shoes on in case we had to make a hasty exit. Some sleep! About the time I'd get to sleep the big guns would start firing and I'd keep listening for the one with my name on it. Daybreak came; none too soon, and I did feel better after splashing cold water on my face. The mother made some much-hoarded coffee and liberally fortified mine with Calvados, that good old American anti-freeze that put a charge in my stomach and confidence in my mind.

The road out of the village was a small narrow winding one bordered by hedgerows and trees, and it was filled with branches and leaves that the shells had knocked off the trees. Shells from both British and German guns were whizzing over my head. So this is no man's land, I thought. A most uncomfortable feeling.

Riding was hard and I was doing more pushing than riding. A little more Calavados and I exhilarated on.

Shortly before reaching Fontenay I ran head on into two young German soldiers who were carrying one of their wounded comrades. Their eyes lighted on my bicycle and I could see the "mama-papa" act wouldn't work, so when they demanded the bike to put the wounded boy on, I got off and let them have it at once. Thank you, Odette, for a very lovely trip. However, before letting me leave one of them frisked me thoroughly and came out with the knife Jean had given me. He also put one hand inside my shirt, at the neck, and felt under my arms. If I had been wearing my dog tags he most certainly would have found them and my game would have been up. At best I would have become a Prisoner of War or at least that's what they said at Geneva.

I walked on toward Fontenay and now was seeing quite a few Germans around on the roads and in the fields, all in camouflage type helmets. I noticed a lack of vehicles and self propelled funs and realized this must be part of a rear guard action and that surely I couldn't be far from my objective. I walked on into the village, which seemed strangely quiet.

Some damage was evident but appeared to be from small arms and field artillery shells, instead of bomb damage like I had seen in other town. In the town square some German soldiers were milling around working on various pieces of equipment, others, cat napping. I saw two soldiers trying to get an American Jeep started but I didn't have my rotor in my pocket at this time, so couldn't help. A few Frenchmen were also milling around but the Germans didn't pay them or me any attention. I did not hesitate but kept walking on north through the outskirts and out again into open country.

I walked on a mile or so and came to a point where the trees stopped and the road ran off through a clearing. As I was just about to step out into the clearing I heard voices over to my left and saw some Germans entrenched in the tall grass right at the edge of the clearing. I could tell they were yelling at me and motioned for me to get down. I promptly fell to the ground and one of the soldiers crawled over my way and motioned for me to follow him back into the grass. We crawled a few yards and came up to a group of them lying around in holes. Several near me started asking questions in German, which, of course, I didn't understand. I couldn't pull my deaf act with the shells going overhead and hitting the ground every now and then nearby.

One of the soldiers asked me in English if I spoke English and I put on one of dumbest don't understand a word you're saying faces. Thank God no one spoke French to me. We laid there for a while until one of the soldiers near me was a hit in the leg and stomach with shrapnel. I readily caught on they wanted me to put the wounded soldier in a wheelbarrow, which was out in the ditch by the road, and wheel him back to a first aid station that luckily I had seen back on the road just after leaving Fontenay.

I dragged him through the grass, put him in the wheelbarrow and started wheeling. The wheeling was easy at first but it soon proved to be real labor. The wounded kid didn't seem to be over seventeen years and he was in great pain and had me stop frequently. I felt sorry for him in a way and looked to see if he had any medications on him to ease the pain, or cyanide to completely get rid of it.

I struggled on with the wheelbarrow and was finally able to deposit the boy in front of the first aid station that I supposed to be something like what we would call a field hospital. Some medical men came out and took him in and I turned to walk back into the village. Someone from the door yelled, like we would say "Hey". I froze in my tracks, afraid to play deaf and keep walking, turned around and saw a medic motioning me to come back. When I got up to him he gave me the surprise of my life, two cigarettes and some kind of candy bar. I thanked him in my best French and bowed out and took off walking toward the village square, as I certainly didn't want to retrace my steps back to the clearing.

I was now somewhat at a loss as to what to do. That feeling of near and yet so far. I was off my beaten memorized tract, but knew that Hacux could not be very far. So when I reached the square I turned west and walked on out of town without incident. Not too far out I saw two boys, young teenagers, standing by a gate leading up to a farmhouse. Because of the horse and plow there I figured they had been working in the field and were now just resting and talking. They eyed me as I was coming up the road and I was eyeing them back.

As I came along side they gave me a friendly greeting "Bon jour Messieur". I took a chance and said 'Allemands?' They pointed northwest. Naturally my accent put very curious looks on their faces.

I then told them that I was an American aviateur, and they momentarily gasped but came on with broad grins. I tried to put over what I was trying to do, and they caught on. One got a stick and scraped on the dirt where we were, just outside Fontenay. A line to the west a few miles was Tilly and just before I got there was a small dirt road headed north and the British were entrenched less than a mile up the road.

I gave them a few francs and started off following their directions; now wishing I had a few more slugs of Calvados.

I noticed the country was beginning to open up, not as many trees, and more open fields. I could see farther in the distance. I also saw several large gun emplacements but very few soldiers around. Some Spitfires came over low, probably looking for targets to strafe and I saw the Germans hit one and he went smoking to the north.

At the intersection of the road where I was to turn were knocked out British vehicles, a few tanks and trucks. Some had been knocked out by guns and a few up my road appeared to have been wrecked by mines.

I turned to the north and started down the small open road, watching carefully for mines. I have often thought how funny it must have looked to see a poor dumb French farmer out on this road jumping over places and side stepping other places, but I had to be careful where I placed each foot.

About a quarter of a mile farther I approached an intersection of hedgerows. I heard several Limey voices—"What the bloody hell is a French civilian doing out there?"

I then saw the good old British helmets.

I Had Made It: VIVA LA FRANCE!

As I hit the intersection one of the Limeys yelled at me in French. I yelled back, "Sorry, Tommy, I don't speak French". He looked surprised, took a tighter hold of his gun and said, "Don't pull that stuff around here," and motioned me with his gun to get over there. I hurriedly explained that I was an American pilot who had been shot down and had been working my way out of enemy territory. His look of 'Oh Yeah' showed that he didn't believe me one bit. I asked him to call his sergeant, or whoever was in charge, as I wanted to be taken back to the headquarters of this outfit.

A sergeant did appear, was given a brief explanation, kept his gun on me and we walked several hundred yards back to a tank. He ordered several soldiers to strip search me while he climbed in top to use the radio.

It was a cold day in Normandy to be standing there without a stitch on. One of the soldiers threw me a great coat and another handed me a mess kit cup of hot tea. I almost thought it was delicious but started to sweat at the thought that I might also be in for a procto search. But no, the sergeant got out of the tank, got briefed on my search while I put back on my clothes and we got in a jeep and drove several miles to a large headquarters house.

I was taken into a large room where several serious looking British officers, one a colonel, and an American major liaison officer, were waiting to see and talk with me. They seemed quite upset that I didn't have any identification on me except my forged French identity care, but agreed that the picture on it was I. Being an evadee seemed to present a new and difficult problem to them. The American major asked all kinds of questions attempting to establish me as an American. With each answer all the gentlemen present began to ease up, relax, and even start to smile. One clincher answer I gave described my life as a student at Texas A & M, and the fact that we had won the Southwest Conference two years in a row, '38 and '39, playing in the Sugar Bowl Jan. 1, 1940. My memory was poor on the game because I had been too sick on Slo-Gin Fizzes.

He had already mentioned he was from Dallas, which jogged my memory when he asked, "What prominent building in a large Texas city has an animal on top of it?" I had worked at the 1936 Texas Centennial Fair in Dallas and knew the tall Magnolia Oil Corp. building had a large flying red horse (Pegasus) atop it. When the major said, "My God! He's got to be an American, a fellow Texan and a fellow Aggie," the rest of the group burst out laughing and a bottle of scotch was produced, over which they shook my hand, slapped me on the back and repeatedly said "Good show, good show."

Back to England

The major took me in charge and drove me in his jeep to a newly established airfield for P-47s. Luck was with me again as I knew some of the pilots. After they tired themselves of laughing at my story and costume, they arranged a flight for me on a hospital type aircraft back to England.

We deposited the wounded at a base in England and the pilots were good enough to fly me back to King's Cliffe.

I was a mild sensation when I walked into our pilots operations office as Jacques Robert and later at the officers' club where I got pretty drunk that night.

Jack Ilfrey & Jacques Robert are pictured above.

Next step was to report to Military Intelligence Service in London, Headquarters European Theater of Operations from which evolved Escape and Evasion Report No. 759 dated 20 June 1944.

The interrogation was one to make the Spanish Inquisition look anemic. The colonel, who was short, fat, and brisk could ask questions as fast as an adding machine can click. No detail was too small to be gone over with a microscope. We finished at last and I felt like a mildewed rag. The colonel said I had acted coolly and skillfully, but that I had not really used my head. In this regard, the colonel stated my indiscretions: (1) I had thrown away my dog tags; (2) I could have been shot by the Germans for not having any kind of identification; (3) I was very foolish not to have kept my G.I. Shoes. (The colonel considered these shoes important for walking. So did I. Jean slipper caused my feet to holler, scream, and groan with pain.); and (4) I did not go the accustomed route of airmen, i.e., across the Pyrenees into Spain.

The colonel then pointed out the French underground would have helped me to the Spanish border, where other members of the underground would have carried on. (I wanted to tell the colonel of the airmen who had died on the torturous ordeal of crossing the Pyrenees. I may have chosen the easier way, but I rightly thought I had a chance to live according to my plan.) The colonel further said I had not been so clever after all; that if there hadn't been so much front-line confusion, more attention would have been paid to a young "French" civilian wandering down the roads.

I was told by His Nibs, I would remain in London for an indefinite period. He said, as I already knew, anyone shot down in enemy territory was not usually permitted to fly again in that theatre of operations. He added, significantly, such airmen were sent home. (I caught my breath on this one. But I kept my mouth shut. Often you can foul everything up in the army by saying just one word.) I was dismissed and told to report at headquarters each day.

Back to business

Normally most everyone who evaded capture as I did, or escaped prison and got back, would be sent home for duty in the states. However, I returned to flying active combat missions. I didn't learn until years later that German Intelligence had a dossier on me and practically every other American fighter pilot in Europe and had I been shot down a second time and captured. I would have immediately been shot as a spy.

I cannot now recall the circumstances of my returning to combat.

Jim Bradshaw told one story to me at our 1980 Orlando reunion. He said I did receive orders to go home, but didn't want to go, so I borrowed General Anderson's P47, flew across the field scattering pieces of the orders out of the cockpit.

I do recall General Anderson calling me in for using his P47 for an unauthorized flight and damaging the landing gear upon return. How did I know that Jug had bricks in it's belly; it was one heavy bird. Brigadier General Edward W. Anderson was then Commanding General 67th Fighter Wing, 8th USAAF. He was one good Joe and had earlier been C.O. 29th Pursuit Group.

I was later to cause him more severe trouble, but that's another story.

Printed with permission of Jack Ilfrey.

Jack Ilfrey's book is a detailed and exciting piece of work. It is of 125 pages and includes more than 200 high quality pictures.

Highly recommended!

For ordering the book, "Happy Jack's Go Buggy", please contact the author, the Pilot himself:

Jack Ilfrey
1409 Nacogdoches Rd.
San Antonio, TX 78209-2751
Phone: (210) 805-0231

"Man O' War"

◆

A story about a B-17 crew on their final mission

8th Air Force, 401st Bomb Group, 612th Bomb Squadron
Edited by Erik Dyreborg

The crew

From L to R:

John H. Crowley Waist Gunner. Bailed out and died from his wounds that same night in a hospital in Reims, France.

Walter R. Rusch Ball Turret Gunner. Bailed out and became a POW.

John Katsaro Waist Gunner. Bailed out, evaded and escaped to England via Spain and Gibraltar.

Henry Kane Co-Pilot. Bailed out and became a POW.

Jack A. Dunaway Pilot. Bailed out and became a POW.

Theodore J. Krol Bombardier. Bailed out, evaded, escaped and made it back to England.

William G. Mock Navigator. Bailed out. His body was later located by the French underground where he had landed.

Marvin H. Benz Tail Gunner. Killed instantly during the attack of the German fighters.

Sterling J. Nichols Engineer & Top Turret Gunner. Replaced by Harry Horst (not pictured). Killed instantly during the attack of the German fighters.

Frank J. Mastronardi Radio Operator. Bailed out and became a POW.

Introduction

On that fateful March afternoon in 1944, the "Man O' War" and its ten-man crew were returning to the base of the 401st Bomb Group at Deenethorpe, England following a mission over Frankfurt, Germany. Mastronardi, then age 20, was the crew's radio operator.

Suddenly three German fighters attacked the lone bomber, riddling it with bullets, setting two of the engines on fire, killing two of the airmen, and wounding most of the others. The order was given to bail out.

The story of those anxious moments as well as the days and the months that followed are one of loyalty, courage, and fortitude. It's a story, too, that has been pieced together only in recent years, because none of the surviving crewmembers saw or knew the fate of the others until 1984.

The Last One Out

By Frank Mastronardi
Edited by Erik Dyreborg

Frank Mastronardi, August 1945, is pictured above.

Introduction

In October 1987, Frank Mastronardi and three fellow crew members of their World War II bomber "Man O' War" returned to Europe to retrace their steps of 43 years ago when they were shot down over Nazi-occupied France.

Mastronardi, along with fellow crewmembers John Katsaros, Ted Krol and Walter Rusch, returned to Europe in October 1987, each man tracing his steps of 43 years ago.

The trip also added a new chapter to the story when Mastronardi received the U.S. Air Force's Distinguished Flying Cross in ceremonies at the U.S. base at Alconbury, England. The medal honored Mastronardi for his "outstanding heroism and selfless devotion to duty" for helping Rusch and another airman bail to out of the plane before jumping himself.

In describing both the German attack in 1944 and the trip in October 1987, Mastronardi speaks modestly about himself, emphasizing instead the stories of all four men.

March 20, 1944, 1:30 p.m.

"The pilot, co-pilot, bombardier, Ted Krol, and the navigator, Bill Mock, were all up front," said Mastronardi, as he begins the story. "Behind them was the flight engineer in the upper turret."

"From my radio compartment behind the bomb bay, I could see the two waist gunners, John Katsaros and John Crowley. Walt Rusch was in the ball turret in the middle of that area," he said. "In the extreme tail was the tail gunner."

When the German fighters attacked, the tail gunner and the engineer in the upper turret were both killed. Katsaros and Crowley were seriously wounded, and Rusch received a leg wound and dust fragments in his eyes. Mastronardi picked up some shrapnel.

"We could not see up front, but we now know that the pilot and co-pilot got out and the navigator was seriously wounded," Mastronardi continued.

"Ted Krol pulled Bill Mock's parachute open inside the plane and pushed him out, but we found out later from the French Resistance that he was dead when he hit the ground. Ted then bailed out and hurt his ankle when he hit the ground, but he was not wounded".

Meanwhile, in the plane's waist section, Rusch was trapped inside the ball turret. During the attack the pilot dived the plane 1,000—1,200 feet to escape the enemy.

"Everything went topsy-turvy, and the loose shells from our mission resettled in the ball turret, the low point in the waist of the ship," Mastronardi said. "As a result, 50-caliber brass casings had worked down into the ball turret's door mechanism."

Katsaros and Mastronardi worked to clear away the casings. Thinking they had the door fixed, Mastronardi told the wounded Katsaros to go ahead and bail out.

"In turning back to help Walt out, I found out the door would only open a little further," he said. "The casings were jammed in—two or three of them—which were enough to keep the door from opening." He continued.

All this time, the men didn't know if the plane was about to explode or how much time they had before it hit the ground.

"I told Walt to close the door, and I used a screw driver or some instrument around there to clear out the shells," he said. "When that was done the door opened and Walt got out of the turret."

While Rusch got to his feet, Mastronardi saw the other waist gunner, John Crowley, move and realized that was alive. He got the severely wounded gunner up, clipped on his parachute, and when Crowley indicated he could pull his ripcord, Mastronardi pushed him out of the plane.

Now out of the turret, Rusch faced another problem. Bullets from the German fighter had torn open the canvas bag that held his parachute. The silk chute itself had some holes.

"It would still clip on Walt's harness, so we gathered up all the silk in his arms and he bailed out. Of course the wind immediately sent the chute up, and silk, being what it is, did not tear—the holes did not rupture."

Mastronardi bailed out soon thereafter. As he floated down, he saw the "Man O' War" crash and explode.

Every man a different direction

When the bail out order was given, the pilot put the disabled bomber in a flat spin so it descended in a wide flat circle. The large land areas covered combined with the time each man jumped and pulled his chute caused them to land in different spots and hence, not see each other again.

For Mastronardi, his jump set him over an open, newly plowed field. As he descended he realized he wouldn't be alone.

"A German ME-109 pilot was radioing my position, and I counted 10 Gestapo soldiers coming toward me."

Taken to a nearby German camp, Mastronardi was treated for his wounds and given a tetanus shot. At midnight he rode by truck to Reims where he was placed in the town's bastille for 14 days of solitary confinement.

Moved to the Frankfurt interrogation center, Mastronardi was questioned and again kept in solitary confinement before being transferred to Stalag 1, the German's POW camp on the Baltic Sea about 130 miles north of Berlin. There he remained until the Russians freed the camp in late April 1945.

Krol landed near a forest, and by hiding his parachute and walking into the forest, he avoided capture.

After spending the night, Krol continued to walk some 15-20 miles before collapsing. A farmer rescued the airman and took him to his home. As a member of the French Resistance, the farmer had Krol taken by the underground to Paris. There he hid with other Allied soldiers in the apartment of Bertrann Auvert, a 25-year old medical student and active member of the Resistance Movement. Eventually Krol made it back to England.

Katsaros also received help from the French Resistance. The owner of farm where Katsaros landed took the wounded gunner into his home where he remained until he could travel. While the severity of his wounds makes the memory of that period a little blurry, Katsaros did remember seeing a little girl no more than five years old in the house.

Once strong enough to travel, Katsaro also safely returned to England by way of the French Underground.

Rusch, wounded in the air attack, landed on a picket fence and suffered further injury. Captured by the Gestapo, he was taken to the Reims hospital where he had surgery and remained for 50 days. Like Mastronardi, Rusch was sent to Frankfurt for interrogation before arriving at the Stalag 17 camp near Vienna, Austria. Fifteen months later, U.S. Army General Mark Clark's division freed the POWs.

John Crowley was also captured and sent to Reims hospital where Rusch saw him. Crowley died that night in surgery. John Katsaros, however, believed for 40 years that his fellow waist gunner had died in the plane because he did not see any movement from Crowley before bailing out. At the group's first reunion in 1984, Katsaros finally learned from Rusch that Crowley did not go down with the plane.

Together again, 40 years later

Katsaros, Krol and Rusch were reunited in Orlando, Florida, in 1984, but they were unable to locate Mastronardi. The pilot and co-pilot had both died of natural causes since the war.

A determined search for Mastronardi by Krol's wife, Virginia, led to the four friends' get together at a reunion of the 401st Bomb Group of the Eighth Army Air Corps in Savannah in 1986.

Rusch had nominated Mastronardi for the Distinguished Flying Cross but learned in Savannah that he had not received it. Upon renominating his friend for the award, Rusch discovered the original recommendation had been lost by the Air Force.

Mastronardi received a letter from the Air Force in August 1987 notifying him of the medal and asking the question, "Where would you like the medal to be presented?"

"I sent the guys a copy of the letter, and they all wanted to be at the presentation," Mastronardi said.

With Katsaros in Massachusetts, Krol in Indiana, Rusch in Wisconsin, and Mastronardi in Mississippi, the crew decided to make the presentation a part of their already planned trip to England and France in October 1987. The base at Alconbury, just 15 miles from the crew's WW II base at Deenethorpe, provided the perfect setting.

"They seemed extremely pleased that we selected their base," Mastronardi said of Alconbury where 4,000 airmen and five colonels were stationed.

Coming full circle

The European trip had an itinerary of which, Mastronardi said, "everyone had his day in the sun" with the other three participating in the background.

On Monday, October 9, 1987, the four men arrived at Alconbury and spent Tuesday touring the Deenethorpe field. Some of the buildings, including the one in which the crew was briefed on their Frankfurt mission in 1944, still stand although time has greatly deteriorated them.

That evening, Mastronardi was presented the Distinguished Flying Cross in ceremonies attended by his fellow crew members, base personnel, and Jim and Trudy McGuire Jackson, friends of Mastronardi's who made the presentation their first stop on their European vacation.

The citation describing the events of that afternoon states in part, "Sergeant Mastronardi displayed tremendous courage by total disregard for his own safety to save fellow crew members." The bronze medal also includes the ribbon one would wear on the uniform and a smaller decoration that the civilian Mastronardi may wear on his lapel.

"The base made a videotape of the total presentation and our tour of the old base and presented it to me," Mastronardi said.

On Wednesday the group toured the Alconbury base before going into the town for the night. The men had dinner at a 12th century pub with three British historians, who Mastronard said, knew more about the 401st activities than they.

That evening the four veterans no doubt added the historians' knowledge.

Thursday took the group to Paris where they visited with Bertrann Auvert, the young medical student and French Resistance member who had aided Krol. She had been at the Savannah reunion in 1986, so this was their second meeting. Now a retired surgeon, she and her husband, also a doctor, live in downtown Paris.

Krol saw another friend from the Resistance on their trip. Travelling to a village near Reims, the group visited with the wife of the farmer who had rescued and protected Krol 43 years earlier.

In Reims, Walt visited the hospital where he stayed for 50 days and Crowley where died. Mastronardi saw the bastille that imprisoned him for two weeks. Katsaros visited with French Resistance members who helped him escape the Gestapo.

One of those persons was the then 5-year-old girl the wounded Katsaros vaguely remembered. Now years later, the girl-now-lady, her husband, and two teenage sons joined in the reunion.

"There were all these people," Mastronardi said, "some still living who remember this bomber falling on them and burning and exploding. They remember the chutes that fell on their property; remember very well."

The trip enabled each crewmember to come full circle with the events of March 20, 1944, and share those memories with his friends.

Printed with permission of Frank Mastronardi.

The Long Escape

By John Katsaros
Edited by Erik Dyreborg

The French

During the attack of the German fighters, I was badly wounded in my right arm and my leg. I suffered six or seven broken ribs, back injuries, and two twisted ankles.

I landed at "La Bonne Maison", which is a farm including the land surrounding it. This was located near the towns of Courville, Unchair and Fismes. Henri an employee of La Bonne Maison spotted me and immediately contacted the French Resistance in Reims. Henri hid my parachute while waiting for the French Resistance to arrive.

Not long after the French Resistance arrived and drove me to Rene and Madalene Felix's house in Reims. Later that same day the Germans arrived at the Chauvin's house and questioned Mrs. Chauvin about me. Mrs. Chauvin gave the Germans the parachute. They were more interested in the silk the parachute was made with, than where I might be.

Reims, France

The first night in Felix home was a very painful one for me due to my wounds and loss of blood. An English speaking woman, Madame Ramoge, warned me the Germans were stationed next to the Felix home and I would have to stop groaning/making noise or be turned over to the Germans. I asked to be muzzled and a cloth was provided…which I bit and chewed on all night.

Next morning I was driven by a man named "Polo" a cab driver, with horse and buggy to the clinic near the Reims Cathedral. A Jewish doctor, also in hiding, operated on me two times. The second time, because he thought I had gangrene in my right arm, and was considering amputation. The doctor was married to the head nurse of the clinic who also helped me considerably.

The night after my second operation, I apparently rang for the nurse in my delirious state and with no pain killing medicine. They quickly dressed me in my flying clothes and said I had to get out of the clinic because no one was supposed to occupy this room and the desk clerk had become suspicious. This made it dangerous for my helpers in the underground.

I was told the doctor had been kidnapped from his home in Paris, and was forced to operate on me at gunpoint. Apparently this was not true, as on my visit to Reims in 1987, friends who helped me in Reims recalled that he was Jewish and was hiding in the clinic basement throughout the war. It was also at this time his name was revealed as Dr. Levy.

On the street near the clinic, a young man and woman whose names I never knew…helped me and eventually I was taken to a room above the circus in Reims. An old Gendarme (French Police), Mr. Dumas, lived there. I would see him a few moments each night and Madame Ramoge, who cooked for him but did not live there, would feed me once a day.

After a few days, a man who was dressed in a riding outfit similar to an equestrian or what could have been a French officer's uniform visited me. He was a strict disciplinarian. He told me to prove that I was an American, as Germans would purposely disguise themselves as English and Americans to infiltrate the underground movement. I had no idea who this man was, and I distrusted him, and thinking he may be a German, I would only give him my name, rank and serial number. Later that day, I was advised by Madame Ramoge (whom I trusted) that he was a powerful man and that he would have me shot if I did not identify myself and my bomber base better, so my story could be proven. I now felt as though I was being held prisoner, and I was still bedridden.

Soon after, I gave Madame Ramoge a description of how my air base at the 491st Bomb Group in England looked like from an airplane. It resembled a pistol with three lakes—looking like bullets protruding from the front of a gun. Many days later I was advised that they corroborated my story. I then felt more secure. I stayed in my present room in the circus for several weeks.

Easter Sunday was my first day out and I was taken to the church of St. John the Baptist to receive communion. Afterwards we celebrated Easter at the Felix house, where many gathered for the occasion. I had too much champagne that affected me for several days, because I was still very weak and undernourished. Polo and his wife drove me back to the circus after curfew with the Gestapo chasing him but Polo talked his way out of trouble. The British bombed the Reims marshalling yards that night.

Among others who helped me was a butcher and his wife and children, I believe their name was Petit-Bon. He had a friend who was a deaf man who I was to go to in case of trouble, and another man who was a wrestler (I never got their names).

Chaumuzy, France

A couple of days after Easter I was visited by a nurse who also administered shots with the largest needle I ever saw. Shortly after the two injections I was taken to Chaumuzy, France and stayed at the house and bakery of Pierre and Juliana Des-Marchez for about 30 days.

Behind his chicken coupe he had dug a large tunnel that was filled with guns and ammunition etc; waiting for the invasion to come so the underground could be supplied. Pierre blew up a P-51, which had landed nearby and was in goog condition with a bomb he planted on it. I understand that someone turned the Des-Marchezs over to the Gestapo the same day I left Chaumuzy for a safe house in a forest with a Mr. Bronos and his family.

I stayed with the Bronos near a German ME-110 air base, which was bombed by the allies. The Bronos had a son called "Le Petit Gorilla". The house was located on a former battleground. The French trenches were still visible.

Mrs. DesMarchez, I learned was tortured by the Gestapo in Reims but they never got any information out of her. She was imprisoned in Regensberg Concentration Camp, Germany, and survived until WW II ended. She and her husband Pierre were both decorated by the American, British and French governments. They both live today in Boulogne S/Mer.

Jack Hoad, a British Lancaster Bombardier was soon brought to the Bronos house. He and I stayed there for about 10 days.

Jack Hoad and I once hid from the Gestapo, in Bronos' abandoned well while Bronos and the Gestapo talked for 15-30 minutes above us. Bronos had a famous saying when he wanted to go somewhere with his motorcycle. "Moi Partee Bourgouyne"—(I'm off to Bourgouyne). The town of Bourgouyne was near Reims and not too far from the Brono's house.

One night we spent with Mr. & Mrs. Ehrhart, his children and friends in his café and bar in Bourgouyne. He actually had one of my dog tags placed in the corner of a mirror behind his bar. I was also introduced to several of the German pilots, from the nearby air base, as his nephew from Paris who was wounded during a British bombing raid on Paris. We also visited a champagne factory in Reims and were there when the 8th Air Force bombed the marshalling yards. The owner of the factory was with the underground but I do not remember his name.

I understand that Mr. Erhart or a friend was caught by the Germans, close to the end of WW II, while cutting wires on a telephone pole, and he was shot to death.

Before departing by train from Reims to Paris, I spent a couple of days with Mrs. Ramoge, and I had the cast on my right arm removed by the nurse, Mrs. Levy. I met a druggist friend of hers, and her daughter and friend brought me books. It was at this time I got my first bath after my arrival in France.

Paris

I arrived in Paris by train and stayed with a Gendarme (French Policeman), his wife, and his Gendarme friends. They were Mr. and Mrs. Marcelin (they are now both deceased). His neighbor took pictures of me including one of me in a Gendarme uniform. I still have them.

While in Paris I had to have a new identification card because the one issued to me in Reims was no longer valid. I was taken to a Jewish woman photographer who wore a Star of David. I was not given her name. My name on the I.D. card was Jean Gauloise (like the French cigarettes).

I was only in Paris a few days Jack Hoad and I left by train to Toulose with several other escapees. At Toulose I hid in a woman's home for a day.

Toulose, France

The next day we all arrived by separate guides at the Toulose train station, the Gestapo was everywhere. Jack Stead and I, were left by ourselves for what seemed like a long time. Finally a guide spoke to us and said the Gestapo had captured the man and the woman we were to follow on the train. Someone else took their place and we boarded the train without further incident.

To Spain, and back to England

We arrived at the border town at the French/Spanish border—I don't recall the name. There were 17 of us by now, including me; seven Americans, two British, one Australian and seven Jewish people.

We were furnished a male guide, while walking at night in a valley, we were spotted by Germans, when their dogs barked. Spotlights were darting through the dark sky, but fortunately in the wrong direction. It was pitch dark; no stars, no moon shown. The guide certainly knew his way. We crossed a stream and then headed straight up the mountains of the Pyrenees. We climbed four nights and four days, avoiding the German spotter planes and arrived in a Spanish town called Les.

From Les we went to Lerida, and Madrid to Gibraltar. There the RAF flew us back to Bristol and then London, England and finally our air base.

45 years later

Jack Stead climbed over the Pyrenees with me, I saw him again 45 years later at the AFEES Reunion in Pittsburg, PA in May 1989. Jack's wife and my wife Mary, as well as Ted and Virginia Krol, also attended this reunion.

I made it thanks to Jack Stead and an American pilot whose rank was Major. They helped me over the mountains because of my poor physical condition. I was down to 87 pounds upon arriving in Les, Spain.

Printed with permission of John Katsaros.

Missing In Action, Killed In Action & A POW

By Walter Rusch
Edited by Erik Dyreborg

Walter Rusch was first reported missing in action, later he was reported as killed in action.

The landing

After Frank managed to open the door to the Ball Turret, I immediately bailed out. I was wounded during the attack of the German fighters.

When the chute opened, my fur line flight boots fell off, so did my GI shoes, tied on the harness. Near the ground, I hit a high voltage power line and landed on a stone wall with a wire fence on top. I had landed near the town of Unchar, France.

Not long after an older man and a young boy were trying to remove me from the wall. They also had to get rid of the parachute, harness and life jacket. I had serious injuries form 20 mm cannon shrapnel fragments and had taken new injuries from the landing impact. I was unconscious at times and bleeding from my mouth.

The older man and the boy finally removed me from the impact area and put me in a wheelbarrow. The older man on the barrow handles and the young boy pulling the barrow with a metal tongs, and they took me, still in the wheelbarrow, to a woodshed nearby.

Later an English speaking man entered the woodshed together with the older man. I believe the English speaking man was an OSS officer from Canada. He told me the serious injuries I received in the plane and also landing on the wall were too extensive for the local people to handle. He then advised me that they would turn me over to the Germans so I could receive the necessary medical attention in a hospital in Reims, France that was not far from Unchar.

It was daylight when they moved me in the wheelbarrow to a hay shelter out in a farm field. They then removed me from the wheelbarrow and laid me down under a small haystack. I was told that later the Germans would pick me up, after they were told that a young boy noticed me in this shelter.

The Germans

After I had been there for some time a black car with two men wearing civilian clothes arrived. I believe they were German police (Gestapo). After a short time, two soldiers on a motorcycle with a sidecar showed up and they both got off and walked to the hay shelter with caution. One went around to the rear and the other stood in the entryway. It wasn't long when a machine gun barrel was stuck at the back of my head and a voice hollering: "AUFSTEHEN" (German for GET UP). I started to crawl out from under the hay but I just couldn't get up.

When they found out that I was not a danger to them, they grabbed me under each armpit and dragged me out and over to the grass area near the farmhouse and let me lay.

One stood back watching me, and other one walked over to the two men with the civilian clothes and talked to them.

I started choking on blood coming out of my mouth and the young boy held my head up on his knee and wiped my mouth so I wouldn't choke. At that time I slipped him my escape kit and he tucked it into the large blouse he was wearing.

Many years later and through a French friend, John Sarot, I received a picture of the young boy who helped me when I landed. He also told me that they built an addition to their school with the 10,000 Francs from my escape kit.

The men in the civilian clothes (probably Gestapo) instructed the two Luftwaffe soldiers and they carried me to the motorcycle and sat me in the sidecar. They both got on and drove me to the Bastille (jail) in Reims. When we arrived at the Bastille, they carried me inside and laid me down on the floor in an interrogating room. I don't remember too much of what was going on at this time.

Another man in civilian clothes came in and spoke to me in German and took my dog tags. I guess he thought that I was of German descent.

Some time later a Luftwaffe officer and the two men that originally picked me up came into the interrogating room, where I lay with a stretcher. The officer who was a pilot with one arm gone argued with some Gestapo people for a short while and then the two men put me on the stretcher and carried me out to a car. Three Germans and myself then drove to a listening base that checked on bombers from England crossing the Channel and checked their direction of flight.

There a woman doctor (I think) gave me a shot of something in the rear buttocks. They removed my flight suit and heated suit and all that remained was my long underwear, GI pants and shirt plus a turtle neck sweater. On my feet I had wools and heated inter shoes. They then took me out of the building to a small sedan delivery type vehicle and put me inside.

Crowley and the hospital in Reims

To my surprise there was another man inside and with my vision I couldn't se who he was, until he spoke to me in English and said: "Walt, is that you?" I said: "Crowley, where did you come from?" and he replied that he laid in a field of high grass until a French farmer went by with a wagon and spotted him. He said that there were three German soldiers right behind him, so they loaded him into the wagon and hauled him to this vehicle we are in. Crowley also said he was not doing very well and stated that his stomach was hit very hard with fragments.

After I was on board we left the area and a short time later we arrived at the hospital in Reims.

They carried both of us into an operating room and laid us both on tables. Two doctors looked us over and after our clothes were removed, they placed a few bandages on me and the two doctors started surgery on Crowley. After a period of time, the one doctor came over to me and laid his hand on my shoulder and said: "Comrade fini". Crowley was dead. As far as I could tell Crowley must have had severe wounds in the stomach area.

I am ashamed to admit this, but I was crying for Crowley and the whole ordeal up until this time.

Shortly after, two hospital women put me on a cart and took me to a room on the 3rd floor for recuperating. There were two others in the room and one was an American who was injured in a crash landing not far from the English Channel. We did not discuss any of our military involvement while hospitalized. Several days later, he was removed from the room and I stayed there for about five weeks.

When I needed to go to the toilet room, a big Russian prisoner would carry me. About two or three days later he carried me again and took me to a window and pointed to the ground, where fresh ground had been dug and then he said: "Comrade Kaput". This is where Crowley was buried.

The Nazi Concentration Camp, Buchenwald

After having been in the hospital for four to five weeks, they were looking for means to remove me to a permanent prison. The morning I left the hospital, I had some mashed rutabagas and fake coffee. I was then picked up by two German infantry soldiers and taken to the Reims railroad depot.

From there we boarded a train going somewhere. I laid on the floor between two facing seats. Four soldiers had the seat and I laid with my head between the soldiers and another soldier's foot separated my legs.

We travelled a long time stopping occasionally for people getting on and off. During the trip, I had to go to the toilet room real bad, but they wouldn't let me up. I am embarrassed to say this, but I finally urinated in my pants.

When we arrived at our destination, the soldiers turned me over to guards at The Buchenwald Concentration Camp, some where near to Helmbrecht. There I was turned loose in a large room with quite a few people, who looked very despondent. I asked around in English of course, but nobody responded.

The next day, very early, I was taken to a delousing area, then got my hair removed. I then dressed with the same unwashed clothes I wore, when I left the base in England and they were raunchy to say the least, but I did finally talk to a man that spoke English. He was from Australia, I think. He wondered why I was in this camp and I told him that I had no idea why.

Some time during this period and with no identification on me, some one in authority must have come to the conclusion that I didn't belong there.

Dulag Luft, Frankfurt

Several days later they put me on a train with a few civilians and three or four guards and we travelled to Wiesbaden, Germany and then by truck to Dulag Luft near Frankfurt.

There I was put in a large room with other Allied inmates, but separated far enough apart that we couldn't communicate with one another. With my name (Rusch—German like), they spoke to me in German during the interrogation (maybe testing me as they had no identification of me at all as my dog tags were long gone).

The missing dog tags were the reason my father was notified after the missing in action telegram with a killed in action telegram and of course my GI insurance, 6 months gratuity pay and my back pay which is another story in itself.

Attempt to take off

Finally they realized that I could not speak German and an interrogation officer now spoke to me in English and found out that I was captive for two months. Two days later I was herded into a boxcar in the railroad yard in Frankfurt, together with ten or twelve other air Corpsmen.

From there we traveled for about two to three days as we were detained once or twice by air raids. At one of these locations we stopped and the guards disappeared when the sirens were blasting. At that time, myself and another fellow named Glen, decided, this is the time to take off as we thought by traveling West for this length of time, we had to be close to the West German border.

Another fellow joined us and outside of the car I was in front and I didn't see any guards. My mistake, as one was standing on the other side of the wheel so I couldn't see his feet or legs. When I stepped around the end of the car, he clobbered me in the face with his rifle butt and he did break my nose. He then had the two fellows with me lift me up and back in the boxcar we went. Some of the other prisoners in the car didn't think it was such a good idea trying to take off.

Stalag 17 B and the forced march

We finally arrived some where close to Munich, Stalag 7 A I think it was. We were there briefly, and then a larger group was loaded in boxcars and taken to Krems, Austria and Stalag Luft 17 B. I was there until the end of March 1945, at which time we started the forced march.

We marched from Krems (just outside Vienna, Austria) through the towns of Maulhausen, Linz and Wels, along the Danube River until we arrived at Braunau, Austria, on the Inn River.

Liberation and back to the States

We lived in the woods until General Clark's Tank Division liberated us. We were then moved to an abandoned aluminium plant until they finally moved us to Camp Lucky Strike, near Le Havre, France on May 7, 1945 and then by ship, back to the States.

They gave me temporary medical attention in Boston and then sent me home for 120 days recuperating leave.

I returned to Coral Gables, Florida around September 15, 1945 for surgery on my legs and the removal of pieces of shrapnel. After recuperation I was discharged and sent home on November 3, 1945 and finally received all my back pay, after being finger printed by some government agency.

What a joke, all of that time they thought I was some one who took my identity to get to the States. Who did they think I was when they sent me home on 120 days leave? Maybe because I went into the service from 1354 El Camino Road, Menlo Park, California and I was going home to the little town of Thorp, Wisconsin. Who knows, I might be an alien?

Printed with permission of Walter Rusch.

Joe, We've Only Got A Little Way To Go...

Narrated by Joseph P. O'Donnell, B-17 Ball Turret Gunner
15th Air Force, 483rd Bomb Group, 815th Bomb Squadron
Edited by Erik Dyreborg

Introduction

I am Staff Sergeant Joseph P. O'Donnell, Service Number 32751328. Prisoner of War number: 1414.

I was born September 28,1923 in the small town of Riverside, New Jersey along the Delaware River.

I have a degree in Applied Science. The company I worked for, Trans America De Lavalle, sent us to night school. We attended two nights a week, taking five and a half years to complete. Eight of us out of eighty-eight, who signed up for the course finished the course. I started out as a metal finisher in a Kaiser Metal Products, about 1950. I then became a foreman in the same Kaiser Metal Products in the same area where I was a metal finisher, now I was a foreman.

When they closed, I went to Stukholf Aircraft, in Mercer County, New Jersey. There, again, I was a metal finisher and assembler of a cargo plane.

I left there and had different and seasonal jobs. I got a job at St. Regis Paper Company, in Hamilton. I started out as a tester, they made the tops for tables. I would test the material to see if it had the right combination of adhesive or varnish—whatever. Also, that's where they started making the coating of copper foil; as they didn't have the micro chip.

They also started making missile cones. They needed a foreman, I applied for the job and got it. I was a foreman there for quite a number of years. After they closed I went to another place where they made fiberglass boats. I was a toll supervisor. That didn't last long.

Finally, I went to Trans America De Lavale and was a procedure writer. I would write the procedure for the manufacture of parts, including steam turbines. The company also had some of the production in Texas.

I had a good job and I was paid a decent wage. I was more or less my own boss. I had my job to do and that was it. They took part in the pieces and moved that department to Hartford, Connecticut. So I would go up there at least two or three times a month and stay one or two days, just to oversee the manufacture of the parts. This was all new to that company.

In 1984, things had become bad at de Lavalle. I was there for 18 years. One day in November, they said, "At the end of the year, you're finished." Just like that. They released about 20 of us due to our ages. We fought on the grounds of age discrimination and won, settling out of court. I did get a nice lump sum of money, tax-free. All the time I was fighting, I pumped gas for February and March, for my daughter and son in-law who had a service station. After a hernia operation, I couldn't get a job anyplace. Finally the check came through for our age discrimination, and also I applied for service-connected disabilities to the VA, and went from 10% to 100 %. So that's where I stand now. The VA and 100% forced retirement.

One thing about Riverside, the population was 7,500 during the war. Riverside High School took the highest casualty rate from World War II for any town or city in the country.

Enlisting and training

December 7 was my first encounter with the military. Myself and three other fellows were riding to work in an aircraft defense factory when we heard of the bombing of Pearl Harbor.

December 8, we went to Camden, New Jersey, to enlist in the service. We were rejected, because we worked in a defense plant. The recruiting sergeant told us, "We'll get you when we want you." Uncle Sam said, "I want you," on February 6, 1943.

I reported to Fort Dix, New Jersey, where I got clothing and some orientation about Army life.

When I went into the service, I was not military material..I thought that everyone else is going in the service, so why not me. I took it in stride. I did nothing to advance my position or rank. I just let the chips fall where they may.

While Fort Dix, I was close to home and I was with the fellows I grew up with. We went to Miami Beach, and the same thing—some of the fellows that I grew up with. So it was something new, being in the service, but it wasn't that difficult. It was strange, to say the least.

Next, I went to Miami Beach, Florida, for Basic Training. There I found out I was in the Army Air Corps, which later on became Army Air Force, which in 1947 became the Air Force.

From Miami Beach, I went to Denver, Colorado, for gunnery training at Buckley Field and at Lowry Field.

In June and July, we went to Kingman, Arizona, where we were training for aerial gunnery. I had never been up in a plane before, and the first two times, I got sick. We were told that we shouldn't eat too much before we fly, when we got sick.

When we flew, we got up at four in the morning and we wouldn't take off until about nine or nine thirty. A second before I got sick the second time, someone told me, "Well, first of all, when you throw up, if it's in the plane, you have to clean it up, which makes you get sick all over again." "So what you do, you unzip your fur lined flying jacket and throw up in your fatigues. Then, when you hit land, you go right into the shower—well, you take your shoes off—and stand under the shower and take your clothes off and hang them up to dry. I never got sick after that.

There wasn't much to enjoy at Kingman. I guess, if you put it on a positive note, here's a kid from a small town, Riverside, New Jersey, and as far as he'd ever gotten away from home was Providence, Rhode Island, when I was about five years old. There's little I can remember of it. Here I was now, out in Kingman, Arizona, prior to that I was at Miami Beach, and Denver, Colorado, and now I'm flying.

I'd never been on an airplane before, never even stepped inside of one. Now I'm flying in one, not only that, I'm firing a big machine gun. There were also other kinds of weapons that we fired, even down to a B-B gun machine gun. So everything was new.

The friends, the fellows I'd gone in with, went to different places. Now I had different friends and buddies, from all over the United States. We were confined to the air base, and there wasn't much to do.

We couldn't get into Kingman, Arizona, although I did get there once when my sister and brother-in-law moved to California, and they stopped on their way. I got an overnight pass, because they came to visit me.

I graduated, and this is not a pun, with flying colors as an aerial gunner.

We went to Salt Lake City, where a crew was formed. Later on, we went to Rapid City, South Dakota, where we started flying air to ground gunnery missions. I was the waist gunner, one of the waist gunners, and was the first armorer gunner. It was my job to fuse and arm the bombs, to arm the bombs, and to make sure all the armament on the ship was in working condition.

When we got to Rapid City, South Dakota, the ball turret gunner was a married man who had two children and one on the way. So he refused to fly and we had to get another ball turret gunner. A replacement came and he refused to fly in the ball turret. I had trained for the ball turret, so I told the pilot that I would take it so there wouldn't be another guy leaving the crew.

In the ball turret, we were flying air to ground gunnery. I got into the ball turret and the waist gunner came along to close the door. When you're in the turret, it's a little difficult, because you have thick leather gloves on and you have to reach up behind you and pull closed the door and lock it. What he did, he closed the door but he didn't lock it.

When it came time for me to fire, I turned the turret so the slipstream did not hold the door shut and it came off. I got back up into the ship, but part of the hinge on the door was still on there, and it got caught between the ring and the ship. The ring that the turret was on, in the fuselage, we couldn't get the ball crank the ball turret all the way up, which meant that someone would have to land in it. Under any other conditions, except an emergency, would be an immediate court martial.

The gunnery instructor said he would land in it. I said, "No, it was my ball turret, I would do it." In the meantime, someone came up with the idea that they got a screwdriver and somehow got it bent and they pulled the piece that was hanging on the door back into the ship and we cranked the ball turret back up again.

Here again, about the only difference between Kingman, Arizona, and Rapid City, South Dakota, was the temperature. Kingman was up around 102. When we would fly, we would have to get up at 4 o'clock in the morning and it was very cold. We would lie on the asphalt road to keep warm.

Now we're in Rapid City, South Dakota, and it's Christmas time and we're freezing out butts off. Rapid City was not the nicest temperature-wise. We did get a pass, sometimes a weekend pass, and at Christmas Time, a large hotel in Rapid City invited all the airmen there for a dinner and a dance, which was real nice.

From there, we went to McDill Field, Tampa, Florida. Here, we were flying gunnery missions, but it was out over the Gulf of Mexico. We threw a dye overboard, but we couldn't locate it, so we threw an empty ammunition box over. We had a brand new B-17 ship with less than fifteen or twenty hours on it. Every-body fired except the top turret, which means the pilot would have to bank the ship so we could shoot at the box in the water.

After the top turret fired, I had my view plate to the views of the ship, and I happened to notice there was oil all over the view plate. I called up to the pilot and said, "Am I supposed to have oil on the view plate?" I heard him say, "Feather number four engine."

When we got down, there were two bullet holes on the inboard side of the engine and about a foot diameter hole on the outboard side of the engine. So all the brass, generals and what have you, came out to the ship. They were trying to figure out what happened. Well, we were lying on the grass, all the rest of the crew except for the pilot, and I said to the co-pilot, "Look at the two caliber .50 caliber machine guns on the top turret." One was two inches lower than the other. So when he turned the turret to fire, there's a fire control cut off switch that would not fire into the engine or the propeller. With the two inches down, this didn't work.

Going overseas

While we were in Tampa, Florida, we had a little bit of a problem with going overseas. We were getting prepared to go and we were told, which was supposed to be something of a nice trip. You fly to Africa, on to South America, then to Ascension Island, then to Africa, then on into Italy. But we were told that we were going to be replaced by the Mess Sergeant, by the Supply Sergeant, the bakers and cooks and whatever have you, because they were to get the first to get everything prepared for the rest of us.

This wasn't just our crew, but other crews also, told them we refused to fly. They couldn't make us fly. Whatever the consequences, we would take. But they had senators, they had generals there, again, we all formed in a hangar. Finally they came up and said, "They would give all the enlisted men a stripe before we went overseas."

We figured, well, that was something anyway. So I became a staff sergeant in the States instead of overseas. We told them that the reason we weren't going to fly was that if we were going into combat after we hit there, let the mess sergeants fly when they get over there in combat and we'll do the cooking.

In March of 1943, we left Hampden Roads, Virginia, on a Liberty Ship and headed for what we didn't know, but found out later was Italy. There was no excitement on the way over. We had a nice ride. It was rough a couple of times. We were going through the Straits of Gibraltar at night and one of the ships was torpedoed and sunk. We could hear the depth charges, the ticking, because we were in bunks right next to the bulkhead.

The voyage overseas was a little bit difficult. We were on a small ship in a convoy, going very slowly. I'd never been on a ship before. It was difficult to get onto the ship; we had to climb up a Jacob's ladder, and we had two barracks bags, one with our flying equipment, and the other with our regular military gear. This was in Hampton Roads, Virginia.

As we were going up the Ladder, the ship would roll. The next thing you knew, you were out about five feet from the ship, and the next thing, you were banging into the side of it.

We were in the hold of the ship. I don't know how many there were—at least a couple hundred. Everything was steel. Steel stairs, they called them gangways, but steel stairs. We ate out of our mess kits. The guys were seasick. They'd throw up on the steel deck another guy would come along with his mess kit, step in that, and slip. All of his food would go all over and somebody else would get sick.

We were in bunks, three high. The guy up in the top bunk, he got sick—you got the rest of it. So it wasn't a very nice trip going over there.

We passed the time mostly reading and in the sack. I never thought of impending combat fear. I'm nineteen years old and when you're nineteen or twenty years old, you're invincible. I never realized that the enemy wanted to kill me. I guess it was a good attitude.

Italy

We landed in Brendezi, Italy, and we took a train to Foggia. From Foggia, we went by truck to the airbase. When we got to the airbase, we went out behind an olive orchard. There were all of these piles of canvas. The sergeant said, "There's your new home."

As a kid, I went camping quite a lot and knew how to put up a tent. So we didn't have much of a trouble there.

They told us we were going to get fed. That's where I got the title for a book of poems, A Time of Great Rewarding, because we were going to get something to eat.

I started writing poetry in about the seventh or eighth grade. I went to a Catholic school up to the seventh grade. Then I transferred to public school.

In one of our English classes, we had to write a poem. I wrote one, I called it A Bum. It started out:

I'm a bum
And a bum I'll be,
I'll eat and sleep
And be so free.
I'll get up early
And come home late,
And eat my food
From a broken plate.

This went on and on and on.

For a kid in the seventh grade, I thought it was great. The teacher gave me a "D." So I gave up writing poetry until high school. Nothing was ever, I won't say published, it was just in a little book, little poems, nothing much.

Well, the chow line was pretty long. It was outside. There was a little hill, a mound, that we went up over. We got on top of it and the line extended for quite a number of yards. I saw that we had our mess kits and saw that everyone was dipping in and getting something out of large garbage cans. When I got there, they handed me a Spam sandwich and a peanut butter sandwich and a cup of water.

The Spam in the sandwich was about a half inch thick and so was the peanut butter.

On our first mission, we had a milk run. It was to a cement factory in East Yugoslavia. There was one anti aircraft gun, and that was about two or three thousand feet from the ship. We called him, "One Gun Charlie."

I didn't see much of anyone who was shirking their duty. It was just that was what we had to do and we did it.

The combat missions

After the first mission, a milk run, I thought, "Boy, this is gonna be a lot of fun." Well, it changed later on.

I thought that this was going to be a snap with the type of flak. But that, as I said, was a milk run. They got you acquainted to flying.
Here again, I wasn't a hero, but I didn't have that kind of fear.

I had my job in the ball turret. It was considered one of the most dangerous, not the most dangerous—it depended on the enemy, how much flak they had and how many fighters they had. But everyone was a target; they didn't pick out any particular one.

The Germans would change their attack. Sometimes it would be head on, maybe ten or fifteen planes. I heard, I never saw this happen, that in order to get to the ball turret, they would come up from underneath the ship and just stall the plane there and fire at the ball turret. Like I say, this never happened to me and I never saw it happen.

On one of the missions, the ground crew would fix up the ship, gas the ship, make sure all the ammunition was aboard, and when they were finished, they were supposed to lock all of the controls. But this one time, on our ship, they left them unlocked. As we got out to the runway, the pilot and co-pilot were checking all the instruments, and instead of unlocking them, they were locking them. By the way, the runway was Pierced Metal Track, which was linked together and was out in a field. And of course, the field wasn't very level. When we could take off, there would be three bounces. We always knew we were off and flying on the third bounce.

But on this particular day, there was a fourth and a fifth and a sixth bounce. We wound up off the end of the runway out in a field. The meat wagon (ambulance) and the fire trucks and what have you came out. Everything was all right. The bombs weren't armed yet, so that was one of the things.

The next was our first mission, to Wienerneustadt, Austria. Part of my job was to count the bombs when they went out. This time, only nine went out. I called up to the pilot and co-pilot and told them we probably had a bomb hung up. As we were coming back, we broke formation and went out over the Adriatic Sea to release the bomb.

We got down out of altitude and I came up on one side of the bomb bay and the bombardier was on the other. If you know the distance between the radio room and the bomb racks, this particular bomb was forward to the bomb bay firewall on the front. The bombardier was motioning for me to come across.

Of course, you can't hear anything. I was telling him to go do something with a four-letter word. He kept motioning me across and I kept telling him. Finally, I motioned for him to get the screwdriver. There are two big screws on there—he just turned them and the bomb went out into the Adriatic.

When we got back, he called me over. In the Air Corps, if no one is around, they always call you by your first name, Joe, Bill, Harry, whatever. But up in the air, it's sir or if we're out accompanying anyone, it's also sir or sergeant.

So he called me over and said, "Hey Joe, what were you saying in there?"

I said, "I was telling you to go for it yourself."

He turned around and looked and said, "You know, I don't believe a damned word you're telling me."

On a mission to Marseilles, France, which was one of the longest missions, except for the ones to Wienerneustadt, we had heated suits. I guess that was the birth of the electric blanket.

My heated suit, the clips that ran from the heated suit to the little felt shoe, didn't make a good connection. When we got up to altitude and the temperature was forty below zero, I could feel my right foot getting numb. Then it would warm up and then it would get numb. What was happening, the connection wasn't right and it would go on for a couple of minutes, then back on again. It was what I got later on, frostbite on my right foot.

We landed at Corsica to refuel. They had to carry me off the ship. I didn't want to report it to the medics or anything like that, because I wanted to stay with the crew. Later on, it wasn't that bad, but it was still frostbite. Today, I'm suffering from that on both feet and both hands.

Shot down

Our thirteenth mission was back up to Wienerneustadt. That was where we got shot down.

We were hit in the number two engine, and it was on fire. The fire was up into the bomb bay. Then we got the order to bail out. The two waist gunners and myself were to bail out the waist door, but what had happened with this old ship that we had, it was a B-17 F, and another crew had completed all their missions in it, so it was pretty well worn out.

Joe's plane is pictured below, with two airmen bailing out (circled). One of them is Joe O'Donnell. The picture was taken from a B-17 flying above Joe's plane. It seems that only #3 and #4 engines are operational.

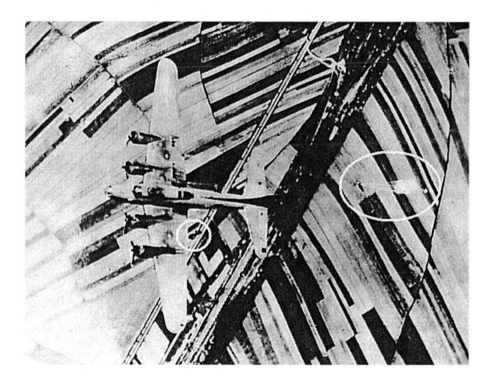

I came up out of the ball turret, and luckily my parachute was right at my side. I clipped that on and I went over to the right waist gunner. He motioned what to do. I told him to pull the emergency release handle. Like I said, the ship was old.

When he pulled the emergency release handle, which had a cable and a pin; the pin was supposed to come out and the door go, the handle pulled out of the cable and the door stayed on.

He asked me, motioning with his hands, what do we do now. Just then, the ship went into a dive. My back was to the front of the ship and I fell forward up into the ball turret, into the radio room. The entire bomb bay was on fire and I bailed out. I was next to the last one out.

The other waist gunner followed me. Since I was off of oxygen, I pulled the rip cord right away. We were up over 20,000 feet. Since I was off of oxygen for so long, I blacked out. When I came to, I was oscillating back and forth so much that I thought the chute would collapse. I saw a German ME-109 circling around me. There were two purposes why he was doing that. He was trying to collapse the chute and he was trying to find out where I was going to land.

I landed farthest from the target than any of our crew. I don't know just how many miles; I have a map that shows where I landed.

The chute got caught in a tree and I swung in and got into the biggest briar patch I ever saw. It ripped my helmet off, my leather gloves; it almost tore my ears off. But I managed to come out of that all right. In that briar patch, that's where I buried the parachute the best as I could.

Then I heard some laughter, chatter, of little kids, and they came up the hill. I was up in the mountains. One of them could speak English and they were saying, "Cigaretten."

I had a pack of Lucky Strikes, in fact I had two packs, and I gave them the one pack and each of them took two cigarettes. He handed me two dinner rolls. I asked him for the underground. They said, "Nein, nein, Gastapo all around." Then they ran back down the hill.

I sat down to get my bearings. I had an escape kit and I was getting the maps out. In each escape kit, there was supposed to be forty-one dollar bills. It so happened that in mine there were only thirty-nine. Somebody in the States was taking a dollar out of each escape kit.

I started walking. I didn't know where I was going. I looked at the map, looked at the compass. Finally, I was getting tired. I came to a small stream. We had a little rubber bottle, container, and some tablets to purify the water. So got some water and put one tablet in. Later on, I sat down and ate a half a roll and I drank some of the water.

I walked until about four or five in the afternoon, and I was thoroughly exhausted. I was on a mountainside. Now these mountains aren't very high or steep, but they were steep enough that you couldn't just walk down, you had to sort of slide. I found a large tree, large tree in diameter, and I braced myself, I sat down and braced myself up to the tree and went to sleep.

The reason I did that, I didn't want to roll down the hill or down the mountain.

It rained that night. It didn't rain hard, but it rained enough to make it miserable. The next morning, I was up early and started walking again. I came to a big gully about the size of a football field.

I could hear someone chopping wood. I got up to the edge of the top of the bowl and I could see a little house down with smoke coming out of the chimney straight up. I kept hearing this chopping and I looked, it was to my left, and quite a distance away was a fella with knee boots on with a tree that was down.

In this bowl, there was all scrub oak, maybe four of five feet high, even on the top where I was. I crawled underneath of it. I saw him, and right in front of me was a deer. The deer saw me and took off. The fellow chopping wood turned and looked. He saw the deer and he went back to chopping wood again.

Now, would you believe it? There was another deer and I took a hand full of sand and threw at the deer. The deer took off. The guy chopping wood turned and looked and saw it was a deer, but right after that, I took off, too. I ran across to the other side. I turned around and he was still chopping wood.

So I kept on walking. I saw a pine forest then. I was going down a sandy road with two ruts. I came around a corner and what was there but a radio lookout tower for spotting, an aircraft spotting tower. I froze right there and turned around and ran like hell. I thought that any minute I'm going to hear shots. But nothing happened. Either those who were up there were asleep or it was empty.

I came to open land, farm land that had just been plowed. A JU 88 went over. I was standing at the edge of the woods. I could see the pilot's eyes. I knew damn well he saw me. I thought, well, he's going to radio someone my location. I thought if I ran back into the woods, it's the obvious thing to do.

Out in the field was an island of a lot of brush and a briar patch that they never plowed around, so I ran to there. I hid. I stayed there for about fifteen minutes.

When I came out, who is standing there but a German soldier. He didn't have a uniform on, he had something like the coveralls. So I said, "Comrade?"

He said, "Ja, ja."

I looked and I saw on his lapel, on the flap of his pocket, there was an eagle with a swastika on it. Here again, with a four-letter word, I said, Yeah, you're a comrade all right.

He motioned to his mouth and said "Essen."

The only word I knew in German was Glockenspiel. I thought, well, he's pointing for something to eat of drink, so I said, Yes."

I had a walking cane, or a walking stick, which was about ¾ of an inch in diameter. He was walking in front of me, unarmed, and I never took the .45 with me. That was back in the tent in a barracks bag. So I thought, something is very strange. Here he is. He's the guard, unarmed. He's in front of me. I thought well, I could hit him in the head. I said, "No, no." Something told me different.

Captured

There was a line of trees ahead. We walked up to them and there were twelve German soldiers with rifles. There was a German officer that came up. He could speak very good English. He said, "Follow me."

I was taken to a huge barn, which was a radar detection station for aircraft. I mean a huge barn. It was converted and very clean. The same officer went into a very large room, more like a mess hall with long tables and long benches like picnic benches. He sat down across from me and started in with the interrogation. I told him I could only tell him my name, rank, and serial number.

We were talking and he wanted to know my age. I said, I can't tell you. He kept asking and asking and asking. Finally he got mad and he had this German Luger,

I never knew what it was before, but a German pistol. He picked it up and cracked me on the side of the head and the ear. He knocked me off the bench. I got up immediately. I told him, "I'm still not going to tell you my age."

Today, I have a perforated ear.

So he got real friendly then. One of the things I heard later on was that when they interrogate you, they'd put their pistol on the table with the handle toward you. The pistol was empty, no ammunition in it. They were enticing you to pick up the pistol, which would give them a chance to shoot you.

In the escape kit there were three silk maps, one of Austria, one of Germany, and one of Italy. He wanted these maps. He wanted me to give them to him. I told him," I'm the prisoner, you have the gun. You take them."

He said, "I can't. If you give them to me, then it's legal."

So I said, "I'll tell you what I'll do. You walk me down to the woods. I'll hand you the three silk maps. You turn around and leave."

He said, "I'll tell you what I'll do. I'm going to do you a favor. I'm not going to take you down to the woods. You're only a half a mile or so from the Hungarian Border. If you get across that, they'll kill you right away."

Then he wanted to know if I wanted some coffee. I said, "No," although I did.

He said, "We're not going to poison you. How about something to eat?" I said, "OK."

They came out. They had a big plate of mashed potatoes piled about five inches high with a stew all coming down. I ate about two spoons full. I guess, I was very hungry, there wasn't any doubt about that. I didn't have anything to eat since the day before at 4 or 5 o'clock in the morning, except for that half a dinner roll that I had. And I ate a vitamin bar.

I think, what it was was that everything was so strange. Strange people, and strange voices. I just didn't realize, and it didn't dawn on me that "I'm a Prisoner of War." These guys can shoot me, they don't have to have any reason, all they do is say he tried to escape and we shot him, so it's legal.

But deep down inside, I think it was extreme fear. It didn't show on the surface, but I think my stomach told me what it was all about. Later on, I wished I had been able to take it with me. That wasn't the case.

Then they got a guard with a rifle and they walked me down the road to a main road. A truck came along and there was enough room for three of us in the front. The guard was there with his rifle. I told him, "You don't need that rifle, and I'm not going anyplace."

The driver said, "He doesn't have the rifle to keep you here, it's to keep the civilians from getting you."

We went into the town of Wienerneustadt. We went right by the aircraft factory that we had bombed. The railroad tracks were all twisted and up in the air. They stripped me down of the heated suit. All I had left were the fatigues.

We walked into another building. They were all young women in there at typewriters. When I walked by, the knee of my fatigue was torn. This one young girl pointed it out and said something to another girl, I guess in the effect of what a poor soldier this guy is.

I thought to myself, "You'll be the one who's going to pay, not me."

When I got through there, they just took my name, rank, and serial number. They marched me down the street. It was strange. There weren't any people on the street. We walked by a three-story building. Come to find out, it was a school building. Here these guys are hanging out the window, all Americans, shot down. And they were yelling, "Watch out for the hook, watch out for the needle, and this type of thing."

They had the officers on one floor, the enlisted men on another. And food was very, very scarce. There was hardly anything to eat at all. We were there several days, then they put us on what I call a Tinker Toy Trolley. We went down to the train station. The station was mobbed with people.

The forty and eight boxcars were backing into the Station. Some of the fellows still had their A2 jackets, with some painting on the back. One fellow standing next to me said to another fellow, "Hey, we're in Vienna, and started humming the Vienna Waltz and dancing." The mob of people started coming towards us.

The guards were loading into the boxcars, just pushing until there wasn't any room for anybody else.

I was one of the last ones in the last car. Because I didn't move fast enough, the guard took his rifle butt and hit me in the back.

Today, I have four inflamed discs in my back and something wrong with my neck. Other than that, I'm in pretty damn good shape.

It was a long ride. We went to Frankfurt on Main, the Dulag Luft, where they did all the interrogation. On the way, we never got anything to eat or drink. It was cold. My waist gunner, the one that survived, had the leather jacket. He was trying to get rid of it. Of course, nobody wanted it.

We arrived at the interrogation center at Frankfurt on the Main and went into like a mess hall again. The Germans gave us a form to fill in. Would you believe, some Jackasses were going to fill that form out. But they stopped and just name, rank, and serial number.

We were at the interrogation center for three or four days. Back onto the forty and eight and shipped out to Stalag Luft IV, Pomerania, Germany.

POW-camp, Stalag Luft 4

On the way there, we passed on the outskirts of Berlin. There were at least fifty engines, train engines, all shot up and rusted. I thought to myself, "That's a lot of engines that we're shooting up."

We arrived at Stalag Luft IV at the end of May. The camp opened on May 14. I probably got there a week later.

One thing about traveling on a forty and eight boxcar, you never got fed and never got any water. From Frankfurt on Main to Stalag Luft IV was two or three days. Like I say, nothing to eat and no water.

When we arrived at the camp—one thing I did keep out of the escape kit was the tiny little compass, a little bit bigger than a pea. Any time we'd come in contact to be interrogated or anything, I'd put the compass in my mouth. I still have that today, but you can't read it because of the corrosion.

When we entered the camp, there were very few people. We were interrogated again at the camp. There were very few Prisoners of War there. We were assigned barracks and a room. They gave us a paper, what we would call particulate, mattress. It was made and was woven out of paper but looked like a burlap bag. We filled it with excelsior or shaved wood. After about a week of that, it crumpled up and became just a mattress with nothing in it. Once in a while, they would bring in excelsior in to refill them.

At the time, I was in "A" Lager. There were to be assigned to each room, sixteen POWs.

I was moved from A Lager to B Lager after about a month. Instead of sixteen, it became eighteen men to the room, then twenty, then twenty-five, eventually, it went up to thirty-three. They were sleeping on the floor, on the table, out in the hall.

The first couple of weeks, I thought, wasn't too bad. We got a full Red Cross parcel. But every time a city was bombed within 100 miles of the camp, we wouldn't get anything at all. They said the bombs hit the train that was carrying the Red Cross parcels. Actually, what was happening was they were giving Red Cross parcels to the civilians of the towns that got bombed.

Our breakfast consisted of a pitcher of hot water. Sometimes it was a mentholated tea. We had the black bread. I have the recipe for it.

This came from a German, from the Hitler's War Crimes Commission:

Prisoners of War in Nazi Germany, may be interested in this recipe for World War II Black Bread. This recipe comes from the official record from the Food Providing Ministry of the Top Secret Berlin 24.11.1941. The Directory of the Ministry, Herr Manfield and Herr Moritz, it was agreed that the baked black bread was:

50 % bruised rye grain
20% sliced sugar beet
20% tree flour (saw dust)
10% mixed leaves and straw

From our own experience with black bread, we also saw bits of glass and??, so someone was cheating on the recipe. That was the black bread. After a while, you got used to it, and it started in to taste good.

The noon meal consisted of a watery soup. We had, they would issue one loaf of the black bread for four men. This was divided—the person that cut the portions for rations was the last one to get his choice for a slice of bread. What we did was, we had homemade cards. We would place the bread on the cards, and whatever card matched that, that was the slice they got. But the guy who sliced it, never got a choice. It was always someone different.

Suppertime was potatoes. Boiled potatoes. If we had Red Cross parcels, we would mix different concoctions with the mashed potatoes. Sometimes, I never see them any more, but they had these soda crackers that were about 3 inches in diameter. If you soaked them in water, they would swell up and get real thick and expand. We had a little stove and we got about two or three coal dust bricks, briquettes, for eight, and we would fry the crackers on the stove.

Getting back to our first arrival at the camp, we were issued a bucket of unpeeled potatoes. When you peel a potato, there is a lot lost, so a lot of the guys from Brooklyn or New York or other large cities, and they never knew how to peel a potato. What had happened, you took a bucket of potatoes back to the so-called mess hall to boil them. Then they would give you a bucket of boiled potatoes back. But the thing is, there were never any potatoes left for at least a half a barracks. So they had to cook some more. We found out later on that you were not going to peel potatoes.

If you wanted it peeled, you did that yourself. Actually, we ate the skins, anyway. That was suppertime.

Recreation consisted of what we made ourselves. We made a deck of cards out or cardboard. The deck of cards was about six inches high. You had to shuffle them piecemeal, three or four at a time.

We made a softball of the flying boots that were worn out. In the Red Cross parcel there was a can of powdered coffee. Inside the lid was a rubber ring to seal it. We would go around to all the barracks and get the rubber ring. We would get string out of sweaters, or whatever you could find, and we'd cut the flying boot. We had all kinds of occupations in the camp—barbers, tailors, and shoemakers.

So they cut out the pattern from the flying boots and they made a softball. But what we didn't have was a bat.

We asked the Germans if we could go out into the forest and cut a sapling to make a bat. They said no one was allowed out of the camp, but they said they would get one for us. What they brought in was a four inch log and it was about six feet long, a pine log. It took us about two weeks for us to get the log down to the size of a baseball bat. It was one of the heaviest bats in the world. It would have gone down in the Guiness Book of Records.

Our first baseball game, the first pitch, a POW hit the ball and it was made out of such flimsy stuff and the baseball bat was so big that the ball literally exploded. It just—there was nothing left of it.

One of the other things that occurred in the camp was the rumor mill. The rumor went around that they were trying to get some cheese. Rumors are always rumors. But this time, we knew that we were getting it, because we could smell it coming into the camp. Each barracks group got an issue of a small piece of cheese wrapped in some sort of foil paper.

When we opened it, it was filled with holes and had maggots. When I was growing up, as a child, we weren't far from the farms of the little town of Riverside. When the corn was ripe, then, they didn't have pesticides or insecticides, and each ear of corn had a worm in it. What my mother would do, when she husked the corn, she would put the ears of corn into a pail of water. The worms would swim up to the top and we'd scoop them off and clean the corn.

I thought of that, so everyone was throwing their cheese into water buckets. I took it outside and pumped water in the bucket, and all the worms came up to the top. I scooped them off and the water washed the cheese off, and I started in to eat it. When the guys in the room spotted it, they all came running out and wanted their cheese back.

But it started a domino effect, and after a while, there was a big line up at the pump to wash the cheese off.

In late September, we were issued GI clothing through the YMCA, coats, pants, gloves, and scarves, getting prepared for the winter. What we still didn't have was shoes.

We did get issued a pair of shoes earlier. They were made in Boston. One of the first roll calls, Appell, we were standing outside, wherever you would form up, if it was in a mud puddle, that was where you stood. Well, all of the shoes, the soles were made of cardboard, and they soaked up the water and fell off. So we were still without shoes.

The Shoe Leather Express

In middle of January, we got word that the camp was to be evacuated. We were told that we were going to move to another camp, a three-day walk, and to get prepared.

So we started walking around the compound daily to get our leg muscles, our so-called leg muscles, in shape. We also made backpacks out of an old shirt by sewing up the shirttails and attaching the sleeves to the sides of the shirt. It made a nice pack.

When we left, it was February 6, 1945; it was bitter cold. It was below zero. We were all issued a full Red Cross parcel. We were taking all of our belongings, everything we had. Some of the fellas got issued two Red Cross Parcels. The Red Cross Parcel weighed eleven pounds. Even eleven pounds was too much to carry.

Two days or a week before we went out on the march, we were issued a pair of GI shoes. What they would do was just hand anybody a pair of shoes, whether it was their size or not. Then, they were to go around and trade for their correct size. I was issued a pair of shoes—I took 9 ½—and I got size 9. It was a half size too small. I could not trade with anyone, because 9 ½ was a common size. After one day of marching, I had fourteen blisters, seven on each foot.

Getting back to the Red Cross Parcels, after we walked for about a half hour or so, we were allowed to rest up a little bit. We took all the items that we thought we wouldn't be able to use like soap and toilet paper and we threw it away. There were women out in the field picking up sticks for fires and they thought this was manna from heaven, getting food and toilet paper and soap.

Around mid afternoon, we stopped and went into barns. In Germany, the barns are enormous. We formed a combine, which were either three or four fellows. We'd fold our blankets and our food and one fellow would be out trying to trade with the natives for eggs or anything else he could barter for.

Along the way, we'd pick up sticks and would build a fire so we could cook.

The fourteen blisters now turned into sores. I tried to wash my socks all the time so I wouldn't get infected. The blisters were bleeding all the time.

I still have a problem today, two things: One is the blisters that never properly healed. There's some discomfort in my toes. And then two, I had frostbite once in the air from the improper connection of my heated suit to the felt boot on my right foot and on the march, it would rain and freeze and rain and freeze, and you couldn't take your shoes off while you were walking. When we reached the barn at night, we'd take our socks off and put them under us to help dry them out.

Today, I have to go to the podiatrist at least every five weeks, otherwise I won't be able to walk.

One thing, in the camp, we did stay clean. We didn't have any lice. But I saw guys take their shirt off and they started picking at things.

I said, "What are you picking at?"

He said, "Lice."

I said, "Oh. I'm glad I don't have them."

But that morning, I felt something crawl. And I had them. One of the things we found out about the lice. You kill one and a thousand would come to its funeral.

We walked from daylight until dusk. We slept in barns, some of the times we slept in fields or snow banks, whatever.

On February 14, we were roused out of a barn and it was dark. It was five o'clock in the morning. We were given a big boiled potato and we started marching. We marched until eleven o'clock that night to a place on the Baltic called Schwinemunde. It was the mouth of the Oder River.

There, there was a forest, a clump of woods that was cleaned out. All that was left was the branches. Also, a group had been there ahead of us, and everyone has dysentery. When you have to go you go, so no matter where they were, they just squatted and went. Which means that you were stepping in that stuff all night long.

As a young fellow, I went camping quite a number of years and I knew how to get along in the woods. So I got our combine to put some of the branches in a pile on the ground and we put our blankets down. Then we put branches alongside of us. When we crawled into the so-called bed, we pulled other branches over the top of us. It had a drizzly rain that night. The next morning, the entire area was covered with ice.

We walked to the mouth of the Oder River and were going to cross over into Germany proper. We were out on a peninsula type spit of land, and we were going to cross in a barge pulled by a tugboat.

As we got out on the spit of land, there were no trees, nothing. It was more of a marsh than anything, and a British fighter plane came over. He started to make a run for strafing. We did form the initials POW. We waved and hollered and whatever. On his second run, he wiggled his wings and off he went.

Some of the things while on the road......

When we got to small towns, the Gestapo would go in ahead of us and tell the people that the Luftgangsters were coming and also what they would do. The German guards, or the German command would give us a break, a toilet break, in the town itself. When we did this, women would come out, mostly women and old men, and would start spitting at us and hitting us and throwing stones.

It wasn't always that bad. In another small town we were going through, the guards were quite a distance apart and when we turned two corners, there was an area where the guards couldn't see us. This woman came out as we were going by, making believe she was hitting us with a cane if a guard came by, but after we were where the guards couldn't see either end of us, she pulled up her apron and gave us two loaves of bread.

I read in several books and articles that fellas called this the Death March. I called it the Shoe Leather Express. People would say, "How many were killed? Or what was the casualty rate?" I don't know if they were talking about this march or all the marches. But there's a figure floating around—like one thousand eight hundred and sixty.

The group I was in, there were about two thousand. There were ten thousand in the camp all together and the entire camp was evacuated in three stages.

After about fifty-three days on the road, it was a miserable, cold, rainy day. It wasn't heavy rain, just a misty rain. I got some sort of a sickness, I don't know what it was. I just couldn't make it any more. I sat down alongside of the road. What would happen is, with regard to casualties, we really didn't know any, because after the column would pass, anyone who would drop out, you would hear shots and you wouldn't see the fellow again.

So I was sitting there, and two fellows came along and picked me up. They said, "Joe, we only got a little ways to go to be at a barn." So we got to the barn, they built fires and made some hot coffee. They covered me up pretty good. The next morning, I felt pretty good. I was off and running again.

The blisters kept getting worse. The facilities for cleaning were limited. As the war progressed, the war got worse for us. It got worse for the Germans. We were marched longer and less food.

Finally we reached a town where we got on boxcars. The name of the town was Uelsen. It's around the Hannover area.

They kept us on those boxcars for thirty-three hours. No water. No food. No facilities for the bathroom, not even a bucket. But fortunately, the car that I was in, there must have been a shell that went through the top of the roof of the boxcar and through the floor and made a hole. That was our toilet.

There was a pump right outside; they wouldn't let us have any water. The train would move, back up, and go forward, move, back up, go forward. But we never went anyplace.

Finally, after thirty-three hours, we got out and marched and were going to another camp. We could smell the smoke and stink coming from the camp. It was ironic. The ones in the camp wanted to get out; we wanted to get in the camp.

They put us in a tent like a circus tent, threw some straw on the floor, and that was our home. The food was very limited. At one time, there was a Russian—there was a break in the fence between the Russians and the others. It was an International Camp.

The Russian was walking peeling a kohlrabi or a big turnip. I was picking up the skins after him, picking up the skins and eating them. Then it became very desperate.

One of the fellas that were next to us could speak Russian, so I wanted to sell my watch. He said he would barter with the Russians. So I got seven loaves of bread for the watch. I was told that, actually, I'd gotten eight loaves, but the fellow took one loaf for himself.

Our combine, at the time, consisted of a fellow and myself by the name of Jim Cox, the two of us. Here I had the seven loaves of bread and was going to share them with Jim. They moved us out the next morning, so I had seven loaves of bread I had to carry, this bread, black bread, was very, very heavy and I was very, very weak. So I gave Jim half of the bread and we bartered with the other POWs for some food.

At one place, they put us in a big barn. There were two enormous barracks and we thought it was time to escape. There was myself, Jim Cox and Green, a fella by the name of Green.

We snuck down to the other barn and went up into the hayloft. Now it was mid April and it was kind of warm. We had on all these heavy overcoats. We got up to the top of the loft—Wilbur Green that was his name. I talked to Jim Cox and I said, "This is a bad idea. The Germans are taking us where we want to go. We don't have any food and we don't have any water."

So Jim Cox and I came down and went back up and joined the rest of the party.

Going back to Stalag Luft IV, when we were issued the clothing, they didn't issue by size, they just handed out anything. Wilbur Green got a pair of pants that were six inches too long, so he folded them up. One day on the march, it was difficult for him to walk, because he kept falling down. So he took a knife and cut the pants off, but he cut them off about four inches too short, and after a while, they started to unravel. Well, this was part of the thing when we tried to make our escape, the next morning, we marched out with the rest of the group and Greenie stayed behind.

When we arrived at the next farm, we were at the fence trying to barter with the natives for food and we heard this commotion.

We looked down the road and here came Greenie with two guards. His pants were raveling and hanging down, he was dirty looking and filled with straw.

Finally, we asked him what had happened and how he got caught.

He said the guards saw us go into the barn and they just waited for him to come out the next day. So they nailed him. At that barn, someone killed one of the farmer's prize rabbits and they had a pot and were stewing the rabbit. The farmer complained to the guards or the German in command, and he was going around to all the fires to see who had the rabbit.

We found this out and we took some socks that we had and threw them in the pot to cover up the rabbit. There weren't any onions or anything in there, so there wasn't much of an aroma coming out.

Another time, at a barn, a young girl, a slave labor girl, was carrying some mush or something to the pigs. One of the fellas grabbed the bucket. It was an oatmeal grain type of mush. We always fed the sick first. They cleaned out the bucket and took it back to the girl. She was sitting on a bench and she was crying. They asked her what she was crying about. She said, "You are proud Americans and you steal food from the pigs."

One fella said, "Well, the pig ate yesterday, we didn't. The pig will eat tomorrow and we won't."

The girl took the bucket back inside. About five minutes later, the farmer and his wife came out. The farmer had a shotgun; his wife was carrying the pail. He was saying something in German as much as to say, "Now, try to steal this."

We looked up into the kitchen window, which would have been the kitchen window of the farmhouse, and here was this little girl with the lace curtains pulled apart, with a V for victory sign. We knew we had it made.

Stalag 11 B

At Fallingbostel, Stalag 11B, the section we were in was known as section 357. We were told we were going to get deloused and a hot shower. They were going to take us to a building. It was about fifty or sixty of us. We marched down to the building. It was a small building.

They told us to strip down and put our clothes, tie them up in a pile, and they were delousing (them). And then they told us that ten could go in to get a shower. Well, we'd heard about the concentration camps and we told the guards and the Germans in command that ten would go in and that we wanted to count ten coming out on the other side before anyone else went in.

So we got ten volunteers for the first ones. But it was the truth. We got a nice hot shower. Our clothes were deloused and were nice and warm and clean. We went back to the camp.

But it wasn't long after that we had the same little lousy bastards back with us.

The Shoe Leather Express goes on

We marched out of Fallingbostel and were on our way back across the Elbe River. This is the second time we crossed the Elbe River. It would eventually be a total of three times.

This time, we marched northeast. Not the same direction that we came, but headed back into Germany proper, again.

At one of the barns, we stopped at, the German in charge said that he was going to shoot a cow so we could have some meat. He had to empty his revolver in order to kill the cow. As they were butchering the cow, someone came along and we had to pack up and get ready to move.

I had an empty Red Cross box and as we went by the cow, I grabbed the heart, because I thought that would keep longer. We only marched about ten miles to another barn. When we lined up, there was about fifty of us. I was in the front row, along with Jim Cox, and the guard asked if any one of us could cook. I stepped out immediately. I could cook at little bit, because when we went camping, we did most of the cooking.

He (the guard) wanted two and I grabbed a hold of Jim Cox. I said, "Come on."

He said, "I can't cook."

I said, "Ya dumb bastard, you're going to be around food. Whether you can cook or not, you can eat."

So he came, it was just the two of us. We went into the part of the barn where they had a big stove, boiler type thing. We built a fire. All we cooked was potatoes. But I had that cow's heart and I was wondering how I could get that cooked. So again, here was this slave labor girl. She was showing us where the wood and the potatoes were.

I motioned to her if she would cook the heart, and she did. Jim and I had a slice of it. We cut the rest of it up and gave it to the fellas in the sick bay.

Later on, we were issued a nice big can of sardines, the big sardines, not the little ones. They said we were going to march out again.

But this time, May 2, 1945, we were going to march out again, we were told to march down to the main road, and there we would be liberated.

As we did, as we were going down the road, I heard a lot of shouting and a lot of noise behind me. I turned around and looked, and here was Jim Cox on one of the farmer's horses.

The farmer was coming after him with a pitchfork. So I stopped Jim and told him, "Look, you only got another hundred yards to freedom. Why risk your life now?" So he got off the horse.

Liberation

When we reached the road, it wasn't long before the British came up in their recon cars. The German officer told us to grab the rifles from the guards. Well, it was just about the end of the war. We told the British officer that they, the Germans, haven't shot us yet, and that we didn't think they were going to do it now.

But we did take their rifles. In fact, the guards that we had then were elderly men, they were up in their sixties, close to their seventies. They cared less about the war. In many instances, we carried their rifle for them. But we knew the war was just about over, so it didn't matter one way or the other.

As we were going through a small town, there was a cheese factory. One of the fellows got in there and got a wheel of cheese. They got these, I guess, five-gallon cans of milk they put out on the platform as we went by. Each of us dipped our cans in to get a drink of milk and we got a slice of cheese.

By the way, we got powdered milk an they called it KLIM. It was milk spelled backwards. We had three cans, pint cans, that we carried with us on the march. One was for drinking water, one was for cooking, and one was for getting food. You can imagine two thousand POWs walking down the road, three tin cans hanging down from their side, the noise that it made.

The march was about 600 miles. You measured from Gross Tychow, Stalag Luft IV, in a straight line. That would probably be about 400 miles. But we went up to the Baltic, then started southwest, then we'd back track. You come around, circle around, and came right back to the barn that we left that morning. That doesn't show on any map.

Also, after we got to Stalag 11 B, we were in the section of the camp called 357. This is at Fallingbostel. We were there two or three days, maybe a week, and they moved us out again, across the Elbe River, heading east, then we turned and headed north. We were 10 or 15 miles east of Hamburg, Germany, when we were liberated.

POWs just liberated. Joe O'Donnell circled.

When I went in the service, I weighed around 150-155. When I was freed, I imagine I was down to 120-123, or something like that. We had a way of measuring how thin we were. We'd take our right hand and put it around our left wrist and see how far we could go up the arm. The thinner you were, the farther you could go up the arm. I could go maybe three or four inches. When I check now and I can't get my fingers around my left wrist unless I squeeze.

We got into the small town of Gudel. There, the British were stripping the German guards and other guards of all of their possessions. They were pushing one guard around, one fellow we took the rifle from. So I went up to the English officer and told him, "Aren't you being a little rough on these fellows?"

He said, in his English accent, "One of your blokes held one of them upside down in a well." And they pushed me out of the way.

They drew a map—that night, we slept in a nice abandoned home. It was brick. The corner of it was knocked out as if a tank went around there and didn't make the turn. We slept on the floor.

The next morning, we were given instructions where to go. We were to go to Hamburg, Germany. We crossed the Kiel Canal by a Canal Boat that was lodged sideways. We got down to a road. It was a motor pool. I told Jim Cox, "I'm not walking any farther. This is it."

As we were sitting there, a British truck came out of the motor pool. He asked us where we were going. We told him. He said, "Hop in." A Looie rolled down the window and lit a cigarette. I think what it was, even though we had gotten a shower, the first of April, this was the first of May, and it was hot. And I guess we stunk pretty badly.

But it wasn't long before we got to Hamburg. We were stripped down of all our clothing and they made a big pile and set fire to it.

There, we were deloused again. We were deloused with DDT and we were given new uniforms. But they were British. What I had were hob nailed shoes. We stayed there for several days, and then they trucked us down to the town of Celle; it was a British airfield. We were put in tents and we were told to prepare to leave at any time.

The worst time, emotionally, was when I sat down alongside the road. I had some sort of sickness I don't know what it was. But I was shaking, cold, damp, wet, and hungry. I just couldn't put up with it any more. But as I said, your buddies help you along. A couple of my buddies picked me up. I would say that was the worst part, emotionally.

Physically, we were actually strafed. That wasn't anything emotional. That was save your ass type of thing. Twice there was an attempted strafing job by the British and the Americans. But they recognized that we were Prisoners of War and they waved their wings and off they went. But this time, the Germans set up a tripod machine gun and started firing at the plane. The fighter plane, I forget whether it was American or British, fired back. That's when we dove into the barn.

About three in the afternoon, someone shouted, "Any of you Yanks want to go home?"

I was in the rear of the tent and instead of going out the door, the flap, like everyone else did, I went out the back. They were loading up the trucks and said that's all. I was the next one to get on. They said, "One more." So I got on the truck.

They took us to an airfield. Instead of going to Camp Lucky Strike at Le Havre, France, like the other thousands went, we went directly to an airfield in England. We were given tea and biscuits and trucked off to a hospital in Oxford, England.

Here again, we were issued pajamas, clean sheets. It was like a different world. That night, they told us we could have anything, all we wanted to eat. One of the things was chicken, some kind of chicken, and mashed potatoes. Well, everyone just gorged himself, and of course, they all were sick. So we learned a lesson.

The next morning, was oatmeal and tea and coffee and toast. We really had it made.

We left there and went into London. I think I over drank every night. I couldn't hold down any beer, anyway. Three or four glasses of beer and I was out.

We were put up in an apartment building, and we were told, every morning, to go to headquarters and check to see if our name was on the shipping list.

We could go wherever we wanted to go, but if you missed the day for shipping back to the United States, you were put on the end of the list. So we made sure we were available every day.

While in London, we did some sightseeing, but not too much. I was there about two or three weeks.

We came back on an LST. A chum of mine from high school, we graduated together, was one of the bakers, and I met up with him. He told me, "Joe, ten o'clock tonight, come on up to the bakery."

I went up there and had hot coffee and cinnamon buns right out of the oven.

It was an uneventful ride home. We landed at Camp Pat Henry, Virginia. Stayed there for a couple of days; got washed and cleaned up again, and went home on a furlough for sixty days. Then I went down to Atlantic City, then to Greenville, South Carolina, just to await discharge, or to get enough points to be discharged.

Not the returning hero

From there, I went to Newark, and got my discharge papers. They were handing out the medals. Captains were doing this.

They'd read off your discharge and got to the end of the line this kid got all the other medals and the Captain read off the Good Conduct Medal. I stuck out my hand, and the Captain said, "You don't get it, it only says you—it doesn't say you're entitled to the Good Conduct Medal, it just says Good Conduct Medal."

I told the Captain that I had one more stop to make to get my discharge. When I get that in my hand, I'm going to come back and tell you what to do with that medal, with the clasp open.

I went home. One of the things I found out that we were not, in some cases, not the returning heroes. A so-called friend of mine, a girl, I went swimming. On my swimming trunks, I had the Air Force insignia. She said, "Oh Joe, were you in the service?"

My mother had put everything in the paper, photographs and everything.

In another instance, one of the fellas, a 4F I'd grown up and went to school with, he told another fella, I wasn't there at the time. They were talking about me being a Prisoner of War. This 4F said, "Yeah, he's a Goddamned coward." The other guy kicked the living hell out of him.

Looking back

So everything wasn't the hero type—which I didn't expect. I did expect to have a job and continue on working. I was promised a job when I got back. It lasted one month. And I was out of a job. I went on the 52-20, fifty-two weeks of $20.00 a week.

My buddy and I bought a car, of course a second hand car, and he and I went out to California to my sister's, and I bummed around for quite a while. Then I went to school on the GI Bill of Rights and finally settled down and got a job. I went to college and retired back in 1984.

The best thing that happened to me during the war, was on May 2, 1945, when they told us to march down the road about a quarter of a mile and you will be liberated. I guess you couldn't expect anything better than that. Everything else would be mediocre. You just can't realize just what it's like to be able to eat again or to be able to do whatever you want again without somebody standing there with a gun. Simple little things like going to the toilet. I know in school you had to ask permission, but you'd think a grown person wouldn't have to ask an armed guard if they can go to the bathroom. These are the little things that returned.

So it was a great day of jubilation. To have your stomach full again, to be able to drink clean water, to have a hair cut, a shave, to be able to brush your teeth, whatever the things that we now take for granted came back. Even today, I don't take things for granted. I look at things from a positive side, I don't like negative things. I don't like crowds. I haven't been to a movie since The Sound of Music, and that was back in the 1950s.

If we go into a restaurant or into anyplace that there's a crowd, they could be watching something like the Air Force Band at the Convention Center, I always make sure I sit on the end of the aisle. If we go into a restaurant, I want to make sure, if it's a square table or a round table, that I'm on the aisle end of it, never my back up against a wall. I don't like to be closed in. I don't like people hanging on me, unless it's a woman.

Printed with permission of Joe O'Donnell and The Oral History Archive of The American Airpower Heritage Museum,

From A Different Point Of View

Some thoughts of someone who was a boy when World War II ended
Narrated by Gerhard Rühlow
Edited by Erik Dyreborg

People may ask what a German boy of ten, during the war, could possibly remember of the prisoners of war, or how could he imagine what it was like to be a soldier. At first glance perhaps it appears questionable, but there are things that happen in our lives we never forget, and this is one of those. There are also many similarities between the POWs and civilians.

I was born at Gross Tychow in Pomerania, the province in East Germany, which now belongs to Poland as far as the part east of the Oder River is concerned. About five miles west of Gross Tychow there was a large POW camp in the forest during the last months of World War II. It was the "Kriegsgefangenenlager der Luftwaffe 4" and when it was evacuated in February 1945 there had been about 10,000 POWs in it, most of them US airmen. I had been there once in the late summer of 1944, but did not see too much except the fence and some barracks.

Some months later, the allied military front reached Pomerania, the Soviets conquered the east German provinces, the Poles followed and we Germans had to leave our homes, were expelled in an inhuman and brutal way. After four months on the roads, in cattle trains and in refugee camps we arrived in the western part of Germany.

Many years of silence followed. The "Cold War" between the political blocks in Europe did not allow any private visits to the former German provinces. The campsite of "Stalag Luft 4" near Gross Tychow (now Tychowo) and its environment had been taken property by the Soviets immediately after the end of the war in 1945 and nobody except members of the Soviet army was allowed to approach that region. That's why the former POW camp was gradually getting the touch of secret and suspicion. Rumors were heard about the past, some people said it might have been a concentration camp, some spoke of "thousands of people" were killed there, which was not true.

Stalag Luft IV with some of the barracks and the barbed wire, is pictured above.

Truth returned when the political situation changed and the former German residents were allowed to come back to their homes as tourists about 30 years after they had been expelled. Also when former POWs, as individual tourists or in groups, came to see the camp site 45 years after they had left it in that painful march in February 1945, called "Death March." Those who survived the march were liberated. Among the ExPOWs who came back to Gross Tychow/Tychowo was Joseph P. O'Donnell from Robbinsville, NJ. On his first visit in 1993, he left a drawing of the camp together with his address. I happened to see his information when I was also there. I got into contact with Joe and some other former POWs. The result was a sincere friendship. We've met in the USA, Berlin, and also Groß Tychow/Tychowo several times whenever a group of former US airmen returned to former Stalag Luft 4. Of course, "life in the camp during 1944/45" was much discussed, many interesting conversations began with "do you remember....?"

People often make the mistake of assessing events of the past from their present point of view. By using the past point of view, gives a better understanding between people who had been enemies during a terrible war. The POWs in Stalag Luft 4 suffered a lot, but—as far as I could tell—they were not and are not filled with hatred against the Germans. They knew to differ between those who maltreated them in the camps and the German people who had to suffer as well during World War II. By the way, a German friend of mine, some years older than I, was a POW in the Soviet Union. When he read some of the books, written by POWs of Stalag Luft 4, he said: "Compared to us, Stalag Luft 4 sounds like paradise."

When we read today that POWs, members of the US Air Force, were threatened by civilians and sometimes spat at, we are shocked and ashamed. How could that happen? Incredible today, about 60 years later! But what was the situation during the war? Six hundred thousand Germans were killed by bombs of allied planes, almost a million were injured, and hundreds of thousands lost their homes because their houses had been destroyed. No wonder German civilians were receptive to political propaganda and ready to look upon the airmen as the "Terrorflieger", the "bad men" who bombed non-military and non-industrial targets in order to break the morale. By the way, the opposite could be seen: The morale of the civilians could not be broken. In contrary, the will to stand the pains of war increased.

No doubt, laws, rules, and regulations, especially during a war, must be obeyed. They are necessary on either side. But to watch POWs obey them is a matter of the individuals, the leaders, and guards of the camps. Did they always act, react and behave as human beings are expected to? I am sorry to say several did not. So dislike or hatred always aims at individuals, not at the whole people generally. In the POW camp Gross Tychow and on the way to it many inmates fell victims to guards who disregarded the rules of the Geneva Convention and even the human rights. Joe O'Donnell put it like this: "There were those who enjoyed what they were doing, and those who just did their duty and would have rather been home with their families."

One of the latter was Hermann Glemnitz, the German commander of Stalag Luft III at Sagan/Schlesien. David C. Lane, a US POW, had an experience with him that is worth describing here. I should mention in advance that prisoners were not allowed to have radios. But they were inventive and there were many experts among them. Within a short time they built a radio of primitive material, and when a guard approached they dismantled it and hid the separate parts.

Lane: "On rumor that the Russians were coming and we were going to be moved I started to make a packsack out of a GI blanket though I knew that it was not allowed. I was caught red-handed when Glemnitz walked in."

Glemnitz, (in his not too good English pronunciation): "Vot are you doing?"

Lane: "I'm making a packsack."

Glemnitz: "You know dot's illegal!"

Lane: "Yes, I know. What do you suggest I do with it?"

Glemnitz: "Put it vid de radio. I can't find dot, either."

As everywhere in the world there are "those and those." After the war Hermann Glemnitz, the former commander of Stalag Luft III, had been a frequent guest at reunions of the former POWs before he died in 1988 at the age of 89.

As I mentioned in the beginning, the Polish who became the new owners in Pomerania as well as in the other East German provinces expelled us Germans. As many POWs come back to their former camp site, I and many refugees go back to our former homes which are now part of Poland. Steps to international under-standing! But this is not the only thing I and most other refugees have in com-mon with the POWs. Those from Stalag Luft 4 had to march from Gross Tychow to the west and suffered from nearly everything man is able to imagine. The term "Death March", hits the nail on the head. When we had to leave our home and were expelled, we had to cross the Oder River, we also had to march in the winter of 1946/47. We sometimes were also put into cold cattle trains, had to pass camps, and after four months finally reached West Germany.

As far as I can say the former POWs don't feel any hatred for us Germans now. Most of my countrymen as well as myself don't feel any hatred for the Poles when we go back to our homes in Pomerania. The way we had to suffer was neither the fault of the generations that have been born there since 1945, nor the fault of the Polish people generally. I could read and I was told that many US POWs have given up speaking about their times as a POW, because most of their countrymen don't know what they are talking about, they are not understood. Real conversation is only possible among men who had been POWs. I as a refugee have given up talking about my experiences after World War II because people who have not lost their homes and property and who did not suffer from starvation and thirst, from fear of being killed don't know what I'm talking about, even more: Most of them don't even listen.

The ten-year-old, and the present Gerhard Rühlow are pictured above.

So after all we have several things in common. The POWs are the deeper background for the good relationship between us. And in spite of all the pain, suffering and bad experiences we should agree that positive thinking is the only way to go: Without reunions, without visiting tours to former camp sites, and writing about life in a POW camp, I would never have made friends with so many people in the USA. "Volksbund Deutsche Kriegsgräberfürsorge" is a German organization that takes care of German soldiers' cemeteries in foreign countries, for example in France or in Russia. Young people who go abroad, working on the cemeteries, meeting with foreign young people. Taking care of cemeteries may have been the basic idea of this organization. But their central idea now is establishing friendship between young generations, shaking hands above the graves for a better, a peaceful future. I think that's a great step toward friendship between peoples after two terrible wars. The contact to former POWs has got in some way the same idea: To shake hands on a former camp site and forgive—for the sake of a better, a peaceful future.

Printed with permission of Gerhard Rühlow.

The Never Ending Search

◆

A story about Glenn Dorwin Woods, B-24 Right Waist Gunner & Radio Operator

8th Air Force, 492 Bomb Group, 859 Bomb Squadron
Narrated byPat Houser, daughter of Glenn Dorwin Woods
Edited by Erik Dyreborg

Background

I still remember holding her hand, speaking the words I knew hurt her so very much, and I remember thinking how sad I was that all her hopes and dreams, as well as mine were gone. I am thinking of the day I told my dear Mother I had heard my father was dead. Her hand went limp and I thought she would faint, she became so ashen and then the tears began for both of us. She was crying for what might have been, and I for the Father I never knew.

My Mother and step dad had been on a trip to the east coast, I remember asking my Mother why this trip was so important to her. It always felt to me like she was saying goodbye to everyone, as she was going to the places that had been important to her during her life. Most of all she said she needed to go to Florida one more time.

So many reflections flashed before my eyes as I held her hand, was the reason she pushed so hard to return to Florida (my place of birth) because she had some inner feeling my Father might be there? Did she feel some sort of pull again the year my Father died in Florida, which prompted her desire to once again return? Or did she have an inner feeling of her own mortality? Questions I wish I had asked, as I have so many questions now about my Mother and Father.

Last year I once again felt I needed some answers, a friend was deeply into her family genealogy and with the progress of the Internet was telling me how much information I might be able to find on line.

She gave me a web address and her password, I was absolutely shaking as I opened the site, put in her password and clicked on military information. Oh, there was so much to chose from, I had no idea where to go, so I closed that site and went to Florida Birth and Death information.

I knew my father had died in Florida, and I knew the year. Once again shaking I typed in his name and year of death. I couldn't believe it there he was, for the first time in so many years he was there in front of me. OK, now I am committed to the search let's see what else I can find.

Now to back up some, about ten years ago I also went on a quest to find out about my father, I only had one person to ask and she was my dear Aunt Lurilla. I didn't want to cause her pain, I didn't want to pry, but I posed a question to her asking if she would mind if I asked about some information on my father.

She immediately wrote back that she had many pictures, letters, even a diary she had kept during WWII and would be thrilled to not only share it with me, but to give it all to me. I wasn't sure I was ready for all that at once, but I took her up on her offer.

She began to write me massive amounts of letters, sent me family charts of who was who and what was what. I must admit it was more painful than I thought it would be. Yes, it was thrilling to see all this, but it was hell to see what I had missed in my life. The following is what I found out, and yes, I did miss out on knowing a wonderful man.

I also contacted and joined the 8th Air Force, I begged to have something placed in their newsletter that I was seeking information on my father, they never did, but now I know why, there are thousands of people looking......

My Father, Glen Dorwin Woods, was born October 6, 1920 in Portland, IN. His parents were George "Doll" Woods and Lizzie Votaw. My Father's mother died shortly after he was born, and, as was the custom in those days, my father was sent to live with his Mother's sister and her family, while his brother Washington remained with their father and moved to Ohio.

I always referred to his Mother's sister as Grandmother Sherburne, and her daughter was my Aunt Lurilla, whom I called Auntie L. It is my understanding my father was a good student, good person, causing no problems at home or school, and he went by the name of Sherburne while in school. Auntie L said he loved to draw and spent many hours drawing at the kitchen table.

Florida

My Father entered the army air corps on January 4, 1940 and received training as a radio operator and mechanic at Scott Field, IL. He completed his combat training at a Texas air base and left for overseas duty spring of 1944. My Father was a radio operator on a B-24, and during this time was a Technical Sergeant.

I've always wondered what is easier knowing your father is alive and you can't find him, or dead and no chance of ever meeting him. All my life I wanted to see my father, to find out how he could blot me out of his life, to see how much like him I was. To find out why he and my Mother divorced, but most of all to just see him and touch him. I mentioned before my Mother had this overwhelming desire to return to Florida, the first time was in 1958.

For me to relocate from my "hometown" was absolutely devastating. I hated Florida, I had been raised in the Eastern Sierra of California, I was raised with no idea what prejudice was. I was raised in the mountains, a place when it rained it turned cool. I was used to snow in the winter, fall colors, and spring wildflowers. When we arrived in Florida, it was always damp, warm and flat. I hated it; I went from a high school of 400 to a sophomore class in high school of over 1000. The hardest thing was the prejudice. I was told in school I could not be friends with other than white kids......strange, I was raised with Native Americans, Mexicans, and who knows what else, and they were all friends.

What I didn't know was my Father was less than 100 miles away. I so clearly remember one day while waiting for the bus seeing this tall man at the bus stop and thinking he looks so much like the pictures of my Father, only less hair. I remember the look on my Mother's face when I told her; there was a smile, yet a look of fear.

I was able to confirm before my dear Auntie L died it probably was my father, as she had told him where we were. She also explained the reason he never made contact was not "wanting to confuse" me, since I had a stepfather. Had he known of the abuse my Mother and I suffered at the hands of my step dad, Auntie L says he would have been there in a heartbeat.

My parents were married in Florida in mid September 1942 I was born the end of June 1943 in Florida. We remained in Florida until I was almost eight years old. I have no idea how my parents met, but I think it was while my Mother was doing some volunteer work for the military spotting enemy planes and submarines or perhaps while she worked at the air base in Southern Florida. I always got the impression from my Mother it was love at first sight, and they married soon after they met.

Looking for information about my father, the airman

As I mentioned earlier, my Father went overseas in the spring of 1944, he was based at North Pickenham, England, with the famous 8th Air Force. I have tried to obtain his service records from the NARA, but evidentially his records were burned in the St Louis fire.

Back to my quest for my father, thanks to the Internet I started poking around, looking for the 8th Air Force, success! Next I looked for the 492nd Bomb Group, more success! Next, the 859th Bomb Squadron. I found a fantastic website for the Army Air Force, again shaking I entered my name to join the group.

Once I was accepted I asked my question on every message board they offered. I then went to the Bomb Group and did the same. I truly NEVER thought I'd hear a word, sure enough, not only did I find out when my father went down (July 7, 1944), where he was a POW (Stalag Luft IV), but met several people who are very important in my life today.

Next I looked up the Stalag Luft IV where my father was as a POW. I posted asking for information on my father or anyone who might have been interned with him. I met yet another incredible man, Carrol F. Dillon, whose twin brother had been in the same Stalag Luft.

Glenn Dorwin Woods is pictured above.

Next I got an email from a man, Erik Dyreborg, in Denmark telling me about a book he was writing on the 8th and 15th Air Force and he'd like me to write my father's story. He also said he had a connection with the 492nd BG and her name was Karen Cline. I wrote Karen telling her as Erik had suggested, saying she might be able to help. Karen was generous enough to send me a copy of my Father's Casualty Report. Yes, it hurt!

Somewhere in this I met Joe O'Donnell who was also in Stalag Luft IV. What an absolute joy this man is, what he endured, and what he has done with the hell he suffered. Instead of being bitter, he spends time helping other soldiers who need help to use the benefits the military promised them. He has also written several books about the forced march, poetry and general information about Stalag Luft IV.

The crew.

Front row L to R: Nose gunner SGT.Vince J. Brdecka, Right waist gunner & radio operator T/SGT. Glenn Dorwin Woods, Ground crew chief SGT. Red Dieso, Tail gunner SGT. Sam Stammerra & Belly gunner SGT. Bob Kohout.

Standing L to R: Pilot LT Bill Keeler, Co-pilot LT Henry Meyer, Bombardier LT Frankie Benton and Navigator LT Sam Turner.

From the casualty report Karen sent me, I can tell what brave men fought for our country. It says "Sgt. Stamerra was badly injured or killed in air, his chute was torn apart. Sgt. Brdecka was apparently unable to get out of the nose turret; he was not wounded at the time. The B-24 circled around for about five minutes before it crashed. Fighters kept making passes at the plane until it hit the ground. Sgt. Brdecka continued to shoot at the fighters until he went down, even though he knew he was the only one onboard." They were enroute to Bernburg, Germany. They went down on July 7, 1944 at 09:47 four km. west of Westerageln, as a result of flak.

I've read several books as well as the website about Stalag Luft IV. I've read about the forced march, over 600 miles, little food, no stopping except to sleep at night. Sleeping in fields where other prisoners had already camped, and used the ground as the only bathroom. I have no idea if my father was captured as soon as they landed, or did they hide? I know my father who was 6' 2", lost almost 100 pounds while interned, he was down to 86 pounds when he returned to the states. I also know he suffered from many of the maladies I've heard many POWs have suffered from. Is this what killed him at such a young age, only 57?

My father hated cold, yet he was a POW in one of the camps who suffered from little or no blankets, lack of heat and food as well poor medical care. Did you know the Germans would open the Red Cross parcels because they feared if too many parcels were handed out, the prisoners might try to store them for escape? And, escape meant death for the Commandant.

Excerpts from a diary

Lurilla Sherburne's Diary, found in box with my father's things. Original was handwritten and then typed by Auntie L. about 1993.

Muncie, Indiana June 6, 1944

Mark this date well. For today is a day that will go down in history. Today is D-Day—Deliverance Day—Invasion Day. The Allied troops landed on the Normandy peninsula in France this a.m. The radio has been broadcasting news every few minutes all day. Special programs are on with prayers offered by different ministers. President Roosevelt led the nation in prayer this evening. I have never known prayer to be so universal. Churches were open to the public all day. Everyone has stayed by the radios all day. It is hard to describe the feeling one has. Somewhat of pride that we are having a part in an enormous task; yet not of pride in a gruesome, pagan way to decide who shall rule the world. It is too early to feel anxiety for individuals involved, but a breathless waiting as in a basketball game when a player is ready to shoot for a goal from the foul line—it remains to be seen who will get the ball and what the next play is to be. There is no cheering along the sidelines, just waiting.

August 13, 1944 Sunday, 7 p.m.

It was about this time July 22 (Saturday) that we got a special delivery letter from Dorothy's mother. They had received a telegram from the War Dept. on Thursday evening that Glen had been reported missing in action over Germany since July 7. The news at first was stunning, just as thought it couldn't happen to him. We had crowded into the back of our minds the thought that Glen would be spared while others fell. The folks took the news very well. I expected them to go to pieces; but they didn't seem to realize all it might mean, except that it might be a long time before we heard from Glen. We have since heard from the Group Chaplain and the navigator's wife that there is a chance they might have parachuted to safety and were prisoners of war. The worst thing is to have our letters returned. I don't suppose he received the fudge he wanted so much, that I made and sent to him. I hope he at least received the letter telling him I was sending it. I keep feeling his is safe. I wish I could realize a little more that he might <u>not</u> be, so I won't be too shocked by any bad news.

September 6, 1944 Wed., 6:15 p.m.

Had a letter from Dorothy today saying she had a telegram from the War Dept. saying that Glen was a prisoner of war in Germany. That is that much at least.—Just three months today since the invasion. U. S. troops from three points—north, west, and south of France—are converging at the Siegfried Line on the German border. Everyone feels sure the war in Europe is only a matter of days, or weeks at the most. I wish I could feel as optimistic. Of course practically all of France has been occupied in a very short time, from Marseille to Belgium in two weeks. But I have a feeling the Germans are just waiting till we reach their border! We shall see!

January 1, 1945 Mon., 7:30 p.m.

And almost four months later, my "feelings" have proved correct. In Alsace-Lorraine and on the Belgium and Holland-German borders the Allied troops met stubborn resistance. The last 3-4 months have shown only a few miles progress. There was a bloody battle at Aachen. Then a few miles from Cologne the Germans surprised the Allies, and our troops were driven back in 3-4 days as much ground as it had taken several months to gain. There is bitter fighting in snow, mud, and ice.—Very little progress is being made in Italy.—Revolution and civil war rages in Greece.—Budapest is about to fall to the Russians.—Politics seems to be uppermost in Allied high circles. Churchill is somewhat in disfavor with the English because of his interference in the Greece revolution. As for the eastern front, there have been the battles of Saipan and Leyte. MacArthur has returned to the Philippines as he promised. B-29's—super—fortresses—are steadily bombing Tokyo. My feelings regarding this front is that we will be well into 1946 before there will be a beginning of an end in that affair.—Dorothy had a letter, and we a post card, from Glen in October that he had written July 28 shortly after he was reported missing. We have no other word from him. According to the Prisoner of War Bulletin published by the Red Cross, Sta-lug Luft 4 is in the northeastern part of Germany, in the Pomerania province, close to the Polish border. It is very cold there, and Glen hates the cold so.—The New Year is being ushered in by a cold wave. It is blowing a terrible gale, as well as being very close to zero. We have had ice on the streets constantly for almost three weeks now.—Our Sunday school class sponsored a watch party at the Dotson's after church last night. We invited the intermediate boys and girls. Had about a dozen. Mary had the table fixed nice with candles, place cards, etc. Had chili. I had the same gang here at the house for a Halloween party.

January 29, 1945 Mon., 5:15 p.m.

The news, since last I wrote, has been filled with the rapid advance of the Russians through Poland. They have crossed the German boarder in several places, are deep in the Selesian province, and have taken Breslow and Poznan. Tonight's news says the Russians are into Pomerania and have taken Schneidemuhl. Should be getting close to Glen. They are just 93 miles from Berlin, came 70 miles in less than two weeks. Is just another calm before the storm, like the march through France, only to be halted at the border? There are those who are optimistic, as before, and believe the Germans will be licked in a matter of days or a couple weeks at the longest. But we shall see!

April 15, 1945 Sun. 6:40 p.m.

The nation, yea, the whole world, is in mourning. A great man, Franklin Delano Roosevelt, our president, died at his "other home" in Warm Springs, GA., Thurs., April 12, at 3:35 p.m. In spite of the things he did with which we did not altogether agree when he was living, in death no one can deny he was a great man; no other would have dared to have done the things he did. No other would have attempted the reforms, the projects, the undertakings, he has attempted and accomplished. No other has been paid the tribute of being four times chosen the leader of his country. Only three months of that 4th term was served. He could not have helped by known when he consented to run that he would never be able to complete this term. Yes, that accepting such a task would shorten his health and very life. "Those who knew him could see the light of death in his eyes," but he refused to look at it. "But he was not one to give up when there was a task to be done." He will go down in history with Washington and Lincoln, a man who worked against great odds, being a victim of infantile paralysis in 1921.—There was a 25-minute funeral service in the East Room of the White House, a simple, punctual affair that marked his whole public life. He was buried at Hyde Park, N.Y., his home today. The whole world pauses to pay tribute to a great leader. But there is only a pause; he would want us to carry on from here, because there is much to be done.

May 8, 1945 Tues. 11:10 p.m.

At 9:05 this evening the folks got a cablegram from Glen: "Am well. See you soon."

July 3, 1945 Tues. 6:45 p.m.

We had a telegram from Glen this noon. He is at Camp Patrick Henry, Virginia! Said, "Dear Folks: Back in the Good Ole USA.

Furlough Soon. Going to see Dot first. Write later. Love. Glen."

We were more or less expecting him. Most of the prisoners were returned the last of May. At that time they said the rest would come the last of June. And then Dorothy had a telegram from the War Dept. saying Glen was being returned soon. That was two weeks ago, and if he came by boat that would just about come out right. So we weren't surprised. We all rather expected a phone call yesterday and Sunday.—After we had his cablegram, we had a V-mail from La Havre, France. It wasn't dated, but was possibly the middle of May. Then we had a letter, written May 3, apparently right after he was liberated. It was on Britain stationary. Then I had one written on V-E Day, 5/8/45. He was in Brussels, Belgium. Dorothy had several, the last on May, 30. It is a great day for us, but so many won't be back.

July 7, 1945 Sat. 9:30 p.m.

Dad had a telegram from Glen saying, "Am home. Found a beautiful wife and wonderful daughter. Wire back. Haven't heard from you in eight months." Dad was afraid to answer it for fear he wouldn't say the right thing! So we phoned a telegram:

"Your telegram just received with better news than one a year ago today. Glad Army's best Sergeant home. Love from the home folks. Sherburnes"

August 15, 1945 Wednesday

Today and tomorrow has been declared V-J (Victory in Japan) Days. Yesterday there was a pretty authentic rumor that Japan had surrendered. Last night President Truman proclaimed a double holiday. About 4:00 a.m. yesterday, when the rumor first came over the radio, the factory workers just walked off the job, and the day shift just didn't show up for work. Places of business did start opening.—Glen and Dorothy met me at my office at 5 o'clock. There was quite a crowd up town. We ate, and at 6:00 the president proclaimed a holiday. In accordance with orders, all the "joints" closed up tight. We went to the drug store for a coke, and they had closed! We thought we would go to a movie, and <u>they</u> were closed. So we joined everyone else on the streets and watched traffic. And what traffic! It was really tied up. Horns were blowing, and anything that would make noise was being used for that, including garbage cans tied onto the back of cars. All this in the pouring down rain, mind you! Finally Glen, Dorothy and I walked home, 30 blocks. My shoes weren't dry even the next morning! We were really soaked. But in spite of the hilarity, there was a deep feeling of gratitude that the whole thing was over, and that we might once again have the opportunity to live a normal life.

October 28, 1945 Sunday, 7:30 p.m.

Well, Dear Diary, you have been so sadly neglected. Ah, the pity of it all, with so much news to be recorded. July 31, about 1:00 a.m., Glen and Dorothy walked in on us, we were surprised!

December 31, 1945 7:30 p.m.

New Year's Eve! Yes, the closing of a full and eventful year; the beginning of a new lease on life. 1945 brought victory on the battlefronts. 1946 will determine whether we shall win the Peace. Hostilities ceased in Germany and the boys are slowly, but surely, returning home. The Army of Occupation is beginning to settle down to a smooth running machine.—(Gen. Patton, leader of the 5th Army, and the Battle of the Bulge, died last week as a result of spinal injuries received in an automobile accident.) How "successful" the Victory was to be determined by the success of the Occupation.—To all outward appearances, Japan has been subdued. How many years or *generations it will take to reeducate the Japanese is mere speculation. Today, Hirohito announced to his people that he was <u>not</u> divine, thus carrying out the first of Mac Arthur's orders to do away with Shintuism, the worship of the emperor as divine and a direct descendent of the Sun God, and the belief that the destiny of the Japanese is to rule the world. It will not be an easy task to uproot such belief and superstition. We will have to offer a substitution. There is much unrest and dissatisfaction in the whole world. There is war in Palestine. China is having a civil war (Nationalist Party led by Chiang Kai-shek vs. the Communist Party.) The Russians, self-sufficient and coming world power, doesn't trust anyone, nor does she have to. But the last meeting (this month) of the Big Three in London, indicates a little closer understanding and agreement. They have decided to turn the Atomic Bomb problem over to the United Nations Organization (UNO) for one thing.—In our own country, the year ended in a lot of doubt and fear. The General Motors strike is going into it's 7th week. There is hope of an early settlement, but management and labor seem to be still as far apart as ever. Labor wants a 33 1/3 % increase in pay (a minimum of 94 cents per hour when the average laborer makes 70 cents!). Warner Gear went back to work the 26th, just three months to the day they walked out. What they have gained is doubtful. How long will it take to regain what they have lost, even at increased pay? These men have spent all their earnings and cashed in all their war bonds, and some are in destitute circumstances. Labor has held the whip hand for so long, it is hard for them to realize that man does not always get what they ask; and management is perhaps taking advantage of the fact that she is in the drivers seat again.*

There is a steel strike threatening which may tie up practically all industries. And, of course, many others, such as telegraphers, telephone operators, Greyhound Bus drivers, etc. Prolonged strikes could well put us into a deep recession. But, as at all New Years, there is a hope and faith that 1946 will bring full employment, prosperity, a "bloom" of production of <u>civilian</u> instead of war goods. It is remarkable what Jan. 1st can do to our morale!

Not the only one

The biggest thing I have found out in my quest for information on my Father is there are hundreds, perhaps more also looking for information for fathers, grandfathers, uncles and so on. I see on the various Internet boards how people ask "any information on so and so, anyone who served with him, knew him in the POW camp" etc. It is the never-ending search.

I've also learned this truly was the "Greatest Generation", how sad for my generation to not have known them better. They lived through the Great Depression, they knew how to stretch a dollar until it was paper thin, they knew not to waste, and they had such integrity. To this day when you make a deal or shake a hand with this generation they mean it. They have been so brave, and we are losing them at such a fast pace.

Whomever is reading this, if there is one of these incredible people in your life, ask them questions, do an oral history, not just about the war, but about their life. Ask them what their dreams were, what they did for play as a kid. Ask them anything that is important to you, as you can bet it is close to what was important to them.

Oh how I wish I could have known my father, seen some of his drawings, found out how he met my Mother, what their dreams were, why did they divorce? Was he happy in his life?

Is there anyone out there who might have known my father? Served with him, knew him growing up? Knew him when he lived in Florida?

I am only one person on this quest; imagine how many others are also seeking knowledge on family, friends of family, those who served together, on and on. Thanks to the Internet it is easier, but it is still hard to know where to post, where it is safe, and where you might get the most information. The largest obstacle is time, finding the right place before those with the information are gone.

If there is anyone reading this who has information on my father, please contact Erik Dyreborg, and he will get the information to me, it would be greatly appreciated. For those of you searching, I wish you all the luck in the world. Don't ever give up; you never know where you might find out something else you didn't know.

I'd like to thank Erik for the inspiration and encouragement to put this into words. I wish I knew more to make it a more interesting and exciting story, but perhaps I will be lucky, and someone will know something that may lead to yet another door opening and possibly more chapters in another book. I also want to thank all these brave men and women who have given so much, asked so little, and given us the freedom to enjoy today, to be free and to be able to write and read books about the history of our lives.

Since meeting Erik, and helping with this book, I have become a transcriber for the Army Air Force Historical Group, transcribing oral histories such as those in this wonderful book. You just never know where a quest will lead you, and it is never too late to find some passion in your life. I may never know more about my father, but you never know. I may find someone through this oral history group who did know him.

Printed with permission of Pat Houser.

Freed At Last

Narrated by Henry C. Paris, B-24 Ball Turret Gunner
15ᵗʰ Air Force, 455ᵗʰ Bomb Group, 743ʳᵈ Bomb Squadron
Edited by Erik Dyreborg

The mission

This is the story of a B-24 Liberator heavy bomber of the 15ᵗʰ A. A. F., manned by a battered crew which refused to bail out and leave an injured buddy behind.

It was a sky battle in an attack by a B-24 on the Trieste Harbor installations and shipping, on April 20, 1944 that sent the Liberator on it's dogged journey. About forty ME-109's closed to clash with the formation, ten of the fighters at first and later others, concentrating their attack on the tail turret of the Liberator piloted by 1ˢᵗ Lt. Robert Cook, 24, Harrisburg, PA.

S/Sgt. Leslie H. Stockdale, 20, of Blue Springs, MO., who shot one Nazi down for sure, manned the tail turret position and he saw another in flames but the victory was not confirmed. Nazi fighters kept swooping and zooming. Their aerial rockets, 20mm cannon shells and machine gun bullets wrecked the turret, severely wounding Stockdale and put his guns out of action.

Other gun positions on the Liberators were having their troubles as well. With a good start the Nazis apparently decided to keep concentrating on this one B-24.

Pictured above: Front row L to R:
F/o Richard Haney, Co-Pilot 1st Lt Robert Cook, Pilot 2nd Lt David
Woodlock, Navigator 1st Lt. Paul Guild----Bombardier.

Back row L to R:
T/Sgt Abe Aziz Engineer Gunner, S/Sgt Ralph Friese Right waist Gunner,
S/Sgt Clayton Brewer Radio Operator Nose Gunner, S/Sgt Leslie
Stockdale Tail Turret Gunner, S/Sgt Henry Paris Ball Turret Gunner and,
Sgt Grover Jenkins Left Waist Gunner.

The top turret T/Sgt. Abe Azie, 24, Lawrence, Mass., engineer-gunner, escaped injury. Flying shrapnel hit the left waist gunner, Sgt. Grober W. Jenkins, 24, Opelika, Alabama, on the face and right arm, but he kept firing. He also called over the interphone to F/O Richard J. Haney, co-pilot, 21, Big Beaver, Michigan, for permission to look after the wounded tail gunner, but was advised to keep firing and wait until the Nazi attack had ended.

The battle continued with the swirling Germans becoming more respectful until they finally stopped attacking altogether, and allowed the Liberator, which had dropped behind its formation in the melee, to limp along unmolested.

Bullet-torn and rocket blasted from a vicious air battle, the B-24 Liberator heavy bomber staggered back victoriously hundreds of miles to a flapless, brakeless and almost rudderless to its home base.

Every member of the crew survived the attack with the ball—and tail gunners alone sustaining serious injures. The crew's numbers just weren't up.

More than a thousand holes of all sizes are estimated to have been blown through the cabin, the wings and other parts of the plane. The tail turret and top turret were completely shot out of the ship. The fluid from the wrecked hydraulic system, sloshing around the bomb bay, caught fire while the bomber was in flight 2nd Lt. John Greco, 24, bombardier, of Everettville, West Va., and Sgt. Jenkins immediately went back to assist Stockdale, despite his own wounds. Sgt. Jenkins took off some of his clothing to put around the injured tail gunner, while Lt. Greco administered first aid.

The engineer started taking stock of the damage to the plane. The hydraulic system was completely shot out.

The wheel brakes were unworkable. That meant if a landing were successful the heavy bomber would have to roll until it stopped of it's own accord.

The landing flaps would not work. That meant the landing speed of the plane could not be cut down safely.

The rudder control cables had been severed. The engineer spliced them with a bit of string.

Two turrets were gone. That lightened the load a little. Then there were the thousand or more bullet holes of all sizes.

The crew was aware of the danger in an attempted landing. A quick check showed nobody wanted to leave under the circumstances. "What about Stockdale?" they asked. The pilot said later that if it had not been for the tail gunner's injuries the order to abandon ship would have been given unhesitatingly.

T/Sgt. Clayton A. Brewer, 36, radio operator and nose gunner, of Mansfield, Pa., opened a hatch before the landing. "Just in case." This proved to be a lifesaver for some members of the crew because the crash almost sealed the door.

The landing was good, although a trifle fast because the flaps couldn't be put down. The big Liberator settled on the runway at well over 100 miles an hour. There was nothing the crew could do but wait. The wheel brakes wouldn't work and there was no way to steer or slow the speed. The pilot could not even attempt a ground loop. He cut the switch.

Off the end of the runway the bomber rolled, and kept rolling for 300 yards. Then plunged down a 50-foot embankment and crashed into the unattended gasoline truck trailer. The trailer was carried an additional 100 feet before the plane partially buried itself in the ground.

All of the crewmembers except the pilot managed to get clear of the wreckage. The pilot was half pinned down at his controls. The co-pilot helped evacuate the navigator, 2nd Lt. David J. Woodlock, 27, of St. Louis Mo., who was slightly dazed. They both crawled through a hole caused by the accident.

In spite of the fact that my left foot was broken in three places I helped to assist critically injured Stockdale, the tail gunner, from the wreck.

Slightly wounded, the right waist gunner, S/Sgt. Ralph W. Friese, 33, of Beverly Hills, Calif., and the other members of the crew made their way through the hatchway that had been opened by Sgt. Brewer, radio gunner, just before the landing.

Lt. Cook, pilot, was still trapped in the cockpit and flames were leaping around him. During this time the ammunition was exploding constantly and there was the added danger that the gas tank would blow up. Lt. Woodlock, the navigator, rushed to help his pilot, whose clothes were already aflame. Woodlock's condition, however, left him without sufficient strength to properly aid Cook.

At this point Captain Harold F. Schuknecht, flight surgeon, 28, of Chancellor, South Dakota, who had been waiting with an ambulance, arrived on the scene. Without hesitation he climbed up to remove the pilot.

The fuselage was enveloped in flames and fire was spurting out the waist window and the cockpit. Captain Schuknecht grabbed Cook and yanked him out through the cockpit window. Cook fell head first toward the ground. Cook landed squarely on top of the navigator who was standing by, half dazed, trying to help. Cook states he would have been seriously injured if the navigator had not broken the fall.

The flight surgeon and the navigator dragged the pilot, his clothes burning briskly, away from the spot, and rolled him on the ground until the flames from his flak suit were smothered. A minute after they had gotten the pilot to safety the gasoline tanks exploded and there was little left of the plane or trailer.

Cook later said he had been pinned around the control wheel at the impact and part of the instrument panel had jammed forward hampering the movement of most of the arm. His legs were wrapped under the seat, which had gone forward. He could not move them.

"The fire was getting hot," he said, "and I was getting desperate. I figured it would be better to injure my hand than burn to death so I gave my hand a good jerk. It came clear but the jagged metal tore huge gashes in my flesh. I struggled to get my feet clear, but it was no soap. My clothes were on fire but I only felt the heat and not the flame. My flak suit was absorbing most of the punishment. It was Captain Schuknecht's help that freed me."

After the mission

The pilot R. L. Cook was promoted to Captain. He finished his missions came home. I haven't been able to find him.

The Co-pilot Richard Haney later took over a crew that needed a pilot. He completed his missions. He stayed in the Air Force after the war and retired as Lt. Col. He and I get together occasionally, we have tried to find the other crew-members, but no luck.

Lt. David Woodlock finished his missions and came home.

Lt. John Greco was flying with our crew on this mission, our regular bombardier Lt. Paul Guild was sick. Lt. John Greco completed his missions and came home on leave. He came back to our group for a second tour. I've heard that he was later killed on a mission.

T/Sgt Abe Azie completed his missions came home.

S/Sgt. Leslie Stockdale was wounded on this mission. He was sent to 26th general hospital in Bari, Italy, and stayed there for several weeks. He later returned to the squadron, recuperated more then went back flying. On a later mission he was flying with Col Graff of Headquarters they got a direct hit from flak in the front bomb bay. The pilot Col Graff and the Co Pilot were able to bail out, but the rest of the crew went down with the plane.

I, S/Sgt Henry Paris, was sent to the 34th field hospital in Cerignola, Italy but they couldn't help me, so they sent me to the 26th General hospital in Bari, Italy. I stayed in the hospital for about three months. Then I returned to my group, the 455th & 743rd Squadron. I recuperated some and went back flying.

Most of the time I flew with the group commander Col Snowder. I came home to have a leave. When I left Italy, I left T/Sgt Clayton Brewer—S/Sgt Ralph Friese in Italy. I think Sgt. Grover Jenkins became very ill was in the hospital or had been sent home. After my leave I reported to Sioux Falls, South Dakota for B-29 training.

When I went through processing, I had enough points to be discharged, and so I was.

Printed with permission of Henry Paris.

Payment To Julia

Narrated by Keith Abbott, B-24 Pilot
15th Air Force, 459th Bomb Group, 756th Bomb Squadron
Edited by Erik Dyreborg

Keith Abbott is pictured above.

Introduction.

The following is the crew I trained and flew over the Atlantic Ocean with and with whom I flew most of my 15th Air Force missions. All these events occurred in 1944.

2nd LT Gerry St. Hilaire Co-pilot
2nd LT John Vig Navigator

2nd LT Charles McCoy Bombardier
T/Sgt. Orral Archer Top Turret Gunner and Engineer
T/Sgt. Frank Dolce Radio Operator
S/Sgt. Richard Simerson Right Waist Gunner
S/Sgt. Joseph Mowrey Left Waist Gunner
S/Sgt. Ed High Lower Ball Turret Gunner
S/Sgt. Walter Hoyt Tail Gunner

What happened to these poor chaps on that fatal day, when our plane caught fire and we had to abandon the ship and what happened when their long-floating parachutes hit the ground? Here's a rundown:

Gerry St. Hilaire, Charles McCoy, George Sands and myself, all evaded capture, thanks to our partisan benefactors.

Orral Archer, Frank Dolce, Richard Simerson and Walter Hoyt were all captured by the Germans and/or their allies and became POWs.

Harold Levine, who was on this mission, was shot by Hungarian soldiers on his way down and wounded as a result, incarcerated for the night, then shot the next day by LT Walter Krüger of the hated SS for no other reason that he was Jewish.

The fatal day

It began with black puffs of smoke emitting from the #2 engine exhaust. The puffs became a contrail of smoke that quickly flickered into flames, and then, within seconds, bursting into a brilliant white sheet of flame extending many feet behind the twin tails.

The stricken plane in my hands had left at dawn from its 459th Bomb Group base nesting near Foggia, Italy. I, 1st LT Keith Abbott, was assigned to lead this crew of eleven and a flight of two B-24 Liberators to bomb the massive, and heavily defended oil refineries at Bleckhammer, Germany, on the western Polish border. The navigation and bombardment tasks were to be handled by a new top-secret device called a Mickey.

Mickey employed sound waves to literally stitch a blip bath on a radarscope through the clouds along sea or land to a specified target, and then, to cut a hole through the undercast and enemy smoke screen over the target.

With the advent of Mickey, the Flying Fortresses and Liberators, the main destructive World War II power of the 8th and 15th Air Forces flying missions from England and Italy, could now bomb day and night in good weather or bad. There would be no "standing down" anymore.

Because of my extensive night and instrument pilot flying hours, I and my crew were chosen to man our squadron's only altered Mickey-equipped four-engine B-24 Liberator bomber, camouflaged externally with dove-grey paint, the plane was barely visible, when it took off on the morning of December 12, 1944 against a background of low-hanging dark clouds.

LT Harry Levine, our reckoning navigator, had given me a northerly heading as we climbed through layers of clouds, breaking clear at our pre-designated altitude of 23,000 feet. My tail gunner, Sgt. Walter Hoyt, reported my wingman's plane had negotiated the poor visibility, too, and was trailing a few minutes behind as he was supposed to do. A last-minute plane-switch before take off put the wing-man's crew in my 756th Squadron plane, and my crew in a 759th Squadron plane, nicknamed the "Blushing Virgin".

We flew for a short while on top of a solid undercast, but the sky ahead had taken on the bruised and fragile look a of a monumental storm. That's when I received an urgent intercom call from my left waist gunner, Sgt. Joseph Mowrey, that #2 engine was starting to spew flames dangerously close to the tail. Most engine fires are extinguished with proper procedure, but I had a premonition that this fire was going to prove different from the norm.

On many of my previous missions, I had prided myself on always being able to channel nervousness to my advantage, using it to heighten my senses and give me an edge, but not this time, for I knew immediately this emergency was going to squeeze my butt into a tight ball—a good thing—also a healthy twinge of fear had come over me.

Avoiding a complete collapse, it was time for some quick remedial action! I automatically called on a memorized "engine fire" check list, and with 2nd LT Gerold St. Hilaire's help, we feathered #2 propeller, and shut down all fuel and electrical feeds to the affected engine. The pull-chain for the carbon dioxide fire extinguisher was under my seat, but lo and behold, a thick coat of new paint had made the system as useful as a screen door in a submarine.

What do I do now? I had heard of pilots diving their plane to try to blow out an engine fire—an emergency procedure usually resulting in failure—and coupled with the danger of flying through a range of cloud-shrouded mountain peaks, was a risk I was not chancing.

I was left with a final resolution; abandon ship.

Without further delay, I hit the bell-alarm switch the required three times, and simultaneously announced in the calmest voice I could manage, "let's blow this damn firetrap before it explodes!"

I glanced to the right. LT St. Hilaire was rising to his feet. We both reached for our tied-together combat shoes, then I followed him back toward the bomb bay where the opening ominously waited. LT Levine stood in front of me nervously. He was looking for his chest-pack parachute, which, when found, needed a hook-up to his chest harness. In what seemed one quick, continuous motion, LT Levine was harnessed, turned around, and went out the opening with me in hot pursuit.

The momentary flight deck excitement made me forget to count off some seconds before I pulled the ripcord. This count down is necessary for two reasons: You want to prevent an inadvertent entanglement of chute and tail, and you want a slower velocity to 130 mph from 300 mph, so when the canopy pops open, the harness straps between your legs won't cause an immediate sex transformation like it almost did to me.

Before I entered the undercast, I thanked God and became disappointed at the same time. Two parachutes were coming down behind me, meaning I hadn't traditionally been "the last man out" as the captain is supposed to be.

As I entered the clouds, the stillness and the loneliness befuddled me momentarily, but my vomiting blood quickly drew my attention. I had been taking off flying status by the flight surgeon for two weeks prior to this mission, because of bad head cold. (My co-pilot had given me a couple of aspirin to satisfactorily relieve a sinus pain I suffered about an hour into the flight.)

The flow of blood stopped along with the snow that turned to a steady rain, which ensued until I broke out into the open—only at about 500 feet above the rapidly approaching freshly-plowed field of "dreams"—like an oasis in a desert of despair. Poor fortune could have had me dangling from one of the ominous trees that surrounded me. After folding my parachute hurriedly, I entered the woods anyway, only this time my way!

I immediately came upon a deep ravine that had a flowing brook at the bottom. Improvising, I slid on my back easily on the wet ground. Crossing the brook in two electric slippers and one fur-lined flying boot (one flying boot and two hand-held leather high-top shoes deserted me during the descent's initiation jolt).

It took me only a few brush-penetrating steps to find what I thought was a good hiding place, snuggled in the brush and trees. I was following suggestions laid down by our predecessors in what to do in such circumstances as I found myself. It was suggested to hide out for twenty-four hours, and since it was around 10:00 now, I had until 10:00 the next day to stay put in a wet, small clearing in the middle of nowhere. (Not one of the three navigators had furnished a ground position before we hit the silk). The silk map I discovered in my small survival kit would have to do instead.

I sat down to see if I could determine where I had come down. The countries depicted on a small map all looked the same. I settled on Austria, probably because it was closer to Italy, and if eventually, I had to walk home, I wouldn't have so far to go. The kit also had some candy, a water purifier, a compass, fish line and some brand new American dollar bills.

I sampled the very limited rations, wrapped the parachute around me, and although the canopy nylon was wet, my heavy nylon flying jacket and pants kept me reasonable comfortable during the long, quiet and wet night. The only disturbance was when mother-nature told me to get up quick to find a "bathroom", I settled for a nearby grassy spot, and when finished, cut the small pilot chute from the top of the main chute, placed the small one over the "embarrassment", and returned to my nocturnal blessing.

Meeting the Slovakians

As departure time approached, a small band of civilian-dressed men appeared surprisingly at the top of the rise. Bearing rifles, they seemed to be coming down the embankment menacingly, and alarmed—I need a machine gun quick—I threw up my hands reluctantly. Their threatening manor turned into a sea of smiles and a cherry greeting in Slovakian, which, because I thought I was in Austria, I attempted to carry on the conversation in poor German, a little of the high school

German that I had learned—then I remembered to drop that language in case they mistake me for one. I spoke only English from then on.

They soon convinced me that they were friendly, and were out searching for any survivors from my plane. To break any remaining tension, one of them made a grab for the pilot chute that was still covering my nighttime deposit. I quickly, but gently pushed him aside while revealing what lie underneath. We all joined in the resulting laughter. I knew then I was in good hands. For the first time since the uncontrollable fire, I was able to relax a little, and I was already feeling that everything would come out right.

We gathered up my meager belongings and headed out. Destination? My parachute landing in the furrowed field made me think a farmhouse was somewhere near by, and my hunch bore fruit. And who made themselves known the moment we all crossed the threshold? 2nd LTs Kenneth Faulk and Charles McCoy stood before me, sheepishly grinning from ear to ear. There followed handshakes and hugs in a sincere effort to show each other how we felt about being alive, and our present good fortune of not having fallen into the hands of the omnipresent Germans occupying the nearby village of Velka Luka, where some of the villagers were determined to resist the German rule, and some choose to abide, so fearful of the consequences.

Our new home

A final decision was made that the widow, Julia Priboj's house close to the center of the town gave the best sanctuary for the three of us, even if it was right under the noses of Germans themselves, so under cover of darkness, we traveled to what was to become our questionable safe haven for the next 30 days.

She made us feel so welcome from the moment we all met, and proudly lead us into one of her bedrooms in the rear of a big house. Her native language proved to be a definite obstacle to hurdle at first. Julia was fluent in seven languages; unfortunately English wasn't one of them. With the ancient art of sign language, and my remembering a few words learned in a high school German class a few years prior, we managed as best we could.

Julia Priboj, age 33, pictured with her daughter Bojena in late 1944.

While Julia directed, we were all too happily willing to comply. We placed two double beds close together, but still leaving a crack that one of us would be forced to endure. We made an "on the spot" agreement we would take turns sleeping in/ on the crack. I did not pull rank, and neither did the crack. We shared the discomfort, and that was that.

A slop bucket was set up in an unattached garage in the rear meant going outside, of course, but Julia was worried that exposing ourselves to unfriendly neighbors who would like nothing better than to score points with the Nazis by telling them the three American flyers, they were searching for, were at Julia's house.

To make a hasty exit in case of impending trouble, we would be required to sleep in our civilian clothes. Of course, this means execution as spies should we be captured. We tried not to dwell on that grave possibility; we were well aware of retaliatory treatment meted out by the Nazis for aiding the enemy. Julia and her friend's safety were as important as ours.

Only a few partisans who kept Julia apprised, knew our whereabouts and what was going on in the German camp at all times.

The days and nights passed quickly, and mainly without incidents, while a small Russian army, only 14 miles away, was moving too slowly toward us from the south. We busied ourselves playing an American card game called hearts, eating barley-stuffed sausage, drinking rum-spiked tea, meeting nice friends and relatives including two beautiful sisters, all of whom were allowing their curiosity to overrule good judgement.

A well-attended Christmas party—how we all managed to squeeze into that small bedroom was miraculous, and even fairly safe; the enemy was not too far away, but too busy celebrating the special event in their own way—in a drunken stupor. (Did you ever hear Christmas carols sung under the influence?) The starlit, snow-covered landscape forgot there was a war, involving half the world, going on, but not that night in Velka Luka, Czchecoslovakia.

The next day we started the same routine all over again, except for Julia who began carrying the slop buckets outside for disposal. She thought it was too dangerous for us to venture out for any reason. We welcomed her over-cautiousness, but to take on the role of a wet nurse, was duty beyond belief!

A scary incident occurred when Julia relaxed her usual vigilance, she decided to take a stroll with me down the street in front of her house, and after the 8 pm curfew time! Our promenade lasted well into five minutes before a German armed sentry was on us like white on rice. Julia immediately engaged the young soldier in light German banter that was so effective that the guard forgot all about checking our identification papers—I had none! I couldn't translate any of the exchange, but it worked, because we were back in our safe haven without further adieu.

Julia was still composed but I remained apprehensive for days afterward. To break up the monotony, we started visiting Julia's tenant residing in the front part of Julia's house, the fearful Andre Buchholzer, his young wife and their infant son. With thick, soundproof walls, there was little danger of our being discovered, so we listened to the British Broadcasting Company sending out short radio waves on what was going on in the real war. The Battle of the Bulge was in full swing, and Glen Miller, a popular American bandleader, had disappeared on a flight to Paris.

So worried was Andre about the safety of his family, he persuaded Julia to stop the visits. (The four walls of our bedroom inched in closer.)

Julia had been sleeping in the kitchen since her flyboys had taken over her bedroom about two and a half long weeks ago. The status quo came suddenly to an end with a knocking from the outside on Julia's kitchen door. Three German officers stood at the threshold when Julia opened the door. In German they explained they were looking for temporary billeting. Ever the actress, Julia apologized that all her rooms were occupied, but they could move into her large kitchen, if they wanted to use her kitchen. They didn't want to take away her quarters, and they objected vehemently to this arrangement.

Julia convinced them that she would move into one of her relative's bedroom. She was thinking what could be better having her boys sleeping almost in the laps of the enemy, thus avoiding future search parties. Julia also declared she loved doing things for the Germans. And so the enemy moved in, glad to find something in this hostile environment.

This feeling of extra security from the enemy living right under our noses was short-lived because rumors spread quickly over the village that the Gestapo was about to search all premises for men, young or old, fit and unfit, to serve in their army or labor camps, a move being carried out all over Europe.

New quarters

Julia sprang immediately into action to protect her American flyers. She enlisted her small covert force of supporters to get her three men out of the harm's way. She chose three, one of them being Andre Bochholzer, of all people, to escort us out of town to a mountain safe spot.

Before we crossed the village boundary two at a time, one mile apart, we passed by a small observation plane field, and further down, a ME-109 fighter plane base. All planes had an inactive, closed-down-starved look, like they needed petrol or something. I saw first hand what our strategic bombing was doing to Görings once-mighty Luftwaffe.

We continued, but not too merrily along, because the path was lined with 12-foot deep snow drifts. The footing became very slippery and treacherous from unkindly rocks, and the cliffs we had to scale in the dark prevented us from making good time. Finally, late at night we came upon the partisan camp we sought in the mountains someplace. In the middle of a large clearing sat a fairly good-size log cabin with welcoming smoke curling from its chimney. Our guides could have gone another 12 miles easily, but we three flyboys, immobile for a month, were completely exhausted and utterly devastated. We needed a bed, and got one; unfortunately, we had to share it with 35 other evadees trying to get back to their own countries; we forgot pleasantries until morning.

Next morning we jumped out of bed with complete strangers. We knew there would be a language barrier; none of them spoke English. Since the beginning of time people finding themselves in similar circumstances have banded together in a common bond to improvise in everything they did, including the communication one. After all, freedom was just around the corner (if around the corner, when translated, means 15 kilometers away down south with the slow-moving Russian army).

We began our steady diet of potato bread, potato skins, boiled potatoes, baked potatoes and whatever our culinary cook could come up with, as long as it contained some form of the almighty spud. One lucky week we enjoyed a by-product of a skirmish between resistance militants and their German adversaries including artillery fire. We welcomed the delicious horsemeat addition to our limited diet.

The next two weeks went along in a routine-like manner. The few paths had six-foot high walls of snow with evidence of the many frequent trips to the bathroom. Some evening hours were spent listening and comparing the various nationalities folk and marching songs. The mixed group enjoyed our effort to entertain, especially our unusual sound effects. There was one program interruption when the sound of flatulence came loud and clear. Then some one yelled, "die luft ist smutzig" (the air is dirty). Everyone knew what that meant, and a loud guffaw broke loose in the log cabin from the forty-foot long bunk.

The mystery of "the last man" from our burning plane was solved during this "exciting" time. When LT Faulk and LT McCoy were fanatically trying to open their nose wheel escape hatch, after I had rung the alarm bell to abandon ship, they chose to use the open bomb bay to the rear. They followed me out, and subsequently, became attached to the opened chutes behind me. Was this a proof that the plane was jinxed before we left Italy six weeks ago? It seems like it.

We were settling in to a monotonous existence, when who wander into this tranquil camp? Julia Priboj, in the flesh. She missed her "boys", and used the excuse that it was my birthday, January 26, to make the long, treacherous journey with friends, to show us all how much she cared. She had brought cigarettes, kielbasa sausage, schnapps and news. She surprised us, with a little of the latter, to disclose that it was Andre Buchholzer who had told the Gestapo that Julia Priboj had three American flyers hiding out in her bedroom. But when they came stormily knocking with their armed search party, we were already in the mountain sanctuary, and Julia felt that she could call the Nazi expletive names for accusing her of harbouring the enemy. Because Julia had been a cooperative village citizen in her dealings with the German occupiers, they let her walk away while they apologized, profusely, to Julia's inner delight.

Although Andre Buchholzer seemed to be working both sides of the fence at the same time, he waited until the Americans were safely up in that mountain hideaway, before informing the Nazis, and insured he and his loved ones would be safe. Julia's suspicions of betrayal by Buchholzer were true, but because Buchholzer had waited until the Americans were gone before tattling, he absolved himself with Julia, while at the same time protecting his family.

After Julia reluctantly said goodbye again to Faulk, McCoy and me, we promised her to fulfill her dream of coming to America when we, ourselves, got back. We tried and failed to oblige her other whim of learning English while she was our presence. (We tried to learn Slovakian and had the same success.)

A sudden appearance of the powerful schnapps in our midst, left us gagging for breath. One foreign evadee shooting a toe off, and another being tied to a tree after swallowing a liter of the pinecone derivative. It was clear white poison!

A few days later we went out hunting with a few of our newly-found friends, one of them carrying a Russian sub-machine gun. Soon we came upon a herd of five deer grazing quietly in a clearing. A few single rifle reports echoed throughout the forest; the errant shots brought the machine gunner to the fore. His indiscriminate volume of bullets produced a wipe out of the herd, and it was back to the cabin with our prize.

How can such a beautiful animal like a deer provide a week's worth of horrible-tasting meat? I was told to blame the cook, because properly-cooked venison is considered delicious. Frankly, I liked the horse meat we had a couple of weeks ago better, but anything was better than a steady diet of starchy potatoes.

Before we went out on patrol and were shot at, we were attacked by cooties. It only took one individual to infesting forty of us sleeping so close together, to cause such an exasperating, long-lasting misery. When we removed our clothing to boil them and freeze them in the snow outside, our white-naked bodies resembled blueberries in pancake batter.

Of course every one of us had an intriguing story to tell. We could all talk about recent encounters with life-threatening dangers. One such story really stood head and shoulders above the rest. A 6'-4" Russian fighter pilot, flying our lend-lease P-39 Air Cobras, had been shot down three times over Berlin, and escaped three times from German Luftwaffe prison camps. Incredible! Sometimes, all they had to eat was each other. And we're complaining about our meager rations being unpalatable!

The shooting incident happened one day as two separated friendly bands became aware of each other while trampling through the dense woods, but not certain of it being "friend or foe", started firing live ammunition in the other's direction. Not familiar with the sound of the whistling bullets, close to my precious head, I momentarily suffered sheer terror. Appropriate yelling by both sides finally brought the gut-wrenching panic to a peaceful end, especially to the great relief of three pounding hearts…With so many soldiers that had been forced to serve in the German army, deserting and then trying to make their way back to their homeland through these Slovakian mountains, our plight took a new undefined mean twist.

The Russians

In the first week of March 1945, our welfare and protection was taken over by a band of Russian army guerrillas. Before this transfer, I paused and reflected of how the ordinary people of this Slovakian region have cared for us in the two and half months. From the time I joined up with my two crewmates, one incident after another revealed the terrible risks these strangers were taking to protect and provide for our every days needs. It also demonstrated the depth of the dedication and length they would be willing to go to achieve that end. Of course, Julia Priboj's leadership, her unselfishness and purpose were outstanding, and deserved whatever thanks we could send her way.

I think at the time everyone in Europe was aware of the American proclamation that anyone aiding downed US airmen, would be rewarded with 2,000 Dollars per man helped. Some of our helpers may have been enticed by this promise, but we were certain Julia was not one of them.

The guerrillas were garbed in civilian attire, and their commander was a twenty-five year old Russian army captain, who looked sixty-five, and who taught school before the war. He was just as mean as he looked, and his control over his men primarily consisted of a blow on the back with his heavy cane. He sat us behind him while he pointed his pistol at German and their forced foreign allies, who were leaving the German army like the proverbial rats leaving a sinking ship. If they refused to join his band and opted for their homes instead, he ordered them taken out and shot.

This was the scenario for about three weeks until the slow-moving liberation army coming up from the south finally arrived. When we were turned over to the Russian "regulars", a Russian colonel and his English interpreter immediately interrogated us. The next morning we were escorted by armed guards to the intersection of a couple of main streets, and turned over to a young Russian soldier wearing a patch over one eye.

The long trip home

The one hundred-day ordeal behind enemy lines had ended, but now we were in our ally's hands, wearing cheap Russian uniforms issued that morning. There we were, the four of us standing in the middle of the road, with our thumbs outstretched, trying to hitch a repatriation ride to Odessa, Russia, which lay 500 miles away across Hungary and Romania. We knew we were going to have trouble along the way when American Studebaker trucks with their Russian drivers kept passing us by as we walked for 24 miles, me, without proper hiking boots—I was still wearing the Czech flying boots given to me over three months ago, and which caused massive foot blisters. Finally we were given a ride to a Hungarian train station, at which time Charles McCoy decided to take off on his own for the American Embassy at Debrecen, Hungary, where he hoped to hasten a trip to America. He had no identification, he had a definite language barrier, but above all he had no permission from me or the poor Russian guide, who had been given the responsibility of getting us safely to Odessa.

Before boarding the awaiting train, the guide managed to track McCoy down, whereupon McCoy really got a deserved tongue lashing from me for doing such a stupid thing, and a worried guide, who had one teary eye, accepted our profound apologies in some made-up language. We assured him such a fool-hearty stunt would not to occur again!

Our "rapid" express train did not move at night; had pull-down slabs of wood for sleeping; had hard sausage, sour brown bread, and lard and sugar "cuisine" meals—the Russians were given canned beef made in America. After nine days of these "luxurious" accommodations, we pulled into the station at Odessa.

Two diversions, from an otherwise unpleasant trip, were a flyover of German V-1 planes and a first hand-view of the damage done to the infamous Polesti oil refineries in Romania. Flattened oil storage tanks, rusting and bent steel frameworks, demolished buildings, bomb craters and strewn plane parts came into view as we passed through the devastated site.

When we exited the train, Russian officials were there to greet us, then lead us to an official-looking building, where we were immediately interrogated and physically examined by a Russian nurse. An American cargo ship was being readied for departure; hence, a speedy repatriation-process procedure was in effect.

We were supposed to get de-loused, but time didn't permit this important service, nor was a change of uniform to take place; so there we were, three Americans in Russian clothes, marching with a contingent of other Americans dressed in American fatigue uniforms, causing a look of startling disbelief on the faces of civilian onlookers. The ship's personnel were flabbergasted as well, when we arrived at the boarding gangplank.

Because they knew they were on their way home at last, these evadees, escapees and released prisoners of war, eagerly and cheerfully climbed aboard. Their part of the war ended, except for floating mines and German e-patrol boats encountered as we sailed across a portion of the Black Sea, near Istanbul, across the Sea of Marmara, across the Aegean Sea and the eastern end of the Mediterranean Sea to Oran, North Africa. Orders were for airmen evadees to get briefed at the 15th Air Force headquarters located in Bari, Italy, upon their return to allied control, so we got off the nice American Liberty boat at Oran to await passage to Bari. Too bad, because the departed ship was scheduled to sail to America, taking twenty-one more days to add to the twenty it took to reach Oran.

In that twenty-day time period, because I was the ranking officer among the new passengers, I received preferential treatment by the merchant marine crew. I ate at the captain's table and slept in a single room. I got sunburned while lying naked on a top deck (this was my crazy attempt to remove cootie sores, which I did, but got a bad dose of sunburn in their place.) The food was spectacular, and I gorged, but can you blame me?

The ten-day stay at Oran, which was home to an American Military Air Transport Service (MATS) unit, provided food, sleeping quarters, a haircut, PX goodies, money, and at last, if not best, a makeshift American uniform including rank insignia. The European war ended in early May 1945, and here we were stuck in French possession, and not even at our 756th Squadron base.

Finally, our orders came though to proceed to Bari, Italy, and we hitched a ride on a MATS plane, got interrogated by British intelligence officers, went to our old 459th Bomb Group base by truck, where a change of personnel confronted us. We traveled by plane to Naples, Italy, then by a C-54 MATS plane to America, with stopovers in Casablanca, the Azore Islands, the Bahama Islands: thence to Miami, Florida, touching US terra firma for the first time in nine months.

Faulk, McCoy and I said goodbye at the train station, each taking separate trains to scattered destinations. We waited a long time to get back home, and I for one, found out when I got there, it was well worth the wait!

While with Julia at Christmas, 1944, a promise was made by Kenneth Faulk, Charles McCoy and myself, that we three rescued Americans would see that Julia would spend a Christmas with us in America, and she did, when she and her daughter joined us in Canton, Ohio on Christmas Day, 1950.

To America

While we were hiding in Julia's house in Slovakia in 1944 and 1945, Julia's daughter, Bojenna (Slovakian for Betty), was kept safe with relatives. What happened to Julia and Bojenna after the war ended follows:

Julia and her daughter spent three years living under Russian control, behind the Iron Curtin. They were not trusted because Julia believed in the American way of life, which was so different from what she experienced in Slovakia.

We three American benefactors of hers were not able to communicate with her until she and Bojenna managed to escape Slovakia and into freedom in Austria in 1948.

Upon arrival in Austria, they were placed in a refugee camp, a former NAZI camp for displaced persons, and soon after the letter writing started from both ends.

Julia was writing to officials in Europe, and the three of us, all from the State of Ohio, were writing to President Eisenhower and his wife, Mrs. Roosevelt, US Congressmen, and even the Governor of Ohio tried to get permission to bring them to America and become citizens. We even mentioned her commendation from Eisenhower himself while he was still the Supreme Commander of the Allied Forces.

After two long years in the camp in Austria, our efforts and her determination paid off.

Her arrival in New York and Canton, Ohio was played up big in the New York and Ohio papers when she arrived at the Canton Train Station, where her three "boys" were waiting, along with hundreds of other Ohioans.

Our Christmas of 1950 was a tearfully joyous one, and The Ohio Bell Telephone Company considered it such a momentous occasion and a good war story, they made a radio broadcast called "Payment to Julia" in the Spring of 1951.

Julia and Bojenna lived in Canton, Ohio for awhile. Julia then moved to Chicago where she died in 1957, at only 46 years of age. Her early death was probably caused by tuberculosis she was suffering from in 1944.

Later Julia's daughter, Bojenna, settled in Denver, Colorado with her American husband. Five children were born to this happy couple, and they all came to New Jersey to visit my wife and I in the 1970s. When I tried to visit Bojenna in the early 1980s, I missed them as they had left for a visit to Slovakia.

After many years of correspondence, Bojenna suddenly died in the year 2000 of a heart attack at an age of only 65.

I hope Julia and Bojenna both enjoyed America while they lived among us. Kenneth Faulk and Charles McCoy have reunited with them in heaven. I will have to wait my turn.

Printed with permission of Keith Abbott

Ground Crew

Narrated by James T. Kay, Jr., Engine Mechanic
8th Air Force, 55th Fighter Group, 343rd Fighter Squadron
Written by Karen Esberger (Daughter of James T. Kay, Jr.)
Edited by Erik Dyreborg

Introduction

In the early morning of 24 May 1914, I was born near Winona, Texas, north of Tyler. My two older brothers, my parents, and I lived on my Mother's farm, passed down from her father. Dad ran the farm and taught school at Harris Creek. I graduated from Winona High School in 1931 and received my Bachelor's degree in agriculture from (then) Sam Houston State Teachers' College in 1938. Jobs were still scarce because of the depression, so I attended one semester at Texas A & M before getting a teaching position at Midlothian, Texas, High School. The day I began work there in February, 1939, I met the Superintendent's secretary, Phama and married her, on 28 Sept 1940.

We continued to live in Midlothian and work at the school. About the end of 1940, I became a rural mail carrier on Rt. 1, out of Midlothian. A year later we were, of course, horrified by the attack upon Pearl Harbor, and my wife was filled with dread.

The Army

I was inducted into the Army in Dallas, Texas, on 18 June 1942. Phama was appointed temporary rural carrier on my route, and she continued towork at school in the afternoons.

Another Midlothian man, nicknamed "Tedo," was in basic training with me at Sheppard Field, Wichita Falls, Texas, The Texas summer was as hot as usual and kept us miserable. The "Yankees" had an especially hard time adjusting to the heat. The barracks were quite crowded, with only a few inches between the bunks. Our sergeant drank on many nights and would then awaken us around 2 a.m. to do calisthenics. Tedo and I made a pact with each other to make a point of keeping each other's spirits up. That really helped us survive the time there.

Later I was stationed at Squaw Valley, California, a city of tents and mud. My photographic collection began there. I carried a camera throughout the rest of the war and sent home many interesting photos of scenery and our planes—views that were approved by the censors.

A long train ride took us to McChord (Washington) Field to join the 343rd Fighter Squadron, 55th Fighter Group. Most of my time in Washington was spent at the Tumwater Base, near Olympia, where we trained at Olympia Airport that the Air Corps had taken over.

My mother passed away on 14 Feb 1943. The Red Cross failed to locate me in time for me to attend the funeral, but I was granted leave soon afterwards and spent two weeks with my wife, my dad, and my brothers.

During the summer, 1943, Phama came to visit me in Olympia. She thought the city was so beautiful, and we greatly enjoyed the time together. Also during that summer, I earned an "expert rifle" rating and finely tuned my skills at maintaining P-38 engines.

England

In early August, we left McChord for Camp Kilmer, NJ, the shipping out point for all AAF Units to the ETO or MTO. The train stopped twice a day for exercise, and I took photos at Boise, Idaho, and of McKennon Park in Sioux Falls. After a week at Kilmer, we proceeded to Pier 86 to board "HMS Orion" on 4 Sept 1943 and pulled out on the fifth. This ship was meant to carry 1500 people, but 300 officers and 6200 enlisted men were loaded aboard. Our bunks were built three high, and most of the men didn't like the food prepared by the British cooks. The ocean got rougher, the farther we went; but we celebrated when we heard that Italy had surrendered!

We arrived at Glasgow, Scotland, on 12 September 1943 and immediately boarded a train to go to Nuthampstead, near Cambridge. We lived in metal huts with one small potbellied stove in each. I had never liked chilly, rainy weather, and we had plenty of that in England. Before our P-38s arrived, we had lectures on security, what could be written in letters, and about our conduct, in general, in the ETO.

We became lots busier when our P-38s began arriving. On 21 September I was assigned to D flight, to planes designated CY-Y. My crew chief was Walter Harris from Vermont, the armorer was Payton Shrum from Missouri, and Fitz from Michigan also worked with us. One of my early pilots was Capt. Dick Stanton. He had his picture taken in a kilt and full Scottish regalia, and gave us each a copy. I also snapped a photo of him standing in front of his P-38.

Pictured above, L to R: Shrum, Fitz, Harris and Kay

The MIDLOTHIAN MIRROR, our hometown newspaper, reported in October that "Cpl. J. T. Kay, Jr. of the Ground Air Corps has recently arrived in England."

We rode English bicycles from our huts to the hardstands where our planes were parked. Actually, we rode them everywhere we went. The mud made this a difficult trip on some days, and we often referred to the post as "Mudhampstead."

The P-38s were extremely closely cowled engines with much piping and no space. We spent long hours fixing coolant leaks, rough engines, and leaky shocks on the landing gear struts. The leaks got worse as the weather got colder.

We on the ground crews were always concerned about our pilots. We'd be standing out on the runway watching for them, "sweating them in" as was commonly said. We'd strap a boy into the cockpit and help a man out of there several hours later.

Several of the ground crew became my good friends, and we made trips together around England when we got leave. From Nuthampstead, we bicycled into Cambridge several times to visit the Colleges and go boating on the River "Cam." This was a good location for more photos.

Other activities available to us were the church services conducted on base by the Chaplains. Sal and I found that our religious convictions were pretty much the same and took comfort from our ability to discuss those topics. My wife and his fiancée were also frequently mentioned.

At Nuthampstead, as was common on most of the English airfields; we worked around the farmers with their cultivated fields, haystacks, & thatched roof cottages.

On Friday night, 11-26-43, I wrote a letter to Dad. "Dear Dad, I got two letters from you tonight; an air mail written Nov. 11, and yes, a v-mail written Nov. 14. I had a v-Mail from Louise [my sister-in-law]. I have less work to do here than in the states. I mean I put in fewer hours. But I gotta go on guard duty tonight, from mid-night till daylight."

"Say, I spent Wednesday night, Thursday, and Thursday night in London. I went to see Irving Berlin's famous production, THIS IS THE ARMY on Wednesday night. Then I went to Thanksgiving service at Westminster Abbey Thursday, ate a very good dinner at the Red Cross free of charge. I saw quite a bit of the town, such famous places as Piccadilly Circus, Leicester Square, Oxford Circus, Covent Gardens, etc. Also, I saw Churchill at the show THIS IS THE ARMY, Wednesday night."

"I went to see an English movie Thursday night. I rode the double deck buses as well as the underground. See, they call the subway (the underground)."

"It was all very interesting and well worth the money spent."

"Dad, I'm enclosing what they call a key chain. You may use it for a watch chain till it turns brass. The only gold watch chain I found was priced "18 guineas" or about $95. Yes, that is hard to believe but that is what he asked me for it."

"I guess that is all the news I know so I'll sleep a little before I go on guard."

The program I got at the "Thanksgiving Day Service for The American Forces" reminds me that it was held at Westminster Abbey, at 1100 hours. Hymns we sang were "Come Thou Almighty King," "Come, Ye Thankful People, Come," and "Lead On, O King Eternal." The Army Choir did a real good job.

While in London, I had my photograph taken and enough copies made for Phama, my dad, aunts, and brothers, neither of who were in the service.

December found flu going around the base and snow on the ground.

By this time, each ground crew had built themselves a "shack" near the line to try to stay somewhat warm when not directly involved in working on the planes. Most of us built them from the frames that the P-38 auxiliary gas tanks came in. Harris and I had a relatively snug little shack about a mile from the barracks. Lots of good visiting went on in these shacks to pass the time while waiting for our planes.

Bud Daugherty was the instrument mechanic who serviced our CY-Y, and he really teased me about my rosy cheeks. Charles Killion visited us often and was one of the buddies on several bicycle tours of the area. Floyd O. James was another buddy, as was John Wuebbens who teased me with a comparison to Sammy Kaye. I got acquainted with J. F. "Dusty" Rhodes from Gladewater, Tx, very near my hometown in East Texas. When I took an air conditioning correspondence course, I spent a good bit of time studying and had less time to visit. John Rydberg particularly noticed this.

On Christmas Eve, 1943, I had seven packages from home to open. My sister-in-law Bonnie sent a big box of cookies. The guys were complimenting my wife's cooking, but I had to admit they were from my brother's wife. Both my brothers sent photos of their kids. On Christmas day, I got to sleep an hour later, went to church and got a real good turkey dinner. I told the boys that they are good fellows but I hope we are not together next Christmas. I did have to work late that night, however.

Sal and I visited Stratford-on-Avon. We found that east England where we were stationed had been more touched by the war than had the west part of the country. For example, we could get ice cream at Stratford.

Sal received one of the first bronze stars earned by our crews. His fiancée sent a copy of the nice write-up and his picture in their hometown newspaper.

We visited Rothhamstead Experiment Station, including its big manor house, remains of a Roman temple, and the field where super-phosphate was invented. We visited Midland Agricultural College, as well as the National Dairy Institute where the Director was Dr. H. D. Kay. [I wondered if he and I were kin.] Besides my being raised on a farm and teaching agriculture, Sal owned a farm in Oregon. One of his brothers was running it while we were overseas. Carl Wilson, from Oklahoma, accompanied us on these trips concerning agriculture.

February saw more action. During "Big Week," our fighters flew escort for the bombers to the German aircraft plants. One night a 500 lb. bomb exploded on our runway, and many incendiary bombs were scattered around.

In April 1944, we were moved to Wormingford, 5 miles northwest of Colchester. The Colchester Castle was an interesting place to visit. Sal, Killion, Hank Misura, and I rode over there on our bikes. We toured the castle and its gardens, again taking many photos to send home.

The following month, we were told that paratrooper suicide outfits might be dropped there, so we had to wear masks and side arms. The field was closely guarded.

We knew the invasion was coming when, on June 5, the ground crews were told to paint black and white stripes on our planes, the wings and tails. That evening our P-38s escorted invasion ships. The next morning we were awakened shortly after 1 a.m. Only a few thin clouds lighted the moon. We heard bombers passing overhead by 3 a.m. Our planes patrolled the Channel from ½ hour before daylight to ½ hour after dark for several days, in spite of intermittent rain.

Wormingford was on the path of the buzzbombs to London and other targets. At first, we would quit work and take cover when we heard them, but they interrupted us so often that we soon began ignoring them.

In July our group switched over to P-51Ds. They flew in the P-51s and flew out the P-38s. We were left with English wrenches to work on metric engines.

We received a Distinguished Unit Citation for missions flown on September 3-13. Our planes flew eight missions and destroyed 106 enemy planes while protecting the bombers and strafing airdromes.

Those winter days were so short. In December 1944, I took a picture of sunrise on the base at 9:15 a.m. and the same angle at sunset, 4:30 p.m. We had an unusually large amount of snow this month in England and on the continent.

On Sunday, Feb.11, 1945, I wrote Dad again. "Yeah, I'm in the barracks all alone tonight. Everyone else has gone to town or somewhere. I have a good fire going and am taking it easy. I just finished a long letter to Phama. I got five airmail letters from her tonight-dated Jan 15, 18, 22, 23 & 25. I got one from her yesterday dated Jan. 30. That is very good."

"Well, I worked all day today. It was bad weather but we pulled the plane in the hanger. We had ice again this morning. It is cold and misty tonight. I took time out to go to church this morning. Last Sunday was the first Sunday morning I've missed in quite awhile. I was very busy and hated to beg off. You know lotsa guys would say I went to church just to get out of work and I have seen guys go when I thought they went just to get out of work. Anyway I liked a piece about "friendship" in the church program this morning so I'll mail it to you."

"Say, did I tell you that I finished a ten lesson correspondence course in "Air Conditioning?" Well, I finished it quite a spell ago and my final grade was 91. I am now taking a course in book keeping and accounting. I have finished six lessons."

My cousin Earl Shank was also stationed in England. He was a C-47 pilot. On 20 March 1945 he had to fly to Paris, and I received permission to go along. We landed at Le Bourget where we saw captured German planes. There was a problem with one of Earl's tires, so we had time to go into town, see the main sights, and take a break at a sidewalk café.

To Germany and then home

In July 1945 the ground crews were loaded onto B-17s, to fly to Germany. The 55th was stationed at Kaufbeuren, southwest of Munich. This area had been relatively untouched by the war; so all the facilities were first rate. This had been part of a primary flight-training field, and we lived in the barracks of German airmen. They were good dorms having red tile roofs, steam heat, and decorated with parquet floors & marble. The mess hall was decorated with fancy German lettering on walls. There was even a swimming pool, but it turned out to be a very cold spring-fed pool. That is, it was cold even in August.

Bob Hope came to Kaufbeuren to entertain several thousand soldiers. Since our field was the only place for his plane to land, we got to see him, too. An ammo dump, which Floyd described "as big as a hotel" blew up during the show creating quite a commotion.

On 2 September 1945 my ASR score was 85—the number needed to go home. I described the excitement in this letter to Dad. It was a very happy letter on Sunday night, 9 September 1945 from <u>Stone, England</u>. "Hi Dad, We got here at five p.m. yesterday. First thing, we set our watches back to five o'clock. Yep, be glad when I can set it back about six more hours."

"See, we were alerted Tuesday night for shipment early Wednesday morning. Well, Wednesday, we sat around all day and no planes showed up. Thursday, it was drizzly, so we didn't expect any planes. Friday, it was cloudy and foggy in the morning but cleared off in the afternoon, so we were expecting action Sat. Real early, the loudspeaker called for flights 1 & 2 to report by 8:30. Well, about 8:30, some C47s started arriving. That is the same kind of plane used on commercial airlines in the U.S. before the war. Pretty soon, they called for flights 3, 4, & 5. Well, I was in the last flight, no. 11. About 9 or 9:30, they called for ALL personnel going to England and boy, did I hustle my bags out on the line. By 10 or 11 in the morning, only 8 planes had come in so they came on to England."

"It was rather a gloomy bunch that ate dinner <u>one more time </u>in Germany. Then, a little before one o'clock, two more planes came in. That took everyone but 12 of us. Aw, it was nearly 1:30 before the 11th plane came in. Yes Sir, we were glad to see it. While the crew went to eat dinner, I crawled up on the wing and filled up the gas tanks. Yes, I was gonna ride that ship, so I didn't want her to run out of gas."

"Just before two o'clock, we took off. If we had come Wednesday, as scheduled, it would have been two years to the day since we sailed from New York. I slept for about the first hour of the trip. Then I awoke. The bucket seats in the plane were about to break my back. I walked around awhile and laid down on the barracks bag. See, we hit an air pocket and the plane dropped. I wasn't asleep, but I was deep in thought. I really came alive grabbing for something. Several guys saw me and almost laughed their heads off."

"Well, when we got to the airport near here, we set our watches back to five but it was six o'clock before we got ourselves and our luggage over to this base. We then ate, and registered, and were assigned rooms. Finally having nothing to do, I went to see a picture show. It was a pretty good show. I moved into the room where two men were shipping out last night at 10:30. There are now three of us in the room; the other guys are from Alabama and Pennsylvania. They took me in and made me one of them. The guy from Pa. leaves tomorrow for the U.S. Most guys get out of here in about a week but some have bad luck and stay longer. I see no reason for me to be here over a week."

"This morning, we checked our bags, turning in surplus property and signing up for stuff we need. This afternoon, we were off, so I slept. I hope to proceed with the rest of the essentials tomorrow, mainly, a physical examination, and then I'm ready to go. (home)....P.S. I guess you need not write me any more letters. I probably won't get 'em."

I was in the group that came back to the U.S. on the Queen Mary. When we left England, there was a storm on the North Atlantic that caused the smaller ships transporting troops to stay in port at Liverpool several more days. The Queen was large enough to plow right through the storm. We arrived in New York on 4 Oct. There were huge banners hanging on the docks saying, "Welcome, Victors," and the Statue of Liberty never looked better.

On Saturday, 6 October 1945, I wrote Dad this. "Well, we (group going to Ft. Sam Houston) eat at 12 o'clock and meet a formation at 12:30 so I feel we'll be on a train not later than 2:30 headed for "Deep in the Heart of Texas."

"Maybe you have read of the big steak dinner promised to all returning overseas veterans. Well, I had mine yesterday. We had a big hunk of steak, well-cooked, mashed potatoes, brown gravy, and lettuce with dressing, fruit salad, light bread, rolls, asparagus, cake and ice cream. I almost <u>busted</u>. Then I went to bed and slept till 3 or 4 o'clock."

"I got up and went to the P. X. with some of the guys and ate more ice cream. Then I went to supper last night to find good pork (not greasy) plus fruit salad, ice cream and cake. What I ate yesterday would sell for $10 in England or $50 in Germany....cloudy today...yesterday they checked our bags for guns, liquor, etc. Then they issued any clothes needed. That concluded our business at Camp Kilmer...."

Written in Pennsylvania (I think) Sunday Morning, 8 o'clock, 7 Oct '45.

"Hi Pop, I hope you can read this. This old train is kinda rough. But Oh Boy, as long as it's rollin' I like it. We left Camp Kilmer a little after two o'clock yesterday afternoon. We cut up the Lehigh Valley in Pennsylvania to New York. We hit Buffalo late last night. The porter says we'll be in Cleveland, Ohio by 9 o'clock. I'll get him to mail this there. This is a whole trainload all going to Fort Sam, Houston. We are in an air-conditioned car. I slept alone in the top berth last night. It is all very comfortable. I'll see you next week at the latest."

I was officially separated from the service at Fort Sam Houston, San Antonio, Texas, on 13 Oct 1945.

Printed with permission of Karen Esberger.

American Airmen In Buchenwald

Narrated by Frank Lewis, P-47 pilot
9th Air Force, 406th Fighter Group, 514th Fighter Squadron
Edited by Erik Dyreborg

Introduction

When P-47 "Thunderbolt" pilot Levitt C. Beck crossed the English Channel into France on June 29, 1944, little did he dream that he was about to make his one and only aerial combat kill. He would meet an FW-190 German fighter head on, each pilot taking serious hits from the other, shooting each other down. Rescued by the French Underground, then betrayed to the Gestapo, with 167 other American and British airmen, his life would end in a Nazi concentration camp.

It was common among aircrew men to believe that, if shot down and captured, they would enter survivable POW life in a Nazi stalag or dulag, administered, for airmen prisoners, by the Luftwaffe under the Geneva Convention. These camps, years later, would be depicted with questionable accuracy by "Hogan's Heroes," on TV, still in reruns today. Tragically, Beck would not be that furtunate.

June 29, 1944

On that fateful day, three weeks after the Normandy invasion, a flight of P-47s of the 514th Squadron of the 406th Fighter Bomber Group were on armed reconnaissance in northern France, in support of General Patton's Third Army. While looking for bridge targets over the Seine River, they were bounced by a flight of FW-190 fighter planes. Beck was attacked head on by one of the 190s, both of them spitting bullets as they zoomed toward each other at what must have been at least 600 knots.

Both took strikes, and Beck chortled to himself about which he wrote in a final autobiography three weeks later) "Becky, there's your first victory!" Unfortunately the FW-190 pilot also got a kill as Beck's engine took fatal strikes, and he headed for a crash landing.

On the way down, another FW-190 attacked him and, carelessly overestimating Beck's gliding speed, ended up in front of the powerless Jug. With typical fighter-pilot-quick reaction, Beck centered the 190 in his gun sight and hosed him roundly.

He thought he must have hit the 190, but could not be sure that the German went down due to oil obscuring his view through the windshield and his need to pay attention to gliding his lead sled down to a belly landing. It is possible, however, that his final flight gave him two unclaimed, unawarded victories.

Betrayed

He bellied in successfully, and was immediately scooped up by members of the French Underground. They took him to a nearby town where he was hidden on the third floor of a café. There during the next two weeks, he wrote his autobiography on the backs of café menus.

In the meantime, the French Underground was arranging his pickup and transportation to an airfield for return to his unit. They were unsuspecting of the infiltration of the underground cell by a turncoat by name of Jean-Jacques Desoubrie.

He, Desoubrie, had an automobile, and, with a pretty red-haired girlfriend, volunteered his services as a taxi to take the hidden Allied airmen to their departure point, most of them supposedly to an airfield in France, others to the Spanish border for crossing of the Pyrenees into neutral Spain and eventually back to their unit.

Gestapo

Instead, this traitor took the airmen to Paris; there he turned them over to the Gestapo, to be assembled in Fresnes Prison on the outskirts of Paris for further disposition.

Jean-Jacques Desoubrie, a Belgian electrician, during summer and fall of 1944, betrayed as many as 150 Allied airmen. The number of underground personnel whose lives he cost must have been enormous. Jean-Jacques Desoubrie was executed after the war; however, his lady friend got off.

In the Fresnes Prison, the airmen had their first taste of life to come, such as starvation, torture, beatings, rats, lice, fleas, and unbearable living conditions. But they would look back to Fresnes as luxurious after a few days in their soon-to-be home in a Nazi concentration camp.

Trip to Buchenwald

On the 19th of August they were rousted out of Fresnes to a railroad station where they were loaded into 40-&-8 freight cars, about 90 of them jammed in each car. There were some 2,000 other prisoners: Jews and "politicals", men, women, children, all bound for the Buchenwald Concentration Camp, and death, as the readers have seen in movies of the Holocaust history.

Ironically, Paris was liberated a few days later, on the 25th of August 1944.

For five miserable days the train lurched along, the prisoners crowded so tightly they could not lie down. They had little food or water, and only a bucket to use as a latrine, which was soon filled and overflowed. The fetid air was almost unbreathable, for there was virtually no ventilation.

At a stop, a few of the prisoners escaped from one of the airmen's cars by tearing boards out of the floor. A young French boy put his hand through a barbed-wire window and a German guard shot it off. He was then driven from the car and chased down the track embankment. Finally captured, he was beaten, then shot to death and left lying. He was buried by two of the airmen. The inmates of this freight car, mostly airmen, were stripped of their clothing and forced to make the rest of the five-day trip nude.

The train was attacked a couple of times by fighter-bombers; another time, it was halted at the Marne River where the bridge had been bombed out of existence. They all had to detrain and hike to a river crossing to another train, no better than the first one.

While enduring the horrors of this train trip, Beck recognized a B-26 pilot from his hometown in California, Lieutenant Mike Petrich. They renewed their acquaintance and became good friends, and Petrich would be one of the last of the 82 Americans prisoners to speak to Beck before he died in the Buchenwald hospital. But we're getting ahead of the story.

Buchenwald and the German SS

On the 24th of August, 8th Air Force B-17 bombers flattened the Gustloff armaments factory that used Buchenwald slave labor. The last train from Paris before its liberation arrived with the airmen prisoners just in time for them to be put to work cleaning up the debris from the precision bombing, which had destroyed the factory and killed hundreds of camp prisoner workers as well as over 100 SS personnel. Among these were the Commandant's wife and child.

The 168 English-speaking airmen, consisting of equal numbers of British and American prisoners, were housed in the infamous "Little Camp," segregated from, and more horrible than the regular camp on the far side of the electrified fences. They were forced for over two weeks, before being assigned to barracks, to live in an open field strewn with rocks, and to sleep there in the cold fall rain. Many of them sickened because of the savage conditions, Beck was one of them.

I have written to and talked on the phone with some of the Buchenwald survivors, and Mike Petrich reported that Beck was extremely popular with his fellows, cheerful and optimistic. He even started a small jazz band with instruments that came in by train one day from another concentration camp where few inmates were still living to make use of them. They played for other groups of prisoners in exchange for precious food, always in starvation supply and disgustingly inedible to boot. They all soon deteriorated into little better than living skeletons.

The savage treatment they and all other prisoners received from the sadistic German SS guards will not be dwelt on here inasmuch as anyone reading this must already have seen one or more of the myriad movies depicting concentration-camp conditions. They all appeared to be similar in cruelty. Buchenwald was one of the very first and worst, and our airmen experienced and saw the full extent of Nazi depravity there.

Inasmuch as they were in the French civilian clothing and not their uniforms when betrayed to the Gestapo, they were all classified as spies and expected to be executed.

Luftwaffe and the transfer of the airmen to Stalag Luft III

Officers of the Luftwaffe came to Buchenwald soon after the bombing to assess the damage and found this unexpected contingent of English-speaking airmen incarcerated there when they should have been held under the Luftwaffe in their POW system.

The prisoners convinced the Luftwaffe officers they were not spies but were, indeed, bona-fide airmen. Having assessed the unusual situation, the Luftwaffe officers left, and soon returned with questionnaires for the airmen to fill out to prove that they were not spies. Some of the airmen refused, but suffered no retaliation for it.

Satisfied that they were not spies, the Luftwaffe brass pulled the proper bureaucratic strings to get the 168 airmen sprung from Buchenwald and sent to Stalag Luft 3 at Sagan, a POW camp made famous years later by the movie, "The Great Escape", starring Steve McQueen. They would survive the war there, finding it hard to convince the existing POW contingent that they had come from Buchenwald.

This same scepticism would dog their footsteps on into postwar civilian life as they tried to tell of their experiences.

The destiny of 1st Lieutenant Levitt C. Beck

Levitt C. Beck had fallen deathly ill with pneumonia and had been taken to the Buchenwald hospital. He did this reluctantly; as it was well known that few ever-survived the "treatment" they received in these hospitals.

Not known to the 166 survivors, until years later, was the fact that the SS execution order for all of them was in the Commandant's office the day they departed.

The prisoner contingent left the Buchenwald Concentration Camp at Thanksgiving time, leaving behind Beck, soon to die. A British pilot had died a few weeks earlier.

Beck's last words in a note to a friend in the hospital were: "Dear Joe, I don't know how long I can still keep it up. I have no pains. I don't know what my hands write even, because I am full of drugs. Please. Joe, when you get out of here, tell my parents that my last thoughts were of them. Thanks for everything. Beck".

Beck's note was, indeed, eventually sent to his parents.

It is known that other Americans ended up in various concentration camps from which they did not escape or survive, particularly those on behind-the-lines intelligence missions.

The Buchenwald prisoners were unusual inasmuch as they were a very large contingent, and all of them were aircrew, officer and enlisted. My research has unearthed no similar occurrence.

Several weeks earlier, as Beck was leaving the café for Paris and freedom, he completed his autobiography and buried it in a can in the café's backyard. It was sent to his parents in California after the war, and was privately published by his family as "FIGHTER PILOT" by First Lieutenant Levitt C. Beck.

Two books on the subject have been recently published, one being "DESTINATION BUCHENWALD", by Colin Burgess, Kangaroo Press, Kenthurst NSW, Australia; and, "168 JUMP INTO HELL", by Arthur Kinnis and Stanly Booker, published by Mr. Kinnis, Victoria BC. Kinnis is president of the KLB Club of Buchenwald airmen survivors, both British and American. A third book, "FORGOTTEN VICTIMS"—The Abandonment Of Americans In Hitler's Camps, by Mitchell G. Bard, Westview Press, 1994, contains some mention of the Buchenwald airmen, but little detail.

The story of these airmen is not widely known as few believed them when they returned to their units in 1945, and later to their homes. Some were referred to psychiatrists.

This scepticism about the truth of their stories of concentration-camp-life made it difficult for researchers attempting to amass documentation on the strange event. To this day, many find it hard to believe.

The same sceptical reaction has been common among other veterans and non-veterans, alike. It is hard to believe.

I once told a retired three-star general of these men, and he had never heard of them.

I, Frank Lewis, was a Squadron-mate of 1st Lieutenant Levitt C. Beck.

Printed with permission of Frank Lewis.

The "Varga Bell"

Narrated by Marvin E. Andrews
8th Air Force, 446th Bomb Group, 707th Bomb Squadron
8th Air Force, 801/492nd Group, 859th Squadron
15th Air Force, 2641st Special Group, 859th Squadron
Transcribed by Theresa Andrews
Edited by Erik Dyreborg

Introduction

I was born September 24, 1919 in Kansas City, Missouri and have lived there my entire life except for the 27 months I served in the U.S. Army Air Force. After graduation from high school in 1936, I went to work at the Forum Cafeteria as a baker. As a young man, I dated, went to dances, movies, picnics, sporting events and all the other things a person would do in peacetime.

When Germany began war in Europe, a military draft referred to as the Selective Service, was instituted. All men 18 years and older were required to register and take a physical exam at their local draft board. I was classified as "4F" or not physically fit for military duty due to my slightly crooked elbow, resulting from the broken arm I received as a child. After Pearl Harbor in 1941, I wanted to help in some way and went to work at the Lake City Arsenal where 30 and 50 caliber ammunition was manufactured. In May 1943, I was called to report to Ft. Leavenworth for another physical exam and this time I was classified "1A" and inducted into the U.S. Army Air Force. Many of my friends already serving somewhere overseas were married, leaving a wife and children at home. I was not married while in the service.

To England

I received my basic training at Sheppard Field, Texas; Armory school in Denver, Colorado, Aerial Gunnery School at Buckingham A.F.B. in Ft. Meyers, Florida and then traveled to Salt Lake City, Utah for aircrew assignment. As a complete crew, we were sent to Pueblo A.F.B., Pueblo, Colorado. There we trained for high altitude bombing, as part of a bomb group, and for night flying. After three months, our training was completed and in late May 1944, we were sent to Forbes Field, Topeka, Kansas. There we received our final shots, flight gear and orders for overseas assignment. After a train trip to Ft. Kilmer, New Jersey, we were sent to New York where we boarded the Queen Elizabeth with 25,000 other troops for shipment to Europe. The trip took five days. Water was rationed, and no showers were allowed. The food was good and each afternoon, when the weather permitted, we were fortunate enough to enjoy the music of the Glen Miller Band. They were being shipped to England also.

After the "Queen" docked in Glasgow, Scotland, we were sent to Stone, England then to Northern Ireland for a week of additional training. Our crew was assigned to the 707th squadron, 446th Bomb Group, Bungay, England as a replacement crew.

Top secret

Before our crews could fly a mission, we received orders to report to an English Air Base at Leuchars, Scotland. We were to tell no one where we were going because it was classified as top secret. As we departed the train at Leuchars Jct., the first thing we saw was a row of six coffins on the station platform, each draped with a British Flag. This was rather disturbing to us. We were loaded on a truck and taken to a hangar where we met our new C.O.—Col Berndt Balchen.

The unit was called the 1409AAFBU Detachment #1, European Division Air Transport Command. It was a small group of Americans operating from this British Base. The unit had one hangar; one permanent barracks for the enlisted men and separate quarters for the officers. We had six modified black B-24 aircraft, one C-47 transport and one Green B-24 with no armament. This was a top-secret operation using the Air Transport as a cover for our real operations. Colonel Balchen had been assigned to set up two separate projects. One called the Sony Project, which consisted of secret night flights to Sweden in the C-47 and Green B-24. They brought back downed U.S. bomber crews, Norwegian soldiers, high government officials and various other things. Our crew was assigned to the Ball Project. We flew supplies and O.S.S. agents to Norway dropping them to the waiting Resistance forces to aid in their fight against German troops.

The planes were modified Black B-24's. The oxygen was removed because all of our missions were at low-level altitudes. The ball turret and nose turret were removed and replaced with a plexiglass enclosure in the nose turret position and a plywood-hinged door covering the ball turret hole. This hole was known as the "Joe Hole". When at the drop zone, the door would be raised and the O.S.S. Agents, called "Joes" would sit around the hole and parachute out on a signal from the Bombardier. Small packages with a parachute attached were also pushed out the Joe Hole. Special containers with parachutes attached were carried on the bomb racks and dropped by the Bombardier at the drop zone. Flame dampers were installed on the engine exhaust to help conceal us from the night fighters. The waist guns, top turret and tail turret were retained as our armament.

Since our crew was trained as part of a high altitude bomb group, we started flying night practice missions at low altitude over England and Scotland with single planes instead of formation flying. This took exceptional skill in navigation and flying. When dropping supplies or agents, we would approach the drop zone at 500 ft. or lower at almost stalling speed. The reception party on the ground would flash a code signal and after identification, would make three or four fires in a line so we would have something to drop by. After a month of intensive training, we were ready to fly missions to Norway.

The missions

Our first mission happened on the night of August 22, 1944 near Trondheim, Norway where we made a successful drop. The weather was excellent. We saw some light flack and one night fighter but lost him in some clouds. Take off was 9:30 P.M.; landing was 6:15 A.M. on August 23, 1944.

Mission #2 was near Oslo, Norway on August 24, 1944. The drop zone was cloud covered and we were unable to find it. On the way back to Leuchars, we ran into a terrible storm approximately 150 miles from Norway. We tried to fly under it but no luck. With no oxygen on board we could not get above it either. We had no choice but to fly through the storm. Fuel was getting low and we would lose or gain as much as 1000 feet at a time. The entire aircraft was enveloped in an eerie blue light known as, St. Elmo's Fire. I was riding in the top turret and raindrops hitting the Plexiglass dome looked like hundreds of tiny blue lights. We finally pulled out of the storms two hours later. A British Mosquito pilot flying above the storm reported he saw a plane that looked like it was on fire. How that old plane held together I would never know.

On September 9, 1944, three of our crews took off for Norway again. It was our fifth mission and again could not locate the reception party because of cloud cover. Lt. O'Hara's crew did not return to base and we learned later they had crashed into a mountain and all aboard were killed. This was our first experience at losing one of our crews and friends, a very sad and sobering occasion.

We flew mission #6 on September 13, 1944 and mission #7 on September 19, 1944. Both were successful drops.

On September 21, 1944, Col. Keith Allen and his crew were on a shuttle type mission dropping supplies and agents in Norway and going on to Murmansk, Russia. They were successful in their drop in Norway and were cleared to land in Murmansk. While making their approach over the harbor, they were mistakenly fired on by Russian ships and badly damaged. All the crew bailed out except for the pilot, Col. Allen who was killed in the crash. The rest of the crew was returned to Leuchars in about a week.

On September 28, 1944 the Ball Project was cancelled due to the continuous bad weather over Norway and the loss of two of our six B-24's & crew.

During our stay at Leuchars Junction, we had our meals at the British Sergeant's mess. Rank was very rigid in the British Army so we furnished Sergeant stripes to all our personnel so we could all eat together. They could never figure out how we had no Privates or Corporals in our unit. We spent lots of our spare time between missions in the nearby city of Dundee, Scotland. We stayed at a bed & breakfast across the street from a dance hall called "The Palis" and the "MacKay Pub". The Scottish people treated us very well and some became very good friends.

The Carpetbaggers

On October 1, 1944, we flew our plane to our new assignment with the 859th Squadron 801/492 Bomb Group "Carpetbaggers" at Harrington, England. They were flying the same type missions to France, Holland, Denmark and other German occupied countries. Our new quarters were now a tent in Tent City.

The 859th Squadron was to practice night bombing missions and start low-level night raids soon. It was slow going because every night the fog would roll in about time for take off. Before we could start the night bombing, we were advised that the 859th Squadron. Would be sent to Italy to join a group there doing Carpetbagger missions.

To Italy

On December 18, 1944, we loaded our gear into the plane and flew from Harrington to Brindizi, Italy. There we joined the 2641st Special Group of the 15 AAF. Two of our original crewmembers did not go to Italy with us and transferred to another crew in England. One of the two was our tail gunner, so I took over that position and the flight engineer took the top turret. Our new group commander was a West Point man, Col. McCloskey, and was much more military than our former Col. Berndt Balchen. Our Squadron C.O. was Col. McManus, also from Harrington.

We were again sharing an Air Base that was a former Italian Air Base, with the R.A.F. We had barracks that were single story long wooden buildings, which were slightly better than tents. We did have electric lights and made stoves for heating from 55-gallon drums and used gasoline for fuel. That worked pretty well if you were very careful.

Our first mission from Italy was to the Po Valley in Northern Italy on December 31, 1944, New Years Eve. We encountered lots of bad weather on the way but had a clear drop zone and made a good drop. When we arrived back at our base, flares were coming up from all over the field as well as tracers from some of the planes. It seems that some of the troops had been into the "Vino" and were celebrating New Years Eve. We finally managed to land after midnight.

The area around the barracks was muddy most of the time so we decided to build walkways. During the day we would send up planes to look for gravel piles the Italians were using to repair roads. At night we would load into trucks and go out to requisition some gravel. We managed to take care of the mud.

We flew 23 missions out of Brindizi from December 31, 1944 to March 21 1945. Some of these were daylight missions and we had a couple of P-51 Escorts on some of these missions but not always.

On March 24, 1945, we again loaded our planes and flew to a new airfield at Rosignano, Italy. This was in northern Italy in newly liberated country and allowed for shorter missions. A "Count's" castle was taken over for Squadron. Headquarters and we set up tents on the castle grounds for living quarters. A high wall for security surrounded the grounds. The castle was located on a hillside overlooking the ocean and a beautiful beach. We spent the next several days getting everything in order so we could start flying missions again.

On one of our daylight missions to Yugoslavia, we had already been to the target, successfully dropping our load and were flying at about 6,000 ft on our way out. Suddenly, an ME-109 fighter flew in along side of us. He was in so close you could read his lips. Our orders were not to fire unless fired upon so, we just watched him fly along side. After about five minutes, he saluted us and flew off never trying to attack. I think he was so surprised at seeing a lone B-24 so deep in enemy territory that he was trying to find out what we were up to and didn't want to attack.

We flew seven more missions from April 1, 1945 to April 14, 1945, five of which were night missions. April 15 through April 20, 1945 we were given a pass to the U.S. Air Force Rest Camp in Rome. We took in all the historic sites and places to visit and really had a great time before returning to base. April 22, 1945 was back to flying missions again.

Counting our seven missions from Scotland, this was #38. To complete a tour in the 15th Air Force required 50 missions. We needed 12 more to finish and were hoping our luck would hold out. So far, we had never suffered a casualty on our crew and never had any severe damage to the plane. After flying mission #41 on April 30, 1945, we started hearing rumors that the war would soon be over and that German Troops in Italy had surrendered.

Marvin Andrews (right), receiving the Air Medal from Col.McManus, CO 859th Squadron, Italy, is pictured above.

The last mission

On the night of May 6, 1945, our crew was called from a movie and told we had another mission to fly. We were to fly a couple of O.S.S. agents and their equipment to a site in Austria near Hitler's mountain retreat. The agent's job was to capture high ranking Nazi officials before they could escape. No opposition was expected.

The weather was clear all the way. We made three passes over the target area dropping one agent on each of the first two passes and their equipment on the third. We started picking up ground fire after our third pass but received no damage. We landed back at our base on the morning of May 7, 1945 and were told that all German troops in Italy had officially surrendered.

May 8, 1945, V.E. Day—all German troops in Europe had officially surrendered and the war, for us, was over. We were restricted to a base for a couple of days to avoid any conflict with the celebrating Italians.

Between May 8, and May 20, 1945 we spent our time mostly swimming on the nearby beach, writing letters and cleaning the Castle grounds while waiting for orders on what we would do next.

May 20, 1945 we flew to Gioia Italy where our plane was to be overhauled in preparation for flying back to the U.S. On May 21st, the enlisted members of the crew were assigned to help build a new mess hall. This was needed to handle the influx of crews arriving on their flights home. The project was completed in six days.

Flying home

On May 29, our plane was finally ready and on June 2, 1945 we took off for the first leg of our flight; destination Casablanca, Africa. This was no doubt the hottest place I have seen. Even flying over the desert at 8000 ft. was extremely hot.

June 3, 1945 we took off from Casablanca for Dakar, West Africa. On landing at Dakar we were greeted by native troops lined up on both sides of the runway. They stood barefoot wearing shorts, vest and a Fez with rifles held at attention. Quite impressive!

June 4, 1945 we took off for our flight across the Atlantic to Natal, Brazil. We spent two days there while the plane was being checked out for the rest of the trip. On June 6, 1945 we flew from Natal to Georgetown, British Ghana. Most of this flight was over the Amazon River basin and dense jungle. The runway at Georgetown was just a narrow strip cut out of the jungle. On June 7, 1945 we flew from Georgetown to San Juan, Puerto Rico, a real nice base.

June 8, 1945 we flew to Savannah, Georgia where we turned over our plane, The Varga Belle, and went through Customs. There we turned in all of our flight gear. We were then taken to a special mess hall for returning crews where you could order anything you wanted, steak, bacon & eggs, ice cream, etc. We were then given a 30 day leave and travel time with a new assignment station at the end of the leave. I was home on leave with my family by June 13, 1945. This was the last time I saw any of my crewmembers until 1992 when I met our pilot, Lt. Col. Robert E. Brandenburg at a "Carpetbaggers" reunion in Houston, Texas. After my leave, I reported to the Waycross Army Airbase in Waycross, Georgia, a P-51 training base. Points were awarded toward discharge depending on your service records, missions, etc. I had plenty of points and after a short time at Waycross was sent to Jefferson Barracks, St. Louis, Missouri. I was discharged on September 2, 1945. Our plane, which we had named The Vargas Belle, had flown a total of 104 missions. We had a pretty girl painted on the nose. I am sure it was flown to the desert where most of the planes were cut up and melted down for aluminum and other metals.

We flew a total of 42 missions, seven from Scotland and 35 from Italy. 30 were night missions and 12 were daytime. On 30 of our missions we made successful drops, the other 12 we were unable to drop because of cloud cover or unable to locate the ground party. Sometimes the Germans captured the ground parties and they were always tortured and killed. We were fortunate to receive good information from the Resistance forces about the location of German defenses. Our navigator could plot a course in and out of the target area to avoid much of the anti-aircraft fire. The high altitude groups did not have this advantage. One of our worst enemies was the bad weather in the mountains where most of our missions were flown.

Post war

After discharge I returned home and went to work as a salesman for the Graybar Electric Company. I was married to my wife, Stella, and we have two children. My son lives lives in Oklahoma and my daughter here in Kansas City, Mo. Stella and I were married on June 29, 1945 and have been married 57 years. I retired from Graybar on January 1, 1977 after 32 years.

For hobbies I like to fish and hunt. I belong to a group called The Commemorative Air Force, formerly known as The Confederate Air Force. Our purpose is to restore and keep in flying condition the combat aircraft of WW II. I have been a member since 1974. We have our own wing and hangar here in Kansas City built entirely by local members. Several of our members own the planes and take part in air shows around the country. Our group plane is a PT-19 Primary trainer. I also belong to a metal-detecting club and enjoy locating buried artifacts with my detector.

My daughter, Theresa, went to England and Scotland and visited a lady named Nellie MacKay, who, with her husband Bob, had owned the Pub I mentioned in Dundee, Scotland. Nellie had a friend in the R.A.F. at Leuchars and he took my daughter on a tour of the base including a flight in the F-4 Phantom simulator.

My daughter and Nellie really hit it off and corresponded until Nellie's death a few years ago.

In 1994 a photo appeared in the Kansas City Star Newspaper with a photo of four crewmembers in Lt. O'Hara's crew. I called the Star to find where they acquired the photograph and story. It seems that a gentleman named, Birger Smedstat of Seljord, Norway was trying to locate next of kin of Lt. O'Hara's crewmembers. As a small boy, he had witnessed the crash of the B-24 on Mt. Skorve. The co-pilot was from Kansas City and had been married thus, the photo here. To honor the crew, the citizens of Seljord were building a memorial and wanted to notify next of kin so they could attend. The memorial was dedicated on September 9, 1994, 50 years after the crash. The bodies of the crew have since been returned to the U.S. and are buried together at the Jefferson Barracks National Cemetery in St. Louis, Missouri.

In 1995 I met Birger Smedstat and his wife, Anna Alicia, in Minot, North Dakota at the 50-year anniversary celebration of the end of WWII. This was called The Scandinavian Hall of Fame Banquet and people from the Norwegian resistance were guests of honor. O'Hara's crew was also being honored. Birger has written a story about their mission and is now in charge of monuments in Norway.

Printed with permission of Marvin Andrews.

Nellie

By *Theresa Andrews, daughter of Marvin Andrews*
Edited by *Erik Dyreborg*

In my father's narrative he spoke of a Pub in Dundee, Scotland run by a charming couple named Bob and Nellie MacKay. The MacKays had a particular fondness for Marvin and the rest of his crew. For them, the finest liquor was reserved in the back and cakes were baked on birthdays. To my father, they were known as Bob and "Mom" MacKay. To the MacKays my father was known as "Andy". Although their time together was brief, the bond of friendship between them lasted a lifetime. Never a holiday passed without cards, letters and telephone calls between us. And, always accompanied by a gift. The MacKays would send beautiful calendars, lovely embroidered linen hankies and, at the birth of my brother, a tartan plaid woolen toy duck arrived.

I grew up looking forward to each Christmas Day when we would place an overseas call to Dundee, Scotland. Nellie's first words to my father were always the same, "Is that really you Andy?" My father was the only member of his crew to keep in touch with the MacKays after the war. The MacKays had no children of their own which I believe made Marvin even more special to them. I had dreamed of meeting this kind woman with the sweet Scottish brogue, whom I had grown to love over the years. Sadly, Bob MacKay passed away before I was able to meet him.

After graduating from college, I decided to travel to England and Scotland to meet Nellie and visit the airbase at Leuchars, Scotland where my father had been stationed. So in 1979, I began this wonderful trip.

While in England, I visited the Battle of Britain Museum, what an experience seeing all of those planes. I was filled with excitement as I took the six-hour train ride from London to Dundee, Scotland.

To my surprise, a taxi driver awaited my arrival and took me straight to Nellie's flat.

Bob & Nellie are pictured above.

When she opened the door we hugged, kissed and cried. I knew I was exactly where I belonged. Thinking that I would be tired, Nellie had hot tea and scones waiting. The first thing we did was phone my father and mother in the states and all of us spoke to each other. The emotion was overwhelming.

Nellie had planned so many things for my visit. We drove through the Moors, visited the site where her Pub had once stood, strolled down the road to the home of "Celia and Carl" where we dined on smoked haddock. We would end our evenings drinking Gin & Tonics while pouring over old photographs. I felt totally and completely at home. Nellie had also contacted a friend of hers who was an Officer at the still active R.A.F. airbase in Leuchars, Scotland. While there I was treated as a guest of honor.

After touring the base, I was allowed the rare opportunity to climb in an F-4 Phantom simulator. The officers closed the canopy and permitted me an attempt at simulated flight. I did a terrible job of it and all had a good laugh. Before leaving, I took another walk through the grounds of the airbase. One old barracks was still standing. As I looked around for the last time, I could imagine my father's black B-24, The Vargas Belle firing up the engines for another mission. It was hard to believe that I was standing where my father had stood some 35 years earlier. I could not have been prouder to be the daughter of Marvin E. Andrews as I was at that moment.

Saying goodbye to Nellie, this dear woman with her laughing eyes, was one of the most difficult things I've ever done. In her usual kindness, Nellie had arranged for me to have a sleeper car for my trip back to London. As my train crossed the Tay Bridge I watched the lights of Dundee become tiny, twinkling specks in the night. My face was pressed against the window as tears rolled down my cheeks. My journey was almost over and my dream had come true.

We continued to write and call Nellie on all Holidays. Nellie and I never mastered the ability to end our telephone calls without crying when it was time to say goodbye.

Several years later, officials in Scotland notified me that Nellie had passed away.

I will never forget how I felt when I telephoned my father to relay the sad news. Today when bittersweet memories get the best of me, I think back on my most cherished moment with Nellie. On our last evening together, while a taxi waited outside her door, I held Nellie's face in my hands and thanked her for being there for Marvin & his crew and for being such an important part of our family. She told me that we were her family and ended with, "I love you dearie." I love you too Nellie.

Printed with permission of Theresa Andrews.

The Murdering Of Downed Airmen

Narrated by Carrol F. Dillon
Edited by Erik Dyreborg

Carrol F. Dillon is pictured above.

Introduction

My own story is one of frustration and breached promises of the AAF. It is the story of my yet unpublished book.

I was a student at Indiana University and in infantry ROTC at the time of Pearl Harbor. I volunteered for pilot training in the AAF shortly after our entry into war. So many were applying, the AAF could not give me the required mental and physical tests required for Aviation Cadets until June 1942. After being sworn in,

309

I waited along with 50,000 other volunteers for orders to report for active duty as Aviation Cadets.

In February and March of 1943, the AAF called all 50,000 of us into active duty. This created a serious oversupply of men in pilot training—more than the flight training facilities could handle. I trained in the pilot program for a year. Then, I trained as a radio operator and gunner for a year and went through operational combat training on a B-17 crew.

I was on my way to the 8th Air Force in England when five crews out of our group were sent to B-29s. I went through B-29 transition and was with a group being sent to the 21st Bomber Command in the Marianas Islands. However, there was a shortage of Superfortresses and only every other crew received one. The rest of the crews were given an APO number and sent Hamilton Field, California to be flown to the Marianas. We were sitting there waiting, receiving our mail through an APO number when the war ended.

My crew was then sent to March Field, California and assigned to the 458th Bomb Group, 752nd Bomb Squadron, an 8th Air Force group converted to B-29s and on its way to the Marianas. But after a while, it was discovered that the air crews in my group had so many points toward discharge that soon they would have to turn around and send us back, so they canceled the whole thing.

The AAF began discharging all aircrew members; however, they looked in my file for the first time during the war and saw that I had majored in personnel management and pre-law and, in lieu of discharging me, gratuitously conveyed upon me the MOS of Personal Affairs Consultant and assigned me to the March Field Separation Center to counsel the fellows being separated from service.

So, I trained for air combat for three years and ended up counseling the fellows that went to combat and survived to be discharged. There was no crew that was better trained for combat than my crew. The whole crew had extensive, multiple aircrew training and experience; however, we did not get to combat.

The following story is from the book:
"A Domain Of Heroes" by Carrol F. Dillon.

Murder of airmen

The policies of the Nazi leaders pertaining to the treatment of parachuting flyers, created an atmosphere that encouraged the murder of Air Force prisoners by civilians and the military, particularly the SS.

A favorite form of retaliation by avenging German citizens was lynching of American and British flyers by hanging them from lampposts in the bombed cities. There were many reports of lynching of Allied flyers, and most of the culprits got away with it. Staff Sergeant Frederick E. Hutchinson saw several airmen hanging from lamp posts when he parachuted into Bremen on October 8, 1943. He was about to suffer the same fate but was rescued from a mob of wrathful civilians by eight sympathetic German soldiers. A Sergeant Williams in Stalag XVII-B saw his entire crew lynched by German civilians, but somehow escaped the same fate. Being the only survivor left him with a guilt feeling that he never recovered from.

For some inexplicable reason, German farmers were often quite ruthless in the treatment of Allied flyers. An example was the case of Second Lieutenant James E. Hack. He was shot down on the morning of April 24, 1945, only a few days before the end of the war.

Hack was a P-47 pilot. His fighter plane was brought down by ground fire when he strafed military equipment between Buch and Illetissen, Germany. Being forced to bail out at low altitude, his parachute only partially opened and he landed hard in what was described as a "sea of mud." The great impact from the landing drove his body into the mud up to his hips.

Several farmers rushed to Hack and found him helplessly mired in the mud but conscious and still alive. One of the farmers was Hermann Wasler of Buch. The farmer was ruthless. Instead of helping the injured pilot, Wasler brutally kicked the pilot, again and again, until he had kicked the last ounce of life from the defenseless pilot's body. The other farmers stood by and watched. When they were satisfied that the flyer was dead, the farmers and SS soldiers walked away. A Polish slave laborer who worked for Wasler stayed behind and pulled Hack's body from the mud. He carried the dead airman into Buch, looking for a coffin to bury him in. He asked some of the townspeople for assistance in finding a coffin, but none would help. The Polish laborer had no choice but to bury the dead flyer, clothed in his leather flight jacket and flying clothes, in the raw earth. The

Pole made a wooden cross and erected it over the grave upon which he inscribed, "Here Sleeps An American Pilot."

One of the most brutal documented cases of barbarous treatment of American air crews shot down over Germany was that of "Wham-Bam, Thank You Ma'am." The B-24 crew was shot down on Thursday, August 24, 1944, near Hannover. The engineer of the crew, Forrest W. Brininstool was seriously wounded and was sent by his captors to a hospital. Two days after their capture the rest of the crew, Norman J. Rogers, Jr., pilot, John N. Sekul, co-pilot, Haigus Tufenkjian, navigator, Thomas D. Williams, Jr., radio operator, William M. Adams, nose gunner, Elmer Austin, waist gunner, Sidney Brown, tail gunner, and William A. Dumont, ball turret gunner, were placed on a train for Frankfurt.

At 8:00 in the morning, the train came to a stop at Russelssheim, fifteen miles southwest of Frankfurt. The tracks had been blown up the night before by the RAF and the train could proceed no further. The three Luftwaffe soldiers directed the aircrew to climb down from the train. They marched through the town towards the other side where the tracks were undamaged. As the prisoners walked past the Park Hotel in the bombed-out town they were seen by three women who worked in the tobacco store next door. The women, Kathe Reinhardt, her sister, Margarete Witzler, and Margarete's daughter, Lilo, ran out of the shop shouting obscenities and threats, "These are the terror flyers! Beat them to death!" Other people nearby heard the shouting and crowded around the airmen. The hysterical women pelted the crew with stones. Kathe Reinhardt struck one of the men with a large piece of slate, knocking him down. Philip Gutlich, a tavern keeper, joined in the tumult. He beat Dumont with a club and broke his ankle. The guards either could not control the crowd or did not choose to do so. In any event, they did not take any action to protect the Americans.

Dumont was picked up by two of his fellow crewmen, and they all started running down the street with the mob in hot pursuit. Joseph Hartgen, the local Nazi Party leader, joined the crowd and shouted, "Beat the schweins to death!" He then fired his pistol in the air several times to incite the mob. As the flyers ran down the street, they were showered with bricks and rocks. As they turned into a side street, Johannes Seipel, a farmer, who had joined the agitators, ran along beside the crew, hammering them with a club. George Daum, a factory worker, joined in and beat them with a shovel. Johann Opper, a railroad worker, broke a broom handle over the head of one of the men. Three or four soldiers in Wehrmacht uniforms came upon the scene and joined in the rancorous beating.

The fleeing prisoners came to a dead end of the street at a stone wall of an elevated railroad crossing. They had no line of retreat. The battered Americans huddled together against the wall trying to ward off the blows, resigned to their fate.

Three factory workers, August Wolf, Karl Fugmann, and Freidrick Wust, attacked the men from the top of the wall. Wust leaned over the wall and clubbed the men on their heads with a large hammer. Wolf and Fugmann threw railroad ties and large boulders down upon them. The ruthless, sadistic, townspeople continued their frenzied attack upon the beaten men, like a pack of wolves that had tasted blood, intent upon beating them to death. They did not stop their deadly blows until all signs of life were gone from their battered, broken, and bloodied bodies. The Nazi leader then stepped up and emptied his pistol into the heads of several of the motionless airmen.

The bodies, taken for dead, were thrown into an old farm wagon and hauled to the local cemetery. Miraculously, Adams, Brown, Sekul and Williams were still alive. Sekul had his hand on Brown's shoulder. One of the murderers apparently saw some signs of life in Sekul; for, he began beating him on the head with a club. Brown could feel his comrade release his grip as he died. Williams was beaten on the head again and died. Brown and Adams, by the grace of God, although on the brink of death, still lived.

The Germans, believing the Americans were dead, departed leaving the bodies behind for a later burial. Brown and Adams remained completely motionless, afraid to breathe, for about twenty minutes. When certain the Germans had left, they crawled out from under the dead crew members and ran to a chapel in the cemetery. They huddled closely together in a corner of the chapel for what seemed an eternity. When no one appeared and they deemed it safe to leave, they headed west towards the Rhine River. For four days, they trudged through the German countryside, mostly at night until reaching the river. Again fate was not kind. They were spotted by a German policeman and recaptured. The bruised, bloody and exhausted men expected the worst. But this time their luck changed and they were sent to the nearby Oberursel Reception Center and ultimately from there to Stalag Luft IV.

Himmler's order of August of 1943 provided, "Enemy air crews who…offer resistance when captured…are to be shot at once…." The directive gave German soldiers bent on killing Allied airmen an excuse to justify murder; the prisoner was resisting. This became the standard lie used to excuse the killings. For example, when Roy Duncan, Kenneth Ross's co-pilot, was shot and killed on capture, the Germans attempted to absolve the killing on the grounds that he had tried to escape, but it was a lie.

Sometimes, they didn't even bother to make any excuse. In August 1944, a B-17 crew was captured on Borkum Island by German soldiers under the command of one Hauptmann Kurt Goebbel. The airmen were forced to run a gauntlet of German workers during which they were beaten with shovels. The flyers were beaten almost to death. Afterwards, Jacob Witmark, a German soldier, with the approval of Hauptmann Goebbel and his Adjutant, Erich Wentzel, shot each of the flyers in the back of the head, killing them.

German soldiers observed Lieutenant Simmons, co-pilot on John Chapman's crew, land in his parachute. The pilot took off running when he hit the ground. The German soldiers ran after him. Simmons tripped and fell face down in a ditch with the Germans in hot pursuit. When Simmons fell, the soldiers caught up with him and surrounded him. The Lieutenant was clearly in their control with no chance of escape, but as he started to get up, one of the soldiers, without any justification, shot him in the back of the head, taking his life.

When Lieutenant Leslie N. Hauss came down in his parachute in Grossliedern on August 23, 1944, he raised his hands above his head and surrendered to the Germans. He made no effort to escape. This didn't make any difference to his German captors. One Siegfried Utermack shot and killed the Lieutenant in cold blood while his hands were raised above his head.

On Wednesday, June 7, one day after D-Day, Major Paul J. Stach, Second Lieutenant Guido Gelino and Tech Sergeant Albert G. Brenan bailed out in the vicinity of Argentan-Orne, France. They were captured immediately. The Germans, Hauptmann Eugene Knuppe and Feldwebels Robertz and Stockatz, took the airmen behind a Frenchman's home in Argentan and in execution style, shot the three POWs in the head at close range.

One of the most savage acts committed by military personnel was perpetrated by German Doctor Max Schmidt, Commandant of the Luftwaffe dispensary near Marquise, France. He killed a wounded American flyer in August 1944 by giving him a fatal drug injection. A nurse was ordered to sever the dead man's head, boil it and bleach it. Later the weird Commandant sent the head to his wife as a souvenir.

Murder of airmen by Gestapo agents was not uncommon. Usually, however, the dastardly act was committed in a secluded place out of the presence of witnesses, never to be detected. A few of such dastardly acts were brought to light.

One such case was that of Second Lieutenants Gregory W. Collins and Anthony J. Forte who bailed out near Mont-Louis, Indre-Et-Loire, Touraine, France on August 1, 1944. French countrymen saw them come down and went to their aid. The Frenchmen took them to the home of Marie Guipauille near Lussault to hide. Apparently they were seen by one of the neighbors, who informed the Gestapo at Tours. Paul Langden, accompanied by several Gestapo agents or Sicherheitsdienst, burst into the house. Both flyers fled but were captured by the Gestapo and shot.

Another such case occurred late in the war between the 21st and 25th of March 1945. A fighter plane crash landed in a field near Quirnbach, Germany. The pilot, Jack Rivers, was not injured by the crash, but was taken prisoner by local Gestapo agents. In the evening of the same day, he was taken a few kilometers outside the city and shot to death by Gestapo agent Karl Dressler.

The murder of POWs by German soldiers was, more often than not, by the Waffen SS, the military branch of Himmler's thugs, rather than the regular army. One's chances of reaching a prisoner of war camp in one piece were greatly reduced when captured by the SS.

SS units committed a number of major atrocities against Allied military person-nel such as the Malmedy Massacre that occurred during the Battle of the Bulge. Approximately one hundred and fifteen American soldiers were lined up with their hands above their heads at the Baugnez crossroads, outside Malmedy, Bel-gium on December 17, 1944. They were gunned down by machine gun fire from a unit of the First Waffen SS Panzer Division. Miraculously, forty-three survived with multiple bullet wounds.

The SS were quick to seek revenge for the strafing of their forces. On June 10, 1944, four days after D-Day, Lieutenant D. T. Loyd, a P-47 pilot, was flying a mission in tactical support of the beachhead near Rugles Eure, France. He strafed a vehicle column attached to a German Reconnaissance Battery of the 12th SS Panzer Division (Hitler-Jugend). Two German officers were killed in the attack. Ground fire disabled the Lieutenant's fighter plane, forcing it down near Bois-Arnault. He was captured by a near by Reconnaissance Battery. A head wound sustained by the pilot was treated by his captors. But then, Sturmbannfuhrer Bremer, the Commanding Officer of the Recon-Battery, with the approval of Obersturmfuhrer Hirchner, Senior Officer of the 12th SS Panzer Division, turned the flyer over to Unterscharfuhrer Hugo Wolf for "special treatment."

Wolf, accompanied by five soldiers, took the pilot back to the site where the two dead officers were laid out on the ground. They made him walk by and look at the bodies. Then Wolf, turned to Loyd and shouted, "Kaput! Kaput!" The American flyer, aware that he was to be killed, looked the Nazi in the eye and responded, "I understand. I understand." Then Wolf, the evil SS officer, emptied his gun into the body of the defenceless POW. Later, when Wolf, returned to the French residence where he was billeted, he laid the machine gun on a table and arrogantly proclaimed, "It is with this that I killed him. There is one who will not go back to America."

The Germans reasoned in strange ways. They treated the Lieutenant's wounds and then murdered him.

The SS committed atrocities upon Allied prisoners of war in concentration camps as well as upon Jews and political prisoners. An example of such a case occurred just a few days before the end of the war. On Wednesday, April 25, 1945, four members of a bomber crew, were shot down dropping bombs on Linz, Hitler's city of the future. The flyers landed in their parachutes near the infamous concentration camp of Mauthausen. They were taken into custody by the Commandant of the camp and a number of his SS murderers. According to M. de Lipske, a French inmate in the camp, one airman had fractured both legs on landing and could not walk. The injured airman was ruthlessly shot and killed on the spot. The others were tied by their wrists to the Commandant's car with rope and forced to run behind the car several kilometers to the camp.

At Mauthausen, the three were stripped of their clothing and ordered into a cellar used as a gas chamber. This SS interrogated the airmen. They viciously clubbed the flyers in an attempt to beat military information out of them. After they were convinced that they had all the information they were going to get, the Assistant Camp Commandant by the name of Bachmayer, armed with a submachine gun, went down into the cellar fired into the airmen. Methodically he went from prisoner to prisoner, brutally firing bullets into their bodies. After the firing stopped, the executioner was seen coming out of the cellar carrying the smoking machine gun in his hand. He walked slowly away, smiling and whistling the Vienna Waltz.

All airmen knew when the wheels of their aircraft left the runway at the beginning of a mission that some would not be coming home. At the end of the day, the initials "MIA" would be noted after some names on the loading list. Someone would pack up the personal belongings of the missing airmen, the pictures of their wives or girlfriends, letters, the little keepsakes that kept them from going nuts while waiting for the next mission, and send them home. Their bunks would be assigned to replacements, their names struck from the Squadron roster, and they would become forgotten men. There was no time to take the loss personally. That had to be left for the families at home.

If the airman was lucky enough to survive his capture and become a prisoner of war in one of the Stalag Lufts, he had a bleak future to look forward to. A POW won no promotions, no Air Medals, no Medals of Honor, or other awards. No matter how courageously or how bravely the airman may have fought during the air battle of the last mission, or what sacrifice he may have made for his country or fellow crewmen, the acts would go unknown and there would be no medals. Medals were given only to those who returned to base, either dead or alive—in situations where there was someone who could tell the heroic story. A POW could tell the story only to other POWs, and they could not award medals.

The Air Force POWs were usually seen descending in their parachutes and had little opportunity to escape. They were taken to various and sundry places of confinement, where they were interrogated by the military or local police before being gathered into groups to be sent to Dulag Luft.

After capture, Sergeant Dillon was locked up in a shack used by a Luftwaffe anti-aircraft gun crew. Other airmen picked up nearby were also confined there. They were taken by truck to Osterfeld locked up in a "town hall" type building and then were taken to a nearby civilian prison, a collecting point for prisoners. They were interrogated by the Gestapo. The airmen had a strong sense of patriotism and were new at being prisoners of war. They were not certain as to what they were supposed to do and refused to talk at all. A young Lieutenant, a pilot from another bomb group, the ranking officer among the POWs, talked to them about the questioning. He said that there were some wounded flyers among them and that the Germans were refusing to give them medical aid unless they gave them their names, ranks, serial numbers and where they were shot down. He said that he thought it was all right to give them this information.

For four days some twelve new POWs picked up in the area were confined in the dark, cold cell of the prison. They slept on wooden bunks without mattresses, pillows or bedding. The boards on the bottom of the bunks were spaced three to four inches apart making creases on their bodies. Water was distributed only once a day and then in small amounts. The only food they received was some moldy black bread and a soup of unknown ingredients that was not edible. Several times the Gestapo or police attempted to question the airmen. Finally, their German captors gave up. Shortly thereafter, the POWs were on their way by boxcar to a prisoner of war facility. The next stop for the new POWs was Dulag Luft in Oberursel, Germany, ten miles north of Frankfurt.

Carrol F. Dillon spent twelve years talking to airmen who were POWs, researching and writing this book.

His interest in POWs arose from the fact that his twin brother, an engineer-gunner on B-17s, was shot down over Germany and became a POW.

The research compiled in this book is truly amazing. It is a tribute to the 32,000 American airmen of WW II who became Prisoners Of War.

Highly recommended!

For ordering the book: "A Domain Of Heroes", please contact the Author, Carrol F. Dillon by e-mail: attorneydillon@msn.com

Printed with permission of Carrol F. Dillon.

Where Is Lt. John L. DaCrema?

Narrated by Frank J. Finklang, B-17 Bombardier
15th Air Force, 301st Bomb Group, 419th Bomb Squadron
Edited by Erik Dyreborg

Introduction

by Erik Dyreborg

Frank J. Finklang responded to my quest for stories of American airmen of WW II in Don Hayes' newsletter, "The B17 Flying Fortress Association."

Frank J Finklang e-mailed me several excellent stories, mainly about the day-to-day life of American airmen in the 15th Air Force. However, I picked the story about his search for his friend Leon.

Frank J.Finklang writes…

Leon was my friend. We met in late July 1944 at Plant Park, Tampa, Florida. Individual crewmembers reported there and were assigned alphabetically to form B-17 crews of 10. Leon was to be the co-pilot on George Fisher's crew. We then moved south to Avon Park for our actual crew training. It was a multiple task for each of us. First, we had to learn our specific crew position, applying all the technical training we assimilated to that point. Second, we needed to develop the ability to work together as a crew. During the close living, flying, and in general constant association, we all became friends.

Leon & Frank, 1944, are pictured above.

After completing our Replacement Training Unit (R.T.U.) requirements, we each got six days leave prior to departing overseas. After our brief period at home, we were sent to Hunter Field, Savannah, Georgia to get a new B-17 and combat equipment, including a personal .45 caliber automatic and shoulder holster. We all proudly wore our guns for the crew photo prior to our 16 October departure to Dow Field, Massachusetts. We then flew to Newfoundland, Azores, Marrakech, Tunis and finally to Gioia, Italy where we lost possession of our new B-17. We were then ferried to the 301st BG near Foggia. We reported to the 419th BS with all our gear, including 10 cases of K-rations.

Not a plush assignment

We very quickly determined that this would not be a plush assignment. The rows of tents were an ominous clue, plus the request of several old-timers for any K-rations we might be willing to share. This scene did not fit the movies about the USAAF living conditions. It was more like going to Boy Scout camp permanently.

Things didn't improve when we saw our tent assignment. It was leaning—being held up by only the four corner pegs. I went inside and saw daylight from about a thousand small holes that reportedly came from repeated sand storms in North Africa. After questioning our neighbors about how we were to make this tent livable, we quickly determined, sadly, that this tent plus canvas cots were all the help we would get from the government. The rest of any improvements would be gotten only as the result of our own resourcefulness. Since everyone was confronted with the same problems, shortages like wood, flooring, heat, water, a washing facility, etc., were left to our own initiative, resourcefulness, midnight requisitioning, and creativity.

Some weeks later the tent was much improved. The dirt floor was covered with pierced steel planking (PSP) runway section, the same type on which we landed our planes. Our door and frame arrived originally as packing crates. We had a G.I. steel helmet as a washbasin. A Jeep gas tank in an olive tree provided our running water, using oxygen line from wrecked aircraft to transport it in and out through plain gravity.

Biggest Problem

The biggest problem was heating the tent in winter to counter the cold, damp conditions that everyone who ever camped has experienced. We got a 55-gallon oil drum, which was converted, to a stove by standing it on end and cutting a door located about one-third the distance from the top. We then inserted two rods front to back to rest the oil pan from a Jeep we filled with sand and gravel. From the rear, above the oil pan, we inserted oxygen line, running under the PSP floor to the olive tree to a P-38 drop tank filled with aviation gasoline (the same fuel used in our bombers). It took a week to locate a spigot to control the fuel flow. The smoke stack, a 10-foot section of cast iron pipe, was found at night, part of a water line under construction between Foggia and Lucera. Since it weighed close to 100 lbs., we always worried during windy days since it was tied to the center pole.

The procedure for lighting the stove was simple, yet contained all the elements of danger that discouraged most people, especially those who had an unfortunate experience. Self-survival prompted attempts to fake sleeping while enduring the pain from an overfilled bladder. One frosty morning eight beady eyes were surveying the others to calculate any movement that might indicate a weakness in one of the four—crewmembers who would leave his cot to relieve himself, thus obligating him to light the stove. Leon had always avoided this chore, freely expressing his fear, but this time he was elected. Due to his inexperience, he allowed too much gas to collect in the oil pan. He stood in front of the stove in G.I. underwear with knees shaking and lit a match. The following events happened in rapid fashion. A whooshing noise was heard with a four-foot sheet of flame belching through the stove door opening, he yelped while staggering backward, falling through the doorway. He reappeared with soot on his face, minus his dark busy eyebrows and moustache. That was Leon's first and last attempt to light the stove.

Shot Down

Several months later, he, Fisher, the pilot, and Fish, our navigator were shot down on 7 February 1945 south of Vienna, bombing Lobau Oil Refinery. I went over the same target about 10 seconds after they did and was unaware of their misfortune. I returned to our tent and was further depressed when an extra co-pilot sharing our tent was also shot down the following day. I had the tent to myself for a while and was destined to fly for the rest of the war with new, inexperienced crews, which was very exciting, even without any German opposition.

Was Leon murdered by Austrian farmers?

George Fisher, our pilot, survived the Vienna bailout, landing just south of the Danube. He and Howard Fish, our navigator, were captured with the rest of the crew, except Leon DaCrema, our co-pilot. Leon left the aircraft seconds before Fisher, which would position his landing north of the river. He was never reported captured, so his status was officially MIA. He was later declared dead only because of the absence of information. The prison guards were overheard by a German-speaking crewmember discussing how farmers captured 10 downed airmen that day in the area Leon must have landed. They were all killed with pitchforks, stripped, and thrown in the Danube. Since Leon was never heard from after the bailout, it was concluded that my friend was one of the 10 who were murdered that day by the Blue Danube.

We had often talked of home and family to the point we each felt part of both families. After the war, we planned to visit each other" homes to meet our families. I wrote Leon's parents in Philadelphia, and they encouraged me to visit. So in January 1946, I took a train from St. Louis. I felt I almost received the welcome his parents had reserved for Leon. Their warmth and understanding caused me to extend by intended one-day stay to three. As I rode home, I reflected on all that had happened. I was happy I made the trip because Leon's parents seemed to see in me some tangible return for the son who left for the war. I felt then, as I do today, the lack of proof of what actually happened to Leon haunts me to the extent that I write this story with the hope that someone who has the answers will provide the missing facts to this unfinished puzzle.

Leon's destiny

I was reluctant to accept as fact that irate farmers on the outskirts of Vienna on 7 February 1945, killed Leon, but what was the alternative?

On Friday, 11 October 1996, after the 419th BS Dinner at Norfolk, Virginia, I was presented with the first probable different ending to this frightful tale. Bill Rogers introduced me to Jim Maynor, who was attending his first 301st reunion. Jim was a waist gunner on the same aircraft with Bill and Leon. He hadn't seen Bill since their liberation following WWII. He said he read my story, "Where is Lt. John 'Leon' DaCrema?" and wanted to talk to me in private. I sensed he had some bad news, but any information concerning Leon was important to me.

After the meal, I went back to Jim's table and he seemed ready to talk. We moved to the rear of the room and he told me of this sequence of events. After the aircraft left the formation with an engine on fire, Fischer, the pilot, gave the bailout signal. Jim helped Joe Gray, near the ball turret, who was semi-conscious due to a lack of oxygen, to get to the waist door, hooked his chute at the door, pushed him out and followed him. He delayed opening his chute due to the high altitude. As he drifted down, he looked up and saw the plane still under control, so he assumed Fisher was still at the controls. He saw another crewmember close above him who, by his count, was #10 of the 11 aboard to bail out. That meant it should be DaCrema. He saw four or five bursts of flak close to this fellow crewman, apparently killing him. He was so horrified by this scene that he never spoke of it until now. In his mind it had to be DaCrema, since all the other crewmembers were later accounted for.

I was hesitant to interrupt Jim during the telling of this story, which was obviously painful to talk about. I was stunned, because in accepting this revelation never mentioned until now, it closed the door on any possibility of Leon's survival.

I'm grateful to Jim for surfacing the memory of this extremely painful event that he avoided for 51 years. Leon's parents are dead, but he did have younger brothers—Francis, who was in the 7th Army somewhere in Europe when Leon was declared MIA, and Joe, who were only 12. I planned to try and locate them, hopefully in Philadelphia, because Leon was my friend.

Epilogue

Five major events took place following the publication of my original story in the January 1997 issue #30 of The Raven.

First, I received a letter from Jim Maynor who, after further reflection, revised and elaborated on some of the events of that fateful day.

Second, a FAX message from Ted Darcy (whom I do not know) was sent to the 301st and then forwarded to me. He had read the story in The Raven and applied his company records to find that 2nd Lt. John L. DaCrema 0714037 was originally buried in Saint Avold Cemetery, Metz, France. His remains were later interred at Jefferson Barracks National Cemetery in St. Louis, Missouri on 10 September 1952.

Third, I immediately discussed the FAX with my brother Jack, who lives near the cemetery and who is very familiar with Jefferson Barracks. He quickly located the gravesite, providing me a precise location and a typed listing of the 27 Army Air Force members who share the 3 x 6-foot white marble marker.

Fourth, on 28 February 1997, my wife and I drove to the cemetery without much conversation. I was sorting out the jumble of events and wondering how I would react when I personally viewed Leon's grave.

It was a sunny day and there was the marker, exactly where I was told, with Leon's name, fourth of the group. It suddenly dawned on me that Leon had completed his promise to visit St. Louis and my family, as I had visited Philadelphia and his family in January 1946. Perhaps by coincidence, my parents are buried about 300 yards from Leon. I made a rubbing of his name on the stone and shed a few tears as I knelt there. I returned home sad, yet fulfilled, but not prepared for what followed within an hour of arrival.

Fifth, the phone rang and I found I was talking to Leon's kid brother Joe, now 64. He had just received the letter I had mailed to his brother Francis, the only DaCrema listed in the U.S. He was located by a computer search my daughter Mary had initiated on my behalf. As we talked for over an hour, I found out Francis had died in 1986 and his widow forwarded my letter to Joe. It was immediately apparent that we were both fighting our emotions in discussing Leon. Joe had no idea of anything that followed 7 February 1945 except his mother's continuous attempts to get more facts, including a visit to the Pentagon and a letter to the mayor of Vienna. I promptly mailed Joe copies of the information I possessed without waiting for the responses I expected from Ted Darcy and the National Archivist in Washington, D.C.

I owe a great deal to many people who assisted me in my search. The 301st Veterans Association proved to me the value of belonging and sharing one's experiences by writing and attending reunions. One day, I too will occupy a site with a marker at Jefferson Barracks, where I began my military career with Basic Training, Aviation Cadets and flying as part of a crew in a big crusade called World War II. Is this what is referred to as "going full circle?"

Printed with permission of Frank J. Finklang

In memory of the Mackey family who grew up with me. I wish them well. In a few years I'll join Cliff at J.B.

Frank J. Finklang

The Final Flight Of The "Rum Dum"

The story about Earle W. Painter, a B-24 Ball Turret Gunner
13th Air Force, 307th Bomb Group, 371st Bomb Squadron
Narrated by John Painter
Edited by Erik Dyreborg

Earle W. Painter

While the airmen of the 8th and 15th Army Air Forces were waging war with the axis powers in the European and Mediterranean theaters with their missions of hundreds of bombers there was an air war of a different sort being carried out by the allied forces in the pacific theater.

The Imperial Japanese forces had established, early in the war, a perimeter, that included a large part of the south pacific. The allied forces started a campaign of island hopping and chiseling away at the Japanese defenses with aerial bombing in support of ground forces landing on these islands.

Flying originally from Guadalcanal the airmen of the 13th Army Air Forces moved gradually toward their goal of having a base that would put Japan within striking distance of it's B-24`s. one of the bomber groups of the 13th air force was the 307th and it was this group that Earle Painter found himself assigned to in January of 1944.

Born on May the 12th 1924, Mother's Day that year, Earle was the oldest of four children in his family. He had a brother, Jack, seventeen months his junior, and two sisters, Jean and Nancy.

He spent his early childhood in Washington, D.C. and moved to the small town of Staunton, Virginia when he was in his teens. Starting tackle on his high school football team his senior year, Earle left school in October 1942, deciding he would be better off to enlist in the Army Air Forces than to be drafted into the infantry.

Enlisting and training

It had taken him several months to convince his parents he should enlist as neither of them was willing to see their oldest child go off to war. He enlisted in the Army Air Forces and was soon on his way to Fort Lee, Virginia, the local Army Air Forces Induction Center.

From there he was transferred to Miami Beach, Florida, for basic training. Following completion of the Army's basic training course Earle was then sent to Tyndale Field for flexible gunnery school. A member of the class of 43-3, Section 21, Earle completed the course and received his diploma on 19 January 1943.

During the next year the 18 year old from Staunton, Virginia would see more of the United States than most people in his hometown. In the course of his training he would travel to Lowery Field, Colorado, New Cumberland, Pennsylvania, Fort Devens, Massachusetts, Reading, Pennsylvania, Salt Lake City, Utah, and Tucson, Arizona.

Along the way he was promoted to corporal then to sergeant and on 3rd April 1943 he received his diploma for Aircraft Armorers [bombardment] and was promoted to Staff Sargent. His next station was Combat Crew Training School at Pueblo, Colorado. It was here that the "Crew of Rum Dum" came together.

Like many of the bomber crews of World War II, the "Crew of Rum Dum" reflected the complexion of America. Piloted by Lt. Edward J. Rice, married and the father of a young son, from Des Moines Iowa, an able leader and the embodiment of what the Army Air Forces were looking for in a flight leader.

Pictured above:

In the waist window Sol Stein.
Standing L to R: Earle W. Painter, Don Reed and Benny Tampio.
Front row L to R: Tom Silko and Sam Manfredi

The crew:

Lt. Edward J. Rice, pilot, Des Moines, Iowa.
Lt. Kenneth Smith, co-pilot, Albuquerque, New Mexico,
Lt. Marcel Bilder, navigator, Winona, Minnesota,
Lt. Lester Brown, bombardier, Pittsfield, Massachusetts,
S/Sgt. Benny Tampio, 1st Engineer, Ironwood, Michigan,
Sgt. Sol Stein, Ass't Engineer, Brooklyn, New York,
S/Sgt. Tom Silko, Radio Operator, Monongahela, Pennsylvania,
Sgt. Sam Manfredi, Tail Gunner, Chicago, Illinois,

Sgt. Don Reed, Waist Gunner, Buckhannon, West Virginia,
S/Sgt. Earle W. Painter, Ball Turret Gunner, Taunton, Virginia.

Unlike many of the replacement crews of World War II this crew was to fly virtually all of its 60 missions together.

To war

In December of 1943, Earle was given leave before shipping out. He returned to Staunton to spend time with his family and his brother Jack, who was home on leave from Navy Divers School in Washington, D.C.

As he was getting ready return to the Army Air Corp his 12 year old sister Nancy asked, through her tears, why he had to go off to the South Pacific and fight the Japanese. The nineteen year old Earle explained to her that one day she would grow up and get married and have children of her own and that he was going off to fight so that her children would not have to.

Assigned to the 13th Air Force, 307th Bomber Group the crew transferred to the South Pacific in January of 1944. Transferring through Hamilton Field, San Francisco, Hickam Field, Hawaii, and the Phoenix Islands. Finally joining the 307th in New Caledonia.

They were assigned to the 371st Bombardment Squadron and were stationed at Munda, New Georgia by the end of January. Within two weeks the crew was to fly it`s first combat mission.

On February 14th, with a payload of 8 one thousand pound bombs, the crew began their war against the Japanese. The target was a Japanese airfield at Kahili.

They hit the runway with all eight bombs, the ack-ack was light, light and inaccurate. Their plane was not hit and there was no interception. Flying time was three hours and forty minutes.

Bombing targets with names like Borpop, Lakunai, Kavieng,and Vunakanau the crew was to participate in the campaign against Rabual. Flying five missions to Rabual Town between March 2nd and March 22nd the "Crew of Rum Dum" dropped 30 one thousand pound bombs, 12 five hundred pound bombs, and 40 one hundred pound incendiaries on the town. Anti-aircraft fire over Rabual was usually intense but rarely accurate and their plane was only hit once, in the left waist.

After completing their first fourteen missions the crew was given R and R in Auckland, New Zealand.

The crew flew their 15th mission on April 19, 1944 to Satawan, bombing the runway with 9 five hundred pound bombs. The flying time was fourteen hours fifty-five minutes. The 307th was starting the campaign that earned it the name "The Long Rangers".

About the middle of May 1944 the 307th moved to the island of Los Negros and the 371st set up housekeeping at Mokerang Airdrome.

Their attention was turned towards the Caroline Islands and targets like the Sorol Atoll, Woleai Atoll, and the Truk Atoll. The 307th earned a Presidential Unit Citation for it`s missions to the Truk Atoll.

During the months of May and June the "Crew of Rum Dum" flew missions almost every other day to one small island group or another. It wasn't long before they had over fifty missions under their belts.

Unlike the bomber crews in Europe there was no magic number to get you home in the South Pacific. The Caroline Islands were an important stepping-stone for the Allies and Yap Island`s airfield and naval installation were providing defense cover for Palau Island. Thus by the end of June Yap Island's airfield was a major target for the 307th which was by now part of the 13th Air Task Force with elements of the 5th Air Force.

The final mission

The island was being protected by the remnants of the Imperial Japanese Naval Fighter Squadron 261, 61st Kouku-Sentai (Air Combat Group). Attacks over the previous two weeks had greatly reduced the number of aircraft the Japanese could put up.

The 13th Air Task Force command decided that in an effort to catch the Japanese fighters on the ground the attack would be made in two waves. The first made up of aircraft from the 371st BS, the 372nd BS, and the 424th BS would take off at night. This was to be one of the longest missions the 307th would undertake, approximately 1300 miles away. It would require the use of two extra fuel tanks in two of the bomb bays with the other two bays loaded with bombs. During the entire war the 307th only flew two other missions requiring the use of two extra fuel tanks.

They carried fragmentary bombs to inflict as much damage as possible to the planes and personnel on the ground. The rendezvous point was over Sorol Island. Of the first flight of twelve aircraft, only eight made it to the rendezvous point. Among the one's who didn't make it was the flight leader from the 371st.

Lt. Edward Rice and the "Crew of Rum Dum", flying aircraft number 44-40611, assumed the lead. After setting up for the bomb run it was realized that the element of surprise had been lost. The flight of eight bombers was attacked by 28 Zeros of the 261st Squadron. The bombers managed to get their bombs released over target and the fight ensued.

Approximately 15 minutes into the fight the 0611 took a 20mm shell in the #1 engine. Lt. Rice tried several times before successfully managing to feather the prop. The attacking Zeros, seeing his difficulties, immediately seized on the opportunity and attacked the aircraft-making pass after pass.

A short time later the #3 engine began to smoke and Lt. Rice ordered the formation to reduce air speed to 140 m.p.h. and to stay together to provide cover for each other.

When the Japanese interceptors had left Lt. Rice was still losing altitude and air speed but continued leading the formation, staying away from the cumulus to enable the formation to stay together. By now the 0611 had flames coming from the right wing root. Lt Rice made a series of steep dives and pullouts in an attempt to extinguish the fire. It was then that Lt. Rice called to Lt. Johnson over the VHF in a rather bored and slightly disgusted tone, "I'm going to ditch the son of a bitch."

At 2500 ft. five men were seen to bail out of the plane, two from the bomb bay and three from the camera hatch. By now the flames were coming out of the waist windows and the fire was obviously out of control. The plane slid steeply on it's left wing and crashed into the water and exploded violently on impact.

Of the five men seen to bail out all their chutes opened and all were seen swimming in the water. Lt. Howard Johnson, flying a 371st aircraft, dropped a five-man life raft as did an aircraft of the 424th. A third raft, presumably dropped by the 0611 prior to the crash, was observed in the water.

Lt. Johnson`s aircraft and the one from the 424th continued to circle the crash for 25 minutes. The closest raft to any of the survivors was 300 yards. Due to being low on fuel the two aircraft left the crash site and returned to base.

A rescue Catalina was sent to the crash scene about two hours and thirty minutes after the crash. It found much airplane wreckage and three empty life rafts but no sign of the survivors.

On 6 July, 1944 three aircraft of the 307th flew an extensive search for the survivors of the "Crew of Rum Dum" without success. The coverage of the search area was 100 percent at an altitude of 1000 feet.

On July 6, 1945 the military issued a Finding of Death for the 10 men who were the "Crew of Rum Dum" and radio operator Tommy Griggs who was with them that day.

Research

This story started out as attempt to help my aunt find out the details of the loss of my uncle, Earle Weldon Painter.

After months of coming up empty-handed I stumbled across the armyairforces.com website. From there I got the address of Wally Forman who provided me with a picture of the "Miss Jones", the first aircraft Earle and the crew flew in the South Pacific. This picture gave me the numbers of the group and squadron n they had served in.

Wally suggested that I contact Buck Harmon. Buck was an armorer with the 307th. He provided me with the first details of the mission to Yap Island on July 5th, 1944. Buck contacted Jim Kendall, who is the historian for the 307th, and Jim sent me copies of excerpts from Sam Britt`s book, "The Long Rangers".

This contained a report of the loss of a/c #44-40611 and Lt. Rice`s crew. About this time Stu Stein, the nephew of S/Sgt Sol Stein, the asst. engineer of the Rum Dum crew, contacted me. He graciously sent me a copy of the Missing Air Crew Report. My friend Mitsutaka Suzuki from Sapporo, Japan provided the information on the Japanese defending Yap Island.

My aunts, Jean and Nancy, provided me personal recollections, pictures, and some documents. My son Johnny encouraged me through his interest in B-24`s and the air war in World War II.

As you can see the gathering of information for this story involved a group of people as diverse as the crew.

Last but certainly not least is my friend, Erik Dyreborg, who not only encouraged me to write this story but also helped me to realize the importance of seizing the opportunity when it comes along.

Printed with permission of John Painter.

One Sandwich In Five Days

Narrated by Robert J. Starzynski, B-17 Gunner
8ᵗʰ Air Force, 306ᵗʰ Bomb Group, 367ᵗʰ Bomb Squadron
Edited by Erik Dyreborg

Into the Air Corps

I was born and raised in Chicago, Illinois. I left high school in '42, knowing that I would go into the military. In January of '43, I went into the air corps—I decided anything was better than the infantry.

I stayed in a big hotel in Atlantic City, New Jersey, for my basic, first-class accommodations. We had our training out on the boardwalk. It was very cold and damp in Atlantic City. We did a lot of marching and we weren't given any firearms.

From New Jersey, we went to Drew Field in Tampa, Florida. We were trained on how to use a rifle. There was more marching and drilling—that was about all. We didn't have much training. In March, we went from Tampa to Bradenton, a new camp the army opened up just south of Tampa. The army took over an old ball field and put up tents.

From there we were shipped to Jacksonville. I was not being trained for anything specific up till that point. In Jacksonville, we started to be trained in visual signals. That's where white sheets are laid on the ground when there is no other communication with the planes. The planes fly over and would get the messages. We also had some training in Morse code, but we didn't get much of that.

We were shipped to Camp Kilmer on June 1, and went over on the *Queen Mary* to England. I didn't know what I was going to be doing when I arrived. We weren't trained specifically for anything. We were ground crew. From what I understood, we were a replacement pool—a body here, a body there. When I did get to England, we were detailed to the MP's, and to headquarters to work the switchboard for a while. It was all on-the-job training.

While I was a military policeman, one of the American prisoners we were guarding was being held for murder. We would escort him from the temporary prison on the base, to the mess hall, back and forth until he was transferred out. Then, an Italian prisoner of war escaped and killed somebody—an Englishman working on his farm. We searched for him. Other than that, we just handled the gates and checked passes. We also had to guard the bomb dump on the base at Thurleigh.

I became a gunner

There was a shortage of gunners, so I volunteered for gunnery school. I guess I wanted to wear the wings and get a rank. I was a private, a PFC. I wanted to be one of the glamour boys. I finally got a commanding officer to transfer me to the 367th Bomb Group. So I was sent to gunnery school in England for three days. I'm glad my pilots didn't know that. Training was mostly firing at the sleeve targets. After a while, we'd get together. Some of the other fellows knew a lot more about the .50 caliber than I did. We'd take it apart and put it back together. I had no other training for flying or anything.

After that I was, put into the pool of the 367th. I was assigned to several crews where we just kind of flew back and forth on practice missions—more training for the pilots than anybody else. I have a list of all the dates and times I flew in a B-17 as tail gunner. I was a little tall for a tail gunner—about 5'11." But I only weighed 148 pounds, so I was thin.

The missions

My first mission was the first raid on Berlin, March 6. There were missions flown on the 3rd and 4th of March. But one was aborted, and the other was cancelled, but on the 6th we finally made it. My fifth mission to Berlin was pretty exciting, in that it was going to be the first raid on Berlin. Goring said that we'd never bomb Berlin in the daytime. There were quite a few civilian casualties because people wouldn't go to the air raid shelters. Some groups had a rough time, but that mission for us wasn't bad at all. We had flak, but fighters didn't attack us.

The worst mission was my seventh mission over Faufenhafen, Germany. We were on oxygen for six hours. It was a nine hour and thirty minute mission, or something like that. The 306th sent up eighteen planes and lost ten. We got hit really bad. The enemy fighters came in head-on. Being in the tail, I could see the pilot of the enemy plane go right by sitting in his plane. We were flying in the hole position, number four. It was kind of hard to get shots off, because in that position there were a lot of our planes in back of me. I understand the plane on our right got credit for shooting quite a few fighters down. I shot at some planes that day. That was the first time I got a chance to fire.

We'd be just glad to get back. I was not, at that time, permanently assigned to a crew, so I would fly as a spare. There were times when a crew would come in at eight, nine or ten in the evening, and later that same crew would get called up to go on a mission at one o'clock and would never come back. There were times there would be twenty-four in a barracks—and there'd be times when there were only two of us left.

Later on, I joined a permanent crew. Their tail gunner was killed on their first mission, so I was assigned to their crew. Perry Raster was the pilot. The co-pilot was Virgil Dingman, was made a first pilot—and the air corps trained him. So we got a lot of practice flying time—landing and taking off, one-hour or two-hour flights. That was the crew I got shot down with. I flew six or seven missions before I joined them. I flew with five different pilots that I can remember. Perry Raster was a real hotshot pilot. Some fellows just didn't have a natural ability to fly, and others took a little more training. [as a gunner, it was difficult to tell. I just thought, "a pilot can fly," even though he's maybe nineteen years old.]

Shot down

I went down on my seventeenth mission, so I had flown about eight or ten with my crew. The seventh mission was bad, but the other ones weren't. We had flak, but they weren't that bad. I was pretty lucky, because after that disaster to southern Germany where we lost all those planes, we had a lot of short runs to France. There was nothing really exceptional in terms of heavy fighter attacks. This wasn't deliberate, it was just chance.

On the seventeenth mission, we took off on a mission to France and got over the Channel. As we entered France, we got hit with some heavy anti-aircraft fire. It knocked down two of our planes. The number three engine was on fire, and the fire had nearly reached the horizontal stabilizer. The pilot, talking to the navigator, asked, "Which is farther, back to England, or back to our lines?"

The navigator said, "Well, it's about the same distance either way." So in another minute or two, the pilot saw it was pretty bad. We were still loaded with gasoline and bombs. He told the crew to bail out.

So I said, "Tail gunner bailing out." We had broken formation. There is a little escape door right under the horizontal stabilizer, just for the tail gunner. I always carried my small, portable chute. The tail gunners couldn't wear it, because right under us was a piece of steel to protect us from the flak. I couldn't wear the parachute and handle the gun, so I kept the parachute in back of me. During all of this the parachute had fallen back behind the rear—landing wheel. So I took off my oxygen mask and went back to get my chute. I strapped it on, and tried to open the door. I had a hard time getting it open, because it was stuck. I put my feet out, like you're supposed to do, grabbed onto the top, and was about to throw my rear end out. That's when I noticed I had only clipped one side of my parachute on. So I had to go back and hook the other part on, and then I bailed out.

I don't remember anything after that. When I woke up, I was floating down. So apparently in the time it took to get the chute and open the door, I was about ready to pass out for lack of oxygen. I don't know how the chute got pulled. I had never had any training as far as how to jump or anything. I never took any parachute training. Probably, subconsciously, about ready to pass out, I must have pulled it. We were at about twenty thousand feet when I jumped—well above oxygen.

I don't know when I came to, but all of the sudden I was floating down in complete silence, especially after hearing the roar of the four engines. There was a lot of cloud cover. It felt like I wasn't moving, because I couldn't see the ground coming. Then a P-51 pilot came by. I waved to him. He tipped his wing, and I just kept going down. All of the sudden, I was through the clouds. I could see a couple of farmhouses in the distance. With that emergency chute, you come down pretty fast. So just as I was coming down, I picked up my feet so that I wouldn't hit a hedgerow. I landed right on my back. Fortunately, there were no rocks or anything, so I didn't hurt myself.

France

I was in France, near Buchey. I found that out later. I thought, "Get out of the field." I took my chute, went into the hedges, took off my Mae West, and collected my thoughts. I had my escape kit. I never knew what was in it. The army said, "There are things that will help you escape, money, but I never did see what was really in it." When I opened it up I saw there was a little compass, about the size of a dime, and a map of France and a French to English dictionary. All I had to do was point to the words, and the locals could read it in French. I thought about my family and what was going to happen now. I went through all of my personal belongings to see if I had something that might help my captors if I was captured. I had an address book of friends I had met in England, family from the States, which I tore up. I probably shouldn't have been carrying it.

I stayed in the hedge until it got dark. It was quite late. It didn't get dark until almost ten-thirty at night. This was June 17. You know in England, there was what was called "the double summer." Guys would be out playing ball till ten-thirty at night. I carried a pair of my dress shoes to walk. I had tied them onto my belt. But I had slipped them over my shoulder, which was the wrong thing to do, because when I left the plane, the shoes were gone too. So all I had on was my big flying boots, and the electric heated suit.

When it got dark, I walked out of the woods, went to a farmhouse, and knocked on a door. The people inside were all sleeping. I shouted, "American, American." Three young couples in who were in their late twenties or early thirties were living there. The couples looked at me and looked around. I was invited in. I had the dictionary out, and that's when I started showing them. I was given something to eat and drink. I was given some clothes. I wanted some shoes, and I offered the fellow my money for them. Nope, he wouldn't sell his shoes for anything. I did get a pair of shoes but they were a size or a size and a half too small. I had problems with that, but at least I had shoes on.

I asked if they would hide me, and they said, "Beaucoup boshe," [Many Germans] and it didn't ring a bell, because I wasn't familiar with it. I got the map out, and the couples told me where I was. I figured, looking at the map, I could walk towards our lines. They pointed me in the right direction, but they couldn't hide me because there were too many Germans.

The escape

I started walking down the road at night; that's what the intelligence reports told you to do. I got to the little town of Buchey. There was no one on the street at night. I heard the clunk of boots, so I ducked in a doorway and two Germans walked by. This wasn't too good. The Germans walked by, so I back tracked. I remembered seeing a courtyard. I went and sat in the courtyard right at the fence. I heard them walking back and forth again, and thought, "What the hell? This isn't too good." I ducked into one of the sheds near the courtyard. In this shed was an extremely large barrel of cider, so I had some. There was a German car covered with camouflage. I sat down on the floor and heard these two guys coming back again, standing outside. I could hear them, but I put my head down and didn't move. I was afraid to look up. After the Germans left, I could make out that across the courtyard there was a bombed out building. I made my way in there.

The stairway was bombed out, but I managed to make my way to the second floor on the rubble. I stayed there and fell asleep on the floor of this building. I wasn't scared. I was nineteen—that's too young to be scared. Something woke me up. I heard voices. The building had some bricks that had been knocked out. I could look through and see two German soldiers in the courtyard looking at a rifle. I thought, "Oh, geez, I've got to get out of here." But it was daylight, and everyone was walking around. I had to stay in that building the whole day.

I left early the next morning. I figured, "Heck with this walking around at night, I nearly got caught." I walked in the daytime from then on. I had civilian clothes.

So I walked right out of the building, right down the street. I walked right by the Germans. No one said anything.

The next night, I slept in a field. I turned over some wheat that was harvested, and laid in there. That was a mistake, because I ended up with some body lice from that. The next night, I stayed in shack by the railroad tracks. Two couples came in that night and were startled. I said, "American," and the couples got out of there real fast. They didn't want any part of me.

The barbershop

I started toward a village the next morning, and did a really screwy thing. I walked through the village and saw a barbershop. I needed haircut and a shave pretty bad. I had a three or four day's growth. I looked in the barbershop and saw a young fellow, about sixteen, cutting a little girl's hair.

Her mother was there. In the next chair was a young fellow about twelve or thirteen years old. I sat down in the chair, and the young fellow gave me a shave, but he cut me a bit on the side. So I was holding to the cut a handkerchief that I had.

A German soldier came in the door and said something to the barber. I'm looking at this in the mirror. It happened behind me. The barber said something to me, and I said, "Oui." Apparently, what it was the German wanted to get his hair cut ahead of me. The German left. Apparently he was going to come right back. The little girl had left, and the German soldier wasn't back yet, so the barber started to cut my hair. As he started, four German soldiers walked in.

The barber didn't know I was American. I had civilian clothes. I had a jacket hanging over the back of the chair where the German was sitting. All he'd have to do was look down and see the map, and he'd know whom I was. He gave me dirty looks in the mirror, but what could I do? About halfway through my haircut, the barber said something to me in French about my hair. I don't know what I said. I might have even spoken a few words of English. I took out the biggest note that I had, paid him, and I left. I got a shave and a haircut, and I escaped. It was a screwy thing to do, but I felt that the more ragged I looked, the more attention I would attract.

Small shoes and aching feet

When I was walking down the road, the shoes were causing my heels to bleed. The shoes were very tight. I would stop every so often and take off my shoes for a while. I had one sandwich in five days. I would go by cafes that would say, "Soda and beer." I would lay a note down and say either soda or beer. I'd get something to drink, and out I'd go. There was a German soldier on a bicycle, an old timer, in charge of some fellows digging trenches along the road. I assume they were Frenchmen, because they were in civilian clothes. He looked at me, and I kept on walking. Later on I stopped, and he saw me sitting down by the road. He was riding back and forth down the road on his bicycle. He called me over. He said something in French to me about papers. I said the name of the next town, "Balbeque."

He looked at me, and looked at my shoes, and said, "Get out of here." So I got away again. That's one thing we were told. "Don't take shoes with metal buckles, because those haven't been made in France for quite a while." That's one of the first things the Germans would notice, your shoes—if you had a nice pair of shoes on, but old clothes, they'd have an idea. This was just before I got the haircut. I got out of that one.

Then I walked into a farmyard. I asked people if they would hide me. Then, when the people saw my feet—how bad they were bleeding at both heels—they said they would help me. I washed my feet and the people were going to let me sleep in the barn. But the farmer said, "No, no." The people let me sleep in their house. But the people would not hide me because there were too many Germans. At that point, I was thinking if I could get to Le Havre, the seaport, I might have a chance to get back to England. The farmers told me I couldn't get into Lahar, because I needed papers. That's when I decided to go south to see if I could get to our lines.

Finally rescued

I walked into one café. I told the woman at the bar, "American, American." She started laughing. So I walked out. Later on, as I was walking down the road, there was a black fellow, a Brazilian, who was stranded there during the war. He could speak just a few words of English. I told him who I was, and where I wanted to go.

He said, "You can't go because the Germans have the ferry boat across the river." He said, "Come with me."

He took me up to a place where there were some Frenchmen who would go back and forth across the river in a rowboat, to take people who wanted to go back and forth. He must have told the men I was an American. I got in the boat and went across. When we got across the river, the fellow in the boat told me to wait in a café. I had a beer. I waited and waited, and wondered, "What the heck is going on?"

I did another screwy thing. I bought a half a dozen French postcards. I was there for a couple hours, and nothing happened, so I decided to hit the road again. As I was walking away from the tavern, all of the sudden I heard terrific explosions, and machinegun fire. So I hit the ditch. Later on, I found out the American Fighters were trying to bomb the ferryboat, which the Germans had confiscated and wouldn't let anyone use but themselves. I got out of the ditch and saw an abandoned farmhouse just off the road. I went in there and sat down. There was no furniture or anything. It was just a dirt floor. I took off my shoes again. A German soldier walked in and said something in French. I said, "Oui," again.

So he walked over to the corner and took a homemade ladder out that was leaning against the wall, then went back out. I thought, "Well, I'd better get out of here." This was the fifth or sixth day, and I was getting pretty depressed. I thought, "When am I going to run into the fabulous underground, the Resistance?" I was just getting ready to leave and a blonde, blue-eyed guy walks in. A Nazi, if I've ever seen one. He said something to me, and I said, "Oui."

I found out later that he had asked me, "What are you doing here?"

And I had said, "Yes."

I told him I was an American. I showed him my dogtags and everything. He was a Frenchmen, but could speak English. He said, "You wait here, and I'll be back." I thought that this was it that he'd be back with reinforcements. He came back with a woman who had a big basket of food. There were hardboiled eggs and bread and sausage. The man, whose name was Charlie, and the woman took me away from the house to a little picnic area. I couldn't eat; my stomach had shrunk so much. The man questioned me over and over again, "Are you sure you're an American?" Their lives were at stake.

The man and woman took me to a farmhouse, where there were some other people. The man spoke to them for a long time, and finally convinced them that I was an American. Charlie was not with the Resistance. I never asked him what he did, or why he wasn't in the service. He was only a couple of years older than I was. He put me in touch with a couple of people he knew in the Resistance.

Those people took over taking care of me in the small village of Quillebeuf, France. I stayed there, going from house to house at different places, where I was being hid. I didn't meet any other Americans. The people had a hard time getting rations. I understood later that people would give up their rations for me. The Resistance would give me candy and tobacco. Well, I didn't smoke, so I traded the cigarettes for candy; all of the French smoked.

I stayed in that village for two and a half months until the Canadian Tank outfit liberated it. I was working with the Resistance then. We only had one old rifle and a pistol. We'd go out at night and tear a couple of telephone lines down. The Germans had confiscated the cows, so we stole two cows from the Germans, not at the same time. We slaughtered them so that we could have meat. We'd go out in the field at night and dig up potatoes for ourselves. I was sleeping at different homes.

The three fellows I was with were in charge of the Resistance in that area, and they were real whackos. In town one night, those guys were bragging about the American they were hiding. I understand the Germans overheard it, or were told by somebody. That's when Charlie came again. He said, "Come with me. You're not staying with those people any more."

He put me in with a couple with a small child. I stayed in that house for three weeks, almost without leaving. We left a couple of times because across the street, behind some buildings, there were caves that were used for air raid shelters. Because the Germans were there, the French were shelled by the Americans. When the Americans were there, the French were shelled by the Germans. The only time I left that house was to go to the air raid shelter. I was close to Rouen. I learned a little French, not much. The only fellow who spoke English was Charlie. I didn't see him all the time; maybe I wouldn't see him for a week or ten days. It was hard to learn much.

The Canadians

A Canadian tank came into town after the shelling. There were a lot of abandoned wagons. The Germans had quite a few horses in the area, and there were a lot of dead horses. I mentioned to one of the Canadians that I was a GI. He said, "Come on, hop on."

The farmer Joseph Szumanski (L), his little boy, and Robert Starzynski are pictured above. The photo was taken in the summer of 1944.

I said, "I have to get my money." I had sixteen English pounds, plus my map and compass; and the underground had taken my dog tags from me. I never met the underground leader of my particular area. Apparently, he didn't want me to meet him, so in case something happened, I wouldn't be able to point him out. The tank officer said, "Okay."

The guy I was staying with didn't want to give me my money back. I told the Canadian, and he said, "Tell him to give you your money back, or I'll take my tank right through his house." It wasn't long after that when another man came with my money and my map. I got my dog tags back and stayed with the couple one more night.

Picked up and back to England

The next day an American major and a sergeant came in a jeep. His job was to catch all the stragglers like me. I ended up in an English camp for a while. Then we drove to Cherbourg to Schaff Headquarters in London, where we were interrogated. I told them everything I've just said.

I went back to Thurleigh for my clothes. I still had civilian clothes. My dog tags were the only ID. I got rid of the lice when I went back to London. The French tried to give me something for them, but I think the lice fed off it. After a while, it really gets to you. We got back to London, and apparently lice are very common. Because when I told them about the lice, I was told, "Oh, the powder is right there." A lot the GI's coming back had the same problem. So I got a nice room in a hotel, and took a hot bath for the first time in a long time. One application of the powder, and the lice were all gone.

When I got back to Thurleigh, I met my pilot and copilot, who had just gotten back. They had evaded also. Four of us had evaded, and five were prisoners of war. I met all of them again. (One of the POW's is at this reunion. In fact, he was at my home two weeks ago.) The fellows couldn't believe I was back. Because for a while I wasn't assigned to a specific crew, I knew quite a few people. I went by one MP. "I thought you were dead," he said. "We heard you were shot down." Our group only had 41 evadees.

Anyway, I found that my clothes had been shipped back to London. So I had to go back to London, but fortunately everything was there. I got my uniform and everything back. I got a thirty day-leave; it took three weeks to get back on an Italian hospital ship.

Home

I went home. My mother kept the original telegram stating that I had been missing in action. I still have it. She was glad to hear I was safe. The strange part about this was that my mother was pretty laid back. She didn't get too excited about too many things. She said she had a dream one night, a picture of me, and I was pointing to the ground. After I got back, she said, "It didn't dawn on me that you were with the underground." She was a very religious Catholic.

From what I could tell from talking to people later on, she was concerned, but somehow she felt everything would be all right. I was pretty laid back too. At nineteen or twenty years old, things like that don't worry you. Maybe if I had been married and had a family it might have made a difference.

After my thirty days leave I went to Miami Beach for two weeks of R and R [rest and recuperation], one in the Atlantic Towers. Then I was grounded for six months for combat fatigue. But that was all horse shit, you know.

After the two weeks was over, the army needed to do something with me, so I went to the reclassification officer. He said, "Oh, you were with the MP's. We'll make you an MP."

"I don't want to be an MP."

"You're a photographer."

I said, "That's all right." So I was assigned to the photo lab in Shreveport, Louisiana. I was finally separated, just before the war ended. I finally had enough points to get out. I was going to be transferred to B-29's, but I said, "Wait a minute, I've got enough flights to go home," so that's when I got discharged.

I was a police officer for forty years in Chicago. I retired in 1985.

Printed with permission of Robert Starzynski and The Oral History Archive of The American Airpower Heritage Museum,

American Airmen In Slovakia

Narrated by Peter Kassak, Slovakia
Edited by Erik Dyreborg

Introduction

This is taken from my manuscript of a book. It describes all crashes of bombers and fighters in the area of Slovakia, during the years 1944-45.

Many airmen's fates are related to the Slovakian people, and country. The stories of two crashes and the Slovakian POW camp, Grinava, are presented. In these stories, as well as in others, men, very young men, were captured, wounded, killed or died…their mothers received telegrams that announced, their beloved son will never return or is missing in action. It was the war! But due to the courage and help of Slovak people, some sons evaded capture and returned home safely.

On March 15, 1939 Hitler and his Wehrmacht took power over the Czech lands and Moravia, and Czechoslovakia were cut into two pieces. Protectorate Böhmen und Mähren (Czech and Moravia) was under the power and rule of the Third Reich. The Slovak Republic, was a new state of Slovak Nation, and rose with Joseph Tiso as a president. But parliament was only a puppet government ruled from outside by the Germans. The Germans let the Polish in the North and the Hungarians in the South occupy a part of Slovakia.

It is natural that the Slovak nation overlooked this dirty game and was not satisfied with such a situation. It seems to them there was nothing to do about it. But there was a deep feeling in the minds and hearts of the Slovak people, to help anyone who was anti Nazi. To help and battle with them in any possible way. These feelings helped also many U.S. airmen if not to evade, then to survive the war.

The Slovak people carried on with their lives until the month of June 1944.

The 15th USAAF started its offensive on the refineries in Vienna area and Blech-hammer, and thus flew over the southwestern part of Slovakia. Naturally, Luft-waffe fighters defended the air space of the Third Reich, in the southwestern part of Slovakia. Many battles in the sky took place over this part of Slovakia. But the wake up to the reality for the Slovaks came on June 16, 1944 when the capital city of Slovakia, Bratislava, was bombed.

The Apollo refinery situated on the bank of river Danube, the winter harbor and a nearby railroad bridge were the targets for that day's mission. Two of four attacking formations were not aiming properly and thus the city was partially destroyed too.

From this time, the 15th USAAF bombers with fighter escort were flying mis-sions, almost daily over Slovakia.

The following are two events with common features.

In both cases it was the oil refinery at Blechhammer—one of the most bombed targets in Europe. The second target is also binding the fates of the airmen men-tioned in these crashes. The Slovak people, who also saved some of them from the POW camp hostilities, helped them.

The "Rita Ann"

On Friday, October 13, 1944, 144-B-17 "Flying Fortresses" and 183-B-24 "Lib-erators" once again attacked the oil refineries at Blechhammer. Both refineries were hit by a total of 665 tons of bombs. The second target that day was reserved for another group of 106 "Fortresses" from 15th USAAF. It was Florisdorf oil refinery, in Austria. Out of the 106 bombers, which took off, only 93 reached the target and dropped 217 tons of bombs.

The 99th Bomb Group flew on this same day, its Mission Number was 227. The planes took off from Tortorella Air Base and headed for their target, which was the Southern oil refinery at Blechhammer. Within this Bomb Group was the 347th Bomb Squadron with a B-17G 42-32033 nicknamed "Rita Ann." The crew:

1/Lt.	Jonathan K. Shafer	P	0-767669	POW
2/Lt.	John W. Brinser	CP	0-710439	POW

2/Lt.	Gordon C. Wheeler	N	0-2058051	POW
2/Lt.	Thomas A. Michaels	B	0-1540385	POW
S/Sgt.	Arnold T. Wilson	E	33694429	POW
S/Sgt.	Guy R. Haines	Asst. E	6931430	POW
S/Sgt.	Theron A. Arnett	R/O	17099131	POW
S/Sgt.	Eugene E. Yeargin	BT	16146859	POW
S/Sgt.	Edwin J. Zavisa	W/G	36863210	POW
S/Sgt.	Joseph F. Williams	T/G	31378889	POW

An engine problem occurred on 1/Lt. Shafer's plane approximately half an hour before reaching the target. The plane was not able to keep up with the formation and was falling behind. But in spite of that, the crew was able to reach the target and drop their bombs.

Upon completion of the bombing of the target, the pilot of the "Rita Ann" called the formation leader and asked for reduction of air speed for the formation. The leader agreed, and air speed was reduced to 135 mph.

Soon they discovered the speed reduction was not sufficient and the damaged plane was loosing altitude as well as falling behind the formation. One engine had been feathered, and another engine, damaged over the target, could not be feathered and later froze. One of the "healthy" planes reduced speed to the speed of "Rita Ann" and accompanied the crippled plane and its crew.

The Shafer crew is pictured above.

The speed was now so low, that the healthy plane was not able to keep its position along with the damaged plane, so they peeled off, and that was the last contact with the plane of 1/Lt. Shafer. That was in the area of Puchov and Zilina, Slovakia. When last seen, the crippled plane had an altitude 10,000 ft.

Eyewitnesses stated for the Missing Air Crew Report, that the damaged plane was probably not able to fly over the mountains and they thought it crashed somewhere in that region. However, this is not correct the pilots of "Rita Ann" made it over the mountains and reached some other mountains in the area of Hronský Benadik, still in Slovakia. The crew was ordered to bail out and the abandoned plane crashed.

Jan Debnar, teacher from Devicany village, Slovakia remembers this day:

"Dense smog was disappearing in the morning as the sun warmed the air of that October day. Suddenly the air was jiggling by the noise made by hundreds of engines of American bombers and fighters. It lasted for only a few moments, and as suddenly they arrived, as suddenly they disappeared.

One hour later, again the noise of bomber engines attracted our attention. But this time it sounded something different. Few hundred meters over small and young trees flew a giant body of a four-engine bomber. Automatically we cringled, but in a second we were again standing directly to see the parachutes, which started to open on the sky.

The crippled bomber made a wide turn over the veldts, and took direction to the Hron valley. Within a few seconds we lost sight of it, but it was clear that it had to crash somewhere in the mountains in that direction.

Samo Slavik, who accompanied a U.S. airman, visited our chamber immediately after the sunset. He said, that he found him in the vineyard near Pukanec village. Samo, his brother, brother-in-law Zeljenka as well as me, were all members of illegal underground. We all knew our task.

On the next day Martin Klucka brought another airman in. He was collecting corn harvest and found him hidden in the field. We all left the chamber and went out to find the rest of the U.S. airmen. First we headed for Zuhracka, where the old forester with some personnel was accommodated. Forester Ciganek immediately recognized the purpose of our visit and said that one airman was hid in the glade in the woods. We ordered them to leave him there, until we returned. Our route then continued to hay-lofts, scattered on the veldts in the woods. We walked across all of them and searched through all the cottages in the woods, but we found no one.

On the route back to the last cottage we found another airman. Then we took out the fourth one, which was hidden at forester Ciganek. He told us that his name was Thomas A. Michaels and what surprised us was, that he had Slovak roots. His grandfather was from Eastern Slovakia. The airman was not only able to speak Slovak, but also sang some songs in the Slovak language.

Tired, we all returned to the chamber we left that morning. Another surprise was waiting there for us. One citizen and two U.S. airmen waited for us. These were Shafer and Arnett. They were "captured" by a Slovak policeman in the cadastre of Village Rybnik—Cajka. The policeman, being a Slovak, he didn't want the Americans to be captured by Germans, so he took the airmen to Devicany village where they met the others.

The first effort of Jozef Pyry was to move the U.S. airmen via Moravske Kostolany, Terany, and Krupina villages to Zvolen—the center of Slovak National Uprising, failed, so I decided to try to realize my plan.

On Monday, October 16, when the dark covered all country and fog and small rain was falling from the sky, I went with all airmen through the fields to Drzenice village. Partisan Pavol Danis also accompanied us. At the village we went into the house of K. Fojtik, where a dinner was already prepared for us.

Then we continued 200 meters along the road to Zemberovce village, hidden in the dark. Mud was all around making it difficult to walk. The airmen were tired; they were not trained for such a walk. Near Dudince, where German soldiers were stationed, we moved far from the road and approached the village from the side of the vineyards.

Then with only two kilometers left, we were on schedule, but these were as hard as the previous ten. Carefully we arrived at the village Terany and walked to the railroad station. There I learned, the trains were not running from this station. The nearest operating station was 5 kilometres away at Hontianske Tesare. We called Tesare station and after many pleases, wishes, abuses and threatens they sent us one locomotive and one car. In one hour we were in Zvolen, where we took the train to Banska Bystrica and at sun rise we were all safe in Banska Bystrica including the U.S. airmen."

Five members of the Shafer's crew were saved, the son of Adam Komaromy led another four airmen via Zemberovce village to Tesare railroad station. From there they reached Banska Bystrica as well.

Only co-pilot John W. Brinser met misfortune by being captured by German soldiers immediately after landing.

Jean Arnett, the widow of Theron Arnett sent her husbands story. From this story we learned some details about the route to Banska Bystrica, as well as the fate of all the surviving airmen.

The following is the military history of Tech. Sgt. Theron H. Arnett from the time he enlisted in the U.S. Army Air Force in Fort Riley, Kansas, on July 21, 1942; however, he was not called into active service until February 3, 1943.

His preflight training was in San Antonio, Texas. Sgt. Arnett was then sent to Muskogee, Oklahoma, for primary flight training.

The Air Force had an abundance of pilots, navigators, etc., at that time, they transferred Arnett's group to other schools. Sgt. Arnett was sent to Sioux Falls, South Dakota, for training as a Radio Operator and then to Yuma, Arizona for aerial gunnery training. Finally he was transferred to Lincoln, Nebraska, where he was assigned as a Radio Operator with a B-17 bomber crew in the 15th Air Force.

This crew flew their B-17 from Nebraska to Scotland where the plane was transferred to the 8th Air Force. Sgt. Arnett and his crew were flown to Casablanca for further training with the 347th Bomb Squadron. Upon completion of this training, they were flown to Foggia, Italy. After they finished two pretraining bombing missions, the crew started their missions out of Foggia, Italy.

On Friday, October 13, 1944, Sgt. Arnett's final bombing mission started as a "standby" when the 15th Air Force's 99th Bomb Group took off from Foggia, to bomb the southern oil refinery in Blechhamer, Germany. Two of the B-17 bombers had trouble and were returning. Sgt. Arnett's plane replaced one of the troubled bombers. His plane had engine problems and they were unable to catch up with the other planes; therefore, they flew over the target almost alone.

Sgt. Arnett's B-17 was severely damaged by flak, destroying three of its four engines; heavily damaged most of the plane's structure, and part of a wing had been torn off. The remaining one good engine could not keep them high enough to clear the mountains near Hronsky Benadik, Czechoslovakia (at present Slovakia), therefore, they were ordered to "bail out" before the plane crashed.

After landing, Sgt. Arnett hid his parachute and started walking toward a road he had seen on his was down after jumping out of the plane. (Sgt. Arnett could speak some German because he had a couple of semesters of German in college before joining the Air Force.) He found a young man shortly after landing and started asking him directions to the nearest town.

While Sgt. Arnett was talking with the young man, his Pilot was watching from the trees to see if the young man was friendly to Americans and to make sure Sgt. Arnett was not in any trouble. During this time Lieutenant Shafer, the pilot of Sgt. Arnett's plane, joined them.

The young man took them to a farmhouse close by and they received kind attention from the farmer and his family. Some of the other crewmen later caught up with Sgt. Arnett and Lt. Shafer.

The Slovakian people were very good to them and at one farm the family had a wine cellar. Sgt. Arnett was not use to drinking and had a little too much to drink. That night the Underground in the area decided to move them to another place. As they started walking along the road to their next destination, they heard a group of Germans coming down the road singing. The leader had the Americans hide beside the road. However, Sgt. Arnett decided to join the Germans in their song. They spent quite some time keeping him quiet. (Lt. Shafer made Sgt. Arnett the group's official translator.)

Due to the efforts of the Underground, they were able to get through the German patrols of the town of Banska Bystrica, Slovakia.

At one time, they hid the group in mailbags. They found themselves in the middle of a rebellion with the town filled with partisans, part of the Czechoslovak Army and Air Force, a Russian Guerilla Unit, an English spy team, and an American OSS Team. It was the intent of the Czech forces to prevent any German Army Units from retreating through the Tatra Mountains.

Sgt. Arnett and his group were taken to the American OSS Office where he was questioned and briefed, and then told to circulate in the town so that everyone could see the presence of American soldiers.

They hoped to be picked up by a plane and return to the 15th Air Force. However, the bad weather prevented planes from landing or restocking. The German troops were pushing towards Banska Bystrica and the German dive-bombers Ju-87s "Stuka" were attacking daily.

After a couple of weeks, Sgt. Arnett's crew was notified that they and the OSS Team should retreat. They used an old bus to travel to Donovaly, which was located higher in the Tatra Mountains.

The weather was bitterly cold and they used slit blankets as ponchos to protect themselves. They moved high into the mountains intending to go into Poland. (There were many people in the rebellion fleeing across the Tatra's who were also not dressed appropriately for the extremely cold weather.) During the night, Sgt. Arnett was breaking a path through the snow and the blinding blizzard when his group discovered their own tracks. They were lost.

They took their packs from the horses and started down a steep mountainside chopping holes for hands and feet. When they were close to the bottom, and they were exhausted from breaking a trail through the snow and ice, they found their feet were partially frozen, so they tried to warm them by putting their feet together.

The next morning, their boots were frozen and their feet were not much better. They tore blanket strips to wrap their feet. When they found a pond, they broke the ice and put their feet in the water trying to thaw them. Almost all of the supplies had been lost so they found some of the horses, which had fallen and were frozen. They "hacked" off enough meat to eat.

Part of their group volunteered to go down to a small village to get food and medicine. (Many people in the group were ill.) The first time Sgt. Arnett's group (eight men) returned with some supplies. On their second trip, on November 7, they walked into a German SS machine gun trap. The OSS Officer, who was with Sgt. Arnett's group, threw a copy of the "Houseboat plan" (a coded radio message used by the OSS), which landed in the mud near Sgt. Arnett. Along with Sgt. Arnett were Shafer, Wilson, Zavisa and Williams who were also captured. The rest of the Shafer's crew was captured four days later.

This small group was then taken to the local SS Headquarters where they were roughly interrogated with fists, gun butts, etc. They were put into a barn, which was used by the SS Headquarters; it was here they saw Jewish boys and old men being beaten. Four of the SS troopers then escorted them to Ruzomberok, where they were placed in the local jail for several days until they could transport and/or walk them to the main Gestapo Prison in Vienna for more interrogation.

When Sgt. Arnett's group arrived, they were thoroughly searched and extensively interrogated. (Sgt. Arnett hid some gold coins in some very doughy bread, which he held in his hands.) They were then placed in cells with 30-40 soldiers and political prisoners from many countries. (Each had a straw mat, one blanket and lots and lots of lice.) They were fed twice a day, once in the morning with the ersatz bread (a lot of sawdust) and in the evening with the watered "soup."

During one of the many interrogation sessions, one of the crewmembers talked too much and told that Sgt. Arnett was a radio operator.

The Gestapo remembered that the coded OSS message was found at his feet; therefore, the Gestapo was sure that he was the OSS man in the group who had the information they wanted.

From that time on, Sgt. Arnett was harshly interrogated (beaten with hose, fists, etc.) and then put in a small cell where he couldn't sit up or lie down all night. They were trying to break his resistance. He almost starved to death.

This treatment went on for about three weeks. During that time, Sgt. Arnett became seriously ill with amebic dysentery and the Gestapo was worried that he would die before he gave them the information they wanted. The German Doctor in charge sent him to the medical room where he was given charcoal and food.

When Sgt. Arnett was strong enough to walk, he was sent back to the interrogation cell. The next time he was interrogated, he was told if he didn't tell them what they wanted to know, they were going to shoot all of the men in his group. Until then, Sgt. Arnett did not know who was still in the prison from his group.

Sgt. Arnett's group was then brought down to the interrogation cells in the basement. They were aware that the SS troops, who had captured them, were there also. They were told that was their last chance and the SS troops would shoot them all if they did not give them the information they wanted. At that point, the OSS Officer stepped forward.

The Gestapo members were very surprised because they were sure that Sgt. Arnett was their man. (He was the only member of their crew who received such severe abusive treatment.)

The group was then cleared by the Gestapo prison officers and transported in an open train car to a regular Prison of War Camp.

"Paulette" & "Ten Man Bak"

Activity of 15th USAAF in December 1944 decreased due to the bad weather condition. Only a few days had operating status. Luftwaffe, defending the air space over the Reich, sent all units to the West to support offensive at Ardennes. Only two units remained in the central Reich to protect Berlin and other cities. These units were JG 300 and JG 301, whose pilots were trained to fly by instruments in bad weather. However, these two units could not defend the entire area, so the Americans thought that the Luftwaffe had no more fighters. December 17, 1944 changed their opinion.

On that day, the 461st Bomb Group dispatched 31 B-24 Liberators, under the lead of Capt. Mixon, to the oil refinery at Odertal (today Zdieszowice, Poland). The bombers took off at 09:12 and made their rendezvous with the 451st Bomb Group and the 484th Bomb Group. The huge formation was formed with the 451st Bomb Group as "Lead and Low," the 484th Bomb Group flying as "Middle" and the 461st Bomb Group flew as "High squadron." Over Yugoslavia fighter cover P-38 Lightnings from the 14th Fighter Group, joined this force. They all continued over Hungary to Bratislava. They reached the air space of Slovakia approximately 30 km East of Bratislava.

Five planes had to return from the mission due to mechanical failures. Only five planes of the 461st Bomb Group reached their target. German defenders shot down some of the other planes from the force. Nine Liberators were shot down and a tenth was written off after ditching on return flight near the island of Vis. Five planes returned to Italy damaged by fighters and FLAK.

Plane B-24J 42-51324 named "Paulette" of 764th Bomb Squadron, 461st Bomb Group, t while en route to the target; the supercharger on engine No. 3 malfunctioned. The pilot tried to call the formation leader and get permission to return to the base, however, he continued in flight to the target. At 11:23 their crippled plane lost the formation, somewhere in the air space over Bratislava.

2/Lt.	Kenneth B. Smith	P	0-825700	POW
2/Lt.	Chester H. Rudel	CP	0-713554	WIA, POW
2/Lt.	Frank V. Hokr	N	0-2064256	POW
2/Lt.	Harry D. Edmiston	B	0-2061225	POW
Cpl.	Charles F. Foss	R/W	31380952	WIA, POW
Cpl.	Homer E. Hynbaugh	L/W	16073922	POW
Cpl.	Roland W. Morin	B/T	20153518	KIA
Cpl.	Robert T. Trumpy	U/T	16186093	WIA, POW
S/Sgt.	Urbain H. Granger	T/G	36397799	POW
Cpl.	Erwin A. Burkhardt	N/G	33614032	EVADED

The Smith crew is pictured above.

The pilot 2/Lt. Kenneth B. Smith saw, he was unable to remain in formation, he decided to turn the plane to the East, and try to make a landing at the friendly occupied area there. Approximately 20 minutes later, at 11:50 German fighters attacked the formation. One of the first victims of the FW-190 pilots was the lonely plane "Ten Man Back."

Ken Smith remembers that day as follows:

"We ate breakfast at 0430 and one hour later we met in briefing room to hear instructions for our bombing mission. I was told about the substitution in my crew. Lt. Chojnowski, our co-pilot was not briefed to fly with us and his place next to me had to be filled by 2/Lt. Chester "Chet" Rudel.

In the air, enemy fighters bounced us. ME-109s and FW-190s were all around us. I remember it all like in a slow motion movie. Homer Hynbaugh called me on intercom, saying our left wing was on fire. I looked over my shoulder and checked the truth of this bad message. Engine No.2 was covered in flames. I switched off the fuel supply for this engine, but nothing changed and the fire continued. At that time also No.3 engine completely malfunctioned. I checked the damage in the other part of the plane via intercom. The tail turret was shot away during the attack of German fighters. Also the ball turret was damaged and was not operating properly. Guns were jammed. The tail gunner, Granger, was OK, but Morin, our ball turret gunner was badly wounded.

I tried to drop our bombs, but I couldn't open the bomb bay doors. The hydraulic system was broken and the manual opening was seized. I gave the order to abandon the plane. All, except Morin, bailed out safely.

I switched on the autopilot and went to jump out via the back escape exit. The catwalk over bomb bay was damaged and I couldn't get to the back of the plane.

At that time the left wing broke off the bomber. You almost cannot imagine what it did to the plane. It was said that no one could leave Liberator from front board. I did... The plane turned and began spinning, and I do not know which way I left the plane. Suddenly I was falling in the air. I was falling for a long time and waited to open the parachute at the minimum height over the ground. I landed safely.

I was captured immediately after landing. Germans moved me to the SS base at Trencin, Slovakia. I had a few teeth out and a broken jaw after the interrogation by fists and sticks. Then I was transported to the Stalag Luft I POW camp, where I remained until April 1945."

The uncontrolled bomber crashed at 11:50 in the vicinity of village Omsenie at Slovakia in the area called Baracka. Today, this place belongs to the town Trencianske Teplice. 20mm bullets from German fighters hit Morin in the chest and stomach. Charlie Foss moved him to the radio compartment and Sgt. Granger tried to give him first aid there, but it was too late. To ease his pains, Granger gave him shot of morphine.

His body touched the ground together with the wreck of the plane, so his body was strongly burned. Germans took his body out of the plane and tried to put it into the coffin. But the one they brought was too small and Morin's body could not be put inside. So they cut off both of his hands etc. and in pieces they placed his body inside the coffin. Two days later, burial took place at the local cemetery in Trencin. After the war, on June 13, 1945 his remains were exhumed and transported to La Fontain in France where they were put to a last rest at the American military cemetery.

In the closest span of the crash site there is a small memorial of the dead ball turret gunner Cpl. Roland W. Morin.

And what happened to the others? Bombardier 2/Lt. Harry D. Edminston, tail gunner S/Sgt. Urban H. Granger, left waist gunner Cpl. Homer E. Hynbaugh and navigator 2/Lt. Frank V. Hokr were all captured together with their pilot. They were all moved to the barracks at Trencin and after interrogation all ended up in Stalag Luft I. However, the officers were separated from the rest of the crew.

Cpl. Robert T. Trumpy, top turret gunner was wounded and transported to the hospital at Trencin:

"The plane we were assigned to was one that had a record of problems. As a result, we fell behind the formation. FLAK picked us up and we lost one engine. German fighters attacked us and we lost another engine, and a fire started behind our left inboard engine. Our inter-com was also shot out, so I left my top turret position and notified the pilot of the fire behind our number two engine.

Knowing the fire would reach our gas tanks, located in the wings just behind the engines, we could have ended up as one giant explosion, and none of us would have survived. I jumped back into my turret and continued firing. As I observed the fire behind number two engine, it appeared to be creeping forward toward the gas tanks I jumped down again and told the pilot "We're on fire and we have to get out of here". He motioned for me to get out and rang the bell to "ABANDON PLANE."

I clipped on my parachute and went together with the engineer to the bomb bay, which we planned to use as an escape hatch. The bomb bay doors would not open, as the hydraulic system was no longer working. The engineer tried to crank the bomb bay doors open manually, but the doors were stuck shut and wouldn't move.

I knew we did not have a lot of time so I jumped on the doors and tried to kick them off, thus giving us an escape route. I did not succeed in kicking off the doors but apparently loosened them enough so that the engineer was able to open the doors manually with the hand crank.

Normally the engineer would operate the top turret and the armor gunner (me) would man one of the waist gun positions. However the engineer may have been slightly claustrophobic and suggested we trade position, so that's why I happened to be in the top turret.

The radio operator took bullets or flak fragments in his right arm below the elbow, and an amputation of the lower arm took place after his return to the States. The co-pilot was all right until his chute got caught in a tree and he fell approximately twenty feet, and broke his back. He remained paralyzed from the waist down for the rest of his life, but after the war returned to college and completed his degree in geology and ultimately retired from Standard oil of California. He died in his mid sixties.

After the Germans had captured me, I was carried by the soldiers' to a truck and transported to the place, where the pilot, navigator, bombardier and engineer were being held.

While carrying me, they carried me near where our plane had crashed. They said to me that one man was still in the plane. I did not learn that it was the ball-gunner until later.

Since my ankle was shattered I was in great pain, so in the morning the Germans took me to the State hospital in Trencin, where I remained for approximately three weeks. I was put in a room with our co-pilot. The radio operator was also in the hospital room. I remember the Slovak people were very friendly, as several came by to visit the American flyers. Since it was near Christmas, we even received gifts of wine and sweets from the local population."

"From the hospital, I was sent to the Air Force interrogation center in Germany. Next I was sent to a POW hospital in Memmingen, Germany. Everyone there had been wounded or injured in some way. The medical staff was made-up of captured allied doctors. Some were Americans and some were British. I was next sent to a similar hospital at Obermansfeld, Germany. I then returned to Memmingen. I don't remember how long I stayed at each hospital.

My first prisoner of war camp was at Nuremberg, Germany. I don't remember how long I was there. Just before our troops liberated the camp, we were sent to Stalag VII A at Moosburg, Germany.

On April 29, 1945, Patton's Third Army overran the German troops around Moos-burg and we were liberated."

In the hospital at Trencin, M.D. Czongradi and M.D. Elias were taking care of the airmen and tried to protect them against Einsatzkommando 13, which had HQ in the town.

A Slovak, Jozef Poruban, accompanied the flyers in the room and acted as an interpreter for them. Also two catholic nuns—Zofia from Piestany and Filipa Krchlikova, from Banovce and Bebravou—took care of the flyers.

Charles Foss, another wounded crewmember remembers his first and last action during WWII:

"On December 17, 1944 we took off at dawn on our first mission from our base in Italy. Our target was Odertal, Gemany. It seemed as if it took forever to get off the runway and into the air that day.

At some point during the flight we fell out of formation due to engine trouble.

While we were throwing out the ribbons of metal that were used to confuse the ground artillery I saw the tail of a German fighter plane in the overcast below us. I got on the intercom to tell the others we had company.

Homer Hymbaugh, our flight engineer, was assigned to the left waist gun but he was on the flight deck at that time because of the engine problem.

My position was right waist gun. Rollie Morin was assigned to the lower ball turret. We came under fire immediately so Rollie and I grabbed the nearest guns. He took the right waist gun and I took the left.

I'm not sure how many fighters attacked us. When I looked over my shoulder through the right waist window where Rollie was I saw a fighter. He was making a clockwise pass around our plane. I picked him up when he banked and slid past our tail and fired at him until he was out of sight. It was my first time in combat, and I was concerned about firing the gun. I was aware that you had to fire intermittent bursts or the gun could overheat.

After the second or third pass while I was waiting for the plane to come into my range, Rollie tapped me on the shoulder. I turned around and he was pointing to his leg. All I could see was blood and ragged cloth. He had a terrible wound. I motioned for him to go back to the camera hatch because that was where we would have to bail out.

I don't remember getting hit or falling. I suppose I had a near death experience. My whole life did not flash before me but I was thinking I was back in Maine outside our little house in the warm spring sun sitting on a pile of fir boughs. I could even smell the aroma of the fir. When I regained consciousness I was under the right waist gun.

My right arm had been shot in at least two places and was completely limp. I could see that the plane was full of holes. I saw Grainger, the tail gunner, who had come out of his turret. I motioned to him. I saw him grab his D ring and go directly to the camera hatch and bail out.

Somehow I got on my feet and headed for the camera hatch. I felt a severe pain in my midsection that made it impossible for me to stand up straight. My first thought was that I had been shot too. I started to feel around my abdomen and discovered there were no holes or blood. This gave me new hope and I knew I had to try hard to get out.

I saw Rollie and realized he had gone to the hatch and pulled the door open, which made it easier for Grainger and I to bail out. But Rollie hadn't jumped. He was just lying there with his good leg outside the hatch and his wounded leg inside. He was motionless, his eyes were nearly closed and I believe he was dead.

I looked to the front of the plane and could see the sun shining on the flight deck. Through the waist gun windows I saw fire on both wings, like a rainbow of yellow, reds and blues. I stared at the fire, thinking how beautiful it was. I realized that Rollie and I were alone.

I had lost a lot of blood by that time. I realized that I could very likely die here in the plane. For some time I just stood near the hatch.

I remember kneeling down beside the hatch door and wondering what I was going to do. The parachute D-ring was on the right side. So many things went through my mind. How was I going to open the chute? Did I have enough strength in my left hand to pull or push the D—ring? What if the chute didn't open? What if the fire on the wings caught the chute? What if I came down over water?

I could not jump out without knowing how I would open the chute. I knew you should never, ever open your chute in the plane but I had no other choice. I opened the fasteners on one end of the chute and it popped out a little. I did the same on the other end, except this time the chute popped out a little more than I had expected. I grabbed it with my left arm and pulled it close to my chest. I crouched at the hatch door, looked down at the clouds below and at Rollie, and then I went out through the hatch like a shot.

After leaving the plane my head snapped back suddenly. I looked up and saw the chute open. It was ragged but it had opened completely and it wasn't on fire.

It was my first time in a parachute, and it was so still and silent inside the cloud that I began to wonder if I was already dead.

Just before I dropped through the cloud I looked across the top of the clouds and saw the tip of the right wing of the plane. It was at a sharp angle, and I realized that I had probably been thrown out of the plane just as I was ready to jump.

My other fear was that I had bailed out over water. I had a Mae West on and when I was in the clouds I checked to see how I could inflate it in case it was needed. However, when I left the clouds I could see that I was over land. There were fields and mountains below me.

I looked for the plane to see where it was going down for just a moment I spotted it flying low in front of a green growth below the mountaintop.

As I got closer to the ground I could see people walking around. They were German soldiers. I could see the top of the trees coming towards me fast and I didn't know what to expect next.

When I reached the trees I crossed my legs and closed my eyes. I hit the ground hard. I landed right on my backside; my head went down between my legs. Luckily I reached the ground without getting tangled in a tree.

I knew I had a .45 with me but I couldn't find it. It was just as well; it probably would have caused me more trouble. I wasn't there too long, perhaps five minutes, before I heard the German soldiers coming. I could see one in front of me and could hear others behind me and at my side. One soldier yelled out "Stick 'em up!," like an actor in a Western movie. I raised my good arm.

The soldiers stood me up and started to walk me out. We had to go down a mountain; there was a soldier on each side of me holding me up and one behind me. I was starting to feel faint from blood loss and began to black out. I needed to put my head down to avoid passing out, but the soldiers pushed me ahead. Eventually I dragged my feet, which they didn't like very much, but it made them realize I couldn't go much further on my own. They dragged me head first to the bottom of the hill.

When we reached the bottom of the hill, I could see the German barracks. The soldiers walked me into the barracks and sat me on one of the beds. They went through my pockets and took the one cigarette I had left.

Two German officers entered the room and started to question me, asking the usual questions.

Two soldiers walked me out through the door and put me down on the end of a stack of logs. I sat there for a while and could hear the soldiers yelling out commands. I saw six or seven of them running out of the barracks with their rifles. I thought they were going to shoot me, so I closed my eyes and said a prayer. Then I heard another command and they marched off. I was so relieved, but still didn't know what they planned to do with me.

A little while later an ambulance arrived. I climbed in the back and lay down on the stretcher. I started to tighten up all over and shake. I knew it was shock from the blood loss. When we arrived at the hospital, they took me out of the ambulance and left me in the front hall of the hospital on the stretcher.

At the hospital the doctors started to cut off my clothing, and that's all I remember until the next day. When I opened my eyes I was looking at myself. There was a large mirror beside the bed, and I could see a patient in traction beside me. The patient was Chet, our co-pilot. He was not injured during the attack, but his chute got hung up in a tree when he landed, and when he tried to free himself he fell quite a distance and broke his spine. He was paralyzed from the waist down.

Chet and I were transferred to a room with three beds. There was a Slovak soldier in the bed near the window, I was in the middle and Chet was in the bed near the door. The Slovak soldier had been wounded in combat, but was expected to recover fully. He had been hit with one bullet that surely would have been fatal, but his belt buckle had miraculously deflected it.

At the hospital in Trencin my doctor's name was Dr. Czongradi. He was a slightly built man who was always in motion. He had a lot on his mind. He had an operating assistant named Dr. Elias, who was the only one on the hospital staff who spoke English. One day Dr. Elias told me, "Charles, the next time you're in the operating room I won't be here. These are all fine people taking care of you and you'll be all right." I never saw him again.

I was in the operating room several times on one occasion the doctor was picking pieces of bone out of my arm. Every so often he would show me what he was taking out to let me know he was trying to help me. My arm had become infected and it needed to be cleaned often. One time in the operating room, I woke up and found myself alone. I got off the table and crawled up the stairs to the second floor on my hands and knees. I was ready to pass out and I could not see. I crawled to the door of our room and called to Chet. He asked me what I was doing. I told him "I can't see and I want to get back in bed. "He said, "You're almost there, keep coming." I went toward his voice and found the bed.

The sisters who cared for us were wonderful people who were always very cheerful. Towards the end of my stay at the hospital I became very ill and had a high fever. I recall the nurses soaking a sheet in cold water and wrapping it around my chest. I believe I had pneumonia.

Very early one morning in April a ward attendant brought my flying suit and boots to me and helped me get dressed. Shortly after that two German soldiers came into our room. I was pretty upset because I didn't want to leave the hospital and I didn't want to say goodbye to Chet. We shook hands and I left.

The sisters gave me a box for my trip that contained a big roll of cigarettes, some sandwiches, a cup and a bottle of medicine. They showed me how much medicine I should take at one time for the pain, and told me that there should be enough to last until I reached my destination. I didn't know where they were taking me except that it was somewhere in Germany.

We went down to the first floor and out the door. The soldiers put me in an army vehicle and took me to the railroad station. They took me out of the vehicle and motioned for me to follow them. They both walked in front of me. The day before I had been in the operating room, and I was still very weak and frequently blacked out. I could feel myself starting to fall so I leaned up against a column and let myself slide to the platform. I didn't say anything to the soldiers, I figured they would find me soon enough. When they discovered I was missing they started shouting. They retraced their steps, found me, and got me on my feet again.

When we got to the boxcar they rolled the door open, shoved me just inside of the door to the right and closed the door.

It was dark in there. I could hear lots of moaning from people in pain, and I realized I was in a car full of wounded soldiers. I was leaning up against someone. He never moved, and I stayed exactly where they put me. I realized as the night went on that the soldier I was leaning against had died.

The train kept moving, and when we stopped I was taken off the train, walked across the rail yard and put into another boxcar. There was no one else in this car. The two

German soldiers who walked me to the car took me to the front and showed me where they had strewn some straw for me to sleep on. The two soldiers took out a bottle of Schnapps. They took the top off the bottle and gave me the first drink. It was a gesture I will always remember. After that drink I had a sip of the medicine from the box and went fast asleep. The next thing I knew I was transferred to a hospital car with lots of wounded soldiers. The more seriously injured soldiers were on bunks. I was placed on the floor in a stretcher-like bed between two of the bunks.

An older German, perhaps in his 60s, came into the car. He told us he was in charge of our hospital car, and he would wait on us and bring us food. He passed out medication to the soldiers who were in pain, and then he left and locked the door.

One time when the train stopped I could see a chance to get some water. I don't know what possessed me, but I wanted so badly to wash my cup and get some fresh water I risked missing the train to get it. I got the water but on my way back, the train started to leave. I missed my car but managed to hop on the back of the very last car. There were two armed German soldiers standing at the back of the train. For a long time I stood there with my cup of water. When the train made its next stop I got off and went back to the hospital car.

During that trip I remember the train stopping in the night at a train station, and hearing announcements in German over a loudspeaker. When the train was going I could hear the click-clack of the wheels on the tracks. I can still hear that sound to this day.

There were soldiers from all over Europe on the train. There was a Romanian soldier who helped me cut my bread. There was a French soldier next to me and an English soldier who had such a thick Cockney accent I hardly understood a word he said except 'sweets.'

The French soldier was in the bunk on my right. One day after we were given our bread, he tapped me on the shoulder and offered me some of his. I refused and told him I wouldn't take it because he needed to eat it to gain strength. He shook his head no. I knew what he meant although I couldn't understand his words. He knew he didn't have very long to live. He died that same day.

We were covered with lice. Each morning when I woke up I could hear the other soldiers popping lice between their fingernails. The soldiers who slept on the floor would get up and check to see who had died during the night. The Germans came in and took the dead out wrapped in their blankets. A few minutes later they returned with the blanket. We weren't sure what had happened to the bodies. Afterwards there was usually a discussion about who would get the vacant bunk.

I'm not sure how many days we were on the train, but I do know we were there on April 12, 1945 because that was the day President Roosevelt died. When the train stopped that day the old German came to our car and asked me to follow him. We went to his compartment where he told me Roosevelt had died and asked me questions about the President. He also wanted to know who Truman was. I told him I didn't know anything about Truman. The old German washed my cup for me and helped me out the door again. I went back to my car and the train took off.

I remember getting off the train at a big station. We were near the front. I learned later that the town was called Hohnstein. There was an American fighter plane-flying overhead strafing the rail yards. I think it was a P-47 Thunderbolt. I looked around the station for a big pillar to hide behind.

Next we were loaded onto a truck that took us to the hospital section of Stalag 4. I was quarantined and was not allowed to stay with the others that night. I had had good care while at the Trencin hospital. Except for the lice, I wasn't too dirty.

An English soldier took me to another building and put me in a high bunk with slats on the sides. He said he would get me in the morning. I hadn't had anything to eat, but I wasn't very hungry, anyway. This barrack had dirt floors and one little light that you could follow to the bathroom outside. I could feel the lice crawling all over me. They seemed to be as big as flies.

The next morning I was transferred to the second floor of the hospital building. I had a cot in the middle of the floor. They gave me bread with some broth but I couldn't eat that much.

One day I heard a burst of machine gun fire. I went back to my cot, where I found everyone leaving. One of the patients told me, "You'd better come with us." Everyone was going to the cellar of the hospital because they were expecting us to be overrun by the front. We knew it was close because the US Army had dug in that evening a short distance away. I lay down on my cot and I didn't want to move because I was so weak and tired. I stayed on the second floor while everyone else left. A few minutes later I heard shooting and breaking window glass. That shot convinced me to go to the cellar. I remember crawling in the darkness over the other soldiers to find a place to sit.

Later that day we left the cellar. We could see the US Army scout jeep coming down the narrow road followed by our tanks. The tanks rolled in and I saw US soldiers disarming the Germans. I knew then that it was only a matter of time before I could go home.

I was taken by ambulance to a US Army field hospital somewhere in Germany. I remember looking at the cot above me in the ambulance and seeing US ARMY printed on it. When I saw it I felt another prayer had been answered. The trip from Hohnstein to the field hospital was very uncomfortable because of the pain in my arm. I was the only patient in the ambulance. I suspect I was alone because the wound to my arm had developed a very bad odor.

From the field hospital I was flown to Reims, France where I stayed until there was a flight out to London. In London they went through the procedure to find out if I was really Charles Foss. I did not have my dog tags or any form of identification. When they were satisfied I finally got de-loused.

In London I was given penicillin and a blood transfusion. I remember looking at myself in a mirror after the transfusion and seeing pink in my cheeks for the first time in months. I weighed 70 pounds. From London I was sent to a hospital in Glasgow, Scotland where I received the Purple Heart. There was a ceremony, and some Scottish children in kilts gave me a turtle with my name painted on its underside. Shortly after, I was taken to the airport in Glasgow where I boarded a military plane and I was finally on my way home."

Last member of the crew, nose gunner Cpl. Edwin A. Burkhard, who evaded:

"I was falling and then pulled the ring which opened my parachute. Immediately after touching ground I packed my parachute and dig a hole in the snow, put the parachute in it and buried it with snow. It was not a problem, because there was 20 cm of snow everywhere.

I decided to walk to the near forest. At sunset I dug a small hole in the ground and prepared myself for some rest. Suddenly I heard steps and saw a man in a uniform. He passed near me only few centimeters but didn't see me, but he had to hear my heart, it was beating like crazy.

The next morning I continued my walk. By using a compass I tried to walk to the South to Italy. On the third day I observed a nice deer in the woods. While looking on it, three men came from behind. They shouted at me something. Two of them held automatic guns so escape was not possible even to think of. Then they came to me and one searched me. He noted my star on my uniform. All started to laugh and shout "Ruski, Ruski!" and I replied "American, American!" Then they wanted me to go with them.

After a short walk we entered small settlement where I was given some bread and milk. After this refreshment they took me to one Jewish man, who spoke English. He explained me the situation. My comrades were partisans and they wanted me to go with them. Also he said that we are near Trencin in Slovakia.

Next day in the morning one man appeared, said something to my three partisans and motioned me to go with him. We walked through mountains in snow. I was completely exhausted, when we reached the partisan camp at Zavada village. Here I met two Canadian flyers, who were shot down in their Mosquito near Piestany. (October 17, 1944, DH-89 Mosquito FB Mk.VI, 418th squadron RAF, crashed near the village Brunovce, narrators note). Their names were F/Lt. Stuart N. May and F/O Jack D. Ritch. Finally I had someone, with whom I was able to speak English. Both Canadians told me that the life conditions in the camp are bad and hard. But better than POW camp"

Memories of Mr. Burkhard are very detailed, so I deleted them a little, and mentioned the major facts only. On January 13, 1945 they joined a new group of partisans in Klak area. In February all three airmen again moved to another group, which operated at Valaska Bela. After a few weeks this group moved again.

It was in early march 1945, they all tried to cross the front line. This was done successfully on March 19, 1945 near Lucenec. The Canadians and the American were separated. Burkhard's way led him via Hungary, Romania to the Russian town of Odessa. There he boarded a ship to Istanbul on May 20, 1945. Then to Algeria and finally on board a B-17 to Bari in Italy.

After 56 years, five of the crew of Ken Smith closed the circle of their fate. They visited Slovakia again in August 22-26, 2000. In Trencianske Teplice, pilot Ken Smith, Bob Trumpy, Frank Hokr, Charlie Foss and Ed Burkhard with their family members. Their first steps led them to the crash site and to the memorial of Roland Morin. This time was full of emotions, stories, and friendship. It was very nice and for the Americans when they met with one of the nurses, which was totally unexpected. The nurse had taken care of them in the hospital at Trencin.

Also present was the interpreter Mr. Poruban. Tears were present in everybody's eyes.

During this small reunion also a misunderstanding of the name of the plane was cleared. The plane took the nickname "Paulette", because it was the name of Chief mechanic Bowers wife. The plane flew many successful mission. But Ken Smith's crew was a new one and they decided to rename the plane "Ten Man Bak". They had no time to repaint it, so it had to carry name and picture of ten men sitting on a bomb. Optimism of this plane's name they didn't realize…

Printed with permission of Peter Kassak.

So We Walked And Walked And Walked Some More

Narrated by P. Joseph DeLio, B-17 Radio Operator
8th Air Force, 95th Bomb Group, 334th Bomb Squadron,
Edited by Erik Dyreborg

Enlisting and training

I'll begin with Pearl Harbor. I remember Pearl Harbor day, because I was working in the Douglas Aircraft plant in Santa Monica, CA. Some of my friends had gone with me to Long Beach to look at the B-19, the forerunner of the B-29. When we got home, Bud Cole's grandfather met us at the door and told us, "I want you to listen to something." We went on into the house and heard the news about Pearl Harbor. We could hardly believe what had happened.

My friends and I decided right away we wanted to go into the service; we were all eighteen and nineteen year-olds. We signed up for the Army Air Corps and took all of the exams. Going into the Air Corps seemed like the thing to do. Our country had been attacked, and we felt we should do something about it.

In those days, there was no such thing as protesting; you didn't protest against what your country was involved in. We didn't even think about such a thing. We wanted to go take care of the guys who had attacked our country.

I went to school at Santa Monica Junior College and took math and other things I thought would help me become a pilot. When we'd (by we, I mean my friends and me) finished up with school, we took and passed the examination for pilot training, and were put in the reserve.

Cpl. P. Joseph DeLio, 1942 is pictured above.

I was in the reserve until January 23, 1943, when I went home to Fort Lupton, Colorado. I came back to my folks, was inducted into the service the last of January 1943, and shipped to Randolph Field, Texas, for preflight pilot training. I had no basic training; I received officer's training at Randolph.

I went through preflight training for eighteen weeks, or something like that, then on to the next phase of pilot training at Muskogee, Oklahoma for about eight weeks. I flew PT-19s, primary trainers. Ninety-three percent of class 43-K, my class, the last class scheduled to graduate in 1943, were washed out; I was one of those. Pilot training was geared to plane production. In other words, there were too many pilots. Instead of cutting back the pilot training program, the air corps just washed the trainees out and used them for aircrew.

From Muskogee, I was sent to Shepard Field, Texas, for basic training all over again—real basic training. From Texas, I went to Sioux Falls, South Dakota, for six months of radio school.

In radio school, we learned code and voice, radio mechanics, how to operate radio equipment, direction-finding equipment—those kinds of things. It was easy for me. School was always easy for me; I didn't have any trouble with radio school.

After we graduated from radio school—it was in the winter—we went to Yuma, Arizona, to gunnery school. That lasted January, February, and part of March.

First we went to the skeet range, where we learned to lead a bird, a clay pigeon, using shotguns. In the second phase of that training, we got aboard trucks that drove around in a big circle past the skeet towers, and shot clay pigeons. It was easy; it was fun. I'd done a lot of hunting when I was a kid. Gunnery school was no problem.

Next we went to .50-cal. Machine guns. We had to learn how to take those things apart and put them back together while blindfolded. That training lasted into March.

From Yuma, we went to Hill Field at Salt Lake City, Utah. That was where I met my crewmembers. The pilot was Bert Powell; the ball gunner was Curly Covel; the waist gunner was Hank Schneider (from Pennsylvania); the tail gunner was Willy—I can't remember his last name; the upper turret gunner and engineer was Bunny Steffans (from Greeley, Colorado—his name was Eldred, but we called him Bunny); my nickname was Sparks, from electric sparks and all that kind of stuff; Frank Conners was the co-pilot; Frank Whalen was the bombardier; the navigator was Donald Overdorf.

After the crew had gathered together in Salt Lake City, we were shipped by train to Rapid City, South Dakota, for transition training. The train was just a regular troop train.

Flying overseas

At Rapid City, the crew lived together; the officers lived in one place, the enlisted men in another. We trained for three months, almost until the end of June, 1944. Then, when we were ready to go overseas, we were flown down to Carney, Nebraska, where we picked up a brand new B-17. In early July, we flew overseas. We went from Carney, Nebraska to Bangor, Maine; to Gander, Newfoundland; then across the Atlantic to Prestwick Isle, Scotland. That trip was rather an exciting experience.

When we got to Prestwick, the entire British Isles were socked in with 10,000 feet of overcast. We had to contact the tower—there were sixty of us in our flight—and the tower had to talk us down. My pilot wasn't able to modulate his set, so I had to take the instructions from the tower on my radio, then tell the pilot over the intercom the maneuvers he had to perform to get us down. This all took quite a while. When we finally got down through the overcast—we broke out at 1,500 feet—I went up to talk to the pilot. I'll never forget it. This guy was sitting in a pool of sweat; it was dripping off the end of his nose, off his ears, and off his chin. He was dripping wet. He was the pilot, but he wasn't really in control because he had to take instructions and hope they were right. As it was, it worked out.

I'll never forget going down through that overcast. I had to sit by my radio while all the other crewmembers sat back by the door with their parachutes on, waiting to see what was going to happen. If we hit another plane, they were all going to bail out. I remember saying, "what am I going to do if we get hit?" I'd never have gotten out of that plane.

Anyway, we landed on the runway at Prestwick. We had to relinquish our new airplane. We'd flown a reserve plane over; it was not our airplane.

The 95th Bomb Group and the missions

We were assigned to the 95th Bombardment Group of the 13th Combat Wing of the 8th Air Force, stationed at Corham AFB, between Eye and Dyss (north of London about eighty or ninety miles, and below the Wash). This was in eastern England.

We weren't scared; we didn't think much about combat. We were young, and when you're young, you don't think much about those kinds of things. You're ready to go.

We had to go through about a month of combat training after we got to England. We'd take off, form up and fly around, do simulated runs on targets, and things like that. We had to train with the group. A green crew that hadn't gone through the procedures would not be put into combat. Ordinarily, when you flew, you had to climb and form up the formation—that might take an hour. You had to be in formation before you could do anything else, before you could take off on the combat mission. This sort of thing was all part of that training.

Our first mission was to Munich in either late July or early August, a one thousand plane raid. We were the last plane of the last group on the way home. That meant that I, as the radio operator, was the one who monitored the distress calls and all of that business. But I didn't pick up any. If planes were shot down, and if they could, they'd send out distress calls, If we saw somebody down in the water, we'd radio ahead that they were down.

You have to remember that we were young kids; this was kind of a lark. We didn't really realize what this was all about until we got to Munich—then we found out. The Germans shot down forty of our planes that day. It's strange how airplanes at twenty-five or thirty thousand feet look when they explode. At that altitude, a plane doesn't explode like a firecracker, it explodes in slow motion; it just comes apart slowly. I counted five planes going down at one time over Munich. The antiaircraft fire was really bad. We didn't encounter any German fighters, because at that stage of the war, German fighters were pretty scarce and we had P-51 Mustang escorts. To me, the P-51s were the best escorts. Whenever we had those planes with us, German fighters wouldn't bother us.

The accuracy of German flak was incredible. Later on the shoot-down day, flak got more planes than it did this day over Munich. It was just incredible how many planes were knocked down.

When you have 1,000 planes flying at 180 miles-an-hour, they're like sitting ducks. It's not like modern days when planes travel two or three times the speed of sound. At such high speeds, it's hard to make contact with antiaircraft fire. But in those days, it was different. Planes would seem to drone on forever over a target; your chances weren't very good.

The antiaircraft fire over Munich was really bad. I finally realized, "Jeez, they are shooting at us." Then I really got scared. That was the first time I was really scared. I thought we were going to get it like the rest of those guys.

When we got back to base, we got a debriefing. In the debriefing, the interrogating personnel tried to find out everything that had happened. The reason they did was that it our commanders could figure out a way to prevent all the aircraft losses, they would.

The ceiling on a B-17 was about 24,000 feet. Our pilot sometimes took us up to 26-28,000, but when you get those old planes up that high, they sort of just wallow along like a stuffed duck. They're slow and weave around; they don't hold a course very good. We flew so high in an attempt to avoid the antiaircraft fire. But that was almost impossible; the Germans had it perfected to the point where they were very effective. I don't know if their guns were radar controlled or not.

We had a radar ship with us, the Mickey Ship. That was the plane that found the target through the clouds and all that. I'm sure the Germans also had radar. Whatever it was they had, it worked very well.

We really got an initiation on that Munich mission. After that, we did several missions, then were called in and told we had two days to get ready for a big mission.

We continued to train. Then one day we were called in for a briefing and told we were going to Russia on a shuttle bombing. This was the second shuttle bomb mission; there had been one previously. The shuttle bombs in those days would go from England in Kharkov or Poltava, Russia, fly over Poland or Czechoslovakia to bomb a target, and return to Russia. Then the planes would fly to Italy, bombing targets on the way. From Italy, they'd fly back to England. One of those trips took ten days.

On the shuttle bomb we went on, we flew aboard Old Mirandy, a wreck with about a hundred missions on it. We were on the way to Russia, getting ready to bomb the rocket manufacturing installations in Germany, when the bomb bay doors stuck open. Some of the crew members said, "Hey, head for Sweden." They were joking like that. We finally had to crank the bomb bay doors closed by hand.

Over east Prussia, we were attacked by FW-190s, the prime German fighters at that time. They passed through the formation head-on. We didn't get a chance to shoot because they were too quick, but our escorts, P-38s, I think, shot a couple of them down after they got out of our formation.

After we got to the Russian border, we flew about treetop level—a little better than that, actually—down to Poltava, where we landed. Poltava is not far from Krakov, in the Russian Ukraine. At Poltava, there were about sixty American crew chiefs on lend-lease to the Russians. Each American had a couple of Russians to help him. One of those guys and his two helpers were assigned to our plane. They worked on our bomb bay doors, I think.

While at Poltava, we stayed in tents. It was strange, because we were told not to go into town alone. We were all excited about going to town, but even in those days, the Russians didn't trust us. We had to go into town four and six at a time. Nobody went alone, because if he did, the Russians would beat him up, shoot him, whatever. Poltava had a population of about 10,000. There was a town square. I didn't even go in. I didn't care about going in there.

We got our plane ready to go. We were supposed to go bomb someplace in Poland. We took off, but one of our engines wouldn't work, so we had to abort the mission. Our plane turned back to Poltava, and we missed that mission.

We were at Poltava for three or four more days, and got ready to go again. We were to bomb the Ploesti oil fields—which we did. I can't remember whether we bombed the oil fields or the airfields in the oil fields.

The Ploesti oil fields had been bombed earlier, especially by the B-24s stationed in North Africa. Ploesti was the German lifeline, and we had to keep that place shut down or damaged as much as possible.

So leaving Poltava that day, everything was working fine. We were headed toward Italy. On the way, over Rumania, I guess, our Mickey Ship, the plane that was monitoring the German frequencies, picked up some conversation. The Germans told their fighter pilots that if we had P-51 escorts, they were not to bother us, because it was too dangerous to attack us. We had P-51s; they had flown with us all the way from England.

We were able to drop our bombs where we were supposed to; it was pretty much a milk run. It wasn't that bad. We landed at the airfield at Foggia, Italy. Foggia had been devastated by the war; it was a shambles. The only thing we did was swim in the Adriatic on the days we weren't flying.

We stayed at Foggia three or four days, and then headed home over France. We were to bomb the south France invasion coast—that was before southern France was invaded. So we hit those targets.

Some funny things happened—maybe not too funny.

Last year our bomb group had a reunion in Colorado Springs, and our crew talked. Old Schneider told me, "I'll bet you don't remember the riot you started in that bar in Italy." I said, "No, I don't remember much about it." Schneider started talking, and then I remembered what had happened.

A bunch of us 8th Air Force guys and some men from the 15th Air Force—by that time the 15th was stationed in Italy—were arguing about who was doing a good job and who wasn't, and I guess I accused the 15th of being junior leaguers. We had a big brawl; a bunch of guys got beat-up. One of the men on our plane, I can't remember who it was, got beaten up so badly he couldn't fly; his sinuses were all broken-up and bloody, so he had to stay in Italy. The rest of us went on home, bombing the south France invasion coast on the way.

We got a bunch of watermelons and other fresh fruit in Italy and took it back to England. Fresh fruit was unheard of up there. It was great, because those watermelons and cantaloupe were ice cold from flying at the cold temperatures at high altitude. When we landed, the ground crew swarmed all over the plane, wanting to know if we had any food. And of course we did and that was great treat for those guys.

One of the other missions that was rather interesting and a little bit different was a mission to the French Alps. We couldn't figure out what could be about. But at briefing, we were told we were to drop supplies to the Maquis—the French underground.

So we flew in across France, and when we got to the place where we could see Switzerland—the lake and Geneva—we turned. We were flying fairly low over the mountains; it was dangerous. But we were flying low because we had to drop those supplies. We looked for and found the bonfires the French had put in lines so we" know where to drop. This was in the daytime. So we went in at six or eight hundred feet, and opened the bomb bays. My compartment was right behind the bomb bay, and I had been told to check to be sure all the supplies went out when the drop was made.

Everything was ready, and the drop went out. I had my parachute on, and I kind of thought, "If I just happen to fall out of here, the war will be over for me, and I won't have to be involved any more." But I didn't; I stayed with the plane. But the thought crossed my mind.

We looked down and could see the people of the French underground gathering up the stuff that had gone down on the parachutes. Then we went on back to England; we went on home. We didn't lose any planes; that's what we called a milk run—we didn't lose anybody and nobody got shot at. It was a pretty good mission.

This mission was about my seventh or eighth. In subsequent missions, we went to Munchafen and some other targets in the French lowlands.

Morale was good. I still felt sick when we landed after a mission, and I'm sure the others did too. The strain and tension were tremendous. You felt great because you were still alive; but you felt bad about the ones who didn't get back. That was just part of it.

We could eat all right. We used to pay two pounds a month into a fund the cooks used to buy fresh eggs and things like that from the British. Usually when we went on a mission, we'd have fresh eggs and a really neat breakfast. I don't know why, but I guess a good breakfast was the kind of thing we felt we should have because we were going on a mission.

I was a tech sergeant by this time.

We flew in Old Mirandy several times, but we also had other planes. There weren't enough airplanes for every crew to fly every day, so crews would be rotated. If you flew two or three days in a row, you'd get some time off. The strange thing was that we'd fly at altitude and have that oxygen mask on for maybe eight or ten hours. After a while, you got to feeling like somebody had hold of you. You felt like someone was—well, not strangling you, but like the mask was grabbing you. It was really irritating. A lot of times I'd open the mask just to get it off my face for a while. You couldn't leave the mask off very long. You have to remember, too, that sometimes the temperature at altitude was fifty-five or sixty degrees below zero.

We had electric suits that worked very well; they kept us warm. We always wore satin gloves under our electric gloves, because at fifty or sixty degrees below zero, if you touched metal with bare skin, it would immediately freeze to it. So if you had to work a gun or anything like that, you didn't dare have bare skin touch it. I think we were told we had maybe a minute with the electric glove off before we were in trouble—even with the satin gloves on underneath the inserts.

In our off time—well, one time we went down to London. The entire crew had a weekend pass and went down. We made the rounds. We'd heard about Piccadilly Circus—that's where what we now call hookers hung out. We'd had a couple of queers at home when I was a kid, but "gay" was not heard of. Homosexuality was never thought about.

We made the bars in London, and did all the things we wanted to do. I'd never seen anything like Piccadilly Circus. I'd never had an experience like that. These gals were peddling that stuff just like they were selling something across a counter. I didn't get involved in it; I wasn't interested in that kind of stuff. I was married, and I wasn't going to have any problems, but some of the other men on our crew did some things.

The English people were just great; I thought they were marvelous. After we got back from prison camp, I remember one old gentleman sitting on a park bench when we were out walking in London. The old man was talking to us, and said he'd sure like to have a cigar, that he hadn't had one for years. It just happened we had some with us, so I gave him one of my cigars. I didn't smoke, but I had some cigars anyway. The old fellow smoked the cigar, then said, "Why don't you come home with me?"

This other kid and I—I can see his face, but I can't remember his name—went to the man's house, and were given tea and stuff. Then the man said, "I have a special treat for you."

He went somewhere and came out with some one hundred year-old Scotch Whiskey. He poured some into two test tubes and gave it to my friend and me. I asked him if he wasn't going to drink any, and he said, "Oh no, this is only for special things, and you Yanks are special. You saved us, and I wanted you to have some." The Scotch was so old it didn't taste like Scotch. It tasted kind of like whiskey, but I don't know if it had any alcoholic content. It was kind of a symbol to the man. It impressed us that the British cared that much.

We had a bar we used to go to near the base but I didn't really drink that much. Not that I was a puritan, I just didn't drink much.

There were always women hanging around the officer's barracks. Officers had rooms; we had only bunks, so it didn't work out too well for us. I remember old Steffan one time. There was a gal who used to come and do laundry for the guys; he used to shack up with her every time he got a chance. She was pretty ugly. I don't know what he saw in her; I guess he was hard up.

You paid the British people for doing your laundry. Gals would come in and do it. That was part of the stuff that went on.

We made several missions after the supply drop. I'll go to the day we got shot down.

The last raid

I had some premonitions that day—I don't know why. We were getting ready to do what turned out to be our last raid. The date was August 25, 1944. We went into briefing. When the map was unveiled and we saw where we were going, everybody moaned. There was a big red mark around Peenemunde, the V-2 manufacturing site. At that time, V-2s were really plastering England. The V-2 was a rocket that went up and came in at about three thousand miles an hour. There was no defense against it. Our mission was to get those launching sites.

We were told everything we were supposed to do at briefing, and reported to the airplane. All of us who were gunners and combination crewmembers had to go get our guns at the shed—they were taken out of the planes after a mission. It was pretty damp in England. Maybe that was the reason the guns weren't left out—I don't really know. We put the guns in the plane. Then there was a pause; I don't know if it was for weather or what.

I felt funny that day. I don't know why, I just felt funny. Here I was in this radio compartment. All that was between me and the outside was an aluminum skin about one-fiftieth of an inch thick. So I thought, "Hey, I need some protection." I got in a jeep, had one of the guys who wasn't flying that day drive me around, and picked up all the extra flak suits I could get. I took them into the plane and lined my compartment with them. Then I felt better.

We all wore flak suits, but the extra one, I put around so I'd have what I thought was protection. They didn't really do any good, but I thought they would.

We took off and formed up. Then we were flying on the way over the North Sea. When we were over the Heligoland, near Denmark, the four German antiaircraft guns there shot at us. Anyone who flew near Heligoland always got four shots from those guns before they sank down into the mud—they were in a swamp. So we got shot at like everybody else that day.

Curly Covel, my good friend who was the ball gunner, always used to ride with me in the radio compartment. We were sitting in there talking, and Curly was kidding me about all those flak suits. I said, "Maybe they'll protect me." He said,

"I just hope we make it back today." So he had funny feelings, too. I don't know much about psychic stuff, but this was really strange.

We didn't have any problem with fighters; we had our P-51 escort. We loved to have the 51s with us. We approached the IP, the initial point, the point where you drop the bombs. We were in the IP for about fifteen minutes, I think. The antiaircraft fire was incredible. We went in, and our group lost seven out of twelve planes. Just before our plane was hit—we were flying about 28,000 feet-I didn't have my parachute on. I don't know why, but even though the pilot had a rule that everyone had to wear a parachute when we were over enemy territory, I didn't have mine on. I just wasn't thinking about it, I guess. I reached down and snapped the parachute on one side so it was beneath my arm. I always did that, because I couldn't operate the radio or anything comfortable with the chute on my chest. So I just hooked the chute on the left side, on the left ring. Chest packs were about half as big as a pillow. Anyway, the chute was hooked on.

Blown apart

In the meantime, Curly had gone down into the turret, into combat position. When the plane was hit, I noticed four bursts. I guess there was one burst forward, but I counted three or four more inside the fuselage from my door back to the tail. Apparently, the plane just blew apart and we were thrown out. I figured that was the end; it was the end of the ball game.

We'd been praying we wouldn't get hit, but we were. That's part of it.

I was knocked unconscious. When I came to, I was falling through the air, spinning like a top. I realized I was out in the air and that I'd better hook the right side of the parachute up, that I couldn't pull the ripcord with the chute hooked on only one side. I knew if I did, I'd probably go in at an angle and break a leg or something. My helmet had been blown off, but I still had the electric gloves on. I took time to rip the gloves off—I thought I had plenty of time. I hooked the chute on and pulled the ripcord. Nothing happened. I started shaking the thing and grabbing, and the chute finally went out. When it opened, I was over trees.

We decided later I was probably at only about three thousand feet by then. When I looked up, I saw the yellow parachutes from our plane—the pilot and co-pilot had yellow parachutes—and those chutes weren't much bigger than the head of a pin. They were yellow and they were way up there. The reason I know I was close to the ground was because the pilot and co-pilot had been trapped in the cabin for fifteen thousand feet, and had watched the altimeter unwind; they'd been in a free-fall for fifteen thousand feet before they could get out of the cabin. So we knew I was very close to the ground before my chute opened.

I went into the trees. I'd heard about slipping parachutes, and I didn't want to get hung up. I saw a little clearing and thought I was slipping the parachute. I was over a flak battery, and could hear the shells going past me; I kept hoping one wouldn't hit me in the butt on the way up. None did, so that was good. I could look right down into the muzzles of the guns and see the batteries operating.

The landing and the escape

I got over the forest and slipped my parachute enough that I landed in a clearing in some moss. It was an easy landing. I did a front roll, and when I got up, I grabbed my chute and ran like hell; I knew the Germans would be in there after me. I got to a place where it was pretty brushy and ripped the parachute off and hid it so the Germans couldn't find it.

Then I started running again, moving away from there as fast as I could—remember, I was in a big, thick forest. I got to a place I thought I'd like to rest. I was hot. It was August, and I was sweating. I had a wool suit on, and I was scared to beat hell, I'll tell you.

I figured I was alive and maybe I'd get out of this, but I didn't know how I was going to do it. I sat down to rest. All at once I heard voices. I lay real still—I was in some tall reeds and some weeds. Eight Kraut soldiers came walking into a little clearing. They were supposed to be hunting for us; they had seen us go down in the forest. I knew what the deal was.

The soldiers sat down and smoked cigarettes and talked and joked. Every once in a while, one of them would stand up and yell, "halt, halt Amerikaner."

They were just like our GIs—goofing-off. Hell. They were told to do something, and didn't do a damn thing but sit and goof-off and smoke cigarettes. They didn't even look for us. I sat there and they sat there—for about two and one-half hours. I knew they were pretending they were hunting for us. Finally, they got up and left.

I sat there for a while and wondered what the heck I was going to do. Then I heard rustling in the bushes! What the heck was it? I saw the bushes moving and a man crawling. It was Frank Whalen, our navigator—Lieutenant Whalen. He was crawling along through the bushes and went right in front of me. I went, "psst!" Frank jumped about forty feet in the air. He thought he'd been hit. It was great. The best thing of all was that I had somebody I knew with me. Now we tried to figure what the hell we were going to do.

This was the beginning of our ten-day evasion.

Frank and I sat down and talked about how we were going to get out of this mess. We knew we were south of the Baltic Sea, so we thought that maybe we could get a freighter and go—we were dreaming. We didn't realize what we were up against.

We decided that the best thing for us to do was to travel at night and sleep in the daytime. That was complicated, because I snore like hell. Frank would stay awake while I slept and punch me so I wouldn't snore; I'd stay awake while he slept. There were some rather bizarre adventures on this little jaunt.

The first thing we had to do was to escape from that forest. We knew the Germans probably had the thing surrounded, so we laid in the grass, waiting for dark. About dusk, some Germans came by. There was a road around the forest, part of the compound for the antiaircraft battery. Soldiers were dropped off a truck about every fifty feet to stand guard and catch us when we came out of the forest.

After dark, we sneaked through the guards, crossed the road, went to another part of the forest, and walked and walked and walked. We were thirsty and we were hungry. I had an escape kit I'd kept from the Russian mission. Inside the kit were malted milk tablets and some dehydrated stuff-I don't know what all, but there was a bunch of stuff in there. But we didn't have any water, and didn't know what to do.

The swamp we were in was kind of a dry swamp; the water level was very low. We took the water kit from the escape kit, a plastic bag, put moss in a handkerchief I had, squeezed the water out of the moss into the bag, and put halizone pills from the escape kit into the water to purify it. The water looked like chocolate milk it was so black, but we drank it anyway.

Then we thought, "Well, we're going to have to travel." Our objective was to get to the Baltic. We had to get out of the area we were in. We were two hundred and fifty miles from our lines, we knew that.

I had regular flight boots, which were good. When Frank parachuted out of the plane, his fall had been stopped so suddenly that he had lost one of his boots. So he had one flight boot, but all he had on the other foot was the felt boot inner liner—that was what he walked on. It was pretty painful for him.

We decided to continue moving. The first night we started walking through the countryside, and lo and behold, we walked into the aircraft battery that had shot us down. We walked in and could hardly believe where we were—right in the middle of the thing. There were soldiers around us. I looked up toward the sky, and saw a gun muzzle. I looked around—our eyes were used to the dark—and I could see we were right in the middle of this ninety-gun flak battery. We found out later it was a ninety-gun battery.

So we backed out and nonchalantly walked away from there. The next day we were in a swamp, a low-lying area, and had to hide out. We lay down in the bushes and slept in shifts. Near midday, two Germans came by in a boat. They were fishing, and went right by us. We just lay quietly and waited for them to leave. We started walking again at dusk.

Our objective was to find a railroad. We heard trains north of us. We had a primary plan and an alternate plan. We could either try to get to the Baltic or find a train, a railroad that went to the Russian lines; maybe we could get through that way. Of course that didn't work. I guess we weren't thinking very good.

Our main objective was escape. We'd been indoctrinated to escape, and that was the way it was. That was what we were trying to do.

Frank and I were both in pretty good shape. We weren't hurt too bad. I had some cuts on my elbow, and Frank's face had been burned a little bit and was cut a little, but otherwise, we were okay. We weren't hurt badly enough to be debilitated.

We found the railroad and walked into a marshaling yard. We were walking along, sneaking through there quietly along the tracks. We came to the end of the railroad yard, and just as Frank was about to step in front of me, I grabbed him and pulled him down. He asked me what I was doing. I said, "That's an electric eye." There was enough light that I could see the eye. When trains passed through this area, the electric eye would turn the lights on in the marshaling area; when trains left the area, the electric eye would turn the lights off. Had we walked through that electric eye, the Germans would have known somebody was in there, and would probably have come after us.

From there, we went into a village. We wanted to get something to eat. The Germans had apple trees and corn in their gardens and stuff, so we ate that. We stuffed our pockets full of apples and raw corn, then walked on.

Eating the apples and raw corn didn't bother us. I guess the human body is a lot more resilient than we think it is. I think our bodies adjusted to the conditions we faced. I think your body adjusts as much as it needs to survive. I really believe that.

Frank and I kept close together, because we knew we could probably find something to eat. The next night we went into another village. All at once we saw a German soldier walking along on the other side of the street. We decided we couldn't run. It was dark and we had uniforms on, but we didn't have hats on. We kept walking; the German stayed about a block behind us. We came to the end of the street; it curved to the right. I looked up at the house at the end of the street, and saw a woman standing in the window.

When she saw Frank and me looking at her, she closed the window and the curtains. We just kept walking; we just toughed it out. The soldier was still behind us. We went around a corner and got beneath a dock beside a place that looked like a garage. Suddenly the garage doors opened, and Germans came out. They'd been in a briefing, but we hadn't known that. There was a mobile flak battery in the town—there were trucks and stuff. We looked around then, and saw a lot of equipment. We hid under the dock until the Germans left.

We watched the Germans come out of the briefing. They jumped into their trucks, and the entire mobile unit took off for wherever they were going to go. We decided we'd better get out of town, so we walked out the same way we'd come in.

I guess we were pretty brazen—or stupid; I don't know which. Anyway, as we walked down the main street of another little village, we heard somebody talking. We stopped behind a big tree, and there, only a few feet from us, were a German and his girl friend. I don't know how they kept from smelling us; we hadn't had a bath for days and had both been smoking.

We moved on out of town and into a field. Daylight came and we slept while we waited for dark.

The next night we went into another village and into a half-finished garage or warehouse. There was a scaffold in there the bricklayers had used, so we went up onto that and stayed there. This was one of the scariest things.

We were up there sleeping in the daytime; one of us sleeping, the other watching. All at once a little fox terrier came in the building and started barking. He was barking and looking up where we were. Like I said, we were in a big open warehouse with a big open door. A Kraut came to the door, but not into the garage, and screamed at the dog. I guess the guy thought the dog was barking at a mouse or something.

If the guy had come in, he'd have seen us up on that platform if he'd looked. The guy got hold of the dog and took him out of the building. That was pretty narrow on that one; the Germans almost got us that time.

We're into the fourth or fifth day of our evasion. I don't remember which day it was exactly.

When nightfall came, we got out of the garage. We spent the next several days sleeping and walking, following the railroad, waiting for a chance to get on a train going east so we could get out of Germany.

One day we were in a pretty dense forest, and we were tired. We decided we'd walk in the daytime. So we started walking—this was the eighth or ninth day. We were walking along a seldom used road through the forest. We went around a corner and looked back; a woman in black was walking behind us.

We kept walking and she kept walking. You've got to remember there were a lot of laborers in Germany, slave laborers and Italians. By that time, we probably looked like Italians; we had beards and dirty clothes. We probably resembled the workers the Germans had on farms and in their industries.

So we kept walking. Every time we'd turn in the road, the woman would turn, too—she was maybe two blocks behind us. We were starting to get panicky. We were parallel to the railroad, and didn't know what to do. All we really knew was we had to keep moving. We came to a spot in the road where we could look ahead, and there, coming toward us, was a farmer with a horse and cart. We didn't know what to do. What should we do now?

Just as we started to panic, we came to a little trail to the right. We walked nonchalantly into that, and kept going until we got out of sight of the people on the road, then got down. We were almost to the railroad; we could see the tracks. We lay down in the bushes and waited.

Apparently we hadn't sounded any alarm; the people didn't seem to think anything about seeing us. Nothing happened. Later in the day while we were waiting there, we heard kids laughing and talking.

Looking up through the bushes, we saw a Hitler Youth Group with some leaders out for a walk. We were lucky the group didn't have dogs with it. The kids passed within a few feet of us, and went on their way. We continued to wait. We decided this was the spot from which we'd try to get on a train.

As luck would have it, a train came by going slow enough that we could jump aboard. The boxcars on those trains were a little strange. They had kind of a little alcove or little house at the end of the car with a place for people to sit. Not all of the cars had those, just some of them. We got into one of those little houses and sat down. Now, we thought, we're going to make it.

The train went along, in and out of different parts of town and through other little towns. The Germans didn't search the train; they didn't have any reason to. But what was really bad about this—its kind of gross—was somebody had gone to the bathroom, they'd had a bowel movement in this little house. The little house was kind of like an outdoor toilet, only much smaller. Frank and I sat side-by-side, and of course, we both sat in the excrement. Now we really smelled great—that plus all the other stuff we were stinking from.

It's funny now, but it sure as hell wasn't funny then.

We still had our Russian identity cards from the Russian shuttle bomb, and thought maybe we could use them for something.

The train backed into a kind of defense plant. We were really scared; there were floodlights all over the place. The train was finally switched out of there. It moved to another place and pulled into a little siding in a town and disconnected our car, a coal car. So here we were, stranded.

The freight train was gone and we were no longer hooked to it. We were sitting in a little house at the end of a boxcar in the middle of a railroad yard. We didn't know what we were going to do now. It was about five o'clock in the morning.

The town was very small and very quiet. We heard voices. We looked out a little hole in the wall, and saw Russian laborers—I guess they were POWs—emptying the boxcars. We thought, "Jeez, what are we going to do? They are going to find us."

We decided to walk out of there. We looked around and saw some woods not far away. And there were really three little towns—our town, one to the right, and one to the left—on different sides of the woods. We walked away from the boxcar like we owned the place, right through the rail yard in broad daylight. All at once we heard somebody screaming at us. "Oh crap, here it comes!"

This guy screamed, "Italiano? Italiano?" We said "Yeah, yeah."

But the guy couldn't speak Italian. He motioned for us to wait by the railroad station while he got someone who could speak Italian. We had those plastic water bags around our necks, and the guy didn't know what they were; he didn't want us to touch them.

All my life I'd ridiculed my grandmother for speaking Italian; those dumb people who speak a foreign language and al that. For once in my life, I wished too hell I could speak Italian. I knew the cuss words, but that was all. The Italian started spouting Italian. We said, "No capice."

Then the men surmised we were escapees, took us to the railroad station, and made us sit down above a grill over a basement window.

Frank and I still had the Russian identity cards and all that other stuff we'd had on those shuttle bombs. While I waited for the German military to come and pick us up, I shredded everything I had on me; I got rid of everything. If the Germans had found the papers, it would have told them something about the shuttle bombs. I understood later that those shuttle bombs were really a damaging thing to Germany. Our planes would come from the west and go to the east and not fly back to England. The Germans never did figure out just what was going on.

Captured

The Germans picked us up and took us to the Stettin Air Base. We were treated all right. You have to remember that some of these people had never seen an American; we were kind of a curiosity. They told us, "Kaput." That means it's over with. I was taken to an enlisted men's barracks on the air base and put in the barracks office; Frank was taken to the Officers quarters.

The Germans asked us our rank. I told them I was a sergeant, so that was pretty good. A sergeant in the German army wasn't at the bottom of the heap. There was a bunk in the office on which I was to sleep.

During the day the Germans would come and talk to me. "Are you nort or sout American?" They didn't really know. I told them north. I was surprised the Germans were as knowledgeable as they were. I stayed in the orderly room that night. I was fed regular army food—soup, bread, and coffee. It was the same thing the German troops got. It was good; it was great! It was the first food we'd had in a while.

That night I was supposed to sleep on the bench, the bunk. I had one guard. He had a big gun on, and when he got tired, he took the gun off, laid it on the counter, the desk, and walked away to get something.

Here I was, all by myself. The gun was lying there; I was in this orderly room in this barracks while the Krauts—there was nobody around; everybody was asleep. I thought to myself, "I could get away from here." But I was so tired. I didn't feel too good because we'd gone through all that other junk trying to get away.

While I was thinking it over, the sergeant of the guard came in. He looked at me; he looked at the gun; he looked around and there was nobody there. He looked at me; I looked at him. Then he started screaming like somebody had stuck him with a hot iron. He screamed for the guard who had left his post to go get coffee or something. The guy came running. When he came into the room, the sergeant beat the hell out of him for what he'd done. Then they put a guard on me for sure—a real guard, a wide-awake guard, a special guard. But I wasn't going any damn lace.

The next day after breakfast, some little guy, an older soldier, came in—I still hadn't had a bath—and marched me across the air base. I had on a cameo ring I'd gotten as a graduation present, a man's ring with a black cameo in it. The guard pointed to it and said, "For me, for me." I said "No." He said "They shoot you. They shoot you."

I thought, "Well, you can't have it. Shoot me, but I'm still not going to give you my ring." It was a gold ring.

Interrogation in Frankfurt

The guard didn't say any more. He took me on into a building. Frank was there. The Germans told us we were to be taken to the interrogation center at Frankfurt, Germany. That was a long way away—clear across Germany.

So there was Frank and me, a sergeant, and a private. The sergeant was Baron von—I can't remember his name—but he competed against Don Budge in tennis in the 30s. I was at my mother-in-law's house many years later, and found a newspaper that showed a picture of this baron as a tennis player. It was an incredible coincidence.

The Germans told us we'd be transported by train to Frankfurt on Main, way down in southwest Germany. So we got on the train and traveled in a regular passenger car with civilians. The guards made us sit in regular seats on the train until it got crowded, then we were forced to ride in the vestibule between the cars. Our guards were out there with us.

On the way to Frankfurt, the train stopped in Berlin. We were in the railway station there, and water was running everywhere through the basin. That meant the bombers had really done a job on the town; pipes were broken.

When we got off the train in Berlin, the civilians didn't say much to us; apparently they'd seen a lot of captured people, because they didn't pay much attention to us. We didn't have any arguments or anything—no problems. The German civilians weren't friendly—they didn't have any reason to be.

We got off the train in Frankfurt and were just standing there, waiting for transport to the Gestapo interrogation center. We, the two guards, Frank, and me, were still on the train platform when some civilians came by. They shouted at us; they were very angry with us. They spit at us and called us "scheissen fliegers." Of course, you know what scheissen means.

How did this make us feel? By this time, we'd been through so many prob-lems...The thing is, you never give up hope; that's part of the whole game. You're not smart enough not to give up hope.

We figured we'd just take each stage as it came. We were scared. We hoped the Gestapo wouldn't beat us up. You don't know what will be done to you. The guards protected us from the civilians. And about that same time, guards from the interrogation center got there and took us, by truck, to the interrogation cen-ter.

This was a very sad time for me. I was put in solitary confinement for three days, in a room about four or six by eight—don't remember exactly; it was very small. There was a bench to sleep on and a window. The window was closed so you couldn't see through it. The room was on the main floor and had a light that was never turned off. On one of the days, I wanted to see out. I don't know how I did it, but I got the window open and looked out. Guess what I saw? Right outside my window was a Nazi flag on a flagpole. Then it really hit me. "Man, you're a long way from home, and you're it." That was a real chock.

All of a sudden, everything came into focus. You're down, and you're it. I was twenty-one years old. That was a very bad time for me. You're so used to looking out the window and seeing the American flag, you take it for granted. When you look out a window and see the enemy's flag, that's another story, believe me.

After three days in solitary, I was taken before a Gestapo officer. I was frightened; I didn't know what was going to happen. The officer was a little short guy with a friendly face and gentle manner. He said, "Where are you from, sergeant?"

"I can't give you anything but my name, rank, and serial number."

Apparently someone from our crew had been through there, because the Gestapo officer had all the information on me. He told me all this stuff; I didn't verify it, I just looked at him.

Then the officer said, "Where are you from, sergeant?:

"I'm from Colorado."

"You're from Colorado? Ah, have you ever been to the top of Pikes Peak?"

"No."

"I've traveled in America. I've been to the top of Pikes Peak."

I don't know whether he was giving me a bunch of crap or whether it was true. This was probably part of the technique he used. I never gave him anything but my name, rank, and serial number. I told him I was from Colorado, but that was all.

I was surprised that somebody on our crew had given the Gestapo so much information about the crew. Some of my crew had been captured the day after we were shot down; they'd gone through this center a long time before I did.

I was going through here two weeks after the rest of the crew. The Gestapo had our names—they had everything. That was scary. We'd seen movies about the Gestapo, and we didn't know if they were going to shoot us or what.

I didn't tell the Gestapo anything. After I heard what that officer had to say, I realized he'd already gotten all the information he was going to get anyway. I was not maltreated. I was just locked up.

Going to Stalag Luft IV

An entire train made up of captured personnel was prepared to take us to prison camps. There were ground forces, air force, tank personnel—everyone who had been captured at this time. There were several cars of prisoners and their guards. We didn't know it, but the prison camp we were headed for was near Peenemunde, at Gross Tychow.

The prison trains were marked with a red cross on top so our flyers wouldn't attack them. It worked, because we weren't attacked. We rode in regular passenger train cars. When the train stopped, we got off and went to the bathroom alongside the tracks, then got back on the train.

We stopped at one station I can't remember the name of it. Maybe it was Berlin. We were in the railroad yards, and a train made up of many boxcars came by. There were fifty people in each of those cars—refugees of some kind, we thought. We found out later that the people on those cars were probably some of the Jews being transported to camps. I asked one of the guards who could speak a little English who the people on the train were. He said, "Kaputt, kaputt."

The Germans weren't as innocent of the Jewish situation as they want us to believe. How would an ordinary soldier know about it if it was all so secret? Those people were taken off the train and marched somewhere; they had all their belongings in a little handkerchief or little rag they carried. Some of them didn't have coats or anything; their clothes were just rags. They all had a P marked on their backs—I can't remember what that meant.

Our train left that station and traveled for several days. We got up into east Prussia, and the train stopped at the prison camp. We were marched from the train to the camp on a road between guards with machine guns. It was probably a couple of miles.

Stalag Luft IV and POW life

We marched into Luftwaffe Stalag number four. So many planes had been shot down and the Germans had taken so many prisoners, there wasn't enough room in the barracks for everyone. Tents had been set up in the infield, and that's where we were put. We were issued two blankets. We stayed in those tents for about a month, sleeping on the ground. We were fed normal fare; in the morning, coffee; at noon, soup and two slices of black bread; at night potatoes. We were on that diet for quite a while. After the addition to the prison camp was completed, we were taken to "C" Lager.

There were thirty of us to a room about 12 by 12; we slept on the floor. There was only room to walk between the rows of blankets the guys had on the floor. After a while, bunks were brought in, and we moved our stuff onto the bunk beds.

Our room did have a stove in it.

I met a man who is still my friend—George Demott, who lives on Long Island. Everybody had to have a buddy, a friend, or your food and anything else you had would get stolen. You had to have someone watch out for you. So George and I buddied up; we were friends for the entire time we were in the prison camp.

The biggest cry-babies in our outfit were those kids from New York and New England. I had been a Boy Scout, and I've always felt that Boy Scout training is very good for kids. Boys like me, boys from the Southwest and the West, did pretty well. We noticed that kids from the big cities weren't able to cope with prison life. They were nervous.

I remember the Lucky Strike Orchestra, the Mark Warno years? Mark Warno's son was with us. He got into hypnotism and mind junk. He couldn't take care of himself; he was dirty. He just existed. After a while, most of us got into a regimen where we'd try to keep clean and exercise—to be ready in case we could get away. That's what the whole thing was about, to try to escape.

I played a lot of chess to keep my mind busy. Little chess sets about four-by-four or five-by-five inches and pegs and holes so you could keep your men in place came in the Red Cross parcels from Switzerland.

We had no classes. We were not allowed to gather in groups.

The Swiss Red Cross was allowed to bring in Red Cross parcels. We prisoners were supposed to get one parcel a week that contained canned meat, canned coffee, chocolate—things like that. Survival kits was what they were. The Germans gave us only half parcels; they took the other half for themselves. There were the little chess sets and also some sports equipment with the parcels. The reason I mention that is that we prisoners had a radio. Those radios came in one piece at a time in softballs that were included in the parcels. We knew what was going on in the war through BBC.

I don't know how the guys in camp knew which of the softballs contained radio parts. The radio must have been some kind of crystal set. I didn't see that radio, and I didn't see the receiver itself. It was kept in a room that not many people knew much about except the members of the Sanitary Committee.

The room in which the committee gathered was one I was in only one time. I didn't know what it was until I left. Paddy, our barracks leader, asked me, "Did you notice the radio?"

"No, what are you talking about?"

He said, "The radio was on the table and the parts were in the coffee pot. It sits out in the open like that, and nobody pays any attention to it."

The Sanitary Committee, a group of about twenty-five men, consisted of representatives from each barracks in our compound. Those men were the only ones who listened to the radio broadcasts. Nothing was ever put in writing. The representatives would come around at a certain time before curfew and say, "Here's the report for today." So we knew where the war was even when the Germans guarding us didn't. We knew about the Battle of the Bulge. We noticed the Germans got news about that—something good for them—and really got cocky.

The Germans asked for someone to work in the tailor shop. I'd had some experience in tailoring before the war, so I volunteered. Then I watched the German's attitude, and decided I didn't want to go over there and work after all. It didn't look very good. This was in December 1944.

When we first got to the prison camp, the Sanitary Committee told us not to try to escape, because there had been incidents in which German civilians had massacred air crews. So we decided we wouldn't try t get out, that we'd do as we were told. We didn't do any tunneling. There were some tunnels dug, I think, but we weren't privy to any of that.

By combining the rations from the Red Cross parcels and the German rations, we were able to survive. We lost weight, but we were able to survive.

The bad part about the German diet was that it was mostly black sauerkraut. It looked like chocolate, but it was sauerkraut. I don't know what the Germans did to that stuff, but it was terrible. But we ate it because we had to eat. If you had any problems with your bowels, it really worked on you. A lot of the guys did have bowel problems.

Life in camp settled into a routine after we moved into the barracks. We didn't really have much problem with people who wouldn't conform; most kept clean and tried to exercise. We were aware of the fact that our emotional state would be better if we kept a positive outlook. If you were positive and had hope, it was easier to face the problems you had.

It's cold in northern Germany in winter. There was a stove in the barracks, but we were issued only a certain amount of coal, which could only be burned at a certain time. We burned it at night so the room would be warm when we went to bed.

Somehow the Germans had gotten some American uniforms—I guess they came through the Red Cross. I had an overcoat and some other stuff. We had enough clothes that we could keep warm.

The Germans issued eating utensils to us when we entered the prison camp: a knife, fork, spoon, bowl, and a cup. If you wanted to take a bath, you had to use your damn soup bowl to take a sponge bath with. Then you had to wash it and eat out of it. That was just great! If you were lucky enough to get your hands on a bucket, you could use that water to wash with. There were no showers.

Because of the sauerkraut and the diet we ate, everybody had pretty frequent, pretty runny bowel movements. There was an outdoor latrine; the thing had a lot of seats over a big tank. The Germans had to dispose of that stuff what with all the guys in camp, so about once a week, they'd come in with what they called a Scheissen Scooper. It was a big tank with a flexible hose on it. The Germans would throw the big hose into the tank and light something under the tank they'd brought in; the heat would somehow create a vacuum in the tank on the Scheissen Scooper, and pretty soon stuff would be sucked up through the hose. They took the contents they'd sucked up and spray it somewhere-I don't know what they did with it.

One day, the biggest news of all was when the thing plugged up and the damned Scheissen Scooper exploded. Big News! Big News! Jeez, that was funny.

We had a football game on Thanksgiving Day. The Germans gave us horsemeat hamburgers. That was the only time we got fresh meat while we were in prison. Horsemeat tastes pretty good. They eat horses in Germany; they're not civilized, like we are.

The mail. I never received any mail. I think some of the guys got some, but I didn't. I wrote many letters home. My mother received some of those letters; I still have some of them at home. So the family knew I was all right.

A strange thing happened. When I was home on furlough before I went overseas, my mother's hair was black. When I came home after the war, her hair had turned almost white. I was missing for two months before the Red Cross notified my parents that I had been captured. The Germans took one dog tag and gave it to the Red Cross as proof that we were captured.

Christmas. In the Red Cross parcels, there were raisins and prunes. The guys made applejack with that fruit. It wasn't that great, but we thought we were doing something pretty good. There was a little alcohol in it. Everybody in our compound was a sergeant and above, so we weren't required to work. The Geneva Convention said we didn't have to work; it didn't keep us from volunteering if we wanted to, though. The Germans did live up to that part. The part of the Geneva Convention they didn't live up to was the fact that they didn't give us much to eat. I don't know if you're familiar with the prison camps, but there were the towers, a big high fence, and a warning wire. The warning wire was about a foot high and about forty feet back from the main fence around the camp. You were not to cross the warning wire. If you did, you could be shot—everybody knew that. I never saw anybody cross it.

Morale was pretty good. Major Pollis, the camp leader, was the only officer in our group and the kind of man people would follow. He was able to keep things under control. You have to remember these kids were all young. Morale got bad later on.

At Christmas there wasn't much we could do. We sang Christmas Carols. The barracks were built about two feet off the ground on stilts; they were all open underneath so the Germans could run dogs under them. It was very difficult to tunnel out or get away. The Germans had dogs running through the compound all night.

Word came to me that Steffans, our navigator from Greeley, was in the lager next to ours. Somehow we arranged a time to meet. I stood out behind my barracks near the warning wire, he stood in his compound, and we talked. He was the only one from my crew I had contact with or was able to talk to during the time I was a prisoner. Later, after the march, he went to another camp. But every now and then we talked across the wire.

The forced march

In January 1945, when the Russians started their big offensive toward the west, we were told we were going to march out. We formed everything up; we had everything we could carry. It was cold; it was the middle of winter.

I carried my blankets and whatever food we had around from the last parcel. We went by the storehouse where the Red Cross parcels were kept, and saw shoes, American uniforms, Red Cross parcels stacked twelve feet high. Those lousy Germans had kept those things from us; they had hoarded it all. So we grabbed everything we could carry. You never knew when you were going to eat again.

We grabbed all this stuff, and of course, took more than we could carry. We stopped in the woods that night, and the next morning, we discarded what we couldn't carry.

The march started in Gross Tychow and went across Northern Germany, almost to the western border. We were put on trains and rode to the southern part of Germany, then marched some more. We went through one hundred fourteen town and villages during the eighty-two day march. We crossed over at the little town of Halle at the end of the war.

I took cigarette wrappers apart and, using pipe cleaners, made a book. In that little book, I listed every single town we went through.

The march didn't go through any large towns. We went mostly through small towns and villages in farming country, where we could be put up in barns to sleep.

My weight had not started to go down dramatically yet, not at this point.

We slept in barns and in the woods—ten thousand men. After the war, we found the Germans had had one hundred twenty-five thousand allied prisoners on the march at the time we were making our march. My unit, 750 men, was just a small portion of the total number of marchers. Our group pretty much stayed together. George and I stayed together, and some of our friends from the camp stayed with us. We marched 813 kilometers (487.8 miles).

The march was very difficult. Morale was not very good. We didn't know what was going to happen; we were just hanging on. The Germans would march us several miles during the day, then we'd stop near a barn. We managed to sleep in barns and out of the snow most of the time.

We prisoners helped each other by sharing our food. As I said before, George and I were friends. As we went along, if one of us got some food, we'd share it.

The Germans managed to feed us occasionally; we also had the stuff we'd managed to carry along with us. A lot of times we'd eat whatever there was to eat in the barn in which we had stopped.

At that time, the Germans started their potatoes from seed potatoes, so we stole those seed potatoes and ate them. We'd take the grain stored in the barns, shake the heads out, and eat the grain raw. A lot of the guys got dysentery. This again, is where the Boy Scout training comes in.

Those kids from New York didn't know how to take care of themselves. They would cry—they just couldn't cope with things. If we got dysentery or diarrhea, we knew enough to get a couple of chunks of charcoal out of the campfire and eat it. It would sort of stabilize your system. I'm sure the charcoal absorbed some of the poison that was causing the diarrhea.

So we were managing. I remember going three weeks without going to the "bathroom," without having a bowel movement. That doesn't sound very reasonable or logical, but I did it, so I know it happened.

Your body can withstand a lot more than you think it can. You can stretch it to the limit, and it will go on beyond that.

The most terrifying experience of all on the march occurred while we were marching across northern Germany, when we came near the rocket installation we'd bombed. I don't know whether it was the same installation we'd bombed or not, but the Germans told us to be quiet on that day and to obey. So we started across this section, and about every fifty feet, there was an SS guard with a submachine gun.

It was terrifying. Those black uniforms, the skull and crossbones, and all that stuff—they just stood there waiting for somebody to fall down. But none of our guys fell down; we helped each other. We got across that area and out of there. It worked out okay.

Some strange things happened during the course of the march. We were marching through a village. You must remember that we were a pretty bedraggled looking bunch by now—thin, dirty, unshaven; we looked like bums. We were walking through this one little town, and I looked up on the porch of a house we were passing. Here was an old German grandmother rocking in her rocking chair with tears in her eyes as she watched us going by. I thought, "Now isn't that something. Here's one that has a little compassion."

A guy named Isenberg, the only survivor of his crew, had been in our camp and was walking with us. His plane had been shot down in Hungary, and everyone except him had been massacred because he was a Jew.

We were walking along a narrow street in a little town when a shutter opened and a woman's arm came out holding a piece of fried chicken. This happened right in front of Isenberg. He reached up, took the chicken, and started eating it as he marched along. I thought, "That's the damndest thing I've ever seen in my life."

We were beginning to see that some Germans had some compassion for the allies. It was near the end of the war. I saw both sides of it. I think many Germans were aware of the holocaust situation, and then there were others who didn't want war, had never wanted it—including some of those guarding us.
Our guards were old guys, fifty-, sixty-, seventy years old, members of the Wehrmacht in army uniforms. They weren't fit for combat, but they could watch us.

At this stage of the game, they'd known us a long time, and would talk to us and be friendly. I remember one—I can't remember his name, but I can see the face—who said to us, "Kommen Sie hier." He told us Roosevelt was dead. This happened on the fifteenth of April 1945 or something like that.

We told him that couldn't be. He repeated that Roosevelt was dead. We didn't believe him; we thought it was propaganda. This was near the end of the march.

Our guards treated us pretty well. They, like we, were waiting for the war to end.

We were in one place at the end of the march, and wanted to get some water. German civilians ran out and pumped the water for us. This was very near the end of the war. The Russians were taking towns and farms four hours after we'd left them. I was afraid the Russians would get us. We knew the Russians were not cooperative, that they were bad news.

Some of our guys who were liberated by the Russians had to get out through Egypt. It took them months to get out of Europe. The Russians just didn't care. They were still under Stalin and suspicious of everyone. If it hadn't been for us (the United States) and the tanks, planes, and other stuff we gave them, the Russians would never have been able to drive the Germans out of their country. The Russians were a different breed altogether from us.

By now, our physical state was not too good; we'd lost many pounds; I'd lost forty or fifty, and so had George. The only way we could keep going was knowing that sooner or later, we knew we'd make it out of there.

We were near the end of the march in a small town with many other allied prisoners of war. At that time, we had some Sikhs and Hindus, British troops from India, who had also been prisoners. George and I didn't have anything to eat. We'd made friends with two of the Indian colonial troops, and they gave us some of the food they had.

After we'd eaten, we asked them why they'd shared with us. They said, "This is called dost."

"What does that mean?"

"It means that we will share with you because you do not have and we have." Bear in mind that these were Islamic troops. This was a custom we'd never heard of; we were very pleased that they'd helped us, that they'd given us food so we could get through to the end of the ordeal.

Meeting our own troops

A bunch of us came to a town called Halle. We were walking along, and the guard who'd told us about Roosevelt said, "Maybe today, maybe today the Americans come."

This was the 26th of April. We'd marched about five miles that day. We came around a curve to a level area, and here came an American jeep with a white star on it. A major and a couple of GIs wheeled up gave us the old "Hi" sign, and said, "Follow us."

George and I and a bunch of other guys said, "Hell, we're not going to march anymore." Some of the guys got in front and were going to march four abreast like they were on a damn parade.

We were so damn sick of everything—we stole a big old bus and drove around and waved at the guys marching. We drove on by the boys and got to the American lines ahead of them, dumped the bus, and walked across a river—maybe the Elbe, I'm not sure—on a broken-down bridge that had been blown up. There was a walkway—that's how we got across.

Military newsreel cameramen were there filming everything. They filmed us jumping off the bus and everything. We had a great time.

We went to a field hospital set up on the American side. There were a lot of American nurses there, the first American women we'd seen in a long time; they were just like angels.

Medics were checking the guys out; the hurt and wounded were treated. George and I were lucky; we weren't hurt. By this time, I had lost about sixty pounds. I weighed 105 pounds.

There was K rations all stacked up at the hospital. K rations come in boxes and look like Cracker Jack boxes. We were so used to stealing and scavenging and grabbing, that we stole the rations. We opened up the fronts of our uniforms and stuffed them full of food. One of the nurses standing there—I'll never forget it—was crying. She was standing in front of me and didn't say one word to me about what I was doing or ask why I was taking all the food. She just stood there crying. We were loaded on trucks and taken to Stettin Air Base, one of the main German air bases.

We all went through delousing; we all had fleas. I'll never forget the delousing room. DDT must have been four inches deep on the floor. We went in there and threw that powder all over ourselves like we were kids playing in the dirt. It was the damndest thing you ever saw. Some guys got down and rolled in that stuff. We'd had to put up with the fleas so long; it was just great to get rid of them. We got a shower and clean clothes. It sure felt good.

We were housed in some pretty good places, because this base had been Goering's headquarters for a time. The floors were marble. It was pretty nice.

But let me tell you what happened.

We had been without decent food for so long that we gorged ourselves. Then, of course, we all got diarrhea. The bathroom floors were two or three inches deep in bowel movement; it was a mess. The medics decided to take away all our food-no more C rations, no more K rations, nothing. We were put back on German rations: bread, soup, potatoes, and some fruit. We had to stabilize. So we were at Stettin for quite a while. This was the 26th of April 1945.

One funny thing happened while we were at Stettin. George and I had heard about Hermann Goering's warehouse, and decided we'd go over there and get some stuff. Some of the guys had been over there and gotten champagne and stuff, and we wanted some too.

So George and I went into this warehouse. There were mountains of chocolate, Turkish cigarettes—you couldn't believe the stuff in that place. We loaded up: champagne bottles in our hip pockets—but we never got a chance to drink it. We started out carrying all this stuff through the opening in the fence, and ran into an American GI standing there with a pistol—which he pointed at us.

"Where are you going? Who are you?"

I told him, "We're ramp tramps, recovered Allied military personnel. In other words, we're ex-POWs."

The guy looked around and said, "Listen kid, go down that way. That chicken-shit lieutenant will get you if he sees you. Just go down that way."

So we got out of there with our loot.

The stuff we'd taken was heavy; we had sacks full of stuff. We were still pretty weak, and when we got tired we went to a farmhouse.

An old German couple was there, and we told them we wanted a wagon to haul our stuff in.

"Jawohl." They said.

About that time, some Kraut wearing leather leggings and a black hat came by and said, "You komm."

He was going to show us where to get the wagon. We had to climb over a fence to get into the yard. He told us to come around back with him.
We put our stuff down. All the loot we still had was what was in our pockets. As we started to climb over the fence, George noticed that the Kraut had a pistol under his coat. "Pep, let's go Pep." (The P. in my name stood for Peppe. I had this name changed.)

So we ran like hell. We left everything and ran down the road, right into some American MPs. We told them that bastard was going to shoot us.

The MPs went to the area we'd just left, found the Kraut, and beat him up, but it didn't do any good. He wouldn't say anything.

We went back to camp with a little chocolate, some cigarettes, and I had a couple of bottles of champagne in my hip pockets. But we had enough stuff to have a party that night.

We were still thieves. A couple of days later we went to the mess hall. We ate, and then as we were leaving, we noticed the door to the basement was open. We knew there was food in the basement, so we went down there and stole a bunch of it. Who knows why we did this but we just had to do it. I got out of there, but some of the guys were caught. I guess we ate the stuff. I can't remember what we did with it.

At this camp in Stettin, we were on a bland diet-canned turkey and stuff, but we were still getting German black bread. We finally got to where we could eat regular food; the medics decided we were ready to go home.

Camp Lucky Strike and back in England

We were moved, by train, to Camp Lucky Strike in France.

Ike came and talked to a bunch of us ex-prisoners. At Lucky Strike we were still on our bland diet. We decided we wanted to get back to England, and made inquiries. We were told that the army would contact our base in England, and that a plane would be sent for us.

The 95th did send a plane, and we rode aboard it to our old base in England. We shook hands with the guys who did the parachutes and all. We inquired about the personal belongings we'd left the preceding August—everything had been shipped home. There was no mail for us. Everything had been returned to our parents.

There was an opportunity to take a flight to Ireland, and some of our guys went; I didn't want to fly any more. We were also asked if we'd like to fly back over Europe and take a look at it.

Some of us did decide to go to Scotland on a kind of holiday. Snyder, our waist-gunner, and I had run into each other at Lucky Strike, so some of the other guys, he, Steffans, and I went to Scotland by train.

We returned POWs were given temporary service records so we could go to a base anywhere and get money if we needed it. There were so many people trying to get home that the army just couldn't accommodate everyone. Many of us were turned loose for a furlough.

Snyder got sick on the way to Scotland. Steffans went on, but I took Snyder back to our old airbase. He was really sick—strep throat, or something.

Home in the States

We went to Southampton to board ship to come home. We were processed through, got on the Queen Elizabeth, and landed in New York in June. We went to Camp Kilmer where we boarded a troop train to fort Logan. I was given a sixty-day furlough.

I went to California on that furlough and visited Aunt Virgie for a while, then visited the folks in Colorado.

I was reassigned, because I didn't have enough points for discharge. I wanted to go to Wright-Patterson field in Ohio, because I was married to Joyce at the time, and she lived with her parents in Kentucky. It was a commute deal on the weekend.

I was assigned as the mailman at Wright-Patterson, and had a WAC driver. I could do all of my work in about two hours each day. The army was just holding me.

I was on my way down to Kentucky one day, and the train was full. I was riding between the cars, and looked into a car labeled Jim Crow Car. I looked in there, and saw about five black people and seventy empty seats. So I went in and sat down.

The conductor came through and looked at me, but didn't say anything. Finally he said, "Psst. You can't stay here."

"Why not? I'm not going to ride between the cars. I need a place to sit down."

"You get out of this car, or I'll send for the MPs and have you arrested." In other words, I was white and had no right to be in a car where the blacks were. Stupid. Here we'd fought this war and there was this kind of thing going on. But I did get out of there and did as I was told.

Truman decided it was time to get the POWs home. He issued an executive order that we were all to be processed and released from the army.

I went back to Lowry Field, and was honorably discharged from there on October 26, 1945. I went on home.

I'll never forget

I'll have to admit that it did take a while to adjust after I got home. I remember—it must have been the third or fourth day I was home at my mother's house in Fort Lupton. We were sitting at the dinner table, when there was a very loud clap of thunder. I dove under the table and rolled up into a ball. It was a natural reaction. I must have thought it was some kind of bomb or explosion; I'd reacted without thinking.

My adjustment was easy, because I was still in the service. I traveled to California and Ohio. I was on furlough, and so glad to be out of the mess. I think that' part of the reason I recovered easily.

For a time, it was almost as if all of this had happened to somebody else. We knew at the time we were in prison—George and I talked many times; he's pretty bright—that we would forget the physical part, but that the emotional part was what we would never forget. You are so glad to have survived the experience, so glad to be alive, that that alone is sort of a cleansing thing.

I knew I couldn't be bitter all of my life. Bitterness just breeds more of the same. I was not bitter then, and still am not toward the Germans.

Most of those people were saddled with a situation they couldn't do anything about, and I saw that. There were enough people in charge that there wasn't much ordinary people could do. I think the training and upbringing I had at home was unusual.

The best thing, of course, was when we were liberated; we were out of it.

The very worse thing was when I first landed after bailing out. I realized I was down 250 miles behind the lines and on my own. I remember looking up at the sky and wondering what effect it would have on my mother and my family when they were notified that I was missing in action. Almost as bad as that was the time I was in solitary confinement.

This wasn't the foremost thing in my life. Of course it wasn't. It was just a thing along the way. The fact that I was able to get an education was a tremendous thing. I was the first DeLeo to get a college education.

The main part of my life was that Peg and I were married and raised a family. And, now with a grandson, it's just great.

Towns passed through on the 487.8 miles march through Germany from February 6 to April 26, 1945:

Gross Tychow-Kiefheide-Bad Posen-Solzenbert-Rustow-Greifenberg-Stuchow-Kummin-Konigsberg-LudwigsBad-Gorke-DobberPhul-Wollin-Swinemunde (Feb.14)-Kilzow-Usedom-Pinnow-Anklum-Rustow-Postlow-Breest-Gultz-Fahnbarh-Schmale-Schossow-Tarnow—six days layover)-Mollenberg-Kargow-Warren (March 3)-Knink-Peptin-Lebbin-Malchow-Karow-Penzlin-Callin-Zahren-Darze-Belgrade-Lubbey-Zeisbulle-Damm-Maltzow-Brenz-Blienenstorf-Muchow-Zierow-Balow (seven days layover)-Kremmin-Wanzlitz-Eldene-Bresegard-Karent-Malliss-Beisdorf-Domitz-Riverglbg-Dannenberg-Tripkau-Melzinger-Gohrde-Devington-Bevensen-Barum-Ulesen-Stetlin-Loburt (train ride)-Madeburg-KGF 11-A-Altengrabow-Gorzke-Benken-Lubnitz-Belzig-Dansdorf-Niemeok-Hohenwerdiggo-Zeuden-Marzahna-Schonefeld-Kurzlipsdorf-Blonsdorf-Seehausen-Mellnitz-Seyda-Luttchenseyda-Gentha-Rulesdorf-Rehain-Jessen-Annaburg (Pottery factory bombed A-26s)-Naundorf (Kolonie)-Naundorf-Labrun (Elbe River)-Prettin-Dommitzsth-Dahlenberg-Trossin-Falkenburg-Cossa-Durchweana-Sollichau-Tornau-Krina-Ploddo-Schlaitz-Bitterfield-Halle.

Printed with permission of P. Joseph DeLio and The Oral History Archive of The American Airpower Heritage Museum.

Looking Back At Those Great Days

❖

It wasn't all death and destruction

Narrated by Frank Lewis, P-47 pilot
9th Air Force, 406th Fighter Group, 514th Fighter Squadron
Edited by Erik Dyreborg

Introduction

Many memoirs of the wartime experiences of P-47 (Jug) pilots have appeared in print as we pass our 80th birthdays and time seems to be running short. Most of them appear to concentrate on mission-by-mission stories of combat.

When I look back, the raw fighting seems to fade away, and I recall some of the things that characterized our day-to-day living that were not necessarily associated with combat and endemic death and destruction.

Many fine men, our buddies, were lost; but life went on, we lived from day to day, and strange things happened, too often tragic, sometimes humorous. I'd like to tell of a few that I remember.

What? Girls flying our birds?

Once graduated from flying school, we new Second Lieutenants found ourselves in transition schools to upgrade to the fighter that would control our destinies; in my case, the P-47 Thunderbolt, at Bradley Field, Windsor Locks, Connecticut, in the Spring of 1944. Little did we know that we were training specifically for the coming invasion of France, cannon fodder, as it were. We were needed in combat, and how badly we found out one fine day.

413

Our class, 44-B, had already experienced special attention in that only one cadet had washed out of advanced training at Williams Field when usually, a large percentage failed. We graduated with just enough time before D-Day ahead of us to complete fighter transition. Classes after ours were ruthlessly pruned as 1944 progressed and the loss rate was far less than estimated.

School had progressed, we were checked out on and actually flying the seven-ton monster, making rough use of a fleet of war—and trainee-weary OD-colored razorbacks. Word came down that a new Jug was due in, the latest model, brand spanking shiny new from the Long Island factory. On the appointed morning we were all on the ramp to welcome the inbound Jug.

There she came, glinting silver in the morning sun, roaring into a tight 360 pattern, gear and flaps down at just the right spot and altitude, smooth as silk, far more competent than our schoolboy efforts. A grease job right on the runway number was very impressive.

We conjectured that this must surely be an ETO returnee ace, come to teach us how to splash Krauts in ME-109s and FW-190s. Tail wagging behind a "follow-me" jeep, the Jug pulled into a parking slot right in front of the assembled observers and shut down.

Back rolled the motorized bubble canopy, new and wonderful to us, off came the helmet, and out streamed a mane of blonde, wavy hair, immediately assailed by a comb, and we were treated to a winsome grin by the fair pilot. ETO Ace? No way; this was a LADY pilot, flying our bird, showing us a landing pattern that put ours to shame.

This was a shock. Here we were at the pinnacle of young men's desires, flying a 2000—HP fighter, and now we were treated to the fact that it could be competently done by girls. We had never heard of this, and some found it hard to accept.

We soon found out that there existed a cadre of some 1100 young women pilots known as Women Air Force Service Pilots (WASP) who trained as we had done as cadets at Avenger Field in west Texas, and were efficiently flying every type of aircraft in our military inventory to release male pilots for combat. In fact, they did so well as fighter jocks that they would take over all ferrying of Jugs from the Long Island factory during the fall of 1944.

Needless to say, we Second Balloons were allowed no contact with the lovely WASP, who was whisked away by the brass, leaving us to contemplate the thought: If women can do it, what's so special about being a fighter pilot? When we found ourselves in England in a combat unit soon, we would find out that women pilots were doing similar duty there as the Air Transport Auxiliary (ATA).

And so we were left with a new Jug and the knowledge that our sisters were joining us in our craft and we had better get used to it. History would eventually show that the WASP performed admirably in all stateside flying tasks assigned. And we gentleman pilots, for the most part, accepted them as honored and valuable members of our exclusive fraternity of the sky. They suffered the same deaths that we did: 38 of them lost their lives for their country.

We had it better than the bomber trainees

The lady pilot on her way to her home base, and our new silver Jug, with the motorized canopy and paddle-blade Hydramatic prop for more horsepower, begging for action, life as trainees went on. Day by day we honed our flying skills in constant practice, a tough regimen of a half day's ground school, then practice missions in formation, instrument flight, in the air and Link trainer, gunnery at a nearby Long Island range, aerobatics, and dive bombing. Our class was fortunate: no accidents occurred other than a couple of nose-ups from running off the runway, and we all graduated. But things were different at the bomber training base 20 miles away at Westover Field, where losses were tragically heavy from all-too-frequent crashes of the big four-engine birds.

We learned of events at Westover from the young ladies of the nearby towns of Springfield and Chicopee Falls, many of whom had lost boy friends at the bomber base. One lovely who had lost two fiancés to crashes let it be known that she and her friends had given up on Westover dates and looked to the fighter jocks at Bradley Field as more reliable in longevity.

As our class of 44-B graduates completed our Jug transition and moved on to embarkation via troop ship at New York, many of the girls we left behind joined us in the uniformed services, the ladies' branches, such as the WAVES and WACS. One of our young ladies qualified for the WASP and subsequently became a Jug pilot. Years later we found that the Russians also utilized women as combat bomber and fighter pilots, some of them becoming aces.

Fresh meat for the 406th

On our transatlantic journey aboard a forlorn and rusty example of the worst of troopship art, we endured a week of boredom and daily scares of U-boats in our way. Our lumbering convoy never was attacked. We played a lot of cards, mainly hearts, and oftentimes removed our rank emblems and joined our enlisted colleagues in their mess below-decks, judging their hot dogs better eating than the junk our own mess provided.

Our floating palace duly deposited our contingent of soldiers and airmen at the port of Liverpool from whence we were entrained in those weird, to us, British railway coaches with the outside doors, to a Replacement Depot (repple-depple) base at Atcham, to become acclimated, if that were possible, to flying a Jug in typical British lousy weather.

Here we were divided up into groups and assigned to various fighter units in need of replacements, and this is where those who would have a chance for ace glory were selected, by some arcane reasoning, and sent on to 8th Air Force bomber escort units.

The rest of us became ground peckers, fighter-bomber pilots, funneled to units of the 9th Air Force, fighter-bomber units destined to cross the Channel to lodge behind the advancing armies across France to Germany, virtually never to catch sight of an enemy aircraft except as strafing targets on an airdrome. Few aces were spawned in the 9th Air Force. In my 70 missions, I never saw a German aircraft in flight, though I did get to strafe a few of them.

Four of us, George McKeand, Alvin Meireis, Clyde McFrederick, me, had managed to stick together through flying school, then RTU, and now were assigned to the 406th Fighter Bomber Group and the 514th Fighter Bomber Squadron at a place in south-eastern England called Ashford. Our stay there would be very short inasmuch as the Group was then in process of moving across the Channel to take up residence in Normandy at a hastily constructed, pierced-plank-runway forward airbase numbered A-13, near Bayeaux, in direct support of General George Patton's Third Army.

Assignment to the 'hot sacks' of recently MIA or KIA pilots

The Normandy invasion had occurred a month before, and losses in our Group had been heavy, thus our arrival as replacements was welcomed.

We found that one hot sack had belonged to a pilot who had been badly wounded on a dive-bombing run in Normandy, and was unable to either control the plane or manage a bailout, and had heroically dived his aircraft directly into the flak batteries and wiped them out. We newcomers would find that this kind of heroism was not unusual. Being young and indestructible, little did we four dream that only two of us would return to the states at the end of our combat tour.

How long in months or in missions or time a tour might be we were not informed. As I moved my stuff into my new canvas home, friends of the departed were quietly packing up his possessions for shipment home to his family, a sad duty all-too-frequently required.

For others, of course, I had no intention of it happening to me. That was the overriding philosophy of all of us. We were personally going to win the war and go home to a hero's welcome. Our fears were not so much of death in battle but rather of simply screwing up in some stupid way to lose face with our colleagues. We were more worried about lousing up the taxi sequence on a mission, or of doing a sloppy job of formation flying than we were of combat.

We got an immediate and graphic idea of what we were getting into as our 6 X 6 truck full of new pilots arrived at Ashford airfield. We were forced to stop and park for a while since the approach road crossed the end of the runway, which appeared to be of some kind of heavy mesh steel matting buried in the grass.

Incoming Jugs passed in front of us and turned onto a taxiway to go off to their parking spots. And what a parade it was to our combat-innocent eyes. Several of the birds showed battle-damage areas on wings, or tail surfaces, or fuselage.

The last one, showing evidence of serious battle damage, came rampaging down the runway much faster than all the others, making no sign of slowing for the runway's end, and we could see that it still carried bombs under the wings. The excited comment could be heard from one of us, "Hell! He's going clean off the runway!"

Sure enough, the Jug flashed past us onto the runway overrun and nosed over onto its back in the grass. But at least it did not explode or catch fire. Emergency vehicles rushed into action, and as we went on our way to our squadron areas. We found later that the pilot was rescued once the fuselage was lifted.

Thus our welcome to combat! Little did I dream that, in a very few months I would belly land a Jug with so much wing gone that, technically, it was not supposed to be able to fly. More on that story later.

We found our group in the throes of packing up for the move to a Channel port for water transport across to Normandy and a new airbase. Housing was changing rapidly from day to day as the normal six-man pyramidal tents were taken to be packed and trucked to the Channel, we occupants relegated to two-man pup tents. The enlisted men were already in the pup tents while pilots were gradually moving to them.

Here, American ingenuity reigned as each pair of occupants (Army pup tents were called "shelter halves" as two of them were buttoned together too make one small two-man tent.) vied with others to modify their tents for maximum liveability.

Basically, these were deep excavations under the tent roofs with sleeping ledges cut into the side walls, scrounged materials used as carpets and wall coverings, wall excavations to house personal gear, each tent demonstrating imaginative treatments aimed at outstripping all others in elaboration.

We newcomers were lucky to be assigned to six-man pyramidals for a time, and we dispersed to locate our assigned sacks and meet our tent mates. It was explained to us that the pilots would be the last to go, landing at the new Normandy base after a mission, tents and packed gear all set up and ready for us among the hedgerows.

In the meantime, we could expect two weeks or so of Ashford living before the final move. It was a slow, laborious process. So, we settled into our new life in a combat unit, armed with the finest fighter known to man.

July's first two weeks gave me three training flights and, glory of glories, my first combat mission on the 12th, a milk-run B-26 escort mission. The bombers dropped through an undercast and we escort fighters were unmolested by the Luftwaffe.

Seven more dive bombing and armed recce missions passed into history, but my last one on the 28th had a cryptic Form 5 entry, "Return from France." Strange. Well, as it transpired, this mission was somewhat abnormal. You don't become a skilled dive—bomber short of a bit of practical experience and instructions from more experienced pilots. I'd had the instructions alright, but needed experience. I was getting it, slowly, but mistakes were made.

On the 28th's mission, my flight had a target in a mountainous area. I was tail end Charley, the last to go down, with two 500-pounders. I guess I got a little excited because I prolonged my dive beyond safety, let the bombs go, and then looked at too little altitude for a normal dive recovery. As I frantically initiated pullout, the hills got closer and closer, and it looked as though I had fatally miscalculated my pullout clearance. But, nothing daunted, I horsed that stick back with both hands and all my strength, slowly greyed and then blacked totally out, and recovered consciousness zooming straight up, out of control, about to stall, not a friendly aircraft in sight.

It appeared later that my comrades had thought I had augured in. Regaining control I headed home on our emergency heading, but noted that my fuel available looked to be insufficient to make it back across the Channel to Ashford with any reserve.

Discretion overriding valor, I landed at the first forward strip I ran across and picked up fuel from five-gallon jerricans, administered by a pair of disgruntled GIs not happy with the slow process. It was enough to get me home to Ashford to a serious discussion with my flight commander about my lousy dive-bombing methodology. I learned. You learned or died, and I intended to avoid dying.

Ground life at Ashford

Missions were scheduled less than every other day so we pilots had plenty of loafing and recreational time, while our hard-working crews worked their butts off keeping our Jugs in good shape for combat, clean and shiny.

One sunny July day, with nothing scheduled to occupy us, one of my buddies and I borrowed bicycles and headed off down the road to town where we had heard there might be a golf course, of all things. Sure enough, there was, a nine-holer with a small farmhouse for administration. We dropped in to find a cordial English gentleman on hand to loan us a couple sets of clubs, old-fashioned wooden shaft types unlike anything we had ever seen at home. He warned us to watch out for his sheep on the fairways, his mobile grass cutters. He had no fuel to run a regular fairway mower. The sheep did nicely, although they got in our way from time to time, and we had to drive them off the fairway to make our shots. But this was a nice touch to lighten the load of combat.

When we finished our nine-hole round, the grounds keeper invited us to sit for a while under his apple tree. While we sat he windlassed a rope up from the depths of his well, and, miraculously, dangling from the end of that rope was a pail containing several bottles. "Here, boys. Have a sip of good English apple cider." Which we did, and it was delectably cold and delicious. What a welcome by the generous English for us invading Yankees. We parted that day with the most cordial of relations between our two civilizations.

Here was a real British gentleman who would never mouth the unfriendly complaint: "Over-paid, over-sexed, over here." It was our misfortune that our move across the Channel precluded our enjoying the golf course again.

Doodlebug Alley

Ashford was located in southeastern England right smack on a line from the Kraut buzz-bomb launching spots on the south Channel coast to England and on to London.

Every V-l pilotless bomb, or doodlebug, or buzz-bomb, as they were variously called, checked in with us on its way to blast some defenseless neighborhood of women and children in London. Some were damaged in flight by coastal anti-aircraft guns, the wounded bird often staggering far enough to crash near, too near, our airfield. We made a game out of estimating how far the crashes occurred in our vicinity.

I had a fancy chronograph watch with a lot of buttons controlling various time functions. One function measured distance by timing the seconds from seeing an explosion compared to the time the explosion was heard. The watch then displayed the distance, the closest one being only one-half mile.

A fair amount of money changed hands from day to day in this game as each participant registered his estimates to match against the watch's figure. After a few days of doodlebugs we got pretty good at it. Fortunately, none exploded on the airfield, though the dread possibility certainly existed. It was a relief to get free of them when we moved.

We had other troubles with the buzz bombs. The P-51 Mustang and the British Tempest aircraft could catch the bombs if they had a chance to dive on them to pick up speed. We had the squadron marshalled on the end of the runway one day, loaded with two 500-lb bombs each. As we waited for takeoff time, we became aware of a buzz bomb heading directly towards us from down the runway, at only a couple hundred feet altitude, with a Mustang on its tail, hosing it with 50-caliber bullets, the spent bullets landing in our vicinity.

The pilot seemed totally unaware of our Jugs in his line of fire. Several pilots panicked, set their brakes and bailed out and ran, for it looked like the buzz bomb would crash among us, thus wiping out the squadron in one fell swoop. We saw strikes on the buzz bomb and, wounded, it reared up right in front of us, stalled, and crashed a few hundred yards past our assemblage of Jugs. That was a close one; nearly an entire squadron wiped out but for the good fortune a kind God meted out to us.

The flag officer, sitting in his jeep waiting for takeoff time to flag us off, facing down the runway, had one of the spent bullets bounce off his hood and ricochet up through the windshield, most of its energy gone, and bumped the officer's forehead and tipped his hot pilot cap into the back seat.

Another day a buzz bomb came by, a Spitfire on its tail, getting strikes, to blow up the bomb in midair, the chase plane too close and flew through the burning detritus. The Spitfire had fabric on the control and flap surfaces, and this cloth material caught fire and burned off, leaving the pilot in a precarious position. However, the bird was kept under control and the pilot landed at our airbase. The Spit was pulled to a parking space to await maintenance personnel to come to repair the control surfaces.

The lovely little Spitfire attracted a lot of us admiring visitors, all wishing that we could fly her. The repair crew came in due time and repaired her, and a ferry pilot soon came and whisked her away. And so we lost our badly scorched visitor.

A rare air battle and a pilot lost

An unusual mission occurred on the 29th of June, just before our group arrived.

On that day, my 22nd birthday, the squadron went looking for bridges behind the Normandy beachfront. They were jumped by a swarm of FW-190s. First Lieutenant Levitt C. Beck was reported at debriefing to have met one of them head on, and both his plane and the FW-190 went down. Beck was classified as MIA for months until late in the year he was reclassified as KIA, but the story of his survival into the French Underground, betrayal to the Gestapo, and death in Buchenwald concentration camp was unknown.

Fifty years later I would research the fate of Beck and several score of other American and British airmen who found themselves in Buchenwald for a few weeks in 1944. That story will be found in detail in this book. (Beck had an interesting experience earlier that month when he crash-landed near Cherbourg. His squadron mate landed and took Beck aboard on his lap and they flew back to Ashford, where Beck logged P-47 co-pilot time.)

Life among the hedgerows

Early August found us taking up tent residence at A-14, near Creteville. Our pyramidal tents were set up around the perimeter of a hedgerow field, the thick hedgerows 10-to-15 feet high, and the selfsame hedgerows that gave Patton's tanks difficulty in passage from one field to another. The pastures featured a mound or berm of earth raising four or five feet with the hedgerows planted on top, encircling the field, making an almost impenetrable fence around each field. Some brainy GI invented a brush cutter apparatus to weld to the noses of the tanks that, when rammed into the hedgerow, would cut a swath through it wide enough to allow unrestricted tank passage.

Tents were occupied by six-man flights around the circumference of our particular field, and so we settled down to life bounded by hedgerows, and tried to achieve some measure of normal living between missions, which came thick and fast with good summer weather and the needs of Patton's army in its eastward sweep. We set up our own little field kitchen where the five-gallon jerrican became indispensable for keeping each tent supplied with water, dispensed by a water trailer.

This was situated outside the door to the officers' club tent some 300 yards away down a pathway swamped through the intervening hedgerows. Lugged that far, the can of water appeared to gain a pound every 10 feet and became an intolerable burden to those stuck with the chore, for which we all took turns daily. One evening as the light faded I returned to our tent from the flight line. No one was about. It was my turn to lug water, but our jerrrican was missing. Inasmuch as thieving was common, I suspected that we had been victimized by a thief, GI or pilot, one as possible as the other.

Cussing to myself roundly, I headed for the club tent to see if I could find our guys. At the tent and the water trailer, pitch dark by now, I saw none of our tent personnel but did, to my joy, spot a jerrican tucked away behind the water trailer. Opportunity plus necessity blew away my scruples. I sneakily snatched up the errant can, heavy as hell, and headed surreptitiously back to our tent, avoiding the regular pathway through the hedgerows for fear of someone seeing the can and recognizing it as theirs. We made a practice of painting emblems of our possession on our cans, but I had not seen any in the dark night on this one.

The route back to our tent off the path was onerous, rough, through several unbroken hedgerows, over a creek which soaked my feet, fell down twice, got scratched crossing a wire fence, but finally, triumphant but exhausted, arrived at our tent's back side. I put the can down and entered our tent.

The guys were back. "Hey, Frank, where you been? Some SOB stole our jerrican, down at the trailer!" Oh, surely not! I retrieved the can from outside and brought it in. Sure enough, all the others and I could see that it was plainly our own can that I had stolen. My tent-mates had taken it to the trailer ahead of me, filled it, left it by the trailer while they played some cards in the tent, came out to find it gone, courtesy of me. Talk about stupid. It took a few weeks of ribbing for the jerrican kid to live it down.

In the meantime, the war went on full bore, with or without jerricans. Patton moved so fast he went clear off his maps while we cleaned out Tiger tanks ahead of him. We participated in the massive bombing of St. Lo to give him some manoeuvring room, at the cost of an Army general, lost to bombs dropped off target, the tragic fault of straight-and-level bombers, not fighter bombers. We were thankful for that.

We also participated in the carnage of the Belfort Gap where, with better-Allied coordination, we might have shortened the war considerably, there would have been so many more Germans killed or captured. But they were able to retreat in large numbers eastward to fight another day. Our Group earned a rare Distinguished Unit Citation for this action, and contributed to the surrender of a 20,000-man German unit because of our specific aerial action. How the German soldier feared and hated our "Jabos."

The chow situation was not exactly epicurean. We endured it while attempting to set up our own individual kitchen capability in our tents. Mainly, this was made possible by scrounging 10-in-one ration cartons. This wonderful facility provided three meals for a day for ten soldiers, and it included such goodies as canned bacon and butter, powdered eggs, jam, canned meats and chicken, cigarettes, candy bars, a cornucopia that made life bearable.

The large cartons were acquired by scrounging a jeep to the huge mountain of such cartons piled in some hedgerow field nearby and guarded by a soldier with M-1 rifle. He might be bribable with whiskey or cigarettes to make him scarce in back of the pile for ten minutes while we loaded the jeep from the front and scampered on our way.

These fine rations, supplemented with goodies from home, sometimes a delicious birthday cake, allowed us to eat reasonably well in spite of what we might find at the mess tent. Now and then we would convene an "ooffs" party. This was a gathering of a group of pilots with their mess kits and as many eggs as each had scrounged from the local farm populace by trading cigarettes or Hershey bars for the "oeufs" (not sure of spelling) as they were called in French. It was not unknown that a local farm girl or two might be invited. It was amazing the goodies that could be procured by bartering candy bars and cigarettes.

These picnics somewhat alleviated the ongoing strain of tough tank-support missions and high losses. Anti-aircraft resistance steadily intensified as the Germans constricted their lines as they retreated eastward. Much of our activity was directed to close front-line support of one or another of General Patton's units, but we also hit other "targets of opportunity," as they were called.

Trains were favorite targets for our bombs, rockets, and strafing, either in marshalling yards, when the entire Group of three squadrons might congregate, or trains caught on the move.

One early August morning, we caught a juicy train at daybreak scuttling towards a tunnel. The flight leader let his two 500-pounders go at a road-track intersection half a mile ahead of the bustling locomotive. A huge hole appeared in the tracks and, unable to stop, the engine toppled into the shell hole and the train crashed to a stop, giving us easy pickings to tear the cars apart with 50-calibre bullets. Whatever flak cars the train might have contained were useless to them tipped on their sides.

This was an outstanding target of opportunity, and most important to discover and destroy, for a shortage of transportation was immediately felt on the front lines by the enemy. Fighter-bomber interdiction of rail lines behind the Normandy beachhead contributed significantly to Allied success in establishing that front in June.

Other incidental targets of opportunity were often vehicles scuttling down the road (Rommel was strafed in such a situation), tanks and other military vehicles on the roads or attempting to hide in the woods, and rarely, airdromes with many parked aircraft.

In 70 missions I participated in strafing but one airdrome, at Metz. Perhaps I was fortunate in that, for 20, 40, and 88-mm flak batteries always heavily defended them, and the casualty rate against such targets was heavy.

The Big Bertha that wasn't there

We were all becoming skilled dive-bombers as the missions piled up and we gained invaluable experience. One rare skip-bombing mission was handed to us as the summer waned.

It seems that a Big Bertha railroad gun with some 20 miles of range was harassing our ground troops during the night, and then retiring to a short tunnel in the nearby hills to hide during the day.

We were armed with under-wing 500-pounders with 15-second fuses, the usual for skip bombing to allow the bombing plane time to get back to altitude before the bombs went off. The tunnel sighted, our number one took the first pass; right on the tracks he skimmed straight at the tunnel mouth. At the exact right spot, he toggled off his bombs and began a climb up and over the tunnel mountain. It wasn't much of a mountain, more a small hill. The bombs entered the tunnel and should have stopped inside as they hit the railroad cars.

Unfortunately, the Krauts had changed their tactics overnight, had moved the Big Bertha out of the tunnel to some other location, and the two bombs tumbled right on through the tunnel, to explode in the open on the far side.

Unfortunately again, the pilot had not expected this and was surprised by the bombs exploding outside the tunnel, giving him a slight boost back to altitude. It could have been worse. With minor damage, he was able to fly the bird home.

The Third Army continued eastward at breakneck speed. We were hard put to keep up, necessitating moving from one airdrome to another as we closed in on Belgium, Holland, and eventually, Germany. September was well along and we had moved from A-14 at Cretteville to A-36 at Louplande near Le Mans. Our armies were moving steadily eastward through France, but an attempt to force a Rhine crossing at Arnhem, in Holland, was a dismal failure. Inept planning brought about failure of two American and one British airborne division to coordinate competently on their drops into Holland. Added to this tragedy was the unanticipated appearance of a German tank division that threw them back from the Rhine Bridge they were attempting to invest. The Rhine crossing would have to wait several months until we took the bridge at Remagen.

The Group had occupied three primitive airfields since leaving Ashford, spending less than a month at any one of them. They all featured similar facilities, i.e., short pierced-plank steel runways, tent living, surrounded by hedgerows. The whole of northern France appeared to be of this bocage-type country for the benefit of small farmers and their cattle, with every hedgerow pasture featuring its quota of swollen, putrid smelling dead cattle and horses.

The hedgerows did, indeed, contain the cattle in neat pastures without need of expensive fencing. But it made hard going for our troops, and the Germans found it easy to set up effective snipers' positions buried out of sight in the hedgerows. And, the Germans were past masters of rifle design, manufacture, and sniper-quality marksmanship among its male citizenry, characteristics that German emigrants had established in the gunsmithing and schuetzen rifle clubs in the United States.

Souvenir-addicted soldiers and airmen

The American fighting man was very young, mostly from small rural towns, had been raised in the frontier spirit, a hunter and fisherman, and used to the outdoors. Three things fascinated him: young women, cars, and guns.

The jalopy acquired at age 16 got him the girl. The guns satisfied his frontier heritage. There wasn't a farmhouse in the breadth of the United States that failed to display a Marlin or Winchester lever-action thirty-thirty deer rifle in the corner behind the kitchen stove. Wartime gave him ample opportunity to indulge his craving for exotic guns, a Luger or P-38 pistol, or a Model 98 infantry rifle, or a beautifully made—and—decorated target rifle, single-shot, inlaid with gold and silver. A War Department Circular allowed him to collect souvenir weapons as long as they were not intended for commercial purposes back home.

And so, we became gun collectors, some of us in a big way, for it was a piece of cake to acquire every imaginable type of German gun by trading with army troops who had picked them off a battlefield, or confiscated them from captured Germans, or collected them from the citizenry. A Luger was the most-wanted item, or a P-38, for either could be worn in place of or substituted for the clumsy Colt .45 auto.

When one saw the maker engraved on a .45 to be Underwood Typewriter, or Singer Sewing Machine, the tendency was not to trust the reliability of that war-industry product. Besides, there was just some aura of machismo in sporting a fine German pistol in its black German leather holster.

As the army units moved through, Quartermaster troops confiscated all firearms from the populace, cleaned them from battlefields, or from captured enemy, and collected them for disposal in large piles, outdoors or in tents or warehouses, when available.

There, they were open to trade, and particularly liked dealing with fighter pilots who seemed to have inexhaustible supplies of cigarettes, whiskey, even Hershey bars, all worth their weight in gold in trade, deals that had to be expedited, for the confiscated weapons were officially ordered to be destroyed by burning.

It was not unusual to jeep to a rumored large collection at one or another army unit, and arrive to a large smoking pile of hundreds of burned rifles, pistols, shotguns, many of them rare and expensive hand-made items, selling for thousands of dollars back home, and the sad greeting: "You should have been here yesterday!"

Despite many such disappointments, I soon found myself the proud possessor of several pistols and a couple of battlefield Mauser rifles, one of them a sniper version with a four-power scope sight. I was well on my way to my eventual name: "The junk dealer of the 514th."

I was not alone in this predilection. Several other pilots became collectors, to the point that, months later during our occupation of northern Germany, we formed a shooting club and had weekend marksmanship shoots with our "liberated" .22 rifles and pistols.

Winter quarters at Mourmelon le Grand

As a cold fall faced an oncoming very cold winter, our Group left tents behind, on the 24th of September, and moved forward to Rheims, a major command city, with an excellent airdrome nearby called Mourmelon le Grand, numbered A-80, consisting of solid, permanent structures, what had been a French cavalry camp in historic times.

This was comfortable living, far removed from the crude conditions of our tent hedgerow cities. We all prayed that our good fortune would be long-lived. Actually, it was. We were to stay there all through the coldest winter in decades, according to local citizenry. This was a blessing for we were able to keep our barracks buildings reasonably warm with little oil-fired stoves.

Unknown to us grunts, the high brass were planning a vast airborne enterprise in Holland that, if successful, would gain a Rhine River crossing at Arnhem. Our Screaming Eagles, the 101st Airborne with our 82nd Airborne and a British airborne unit would drop onto and take the bridge at Arnhem, and, some 20 km back with other crucial bridges, Nijmegen and Eindhoven, with British ground support. I

It was a poorly planned debacle from the first hapless paratrooper out the door of his C-47 carrier. Half a century later, it would become the subject of a best-selling book and a movie, A BRIDGE TOO FAR. The plan failed; the Arnhem Bridge was not secured, and initial crossing of the Rhine would take place many kilometers away at another bridge at Remagen. All of the airborne units were badly mauled by the German tanks that had not been anticipated in the flawed planning, whose appearance was an unpleasant and fatal surprise.

At Mourmelon, we learned first-hand of all this when there appeared in our midst, camped on the far side of our runway, the remnants of the weary 101st Airborne, to rest and recuperate, and resupply in readiness for their next jump.

They needed everything. Many of them were armed with German rifles and pistols, having lost their own, and were more than eager to do business with we fighter jocks, appearing with varied and valuable trade goods. In the process of dickering for a small Mauser pocket pistol, I made an almost fatal mistake.

The gun's owner assured me that it was unloaded. I believed him. Somehow, the trigger was pressed, the pistol fired, but up and through the roof, affording a little unexpected ventilation. When ruffled feelings had been smoothed out, we completed the trade, and I added a nice little pistol to my burgeoning collection. The souvenir-collecting many in our Group did a lot of business in the few weeks the paratroopers lived with us.

The jumping 101st into battle in 6 x 6s—surrounded at Bastogne

Under cover of bad weather that grounded most fighter-bombers, General von Rundstedt launched a massive retro movement towards Antwerp on the 16th of December.

He caught us flat-footed, mauled scores of army units, took thousands of prisoners, cruelly executed many of our POWs, and sent hundreds off to the horrible conditions of concentration camps. Our Group lost 10 pilots, I lost one of my pals, and had my Jug shot up to the tune of a belly landing and a junked airplane.

Our visiting friends, the 101st Screamin' Eagles, were suddenly called to action, only this time on the ground, in trucks they were so far from full recovery from Holland's debacle. At the road center of Bastogne in Belgium, the 101st found themselves surrounded by the rampaging Germans, with no help from we Jug jocks because of the lousy weather. For days, they suffered siege while desperately looking for the weather to clear, which it finally did on the 23rd just in time for Christmas.

The skies were blue and filled with fighter-bombers, supporting the recovery of the ground lost to von Rundstedt in the preceding two weeks. It was costly for our Group.

We heard at aircrew level that our Group Commander and the 101st commander, General Tony MacAuliffe, were old friends, and, as a result, our unit was particularly called upon for support, which we gladly gave the friends who had shared our airbase and traded war stories and souvenirs with us. For five continuous and intensive days our Group attacked the hundreds of gun positions surrounding Bastogne, losing 10 pilots in the process.

Returning from one mission with serious battle damage, my flying school buddy, Mac, was faced with bailout. Apparently he was unable to roll onto his back and drop out, as we normally tried to do, but elected to go over the side and off the left wing.

This was bad move. He didn't clear the horizontal stabilizer and was injured to the point that he was unable to deploy his chute. A close look removed any doubt that there was any fault in the chute whatsoever, that he was simply unable to pull the ripcord. And so the first of we four pals from flying school days was gone, a good ol' boy, a fine pilot, well liked by everyone. I soon had my own chance to join him but was blessed with more luck.

Soon after Christmas, I was leading a flight of four to destroy flak positions situated around Bastogne, supposedly over 700 sites, a mix of 20, 40, and 88 mm guns, mostly quad 20s as far as we knew. My own plane out for maintenance, I was assigned a brand-new P-47, belonging to our fearless squadron commander, who had just gotten his lady's name painted on the nose. Needless to say, I was careful with this precious bird, to no avail.

Pulling up off a strafing pass at a nest of quad 20s, suddenly, a loud WHOMP, and I was rolled precipitately onto my back with almost five feet of the left wing outboard of the pitot tube missing as though band-sawed off neatly. This was not good. I managed to roll out in my climb, but while upside down, another loud WHOMP, and a direct hit on my left horizontal stabilizer, shredding it and the rudder, and forcing the trim tab into full UP position.

The engine seemed fine, the Jug flew OK, but with very heavy UP pressure on the stick that I had to counteract by holding it forward with both hands braced against my knees and all the arm and shoulder strength I could muster, with some 80 miles to get back to Mourmelon. Advice to bail out came thick and fast from well-wishers who could see how badly my bird was hurt, but I elected to get home if at all possible.

And so, home to Mourmelon, where I was again advised to bail out. This was not an option. Letting go of the stick would immediately pull the plane up into a steep climb and stall, pinning me in the seat. No go. I respectfully declined and elected a belly landing beside the runway in the snow. With a wingman calling airspeeds and holding 30 knots or so higher than normal, the plane was not difficult to control into a smooth belly landing. I tried 10 degrees of flaps, and, to my wonder, all the UP pressure from the damaged trim tab evaporated and the stick felt normal.

As a crowd gathered around to take pictures and consider my good fortune, comments were heard from tech rep/maintenance types, "With that much wing gone this bird should not have been flyable." Well, they tell the bumblebee that, too, and he flies anyway. Jacked up and on its gear, my commander's new Jug was towed off to the Class 26 bone yard to suffer as a cannibalised hangar queen. I, somewhat frazzled, wrote it off in the Form 1, "OK." This inaccurate entry was called to my attention later. Fifty-some years later I wrote to Colonel Kelly and apologized for trashing his new bird. He wrote back, generously, and suggested that I not do that any more. He was a truly fine gentleman.

Frank Lewis with the not so brand new P-47 is pictured above.

Returning one day from bombing in the Ruhr Valley, I had the bad luck to have one of my 500-lb bombs hang up and defy all my efforts to dislodge it. Over the mountains somewhere near Trier, I gave one last haul on the manual release and the bomb finally let go and dropped. I rolled up on a wing to try to see it hit the ground and observed a large truck with a snowplow laboriously making its way up a mountain road.

I lost sight of my bomb, but when I rolled up to look again I saw the snowplow disappear in a large explosion. To my horror, my errant bomb had apparently made its way onto the snowplow to explode, for we were over enemy terrain and I had dropped the bomb armed. I have felt bad about that tragedy until this day, for I can imagine that the occupants probably were innocent civilian road workers, not enemy soldiers. That was one fortune of war that I would like to have avoided.

Used car dealers

In his mad dash across France, General Patton's tanks and other gas-guzzling vehicles were too often short on fuel. It was common knowledge that one source of shortage was black-market sales from gas trucks along the Red Ball Express route from the ports to the front lines.

Military Police were taking care of this criminal endeavor.

Another source of shortage, however, was close to home for us: the fuel used by the many incidental, unauthorized vehicles scrounged by both GIs and officers of units such as ours. At one of our bases as we moved across France two American cars showed up, liberated from the Nazis who had also used them as staff cars.

One was a 1939 Mercury four-door convertible, the other a Packard four-door. They had been modified to military uses by removing the plush seats and the doors, replacing the latter with a safety strap, and the seats with military-style wooden bench seats, with rifle boots beside. They did make fine staff cars for brass lucky enough to scrounge them, but they also used a lot of precious gas and oil.

It was possible for fighter jocks to acquire battlefield vehicles at the junkyard assembly fields, crowded with hundreds of after-the-battle military vehicles in various stages of disintegration. We climbed up onto a Tiger tank one time and pulled open the driver's top hatch. The driver was still in the seat, a cremated blob hunched forward between his knees, a terrible sight. We didn't look into any more combat vehicles.

The yard guards could be influenced to look the other way for suitable trade goods while a German Kubelwagen (Jeep), or Schwimmwagen (amphibious Jeep), or Kettenkrad (tracked motorcycle) or virtually any other running or repairable vehicle was driven or towed away.

Our young men were geniuses at field repair of small vehicles, German or American, and, in our dashes from airfield to airfield across France, quite a variety of strange vehicles showed up. We moved from one airbase to another one time with our gear packed into a scrounged American Weasel, a small tracked amphibious jeep. The voyage killed it for a track broke and there was no replacement available.

At one time before the winter, order to cease and desist unauthorized burning of precious fuel filtered down when our squadron personnel were driving at least one Kubelwagen, one Schwimmwagen, and a Kettenkrad (featured in the movie SAVING PRIVATE RYAN); while there were many other such vehicles scattered around the Group. Later, while in the occupation, German aircraft would appear for a while, such as two primary Junkers Jungmeister biplane trainers, a HE-lll bomber, and a ME-ll0 twin-engine fighter, whose gear collapsed, ending its usefulness.

1945 and the war winds down

The Battle of the Bulge successfully concluded and the Germans on the run, we moved closer to the action, eventually into Germany itself. Our first 1945 move was to the city of Metz, Y-34, where we had strafed the airdrome four months before. Our quarters there were unusual in being a multi-storied hotel with an elevator that sometimes worked. Other personnel were housed in an apartment complex, quite an improvement over what we had endured crossing France.

We enjoyed this for only a week before moving on to Y-29 at Aasch in Belgium near Liege. Here we were in tents again, but enjoyed hot baths in a public bath building provided for the comfort of coal miners in the vicinity, a place to relax after a hard and dirty day, down a brew, socialize, and luxuriate in steam rooms and hot baths.

For us, this was magic, and we took full advantage of the town's generosity. This made up in part for our being in tents again. That would change when we reached Germany and could commandeer houses from the citizenry, the right of the conqueror. And it was beginning to be plain, as the Battle of the Bulge petered out late in January, that we were the conquerors.

Several pilots had been sent home for R & R, "Flak" leave as we called it. That had started in December with commanders enjoying the privilege first.

Terror Fliegers—the loss of my best friend

With the Battle of the Bulge bringing the Germans to desperation and the atrocities of the murders at Malmedy and other places where our prisoners were mistreated, we were faced with Hitler's "Terror Flieger" order that classified fighter-bomber pilots as terrorists, to be summarily executed on the spot if captured. Two pilots in our Group suffered this fate, one of them my best friend, George McKeand.

At the height of the December Bulge action, in the vicinity of Trier, George suffered severe battle damage and had to bail out. He was seen to land safely and run into nearby woods.

Our ground forces several days later found his nude body, a small-caliber pistol bullet in the back of his head. There was known to be an SS tank unit in the vicinity at the time.

Major Gordon Fowler of the 513th crash-landed near the Rhine, and his body was found a few days later by ground forces. He had been bayoneted in the back. After the war, the War Department classed these events among the atrocities being investigated as "War Crimes." Investigations proved that there were many aircrew men shot, pitchforked, beaten to death upon capture. A little-known event during the Bastogne action was the segregating of hundreds of American prisoners by circumcision, and those displaying this condition were sent to concentration camps, such as Buchenwald and Berga, to work out their short remaining lifespan underground in unsurvivable mining work.

My war ends abruptly

Out of the blue in February, I was told that my ETO war was over, temporarily. I had just flown my 70th mission, one of only five for the final month, and was looking forward to the war ending soon, possibly another 15 to 20 missions, and probably transfer of our exceptionally fine unit to the Pacific to fight the Japanese.

I liked what I was doing; I looked forward to a military career. (Which did, indeed come about after two combat tours in Korea in 1951, I did advance and succeed with my military career). However, now it was time to go home.

Ever the junk dealer, I shouldered my Mauser 98 battlefield rifle and my B-4 bag and obeyed my orders, taking one last photograph of my Jug, Number 07-F, and said "Goodbye."

I did return almost three months later, landing at Orly Airfield on V-E Day; but the war was over, we did not go to the Pacific Theatre, and occupation duty was another, far different story.

Erik Dyreborg: Saturday, Februar 15, 2003, I realized that Frank Lewis and Ken Glemby both served in the same Squadron at the same time in France. I called both of them and the two squadron-mates were reunited after almost 58 years.

Read Ken Glemby's story: A Jug Jock's Story

Printed with permission of Frank Lewis.

A Jug Jock's Story

Narrated by Ken Glemby, a P-47 Pilot
9th Air Force, 406th Fighter Group, 514th Squadron
Edited by Erik Dyreborg

Enlisting and training

When Pearl Harbor was attacked, I was in college and was living with my mother on Ocean Avenue in Brooklyn. I was coming back from school and when I hit the apartment, the word was out, and I heard it then. My mother had the radio on, and she was very shocked. Who wasn't?

When we heard the announcement, the first question was, "Where's Pearl Harbor?" And then, "Why and who attacked us?" Eventually, feelings of outrage just built and built until most everyone in the country was enraged, and I suspect my reaction was typical. I was not yet nineteen when that happened, and we were "gung ho" to do something to somebody, whatever that was going to be.

I enlisted in the Air Force on the first anniversary of Pearl Harbor. I was just finishing the first semester of my senior year in college. At that time, the Air Force had a program whereby if you had only six months or so to go until graduation, and you enlisted right away, they would allow you to finish college. I was in ROTC anyway and qualified for this program. It was, "Come on in NOW fellows and we'll take you at the end of college, when you graduate." But thirty days later, I was in the Air Corps.

I was in Atlantic City in no time. The Army at the Senator Hotel in Atlantic City welcomed me, which was an elevator serviced high-rise hotel. And they had this joyous rule that if you lived from the 7th floor down to the ground floor, you were allowed to use the elevators. But if you roomed above the 7th floor, you had to walk up the stairs. I never could quite figure that one out, but that's the way the Army operated.

437

In Atlantic City, we were given some basic training. I remember a huge parade ground. I also remember that we had a fire drill every night—and that's why I remember the steps going up to my room so very well.

Basic training was, basically, teaching you your left foot from your right. I'll tell you a cute story about that time.

The first day I was there, they had us lined up, and we're now in uniform, feeling really good. The sergeant asks, "Who would like to fly the China Clipper?" The China Clipper at that time was this Pan Am flight across the Pacific. So I raised my hand. "Me, I'd like to fly the China Clipper!" So the next three days, I spent on the dishwashing machine learning not to volunteer. It was a huge dishwashing machine at this hotel. All the dishes went through. You swabbed them, you loaded them, and you sweated. It was a great experience. Never did get to fly the other Clipper.

After Basic, I was sent to Michigan State at Lansing. They had a college course program for guys who were headed for pilot training. Pilot training was something you had to volunteer for. You spent from one to perhaps four months at the college. I spent only thirty days there, because as a science major, my math was up. I had taken math through calculus, and everything else that they wanted us to know, I knew. So I only had a short stay there. It was a very beautiful campus with a winding brook through it. The first night we were there, the co-eds came out and serenaded us. It was really so very nice.

I did get some Cub time, a two-seater, at the Lansing Airport. I don't know why they did it, perhaps for orientation or to see if you got air sick, but these Cubs were so underpowered that they could hardly fly across the field if there was a slight headwind. It was like you were standing still. But it was enough to convince me that I wanted to fly.

From there, I went to San Antonio, Texas, for my Pre-flight training.

There, I really learned where my left foot was from my right foot. San Antonio was a huge staging area from where they eventually sent us out to the various flight training schools.

But that's where you got your physical training, and that's where you became a cadet. You ate on a "square," and you learned discipline. And you got in pretty good physical shape, because you did cross country (running) and P. T. every single day. I don't remember how far we ran. It was just sort of between here and forever. Obstacle courses were included. It was long. You really got into good shape. I used to fence in college and I boxed a little bit, so I wasn't in bad shape, but you don't know what shape is until they put you into it.

All the time I was at San Antonio, I don't think we ever got a day off, and up until the very last day or so, were never off the post.

At the very end, they let us go into San Antonio to see the sights, just so that we could say that we saw it. From there, I went to Cuero, Texas, for Primary Training.

Cuero was a Primary Training school run by civilians. For Primary Training, we flew the PT-19 and were taught by civilian pilots. That was the start of knowing a bit about airplanes.

I had a couple of interesting experiences at Cuero. When we had our graduation night, my instructor, Max Holderness, and his flight of six cadets went out to the USO dance in downtown Cuero in the Fire Hall. They had pulled the fire engines out to have a dance floor. But when we got there, there were loads of cadets but very few girls and not much going on. So we decided we'd take a ride in one of the fire engines, which we did. We drove it around town and finally parked it in some lady's driveway. I assume we may have had a beer or two.

She looked out the window at us, but the fire engine was higher than the window. We left the fire engine there and thought we were home free.

We got in the car and drove to a roadhouse where it was very crowded. There was a table for us, but we were short one chair. A cadet named Royal Heath, who was in our group—you're alphabetically grouped—saw a chair that he wanted, but some older gentleman had his eye on the same chair. They had a little bit of a tugging match, which Royal won. But it turned out the guy was the Justice of the Peace. So he called the troopers and the trooper came over to the table to find out something about the chair pulling.

Royal Heath very honorable stood up and said, "Sir, I stole the fire engine. They didn't have anything to do with it."

Now, we were all in the clink. I walked 100 hours of tours because of that. Royal was killed in the war. I'll never forget him.

Max Holderness was a very fine instructor. He was very important to us, because he could flunk you out or pass you on. The flunking process started right there in Primary school. If you didn't have it, out you went. I know of one guy who knew he was on his last flight. They give you a check out flight, an elimination flight, really, and he knew he would be gone the next day.

The PT-19 is an open cockpit airplane, and one that recovers from a spin. The recovery procedure is to pull back the throttle all the way, kick opposite rudder all the way, and shove the stick forward. The tail comes whomping up and you find the plane in a vertical dive. You get vertical in a hurry—like throwing a stick. So this guy goes into a spin, kicks the rudder, pops the stick forward, unfastens his belt buckle and out of the plane he goes. He pulls the ripcord, floats to earth, and the next day, he was an infantryman! We're crazy people!

I was never concerned that I might not make it. I was pretty good. I was in trouble in Basic Flight. I crashed, but that's a different kind of trouble. I was able to fly.

From Basic, I was sent to Uvalde, Texas, for Basic Flight Training.

At Uvalde, they had a clear recollection of my having been party to the stealing of the fire engine. I did 100 hours of tours, which means that you go out on the parade ground, or on any enclosure, and you march when the other guys are having a day off. You march 'till you walk off your tours. You walk with a seat pack parachute hanging from your shoulders that's hitting the backs of your legs. So with every step you take, this parachute goes whack, whack, whack and wears a groove into the back of your leg. But I got through it, as did the other guys.

We flew BT-13s, Vultee Vibrators they called them. They were made by Vultee and they vibrated like hell. It was a fixed gear, metal airplane with a sort of glasshouse of the tandem pilot position. We were taught a little bit of formation flying, instrument flying, and some preliminary combat flying. This is where I had my crash.

There, they used a night landing technique similar to the one used in England at that time, which didn't expose their runways to the German fighters or bombers. This was done by taking the rows of lights running down the runway and putting a can on top of them. Then they would cut a slit in the can and would tilt up the cover. If you were at the right angle, you could see the line of the runway. Although this method didn't give you very good depth perception, you could see the runway lying out in front of you. But you really had to be within a few degrees of the right glide angle to be able to see the dim lights.

Anyway, the night was pitch black. I was in this night exercise and made a nice landing, but the guy in front of me turned on his landing lights in order to see where he was going. The BT-13 is a tail dragger. He was now on the ground coming back to the control group on the right hand side of the runway, and he had turned on his landing lights.

Well, the Vultee Vibrator is famous for throwing oil on the windshield. When those lights went on, I went blind and got turned just enough to head for the control ship. The instructor was sitting there in his airplane. Next to it was a fire engine in case there was a crash—which there was. My right wing ran up on his wing, the other wing swung around and knocked the engine off his plane. The fire engine was standing there, and I whacked the front of that thing, too. I unbuckled myself and hollered, "Anybody hurt?"

I thought I was going to be washed out for that crash, because it was an expensive crash. It was December 19th, my birthday. My wife had sent me a crash bracelet (silver I. D. bracelet with my serial number engraved on it). Sure enough, I crashed.

But at the review board, for whatever reason, they figured I'd be able to survive as a pilot. You have to fly an elimination flight, and they check you out. I was a good pilot. I was a very smooth pilot. If you flew in a circle, if you're doing it accurately and maintain your altitude, you'll hit your own disturbed air and you'll get a bump. I could do that time after time.

From Cuero, I went to Mission, Texas, for Advanced Fighter Training. Advanced was combat training. There you started your gunnery training. They would have a sleeve towed behind a plane and we would fire .30 caliber machine guns at it. The nose of the bullets had paint on them. We each were assigned a different color. So that if you were assigned blue that day, they could count the number of bullet holes in the sock that were blue and know how well you did. There would be red holes, yellow holes, maybe no blues and you didn't hit anything. But you had to be fairly adept at gunnery, because that was your life.

For this particular exercise, we flew AT-6s with a single machine gun. It takes something to hit that sleeve. It takes more to have the guts to sit in the airplane in front of it while some wide-eyed kids are firing at you.

Also, we shot skeet to teach angle, and us lead and we were given instruction on formation flying in pretty good detail, as well as some explanations of tactics in bombing and things of that nature.

When you finished with Advanced, the selection started as to who was to become a bomber pilot, who was to stay and teach, who was to fly fighters. And, of course, we all wanted to be fighter pilots, but there was a rather limited requirement. Those guys who got bomber training were unhappy. Those who got fighters automatically elevated themselves to some kind of "Wow, look what I did." This was a "gung ho" generation.

I was sent to Matagordo Island, a little ways off the coast of Texas. There I was introduced to the P-40.

The P-40 was a totally different kind of plane—also a tail dragger, but an inline engine, a very long nose, and a lot of torque. You have to stand on the right rudder going down the runway in order to keep it on the runway until you pick up enough speed. It was very much faster than the AT-6s. It cruised around 240 miles an hour, and at that point, it passed everything we had flown.

For entertainment, we used to watch the newly trained pilots, the guys who were training in P-40s, trying to land the thing. Everybody went down to the runway and counted the number of landings they made along the way. Jaboom, jaboom, jaboom. It was very funny. It was very difficult, but we all did it.

The P-47, the Jug

At Matagordo Island, we had what they called Advanced Fighter Training, but we were really learning air-to-air combat and gunnery proficiency, and also some dive-bombing. But the dive-bombing technique they taught us was totally unlike what we used in the service. They had not a clue as to what was going on in Europe, or they knew, they weren't telling us. When we finally got to Europe, we were given on-the-job training.

My next station, which was P-47 training, was at a coastal airfield near Richmond, Virginia. It was most interesting how they teach you to fly the P-47. That was a lot of fun. The P-47 was overwhelming to look at. It was so big, heavy, powerful, and massive.

The advanced single engine training at Mission ended with an elaborate cere-mony, where in we received the silver wings, were commissioned as second Lieu-tenants or Warrant Officers, and were given ten days leave to get to Richmond, Virginia, for P-47 training. To beat the rush for airline space, four of us hired an old Cub with its older pilot and set out for a civilian airport about 100 miles away. The pilot and the four of us piled in. I had one new Second Lieutenant on my lap, one sat on the rear seat surrounded by duffle bags, and Lieutenant Pitalla stretched out across the bags with no place to sit.

The plane could barely fly, and we probably never got above fifty feet. That's the way we flew through an army Base Traffic Pattern with Red Flares and com-plaints from Control. We landed at an airport, thanked the Lord, and headed for New York for our ten-day leave.

Vincent Pitalla and I were both eventually assigned to the 514th, and during the Battle of the Bulge, were both flying over Bastogne when he was hit by flak and killed.

At Richmond, we first went to a very intensive ground school to learn about the mechanics of the P-47. But ultimately, the moment comes when they put you in an airplane and the instructor crouches on the wing, gives you some last minute tips, slaps you on the shoulder and says, "You got it." And off you go.

I remember that first flight as such a remarkable experience. You really enjoy the beauty of this powerful airplane zooming in and around the clouds, diving through them. All the things you can't do as a pilot in civilian life. The greatest sensation of speed that you get is in the clouds, the freedom to fly down the val-leys of those cumulus clouds. Really nice.

Another aspect of our training was getting "bounced" by the Navy fliers, or we would "bounce" them. This was good combat training and one that I think was encouraged. Both services wanted the mix-up. It was a sort of on the job training.

Shortly before I went overseas, I was in the Officer's Club in Richmond one night, where they had slot machines. Paula was up in Newark, and I was trying to place a phone call to her. You had to wait in line to use the telephone. Because the phone lines were so jammed, they would page you when your phone call was put through. As they called my name, I hit the Jackpot. I had a hat full of quar-ters, and I said to her over the phone, something like this proposal. I said, "I've got fifty bucks, we can get married!"

I was allowed to go off base during this time, so we set the date. I took some leave and went up to Newark to her cousin's house, and we were married. The owner of Tuscan Dairy gave us a $100.00 gift, and with those hundred bucks, we were rich. Went back to Richmond and found a little apartment. One of our neighbors was a guy named Queen from Brooklyn, who eventually became a surgeon down in Texas.

In the book, "The Fighter Bomber Boys," the illustrations in there are by Captain Queen. He took a lot of those pictures. He, too, was a P-47 pilot. I called him about a year ago when I came across this book. I located him down in Texas and tried to raise his level of recollection, but he couldn't remember me. He and his wife and Paula and I were buddies at the time.

To England and France

After my training was finished, I went over to England on the liner Queen Mary. We landed in Blackpool and were met by the Salvation Army, who I have a great fondness for. They gave us coffee and doughnuts, the first doughnuts we'd had. The last doughnuts, I got for free, incidentally, because when we were in combat, we would send a truck back to the Red Cross base somewhere in the rear and were paying x dollars a month to buy doughnuts from them. To this day, I have distaste for the Red Cross for that and various other reasons. They were making money on the war.

I was based in England for a short period of time, enough to get deathly sick in their very foggy atmosphere. I remember sitting over an inhaler with a towel over my head in a hospital, trying to clear my nasal passages.

From there, I went to France, arriving on November 4th, to what they call a "Repl Depot," a Replacement Depot, and soon found myself on a truck heading for the 406th Fighter Group, which was, at that time, in Mourmelon, France.

The truck transport was called the "Red Ball Express." Most of the drivers were Black. We went tearing through that night, in rain, with little or no light. Seven other guys and I got dropped off at Mourmelon. How, in this storm and rain, this guy knew where we were is beyond me. The Red Ball Express drivers were a really valuable part of the U. S. successes.

Mourmelon, which was a French Army Camp, was a fairly civilized place. The men lived in little hutments, two guys to a little tiny hut about the size of a tent. The camp had very interesting latrines. You climbed up a set of steps and walked across to your selected position and sat down. The barrels were carried away from underneath.

When we arrived that night, some officers were waiting for us at the headquarters of this group. It was interesting how they'd pick you. It's like a kid's baseball team. "I'll take him, I'll take him, you'll take him, you'll take him." They barely read our 201 Files, which we carried with us, and we were selected based on name, impressions, or who needed a pilot. That's basically the way it went.

Combat

At the time I joined the Group, my Flight Leader was Captain Noah Lewin-Epstein, a tall, blond Jewish officer—Israeli Sabra (native born)—with a pretty good record. He was killed on my first mission.

Ken Glemby and his "old" muddy razorback Jug, is pictured above.

Some guys went into combat before I did. In my case, when Lewin-Epstein was not on a mission, he would tell me to grab a lane, and he'd say, "Whatever I do, stay on my wing. No matter what, stay on my wing." And he would try to shake me. When he thought I couldn't learn any more, and he couldn't shake me, that's when he took me along. And as it happened, on my first mission, he got killed.

The 406th Fighter Group consisted of three fighter squadrons and their respective support personnel. The Squadrons were the 512th, the 513th, and the 514th, identified by blue, yellow, or red cowl colors. I was in the 514th, the blue nose. Somewhere between twenty-five and thirty pilots were assigned to each squadron at any one time. The Squadron and Group Commanders and some of their staff were also pilots and led the missions.

Each Squadron generally put up a flight of four planes, consisting of a Flight Leader and his wingman and an element Leader and his wingman. A Group mission consisted of a flight from each Squadron, twelve planes of three flights.

The Squadron radio call sign was Fairdawn, and we were Fairdawn Blue when in radio contact. Fairdawn Leader was the sign of the Squadron Commander. Fifteen Groups were known as the 9th Air Force, 19th Tactical Air Command. From the invasion through the advance across France, in the Battle of the Bulge and in the Rhine campaign, there were, perhaps, 3000 pilots, total, involved in inflicting tremendous damage in support of the various Allied Armies. Our Group worked predominantly with Patton's Third Army.

We weren't really trained for combat, I'll tell you that! Combat really was on the job training. We would have to get a lot closer to the ground than anybody ever taught us. We also learned that the closer to the ground you were, the safer you were. And the faster you were going, the safer you were.

So we would dive, and if it were a bombing mission, we would get speed up and come screaming across from a low position where they couldn't spot us. The enemy may have known you were coming, but, hopefully, they didn't know quite where you were. You'd hop the trees, depending on what the target was. My most frequent targets were vehicles, tanks, trains, and rail yards. Once in a while, you'd catch troops out in the open, but mostly vehicles.

Going across France, our targets, sometimes, were towns. The farms are laid out differently in France. The farmhouses, which were made of stone, are clustered, because in medieval times, they were built close together for defense. All together, they may number a few dozen houses, and that becomes a little hamlet.

It's not like in this country, where you have a remote house on a hundred acres and another one a mile away. These clusters became defensive points for the Germans. They would dig their 88s into the basements, and as our tanks came rolling down the road, they would encounter this resistance.

To overcome this resistance, flights were radioed in to attack the town. Twelve planes: ninety-six .50 cal machine guns, thirty-six bombs (various) would clear the town so that armored columns could advance.

I flew that kind of mission many times. There came a point in time when pilots were detached from flying to become air controllers for these columns. That was an improvement due to the pilot/controller's language, know-how, and familiarization with the planes' abilities. This also worked well when we were sent to attack artillery that was working over our troops. We got there rapidly under their direction and were more readily to identify the targets.

We had three bomb shackles on the bottom of our planes. We would carry 500-pounders, mostly, sometimes incendiaries, very often napalm. Napalm became the more popular one to use when attacking vehicles out in the open.

When you attack an armored column, the strategy would be to hit the first few tanks in the column, which would then be halted. The tanks would then bunch up, one behind the other. Then the napalm would sweep down the column.

That was the nature of the fighting across France to clear the way and also to protect his Patton's flanks, because the Germans would be retreating or trying to get ahead of him and head him off. Our job was to keep the Germans off our troops.

So if the weather was clear, victory was ours…. Once you had air superiority, there was damn little that the enemy ground troops could do except try to defend themselves and retreat.

If it was napalm, you could get down to 50 feet. I had film of myself firing into the second story of a farmhouse because there was a reported spotter stand there. Just coming up the hill, following the contour and firing up into it, I was below the roof level.

We didn't see German planes very often. We were jumped during bombing missions. That's what happened to Miles Jones, my element leader and me. Just before the Battle of the Bulge, Messerschmitts hit us. In preparation for the battle, the Germans were trying to clear the air of our planes.

We were bombing something. I don't remember what, and they came right through our top cover, didn't attack those guys and caught us at a very low level.

I was Jones' wingman, and they shot his left foot and it was my job to bring him home.

I kept him conscious by talking to him, because he was hurting real bad. But he flew all the way home. When we got him to the airfield, I was flying right next to him, reading off airspeed to him. He got his plane down, but he didn't have the ability to brake. He crashed through several engineering tents before finally stopping.

This was when I learned to dislike the Red Cross, because when he was taken to the hospital and had been there a few days, he needed to brush his teeth and write a note, and the Red Cross charged him for supplies. We all disliked the Red Cross after that, but we still bought their doughnuts, because they were really greasy and good—and they were the only ones in town.

We also attacked airfields. I destroyed planes on the ground. They were lined up and we just blew them away.

I was jumped one time by a Focke Wulf. It came right up in front of me after I had been on my diving mission, and he wasn't more than 200 feet away from me. I had him cold, and I had another '47 behind me who couldn't quite keep up and we chased him into Germany. My gun barrels were worn out tat that particular time from firing. I had some rounds left, but they were going all over, every which way. He was one lucky son of a bitch. I had him so squared. If I could have caught him, I would have tried to tip his wing over. But he was a rookie pilot; he didn't know what to do. He just ran. At that time, the Germans didn't have their good pilots out there.

Some guys drew down Ground Control. I didn't have that. One of my wingmen became a Ground Controller. Later, he became the President of the P-47 Pilots Association here in New Jersey. Later, he became National President—Dave Eldredge.

One time we had started to run out of airplanes and were to be issued new planes. In order to give some of us a sort of a rest, we were flown to England and given five days leave. On the fifth day, they gave each of us a brand new airplane to fly back across the Channel. We were flying formation and came across these massive clouds part way across the Channel before we got to France. The higher we flew, the higher the clouds were. We couldn't get under them, because they were so dense.

We got into the clouds. There were five planes and we were all in one group. The P—47s gas tank control is down to the left of the seat, on the floor, and as Gildersleeve, the Captain leading the flight reached to change it, he inadvertently pulled the stick over and stood his airplane on a wing and stalled. The pilot underneath him trying to fly his wing also spun, and the two of them went down.

I had been on his right wing. I had uncaged my instruments, and I was able to get myself squared away. I was flying toward France, and I had two planes on my wing. We had a quick radio conversation, and I said I was going back to England.

They said they thought they could make it to France, and one did get back to the field. The other one landed somewhere in France, and the next day he I went back to England, which was technically the right thing to do. You know, "A careful pilot is an older pilot."

I chose to land at a field in Britain called Manston, which was just a solid mile of concrete. It was designed for planes whose hydraulics had been shot out so they could land there and just keep rolling until they stopped.

So I was heading for Manston. The British anti-aircraft let me know they were there. They started to pound up at me. They were pretty good too. So I dropped my wheels and rocked my wings. We have an IFF system, "Identification Friend or Foe." When you hit that button, it's supposed to send out a radio identification signal. But they weren't listening or didn't care. Anyway, I managed to get down.

And that was an interesting landing, because when I landed, where do you go on this huge field? I'm rolling down 90 miles an hour and a Jeep passes me. The Jeep is driven by a British WAAF—Women's Air Service. And she's standing in the Jeep, driving with one hand and signaling me to follow with the other, and she's going 90 miles an hour. So of course, I followed her and she got me to the hard stand. I tried to date her, but it didn't work. She was crazy! The next day, I flew back to the base.

On a typical mission day, first of all, it was a question of who was going to fly. We would have twenty to twenty-five available pilots on the roster, depending on who was away, missing, hurt, or sick. So we didn't fly every mission, in theory. But certain days, I flew more than one. If the mission was scheduled for early morning, you'd be awakened early. You'd dress in a uniform of some sort. You weren't required to wear any specific uniform. Everybody flew the way they wanted to fly, but the usual choice was leather flight jacket worn over the flying suit. You'd grab your breakfast and go to your briefing.

Mission boards were in the Ready Room. Every pilot's name was printed on a small plastic card. You knew your position and mission by the posting of your card on the mission board.

The pilots who were going out would load onto the back of a Jeep or a weapons carrier and go out to their planes. We would be carrying our parachutes and side arms. I had traded my .45 for a Webley, with an English officer, because I could hit more with that thing, even though it was a six-shooter as opposed to the .45, which had such a kick that I couldn't hit the side of a barn with it.

You got up onto the wing of the airplane. Your crew chief would meet you, give you a boost up, sometimes, if you were heavily loaded, help tuck you into the cockpit. You'd get hooked up with your seat belt. You'd be sitting on your parachute. You'd hook up your oxygen tube, check your radio, instruments, and controls. There you sat until you got the order to start your engine.

At a point in time, I became a flight leader, so I would have to watch the officer flagging the runway, depending on who was taking off first, me or somebody else. We took off in two's. When you got in position on the runway, he would just flag you to go. You'd gun it and take off down the runway. Generally, you made a left bank off the runway. You'd try to cut inside the other squadron who would be circling and at a point in time, you would join up with them. Sometimes we were first off and the other flights would have to join on us.

Our Air Force Intelligence Officer and the commanding Officer generally gave the Briefings. The whole Squadron was briefed, who ever was going on the mission that day. You were not briefed by flight unless only your flight was scheduled.

They would outline where we were going, what the purpose was. You'd have your maps out. We all carried individual maps, generally strapped to the knee. You'd be given your time for takeoff, where we were joining, where we were heading, what altitude we'd be flying.

Your planes would have been loaded with whatever ordinance you needed for that mission. Bridge busting—you sometimes carried a thousand pound bomb. We did a lot of incendiary work when we got closer to the cities. Frag bombs if we had troops out in the open or if they were trying to make a breakthrough. Generally, we would be told what was known about anti-aircraft, where they might be located, if the positions had been visited before. We'd hack our watches so everybody was on the same time schedule. Then we'd get into the trucks and off we'd go.

At the debriefing, they'd want to know details. What did you hit? Where were the guns? What were the targets? What did you observe? You would, basically, describe the results of your mission, and there'd be some critique.

For example, they might say, "You let them to go soon. You overshot." Or whatever. And if a guy hit something really good, the guys behind him were able to report it. But generally, you didn't know how well you did, because you were past it when it exploded, unless you circled around and could look for your hit.

If it were a train, you would know the result at once. If it was a grain, somebody would knock out the engine first, and when it started to spout white steam and stopped, you had a train trapped out in the open. Then, you simply destroyed it. You would generally attack something like that line abreast, three or four guys going in together and hitting various parts of the train.

Every few missions, you were given bottles of Scotch. Because the Flight Surgeon, Doc Grace was lazy but a good guy, rather than our drinks for each of us, he'd give us each a bottle every five, six, or seven missions. Those bottles were our trading material.

In Mourmelon, which was my first camp, we shared the field with the 101st Airborne, and they, being ground pounders, were at times able to pick up good souvenirs. These bottles were like GOLD to the guys of the 101st, and somehow they showed up to trade Lugers, Mausers and what ever for this treasure.

If the mission was a single flight mission, a flight of four might do it. If it were a Squadron mission, it would be three flights. And rarely, if it was a very big mission, we might be able to get as many as thirty-six. It depended, too, on how many planes were available, because we wore them out pretty fast. During the Battle of the Bulge, we were down to three and four planes in our flight, but the mechanics got damaged planes back into service quickly.

The planes got shot up or they needed repair. When I say wore them out, you did wear them out. You wore out your gun barrels. A lot of things can go wrong on an airplane. You don't like to abort a mission, and one of the things that was a no-no was to get up in the air with your Squadron and say my fuel pressure is low or whatever and have to go back. If you did go back, you better be damned sure that your fuel pressure was low, because it was a disgrace. And you were disgracing your crew chief as well. If something happened like that, only that plane went back.

When there wasn't a mission, time went by, I don't know how. You wrote letters, slept, had a few beers. At night, you drank a bit, sometimes we had some wild parties. Sometimes, if you were not scheduled to fly and you had some time off and there was a Jeep available, you could grab the Jeep and go sightseeing. We used improvised gun ranges a lot for rifle and pistol practice.

You had your laundry taken care of. We had French laundresses come in and pick up our clothes and bring them back fresh and clean. Sometimes you'd go out scrounging. What I mean by that is trying to round up something you could use, like fresh eggs.

Another thing we did during the day—one of our officers, Stan Wyglendowski, was also a photography expert. He set up a dark room so we could develop pictures. I have a whole bunch of pictures taken there. That was a nice hobby, taking and developing pictures, and it was something to do.

But basically, you stayed fairly close with your Group. You'd visit the flight line, you'd bullshit with your armorer or your crew chief. Write letters home, things of that nature. Breakfast, lunch, and dinner. It was boring a lot of times. You sometimes actually looked forward to getting off onto a mission.

Each support crew was really two, your armorer and your crew chief. There were other guys who were specialists, whether they would be the oxygen specialist or whatever, who went from plane to plane. But the crew chief was responsible for his plane and was proud of it. If you came back with a hole in it, he'd be very unhappy.

The film from the gun cameras was evaluated at the end of every mission. They showed what you hit as well as proof of where you were. The camera operated when your guns were firing, when the trigger was depressed. It was located in the starboard (right) wing—through a little window. It was black and white and was fairly good film. You could make out what you were firing at and how good your gunnery was.

Most of my memories of missions are a blur of low-level attack, hits and misses, fear and exhilaration, boredom and intense action. It's hard to distinguish the days. We lived like infantrymen in mud and ice from time to time. What we did was very close, low level and lower. However, one mission that I do remember very well was really a mass killing mission.

It was almost the end of the war and the Germans were using Volksturm troops. We were at the Elbe River. There was an old castle at the crossing and a column of our troops was being fired at from the castle. Six hundred Volksturm had been seen going in and taking up position in this thing.

There were twelve of our planes in the air near there, and the troops called us for help. A mission isn't always only one run. When you were finished with what you were doing, you'd be called in for something else, if you had the ordinance or guns that were needed. Twelve of us demolished the castle and no one got out alive. That's one thing I remember, and I found out later on that there must have been a lot of kids and old people in there. Volksturm was the term for their "people's troops." They would grab somebody on the street and tell them that this is the end of the rifle that shoots and send them out. These people were forced to go. They were not prepared to fight.

My plane was hit on occasion, but never so badly that I had difficulty getting back. It was named "Paula" for my wife (of now fifty plus years).

The food was boring, for the most part, until toward the end of the war. And then there wasn't enough of it. We started to get a lot of prisoners and our rations were cut way back. We would go hungry. We were actually almost starving, along with the prisoners.

We had what we called ersatz eggs, powdered eggs, which were no good. We had decent coffee most of the time, but that was in the pilot's Ready Room. Those in the Ready Room were not only those who were going to fly, when we were off duty, we often hung around in there. If you were not going out, you'd be talking about the mission that was out and then dash out to the field to see who was back and how they did. And there we had coffee all the time and doughnuts. Those were the doughnuts that we were buying from the Red Cross.

Basically, we were there for flying. We had Ground Officers, specialists that took care of everything else. For a while, we censored enlisted men's mail.

I was partial to the '47, of course, but that may have been from lack of experience with many others. I only flew a few others. I liked the AT-6, because it had a retractable gear. You could have that same feeling of flying free. The P-47 was just a monstrous airplane, beautiful. It had power. It was the fastest fighter we had, it just lacked range.

I flew both the razorback and the bubble top. When you first get into the Squadron, they don't give you the best airplane they've got. They want to make sure they get their airplane back. There was a plane called, "Try Me One More Time." It was the plane I broke in on. It was a razorback. It flew. It flew fine, but it was an old veteran. By the time I got my own airplane, we were no longer worried about camouflage, and that's why I had a silver plane. Before that, they were all painted dark Khaki.

The most dangerous targets to bomb were those surrounded by hills. 20 and 40 mm guns heavily defended them. For instance, if the marshaling yard was in a valley and there were hills on either side—which there always seemed to be, because the railroad tracks were built in a low area, they would put the guns up at the top of the hill. That means they would be firing almost horizontally at us as we were coming through the valley. They would send up a cloud of anti-aircraft fire. You could see it, but you had to dive through it.

That was the most dangerous time, because they saw you coming. You couldn't secretly approach a valley. And we were always interdicting the battlefields to stop the supplies and troops from getting in or getting away.

We received little information about what we were going to experience in Europe. Much of what we did receive was misinformation.

How do I evaluate the training I received? The flying training was great. It was enough to get us all there and do the job. And we did a good job. It was enough to get me home. No training could have prepared us for what we encountered on the missions. Every mission was different. There's no way to prepare, because the unexpected always happens.

I learned to pray on one of them, I'll tell you that. I was going down on a .20 mm gun position. You have to knock out these guns, because if you don't get them, they'll get you. They had four barrels mounted on a ring. There were two of these rings in this field, and could only get one. After hitting this one, I was trying to climb out of there, and the other German gunner had me bracketed. He had shells passing on either side of my plane and over and under each wing. I was just showing the narrowest profile I had, which was the tail end of the airplane, and he had me bracketed. And I just prayed. That's when you pray, as you're losing speed, going up, and he's pounding away at you. How I got away from him, I don't know.

As far as the quality of the enemy's ability and his equipment, I can't really characterize it. I came into combat the last seven months of the war. The anti aircraft guns were what impressed us the most, because that was what was the most to us. As to their shoulder guns and artillery, I'm no expert. Incidentally, you can sometimes see an artillery shell when you're flying over them. You can see the glint as it rotates through the air. We were targets, but they were not very effective against fighters. What I did see that was impressive were the first jets, the ME-262.

We were flying line abreast somewhere over Germany and somebody called out, "Bogie, 12 o'clock!" And we all looked toward it. It was through us so fast that not one of us fired a shot. We were going 400 mph this way and he was coming 600 mph the opposite way. We were just stunned by the sight. Nobody got a shot off at the guy. By the time somebody yelled break, he was gone. He didn't fire at us, and we didn't fire at him.

For me, the most memorable battle of all was the defense of Bastogne. I have a picture of the C-47s dropping supplies into Bastogne during the Battle of the Bulge. The 101st Airborne was stationed at one end of Mourmelon and we were the Fighter Group stationed on the other side of the field, so we knew them. One night, they were gone!

They took off in trucks. They were sent to the defense of Bastogne. The weather was so lousy no one could fly, but when the weather broke, we were the Fighter Group that was assigned to the defense of Bastogne.

General Patton sent us a rare, "Thank You" and a supply of Calvados for those missions! Our troops were surrounded and we were flying cover, three to four missions a day, whatever we could. You just kept throwing stuff at them. And I lost some friends in those few days.

After the weather broke, one day I saw a line of planes as far as I could see. I was flying over and around Bastogne, suppressing flak and doing ground attack, and here comes a whole group of those C-47s. There had to be hundreds of them, as far as you could see, coming in a narrow line.

As they got over Bastogne, guys were kicking supplies out the door down into the besieged area. The Germans were surrounding Bastogne and were pretty well concealed. They were dug in during the daylight hours. From their positions, they were able to knock these planes out of the sky readily. So the guys behind would see these planes flaming up and falling to the ground, and they still kept coming. Nobody turned back.

They had no self-sealing gas tanks, no guns, and no armor. No way of protecting themselves; just nothing between them and the bullets. And they kept coming. That was the most courageous thing I ever saw in my life. I was almost crying as I saw this. As soon as we saw gunfire or flak coming up, we would attack, but there were just too many Germans, too many positions too well concealed. Couldn't save them all.

I remember the one close call I had during that day. I suddenly went into a left bank, and where my wing had been an instant before, a whole bunch of anti-aircraft shells exploded. Within inches! Had I not moved, fini!

We had no complaints about the equipment we had to work with. There were not too many people to complain to. And in the Air Force, the officers lead their men in battle, like in the Israeli Army. The officers lead. The Commanding Officer got into the same airplane I got into, strapped it on and went.

The Stars and Stripes was the best source of information about what was going on. There was a lot of funny stuff in them, the cartoons were great, and the information was good. We also had Axis Sally.

Scuttlebutt was like all scuttlebutt. But we were a little isolated, so we didn't have thousands of troops around us, except for the time the 101st Airborne was on their side of the field. Only a few officers came over. Big scuttlebutt was, "When are you going home?"

I didn't realize we were going to be destroying our airplanes at the end of the war. I didn't know we were taking our airplanes and dumping them into the Baltic Sea. That drives me crazy.

I came in contact with the French, and I didn't like them. I found them to be the sleaziest bunch of people. I remember being on leave. Every once in a while we would go back to Paris and get a two-day pass. They'd load us onto a truck and dump us off somewhere in Paris, and we'd have time to wander around the city. I went into a bar one day with a couple of friends, and as soon as we came through the door, a half a dozen men got up and ran out. I mean ran out the back. We were startled. We were greenhorns, we didn't know. They were Germans being sheltered by the French. And they told us afterwards, "Allemande, Allemande."

Also, they gouged the hell out of us. To give you an illustration of what it cost to eat when we went on one of these leaves in Paris. A roast beef sandwich, which was really horsemeat, and toast with some jam on it and coffee at that time, was nineteen bucks. The equivalent of a couple hundred dollars, or maybe more, in today's money. That's how they gouged you, but of course, we'd have nowhere else to spend the money.

Once, we found a ham, a horse's ham, in a farmhouse where we were staying in Germany. The farmer had put it up the chimney to smoke. Boy that was a feast. We cut that thing down, covered the windows to hide our good luck, and we gorged on that stuff.

Lieutenant Consta had a little white terrier. He was our Group mascot.

After the Ardennes Offensive, the 406th was ordered to the Airdrome at Metz, each pilot flying his own plane to the field. Lt. Consta could not leave the dog behind. In formation, in close proximity to the battle line, I could see the little white dog sitting on Consta's lap, looking inquisitively out of the cockpit.

The Germans had other ideas about the occupation of their just barely vacated field, and we suddenly encountered .20 and .40 mm anti-aircraft fire in the landing pattern.

The dog decided he wanted out, and as Consta cracked his canopy open to land, the dog decided to leave, scrambling and fighting to get out. Consta needed one hand for the throttle and one for the stick, leaving none for the dog. Somehow he grabbed a leg, or something, and hauled the dog back in and landed.

Consta went back home later in the war, and I assume, as was customary, a new master inherited the mascot.

I had a superstition or pattern of behavior for good luck. Before I climbed into the cockpit, I took a leak at the back of the airplane. Not only a good luck habit, but also it was important, because when you're dive-bombing or whatever you're doing on a mission, increased Gs make it might uncomfortable. There is a relief tube, which they had under the pilot's seat. All it really was a long rubber hose with a funnel at the end. You'd pull the thing out and somehow, if you could get through all the clothing and straps and everything, you could use it. So you never used it. I solved that one by taking a leak at the hard stand at the tail end of the plane, and that was supposed to be my luck.

The war ends

But one time, I was leading a flight to Oslo, Norway. I was leading twelve planes for review at the end of the war, and I suddenly had to go. We had been circling and circling and joined up with bombers. Finally, I reached down for the relief tube, and I couldn't pull it up. No matter what I did, I couldn't pull it up. We're a hundred feet off the Baltic Ocean now with planes on all sides of me. I'm leading this flight and I got to take a leak. So I drop out of formation, tell so and so to take over, and I pull over and I'm fighting this thing and it won't come out. And I'm dying.

Eventually, I get back to the airport and everybody's circling and circling. I'm used to going in, looping almost, and down in a hurry. By the time I get down, I'm desperate.

I land the airplane, and Sergeant Joy, my crew chief, grabs hold of the gun barrels. He's lying on the wing and he's showing me how to get to the hard stand. I pick up the tail and I gun the thing. He looks over his shoulder and panics. Now he's hanging on for dear life. I taxied on two wheels, tail up, down the runway, just short of flying. I get to the hard stand and I burst out of the cockpit and I run to the tail and I take a leak. I'm starting to chew out the sergeant about the "so and so" relief tube, and he's dying of laughter. The war was over and what the hell. So I laughed with him.

Did it get any easier psychologically as the missions progressed or did it get harder? I don't know the answer to that. I don't know if it ever got hard. I think if you want to know something, everyone of us enjoyed the missions. It's a different kind of fighting. Don't forget, we're always attacking, rarely defending. I don't know of anybody who had a horror of missions. We had a couple of guys who couldn't hack it and they were sent home, but that's different.

We replacement pilots became friendlier with the replacement pilots than with the original guys. The originals were sort of above you and they looked down on you. So the original pilots like Lewin-Epstein and other who came from the States, as a group were solid together, and they were the commanders. The replacement pilots, as you moved up, became your wingman and your element leader. Yes, I think you got closer with the new guys.

Then the older guys, who of course were higher ranking, started to go home. They were the majors and they were three or four years older.

The number of missions we flew had no bearing as to when we went home. You were there for the duration. Some pilots went on 30-day leaves and came back, others stayed there for whatever reason. When it came time to send you home, they would send you home.

Tell you another story. At the end of the war, the Russians were supposed to come to the 19th Tactical Air Command and were to be greeted by our Commanding General. The feelings between the two countries were not that great, but the story was that we were supposed to go to Russia on a good will flight, and we were planning on where we would put our uniforms and hot to pack toothbrushes, and so forth. We practiced flying huge formations in the sky by flying in the position that formed letters. We flew USA, and by positioning each plane, you could read the USA letters from down below and the CCCP for Russia. We were very good at it. We became quite proficient, because we wanted to show the Russians. Instead, they decided to come west. They wouldn't let us into Russia at the last minute.

The day before we were supposed to fly the formation, General Quesada of the 19th Tactical Air Command asked us to fly a review to make sure we were good enough. So we flew USA over his head. Beautiful formation. CCCP and USSR, and we were really getting compliments. And we flew way the hell out and came back again and we flew S _ _ T. Headquarters was calling, but we kept radio silence and they called Colonel Grossetta, who denied it was our Group. I don't remember where I was on the USSR, the CCCP, or the USA formation, but somehow I remember being second from the last on the stem of the I of the S _ _ T formation. Lieutenant Clawson, my wingman, was Tail End Charlie. Great flyer who started his own crop dusting service after the war.

I remember a few funny things. We had captured a German airfield in Bremerhaven, a Naval Air Station. The war was over, and we had captured these naval stores. There was this pilot in our outfit called Kiter. We called him "Dynamite"

Kiter. He always screwed around with explosives. The find was a bonanza. We had a whole airfield packed full of them. Underground, we had found German Naval Powder, which comes in the form of long spaghetti. If you broke them up and lit one end, it would go like a rocket, but you couldn't see it, it was so fast. We would go to bars in towns, and wherever we had a crowd of soldiers, we'd light one up and let it fly. This thing would drive people crazy, because it would whiz right past you and then change direction—but you couldn't see it. We had so much fun with it.

The Fourth of July comes and the Commanding Officer and the Brass at Headquarters are having a poker party in their building. Kiter and I and a few others got hold of the German supplies for the 4th of July. The first thing we found were the long empty brass naval artillery shells, and we stuffed one full of this naval powder to see what would happen. Somehow we got it lit without being killed and it drove the shell casing right into the ground. There was that much force. So we gave that up. But we found smoke bombs, all kinds, and all colors—red, blue, and yellow. Oh, it was a great 4th of July! And we lit these things up, but as luck would have it, the wind took the smoke right into the headquarters building, and it was so dense. The Group Officers plowed their way out in heavy clouds of colored smoke. Talk about Redmen—it was hilarious. Kiter got the credit for it. I thought is a great 4th!

On our last mission, there was no shooting. We went out on a reconnaissance sweep heading over eastern Germany. The clouds were very low, and as far as your eye could see, people, like lemmings, were coming toward us to get away from the Russians.

The Russians were coming from the east, and the civilians were fleeing in panic. They had baby carriages, carts—you name it, stuff on their backs, even people carrying people. And they didn't even look up as we flew over their heads, and I was going over their heads at fifty feet. At that altitude, you could distinguish people. On and on they came. That was my vision of the end of the war.

Other times, you might actually see yourself killing people when you caught them. You don't want to remember too much of that. We were virtually flying tanks. Flying over the population that was trying to escape from the Russians. It was a revelation seeing the fright and fears the Russians, bent on revenge, engendered.

Back in the States

I came back to the States in August of '45, before the dropping of the Atomic Bomb. I flew as a passenger on a C-47 coming from England to Ireland, and then Ireland to Iceland. We were ragging with the pilot of the C-47. He was calling us piss-ant pilots and we called him a truck jockey. But of course, they had the advantage. We were sitting on these hard seats, and he waited until I got up to go to the head, which was at the rear of the plane, and he timed it. I got to the bucket, he dumped the rudder, and I'm five feet in the air, hitting my head on the top, then he kicked it, and I couldn't even get my clothes back on.

But it's a long flight, and eventually he had to go to the John. I had my revenge. I made believe I was asleep and I watched till he got up. When he got in there, I sat down in his seat, and I had the co-pilot play along and give me the controls, and I battered the shit out of him.

The war certainly wasn't terrifying. Boredom was the worst thing. It was exciting, but I can't say it was terrifying. There were terrifying moments, but you live for that.

When I got home, I was really just on temporary leave, scheduled to go to the Pacific. My wife and I took a brief vacation up in the Catskills. That's where I was when they dropped the Atomic Bomb. I remember celebrating with Southern Comfort. I used a stack of dining room chairs to demonstrate how to dive bomb from altitude. I didn't kill myself, but I came close!

I used the GI Bill to go to Business Law. I slept through most of it, I'm afraid. Basically, I got a job almost immediately. My wife was in Newark at that time, and she was the secretary to one of the clothing unions. During the war, they had made up a warm jacket and some warm booties that I could wear in my sleeping bag, and they sent them to me.

So I went in to thank them, and they offered me a job. They asked me to work in a store on Branford Place in Newark, selling men's suits. I had been working there about a week, when the two union leaders came into this store and the owner of the store turned sheet white.

It seems that what had been happening was that during the war, these union men had been funneling merchandise to the storeowner who was selling it and giving them a cut back of some sort. After the war, he says, "Hey fellows, I don't need you anymore," and he stopped feeding the cut back.

When these men entered the store, they ignored him and came up to me and asked, "What is this guy paying you?"

I said, "Oh, I'm getting (whatever the rate was) and I get ten cents if I sell this suit, 25 cents if I sell this suit, and the one I'm wearing, I have to pay this much for.

They said, "You're on strike."

The tailors stood up, dropped their work off their laps and left. A picket line was walking on the street. The store was put out of business. A well-known racketeer, who later founded a savings and loan, ran the union.

I've never had a problem talking about my war experiences. Some people were reluctant to talk about it. I'm sure they had terrible times or they did bad things. We had a good war.

Some of the movies of books captured the experience of the war as I knew it. We all had such diverse experiences. That book, "The Fighter Bomber Story" is good. I have another one called, "Grandpa's War." I have a film here, a pilot named Quentin Amenson did a film for the 50th Anniversary of World War II. He filmed his recollections of World War II as P-47 pilot, and he had remarkable success with it because it was so accurate. It is so detailed. I met him at the P-47 Pilots Association. His wife is the most charming Southern lady. His story could have been mine. And of course, Winston Churchill's, "The War Years."

I keep up with a few of the members of my Squadron. Not really the way I should. We went different ways. I remember my closest Squadron friend, Claire Hoffmeister. He and I shared a cabin in Mourmelon and flew together through most of the war. What I remember about the hut we shared was there was a unique way of heating those things.

We had a pot bellied stove in this little hut, and we'd get used oil from the airplanes. Now you either burned wood in it or, if you got lazy as we later did, you found a way to meter out oil through a can with a little nozzle on it to adjust the drip. Once you started a fire, you'd let the oil drip in. Each time it hit, it would go pow, pow, pow, but it heated up red hot. So all night long you'd hear the pow, pow, pow, but you slept through it, because you were warm. Hoffmeister stayed in the service. He retired with a full term of service. He's down in Florida, but he never comes to our meetings.

I've gone to a few of the 406th Fighter Group meetings. I went to the 20th Anniversary reunion, and I didn't recognize the guys, any of them. They were wearing civilian clothes; they had changed. You put a hat and a suit on a guy, and he doesn't look the way you remember him. There wasn't really that much to talk about after a while. We had gone our different ways. While we had a good time together, a couple of riotous nights together, nevertheless, when it was over, I didn't get in touch with them again. It was over.

Erik Dyreborg: Well not quite over. Saturday, February 15, 2003, I discovered that Ken Glemby and Frank Lewis both served in the same Squadron at the same time in France. I called both of them and the two squadron-mates were reunited after almost 58 years.

Read Frank Lewis' story: "Looking Back At Those Great Days—
It wasn't all death and destruction"

Printed with permission of Ken Glemby and The Army Air Forces Historical Association.

The Thirteenth Mission

✦

The 101ˢᵗ Mission of the Swoose Group

Narrated by George W. Guderley, B-17 gunner
15ᵗʰ Air Force, 463ʳᵈ Bomb Group, 774ᵗʰ Bomb Squadron.
Edited by Erik Dyreborg

George Guderley, October 29, 1943 in the front yard of his home in
Chicago is pictured above.

Introduction

The mission history of the 463rd Bomb Group, 15th Air Force, stationed at Celone, Italy, just North of Foggia, reports as follows for the 12th of September 1944."Intelligence reports of Germany's new jet propelled aircraft blossomed into action. The 5th Wing hit Lechfeld, Germany, site of a jet-propelled field. Hangars and installations on the field were plastered.

Heavy flak met the formation. Lt. Milner and crew of the 774th went down over the target, but not before they had dropped their bombs. Returning crewmen reported from six to ten chutes. The last one that opened was supposed to have been a delayed jump. The chute opened close to the ground over a little lake. On the crew were Lts. Milner, Thayer, Seruya and Weitz; and Sgts. Kelley, Herman, Siems, Guderley, Rempelakis and Pakosz." A rather terse description of what transpired that day, and almost correct.

My 13th mission

That day started out inauspiciously enough, for one following the celebrations of the Group's 100th mission the day before. The crew members were awakened by the squadron clerk-orderly with the usual," Good morning gentlemen, it's time to go to war," for which he was rewarded with the usual muttered epithets from men being awakened from a sound a sleep in the total cold darkness, at 5am. Shaking off the effects of the previous day's alcoholic 100th mission celebrations we stumbled off to the mess hall, where we wolfed down our portions of scram-bled powdered eggs, bacon, pancakes, toast, and coffee, being careful not to over indulge in the "life giving" coffee lest we have to get rid of it a few hours later at high altitude where the temperature was 20 degrees below zero Fahrenheit.

The pilot, co-pilot, navigator, bombardier, radio operator and engineer all piled into a truck that took them to the operations building for their briefings. The remaining crewmen (gunners) did the same in a truck that took us directly to the flight line, where we were dropped off at our aircraft. Our purpose was to check out the .50 caliber machine guns and bomb load, and to make use of the oxygen masks in the plane, in order to rid ourselves of the hangovers from the previous day of celebration.

Upon the later arrival of the pilots, navigator and bombardier at the flight line, we learned that we would be having three crew replacements for those men of our regular crew who had been shot down or wounded on previous missions. This was to be my 13th mission, a number that caused me some personal concern.

The pilot was on his 23rd mission our replacement waist gunner was making his 50th. He had been shot down earlier over Yugoslavia, and had evaded capture with the assistance of the Yugoslavian Partisans, and to return to the bomb group where he learned that he was being "allowed" to complete his mission tour before going home. Since we would be flying as the "Deputy Bomb Group Lead" aircraft this day, we had with us an experienced "lead bombardier" who had to his credit a high number of missions also.

Our co-pilot for this day was the least experienced of the crew, and was flying his second or third mission. This followed the usual practice of "breaking up a crew" and assigning the individuals to experienced crews for on-the-job training before they were re-assembled to work again as a crew.

This motley collection of airmen was assembled at the aircraft on the hard stand following the operations briefing, It was now the turn of the navigator and bombardier to brief the crew on weather conditions, escape and evasion details and for the intelligence observations that we were expected to make, so that they could be reported upon during the post-mission debriefing by the intelligence officer. While this was going on the pilot, co-pilot and engineer made their walk around pre-flight inspection of the plane. This was usually described as, "kicking the tires."

It might be worthwhile to pause here and mention that all of what I have described above was pretty much repeated every mission morning, it had been a routine that I had followed for each of the days when our targets were in or near the cities of Vienna, Brno, Belgrade, Genoa, Budapest, and a collection of little mentioned towns all over southern Europe and the Balkans. We were generally bombing targets like railroad yards, refineries, bridges, and airfields, mostly in support of the Russian armies that were advancing northward from Rumania, and to disrupt the flow of oil to the German war machine.

Back to the beginning

My Air Force career began in September of 1942 when I enlisted in the Army Air Forces aviation cadet program in order to become a pilot, I had taken private pilot lessons as a civilian shortly after I graduated from high school. After completing Pilot Pre-flight School and moving on to Primary Flying Training School it became apparent that I could not "fly the Army way," and was "washed out," with the recommendation that I be reinstated and trained as a navigator.

This required training as an aerial gunner first. While I awaited an opening in the advanced navigation school, I was assigned to teach "dead reckoning navigation" to new cadet trainees, and resulted in my being transferred through various Army air bases in Texas, Nevada, Utah and finally back to Texas, where I learned that the cadet program was being closed down due to the rapid progress of the war.

I therefore volunteered to be a "career gunner" in an active crew, this choice was followed by assignment to a newly assembled B-17 crew, and with whom I took eight weeks of tactical training in Louisiana before leaving for overseas. After a short pre-overseas departure furlough, we were assigned to our POE (Port of Overseas Embarkation).

To Italy

We took possession of a brand new B-17G, delivered "fresh from the factory" to our overseas departure airfield at Kearney, Nebraska, by a pair of lady pilots (WASPs). After a week of preparation, instrument calibration, physical examinations and familiarization we set off to Italy, by way of Manchester, New Hampshire; Gander Lake, Newfoundland; Terciera the Azores; Marrakech, Morocco; Tunis, Tunisia and finally Goia, Italy.

On our way over I assisted the navigator in making solar "shots" with the astro-compass, and helping perform arithmetic interpolations in the solar ephemeris in order to establish our en-route positions between Newfoundland and the Azores, using celestial navigation. We were very happy to make our ETA (estimated time of arrival) within two minutes. The long eight hour flight also provided an opportunity for me to get in a little pilot time, which was part of a program to provide cross-training for certain crew members, so that in an emergency there would be someone capable of bringing the aircraft back after the loss of either one or both of the pilots.

Having left Gander Lake, Newfoundland on the 12th of August we arrived at Goia, Italy on the 17th of August, a trip that at today's modern jet speeds would take about ten hours. Our travel time at least allowed a small amount of "tourist time."

The mission

Now back to my final mission and to the beginning of my POW "career."

All over the flight line the crews were finishing up their last minute checks of bomb loads, fuel levels, and the 13 machine guns in each aircraft. Soon the noise of APUs (auxiliary power units) could be heard starting in preparation for providing the added power necessary to start the four 1200 horsepower engines when the "start engines" signal was given.

When this occurred the whine of inertial starters, and the coughing and chugging of radial engines was heard as the 28 B-17s sprang to life. The 463rd Bomb Group had four squadrons, each of which manned seven aircraft for each mission. Each aircraft carried 6000 pounds of bombs in a variety of types and sizes dependent upon the target to be attacked. Inasmuch as today's target was to be a Luftwaffe airfield and jet aircraft assembly plant the bomb load consisted of either six-500 pounders or twelve-250 pounders, the latter size expected to provide a mix and greater spread of damage over the area.

Upon signal the lead aircraft taxied out onto the taxiway followed by the deputy lead plane and then in numerical order by each plane in each squadron to the take off position at the end of the pierced steel plank runway. In order to conserve fuel little time was spent at this point since the magneto check, and full power run-up and propeller pitch checks were all accomplished before taxiing out of the hard stand. As the aircraft raced down the runway and became airborne, their landing gear was quickly retracted in order to cleanup the planes configuration and to reduce drag. With 2500 gallons of fuel and 6,000 lbs. of bombs the rate of climb was not very high, a "clean" aircraft was essential.

This morning we "buzzed" along at about 100 to 150 feet for quite a while, this provided an opportunity to give a "wake up call" to the P-38 pilots in the fighter group whose tent area was located a few miles North of our take-off runway. This was a "pay back" for their earlier similar buzzing of our area when they left on a mission a few days before.

Our group circled our airfield in order to assemble into four separate squadrons. When assembly was complete at about 10,000 feet of altitude, the formation headed off to the north-northeast to continue climbing over the Adriatic Sea, to be at our attacking altitude of 24,500 feet as we crossed the coast of Yugoslavia.

At this point the signal was given to test fire the machine guns, and alertness increased for possible attacking German fighters. Our route took us over the Alps, and north to Munich, which we passed on the east and then circled to the west using the highly visible concentration camp at Dachau as a landmark to then turn south, and begin our bomb run on the Lechfeld Luftwaffe Airdrome.

When we reached the "IP" (initial point) of our bomb run we began to receive heavy "flak" (anti-aircraft fire). During the bomb run, beginning at the IP, no evasive action can be taken, because the bombardier is allowing the bombsight to steer the plane in order to have no deviation in the flight path that would have an effect on the bombs' trajectory. This greatly increased the chances that the anti-aircraft gunners on the ground could predict our position and improve their chances of getting a hit. They did that exactly.

One of our right engines received a hit and the propeller was feathered, we continued to receive hits, and while looking out of the left waist window I could see that the left inboard engine was on fire, and that the flames had succeeded in reaching the fuel cell.

The pilot was in the process of feathering that engine's propeller, and had asked the navigator for a course to Switzerland, it being obvious that we would not be able to get back over the Alps on two engines, and to return to our "home" airfield in Italy.

Simultaneously it became apparent to me that the fuel cell fire was rapidly progressing to an explosion as the engine vents melted from the heat of the slipstream driven flames of the 155 octane fuel. Setting the "intercom" control knob to the "Call" position I announced the wing fire, and immediately began my "bailout" procedure. The pilot then set off the "bailout alarm bell".

The progress of a wing fire to an explosion leaves very little time for decision-making, and we had trained that with the announcement of a wing fire all crewmembers would immediately and automatically prepare to bail out

As the other waist gunner and I began shedding our flak jackets, disconnecting our heated suits, fastening our parachutes, and pulling the emergency releases on the escape door, we noted that the radio operator had inadvertently "spilled" his chute inside of the plane.

We delayed our departure in order to help him re-fold the neatly strung-out pleats of his parachute so that they could be held in his arms and released after he left the plane. It was his only chance. He became completely hysterical and deranged, screaming help me! help me!, but refusing any assistance, indicating that he was going to stay with the plane. At an altitude of 24,500 feet, arguing with a deranged man will soon find all passing out from anoxia. We were forced to bail out and leave him behind.

Later we learned that other crewmembers also had difficulty.

The ball turret gunner was unable to get back up into the aircraft, and had bailed out directly from the turret against the force of the slipstream. Because of this his foot became trapped between the turret seat and the gun sight, he hung by one leg from the turret until the plane exploded, and then was blown loose. He landed with a compound fracture to his lower leg.

The tail gunner bailed out very late and landed in a lake and drowned, despite his wearing a "May West" life preserver. He was the only member of the crew unable to swim.

There were difficulties on the flight deck too.

After the bombardier and navigator had bailed out through the front escape door, the pilot pulled the release of the bomb bay doors allowing them to hang down free in an open position, he motioned for the engineer gunner to jump, which he did, through the open bomb bay doors, while the pilot and the co-pilot steadied the aircraft.

The pilot then motioned to the new co-pilot to jump, but the man went down to the nose door through which the navigator and bombardier had left the aircraft, and in a panic jumped. The open bomb bay doors apparently decapitated him as he left the plane. His headless body was found in a garden later. The pilot had attempted to grab him and direct him out the open bomb bay, which was his appropriate place to leave the aircraft, but this action was misinterpreted as an attempt to get him to stay with the aircraft, leading to his panicked departure and needless death.

The pilot was the last to leave, he went out through the open bomb bay doors just as the aircraft exploded. He fell through the air with tumbling pieces of wreckage; when he was free of them, he pulled his ripcord. Thus one can see that the official historical description of the loss of our aircraft was "almost correct" as I had stated at the beginning of this story. The finer details make it a bit grim; there were seven survivors. At this writing only two of us remain of the original crew.

The pilot

Of the seven of us who bailed out there were two of us who made a start on a successful evasion effort, the pilot and I.

I learned the details of his efforts, when we met a year or so after returning home. It might be worthwhile detailing his story here.

Upon reaching the ground he unbuckled his parachute and began running into the woods, he was being pursued by two men who were gradually overtaking him, he ran ahead and dropped on his stomach to find cover behind a log, it was apparent as his pursuers came toward him they were going to spot him. He therefore drew his pistol, resting it upon the log, and as soon as the first man came close enough, he fired, hitting the man directly between the eyes. The other pursuer seeing this came to a halt and ran the other way, the pilot was now free to continue his evasion.

He traveled for a day or two and began to grow weak from hunger and the effects of a wound, when he spotted a woman working in the field. He watched her for a while to determine if she was by herself, assuring himself that she was, he approached her, and with hand gestures and other attempted verbal communication that he needed help. She understood, and indicated that he should remain whilst she brought her husband.

After she was gone the pilot moved to a different spot, which allowed him to see if she brought the police or military, she did not. He now met the man who signaled that he accompany him to his home, where he was fed and his wound cared for a couple of days. Later the man produced an old overcoat and a bicycle, and indicated that he would accompany the pilot to the Swiss border.

After a day or two on the bikes they arrived at the border zone, where the pilot's new found friend indicated that he could go no farther and that the frequency of border guards required that the pilot proceed on his own, and as stealthily as possible.

The pilot succeeded in getting to the bridge which crossed over into Switzerland, and was crossing over it on the underside, when he was spotted by the German guard and made prisoner. He received considerable abuse from the Gestapo in their attempts to get him to tell the names of the persons who had aided him, but after persuading them that he stolen the coat and bicycle he too ended up in the Stalag Luft.

Years later he learned that his friendly farmer had just been released from the Dachau concentration camp, where he was held because of his membership in the Social Democrat Party which had opposed Adolph Hitler. For several years after the war the pilot sent food, money, and other assistance to his friend. In later years his daughter visited the family in Germany.

A perfect landing and running for my life

The descent by parachute from 24,500 feet takes a long time, time that can be used to plan your landing, and try to recall some of the escape and evasion briefing that you heard that morning.

As I was hanging in the harness my first impression upon looking up at the open parachute canopy was that," this thing is pulling me up and away from earth", there being no reference against which to determine whether I was going up or down.

As I hung there it became apparent that objects on the ground were growing larger, and that indeed I was going down. Now I hoped that I was high enough so that I would benefit from a "friendly" wind to carry me toward Switzerland and freedom.

The last few hundred feet went quickly, I allowed myself to oscillate so that anyone wishing to take a shot at me would have a little more of a challenging shot. I landed in a clearing of a pine forest well up on a hill; as my feet hit the ground, I bent my knees and rolled over to one side, as one was supposed to do, and "voila" I made a perfect landing. Not bad for the first time I thought.

Gathering the canopy of my parachute I realized that four or five men were heading in my direction from the bottom of the hill, near a road, about 200 yards away. They were carrying "sticks" (I thought), but these proved to be rifles. I deduced that from the sounds of bullets whining through the tree branches near me.

Carrying my parachute and running in flying boots with an injured foot did not allow me to make a 100 yard dash in 9.6 seconds, but there was considerable incentive for me to do so. I raced toward a heavy copse, rid myself of the parachute, grabbed the escape kit, and disarmed my .45 caliber pistol by removing the "slide stop" after first putting a round in the chamber, cocking the hammer and leaving it lay in open view. This latter action, I hoped, might cause any one finding the pistol and attempting to fire it to have the slide buried in his face.

Now running in the direction of, and around, my pursuers I was able to get into still another heavily wooded portion of the forest, dropping down I trenched out a shallow "grave" with my knife, laid down in it, face up, pulling the pine mulch over me, and waited until I could no longer hear the shouts of my pursuers and their accompanying dogs. As twilight approached the forest became quiet, and I abandoned my hiding place.

Opening the "escape kit" I found the very detailed escape maps, the compass, matches, pep candy, water purification tablets, and the plastic bladder that could be used with the halazone tablets for sterilizing available water. Orienting myself to direction, I now took off "cross-country" in a West-Southwest direction, using the star Arcturus as a guide, hoping that I could continue until crossing the border into Switzerland.

The escape

The first few days I traveled only at night, my senses highly attuned to the slightest noise or movement, avoiding obviously populated areas and staying mostly in the forests. During the day I curled up into piles of grain or straw, sleeping under my flying jacket. Sometimes I was able to break into "out buildings" of farms. (One day I slept in a small shed that housed several hives of bees.) This was a particularly comfortable "accommodation" as it rained all that day, and I was able to find several burlap bags that could be used as blankets for sleeping.

I took one of the bags along with me, stuffed with hay, to function as a "prop", as my worsening wounded foot began to become troublesome, making it essential that I speed up my progress by walking during the daytime. Carrying the burlap bag "filled with something" made me look a little less "suspicious" to anyone that

I would meet. During my rest stops I treated my wounded foot with the powdered sulfa compound and the compress bandages that were in my pistol belt first aid kit.

Frequently a small river or stream blocked my cross country travel, so I followed along on the bank of the stream until I came to a bridge, I sat in covering shrubs for an hour to observe if it was guarded, and until it seemed that there would be no one else in the area so I could make an unobserved crossing. One day, coming out from cover, I proceeded across the bridge, as I was part way across I spotted a man who was coming at me, going in the opposite direction, we met midway on the bridge.

I tried out my rudimentary, and long un-used German by saying "gute morgen" he responded likewise, and eyed me in a hard manner. We each kept on walking, and with each of us looking around suspiciously over our shoulders.

Now I recalled seeing the Nazi party button on his Alpine jacket so I decided it was best for me get off the road and back up into the cover of the overlooking forest. After walking up a small stream, climbing up into the branches of a tree, and then crossing over into several more, I found a hiding place in anticipation of the arrival of pursuers, and the inevitable dogs. I was not disappointed.

Shortly the sound of a Fiesler Stork observation plane was heard, and several truck loads of German soldiers disembarked, and proceeded to search the area along the road that I had just left. This continued for several hours while I watched from my hiding place in the woods on top of the hill. After a while they gave up and boarded their trucks; they and the plane departed. I decided it was time to travel at night for a while.

By now I had been able to make use of the escape maps and had located myself a few miles North of the City of Fussen, which is the southern terminus of the "Romantische Strasse" the famous tourist route. I was also on the road that ran in view of Mad King Rudolph's famous castle at Neuschwanstein. Noting that I would have to get through the City of Fussen in order to use the only bridge across the Lech River. The terrain was now completely alpine, and the road paralleled the river that ran in the deep valley that it formed. After that it was across the border, and into Austria.

Waiting until late in the evening I proceeded along the road, occasionally stepping into the roadside cover at the noise of approaching motor traffic (that was very light) I found myself in the outskirts of Fussen.

There was considerable foot traffic of German military personnel, many of who were making full use of the town's "bier stubs." I walked along the road, still wearing my Air Force flight suit, with the trouser legs tied down over my flight boots, until I reached the lighted part of the town where such a uniform might be recognized.

I found a garden that was heavily planted with shrubs, laid down and fell asleep. I awakened about two in the morning, the streets were deserted, I brazenly walked along trying to find the bridge, my only way out of the city, and the road to Austria. At one road sign I climbed up on a fence and lit one of my precious matches to read it. I was pleased to find the name Reutte, which was the name of the first town in Austria, it was only 10 km away.

Years later my wife and I traveled back to this town to re-visit the places that were part of my arrival by parachute in Germany. After retracing my evasion route by auto I came to the town of Fussen, where I was determined to see what had made my task of finding my way so difficult. While walking up and down the tangled web of streets I was pleased to observe that I had spent as little time as I had in doing so some forty years earlier.

Now I was across the Lech River, it was 5 am, daylight was fast dawning, and it was time for me to once again get off the road and travel in parallel along the slope above the road. This made walking difficult, I was also getting hungry, my energy candy having been exhausted the previous day, my efforts at milking a cow in the field produced only about a cup of milk, which I caught in the waterproof escape map, and I had eaten two apples that I picked from a tree along the road.

Walking along the un-even rocky ground was also taking a toll on my injured foot, it was obvious that I was going to need food and a better means of transportation soon, or I was going to expire here in the Alps.

Drink, food and transportation

This day (a Sunday) turned into a beautiful sunny one, I observed many German soldiers and their ladies hiking along the road, they were stopping at the ever-present Tyrolean Gasthofs for refreshment. I decided to throw caution away and do the same, by blatantly walking down the road, with the burlap sack over my shoulder, and trying to get a crust of bread and to drink the dregs out of the bottles that were lying on the tables outside of the Gasthofs. In my assumed "costume" I hoped that I would be thought to be one of the many foreign workers in wartime Germany. My "act" apparently was successful, at one of the inns I was given a chunk of bread slathered with margarine.

Having solved the food problem, temporarily, my next one was transportation. The solution to this one came on the following day. As I was making my way slowly along the slope, I noticed a bicycle leaning against leaning a small brick building that was a transformer vault that fed the secondary power to the small community adjacent to it. There was one of these vaults on the outskirts of each community, as the primary power line serving them led further and further up the river valley.

I watched the bicycle for over an hour, timing the actions of the owner-maintenance man, to establish a pattern that he might have in returning to his tool bag which was hung from the handlebars. After assuring myself that he would be inside the building for enough time for me to make off with the bicycle, I crept up, hopped on the bicycle and took off. After going about 100 yards I threw the bag of tools onto the shoulder and kept peddling as fast I could. After about 10 km the front tire went flat, I had to dismount and push the bicycle along in the hope that, somehow, I would find a way to repair the tire and resume my evasion efforts.

Just after entering a small village, where the front doors of the buildings were located right adjacent to the traveled way, I noticed an older woman standing in the doorway, she recognized my plight, and retreated inside briefly, coming out holding up a tire pump, and a tire repair tool that I recognized immediately from my many experiences at repairing bicycle tires. I accepted the tools, turned the bicycle upside down, and proceeded to repair the tire and, to thereafter pump it up to maximum inflation. Following this I thanked the lady and once again took off.

Captured

For the next thirty km I was exhilarated in my progress, congratulating myself on my good fortune at stealing the bicycle, and the little wear and tear on my injured foot. Just as I was thinking that I'd be in Switzerland the next day, I crossed a bridge over the river, four men came up, one from each corner of the bridge abutments, each holding a rifle, or pistol, with the uniformed member of this party yelling at the top of his voice "Halt!"

They advanced upon me very slowly and telling me, in German, to drop any weapons. They were as frightened as I was, but there were four of them, all armed, and all I had was a pair of hunting knives. The uniformed one (of the Gendarmerie) demanded to know my name, where I was going and why I had stolen the bicycle. My response was that I was Staff Sergeant George Guderley, that I had taken the bike as a souvenir of my visit to Germany, and that I was going to Switzerland.

For some reason he didn't appreciate the humor of my response. He locked my wrists together with a chain and lock and, directed me to proceed up the road to the Gendarmerie post in the small village. Thus ended, temporarily, my active career in the Air Force, and the beginning of a new one as a prisoner of war.

Once inside the "police station" the Gendarmerie member questioned me further about things to which I could give no answers. Later after some frantic hand cranking of a telephone, he repeated my name rank and serial number to someone at the other end of the telephone conversation. Next my handcuffs were removed, and I was directed into a small bedroom that was to function as a jail cell.

The policeman's wife came in later and asked me if I was hungry, and how long ago it was that I had eaten. She was shocked to learn that it had been eight days, and shortly appeared with a large bowl of some sort of stew, together with a large slice of apfel kuchen (apple cake), and a cup of "ersatz" coffee. (An unpleasant tasting brew meant to replace real coffee in WW II in Germany.) After this I was pleased to fall asleep until the next day.

The day dawned with my wishing that I could take a shower and shave, but these hopes were dashed by the arrival of a German Army Feldwebel, (Staff Sergeant) who was to be my escort on a small "post bus" to the army base in Fussen. This base was the same one that was the training site of the German "mountaineer troops" that I had observed as I looked down on them on the road a few days earlier.

Upon arrival at the army camp I was locked up in the guardhouse and later visited by a German Army doctor. He inquired, in impeccable English, how I had been tending to my wound? I indicated that I was using a compress bandage that I had carried with me, and was using the powdered sulfa drug that I also had with me, and that my captors had confiscated it during a search. He immediately had the remaining bandage and sulfa returned to me, saying that it was far better than anything that he could do for me.

Once again I was locked in the guardhouse cell. In the middle of the night some of the German troops opened the door and asked me to share some coffee and sausage sandwiches whilst they asked me about the progress of the war. Apparently they felt that this was an opportunity for them to "get to know their enemy", and to learn directly from someone outside of Germany, as to what was going on that was not reported in the official news reports.

With this communication established I took it as an opportunity to ask to borrow a razor and to take a bath. With great reluctance, thinking I would commit suicide, I was given the razor and offered a large container of water and some soap, then it was back into the guardhouse cell, feeling somewhat refreshed, to await the next morning.

The trip to the POW camp

The new day dawned, the guard brought some more "ersatz" coffee and marmalade, and shortly thereafter I was brought from my cell to meet my new escort, a Luftwaffe Unteroffizier (Sergeant), who would be taking me to the Luftwaffe POW camp.

I accompanied him (this time with no handcuffs) out of the German Army Base and in the direction of the railroad station. There he introduced me to his wife, and inquired further where I lived in the USA and other details in order that he could contact me after the war, and I to be his guest in the Gasthof that he owned in the town.

This was a friendly start in communication, so I suggested that perhaps he and I could head toward Switzerland together, rather than heading North toward the Stalag Luft. He indicated that this would probably end in his being shot, so that we had better be off. He said goodbye to his wife, and we entered the railroad station where he purchased the tickets and awaited the arrival of the train.

This "Unteroffizier" informed me that if I attempted to escape he would shoot, he did this while he patted his holstered sidearm. A somewhat small decline in the friendly rapport displayed earlier.

The next stop was the Luftwaffe Airfield at Kaufbeuren. As the train rattled along the tracks I hoped that just for this time it wouldn't be the time for the rails that I had attempted to disconnect by removing the bolts in the connection plates a few days earlier, in my evasion attempt, to choose to come apart.

We arrived without incident at Kaufbeuren, where I was placed in the guardhouse, later being given the usual sausage, bread, marmalade and ersatz coffee. Once again in the middle of the night I was awakened by the curious German airmen and questioned about the progress of the war. Concluding from their line of questioning that they were attempting to get an un-slanted bit of news that was not available to them from official sources, rather than their questions being an attempt to gain intelligence information from me. They seemed to be involved, for the moment, in some sort of exercise that required the use of their gas masks, while the activities swirled about us there was a good deal of the usual banter and joking that probably occurs at most military bases.

After spending two nights at the Kaufbeuren airfield, my Lufwaffe escort brought me from the cell and we proceeded to the railroad station, this time he informed me that we might be spending some time on the train and he carried with him rations that we would share.

The train traveled mostly at night, we rode in the vestibule, apart from the German passengers. I supposed this to be a way of preventing ugly scenes when the passengers learned that I was one of the hated "terror fliegers". Eventually we arrived at the main station of Frankfurt on the Main, it was suffering from substantial damage due to the many air attacks directed at that city.

We walked out of the station a few blocks to the terminus of a streetcar line, boarding the tram we rode to the other end of the line in the City of Oberursel. There I was escorted to a grim looking place that was the Luftwaffe Interrogation

Center. After the large gate closed behind me, my escort turned me over to one of the guards who escorted me to an unfriendly looking place that had several floors of cells.

I was locked up in one of the cells and was told that if I had to go to the bathroom, I was to pull a cord that released a semaphore device next to the door, and sooner or later a guard would appear. The cell was about eight feet long, five feet wide, had a high clerestory type of window at one end, a hard bench fastened to the wall which functioned as a bed, and a door with a peephole, which from time to time opened, and I could see a human eye peering in.

After being on the road for eight days, and under way traveling for several more, I was happy to enjoy the quiet and isolation, and shortly fell asleep on the "bed". I have no idea how long I slept, but was awakened some time the next day by a pounding on the door, the opening of a small trap door, in the bottom of the door, just above the floor, and through it was shoved a tray with the inevitable heavy bread, marmalade and ersatz coffee.

A short time after this I tried the semaphore-signaling device, and in about 20 minutes a guard appeared to take me to the "abort" (latrine). There I met an RAF member who also was a "guest" at the place, we attempted to exchange a few words, but were loudly told that this was "verboten", thereupon I was reinstalled in the jail cell. Once again I fell asleep for quite a while, until being awakened by a guard who took me down the stairs to the first floor, and into the presence of another Luftwaffe member who called me by name, offered me a cigarette together with a form with the "Red Cross" logo.

The form had all sorts of questions pertaining to our mission, unit name and number, names of my crew, squadron commander, group commander etc., etc. it was obviously not a Red Cross questionnaire. Since I did not smoke, I refused the cigarette, this was taken as an omen of resistance. I filled out the spaces for my name, rank, serial number and gave it back to my interrogator. He then indicated that unless I filled out the form completely my family would not know that I was still alive, and being held as a prisoner.

When I indicated that was all that I would tell him he flew into a rage saying that since I had been captured so many miles from our target, which he knew to be Lechfeld, and that I did not have my dog tags to prove my identity, I could be, and probably would be, shot as a spy. He then told me to think about that for a while and then had the guard return me to the cell. Once again I fell asleep for quite some time.

The next day I was awakened by the opening of the door, the guard took me down to the interrogator who once again offered the "red cross" questionnaire, which I indicated I had no intention of filling out. He then said, "Sergeant Guderley, you must think that we are stupid, and don't know all the answers that are required on that form, to show you how stupid you are I will fill it out completely and show it to you." This he did, and all his answers were correct, he then said will you now sign it?" Which I did, but said those were his answers, not mine!

He then said," Guderley, Guderley, that's a German name. Were you born in Germany?" I said no, and then he said, "Were your parents born in Germany? Once again I said no, then he said," were your grandparents born in Germany? I said yes. To which he asked where. I really didn't know, but said in Hamburg. He then said," do you know how much damage you and your Air Force friends have done to that beautiful old city, the home of your grandparents?" I then said that, "My grandparents had been smart enough to get out of this f—country," and it was not my concern."

With that he once again flew into a rage, calling the guard, and telling me that I would now spend three days in solitary confinement to consider the stupidity of my answer.

Dulag Luft POW camp

Three days later (I would guess) the cell door opened once again, the guard now escorted me down to the courtyard where a group of ten or twelve other POWs were standing. The guard told me that I was to be the interpreter for this group, and that we were now going to march to the railroad station. We walked a mile or so and were told to board an old third class rail car, after a trip of 30 or 40 miles we arrived at the town of Wetzlar, which was the site of the Dulag Luft POW Camp. A "Dulag" is a temporary camp where the captured POW airmen are sorted by rank for further assignment to a Stalag Luft. (A permanent camp for airmen).

I spent several days at the "Dulag", during which I was issued a Red Cross parcel, my wounded foot inspected, issued a pair of ill fitting shoes (the back of which was cut out to accommodate my wound) and amazingly had my personal wrist watch returned to me. Later the Senior POW officer instructed us about our rights as POWs, and how we were to conduct ourselves now that we were POWs.

Leaving for Stalag Luft IV

The few days spent at the Dulag passed quickly, and I was able to learn what had happened to a few of my other crewmates who had passed through the place a few weeks earlier. One day my name was called along with ten or twelve others, we were told to gather whatever personal effects that we might have and be prepared for transportation by train to Stalag Luft IV, a POW camp for Air Force non-commissioned officers.

The trip by rail was made in a specially constructed car for transporting POWs, about ¾ of its length was fitted out like a third class railroad coach, complete with baggage racks. This section was separated from the other ¼ by a heavy door with a barred window; in the smaller section there were bunks and a heating stove, together with a small table, obviously meant for the guards.

There were no toilet facilities, apparently it was expected that the passengers and the guards were expected to find relief along the railroad tracks, or if by chance the train stopped in an adjacent or convenient railroad station. This car was coupled to the end of a regular freight train, there were frequent stops and starts with long periods spent in railroad yards.

This latter occurrence caused great concern to both the POW passengers, and the guards, who realized that the German railroad system, and especially the railroad yards, was regular targets of Allied aircraft. The route from the Dulag Luft to Stalag Luft IV went from Wetzlar around Berlin, then through Stettin, on the Oder River, continuing northeast through Stargard, and finally to the small railroad station called Kiefheide, which was merely a station providing service to a country community in Pommerania, and freight service to an adjoining lumber mill.

Stalag Luft IV and meeting "Big Stoop"

We disembarked on a rail siding, assembled in a column of twos, and marched off through the woods for the three kilometers to the prison camp. Upon first sighting, the camp appeared to be a grim and unpleasant looking place, this view was confirmed after entry, when each of us had what ever small personal effects that we had, or residuals of the Red Cross parcel that we had been issued, confiscated. Then we were directed into a small room where three of us at a time were subjected to a body "strip search", with special attention given to an anal search.

The security guards ostensibly were looking for the small "escape compass" that was in each of the escape kits that we had been issued before takeoff on a mission. The instructions to the POWs being searched were given in German, when the POWs failed to quickly respond to the instructions the huge German guard who later earned the nickname of "Big Stoop" beat them.

My particular experience at this time came as the two other POWs who were being searched didn't respond to the instructions to remove their clothing. Inasmuch as I understood German, I told them what was expected of them. For my effort at trying to help the men I was threatened, and told in German to "keep my mouth shut". Big Stoop then removed his heavy military belt and proceeded to beat one of the POWs, beating him about the head with the heavy buckle, causing deep scalp wounds.

When this ordeal was over we were marched into a supply building and issued a pair of thin German made blankets of "ersatz" wool. Following this we met the POW "American man of Confidence" (the elected leader of the POWs) who briefly explained the rules of the camp, and then we were marched off to the "Lager" (compound) and barracks to which we had been assigned.

Our arrival was witnessed by dozens of the POW residents who immediately asked for news about the war, where we were from, and about missing members of their crews that we may have met at the Dulag Luft. With that we stumbled off to the barracks and room to which we had been assigned, met our new roommates, made a sleeping place on the floor, and awaited mealtime. It proved to be not worth the wait as we shared a bucket full of boiled potatoes complete with dirt, with the other 21 room residents. Unfortunately this proved to be the usual evening meal, along with the inevitable "ersatz" coffee, and a chunk of bread.

The "Bread"

Perhaps a description of the "bread" that was provided to POWs in varying quantities from day to day is appropriate here. Each loaf weighed several "kilos", and had the consistency of a concrete block, there were numbers that had been "cast" into it, probably establishing the date that it had been manufactured. (Certainly not baked) After the war the recipe for this "bread" was learned, it had 40% sawdust and ground leaves, another 40% of "groats, and enough rough rye flour to make the entire mass stick together. One of the better ways to make it edible, and almost palatable, was to cut it about ¼ inch thick, and slap it to the side of the small heating stove. When it was "toasted" it fell to the floor and could be eaten.

"Big Stoop"

"Big Stoop" was another phenomenon worth mentioning. He was a huge man, about 6 ft 4 inches tall, weighing about 225 lbs, his rank was that of Feld Webel (Staff Sergeant), he headed up a group of other guards, all small in stature, who had the appearance of the dwarfs in the "Snow White" movie, the group was assigned to the "Abwehr", the special guards in charge of security.

They were as cruel and sadistic as their leader, and were responsible for the occasional midnight searches when the occupants of an entire barracks were ousted from the barracks no matter what the weather, while "Big Stoop" and company would search for "contraband".

This meant that when returning to their rooms in the barracks, the POWs would find their "mattresses" ripped open, and the stuffing dumped on the floor, and mixed with whatever food stuffs they had saved from the Red Cross parcels, rendering it inedible. Big Stoop was the most hated man in the camp, and every POW vowed that when the day of liberation came, he would be hunted down and killed.

This is exactly what happened when one of the columns of POWs reached the Western part of Germany and they were liberated, "Big Stoop's" body was found on a road decapitated, to this day not one of the POWs claims knowledge of who did him in. Most hope that it was done slowly.

POW camp life

The following months proved to be a blur of sameness, greeting newly arrived POWs, visiting other friends who had preceded us in the camp, and in my case I located a man who had lived in the same neighborhood in Chicago as I did and had attended the same high school. His older brother was a friend of mine. We therefore developed a strong friendship that remains at today's writing, 59 years later.

The location of the camp was quite far north in Europe, and about 25 miles away from the Baltic Sea, at about the same latitude as Goose Bay, Labrador, the weather began to become quite cold and miserable. Fortunately a supply of American Army blankets arrived, shipped in by the Red Cross; this allowed us to use one of the two German blankets that we had to be made into a palliasse, by sewing up the three sides of the blanket and stuffing it with wood shavings, This turned it into a "mattress."

With the arrival of the blankets came a supply of German lumber, of just sufficient quantity for us to hammer together four double deck bunks in the room, one in each corner. They were, in reality, sleeping shelves accommodating three men at each of two levels upon which they placed their mattresses, and covering themselves as best they could with the remaining blankets. This was a considerable improvement over sleeping on the un-insulated floor, whose under-surface was only a few feet above the ground.

The buildings were raised to allow the guard-dogs the freedom to roam under them as a means to detect and prevent any tunneling activity. When the temperature would drop below freezing outside, the cold wind blowing under the buildings would make the floors quite icy. At night, after the limited number of "briquets" that we were provided were exhausted from giving heat in the small stove, the room chilled, and the moisture from the breath of the sleeping POWs would collect as a rime of frost on the wooden walls of the barracks.

The next day, if the temperature allowed it, we would ventilate the room to help eliminate the humidity. These were "survival" tactics that we practiced, along with the other boring activities such as playing cards, or reading the limited number of available books. Anything that didn't burn energy was practiced because of our meager diet.

With the arrival of snow came a new event, the sound of distant artillery fire, it becoming clearer and closer each day. At night the flash of the gunfire could be seen on the horizon when we peered out of an open transom above the barracks door. New attention was paid to the progress of the war and to the hand drawn maps delineating the fronts.

The clandestine BBC radio reports and the reports in the few German newspapers that we were given were studied. There were great hopes that we would be left behind by the retreating German guards to be liberated by the Russians, who had been reported as "breaking out" after liberating Leningrad (Now Petersburg), and driving on into the Baltic Nations of Estonia Latvia, and Lithuania.

The forced march

We sadly learned that it was the German's intention to have us march to the West to prevent our liberation. A program of toughening now began with most of the POWs engaging in a daily hiking activity around the perimeter of each compound.

Preparations were also made to prepare "backpacks" out of shirts, these to be used to carry our meager personal items and food from the Red Cross parcels. The Germans intimated that the duration of the march would be about two weeks, and that our destination was some mythical POW camp to the West.

In what was supposed to be a "humanitarian gesture" about 3000 seriously sick and wounded POWs were loaded into cattle cars and sent ahead to a POW camp in the South of Germany and another group to Stalag Luft I at Barth, Germany.

The latter, an officers camp on the Baltic Sea just East of Denmark, neither of these journeys proved to be very," humanitarian" owing to the crowded conditions of 60 men to a cattle car, very little food or water, and days standing in railroad yards in the unheated and filthy cars, and always with the threat of being killed by strafing or bombing Allied aircraft, there being no identifying marks on the rail cars that they contained wounded and POWs. Despite these conditions they were better off than the 6000 remaining POWs who were forced to "hike" some 600 miles for 87 days before they were all liberated.

The forced march (sometimes called The Shoe Leather Express) began on the 6th of February 1945, following a light snowfall with freezing temperatures.

With some consolidation of the POWs from different compounds (Lagers), the groups were formed into four sections, each in charge of a German Lager Offizier, we marched in a column of three or four, mostly over little used roads, occasionally across farm fields and when unavoidable on main roads.

The column stretched for at least two kilometers. The distance travelled ranged from 10 to 50 kilometers per day, and at night sleeping in barns, pig stys, and open fields.

The German guards were anxious to put as many miles as possible between themselves and the advancing Russians. The life span of a captured German POW camp guard in the hands of the Russians was about five minutes. They were quickly dispatched with a pistol shot to the head. The knowledge of this by the German guards caused an incident that most survivors of the "march" will never forget.

It was 14 February 1945 (St. Valentines Day) we were approaching the Oder River, it was about 50 kilometers distant. In their haste to put this natural river boundary between themselves and the advancing Russians the Germans forced the column of POWs forward to cover those 50 kilometers by nightfall. There was no food, no water, and no rest.

By this time most of the POWs had developed dysentery, there was no stopping to relieve themselves. Most soiled themselves as a result of the forced pace. Upon arrival at the Eastern bank of the Oder River, near the Baltic Seaport City of Swinemunde, there were no barns for sleeping. The POWs were led into a field, and we bedded down where we fell.

Some thinking that they were fortunate to find a few bomb craters, from previous air raids, thought they were lucky to get out of the wind, but the light snow that had been falling now turned to rain, and the bomb craters filled with water, the "lucky" occupants joined the rest of the marchers in the mud.

That night the RAF bombed the seaport, and the anti-aircraft guns in an adjacent field opened fire, showering the area with pieces of shrapnel from the exploding "flak" rounds. This day and night has been etched into the memory of every man who survived the march.

The German guards were also required to stay out in this weather and environment in order to keep us together, when morning finally arrived both the POWs and the guards were totally miserable, the guards however had been fed.

We crossed the river on a barge that was attached to a tugboat, once the entire column of POWs and guards were across the march began in earnest.

Being totally miserable it was decided that we would start to sing. One song contained uncomplimentary words about the Germans, which they understood, noting that this angered them the POWs decided to push the anger further, and we began to sing the Air Force Song. With first few words of, "Off we go into the wild blue yonder—" barely out of our mouths.

The guards called a halt to the marching column, whilst they cocked their rifles, announcing that with any more singing they would shoot. This brought a halt to the singing, but the important point had been made that we were defiant, despite our misery.

From this point on until our arrival at Stalag XIB, Fallingbostel, about 30 miles North of Hannover, the memories of each day become one great miserable mess scrounging for any kind of food, and survival were the principal efforts.

Major Leslie Caplan

In a report about the "march" after the war, a Flight Surgeon who himself was a POW wrote, "We lived in filth, slept in barns or fields and dodged aerial strafing. We marched from the Eastern Front to the Western Front, and then doubled back to the Eastern Front We covered 600 miles."

"For food we averaged 770 calories a day of German rations for the first 53 days of the march. (An American soldier gets 3500 calories a day) If it had not been for the Red Cross food parcels we received occasionally many more of us would have died."

As a medical experience, the march was nightmarish. Our sanitation approached medieval standards. The inevitable result was disease, suffering and death. We soon found out what it means to live in filth on low rations and little water."

Major Leslie Caplan who wrote this was awarded the Legion of Merit for his efforts in trying to save the lives of the airmen on the march."

He will never be forgotten.

The death sentence

At about the same time another event that could have made a profound effect upon our survival occurred in Berlin, in Hitler's bunker. Where according to his testimony at the war crimes tribunal General Karl Koller, Chief of Staff of the Luftwaffe was told that according to news reports in the international press, it had been reported that members of the Luftwaffe, and other military had drawn their weapons on German civilians who were going to lynch downed Allied fliers.

Hitler indicated that this was unthinkable, and that the civilians had every right to retaliate against the airmen for the bombing they were undergoing. In the future, any German member of the military that saved airmen from the German civilian crowds would be shot. Further, he said, that all Allied air crews in hand and, those that were shot down in the future, would be turned over to the "Sicherheits Dienst" (Security Service) and were to be liquidated. Essentially it meant a death sentence for all Air Force POWs.

The POW camp at Fallingbostel and the escape

Our arrival at Stalag XIB, Fallingbostel on/or about 30 March gave us some hope that there would be Red Cross food parcels available, but the camp was over crowded with 40,000 POWs of every nationality. There was no food available, except for that that was stolen and brought in from farms where the ground forces POWs were forced to work. They had very little to trade or share with the newly arrived Air Force POWs.

During one of my food hunting forays I walked up to the main POW compound gate, and found an older German guard who had been at Stalag Luft IV, and with whom I had a few spurious conversations. He and two of his sons had been pressed into military service in the German Luftwaffe after the Germans had annexed the Czechoslovakian Sudetenland Provinces bordering Germany. The two sons had been killed on the Russian front.

Because of his loss he had an affinity for the young Air Force POWs in the camp, and would have conversations if he thought that he was not being observed. Since I could speak a little German I was one of those that he trusted. We called him "Pop."

We were surprised to see each other here, each asking how things were going, and each responding in the negative that they were bad. Then, looking about him, he suddenly said to me that in the morning all of the Air Force POWs were going to be marched out of this camp, and once again go Northeast into Germany, and that if I could get out of this compound, and hide out in one that he indicated, (it was filled with very sick and dying troops from many countries, the Germans called them "unter-mensch"—subhumans).

They were to be left behind for liberation by the advancing British Army, whose guns could now be heard in the distance. I would be free in ten days to two weeks. He said he couldn't help me do this, but I was a clever young man and could figure something out. This prospect pushed me to think of ways to do as he suggested.

I noted about 40 rusted pails that had been used to bring our "food"; in this case it was boiled grass. I then questioned a number of POWs who I thought might make be willing to try to make an escape, I finally had about 20. We tore strips of wood from the interior of the barracks, placed them across our shoulders with a bucket attached at each end, peasant-style.

Now this company, in a column of twos, while I counted cadence, approached the gate leading out of the compound, and into the aisle that allowed access to the compound that my German guard friend had indicated.

The guard came to "port arms" and inquired (in German) where to? I now told him in German that we had been instructed to take the buckets that we were carrying back to the compound where the "unter-mensch" were. He wanted to know who had told us to do this, and I explained the Ober-feldwebel (Senior sergeant) had. This sergeant that I mentioned was a martinet, who was always yelling orders at his troops, he terrorized them. Upon learning that this authority figure had given the instructions, he was not going to question our project any further, lest he receive the benefit of "the loud mouth's" (their translated name for the Ober-feldwebel) displeasure. With this we paraded out and marched to the intended compound, where the performance was repeated.

Once inside the compound, upon my calling "halt! 1-2-3" each of our little company dropped their buckets and disappeared into the barracks and tents. This to the accompaniment of the shouts of the guards who asked each other," NOW what were the God damned, crazy American fliers doing?"

This hubbub continued for about half and hour, when they finally decided it would be impossible to sort us out, and besides they still had about 5000 airmen, what loss were 20 or 25? We hid out in this compound for two days.

The morning after our "escape" the entire group of Air Force POWs were marched out, as predicted by my guard friend, to continue the march for another 130 miles and about one more month.

Liberation

We intimidated the old Volksturm guards, who had now replaced the departed regular guards, to permit us to go back into the original compound and in about ten days were very happy to see a British armored spearhead tank crash through the POW camp front gate accompanied by motor lorries filled with the infantry of the Royal Hussars and a Canadian Engineer Battalion.

The liberation celebration was a combination of Independence Day, My birthday, New Years Eve and one of the wildest bacchanals that one could imagine.

The next day a British officer appeared, who took down the names of all Air Force personnel, leaving instructions for us to find all others that we could, and to meet him at that place the next day.

True to his word and our pleasure he appeared with a number of motor lorries that took us to an airstrip, where the RAF loaded us aboard C-47s (Dakotas as they called them), and flew us off to Brussels to a RAMP Camp (Recovered Allied Military Personnel Camp).

There we were de-loused, given fresh British uniforms, paid the equivalent of $100 in Belgian Francs and told to limit our food intake to eggnog and other easily digestible foods. We were informed that we would be allowed to stay there as long as we wished, and when we felt well enough to travel we would be transported further to American military control and returned home.

After ten days there, I was given tickets for a train to Namur, Belgium where the American army people prepared a temporary service record, provided me with a pair of Staff Sergeant's stripes, gave me a typhus immunization and a first class rail ticket to a town near Le Havre, France.

At the station I was picked up by a staff car and taken to the American RAMP Camp, Lucky Strike. After about two weeks I was picked up on the beach by a LSI (Landing Ship Infantry) and transported out to a passenger ship.

Homeward bound and back in the States

We sailed across the Channel, and picked up about 800 wounded American soldiers at Southampton and then departed for New York in convoy. We celebrated VE Day aboard ship while enjoying the gulfstream, a welcoming blimp appeared and two days later we disembarked in New York on 11 May 1945. Thus ended my thirteenth mission.

From the pier in New York we were transported by interurban train to Fort Dix, New Jersey, where we were assured that we would be "processed" for return to our homes on a 24 hour basis, the next day we were aboard a troop train heading for Chicago after 60 days of R & R (rest and recuperation) at home I reported to the replacement depot in Miami Beach, Florida for reassignment.

After two weeks of paper work processing, physical exams, and the issue of American uniforms we were given our choice of assignment and duty any place we liked. My choice was Truax Army Airbase in Madison, Wisconsin, where I had duty as a Provost Sergeant in the Military Police Squadron. Almost every other member of that squadron was a former POW. The "working hours" of 8 "on", and 32 "off" were very attractive, and allowed a 72-hour time off merely by having someone take your place for one 8-hour tour. I remained assigned in Madison until I was discharged four months later.

Post war

My return home found me working for the highway department and attending engineering school, a full schedule designed to make up the time spent in the Air Force. My love of flying also had me engaged in private flying with friends who had been in the Air Force; we even experimented with trying to start an aerial photography business, and it went nowhere.

The love of flying brought my attention to a group of friends who were flying in the Naval Reserve Air Force. Upon inquiry they indicated that I would be welcomed as an aircrew member in a dive-bomber unit at the nearby Naval Air Station. This led to my enlistment in the Navy Air Force and spent many weekend flying periods as a gunner in the Curtiss Helldiver, SB2C, making practice dive-bombing drops on a simulated battleship located on Lake Winnebago, Wisconsin. My ground time duty was occupied as a "plane captain" pre-flighting various Navy aircraft.

With the formation of the Air Force as a separate branch of the Department of Defense I learned that that branch of service was seeking former WW II aircrew, and especially for ExPOWs, whose inter-service transfer was being encouraged. Upon learning of a promised promotion in rank immediately, and later because of my loss of promotions while in POW camp, I would receive a subsequent promotion I re-enlisted in the United States Air Force.

I learned that "the new blue Air Force" was in need of company grade officers, and that I was qualified for appointment to a direct commission. I applied, and in about six months, after testing and meeting a direct commissioning board, I was awarded a commission in the USAF Reserve. Two months later the Korean War broke out, and I was called to active duty, first as an aircraft maintenance officer, and then after it became known I was in civil engineering, I was transferred to the Air Installations Office (Base Civil Engineer).

This assignment was professionally pleasing to me and offered training and experience in my civilian job. I therefore applied for, and was accepted as a competitive candidate for, a regular commission. Following this I was assigned to the Air Research and Development Command, my assignment took me to a basic research facility that was under construction in Tennessee.

The principle project was to be the assembly and reconstruction of the German BMW hypersonic wind tunnel. Many of the German scientists and engineers, who had worked on it in Germany, continued their work in the United States. My part in the project was to assist in the design of a pumping station that provided cooling water for the wind tunnel's test section, and to supervise maintenance and operation of the base facilities and infrastructure as the Assistant Base Civil Engineer.

This assignment was ended by a reduction in force, and by my transfer to the Wright Air Development Center, at Wright-Patterson AFB, Ohio, where I performed research for prefabricated buildings for the Air Force. This required much travel to the Pentagon and other places, which was not conducive to young family life.

Almost coincidentally my former boss at the highway department contacted me, and inquired when I would be coming back to Chicago, and to be part of the large highway design and construction program that was getting under way. This offer made me request immediate release from active duty, which was granted, and I returned to Chicago and the highway engineering business. I maintained my membership in the Air Force Reserve, and eventually became the Commander of a Civil Engineering Squadron. I also became Chief Engineer at the Highway Department.

There was one more interruption in my civilian profession with a recall to active duty for the Cuban Missile Crisis.

This time I was to be the Commander of a composite squadron of Air Force and Army engineers building tactical airfields in Cuba, after landing there on D Day plus six. Suffice to say the "crisis" ended peacefully and I returned to my highway work. I also continued my Air Force Reserve participation completing civil engineering and management training with the Air University and graduating from the Air Command and Staff Course. After completing 21 years of active and Reserve time I retired from the Air Force.

My work with the Highway Department brought me to the attention of a man who became the Governor, and I accepted appointment as the Executive Director of the Toll Highway Authority. My principle effort here was to provide the organizational restructuring and management development of the Authority in its change from a Commission to an Authority, then to provide management guidance in the issuance of bonds for a major extension of 69 miles of the facility. This work capped 25 years of public service, and I went into private practice with a consulting engineer firm, finally retiring completely after 18 years in private practice.

My contact with the Air Force was re-established by my volunteer work with The USAF Office of Retiree Affairs, at this writing I have been volunteering for 15 years, it is very gratifying work providing assistance to military retirees in their dealing with the military bureaucracy.

Over the years my wife and I have traveled to the scenes of my POW and WW II mission experiences. Retracing my evasion route in Bavaria, visiting the headquarters of the modern day Royal Hussars in England, to Fallingbostel, Germany at the former site of Stalag XIB, and to Tychowo, Poland to dedicate a memorial to the memory of the former airmen POWs who did not survive.

This area of Poland was part of Germany then known as the Province of Pommerania. It was also the birthplace of my paternal grandparents in a village about 20 kilometers from the POW camp, they had left there in 1870. The present residents thought it ironic that I had been so badly treated by my grandparent's former neighbors.

The Polish government brought in all the present day residents of the area after the war to replace the Germans who had their properties expropriated and were then forced out.

During my visits, and those of other former POWs, we received the most gracious hospitality. The community participated in the financing and erection of the memorial figures, provide the maintenance and landscaping at the site, and arrange for contact with the Polish Air Force and Army for memorial services when groups of former Air Force POWs visit.

In some instances an almost "family" relationship has developed. From out of some very grim old events have grown some excellent human relations. A fitting climax to a 101st mission, and my 13th.

A well-known public figure once said, "living well is the best revenge", a commentary of what one's efforts should be after adversity.

This thought has crossed my mind from time to time when considering my current life style, family happiness, a past satisfying career, and a happy retirement, that this is all a dream, and that I'm liable to awaken from it and find myself back behind the barbed wire.

A chilling prospect that makes me enjoy and appreciate the creature comforts that I can see, sense, smell and hear, while I say to myself, "thank God I'm free."

Printed with permission of George Guderley.

Going Full Circle

A story about James Alex Stevenson, B-17 Bombardier
8th Air Force, 401st Bomb Group, 615th Bomb Squadron
Narrated by Shirley Stevenson Wallis, daughter of James Alex Stevenson
Edited by Erik Dyreborg

Introduction

I love discovering things! Whether intently scouring a noticeably barren ocean beach finding one of that day's few intact sand dollars, vicariously riding the Colorado River rapids through the floor of the Grand Canyon via a segment on the History Channel, or walking on a recently cooled Hawaiian lava flow realizing, "I might be the first person to have ever walked on this piece of land!" I am truly excited about learning. Finding answers to questions, or better yet, discovering fascinating information I didn't even know to have had questions about inspires and challenges me to learn more. What follows is my story; a story about discovery, history, experiences, and relationships, all of which I would likely have remained unaware, that is, until a somewhat random encounter on the World Wide Web.

Let's face it. Some things about the Internet can be extremely annoying. Pop-ups that seem to reproduce exponentially, banner advertisements floating across the screen, "new and improved" viruses, and unsolicited junk E-mails can irritate the most patient user. However, there is one aspect of the way websites are configured that actually feeds my passion for discovery: the LINK. To the displeasure of my family members I can spend hours on the Internet totally absorbed in research, following links to sites quite unrelated to the point of beginning. Responding only to the whim of my immediate desires and interests I've "visited" places around the globe in "real" time and viewed the earth from a satellite. I've taken virtual tours of world-renowned museums and scoured the online resources of the Oxford University library system. I've viewed the war in Iraq from the perspective of Middle East websites as well as operated a remote controlled web cam that pans the historic streets of Rome. I truly believe there is no end to that which can be learned via the Internet, and yes, I am "addicted".

For years my daughter and my husband urged me to research my family history. Bob suggested we include a stop in Butte, Montana while in route to Yellowstone National Park during the summer of 2001. We could learn a bit about the city where my parents were raised, see where I was born, and do some research at the Butte Archives (an excellent resource, by the way). I'm unsure why I felt so indifferent about this proposal at the time. Thankfully however, my philosophy on life includes striving to have a good time at whatever I do. Sometimes that requires a little research and/or attitude adjusting upfront. To increase the "odds" of the journey being more meaningful and enjoyable, I decided I needed to know as much as possible about my family before we went to Butte, a decision I was not to regret. In fact, had I not invested that time, I likely would not have ever discovered the reason for the inclusion of my story in this book.

My investigation began with an examination of the materials I already had. Studying photographs for clues, I attempted to determine who the people were and when the pictures were taken. Aware my mother and her brother had both been adopted, I searched for specifics that might give me clues about their backgrounds. I read letters sent to my mother between 1935 and 1937 composed by someone I still cannot place. I asked my two older sisters their recollections of our parents and other relatives. I learned about my maternal grandfather's selection as a Rhodes Scholar, his enrollment at Oxford University in England from 1907-1910, and his subsequent participation in a geological expedition to South America. After the expedition Grandpa Thomas took a position with Montana Power, eventually retiring from the company as the Treasurer in 1949. My mother's scrapbooks included Montana newspaper articles about my Dad having been missing in action during WW II. I was already aware Dad had been the bombardier on a plane shot down during the war but I knew no details as he rarely spoke of the event. Amusingly, the one thing I do recall is Dad's aversion to cottage cheese, a food he in some way associated with his experience during his escape.

Summer 2001

So, off we went to Yellowstone National Park via Butte, Montana. We drove from Seattle, Washington to Butte on the first day. Since my preliminary research had provided the family with enough information from which to start, we spent several hours at the Butte Archives looking things up. The only intermission we took was when I begged my family to please go out and find me a Cornish pasty with gravy, a Butte culinary standard I had been anxiously anticipating. Pasties (pronounced with a "short" 'a' sound, lest you get embarrassed and don't know how to say this word) include meat and potatoes enclosed in a suet crust. Very popular in many mining communities throughout the world, pasties are like a full meal in a neatly sealed envelope! My Dad's mom used to make them. Dad learned how to make them, also and then taught me. At any rate, we had a terrific meal and a productive time at the Archives. My daughter even found the paper announcing my birth. For a moment I thought maybe I was a year younger than I've believed because the paper was dated 1952! However, only the first six pages said 1952; the rest were labeled 1951. Oh, well.

The Archives contained numerous resources: school yearbooks, newspapers, a card catalog listing individuals born in Butte, access to other vital statistics, and a helpful, knowledgeable staff. The City Directories, annual publications listing demographic information for city residents, were the most valuable. Names of family members and their (sometimes incorrectly reported) ages, residential and business addresses, occupations of household members, and other useful bits of information were included (I guess identity theft wasn't a big deal back then). When the Archives closed for the day we drove around town locating all the homes where my parents and their families had lived. Most of the homes still exist. It was quite apparent my Mom and Dad came from families with very different social and economic status. I never have heard the story of how my Mom and Dad ended up together.

When we returned from this vacation I was very excited to begin my genealogical search. Okay, I confess. I'd been bitten by the genealogy "bug". The indifference I'd felt prior to the trip had metamorphosed into a persistent quest for information. Do I have other relatives? What was the connection the Thomas' had with Spokane (where my mother was adopted)? Why did they have family portraits taken there when they lived in Butte? When did my Mom and Dad get married? Did the Thomas' approve of my Dad? Why were we living in Butte when I was born since my two older sisters were born in the Seattle area? With all the information I already had about Grandpa Thomas finding specifics shouldn't be too difficult, should it? Ha!

July 28, 2002

Rather late in the evening on July 28, 2002 my family search was as nonproductive and frustrating as usual. Needing a change of pace, I decided to switch topics. "Where shall I 'go' next in my search?" I knew that my father, James Alex Stevenson had been in the military during World War II. I referred back to the newspaper article in my Mom's scrapbook alluding to Dad's MIA status. Luckily, the date on the newspaper was still visible. I was able to determine the approximate date of this occurrence and the diversionary quest began.

In the search bar of the browser I began entering strings of words: "shot down", "May 1944", "England", "escaped", etc. Those combinations of words led me to a military site (the name I don't recall because I didn't stay there long). Transferring from website to website via the links frequently provided (like I said earlier, I love those links!) I came upon armyairforces.com. Obviously a very comprehensive and extensively indexed site, armyairforces.com impressed me with its ability to be searched without having to scroll through uncategorized comments and questions entered consecutively. The content and the forums on the site are neatly divided into topics. Opening the Heavy Bombers forum within the website, I typed "James A. Stevenson" into the search space. With heightened anticipation I awaited the results. Having experienced many disappointments during other searches on the Internet I also tried not to get my hopes up. Was I in for a huge surprise! The results of that night's search have since absorbed most of my spare time, occupied all the nooks and crannies of my brain "space," and consumed money from a budget category that had not previously existed. And what a wonderful journey it has been!

FOUR!

There were four matches! I opened them and they were, indeed about my Dad! Amazingly, all of the entries had been posted within the previous three weeks (it is not unusual to get archived search results from extinct E-mail addresses). Erik Dyreborg (a name you will undoubtedly recognize as the author of this book) posted an inquiry to a member of the forum asking if he knew the date of my father's death and where he might have lived after his return to the United States from England in 1944. That member's records did not go back further than 1968. Another respondent, an individual who was in the process of creating a website specific to Bombardiers of WWII (a good site, by the way), offered that my Dad had completed Bombardier training at Victorville, California late 1943. Erik remarked in one of his inquiries he was aware two members of my Dad's B-17 crew had spent considerable time in 1994 trying to locate my Dad but had been unsuccessful. Erik thanked the respondents, concluding it seemed unlikely any specifics about my Dad would ever be known.

So what if it was about 1:00 a.m. in Seattle! I was so excited I responded immediately. Remember? It doesn't matter what time it is. We're on the Internet!

E-mail to Erik Dyreborg on armyairforces.com website

Erik:

"Hello! My name is Shirley (Stevenson) Wallis and I am one of the daughters of James Alex Stevenson. I can't tell you how excited I was to come upon information about my Dad's group, mission, etc. As you indicated in an e-mail to a member July 9, 2002, my Dad died April 14, 1981. He died of lung cancer that had not been diagnosed until the end of January 1981. The cancer had already metastasized so there was no treatment possible."

"...tonight was the first time I had ever "wandered" onto the site of the Army Air Force. I'm not usually looking up things about my Dad. He's the relative I already knew the most about. I have several of Dad's military items: his separation papers, a letter to his parents from the War Department announcing the end of Dad's missing in action status, a few pins, and his wool hat. When I entered my Dad's name within the search area of the forum, I was directed to your correspondence with others on the Army Air Forces site. I was so excited! Since I usually dead-end, it was wonderful to come upon your messages."

Since my posting was accessible to all forum readers I proceeded to invite anyone who knew any details about my Dad to please write. And boy, did I get a response!

E-Mail received from Erik a few hours later

Shirley:

"I have just returned from Florida today, a 14 hour flight, and how nice it was to hear from you—and do I have information about your Dad! Your Dad escaped with the Navigator, Seymour Ringle. Also, the daughter of your Dad's Danish helper met with your Dad while on Bornholm and your Dad gave her his air force insignia, which she still has. In 2000 I wrote a book about the various crew-members from your Dad's plane, about their two missions and their crash-landing on Bornholm in the Baltic Sea as well as their escape to Sweden. Within the week I will send you some excerpts from the book about your Dad's war time experiences."

Erik also referred me to his website (http://www.usairmen.com) where I was introduced to the story my Dad had never told, the story of his World War II experiences. I was very excited to read the details about my Dad's crew and their World War II experiences. Erik's book, *The Escape from Bornholm 1944* (drafted in English in 2000 but published in Danish in 2001) had sold out. Erik indicated he was in the process of writing another book entitled, *The Lucky Ones—Airmen of the Mighty Eighth,* due to be released October 2002. Because few people had been able to access the Bornholm story in English, Erik decided to include it in *The Lucky Ones,* also. Wow! A book about MY Dad and his crew! The random diversion during my genealogical search was paying off in a much bigger way than I'd ever expected.

The next several days were a blur. E-mails were rapidly exchanged.

Barraged with information about my Dad's World War II experiences that I had known absolutely nothing about, I was totally overwhelmed. As an educator I'm aware that newly learned information, to be truly understood and retained, has to be able to be associated with something the individual already knows. The connection can be logical, parallel, contradictory, or even absurd. I was in BIG trouble! I guess the "file cabinet" in my mind was full or suddenly had no file folders! I couldn't find any place to sort out this new information, anything familiar to attach it to, or anywhere to store it. Since the file cabinet idea wasn't working, it was as if I'd just taken all these "papers", thrown them on a desk, and turned the fan on high. Thankfully, amidst the commotion of receiving all this new data and experiencing euphoric levels of emotion, I had my wits about me to save all the E-mails and have been able to create a written, sequential record of this fascinating addition to my life.

Flashback: April 1943-April 1944

To acquire a frame of reference for the story about my Dad, I'm going to share some background information. Dad joined the Army Air Force in Butte, Montana two days after his eighteenth birthday. He graduated from the Victorville, California Bombardier Training program in October of 1943. B-17 crews were formed and trained in Alexandria, Louisiana. Accounts by the other crewmembers indicate they picked up a brand new B-17 in Nebraska, flying on to Bangor, Maine. The next leg of the journey was to the U.K. via Gander, Newfoundland. Delays on the runway in Gander consumed extra fuel, requiring the pilot to demand their fuel tanks be refilled. A 2,000 pound overload, fierce storms, and the resulting icing on the propellers necessitated a fuel emergency landing at Nutts Corner, Ireland. Other crews were not as fortunate. Of the 62 planes that took off from Gander that evening, four planes crashed in Greenland, and an additional fourteen planes never reached their destinations in the U.K. On April 22, 1944 the crew arrived at Station #128 at Deenethorpe, England.

Flashback: May 23, 1944

The first mission for the crew of #42-31619 occurred May 23, 1944.

Destination/Target: France. Frequently the flights to the target area lasted 8-10 hours. The bombing run itself might only take ten minutes, followed by the long flight back to base. It was on this first mission that my Dad apparently fell asleep as they approached the initial point. Seymour Ringle, the Navigator noticed the aircraft ahead were dropping their bombs. He nudged Dad, who awakened and toggled the bomb load (oops! A slight delay).

The B-17 was an unheated, non-pressurized aircraft; certainly NOT the "comfy" aircraft we are spoiled by today (even though we still tend to complain about lack of legroom, poor food service, and late flights). Our trivial concerns are quite insignificant relative to the actual discomforts experienced by the Army Air Forces of World War II. Even so, everything is relative. Those airmen who endured the extreme cold, flak attacks, ejections, and crash landings feel lucky. They survived. A high percentage of these planes and their crews were never able to return home.

Flashback: May 24, 1944

The second (and last) mission occurred the very next day, May 24, 1944. The Target: Berlin. Seymour Ringle described their approach so eloquently: "The flight itself was a beautiful thing to witness…like a ballet…with contrails streaming back from each airplane (+500 planes) like the long trains on the wedding dresses of 2,000 new brides against the background of a clear cerulean sky." A far different image was projected as they approached Berlin. Heavy flak covered the area like "a big mass of black flies". Just after dropping their bomb load #42-31619 was hit by flak. Engines #2 and #4 were incapacitated, the left wing had heavy flak damage and the inboard gas tank was struck. At any rate, a return to England was impossible. They headed for Sweden, landing on the island of Bornholm at the southern tip of Sweden. However, Bornholm was part of Denmark so it was German occupied. The crew survived the crash landing. Now they needed to evade the Germans and escape to neutral territory! The details of the flight, the landing, and the escape of each pair of airmen are explained in *The Lucky Ones*. The entire book is well worth reading.

July 30, 2002

By this date Erik had already communicated with some members of the crew. A relative of "Shorty" had been found! Or rather, the relative had found them! I received E-mails of introduction and welcome from the Pilot, John (Jack) Whiteman and the Ball Turret Gunner, Nelson Liddle. Radio Operator, Bill Nunn who, coincidentally, lives about 60 miles from me called. Erik informed me that Orlando Yemma, Marwin Carraway and Seymour Ringle were all still alive. Erik had recently seen Seymour (my Dad's partner in escape). Other crewmembers included: Co-pilot, Horace Shelton, Top Turret Gunner, Richard O'Bannon, and Tail Gunner, Jack Culliton. This was so exciting! Each of the three crewmembers I communicated with indicated how nice my Dad was and that he enjoyed having fun. Jack later told me, when they were out to lunch safe in Sweden, Gestapo would sit close to them, trying to eavesdrop. Jack said my Dad would break into some obnoxious (and derogatory) song about der Fuhrer, infuriating the Gestapo. When the song was done, the group of Americans would hoot and holler and applaud further annoying the Gestapo, who would then leave. Somehow, that doesn't surprise me.

James Alex Stevenson, December 1943, is pictured above.

7/30/02

Today I heard from Jack Whiteman for the first time.

"Your connection brings closure for me and I'm sure, Nels, too. I called your Dad Pee Wee. I'm not sure he liked it. He was the only fun one on the crew. He always kept stealing my bike (I didn't mind)."

7/30/02

Today I also heard from Nelson Liddle.

"I feel that your Dad was probably the most loved member of our crew. He was a great little guy."

August 2, 2002

Jack and Nelson told me of their search for my Dad. They had sent out over 800 postcards asking, "Are you related to the James Alex Stevenson who was shot down over Berlin May 24, 1944, crash landing on the Danish island of Bornholm?" They had gotten notes of support from others but no actual connections with or about my Dad. None of the crew had connected with each other prior to 1994 and that story is a fascinating set of coincidences all by itself! Jack, Nelson, and Erik were interested in knowing more about my Dad's life after the war so I obliged.

My Dad was raised in Butte, Montana. His father had been a miner, the common occupation in Butte for many years. Dad and Mom got married January 11, 1945. A newspaper article I have indicates Dad was a Bombardier instructor at Childress Army Airfield in Texas after his return to the United States in June 1944. I believe he continued in this position until his release from military service in October 1945. Dad and Mom had three daughters. Diane was born in Seattle in 1947. Carol was born in Renton (a suburb of Seattle) in 1949. I was born in Butte, Montana in 1951. I still don't know why we were living there as Dad had relocated to the Seattle area after his separation from the service.

Unfortunately, my parents divorced in 1958. I don't think my Dad wanted to do that, but that was the way it was. Dad remarried a nice woman but I'm not sure he was ever really "in love", a sad observation. Dad was a very hard worker. He worked at McKesson-Robbins, a pharmaceutical wholesaler for 25 years. He was amazingly good at calculating math in his head, very rapidly. I've completed a Master's Degree and many credits beyond (not in Math, mind you), but I certainly didn't inherit that innate ability to do mental math. He was just a natural.

After my parents divorced, my sisters and I lived with my mother, stepfather, and three half-siblings. Dad religiously picked us up for visitations. I don't recall him trying to impress us with gifts or by taking us places. We just spent time together. When I was 16 I decided to go live with Dad. I loved his sense of humor! We used to do ridiculous things like have face-making contests in the mirror (something I've passed on to my children. Andrea and Bob are hysterical!). As a 17-year-old high school senior I'd ask Dad if I could go to the grocery store with him on Saturday mornings. Then I'd sneak silly items into the cart that we certainly didn't need (like cat food when we didn't have a cat) just to enjoy his reaction when he'd discover them. As you can tell, I admired him and I miss him.

My Dad smoked cigarettes incessantly. When my Aunt would come over to our house she and Dad and my stepmother would smoke until there were ribbons of smoke clouds throughout the house. I hated it. When I reached the age where I could have bought cigarettes Dad would ask me to go buy him some. "NO WAY! That isn't good for you!" I'm rather proud to say I don't even know how to smoke a cigarette. Ironically, thirteen years later, when Dad was in the hospital dying of lung cancer, the doctors told me to go ahead and buy him cigarettes. It wasn't going to make any difference anyway. Dad's cancer was not detected until the end of January 1981 following a seizure. Metastases to the brain caused tumors resulting in an inability to talk and, it seemed, an unwillingness to eat (even when I took him a Cornish pastie). He deteriorated rapidly and died April 14, 1981.

My communications with Erik, Jack, and Nelson continued at a steady pace over the next weeks. I searched through pictures I had at my house that I didn't even realize I had. These included the very small black and white pictures common of the era with the rippled white borders. Some of the pictures were of the crew-members! Because there were no names written on the back of the pictures (grrrrr) I didn't know who they were. So, I scanned them and sent the pictures to the "guys". They were able to identify most of the people and I was able to share pictures of them they didn't have. It was quite fun!

August 5, 2002

Within a week of this discovery and whirlwind of information, Erik Dyreborg communicated that he was going to be visiting the United States in October. He was going to visit with Jack Whiteman in New York, meet with other airmen who were highlighted in the book he was releasing, *The Lucky Ones*, and take his first ride in a B-17. There was discussion with Nelson Liddle about possibly having a get together in Dinwiddie, Virginia. Would Bob and I be interested in coming and meeting a few of the airmen? Boy, would we! And then…he dropped even a bigger "bomb": Would we be interested in coming to Bornholm? He could show us where Dad's plane crashed, the routes each of the pairs took to freedom, meet some of the Danish people related to those resistance who aided our airmen, see the room where Dad and Seymour hid out, etc.? Of course, I wanted to do both excursions!

August 31, 2002

This turned out to be a SPECTACULAR day! Bob, Erik (our son), and I went down to the Museum of Flight in Seattle. The EEA from Oskhosh, Wisconsin had a B-17 in town. Was this good timing, or what??? I took all of our cameras. I was positioned in a great spot when Bob said, "Shirley, you need to come over here." Being the ornery one that I am, I responded that the perspective I had was quite good for picture taking. "No, you need to come over here…you need to get in line. You're on the next flight!" I was shocked. I started crying and babbling something about Bob not even knowing the whereabouts of the safety deposit box key. Then I said, "Oh well! This is going to be great!"

I used my cell phone to find Nelson Liddle's phone number and called his house from the runway. He wasn't home but I shared my excitement with his wife, Billie who immediately passed it on. I had an e-mail waiting for me upon my return home. I couldn't locate Jack's number at the time.

What an experience! The sound of the plane kind of reminded me of a Harley Davidson. Okay, a reeeeaaaallllly big Harley Davidson. The squealing of the breaks generated a little nervousness. I sat in the belly of the plane where the Waist Gunners, Marwin Carraway and Orlando J. Yemma were stationed. I can't say the "seatbelts" looked any too heavy-duty. We weren't allowed to go back toward the area where the Tail Gunner, Jack R. Culliton would have been positioned. But we could see the area, a spot quite physically removed from the remaining crew. Ball Turret Gunner, Nelson Liddle's incredibly small bubble was better viewed when we took a ground tour later on. How uncomfortable! Through Bill Nunn's Radio Operator area, looking up toward Richard H. O'Bannon's Top Turret position, squeezing through the catwalk I was in awe of the mechanisms. They were so sophisticated for their time. Pausing at the Pilot's (Jack Whiteman) and Co-pilot's (Horace Shelton) area, I took a picture. Past Navigator, Seymour Ringle's "desk", I headed for Dad's position—the Bombardier's seat.

The weather was gorgeous that day. For those of you who have never been to Seattle, August 31, 2002 was that ONE clear, non-rainy day we get each year. Just kidding, of course. The view was incredible. I might have used a bit more than my allotted time in the bombardier's area but I didn't let myself feel too guilty. I sat in the Bombardier's seat and thought about Dad falling asleep. I laughed. The Ferry boats could be seen going in and out of Seattle, the two floating bridges glistened against Lake Washington, the Space Needle seemed to be saluting, the Cascade and the Olympic Mountain ranges to the east and the west, respectively still sported some snow on their tips, and Mt. Rainier was "out" (a local term). They were jumping out as if to say, "Look at me!" I did, for a second. Instead, I found myself mesmerized by the shadow of our plane on the ground, all the doo-dads inside, watching the engines and thinking about two of them not working, the plane shaking uncontrollably, and the fuel having drained out due to the damage from the flak. Wait! Let's go back to those first images. It was a terrific experience I shall never forget.

October 2002

We did make the trip to Dinwiddie, Virginia. It was a bit unnerving as the "Beltway Sniper" was still active and had struck near Richmond, the airport we would be using. Since we had never been to that part of the U.S. we arrived several days before the scheduled date of the B-17 "Fly-In" that would have Erik Dyreborg and Nelson Liddle aboard. Since our son, Erik was missing school, we had him do a report on Grandpa Stevenson. He ended with a large amount of extra information to ingest as we visited Williamsburg, Yorktown, and Jamestown. So, we discussed the Revolutionary War, the Civil War, and World War II. I'm not sure Erik believed us when we told him there were a few wars we'd actually left out.

I couldn't believe it! The B-17 landed earlier than we'd been told so we didn't even get to see it in the air. I'd have given anything to see the landing because, somehow, it ran off the runway and got stuck in the mud. It ended up taking two large tow trucks to pull the Flying Fortress out of the mud. Erik Dyreborg said the company was going to change their slogan to: We tow B-17s and other stuff! In a previous e-mail conversation with Pilot Jack, when he'd announced his health would not allow him to make the trip to Dinwiddie, he added he hoped we'd be able to meet sometime "before (his) plane ran off the runway"! Quick! Call Jack and make sure he's okay! He was.

What a wonderful few days. We met Erik Dyreborg, Nelson Liddle, Nelson's daughter and son-in-law Barbara and Bob Pack, Seymour and Faye Ringle, James Litchford, Bernie Fridberg, Horace Shelton's cousin and her husband, Nelson's brother and sister-in-law, and several other wonderful people. It seemed as if I already knew them and we immediately felt comfortable. Our son, Erik interviewed the crewmembers of my Dad's B-17. We videotaped the interviews and learned so much about them as individuals and as a team. They didn't know each other well. Officers and enlisted men weren't housed together and they'd only been on one mission. But they banded together. It was particularly interesting to talk with Seymour Ringle, as he was Dad's partner in the escape from Bornholm. Aware of Dad having fallen asleep during the bomb run, I smiled in amusement when Seymour said Dad was instrumental in saving his life. How could that be? Seymour, in all sincerity credited Dad with helping him keep his spirits up. He said Dad's optimism encouraged him to have hope. They would not be captured by the Germans. They would make it to safety. And all ten of them did.

The two days went by quickly. The first night a small ceremony was held at a local restaurant while we ate dinner. On day #2 we returned to the airport, toured the Collings Foundation's B-17 and the B-24 again, and visited with each other. I'd taken along some pictures I had of the crew to see if the guys could help with some identification. While seated next to Seymour at lunch he leaned my way and quietly asked, "Did you know your father lost his virginity in Sweden?" I couldn't do anything but laugh. "No, Seymour, I can't say that I did. It just wasn't something we'd ever discussed." I hope he doesn't get mad at me for mentioning this. In those two days, he could already tell it was "safe" to risk asking me that. I continued laughing and declared, "Seymour, I ended up finding all of you because I was on a search for relatives on my mom's side of the family since she had been adopted. Now you're telling me I may have relatives in Sweden????" It was a great time and the best lasagna I've ever had. Who could complain?

November 2002 to the present

My learning curve is still high. I am now the proud owner of quite an impressive WW II European Theater book and video collection. I have my own model of a B-17 (it's cool…the propellers spin.) I educate and refer people to many of the websites I've found useful. I'm still probably boring some people with my story and inspiring others. I continue to be amazed by the coincidence of it all.

I've continued the research on that other side of my family…the one I was studying when I encountered this WW II information that has added so significantly to my life. And I still exchange frequent e-mails with Erik, Nelson, and Jack. Sometimes Jack's computer doesn't work right. One of the other guys will let me know it's on the fritz and that Jack is doing fine. Recently, however, he broke several ribs and has been in quite a bit of pain. I called him and we chatted. We ended up laughing about something (I don't remember what). While he was laughing he was also saying, "Oh, that hurts! But it's such a good hurt." Nelson and Erik both send thoughtful E-mails and also silly animations. I look forward to their communications.

July 2003

By the time this book is published my husband and I will have completed an excursion that will bring this exciting topic full circle. During the summer of 2003 we will visit England and also the Danish island of Bornholm, the site of the crash of B-17 #42-31619. Destinations in England will include Oxford University, where my grandfather attended as a Rhodes Scholar nearly 100 years ago. We will visit the Imperial Air Museum in Duxford. And certainly, not to be missed, will be the site of Air Field #128 at Deenethorpe, Northamptonshire County. The control tower was demolished in 1996. On the site now stands a commemorative monument honoring the members of the 8th AAF 401st Bomb Group.

Erik Dyreborg will meet us at the airport in Copenhagen. The three of us will travel to the island of Bornholm where Erik will proceed to guide us through the experiences of the crew of B-17 #42-31619. From the crash site, to the farms and homes of those who risked their lives to aid these American airmen, to the beaches where crewmembers embarked in "borrowed" rowboats for Sweden, we will trace the routes of my Dad's crew's ordeal. We recently learned we will be able to go into the actual room where Dad and Seymour were hidden before being hustled past the armed German guards to a boat leaving for Sweden. I am anxiously anticipating meeting Vibeke, the "young girl" whose parents harbored Seymour and my Dad and who was the recipient of my Dad's Air Force insignia.

Special thanks

Thank you to the kind people of Bornholm, Denmark. Had they not taken the enormous risks they did to help people, my Dad would not likely have survived (and I guess we know what that means for me!). I am anxiously anticipating our trip to Bornholm this summer.

Thank you to Erik Dyreborg. Had he not paid attention during those visits to the museums with his Grandfather when he was young, he might not have developed the curiosity about the picture of that B-17 crash-landed on the field near Sose, *The Escape from Bornholm 1944* might never have been written!

To my family: Bob, Erik, and Andrea. An enormous thank you to my husband, Bob for persisting about that trip to Butte and for all the support while I neglected other things that needed to be done. Because my kids haven't really gotten to grow up having grandparents, Andrea's insistence that I pursue the family search kept me on the journey. She was the first to decide, since Pilot Jack (Whiteman) doesn't have any children, he would now officially be "Grandpa Jack". And a big thanks to our son, Erik because he was a very good sport all the times I kicked him off the computer so I could work more on this project. And, lest I forget, our Himalayan cats have thoroughly enjoyed cuddling in as I sat and typed and leaping up right in front of the computer screen when they thought they deserved more attention!

Thank you so much to all veterans, to those presently serving, and to those who will serve in our military. It has been humbling to learn specifics about the tremendous sacrifices soldiers make and the camaraderie and lifetime commitments soldiers intensely feel toward each other. A chance diversion on an Internet search one evening nine months ago provided the impetus for me to explore experiences and events I would not likely have otherwise pursued. I have learned about my Dad's experiences as a very young man, been introduced to absolutely wonderful individuals, and intensified the allegiance and patriotism I feel for the United States of America.

This has been an amazing journey. Even though the crew of the B-17 #42-31619 from the 8th AAF 401st BG 615th BS was only together a short period of calendar time, they have been bonded together for nearly sixty years. I am honored to have "met" them. There is no question…they were part of my missing "family" I was searching for all along.

Printed with permission of Shirley Stevenson Wallis.

Only Two Survivors

Narrated by James D. Haffner, B-17 Bombardier
&
John B. Carson, B-17 Tailgunner
8ᵗʰ Air Force, 401ˢᵗ Bomb Group, 615ᵗʰ Bomb Squadron
Written by Helen Haffner & edited by Erik Dyreborg

Introduction

The early years are a mixture of hearsay and more or less established fact. It seems fairly certain that life began on April 3, 1920, in Sigourney, Iowa, county of Keokuk. I am told it was in the middle of a terrible blizzard, about 11 pm at night and Dad had the honor of pulling me out, as the doctor was snowed under.

My parents were Louis John Haffner and Katherine Eldridge Haffner. I had been preceded, by about four years, by my brother, Louis Darwin, and in two years a baby sister, Betty Ann would join us to complete the family. In 1925 the family moved to Seattle, where we lived with relatives for a short time and then moved into a house near Green Lake, at fifty-seventh and Kensington.

After that we moved to 2112 North Forty-third Street, and I got acquainted with some new friends who stood across the street and threw rocks, as I rode my little red wagon down the sidewalk wearing my funny looking "beaver" hat. They were Pete Jonson, Jackie Norton, and Bill Downie, and we had great times playing Kick the Can, Duck on the Rock, football, basketball, and baseball in the middle of the street.

All through high school Sports consumed most of my time and energy, practically living at Lower Woodland Park during the summer. I finally graduated from High School in 1938 without a great deal in the way of academic credentials.

I had been working with Dad as a painter and finished my apprenticeship in 1940,after which I went to Dutch Harbor, Alaska as a Journeyman painter in April of 1941 and came back to Seattle that fall.

I remember, on Sunday, Dec 7th, a few of us fellows were getting together for a game of touch football in Woodland Park when the news came over the radio about Pearl Harbor.

Enlisting and training

I went downtown the next morning to sign up with the intent of doing something "right now" to teach those sneaky little invaders a lesson and end that conflict in Europe pretty fast! I wanted to be a flier but Army Air Corps pilot training required 2 years of college so I joined the Air Corps as an enlisted man.

The wages were 20 dollars a month. I was sent to Boot Camp at Jefferson Barracks, Missouri, where we learned to march, we got shots, and took aptitude tests, then on to Rantoul, Illinois, where the school for airplane mechanics was located. I hardly realized at the time the enormous anxiety that my dear beloved parents must have gone through at this time in their lives.

When I was about half way through the airplane mechanics course, the army announced a waiver of the two-year college requirement if the applicant could pass the same entrance exam as the college applicant. I regard it as one of my greatest achievements that I was able to pass this exam and be accepted as a cadet. Over 500 men took that test at Rantoul and only about eight made it to Santa Ana, California (the Headquarters for the Army Air Forces West Coast Training Center). I was about to become a Fighter Pilot!! How sweet the world seemed.

But first, ground school: We seemed to be at Santa Ana forever, drilling, watching films on airplane ID, drilling, KP, Dress Parades, etc. We did manage some weekends in the lovely Long Beach area but always had to be back for Sunday Parade.

Bombardier and combat training

Finally up to Tulare to show off our "stuff" in primary trainers, more ground school there but a CHANCE TO FLY!!!

And it wasn't so easy. Landings and takeoffs were difficult in the back seat of a two-seater. Time was "of the essence": You were allowed 12 hours in which to become proficient enough to solo and then it was solo or out! My instructor thought I was ready, so we went to a nearby field to shoot a practice landing. He was going to exit and me solo.

The practice landing was bad, I had to circle twice before landing and so instead of solo, it was "OUT". I took my cracked ego and bent dreams back to Santa Ana to prepare for Bombardier school, which I successfully completed, receiving my Wings and Bars as a second lieutenant at Roswell, New Mexico on February 13, 1943.

After stops at Salt Lake, Utah, Ephrata, Washington, and Great Falls, Montana, we really got our combat training at a great, friendly little place, Lewistown, Montana. There our group was formed and as a Lead Crew we were sent to Orlando, Florida for special training.

We trained in the B-17G, the first plane to have chin turrets. Then back to Lewistown where more crews were added to our squadron. We were the 615th Squadron, 401st Bomb Group and Bill Seawell, soon to be a Colonel was our Leader.

The crew is pictured above.

Front row L-R:

1st Lt. Michael R. Walsh, Navigator; 1st Lt. Robert D. Kaercher, Co-Pilot; Captain William M. Rumsey Jr., Pilot; 1st Lt. James Daniel Haffner, Bombardier (POW Stalag Luft I).

Back row L to R:

1st person unknown…then T/Sgt. William W. Carter, radio operator; Herb McElligot, tail gunner; T/Sgt. Donald B. Roberts, Engineer; S/Sgt. Ivan R. Lee, waist gunner; S/Sgt Irving I. Lieberman "Lucky Lieberman", ball turret gunner.

John B. Carson who was the substitute tail gunner on March 26,1944 when Omar the Dentmaker was hit by FLAK over Pas de Calais, France and exploded, is not pictured here.

The name of our good old airplane was "Omar the Dentmaker" B-17 serial #42-37833.

England

We arrived at an airfield called Deenethorpe, north of London about December, 1943 and spent a month with them learning Tactics.

The bombers rendezvoused over an inlet called "The Wash" and then headed for the coast of France accompanied by the fighter planes nicknamed "little friends", our protectors, who often made the difference in whether the bombers ever made it to their assigned targets or went down in flames, forever.

We flew some harrowing missions the next few months to Oserschleben, Berlin, Pas de Calais, Bordeaux, Kiel, etc.

The long mission to Bordeaux (nine hours) was particularly memorable.

We had flack and Fighters all the way, and we could see our planes going down in flames constantly. With great weariness, after dropping our bombs and re-forming, our three Wings grouped into one, and we struggled home with terrible losses.

I was the Wing Bombardier leader on two flights to Oschers-leben, a suburb near Berlin, where there was a fighter plane factory. Our crew had the lead assignment but was unable to bomb because of clouds, so we picked the alternative target of Marburg, which we bombed successfully with "Lucky" Lieberman taking pictures of it from the Ball Turret position.

Disaster

It was toward the end of March when the event happened that would end in disaster for our crew and destroy the lives of eight dedicated and patriotic men. I wonder what their thoughts are today, as they view the remnants of those precious ideals that they fought to preserve, and those souls who are the beneficiaries of their gift.

It was on Sunday morning, March 26,1944, we were called to an early briefing and our crew was to have the substitute lead; that is, if anything happened to the lead crew we would be prepared to take over their place and lead the mission. It meant that we studied the maps and target just as if to lead, and once on the mission, followed through on their navigating and bombing movements.

The target was Pas de Calais, France and the V-1 installations from which the Germans launched their rocket attacks on Britain. It was considered a mild run as serious opposition was seldom encountered, recently, and time wise, it was brief.

And so it seemed to be as we crossed the channel and headed towards the Initial Point. No fighters were in sight, and no flak had been seen. It was just as we were starting on the bomb run that it happened.

A shell exploded suddenly inside our plane behind the pilot. A single burst of flak had hit us squarely. We immediately went out of control and according to eyewitnesses from other planes I talked to later, we flew upside down and backwards through the formation, causing the other pilots to frantically dodge out of our way. The plane began to disintegrate, wings, engines, etc, breaking off.

What I was aware of in the nose compartment was that guns and everything were flying loose. Centrifugal force was strong and one had little control of one's self. I caught a glimpse of Mike Walsh, navigator who was behind me and near the escape hatch for us. A parachute bounced into my arms (it has occurred to me since that Mike may have thrown it towards me).

I had taken it off to concentrate on following through on the bombsite. I folded it in my arms and at that moment the nose sheared off the plane and I was sliding towards the opening.

I hit the air with such force my boots were ripped off my feet and I fell, tumbling wildly, clinging to the parachute pack like it was a football. After some seconds the fall became more orderly with the feet and head skyward and bottom down. Then I began to hook on my chest pack, first one side, then after looking earthward to see if there was still time, hooking the other side. We were taught to wait as long as possible to pull the rip cord, thus enhancing our chances to avoid being seen…but Earth was pretty close by this time, so I pulled, made a good landing, tumbling over a few times, then gathered up the chute and buried it as we were taught to do.

Captured

So far I hadn't seen any other chutes open and felt very heartsick at the doubtful chances of any other survivors. Trying to look nonchalant I headed towards a wooded area but out of the woods came soldiers so I changed directions towards boxcars on a siding some distance away. Soon soldiers came from that direction too. In short I was surrounded.

They drew closer pointing their rifles at me and said "For you de Var iss Oeffer!" (for you the war is over).

John B. Carson remembers

I was the substitute tail gunner on the final flight of "Omar the Dentmaker", March 26, 1944. I replaced Herb F. McElligott, the original tail gunner for Omar's crew, who was grounded.

I told the guys I had this feeling that this would be my third time for a disaster since I had already been shot down twice before, which of course they were "thrilled' to hear and promptly told me to shut my mouth up.

I was wearing my chest chute when everything exploded in flames. I remember thinking the chute wasn't working as I pulled the cord, crashing into a bunch of trees with German bullets zipping up at me.

Dragging my broken knee along, I crawled across a field to a small hut that looked like an outhouse, slowly opened the door scaring a German guard to death, as well as myself.

Was taken to the jail at Lille, then interrogated at Frankfurt-am-Main where I starved for five days. One of the interrogators was a famous German ski instructor we nicknamed "Ben-zie-knees" who knew of my Lying about my age in order to enter the Corps early. He also knew that I was NOT the original tail-gunner for "Omar"'s crew.

I was informed that one other member of that crew had survived, the bombardier, James D. Haffner, who when I reminded him of my earlier prediction, shouted out "God Damn it! I DON'T WANT TO HEAR ANY MORE OF YOUR PREDICTIONS!!!"

We were both shipped in a boxcar with 68 other people to Barth on the Baltic Sea, freezing to death the whole way!

First I was put into the South Compound at Stalag Luft 1 with the English RAF, then later into the North Compound as a "Dog Robber" to wait on the officers, take care of the Red Cross parcels, and cook "whatever showed up" in a big pot in the middle of the yard."

On May 1st, 1945, the 2nd White Russian Front of the Red Army entered Barth, Germany and "liberated" Stalag Luft I.

The assault troops were made up of horrible-looking mongol-like thugs, armed to the teeth with bayonets and scythes, and Russian women who took delight in bayoneting the German babies.

Hours before the "liberation" of the Stalag, we watched the German farmers gathering their wives and children into the fields surrounding the stalag walls, shooting them and then committing suicide themselves, in terrible fear of the Russian partisans' reprisals. I could never forget this sight and the fear.

On my way into Barth I came across a young girl about 15 and her little brother crying over the dead body of their father, the commander of the German anti-air-craft guns who had just committed suicide. I helped her to put his body into a cart and we dug a quick grave at the Barth cemetary.

James D. Haffner's homecoming

U.S. 8th Air Force planes landed about five miles away and most of the Stalag Luft I prisoners marched out to the evacuation field on or about May 5, 1945.

They flew us up the Ruhr Valley to look at how we had destroyed Germany.

After landing in France, we were held in Camp Lucky Strike where General Eisenhower came through the chow line and waved at troops.

Our own Colonel Bill Seawell, of the 401st Bomb Group, 615th Bomb Squad, flew from England and took those of us from his squadron back to Deenethorpe, England where we were assigned to sleep in the hospital. I stayed two months in England waiting to go home.

Finally I sailed on the troop ship, S.S. Admiral Mayo, to Boston, where we got on a train crossing the U.S. for seven days to Fort Lewis, Washington.

Huge crowds of people waved at the homecoming men all along the way. I went to Seattle for one week to see my folks and then down to Santa Monica, California for my medical check-up and rehabilitation, then back to Fort Lewis for my discharge papers!!! Hurrah for the Good Old U.S.A and it's good to be HOME AGAIN!!!

The letters

V-mail from James Haffner to his parents:

(unfortunately no date on this V-mail)

Dear Mother and Dad,

I was flown from Barth to France, day before yesterday by Eighth Air Force comrades.
We are getting "processed" for immediate shipment home. We must be examined; clothed etc. and then we will be on our way.I should be seeing you again in about 3 weeks. I cannot explain in words how wonderful it is to be free again and in the friendly and protecting hands of Uncle Sam. I hope that I will find you all well and happy when I get home and that the last year and a half has not caused you too much anxiety.
Everything is being done to get us home as quickly as possible, so please be patient for a little while longer.

Your loving son, Dan

Letter received from the parents of Donald B. Roberts (Don, the Engineer) who along with seven other crew members was killed on March 26, 1944:

Wampsville, NY
June 10, 1945

Dear Jim,

We received your letter from England and thank you for writing to us. We are happy for you and your family that you will soon be reunited and we hope you are well.

It was an awful shock to us to lose our Don as you know he was all we had. We are trying to carry on as best we can but life will never be quire the same again.

There are many things we would like to know but we don't like to ask too many questions as you have been through so much we know there are many things you would like to forget.

We would like to know just what happened on that last fatal mission. Do you think the boys were killed instantly? It would be a comfort to know that they didn't suffer.

Is there any way we can find out if the were buried and where?

Don was so fond of all the boys and so proud of your crew. He was so sure that you would all come through as your crew was one of the best in the Air Corps.

We want to know more about yourself. Will you be discharged from the service? If not and you should be stationed here in the East and should you have a short furlough we would be glad to have you come here.

Just give us a ring. Our phone number is Oneida N.Y. 1409—RI. We will be grateful for any information you can give us.

Good bless you and your family.

Sincerely Yours,
Berhn & Elsie Roberts

Translated letter from Mr. J. Yaeguemelle, France to Don's parents:

Bouquemaison,
June 1, 1946

Dear Sir and Dear Madame,

Several days ago I received your letter telling me that you were the parents of one of the heroes who met death on the 26th of March 1944, in our splendid skies of France.

I don't know English, therefore I'm sending my letter to you in French.

It is Sunday, March 26, 1944. About 2:30 while we were finishing our noon meal several of American fortress airplanes appeared in the sky to try to destroy the V-1 emplacements and other fortifications that the Germans were busy getting ready about 3 kilometers from Bouquemaison. (1 kilometer=.6 mile).

Then one of the planes under the command of E. Rumsey Folson was hit several kilometers above us by a burst of German aircraft. Thus the catastrophe occurred, The plane exploded immediately with the ten soldiers making up the crew. Two came to earth by parachute and were made prisoners by the Germans. They were unhurt, but unfortunately eight were killed including, unfortunately, you son.

The bodies of the eight unfortunate ones were strewn along the ground for a distance of 1,000 yards. The bodies were damaged, of course, but all in one piece; certainly they have been killed at the moment of the explosion and hurled in several directions. None of the parachutes was open. Consequently they obviously died before coming to earth. The explosion had been terrible. The plane had been scattered over several kilometers; a fuel tank and a wing burned while falling to earth. A lone engine fell less than ten feet from six people who were watching the crash. What a sad thing war is!

I was requisitioned to take a wagon and two horses and to take the dead soldiers to the cemetery of our village the afternoon of March 27. They were buried side by side in their uniforms and wrapped each one in a sack. It was the Germans who ordered us to do this work.

I hope this information will be of help to you.

As for me, I am 48 years old. I am married and we have a daughter Paulette who is 19 and a son George who is 15. My entire family expresses to you, at this time, our sincere condolences. Please accept, dear Sir and dear Madame, our respectful best wishes.

J. Yaequemelle (signed)

P.S. The bodies of the eight airmen were exhumed by American forces on June 10, 1945 will be buried in a military cemetery.

Printed with permission of Helen Haffner.

Jan Pieter Smit, A Dutch Deaf And Dumb Salesman

Narrated by Claude Murray, a P-38 Pilot
8th Air Force, 7th Photo Reconnaissance Group
Edited by Erik Dyreborg

Enlisting and training

I volunteered for the service and was fortunate enough to be accepted into what was called the Aviation Cadet Program in 1942. I was living at the time in Cheney, Washington, my hometown. Then I had to wait about eight or nine months before I was called to active duty.

Every person who came through classification at Santa Ana Army Air Base, California, was asked the same question: "Why did you choose the Aviation Cadet Program?" Many said it was because they had a "burning desire to fly." I'm sorry to say that that was not my reasoning. My reason was that a second lieutenant could make about $240 a month, and if you were successful and graduated from Cadets and were commissioned, you became an officer. I wanted to be an officer and I wanted to be a fighter pilot. That was the glamorous thing to do at that time. I didn't know whether I could fly or not at the time.

I knew that I wanted to go to war. It was the thing to do. I was patriotic; the U.S. was at war. I didn't want to wait to be drafted; I wanted to get in there.

So I was sent to Santa Ana Army Air Base, which was a classification center, and was classified for pilot training. For primary training, I went to King City, California. Mesa Del Rey was a contract air force training base. We flew PT-19s there, a low-wing aircraft by Ryan.

For basic training, I went to Merced Army Air Base, California, where we flew the Vultee "Vibrator," the BT-13, a much heavier airplane than the Ryan.

Pictured above, Claude Murray 1943.

For advanced training, I went to Williams Field, just outside of Phoenix, Arizona (my present home). There we flew the AT-9, because by that time I had been approved to fly twin-engine. The AT-9 is a horrible airplane; it's called the "flying crowbar." Even the instructors couldn't land it correctly.

Anyway, we suffered through that. We had gunnery training in AT-6s, at Ajo, Arizona.

Our transition to P-38s was an airplane that looked like a P-38 but was called the RP-322, a non-supercharged P-38, contracted by Great Britain. The British found this prototype airplane unsatisfactory, and the USAF used the few models built as trainers. (Both props turned the same way, and that is significant for my later experience.) We had a piggyback ride in an RP-322. Then one was handed over to us, and we were told to "Take off." We'd never flown the damn thing. The only twin-engine airplane we'd had in our hands was the AT-9.

Anyway, I'm guessing we got 25 or 30 hours in the RP-322, and then we graduated—in class 43-J, November 1943. I'm now a second lieutenant. I graduated with Dale Rankin, the son of Tex Rankin—but that doesn't mean much. It's just one of the names I can think of. Dale was killed in action later on.

I went back home for a few days and then to my first assignment, to an OTU (Overseas Training Unit), at Ellensburg Army Air Base, Ellensburg, Washington, a fighter-training base. It's December by now, and up there you get some snow and some pretty bad weather. We weren't getting much flying time.

So a bunch of us, a squadron or two, were transferred to Ontario Army Air Base, in Ontario, California. There we started to do some flying and did a little bit of gunnery. We were flying real P-38s now. These had the counter-rotating propellers (I've seen that written "contra-rotating" also). Now I'm not an expert mechanic, and I suppose I wasn't a great pilot, but I'm thinking that the supercharged P-38s could fly a helluva lot higher than the RP-322s.

All of a sudden the whole group received orders to transfer to Will Rogers Field, in Oklahoma City, Oklahoma, for "photoreconnaissance." Most of us didn't know anything about photo-recon, and of course we didn't like the transfer. We wanted to shoot guns. But we went to Oklahoma and went into training for photo-recon. A few of the guys were able to get transferred out of recon and back into fighters, but I myself didn't try. I went along with the orders.

I think I arrived there in about January of 1944, and I was supposed to go overseas in June. But I was stricken with a hernia problem and had to have some repair, so I was out of pocket for about 60 days.

England and the missions

I believe I arrived in England as a replacement pilot around the middle of August. The base was Mount Farm, near Oxford. That was the base of the Seventh Photo Reconnaissance Group. The first squadron had come over in December of 1943, and I arrived in August of 1944. We had four squadrons by this time: the 13th, 14th, 22nd, and 27th. Interestingly, the 14th squadron was eventually given Spitfires, an excellent plane for photo-recon. One of the first photo-recon planes over Berlin, flown by Lt. Walter Weitner, was a spit from our group.

Like everyone else, we had our orientation, to learn the British radio systems, weather, and those sorts of things.

There were two cameras at the side of the P-38, and one in the front, so you could take oblique photos and do mapping. I have to admit that I'm very foggy on some of these details. To be honest, I wasn't a mechanic. As long as all the needles were in the green, I was okay. Damn, if one of those needles had gone into the red, I don't know if I could have handled the situation or not, or known what to do.

These were still cameras. We were doing damage assessment and mapping. Let's say the 390th Bomb Group went to Merseburg, Germany, and completed its mission, maybe through partial clouds; and they didn't know whether they hit the target or not. So right after them, we would go in, individually—alone—at high altitude, try to find the target, take pictures, then have them taken out of the camera, developed, and printed and sent back. Very quickly the film was taken out of the camera and sent up to Eighth Air Force Headquarters, where it was interpreted, and the results sent back through Doolittle, through all the channels, to let the groups know whether they had been successful—whether they could write that target off.

I'm sure the British also benefited from our recon work. I heard the other day that a German general said that the people who had the best photoreconnaissance were going to win the war. Before D-Day, we had mapped all the beaches; and a lot of our guys did what were called "dicing missions"—flying right down on the deck, taking pictures of bridges, roads, V-bomb sites, etc. But most of our stuff was from high altitude, 25,000 to 32,000 feet. So we were in danger of flak, unseen enemy fighters, and weather.

The German fighters were also looking for us. Of course when the P-38s came into the picture; they were so easily identifiable that when the German fighters got on you, they knew whom you were. We had to fly higher and faster, and see them first. If you didn't see them first, you were duck soup.

There were 65 wartime casualties in our group—that is, killed in action. Total personnel in our group at any one time was probably was 1,200, no more than 80 or 100 pilots in our four squadrons. Oftentimes it was "Cause: unknown; midair collision; unknown; weather; crashed; anoxia—asphyxiation (ran out of oxygen); engine trouble; unknown; flak; flak; FTR (failed to return)." For example, when I got shot down, nobody really knew what happened. Probably half of casualties were due to bad weather, or other problems of that type, as opposed to enemy action.

I flew three missions. I can't remember the places—marshalling yards, and various other installations in France and Germany. You were always given milk runs to start with. The fourth mission was to Hamm, Germany, and to other targets in the area.

Shot down

I had left about nine o'clock in the morning, and one of my buddies in the squadron, Lt. Robert Hall, a guy that slept right next to me, had targets in the same area. We took off at the same time, headed in the same direction; he was flying about a mile off my wing, and we were in radio contact. You weren't supposed to do much talking on the radio, but he gave me a call and said, "Bat Crap" (our real call sign was Baylo'—I was Baylo 28, but we had our own sign), "you're off course."

"No, Bat Crap, I'm not off course."

That was the only conversation I recall that we had—until he called in "Bogies." "There's Bogies at four o'clock"—meaning that enemy aircraft were somewhere coming up from that direction.

The P-38 was very vulnerable, because you're sitting there in the pod and can't see underneath you unless you rack it up; so you're constantly racking it up, to see if anybody's coming from down there. And your neck's on a swivel, because you've got to be looking around all the time.

The minute he called in the Bogie, I was hit. Smack!

I didn't see the guy coming or going. Lt. Hall later reported that German jets had attacked us. We had been briefed on jets—the ME-262. What you're supposed to do immediately is to push everything to the firewall, drop your belly tanks, and go into a tight spiral, because the Me-262 was not maneuverable. It was made for fast, sweeping passes; so the idea was to get away from the enemy, so they couldn't make another pass at you.

But he had hit me, and I didn't know where. All I knew that there had been a huge, huge impact—a big jolt. I knew that something had happened, and it turned out that it was my right engine, which eventually caught fire.

Another funny thing happened. In your training, you are trained and trained and trained in various procedures, which come second nature to you. Everything to the firewall! Drop the belly tanks! But I forgot to switch from the reserve tanks (the belly tanks) to the main tanks. And all of a sudden, both my engines were windmilling, because they weren't getting any fuel.

Realizing that, I switched to main and got my port engine started again, but I couldn't start my starboard engine, the one that was hit. So I figured I would go back home.

I'm guessing I was down to 6,000 to 8,000 feet, and you could fly very nicely on one engine. I would go back.

Pretty quick, I'm getting smoke in the cockpit. Boy, if there's anything that scares you, it's fire and smoke in an airplane! I'd been calling mayday, mayday on the radio, the sign that you're going down over water, which I see down below me.

I'm over the Zuider Zee. I'd gone into Germany, and probably had come back over Arnhem, turning back toward England.

So I popped the canopy, and when I did, off went my helmet, my goggles, and my oxygen mask—because I didn't have my helmet buckled. That didn't make any difference, because I couldn't talk to anybody anyway. We had an IFF (Identification, Friend or Foe) system in the airplane, which is wired. You break the wire and push the switch, and there will be an automatic signal that identifies you as friend or foe. So if anybody was on that IFF channel, and I had been in their vicinity, they would know that I was an Allied aircraft.

This is where the counter-rotating propellers come in. When the right engine stopped, I held in hard left rudder, in order to keep the airplane going straight and level. I didn't trim it. What you're supposed to do is trim the airplane, get into a slight climb, slow it down to around 120 mph, slip out the side, and go down between the two tail booms and underneath the horizontal stabilizer.

That's how the book said to do it, but there had been a few people decapitated trying to do that.

I was still holding the rudder in, and I stuck my elbow out over the side, and God, I thought the wind was going to tear my arm off! I said to myself, "How on earth can I get out of this thing?" I'm sitting on a seat-type dinghy, I have a back-pack type parachute (and these are strapped together down below), I have a Mae West over me, which is also strapped to the dinghy—how am I going to slip out of this thing, with all that wind going by me, without getting hung up? Some people had had that experience too.

"I think you've had it," I thought to myself; and I let go of everything. I took my foot off the rudder and started to pray.

The airplane, with the port engine propeller going one way, flipped over, and I fell out. The next thing I know, I'm coming down in a parachute. You're supposed to hang on to the D-ring for good luck—the ring that opens the parachute.

"Have I got the D-ring?" I don't know. Obviously I had pulled it, but I don't remember doing it. Maybe I had blacked out a little, or something. Anyway, I'm coming down in the parachute, and I didn't realize what had happened. Obviously I hadn't trimmed the airplane up so it would fly straight and level on the one engine, and therefore it simply flipped over, due to torque.

I'm an Episcopalian, and I was an altar boy when I was a kid. I wasn't going to church every Sunday in England, but nevertheless I knew what it meant to pray. I had a certain philosophy. Every time I got ready to take off on one of those missions (though it was only four missions), I told myself, "Nothing's going to happen to me. I'm going to get out of this thing okay. I'm going to fly this mission and come back flying." I just felt that confident. So of course you pray to your God that this will be the result. When I got hit, I thought it just couldn't be happening to me.

I'm coming down in a parachute, and below me is the damned water. Here your training comes in again. You are supposed to unbuckle your chest buckle, and the two buckles on your legs, and slide out the parachute just before you hit the water, so you don't get tangled up in the chute harness.

I couldn't get out of one of the buckles. So I'm in the water now, bobbing up and down, and finally I get rid of the parachute. I inflate the Mae West, which brings me up; and it is connected by a little strap to the dinghy, which is floating in the water. You reach down to the dinghy, find the CO-2 cylinder, and inflate the dingy. Now you climb into it.

We'd seen training films, and incidentally, just a week or so before I went down, one of my buddies in the Quonset Hut quarters, John Ross, had had to ditch in the North Sea, and he spent all night long getting in and out of the dinghy, but was rescued the next day by Air Sea Rescue. When he got back, we had a training exercise on his experience, and why the sea anchor should be used.

When I got in the dingy, I'm looking for the equipment that's supposed to be in it—paddles, something to make a sail out of, a sea anchor, a bail-out bucket, a whistle, sea dye (green). And there was nothing—except the sea anchor and the bailout bucket.

The sea anchor is something you string out in back of the dinghy—something small on the front end, and fanning into a sort of a funnel shape. With that thing trailing you on a rope, it keeps you—I guess—going with the waves, instead of against them. And my buddy, John Ross, didn't have his sea anchor out, so the waves kept throwing him out all night long.

This went down in late September, and he survived. In winter, he wouldn't have.

I don't know how cold the water was when I went down, but it was damned cold, I'll tell you that. And of course all I could do was sit there, though there was a flap you could pull over yourself. I couldn't do anything but just sit there and float!

I wondered where I was, where I was going to go, what was going to happen. I figured I would be captured.

This happened about 13:00 hours—about one o'clock in the afternoon. I couldn't see very much, although I was only about a mile or so off shore. I don't remember seeing the shore when I was coming down; I was too worried about how I was going to get out of that parachute when I fell into the water. I don't remember looking around and saying, "Oh, gosh, there's Amsterdam over there, and I'm in the Zuider Zee, and blah, blah, blah." All I know is that I got in the dinghy, and I'm floating there.

The only warmth I had for the next thirteen hours was taking a leak in the dingy, and feeling that nice warm water down between my legs.

It gets to be night. It's going to get dark. It must have been a clear night, because all of a sudden I see on the horizon what looks like the low form of a boat, maybe what a submarine would look like. I'm starting to paddle with my hands now, and I come into shore. I have floated into a little island, which turns out to be the "Fortress Pampus"—an old Dutch fortress, about two and one-half acres in size. (I have obtained a history of Pampus, which was constructed sometime in the late

1800s.) It sort of guards the bay, which I could now see, when I got up onto the fortress. It's only about a mile from shore.

I'm tired by now, after thirteen hours in a boat, and all I want to do is sleep. I crawl out of the dinghy and deflate it, then lay down underneath some bushes and go to sleep.

The escape

At dawn, the next morning, I start my escape and evasion tactics. I start walking and crawling around, to see if there are any enemy troops around. I'd had the usual escape and evasion classes, just as we all had the VD lectures. So you're supposed to reconnoiter, to see if there are any enemy troops, see if you can stay away from them.

When I stand up, I see a sign: "Verboten." I know what that means: it means you are "forbidden" to be there. I discover some chambers down inside the fortress; as I walk down cement steps, I find all kinds of rooms. It turns out it was a fortress to protect the harbor, but it had been stripped of all guns and other uses. It had been used by troops many years ago, but the Germans didn't want anyone out there now. The Dutch in the little nearby village knew they couldn't come out there. But of course I didn't know that at the time.

I had an escape kit, a little plastic box about four inches by six inches, and an inch and a half thick. Inside the box are a couple of tiny compasses (we called them "ass-hole compasses"), halazone to purify water, something to keep you awake, concentrated chocolate, vitamins, some chewing gum, some matches, a razor, a fishhook, a plastic bag for collecting water, and so forth. In addition, I had a little fiber bag about the same size as the escape kit, which contained the famous little silk maps. So I was able to figure out where I was.

Anyway, I went down inside this place and built a fire, to try to dry out a bit. I'm still pretty soggy. Well, what did I do? I ruined my GI shoes, because I put them too close to the fire and left them sitting there; they became as hard as rocks. But I still had my fleece-lined flight boots on.

I went back up on top and said to myself, "Okay, it's about nine o'clock in the morning." Then I see fishing boats, about a mile away, so I wave my hands and start whistling. I can whistle like hell with my fingers. I tore the flap off my dingy and hooked it onto a stick, and I'm waving it, to try to get somebody to come out. By now I'm getting hungry. I want a cigarette. I want to talk to somebody. I want to get captured. How can I possibly evade? I'm sitting out there on an island and no one is going to come out and get me.

I started to accumulate trash and wood, gathered it together, went right to the top of the Pampus, and said to myself, "At twelve o'clock noon I'm going to set this stuff on fire. I'm going to build the damndest bonfire anyone ever saw."

So I built the fire, but nothing happened. The fishermen saw the fire, I know, because I later talked to a Dutch policeman, and he saw it. But they didn't dare go out there, because of the very stringent rules of their Nazi occupiers.

That was decision number one. For decision number two, I said that at three o'clock, if I haven't talked to anybody, I'm going to get back in that dingy (even though I'd sworn I would never do it—I didn't want to get wet again). But I had to get to shore. I could see what I thought were some smokestacks, so I figured maybe there were some factories on shore. And maybe if I get to shore by four or five o'clock, I can start walking. Maybe nobody will notice me. I had a flight suit on, but so what?

Meeting the Dutch

So at three o'clock I blew up the dingy (don't ask me how I did it), got into it with a couple of pieces of wood I could sort of paddle with, and paddled for about fifteen minutes to half an hour. Then here came three kids in a fishing boat: Jan Dobber, his brother and a friend. They came along side of me, got me into the boat, deflated the dinghy, and hid it under some fishing nets. I think my flight jacket was a B-10, which has an air force insignia. So I'm saying, "I'm an American." They didn't speak any English, and I couldn't speak any Dutch.

A German patrol boat came by, and the boys hid me under the nets. They knew what they were doing. When it left, they rowed the boat into shore and pulled up beside a dike, on the water side. Over the dike was a village. One of the kids said he was going to "Haul his fodder" ("Haal zyn vader"). It sounded to me like he was going to go get his father.

I said to him, "Fine, go ahead."

My next escape and evasion tactic is to never stay in the same place. If somebody is going to do something like that, go back a ways, so you can watch the spot where they're coming back to, to see if they're bringing some solders. I told Dobber that we should get back in the boat, and row around a while. I don't know how I told him that, maybe with hand signals or something.

We got back in the boat, and soon I see the kid coming with a man. "Okay, let's go back to shore," I said. It didn't look like the Gestapo to me.

They'd told the father what had transpired, I suppose. He looks me over and then says, "Wacht even"—"Wait a minute."

He goes back to the village on his bicycle and returns with Joh (short for Johannes) Rozendaal, the leader of the underground organization in the little village of Muiden. That was my fourth stroke of luck.

All over Holland, the underground was made up of independent organizations, in this city, that town, etc. They performed sabotage and many other kinds of "resistance" against the Germans. Later, I realized that Operation Market Garden—the airborne invasion of Holland—started about the 17th of September 1944. Queen Juliana and Prince Bernhard were of course in exile in England. They ordered all the Dutch railway workers to go on strike when the invasion started. So the Germans shut off all the electricity as a punishment (except for hospitals and government buildings). One of the functions of the underground was to obtain food and distribute it to the railway workers who were on strike. They distributed food, money, ration cards, and personal permits (I got one of those: they would steal blank cards from the Germans and type in new names—everyone had to have an identity card). But I'm getting ahead of myself.

Joh Rozendaal says, "Kan je fietsen?"—"Okay, can you ride a bike?"

"I guess so. I used to be a paper boy." Now I can't understand what he is saying, but I figure what they're talking about, because we get on bike and ride a few blocks to a house, where I'm given some farm clothes to put on over my flight suit. And they take my escape kit and maps.

They went on ahead, and when it got dark, we all went into the village. I come into a house, and there sitting around a dining table, under a light, is all the stuff from my escape kit laying there. And here are a bunch of young guys, members of the Rozendaal Resistance Group, sitting around a table, and also a Dutch minister—Dominee Douma—who can speak English. They want to know what's the story.

So here I am. I've been out messing around all night and all day long. I've got a little bit of a beard. My face is dirty. I'm in a crew cut. They were sure I was a "kraut," sure as heck I was a German spy, trying to get into their organization or something. They didn't know who I was, and I didn't know who they were.

Anyway, they fed me and cleaned me up.

The next day, Daan Spoor (real name Swen), one of the underground leaders came in. He had been an officer in the Dutch army, but had gone underground. He had become what was called an "onderduiker" (meaning "to dive under and change identity"). Spoor traveled all the time. He never slept in the same house twice. He never went home because the Germans were on his trail.

He spoke excellent English, and he had a written examination for me—a list of questions on paper. They wanted to determine if I was who I said I was and if I were "legitimate." I'd given them my name, rank, and serial number. But they wanted to know the name of my flight surgeon. I told them, because I figured that if I'm going to get them to trust me, I'm going to have to trust them. And I did. My perception was that I was in good hands. I was on the defense, and they were on the offense.

Questions like "What is a meat wagon'?" Well, it's an ambulance. "What is a 'flying prostitute'?" That's a B-26 bomber, because with its little tiny wings, it had "no visible means of support." "What do the Boston Red Sox do?" And other things like that, to see if you can answer very elementary American questions.

It was sort of like the Dutch town of Scheveningen, near The Hague. The Germans couldn't pronounce it correctly, and this would reveal that they were not Dutch.

A day or two later, Daan Spoor comes back, and in the meantime has been in contact with British Intelligence. They had confirmed who I was, but my group never found out I was alive. They said I was MIA all this time. MI-9 (British Intelligence) was very tight, I'll tell you that.

My .45 automatic and my A-2 jacket with my silver P-38 pin on it were back at the base. (I'll always wonder which one of my "buddies" ended up with these items—I never saw them again.)

"Okay," Daan said, "you are who you say you are, so we have orders that you are not to try to escape or get back, and we are dedicated to help you evade capture. We will hide and protect you, but we can't help you escape."

New identity

What had happened during Operation Market Garden, in September, the previous month, of '44, the underground all came out in the open, fighting the Germans, thinking they had had a big victory and won the war. The Germans were all in a retreat for a while, until everything got screwed up and we were defeated there. That was the major allied defeat in World War II, at Arnhem and Nijmegen, at "The Bridge Too Far." The Gestapo was trying to work its way into the escape chains, and so the idea of getting over the lines and the three rivers, into the Comete escape line in Belgium, and out to the free French, was out. "We don't want you to leave," he told me. "We don't want you to try to leave, and we have orders to make you a Dutch civilian for the time being."

They took my picture, put it on the "persoons bewijs" (personal permit), put my fingerprint on it, and my name is now Jan Pieter Smit, a "doofstom" (deaf and dumb) salesman from the province of Edam. The story was that during Operation Market Garden, with all the bombing, there were a helluva lot of refugees, some of them shell-shocked, that got out of there. And there were a lot! The underground was busy trying to find places for these people to live and hide, and a lot of them were Jewish.

I've got civilian clothes now, and they take my dog tags and uniform. This is a very ticklish thing, because if you're captured and have dog tags, this is supposed to be evidence that you're an American, not a spy. If you don't have dog tags, they can shoot you on the spot.

New hiding-place

Another time, Daan asked me if I could ride a bike for about ten kilometers. "Sure," I told him.

The next day, here comes Jan Van Etten, a young Dutch guy about my age (now a resident of Edmonton, Alberta, Canada). He's got a bike, and I've got a bike. We're going to ride our bikes to I don't know where. It happens that we're going to ride to the town of Naarden, not very far from Muiden.

Incidentally, if you tell a Dutchman that you were staying at "Mowden," they'll say, "What? Where is that?"

"Well, it's spelled Muiden."

"Oh, Muiden!" ("my-den"). Talk about linguistics!

We get on the bicycles, and he says, "Now I'm going to be about ten yards ahead of you. If I get stopped, you stop and turn around."

Here we go, me in my civilian clothes, riding a bicycle down the streets. We get to Naarden, and go to the house of Vrouw (Mrs.) Dietz, a widow. She has a nice home, and two sons: Jaap and Peter. I'd say that Peter was maybe sixteen years old, and Jaap fourteen. And they had a Jewish boy hiding out there, Ted Cohen. Vrouw Dietz got extra food stamps for permitting the underground to house the "onderduikers." Incidentally, they could all speak English, including Ted Cohen. Whenever they wanted to talk to me, they spoke English; whenever they wanted to talk about me, they spoke Dutch. That was par for the course.

We got acquainted. Ted and I slept up on the second floor, and I supposed the others slept on the main floor. So there I am, in this house, and I can't get out. I can't go anyplace, not even out in the yard, except one night when they let me walk around in the back a little bit.

This is getting very discouraging. Every now and then, Daan Spoor would come to visit me in Naarden. Earlier on he had brought a pint of bourbon. On his visits, we would each have a jigger of that bourbon. Oh boy, was that ever good! It relaxed me. I am tense. I am under stress.

One day a Catholic priest came to the house, looking for a place to house refugees, but he had nothing to do with the Daan Spoor group. Vrouw Dietz said to him, "By the way, I've got an American pilot here."

"Do you want me to talk to him?" he asked.

"Yes."

So we talked, and he found out the situation. "Do you want me to investigate the possibility of your leaving here? To get back to your lines?"

"I certainly do. Is there any chance?"

"I think there is. I think maybe I can figure out a plan for your departure."

He told me to get some dirty old farm clothes, a shovel, a potato bag and a bicycle. "We'll ride this bicycle down to such and such a town, where you'll be picked up in a Red Cross ambulance. The ambulance will then take you across the bridges."

Well, there are three rivers: the Waal, the Maas, and the Rhine—three places to cross to get to the area of Belgium that had been liberated. I guess the Red Cross had some leeway with the Germans, because this was going to be the system.

"By the way, you've got to have your dog tags and uniform on under these old clothes."

We sent word back to Muiden to bring my dog tags and flight suit. Well, Mother Rozendaal (as I've come to call her) came on her bicycle and had the uniform with her, but she didn't tell us. She came in the house and talked to Vrouw Diets and tried to talk to me. Then she left, without leaving the uniform with me.

The farm

The next day, comes back Daan Spoor. "I hear you've got an escape plan rigged up. You know, you haven't got a fifty-fifty chance of making it out, and we don't want you to try it. We've got another place for you."

He escorted me out of Naarden and back to Muiden and got me a place on a farm at Weesp, only about a kilometer from Muiden.

So now I'm on the farm of Gys (short for Gysbertha) Regtuyt, a great big strapping Dutch farmer, age 27 at the time (I was 22). The deal had been made with Gys that I would stay there, and he being one of the Dutch patriots and a member of the underground group, it was fine. He had a wife and a little boy by the name of Eppie, who was probably about four years old. And then there was a baby.

This is a dairy farm, and I'm going to get outside a bit. I have my klompen (wooden shoes) and work clothes. The first evening there, Gys takes me around the farm. He's very proud of it. The cow stalls are connected onto the house, and the cows are kept inside in the winter. Gys is talking to me in Dutch, because none of his family speak English; Gys is a boer—farmer. A farm is a boerderij.

He points to a horse—paard. "Versta Je?"—"Do you understand?" he asks me in Dutch.

"Nix versta."—"No."

He shows me a chicken—kip. "Understand?"

"No."

He points to a cow—koe. "Understand?"

Mes? (knife).

"I don't understand."

Tafel is the table. Lepel is a spoon.

I didn't know beans about Dutch, but I'd lived at Naarden for about six weeks and in Weesp and Muiden for the balance of the time—a total of seven months in Holland. Pretty soon, by association—"Pass the butter"—and hearing them talk, I could understand Dutch. I couldn't read Dutch, or speak it well. But I could make myself understood. Now these many years later I can speak quite good Dutch.

By the way, back in Naarden, we had a razzia—a house search. I don't know what it translates to, but it means that the Germans come into the town and look for young Dutch people to ship back to Germany to work. The word comes out: "We want 1,500 workers. Come down to the railroad station at six o'clock in the morning, and bring your mess kit and sleeping bag, or whatever. Be there! Anybody between the ages of 18 and 42, you've got to come!"

Of course a lot of people did go down and went into Germany into in forced labor. But the onderduikers and the underground resisters wouldn't go.

We knew the Germans would be coming the next morning, but we had a hiding place in the Dietz house, on the third floor. There was a closet with bookshelves. The top bookshelf folded down, and you could get up into the attic. The books were put back onto the bookshelf, and there we were—all night long: the Jewish boy, twelve Dutch boys, and me. Only Ted Cohen, the Jewish boy, and the two Dietz boys knew who I was. The rest of them didn't know. We were laying there between the rafters.

I don't know what time, but the next morning, here came the Germans looking for us, house to house. They came down the street with a PA system, telling everybody to get out. They went through every single house, and we heard them tromping around. They were rough guys, infantry people, not the Gestapo agents.

Then they left, and that was my one escape from the razzia in Naarden.

At the Regtuyt farm, I had a nice sleeping place up above the house (we would call it an attic) with a good hiding place beneath the floor close by. Gys was quite an entrepreneur I guess we would say. Although there was an eight o'clock curfew, he would ride his bicycle into town with a cheese or piece of butter, and trade these for something, for example, cigarettes. Two farm workers, Pete Samplonius and Jan Grondella, also lived on the farm, and we would all sit in the house every night after dinner. Gys had a radio, and because he had some kind of connections (I think he was paying somebody), he could keep electricity on the farm, and run his radio.

Twice each day the underground was receiving secret code messages from the British over the BBC news. So we would sit and listen to what I suppose was the eight o'clock news. When Gys would come back from the village with his cigarettes, he would get them out and throw one to you. Again, this was relaxing. What the hell! We didn't have any cigarettes there, and when somebody was able to get a package, I'll tell you they are definitely like a drug. You inhale a cigarette after you haven't had one for a while, and man, you're flying high. So it was a real treat when Gys would go into town and pull off something like that.

I wear the wooden shoes, get up every morning with the family, milk cows (I learned how to milk cows), chopped wood, and did other work around the farm.

Of course Holland was occupied during the war, but the occupation forces were sometimes pretty marginal. For example, there was a little bridge between Weesp and Muiden, over a canal or river; the guard there was Polish, whom the Germans had conscripted. People like that would come to the farm and offer to buy a litre of milk; they didn't browbeat the farmer or do anything like that. The occupation forces, in many instances, were fairly decent to the Dutch.

The Dutch treated me with kid gloves. They didn't want anything to happen to me. I was a hero—an Ally; I was winning the war from them; I was a symbol for them. They never let me go anywhere where I would be confronted by a German. In other words, whenever a German came down the road, the Dutch knew it, and I was hiding. We had a hiding place out by the river, a cave. If I was out in the fields, that's where I would go; if I was in the house, I'd hit the attic and go into the hole in the floor. The Dutch didn't want to take a chance—they couldn't afford to take a chance.

There was a weekly ritual. Every Monday, Gys Regtuyt had a gal who came to help his wife do housework. Bear in mind that the family is not using any electricity, except for the radio. So they can't do any ironing, or any kind of normal housework. So they hired a gal to come and help them.

Well, this gal was kind of "iffy." They suspected her of fraternizing with Germans. So when the dore-gal came, I had to get out of there. In the evening, Jan Van Etten, the man who had escorted me on bicycle to Naarden, would come out to the farm from Muiden, have me get on a bicycle, and follow him to Muiden. I would sit there all day long and talk to the Rozendaals and the kids, as best I could with the language difference, using a word book much of the time. Every now and then someone who spoke English would come along. That gave me a little bit of diversion.

In the evening, Jan would come again and escort me back to the farm at Weesp. I didn't know at the time that he was armed. He lives in Edmonton, Alberta, Canada now, and I met with him in Vancouver, B.C., in 1990, for the first time in forty-five years. That's when I found out that he'd had a gun all that time. A tough guy! He had a lot of nerve.

I was eating well, while the people in the big cities were starving. They were sending their kids out all over the countryside, begging or buying food. The Dutch had what were called "central kitchens." In the middle of the town square, there were big vats of soup, just as you think of in communist countries, where people can't buy food. The Dutch couldn't. But when I got to the farm, I was eating well.

Whenever they figured it was safe, I worked on the farm. I wasn't going to go a long way away from the house. I don't remember what some of the chores were, though I did learn to milk the cows, which we did twice a day by hand. I had my own one-legged stool, and my own piece of rope. You'd get your cow, clean off her udder, tie her tail to her legs, and milk. I couldn't strip a cow very good, though I worked at it.

I was in fact a little overweight, because I wasn't getting enough exercise. You'd get up in the morning and have three pieces of bread with cheese and three cups of hot milk. In midmorning, you had a coffee-drink. At noon you had the big meal—a pile of potatoes and a pile of cabbage. That might be it. Then for dessert, what they called "pap." I think it was some sort of gruel or porridge, and they would put some kind of syrup on it. I think it was made out of barley.

One day you'd have white cabbage—wittekool; one day you'd have red cabbage—rodekool; next day you'd have Brussels sprouts. So I was eating a lot of starchy food. Then after the noon meal, they'd go to bed for a couple of hours.

It seems like I'd get up about two o'clock, and everybody would be out working, so I'd go out and mess around, but not work hard. Then in the middle of the afternoon, you'd have tea-drink and at night your bread and cheese and milk, but we had lots of that on the farm, and boy, am I a cheese-head. The Dutch called me "kasskop."

I was very fortunate never to be sick while I was there. I went through the winter pretty well, and the Dutch were liberated on the 5th of May in 1945. The end of the war in all of Europe came three days later. Parts of Belgium were liberated a little before. You see, Antwerp was a free port when Operation Market Garden went into Holland, in September 1944. I guess part of Holland on the east side of the three rivers was liberated early.

The Germans on retreat

Sometime around March of 1945, the Germans were getting pushed back into Holland, and as they were getting pushed, they were breaking down dikes and flooding areas. Some real German troops started showing up in the Weesp and

Muiden area. We got word that the Germans wanted to occupy the Regtuyt farm, so I had to get moved back into Muiden.

The Germans threw straw all over the Regtuyt living room. They bivouacked their soldiers there and put gun emplacements along the river. The farm was right on the river. I had ice skated on that river during the winter—the Vecht River.

So I was moved back into Muiden, but I should tell about the weapons dropping. This was the activity of the 801/492nd Bomb Group, who were called the "Carpetbaggers." Their major function was dropping agents behind enemy lines and supplying the Underground organizations all over Europe.

I call my Underground group in Muiden the Rozendaal Resistance Group. They were expecting a weapon drop, and oh boy, this was the big thrill. They felt, right after Operation Market Garden, that there would be another airborne invasion. That's how they thought they were going to get liberated. So they wanted guns, ammunition, and weapons.

For some reason, the Rozendaal Group got on a priority list and was scheduled to have a weapon dropping. How would they find out the day the dropping would be, and the time of night? At the end of the eight o'clock morning BBC news broadcast, four or five sentences would be said, for example, "It's cold outside….John and Pete are hungry…. I'd like to have some potatoes," whatever. The signal, as I remember it, was "John and Pete are hungry." That meant the drop was coming that night. If it was followed by "It's cold outside," that meant it they would come at ten o'clock; and if there were another signal given, they would come at midnight.

Of course the site had already been picked out.

Then you listened to the eight o'clock evening news, and if it came through again, then you were on. If it didn't come through, cancel it.

Here came the night for the dropping for the Rozendaal group. It would arrive at midnight. All the guys went out to the site with their horses and wagons, to try to intercept the parachutes as they came down. I don't know what it looked like, because they wouldn't let me go. And it was a good thing, because I wouldn't have known what to do—where to run, or whatever, if we'd been caught.

A couple of days later, they did let me go down to the church where they were unloading all the stuff—kegs and boxes of guns, sabotage equipment, sten-guns (a very simple 9 mm sort of a submachine gun, with an iron stock—a very common, rugged kind of gun that anyone could operate), hand grenades. They had all the weapons hid down at the church, under the floor, I guess. Of course they were getting nervous, because here came the Germans, occupying all the villages around there. There's worry over whether somebody's going to find the guns, or somebody's going to tip the Germans off, or something's going to happen.

Then all of a sudden, here came the ceasefire. The Allies had negotiated with the Germans, so that food could be dropped. This would probably have been in late April. There's a book written about this operation. The British part was called Operation Manna; the American version was called Chowhound. So it was called Operation Manna-Chowhound. With this deal, bombers could come over at 300 feet altitude, right on the deck, over an exact route (they couldn't stray), drop their food on various sites, for example, airports. The Dutch were starving to death.

Capitulation and liberation

Shortly after that, the Germans capitulated, and Northwest Germany, Denmark, Norway, Holland were liberated—shortly before V-E Day. We received the news by radio, and I'll tell you, I was fit to be tied. It was just wonderful. We heard about it the night before.

The next day, the Germans were supposed to lay down their weapons. And of course some of them did, and some of them didn't. But the underground took over. They knew who all the black marketers were, and who the girls were who had been fraternizing. The Underground went out and picked them up and were walking around, but of course there were Germans all over the place. You didn't know when someone was going to take a shot at you.

They didn't care, everybody was so happy. This was the 5th of May, 1945, their liberation day; the 8th of May was V-E day.

The underground was well organized. They knew what they wanted to do. There was no shooting, but of course they now have their own weapons, hidden all over the countryside. They came out in the open and tried to enforce the ceasefire. The Germans were supposed to be herded into schoolyards and places like that.

The Germans pretty much cooperated. The underground cut off the hair of the women fraternizers, then put them in cages, and showed them off to the Dutch people. I suppose there were some trials, but I didn't see any of that kind of stuff. I'm sure there was some violence at this time, but I didn't see it. There certainly were SS and Gestapo who didn't want to take defeat very well, and it was pretty tough to communicate with troops all over the area.

Pretty soon here comes the 1st Canadian Army, but they didn't have much force. They had weapon carriers that they were just running around the block, to make the Germans think that there were a lot of forces coming in, but there weren't. The Canadians were pretty well spread out too, and they had to come in and take over occupied countries.

I was given my uniform back. I put it on. I'm a big hero now. They're carrying me around on their shoulders and entertaining me. Now they're telling everyone that Jan Smit is here: "We've had this pilot here for seven months, and nobody knew it." Well, a few people knew it.

Leaving the Dutch

When I was to leave, I got on a motorcycle with a guy, and we rode down to the town of Blaricum. And when I get there, there's Daan Spoor, one of my benefactors from the area. And there I meet Gene Maddox, a B-24 pilot, and two other airman, whose names I can't recall right now. They had been hiding in the same area. We were to go out together.

We don't know how we're going to go out. I guess we had some kind of little goodbye ceremony and started walking. We hitchhiked. We met some Canadian troops, who took us to a town where we were interrogated. Then we were flown to Paris, where we were interrogated again.

It wasn't so important now as it had been while hostilities were still going on. The interrogators had wanted to know who helped you, what the procedure was, how you evaded, was your escape kit right, what do you need, what should we do different? With us, after the cessation of hostilities, it was different, more a matter of identification of us, and of our helpers, because they wanted to acknowledge them with the Eisenhower Certificate, a recognition for Resistance workers.

I've seen, in my research with the Air Forces Escape and Evasion Society, a lot of missing aircrew reports, by the last person or crew that saw your plane come down. These are on file in Suitland, Maryland, and you can obtain one on any airman who was shot down, if you have the facts. I've got many reports on airmen who were helped by the Partisans and the Chetniks in Yugoslavia. Of course many of these men were liberated while the war was still going on, and there were a lot of problems—the wrong kind of stuff in the escape kit, this compass doesn't work, or that doesn't work, we need a better dinghy or this or that. Intelligence got a lot of valuable information by interrogating the escapers and evaders, but our interrogations after V-E Day were pretty routine.

After Paris, we were transported to the famous Camp Lucky Strike, at Le Havre, which had been a staging area for a division during the war. About 40,000 POWs and evadees were gathered. The weather was kind of bad. It was muddy. We were all living in tents and eating peanut butter sandwiches. That was when some guys got in touch with their congressmen. So Eisenhower flew over. He stood on the wing of a C-47 and said, "For you, the war is over. We'll send the sick and wounded first, then you guys are going home."

Back to England

Well, a funny thing happened. Apparently Eighth Air Force headquarters wanted some aerial pictures of Camp Lucky Strike, with all the ex-POWs down there. So my 7th Photo Recon Group over in England was assigned a mission to fly and take photos of the camp. The next day or so, they came over and dropped off the prints. There were four guys there (I didn't know where they were) from our group who had been POWs or evaders, and one guy got hold of the pilot who brought the prints and said, "For God's sake, get us out of here!"

"Stand by," the pilot said.

The next day he came over in a C-47, and somehow all four or five of us got together, from the 7th Photo Recon Group, scratched our names off the roster and flew back to our group. No orders. No nothing. I could be there still, MIA.

We just signed off the roster. This gathering of ex-POWs and evadees happened so fast that our Transportation Corps hardly knew what had happened and were not too well organized. Nobody knew what they were doing, and we just took off.

I don't know when my group headquarters learned we were alive. When we were interrogated in Paris was the first time we could send a telegram to our families. They had only known that we were MIA—no other word.

British intelligence was tight. I'm not saying that our intelligence didn't know, or weren't passing it on to the Group. The Germans had so much information—perhaps you've read about Hans Scharff, the famous Nazi interrogator, head of the Luftewaffe Evaluation Center, Auswertestelle West, located at Oberursel, Germany. One of the guys from our group was shot down, and he was brought to Scharff. He walked into the office, and there was a picture on the wall of his airplane in its revetment, back in England.

That was pretty shocking. It would tell you, "God, if he's got all that, and he tells me when I graduated from high school, and what my mother's maiden name was, why...."

This is how Scharff had got the picture. Some guy had had a forced landing over in Germany. Before he had taken off from England, he had tested his camera, to see if it would work. He caught this airplane. When the Germans captured the airplane that was forced down, they developed the film. And of course all this gets to Hans Scharff, who has catalogs of information.

He was a master interrogator and psychologist. He would be the kind of guy who would bring you in and say, "Here, have a cigarette. I just wanted to get acquainted with you. Would you like to go to town tonight? We'll go out and get some girls and do this and that and the other thing."

He would work you over psychologically and get information from you.

This is why the information on us was so carefully guarded, because this is what the Germans wanted. Maybe they could work their way into the escape line and it would be sayonara for the underground.

I went back to my base in England and fooled around there for a week or so. I still knew a few people there, but I didn't know very many. I'd only been in my group for two months before I was shot down, and then I'd been gone for about eight months. There were a lot of new faces.

Back to the States

I'm also without orders, so in order to get into channels again, I had to turn myself in to a general hospital, where they would write my orders, give me a physical, and get me assigned to a deployment group, to go back to the States.

So I went back to the States, and that was it. I was discharged.

Printed with permission of Claude Murray and The Oral History Memoir of the American Airpower Heritage Foundation.

We Were Lucky... We Weren't Killed

Narrated by Basil Lyle Shafer, B-17 pilot
8th Air Force, 390th Bomb Group, 569th Bomb Squadron
Edited by Erik Dyreborg

Introduction

I was born in Gettysburg, Ohio. My father was killed in a motorcycle accident; he was a road patrolman for the State of Ohio. I was about two years old when he was killed. My mother remarried and I have two half-brothers.

We lived on a farm north of Greenville, Ohio, about thirty-five or forty miles northwest of Dayton, Ohio. I attended a one-room school from the time I was in the fifth grade until I finished the eighth grade. It was great. It was a great experience. There were only seventeen or eighteen children in all eight grades; there was one other person and myself who graduated from the eighth grade. We then went to high school in Greenville. Both of us were very active scholastically and in athletics, and we're still good friends.

We see one another periodically. He still works in Dayton.

He went to Ohio State and became a civil engineer after the war.

After the war, I came back and went to Harvard and got my undergraduate degree. Then I went on to law school and got my law degree at Ohio State University. In 1955, the company I worked for, the NCR Corporation in Dayton, sent me back to the Harvard Business School for its two-year course. I didn't finish that, because during the second year of the course, I was asked to come back to the company. There was an antitrust case they wanted me to work on, and I was working in the law department at the time.

So I went back to the company. I was told I could go back to school and finish, but I never got back. I got promoted and became assistant general counsel of the company and stayed in the law department for about thirteen years. I then became personnel officer for the company, a vice-president of personnel for their employment worldwide services, and stayed in that job for twenty years.

It was quite an interesting career. I spent my entire career in Dayton, where NCR is headquartered. As I said, my friend and I have always been good friends; we've stayed good friends over the years.

The Army Air Corps

How did I feel when Pearl Harbor occurred? I felt pretty much the way a lot of my classmates felt. I was a senior in high school, and I remember all the excitement that occurred during the time the radio broadcast was made and the days following that. Some of my friends in high school wanted to join up and go into the service. As a matter of fact, a couple of them did.

I was inclined to do the same thing, but my folks didn't want me to. Other people were advising me to finish high school. I'd done quite well in high school, both athletically and scholastically, and felt, too, that the better thing to do was to finish school. I graduated from high school, then, in June 1942.

I worked during the summer. In the fall, I went to Ohio State University for a couple of months, until I went in the service.

I went directly into cadets. The requirements for a college education had been dropped. I was right at the time they were lowering those requirements as far as education is concerned. I remember going into the old post office in Columbus, Ohio, when I was in school at Ohio State.

There was one door marked U. S. Army and one marked U. S. Navy. I had to make a decision as to which one of those doors I was going to go in. I wanted to fly; that was my objective. I wanted to get in either the Army Air Corps or the Navy or the Marines, or someplace, where I could take flight training. I reasoned that I would probably be more successful in being accepted into the program in the Army Air Corps than I would be in the Navy. The Navy, at that point in time, had not yet accepted very many people who did not have a college education or at least two years of college.

So I went in the Army Air Corps. I made that decision on the spot, took my physical and the examinations they required. I was told that I was accepted into the aviation cadet program. I could either go into the service as a private, take my basic and to be assigned to a cadet class, or I could wait and be called up later.

My reasoning was that I was going to have to serve in the military in some way or other. I had no aspirations to be a foot soldier, to be in the artillery or in a tank or a submarine, or for that matter, even on a ship. It just seemed to me that flying was something that was going to suit me and something I would like. I hadn't had any flying experience, but when looking at all of the other options that might be available to me, I thought flying would be one of the better ones. And frankly, I thought the Air Corps was being pretty selective in the people being allowed into the program, and I guess it stirred up my competitive juices enough to want to get into something that was difficult to get into. Anybody could get into the infantry, but the Air Corps was being selective; I thought I would like to get into a program where they were trying to weed people out. I thought the training would be good. It was a program in which I'd end up with a commission. It just seemed to me like a good program for a young kid such as myself. I wanted to give it a try.

Training

Rather than wait around, I just went on in. I went in as a private, took my basic training down in Miami Beach, Florida, and when training was over, was assigned to a cadet program.

I was in class 44 A. I graduated in January 1944.

There was still hazing when I went through pre-flight. It was like the hazing that took place at West Point for many, many years—square meals; the upper class, lower class arrangement; having to salute Coke machines before you got a Coke, and that sort of thing. But I struggled through it. It really was contrary to my way of life, but I took it and was probably better off for having survived that period. I've never been strong on hazing. I really think, that for the most part, it's counterproductive. Nevertheless, I went through it.

It lasted two months. We were lower class men one month and upper class men for one month.

After we got into primary flight school, which was two months, then basic and advanced for two months each. All of that went by the boards.

I liked primary training the best. That was where I flew in the open cockpit of the PT Stearman. Most of the guys enjoyed that very much. It's a very simple airplane. It has only three or four instruments and you flew by the seat of your pants. It was where we learned all of the acrobatics and all the great stuff you visualize in flying.

Then we got into the basic trainer. It was much heavier and you have to rely on instruments a great deal more. That took a lot of the fun out of it.

Then when we went into advanced, I went to twin engine advanced. It was the same thing. You had to fly more-or-less straight and level, you couldn't do acrobatics and dog fight with one another and all that sort of stuff.

I did have a choice of single or multiengine. I wanted to go to multiengine, because I thought the opportunities might be a little broader to be assigned to a plane I'd like to fly. I really wanted to fly P-38s or A-20s. Both of those planes are single pilot, twin-engine planes. At that time, the really hot single engine plane was the P-51; it had come into its own.

At any rate, I thought the options might be broader in twin engine.

I always thought I'd probably go to the Pacific Theater, and if that happened, I wanted to have two engines. It didn't work out that way.

When I graduated, 35 of us were sent from Advanced Flying School to Salt Lake City for assignment. Thirty-four of that group went to B-24s. I was the only guy in that group who went on B-17s. My instructor told me that I would either go into P-38s or A-20s; he'd recommended me for them, and I believed him.

Lyle Shafer, 1944 is pictured above.

The next thing I knew, I was in Pampa, Texas, at the operational training base there, called Rattlesnake Base. I was assigned to a crew and then went overseas with that crew.

The crew I was assigned to and came together at Pyote—pilot, co-pilot, navigator, bombardier, and all the gunners. We finished our operational training at Pyote, and then were sent to Kearney, Nebraska, for staging. Instead of assigning us overseas there, the Air Corps sent us to Langley Field, Virginia, to take some radar training.

Overseas

We went to Langley Field, but were only there about two weeks. We were sent to New York, without a plane, to await shipment by ATC (Air Transport Command) to England as a replacement crew in preparation for the invasion. We went overseas in May 1944.

We roamed around New York City for about a week. We stayed in a hotel. I stayed in the Graystone Hotel, which is somewhere around 85th. Three of the crew lived in or around the New York area. One lived in the Bronx, one in Brooklyn, and one lived in Flushing. We met their families and they had some parties. Every day was like the last day we were going to be there.

Well, we were there for ten days or two weeks, and by that time, we were ready to go. We were ready to leave and go overseas and take whatever was going to be dished out over there.

So we were ready. It was a new experience, of course, for all of us; we were all pretty young. I think we weren't too young to be afraid, but really, our world was quite small. We really didn't see out very far. We lived in our own little world. I've often thought about that over the years. When I was at the base of the 390th Bomb Group, I lived in a hut of the 569th Squadron. Of course, the base was dispersed—the planes were dispersed, the Squadrons were dispersed, the headquarters was somewhere else on the base. Things were all over the place.

My world really consisted of my Squadron area, the mess hall, and hardstand where our plane was parked. We went to briefings, of course.

I went back there—I've been back several times—a few years ago. The farmer who was living there, before and during the war, and still lives there, Percy Kindred, asked me if I would like to go back and see the headquarters Buildings there, that some of them were still there. He said, "I want to show you something."

So we went back to the Headquarters area. There were a couple of brick buildings, that were being used as pigpens. He took me down this long row of pigpens and asked me to stick my head around the corner of one of them. And there was a big blackboard that had been used to outline missions and what have you. He asked me if I remembered the Headquarters. I had to admit that I didn't remember the first thing about it.

Pretty soon, I realized that the reason I didn't remember was because I had never been there. I had no reason to be there; I had never been to any of the other three Squadrons. My world was very small. I was only at the base for a short time. We got there around the first of June and went down in September. We were only there three months and were busy most of the time.

We really didn't realize and understand what was going on in the world. We had a job to do and kept pretty busy doing it. But we didn't really have any understanding of what was going on like we do today. Today (young people understand) because of the news and TV; you have to be pretty withdrawn not to be impacted by what is going on around the world. Back then, we didn't seem to be too concerned about it or have much exposure to it.

As I grow older, I have a tendency to forget some things. My memory, at this age, like everybody else's, isn't what it was when I was twenty years old, but I do have trouble sorting out what I've forgotten and what I didn't know to begin with. Some stuff, I just never knew.

Just like being back at headquarters. Well, I didn't forget that, I'd never been there.

The ATC flew us to England. We were assigned to a base.

The missions

I flew twenty-five missions. I was shot down on my twenty-fifth.

My first mission, I flew as a tail gunner. Since I was a co-pilot, I was put in the tail of the lead plane. I was the person the commanding officer was in touch with over the intercom about flying formation, who was straggling, and what was happening back there. I had a ringside seat, of course, as to what was happening. I could tell him which planes were being shot down—all that sort of thing, all the activity.

In the meantime, an experienced pilot was flying with the new pilot who was flying his first mission.

The other fellow I was flying with, Fred McIntosh, came over as a co-pilot, and also flew his first mission as a tail gunner.

It was pretty exciting back there. Of course, I didn't know anything about firing the tail gunner's guns, so I didn't even try. I just tried to take a ride. If a plane had come in shooting at us, I wouldn't have known what to do. I didn't know how to charge the guns or anything; I was just an observer.

I remember the raid was over Hamburg. We weren't the first ones over.

By the time we went over, the smoke was 25 or 30,000 feet high. There were big balls of fire coming up the smoke; it was like it was a big chimney. I don't know whether it was oil or what it was, but it was really hot fire.

It's interesting, too, that one of my roommates in the POW camp, Don Demmert, married a German woman in the early part of the '50s. Her family had come to this country following the war. She is several years younger than Don; I think she was about 15 during the time that I was flying over Hamburg in 1944. She was living there. It was sort of interesting chatting with her at the reunion. I don't remember a lot of the other missions I went on, but I'll always remember that first one.

I still wasn't scared. Most of the guys were dumb enough to think it will happen only to the next guy, I guess. I really never got to the point where I really felt very uneasy about flying a mission. I always felt I was going to get through them.

I know after flying 25 or 30 missions, people started to get uneasy. I suppose that about the time they were getting ready to finish, they might get a little more uneasy, and I probably would have, too. But up until that time, I really felt pretty confident that I was going to finish my missions.

The other fellow flying with me, the other pilot, was on his last mission, his 25th. He was killed.

We did 25 missions, including a shuttle raid to the Soviet Union, to Italy, then back to England.

The pilot I went overseas with refused to fly after our third mission—we were over France. We had gotten shot up pretty badly, and he almost killed us all. He panicked, and when we got back, he refused to fly any more. He had a dishonorable discharge and was sent back home.

I saw him several times after the war. He died of Hodgkin's Disease around 1950, so he's been dead for a long time. I met his wife. She remarried and she and her husband are both retired now. I'm still in contact with her.

I talked to him about being sent home with a dishonorable discharge a couple of times and even tried to help him see if he could get that reversed, because it was having an adverse effect upon his life. He was a foreman in a management position in a factory. He was probably doing a good job in that position, I think, but he felt the resentment of some of the people who had come back and started to work.

I liked him. I'd gone through training with him, and disagreed with his decision not to fly. I did my level best to try to talk him into changing his mind and going on the missions. I mentioned all kinds of options available to him, trying to get him to go so he would avoid having the confrontation with the military, with the government. But he simply refused to do it.

I never really resented him having the feelings he had. I didn't agree with him; I would have liked to see him do something else. But he didn't. And as I said, I did keep in contact with him after the war. We were friends until he died, and I'm still friends with his wife. He wasn't married at the time; he got married after the war. She is a very fine person in my opinion. I think he was very fortunate to have married her. She was probably a big help to him.

On August 1, we went on the second shuttle raid to the Soviet Union.

Our Group was one of those that had been on the previous one. On the previous mission, the Germans came in and shot up a lot of the B-17s on the ground in the Soviet Union. My Group went, but I wasn't with it. I was on the second raid.

Because of the distance involved, the plane was converted and gasoline tanks were put in part of the bomb bay. It really wasn't a very efficient way of doing a bombing raid, but most of it was PR, part of the hype going at the time. It took about half of the bomb bay for gas. Our bomb load was cut to about 5,000 pounds, or something like that. It wasn't very much.

We carried an extra passenger to the USSR, Hagen, an Ordinance Officer.

We bombed a place in Poland on the way to the Soviet Union. It was Rahmel, an Aircraft Repair Depot near Gdynia, Poland.

We passed the lines, and the Soviets shot up a lot of flak when we did. Apparently they didn't know we were coming, at least the front line didn't know. They didn't hit anything; their flak wouldn't go very high, and they were very inaccurate, anyhow. Their guns wouldn't even go as high as we were.

We came in and there was a huge storm coming up. We flew around the Airbase for a little while at a place called Mirgorod. It's near Kiev. There were a couple of P-39s that came up. They were shooting around, flitting around in the formation, Soviet piloted; zipping around.

The United States had given some P-39s to the Soviets. As I understand it, our guys never really liked the P-39. We had some and when they were replaced with P-51s, they were given to the Soviets.

The storm passed over and we landed in a hayfield. There were little haystacks around. The runway had been put down; it was a perforated steel mat runway—we didn't land on the dirt. It was our understanding that the runways had been laid by Soviet women.

At any rate, we landed and parked along the side. It just so happened that the P-39 pilots were women, Soviet women pilots. They came down and landed. We always thought that was pretty great and different. We were sort of amazed by the whole thing.

We lived in some sort of barracks. It wasn't a very fancy arrangement. We ate outside in sort of a chow line.

We ate mostly American food. Almost everything was American over there, except there were some Soviet people working in serving food and that sort of thing, and doing some of the cooking.

There was quite a contingent of American people that had been sent over there ahead of time, to take care of the situation. The soviets really weren't doing very much.

We stayed there a couple of days. We flew a mission out of there to the Synthetic Oil Refinery at Trzebinia, Poland, and came back to the Soviets and landed again. A couple of days later, we went to Italy. We bombed Zilistea Roumania Airfield.

We went to an airbase near Foggia, Italy, and stayed there about a week.

It was kind of different for us, because it was warm. The runway at this American airbase had been put down; it was also a metal, perforated landing strip. We eventually went on a mission back to England. When we did, we bombed Toulouse Franchea Airfield in southern France. It was part of the invasion of southern France; we were coordinated with that.

I'll always remember when we took off from this base in Italy. We were sitting at the end of the runway. The plane in front of us went roaring down the runway and disappeared. We couldn't see it. And pretty soon, here it came up way down the runway and took off. It was because the perforated landing strip had just been put down on the hills and the valley and whatever else was there. No one had taken the time to straighten and level it out. So the planes, when they took off, would disappear for a while. Then pretty soon, they would appear at the other end of the runway at about the time they were ready to take off.

We went back to England and started flying normal missions. The Group also flew missions at the invasion on June 6. There were a lot of missions flown. Planes were flying back and forth all of the time.

The Group flew more than one mission that day. Our crew did not fly on June 6. I think we flew on the 17th or something like that.

I remember when they had all of those German soldiers in what was called the Falaise Gap—thousands and tens of thousands of guys in there. We went over and dropped bombs indiscriminately in that area. It was also a time when one of the generals was killed, one of the American generals. (General) Leslie McNair 25 January 1944). It was a kind of chaotic situation. Planes were coming and going, planes at low altitude and planes at high altitude, bonfires down on the ground. We'd try to target the area, but it was confusing, chaotic. I'm surprised it came off as well as it did.

There were quite a few midair collisions. I read some statistics on this not too long ago. Most of the Heavy Bomber Groups were in East Anglia. Because of the weather in England, it was either overcast when you took off or overcast when you came back. I remember that almost every time we took off in the morning, when we came up through the clouds—just pop up through the clouds—you'd look around and here were B-17s popping up everyplace. They'd get up above the clouds and try to find their group. The Groups were shooting off flares; maybe your group was two red flares, maybe another one was a green flare, and yet another, maybe a red and a green flare. Trying to find the Group, just roaming around up there—hundreds of B-17s. God. I've often wondered why more planes didn't collide than did.

One of the reasons more didn't collide was because the guys were so paranoid about it. They kept watching, watching all the time. It always surprises me. I've been up in the cockpit of planes more recently, that these days the pilots never look around, they just sort of bury their heads and go. It always sort of disturbs me that airline pilots don't look around; they are always looking at the cockpit instruments. They rely on controllers and other people to keep them from running into anybody. It doesn't surprise me that there are midair collisions every once in a while; the pilots don't look out the windows very much.

At any rate, our guys were looking out of the windows all of the time. They also had all the gunners and everybody else watching for planes.

We were in one big collision over in England (actually over the Channel on the way to the Netherlands). We were flying off the wing of one airplane that came up into the belly of the plane above it. Both airplanes exploded and went down. We were able to survive that. But there were a number of crashes and collisions over England.

Then, of course, when we cam back with holes in the airplane, maybe an engine out, flat tires and what have you, especially if it was overcast, we'd have to peel off and come down through the overcast and get under it in order to land. They used to peel us off—there wasn't too much time between planes. If a plane in front of you was letting down slower than it should have been, you were liable to run into it. Or if the guy behind you was going down faster than he should, he was liable to run into you. Guys were always pretty careful to try to maintain that descent speed and the rate of descent as closely as possible. It was very dangerous.

Then when we got down low, we did everything visually. The planes that were coming back, especially if they'd been to Berlin, for example, they were running low on gas. Those were long missions. They'd last eight hours or something like that.

If the plane's wing tanks had been hit or were ruptured and they'd lost gasoline, they wouldn't have any gas to spare. They'd have to land before they got back to base. But those that got back to base got preferential treatment in landing—and those that had gotten banged up. If you got back without being shot up, you sometimes had to fly around a while, while those others peeled off and went on in and landed. It was always kind of a hairy situation.

I think the gas tanks held 2,750 gallons. A mission to Berlin involved seven or eight hours flying time. What we did was—we had to get up at two or three o'clock in the morning and go to breakfast and go to briefing. We'd be out on the flight line with our plane when it got daybreak. As soon as it got light, the planes were revved up and gotten in line. We'd be in line ready to take off, the engines warm. After the planes were on the flight line, gas trucks would be brought out and the planes' tanks would be topped off. Usually, about fifty gallons would be put in. It took that much gas to warm up the engines, taxi, and everything. The gas tanks would be filled with as much gas as they could hold.

I remember many times, especially on the raids to Berlin, when we needed every gallon gas we could hold. We probably used half of the gas getting to the target on those long missions; it might have been more. It probably was more, because today at an air show, you see a jet go straight up and out of sight in the blink of an eye. In the old B-17, you had to climb to about 20 or 25,000 feet before you started over the Channel, and we were based very close to the Channel. We took off through the overcast and found our Group. Then we just kept circling and circling and circling. It took a couple of hours to get to altitude. Then, we'd take off and go on the mission. That took a lot of gas. The gas tanks were full, we had all the bombs, and we were climbing. It probably did take more than half the gas load to get to the target.

The cruising speed of the B-17 was only 160 miles an hour. I think climbing speed was 140 or 150, something like that. It wasn't very fast.

Of course ground speed, when you were up at 30,000 feet, might be 230 miles an hour. Your airspeed was 160. The B-17 is really a very slow airplane.

Some of my young friends said, "Well, were those B-17s pressurized?"

I'd explain it by telling them you could stick your finger through cracks in the plane in a lot of different places. It was a very open plane. And of course, the bomb bays were part of the plane. When they were open, the whole plane was open. It was a very primitive arrangement, by today's standards. Very primitive.

At that time, the B-17 seemed like a very big airplane. And it was a very big airplane, until the B-29 came along.

The first time I crawled into a B-17 and looked down that long wing, I just didn't know how I was ever going to be able to fly it. But after a while, I got accustomed to it. I've always had a lot of admiration for the airplane. It's really quite an airplane.

The 25th mission

Most of the crew had about 25 missions when we were shot down. We were shot down over Nuremberg on September 10, 1944, on a Sunday morning about 11 or 11:30. We had gone in to bomb a factory and got hit very hard with anti aircraft fire. The plane exploded after a few seconds. There were nine people on the crew that particular day. We were flying deputy lead, we were the plane flying off the wing of the lead plane. If the lead plane got shot down, we were supposed to take over. So we had a bombardier and a navigator. By that time, because the Luftwaffe had been pretty well grounded, we took off a waist gunner.

So, instead of having a ten-man crew, we had nine. And instead of having a bombardier on every crew, gunners, usually waist gunners, were trained as toggleers. He'd simply toggle the bombs off the lead plane bombardier. Each plane usually carried a navigator, because if the plane got separated and had to get back, he was needed. But you didn't need a bombardier.

So the crews had been skinnied down by that time. We were flying with nine. Six of the men were killed. Three of us got out—the tail gunner, the navigator, and me.

It was common practice to fly without wearing the parachute on the B-17. My particular situation was a hair-raising situation for me and probably one of the most dramatic things that had ever happened to me during my lifetime. It was something I really wouldn't talk about to people after the war, I just didn't think they would believe what I was going to say.

In my own case, the plane exploded. I looked around, and the only thing behind me was the back of my seat. The reason I survived the explosion was, we were going over the target at the time we were hit, flying straight and level. I had put my arm up along the edge of the window and was leaning down to try to get my flak helmet, which was down under my seat, under my feet. That was when we got hit.

My right arm was shattered. If I'd been sitting up, I'd have been hit in the head or the chest. We always wore a flak vest. We put on our flying suit, then our parachute harness, which had two snaps (rings) on the front and the chest pack just snapped onto this harness (onto the rings). On top of the harness, we wore a flak vest. We put a flak helmet on over our other helmet, so as the flak came up, we had a least some protection.

So I was trying to get my flak helmet when we were hit. As I said, if I'd have been sitting up, I'd have been killed.

The plane started tumbling. It was full of smoke and fire. One guy came flying over me and went up against the ceiling. We were really tumbling quite violently. I, of course, thought I was going to be killed.

Then it occurred to me that I could, maybe, grab my parachute and see if I could salvage something out of this.

When the pressure was right, I released my seat belt and tumbled out of the seat. I grabbed my chute by the handle as I fell free from the airplane. I just ripped the intercom connection and oxygen connection and what have you. I just ripped them off as I fell out of the plane.

So I was falling free. The plane and I separated. We were falling at different speeds. I had that parachute pack in my hand and was trying to put it on. I couldn't get it hooked on.

I realized I had my flak vest on. It's a very simple device to get rid of.

There's a little red cord on one side, and when you pull it, the vest releases.

I pulled the cord and the back floated away. The front stayed there, and I couldn't quite figure that out. Then I realized I was falling on my stomach.

So I pulled off the front of the flak vest. I pulled it aside and it just floated off. I hooked my chute on one hook. I never did see the ground, but I knew I only had a couple of minutes to do all this. It was a long time in one sense of the word.

Landing in Nuremberg

So I hooked one snap and thought, "Well, gee. I don't want to break my leg. I've got time, so I'll hook the other snap." I pulled the ripcord. I was skyscraper high when the thing opened up. I swung three or four times and hit the ground, right in town, in Nuremberg. (Actually the Nuremberg suburb of Schwimmen) I almost landed on a flak battery in an open lot. I was still on my back when a sailor and an air raid warden were right on top of me.

They asked me if I had a gun. I said, "No." We never carried guns on missions. We wore them around the base, but were told to leave them home. It was a good idea, because if you had a gun, the Germans were liable to kill you.

Anyway, I was captured and stayed at this place until about five o'clock in the evening. I stayed right where I was captured. I was sitting on a bench.

I wrote a little article on time about how I felt as I sat there on that bench. I called it, "Worry Priorities."

I used the story to demonstrate human nature, I guess. When I was in the airplane and thought I was going to die, my only worry was to try to get out and try to save my life. That was my only worry. I didn't worry about anything else.

Then I got out of the airplane and hooked up my chute. Now I started to worry about whether I was going to hit the ground too hard if I only had one hook on rather than two. I hooked on the second hook and landed. But the worry priorities kept getting smaller and smaller, until when I was sitting there on the bench in the afternoon, my worries were, "I wonder where I'm going to be tonight? I wonder if I'm going to get any supper? I wonder if I'm going to get any medical aid." The other worries about survival and those sorts of things had all gone by the boards.

These other things were really not worries. They were concerns or what occupied my mind. I distinctly remember sitting there wondering, of course, "What's going to happen now? Where am I going to be tonight? Are they (the Germans) going to give me anything to eat?" Those kinds of things started to fill my mind.

And of course, I was interested in whether I was going to get any medical aid.

At that time, my arm was really sort of traumatized and I really didn't feel too much. My leg was hurting more than anything.

I had used my arm. There are two bones in the lower arm and one of them was shattered. The other one was okay. And I could still use my fingers and my hand; I had movement. I thought, "Well, gee, it's not too bad." I found out later that there were two big fractures there and splinters of bone were still coming out six months later.

The Germans took all of my clothes except my trousers and shoes, they took my watch, and all that sort of stuff, and then put a dry compress on my arm. I'd been hit in the face and it was cut up some, and one of my jaw teeth had been knocked out. When I landed, I thought I broke my left leg. As a matter of fact, I think I did break my leg. It wasn't a compound fracture or anything, but I think it was fractured around the ankle.

About five or six o'clock in the evening, I would judge, some Luftwaffe soldiers came by riding bicycles. They took me over to a police barracks. They tried to march me over there, but I couldn't walk. The soldiers finally commandeered a truck that was going by and took the guards and me to the barracks. At that time, I thought I was the only person to survive the crash. I couldn't conceive of anybody else getting out.

So I was taken over to the police barracks. It was there that I saw my tail gunner for the first time. He had crawled out of the tail. He fell out of the plane and fell away from it. He told me that was at about ten thousand feet when he finally got out. He was wearing a back pack. He parachuted down, no problem. He wasn't injured or anything.

The Germans caught him and just beat the hell out of him. They hit him in the head and on his arm with rifle butts. He suffered from some of those injuries until he died during the '70s.

But it was a situation where here was an airman coming down right in the midst of the city. The bombs were still falling from other planes that were going over, popping all over the place, and here's a guy who is unscathed. The Germans just didn't want to let that happen.

In my own case, I had blood all over me. Probably the fact that I was all bloody may have saved my life, I don't know. I was a long way from escaping from the plane without injury, and that was quite recognizable to the people (around me).

The other thing and I was fortunate, of course, I was captured by a couple of people who were in the military. The air raid warden, I don't know whether he was in the military, then he was paramilitary. The sailor must have been on leave. But they kept me away from everybody else.

There were several hundred civilians around there, people who lived in that area, who came out of the apartment houses and they were quite agitated by the whole thing. I didn't know for sure whether the group would attack me or not. But I was very fortunate in that regard.

My tail gunner and I were taken, by truck—and we were both really beat-up. We wouldn't have been able to get away even if we'd been told to go. There were about six guards in the truck with us—rifles, fixed bayonets, and all that sort of stuff. We were taken to a dungeon in the Hall of Justice.

There is a prison right next door to the Hall. We were put in cells, solitary confinement cells, in the basement. I call it a dungeon, because it's below ground. There's a little slit of a window up at the top of the cell. The cells must have had nine or ten foot ceilings, and there was a little slit up at the ground level. I could tell it was a window; I could see light, but couldn't see out.

I've been back there a couple of times. I tried to get back into the prison to see some of these rooms, but I was never able to get past the lobby, or whatever substitutes for a lobby. It has been remodeled and changed around quite a bit over the years.

I've also been to the courtroom where the Nuremberg trials were held. I thought that was interesting.

The cell had a wooden table about three or four feet high with straw on it. That was it. We were finally brought some soup and a piece of bread.

We stayed there three days.

The first night I was there, a young Luftwaffe pilot and a woman the same age came into the cell. He wanted to talk to me. Apparently he wanted to see what the enemy looked like. He must have really been encouraged when he saw me, because I didn't look much like a fighting soldier. The Germans had given me back my shirt, and I had a pair of wings on the shirt. The pilot wanted to know if he could trade his wings for my wings. I gave him mine and tried to tell him I needed to see a doctor. I pointed to my arm and said, "Doctor."

He seemed to agree. It seemed to me like he was going to try to help.

The next morning, my tail gunner and I were walked over to what I thought was a hospital. It was some sort of a medical building. The people in there refused to look at us, and we were taken back to our cells.

I began to worry about whether I was going to get any help at all. My wounds were really starting to get sore and infected.

Frankfurt

After about three days, we, my tail gunner and I, along with two other people, were taken to Frankfurt, to the interrogation center.

The other two people, a fellow by the name of Jim Hall and the other was Jerry Gilbert—one was a bombardier and one was a navigator—were on the crew that was right behind us. They were also shot down. Only the two of them survived. Just maybe a week or ten days prior to our mission, they had moved into the same Nissen Hut with us. There were seven or eight of us in this Hut. These two crews were thrown together; we didn't really know one another.

So the four of us went to Frankfurt. We were at Oberursel, just north of Frankfurt, for interrogation for about two weeks, then we were all sent to a place north of Oberursel called Wetzlar, sort of a transient camp and the place where we were deloused. And there was a little medical hospital set up there. My tail gunner was sent to one prison camp, and the three officers were sent to Stalag Luft 1 (in Barth, Germany)

I never did get very much medical attention.

After I'd been in the interrogation center for several days, it became evident to me that the Germans were using my injuries to try to put the pressure on me. Finally, I decided that if I was going to die, I might as well go down fighting, and I started banging on the door, kicking the door, swearing at the guards, and told them I wanted some help.

At Oberursel, the first thing that really hits you is that these people are the only ones who know you are alive. You are kept segregated from everybody. You're in solitary confinement. Even though I went up there on a train with three other people, I didn't know whether they were alive and they didn't know whether I was alive. The Germans were the only ones who knew I was alive, so they could do anything they wanted to me with immunity. And I realized that pretty fast.

Then the Germans took the position that the main purpose of being at the interrogation center was to determine whether I should be treated as a spy or as a prisoner of war, and that they needed my help in making that determination, that they realized that the Americans really had people coming out of airplanes disguised as soldiers and who came down to be with the underground for purposes of sabotage and what have you. They said that sometimes people were legitimate soldiers and they would abide by the rules of the Geneva Convention and sent these people to a POW camp. But many times the people were not soldiers and they wanted to make that determination. If they were spies, they were going to be shot. That frightened me.

They told me I had to answer some questions to prove that I was a soldier, a flyer. For example, they'd say, "We're going to ask you five questions. What altitude were you flying when you came in? What was your radio frequency? What kind of bombs were you carrying? What was your target? What was your Group?

Of course, our instructions were that we were not supposed to give any information except name, rank, and serial number. So I went that route. I'd also heard, however, that if you give them any information that you'd be kept there forever, that the only way to get out of there was never to tell the Germans anything, no matter how bad it was, don't tell them anything, and they'd move you out. They won't waste the time on you.

I decided that was what I wanted to do. I refused to answer the questions. The Germans would come back a couple of days later and go through the same process. They'd say, "You're not helping us any. I don't know what we're going to do with you. We may keep you here forever. If you ever want to go to a POW camp, you'd better help us, if you're really a soldier as you say you are.

Finally, the guy would become exasperated and he's say, "Look, you probably think I'm just trying to get information out of you. We know more information about you than you think we do. Besides that, you don't really know any information that is going to be of any use to us, so I'm going to give you the answers to the five questions that I've been asking you." And he'd give the answers.

Then he'd say, "I'm going to give you one more chance. Here's three more questions. Now, give me the answers to these questions, and that will prove you're a POW. Let's get on with this thing.

He'd ask me to give the names of a half-dozen people in my Group, for example. He would usually ask for information he was going to use on the next guy who came in. It was very logical, what they were trying to do, very powerful psychology. In that second batch of questions, there were usually a couple that they really didn't have any answers to; they were trying to add to their storehouse of knowledge. Scharff (Hans) was the Chief Interrogator there for the fighter pilots, to my knowledge. I never met him.

Scharff was waiting for some of the guys; he was waiting for the Zempke's and the Gabreski's. Because they (Germans) have all the newspapers. They told me where I graduated from flying school, where I went to school, what my Group was, who the commanding officer was, what kind of plane I was flying. The Germans knew all of those things. They had a pretty good intelligence system going for them, and they used it very effectively on people.

The information they got wasn't helping them from the standpoint of getting any big army secrets, but it did help them on working on the other guys. Every once in a while, they'd get some little bits of information that was pretty helpful. Like radio frequencies, what kind of planes we were flying, what kinds of bombs were being carried, what altitudes the planes were flying when they came across the coast.

The Allies kept changing altitude, for example, all the time. But any bit of information the Germans could get that they thought might be helpful to them, they were trying to get. What kind of radio were we using now? What frequencies? What kind of homing devices did the planes carry? Was there any new kind of equipment on the plane?

I never knew what the Germans knew and what they didn't know, but I was smart enough to realize that in all those questions they asked me, that there were a couple they didn't know the answer to. Especially, they didn't know who the guys were back at the base. If I'd say well, there's Jack Williams and Howard Brown and old Loren Schwisaw—they're all pilots, etc., etc. and they're in such-and-such a Group. Well hell, when those got shot down, the Germans would have a lot of information.

They'd say to the guy, "Well, Loren, I've been waiting for you. Let's see, you're in the 569th are you? The 390th? Ah, your friend, Shafer, just came through here and just told us everything about you." The interrogator would just go on and on and on, just really dazzle these guys.

I don't know. Maybe they changed their approach on people a little bit.

I remember some of the guys telling me that when they went through interrogation that the German interrogator would say, "Look, Major so-and-so, Major Rogers just came through here two weeks ago. You remember him. He's in your Group. He just came through here and gave us all this information. He isn't here anymore; he's up in prison camp. He got out of here; he's smart enough to know what the situation is. You ought to wise up. You're going to go up there and meet more friends than you've seen since you graduated from flying school." And he was right. There were about 9,000 people up there at Stalag I. There were people we hadn't seen since graduation.

At any rate, the Germans used a very smart psychological approach on some pretty young, scared, green kids.

The longer I was a prisoner, the better my defenses to the psychological approaches became. It doesn't take very long for you to size up the situation and develop your own strategy and your own policy and the approach you are going to take. It happened to me, and I think it happened to all the other guys.

The Germans really did break some guys who went through that center; their self-confidence was destroyed. I think those guys suffered from it all of their lives.

I know a couple, in particular, that I think it happened to. I don't think anyone would admit that it happened to him.

In my own case, I've always felt that the experience was really the greatest learning experience I've ever had in my life. It taught me a lot about myself; it taught me a lot about life in general. It probably gave me more self-confidence than I really deserved—I'm talking of the entire POW experience, now, the whole experience of being in the service, of being in the war, of being a POW. It really gave me a lot of self—confidence, if it really made me more self-confident than I deserved, I don't know. But it's a hell of a lot better than having your self—confidence destroyed. I think it helped me know who I am and it helped me in my career, in my life.

We were very lucky—for three reasons. One, we weren't killed we had survived. Many of our crewmen did not survive, but we survived. Secondly, I think we were lucky that we were shot down over Germany. If we had been shot down over Vietnam or China or some Far Eastern country, I think our fate would have been a lot different. Third, we weren't prisoners long enough to really have great physical or psychological damage done to us.

The guys I was with, roomed with, were all shot down in July, August, and September of 1944, which meant we were prisoners for nine or ten months, not like nine or ten years.

While we didn't have enough food and it was cold and miserable, you can put up with that for quite a long time, before it starts to really do you damage. Now I'm not saying a lot of POWs didn't have a lot of damage both psychologically and physically, but in our case, in the case of myself and my roommates, we weren't there long enough to really be hurt too bad in those regards. So I consider myself very lucky. I think they (my roommates) are too, and that's the way they look at it.

The flak that had hit my arm came in, hit the bone and splintered it, was still lodged in my arm. There was a big lump on top of my arm.

Finally, I got them to take me to the First Aid station. A German sergeant froze a spot about as big as a quarter on my arm and took a knife and a pair of tweezers and took the flak out. He gave me the piece of flak; I still have it. He wrapped my arm in white crepe paper. That was the only thing I had on my arm for another couple of weeks, until I got to the prison camp.

Stalag Luft I

It took four days and four nights on a train to get to the prison camp, very crowded, lousy conditions. We were in a car that had compartments; the compartments usually held six. In our case, ten people were in there, and they were all injured. When we were all in the compartment, two had to be up in the baggage racks, some on the seats, and a couple on the floor.

We were allowed to come out of the compartment to go to the toilet and also, there was big milk can of water out in the aisle and a dipper, and we'd be given a drink. The Germans gave us big, long salami and some bread and some other German food. Most of the guys were so sick and ill that food was really not important to them.

I remember that salami was still there at the end of the trip. It was kind of a smelly bit of meat, anyway. It wasn't really very much food, but there wasn't much demand for it either.

It took us four days and four nights to go from Wetzlar to Barth, which was just north of Berlin, on the Baltic. It took so long, because a lot of the time, we were just sitting around marshaling yards, waiting for clearance for the train, which had the lowest priority of any train in the German system, of course.

We were always concerned about being bombed. I was never in a bombing while I was on the train. I was in a bombing when I was in Frankfurt at the railroad station at night. The British came over and bombed it. The guards took us down into a crawl space under the railroad station.

The British came back and bombed Frankfurt again, but we were at Oberursel that is about five or six miles to the north. We weren't in any of the splinters or anything like that.

But the ride was miserable. In the compartments where there were no wounded, the Germans crowded two more guys in.

When I got to the prison camp, I was put in a hospital barracks, what was called a hospital barracks. It was just a place where a couple of doctors who had been captured at Dunkirk in 1940, were running a little medical First Aid place. In my case, it was a case of getting rid of the infection or losing my life. There wasn't any question of amputation or anything any more.

I laid around several days with arm in a dishpan full of some kind of disinfectant to try to get rid of the infection. My leg was just left alone, and of course my face was healing up.

Eventually, a cast was put on my arm from the shoulder down and they put me out in the compound. I was in good shape compared to a lot of guys coming in there. I certainly didn't have any quarrel with (being out of the hospital).

I wore the case for six months. The doctors kept dragging their feet about taking the case off. They had put two bandages on my arm, one where the flak went in, the other where the flak was taken out. There were the two cloth bandages and then the cast on my arm, a Plaster of Paris cast.

Things started to rot and smell bad. Finally, I just took the cast off myself after six months. The wounds were still open. Now that I think about it, I wonder why I didn't get a very bad infection. But my arm healed back after the war. The last piece of bone came out when I took the cast off. The arm started to heal back and healed back crooked, but it's been strong and there's no disability, and I'm very happy with the situation. I've never had any problem with the arm at all.

The leg healed back. I had some problems with it for a while, but I've never had any real problem.

I had to have the jaw tooth taken out. That was done after I got back home.

When I saw the camp, there weren't the dramatic affects that some felt? I had several days of transition when I ended up at the camp. I was in a hospital bed for several days; I had a chance to get used to the idea that I was in a camp. Of course, I could see the barracks. I sort of took it in stages. But I still have to say that I was happy to get to the camp, because I figured, after what I'd gone through that the camp would probably be a great improvement. And it turned out to be, that that was true.

I got better physical aid or treatment for my arm while I was in the prison camp hospital. Then, when I got out in the camp itself, I was out there with other airmen. It wasn't but a short time before I felt more comfortable being with people I knew and who spoke English and were more familiar with the culture of our country.

Each one of us POWs was given a bowl, a spoon, and a fork or knife—or maybe both. We were given a blanket and a sack with excelsior in it for a mattress. We got a bucket and a couple of pans for cooking. But each room formed what we referred to as a combine. That meant that all the food that was given to each person, that was handed out individually, would be put in a pot, in a common pile. Then someone in the room would cook for the group.

Another guy, Ed Slocum, and I were the cooks for our room for two or three or four months. The potatoes, the rutabagas, the Red Cross parcels, or whatever, would come in, and we would put it all in a common pile and cook for the group.

We didn't have enough pans, enough cooking utensils, we made pans out of cans. There was a milk company that furnished powdered milk called Klim, milk spelled backwards. That was the trade name. The Klim can was like a coffee can and was the biggest can we had. We used to fabricate a cutting tool out of a piece of metal and cut the edges off the Klim can; we'd end up with a flat piece of tin.

We made pans, bowls, and other utensils from that piece of tin. The way the pans were made was rather ingenious; they were watertight.

We took a strip of tin—if you can visualize a coffee can with the ends cut off, just a flat piece of tin. We'd fold over one side of the tin half-an-inch, take another piece of tin and fold over the edge half-an-inch—now you have two pieces of tin with the edge folded over. Now, we'd cut a strip off another can and fold both sides of that piece of tin over about half-an-inch, then take this piece and slide it over the other bent sides of the larger sheets. The two pieces of tin were now interlocked. We also, sometimes, put a little fiber in there to make it waterproof. Once this was done, we'd hammer the heck out of it, really mash it down hard. We'd take a board and a rock or something, and really mash that down. We'd come up with a watertight seal, or something close to it.

We'd repeat the process until we had a piece of tin that was flat and as big as you wanted it. On the one side, there were all these seams with these extra pieces of metal you'd used to pull the pieces together. But if you turned it over, you had a smooth piece of tin with little cracks—but it was smooth. Then we'd just bend up the ends and crimp them. We could make the pan as deep or as shallow as we wanted it.

We were very ingenious about doing a number of things.

One of the things we did, which really worked wonders, was to make a forge out of tin cans and some clay dirt. We fabricated a wooden wheel, put a little spool on it, most generally the wood came from the slats of our beds. The beds were in essence, just a shallow box. By the time the guys got through with them, there wasn't a solid bottom in them any more. The guys took the boards and used them.

Anyway, back to the forge. We'd use a shoestring for a belt, one shoestring inside another one, the wheel would turn a little propeller-like device, that would push air up through a little fire box. We could take a couple of pieces of coal, each about as big as a prune, and bring a bucket of water to a boil within a few minutes using this invention. The coal we got was pressed coal; we didn't have enough coal for heating. We usually had two meals a day, one about ten o'clock and one about five—if you can call them meals.

We only got a couple of bricks of coal a day. Each brick was a little smaller than a house brick and made of pressed coal dust, apparently. If we burned them in the little stove in the room they were just gone in no time. But we broke them up and used them in the forge. We cooked on the forge.

One time, we all got lice, which were quite common in the interrogation center. In prison camp, we tried to keep clean enough that we didn't get lice.

One of our guys was always over meeting new guys that came in the camp. We picked up a bunch of lice and brought them back to our room. We had to shave all the hair off our bodies—everywhere. Then we went to an outside barracks, somewhere near the camp that had big ovens. We threw all our clothes in these ovens and baked them; we were made to bathe in kerosene. Boy, you talk about smarting. It smarted because of the kerosene, and because we had to do it all. The guys still hold it against this guy for bringing those lice back.

There was a lot of irritability around there for some time as our hair started to grow out and sticking under the arms and everything. The guys were laughing about it at the reunion, but they weren't laughing much about it back when it happened.

The guys tried to keep fairly well shaved; they wore moustaches. They weren't supposed to wear beards; I don't remember anybody having a beard except a three or four-day growth.

Nine months is a long time to keep the lid on the little irritating things the other men did.

We were there in the winter, and it was up north. It got dark at 4:30 in the afternoon and didn't get light until 9 o'clock in the morning. The barracks was locked before it got dark; we had to go in the room. When we were in the room, there wasn't enough floor space to stand around. We had to get in bed. So the fellows were in bed early and late. A lot of people did a lot of reading. We had a library there, of sorts, because one of the compounds was British, and some of those men had been there four years. They'd been captured early in the war. The British, through the Salvation Army and the YMCA and the Red Cross, had sent in some books. So we had sort of an English reading library available. A lot of people did read.

I read an awful lot. I set up my own course on English Lit and read from Beowulf right on up to Robert Louis Stevenson and a number of the others. I read all of Charles Dickens works, including the biography on him. I tried to do a biography on each of the authors and then read some of their works.

So the guys tried to stay out of one another's hair that way, by reading.

In the daytime, the guys would get out and walk, weather permitting and if their health permitted. They'd walk for exercise. Maybe there would be two or three of them together, maybe someone by himself. They'd just walk around.

Others were engaged in little things like taking drops of solder off corned beef cans and making little wings that said POW on them, little pilot wings. We did that for a while.

Then, of course, the day-to-day chores of cooking and cleaning and what have you, took some time. Our room never reached the point where the guys were really at one another's throats. There may have been minor irritations and certain people like certain people better than they did other people, or maybe some fellow might have an irritating habit. But all-in-all, we got along fine, stayed in the same food combine—that's one of the reasons we were able to get together and have a reunion. The fellows felt pretty good about it; a lot of bonding took place.

One of the guys who didn't come back is dying of liver cancer; he couldn't come back (for the reunion). And one of the guys that didn't come had only been with us for only about three weeks; he didn't really know anybody. He came in very late and didn't have any of the feelings; he didn't know whom any of the guys were. But the others did (come).

The men wouldn't have come if they didn't have very good feelings about themselves and about the camp.

Most of the guys in my room had survived being shot down and I was the only guy who was wounded. The others may have had some difficulties—one had some frostbite on his feet, and things like that, but they weren't hospital cases. So they started out reasonably healthy to begin with.

I don't think any of them were under weight when they were shot down. If anything, they were probably overweight when they were shot down. So the guys had a little surplus to go on.

There's a residue of healthiness that takes a while to deteriorate and go away. I'd say this takes a couple of months to happen, but then it really starts to bite. When you don't have food and start to lose weight, or if you don't get the right kinds of vitamins, you can have problems with your teeth.

Our guys seemed to survive that without too much difficulty. I don't think any of our guys came out of there with any really serious physical or psychological damage, at least if they did, I don't know about it. Maybe some of that is showing up now, but I doubt it.

From what I can see, I don't think our group was any healthier or any unhealthier than any normal group in our age group of the same size whether they were in the war or whether they weren't, whether they were POWs or whether they weren't. As a matter of fact, our group may even have been a little bit above the norm.

Four or five different groups guarded us. I don't know what kind was there first, whether it was the Luftwaffe or the SS or Wehrmacht, or what. But during the time we were there, during the nine of ten months, th SS, the Wehrmacht, and the Luftwaffe, guarded the last part and us and, by what is called the Volksturm—the people's army. They were in their 60s to 75 to 80, maybe, very old with old equipment. They were the ones guarding us at the end of the war.

We used to deride them some and laugh at the situation, but all-in-all, the guys were pretty kind to them. They were just a bunch of old guys doing the job they were told to do and what they had to do. But they were like not having any guards at all. We could easily have overcome any one of them at any time, but nobody, at that time, was stupid enough to want to try to break out of that place and get killed.

If we'd gotten loose, we couldn't have gotten very far. You couldn't get very far, anyway, but everybody thought the war was going to be over in a few days.

We had a pool in our room the last of November of 1944. We all put five bucks in the pool. We put names and dates in a hat and were going to record all of those, as to when the war was going to end. We had one guy who thought it was going to be over on December 14, 1944; one on December 24; another on December 27 or something like that. A couple of guys thought it would be January, a couple in March. My guess was it was going to be over on June 6, which was just a year from the invasion. That was why I put the 6th. Another guy thought it to over in August.

Well, my guess was the closest. I can tell that this other guy and I really took a riding from the other guys at being so pessimistic. They all said, "You guys are crazy. The Germans can't hold out, they're kaput." But they did hold out, they held out for several months.

The last couple months of the war, nobody really wanted to make an all-out effort to escape. To do so was sort of foolhardy.

The Russians are coming

We really didn't hear the Soviets coming. We had a radio in the camp. It was a secret radio. It had been put together, and we got news on BBC concerning where the various fronts were located. So we knew what was happening to the East. We knew that bombings took place, that our bombers were over there.

So what happened in our case, at Stalag Luft I—we had about 9,000 people there, and on April 30, at midnight, all the German guards left.

Zemke, who was the internal camp commandant, and his staff had negotiated with the Germans to the extent that if the Germans would leave and leave the prisoners in charge of the camp and the town, airfield, and the flak school that was nearby, that we would allow them to leave before the Russians got there. And if they didn't, we were going to turn them all over to the Soviets.

Of course, The Germans were terrified of the Soviets. So at midnight on April 30, the Germans all left, after, for the previous week or two, systematically blowing up all the airplanes, the JU 88s and others over at the airfield, putting explosive devices in anything of value at the flak school. They exploded everything. It was a sort of scorched-earth kind of policy. But they left.

The next day, a Soviet soldier and a girl, both of them riding horses, came into camp. This soldier was just one of the front runners; I saw Gabreski talk to him and try to talk some sense into the guy. The soldier was drunk. Gabreski was throwing his arms around him saying, "Tovarich." Being a Pole, I guess, he could speak some Russian or at least he could speak Polish to the guy.

But the soldier wouldn't have any part of it. As I recall, and as I understand the story, the soviet soldier said, "Why are you people behind this barbed wire?"

In the meantime, Zemke and the other people who were running the camp from an internal military viewpoint, had put Americans in the guard towers. Zemke told everybody they had to stay, because the war wasn't over yet, and he didn't want anyone to get hurt.

The soldier was told that the Germans were gone and that these (guards) were Americans. He couldn't understand that. He couldn't tell whether the Germans were out there with us or not. We all had nondescript clothing on. He said, "I hereby liberate this camp." And nothing happened. He said to Zemke, "You either let these people go or I'm going to kill you."

Zemke was outside and said, "I'm one of them. I'm a prisoner. I'll prove it to you. I'll go along the fence and you'll see when they cheer for me that I'm one of them." He explained (to us) that this Russian was going to kill him if he didn't get some support.

All the prisoners were pretty ticked-off at what was happening. So when Zemke came down and asked for their support, they wouldn't give it to him. They just stood mute.

So Zemke said, "Okay, tear down the fences and the guard towers, but I'll see that any man who leaves here is court martialed.

So the fences were torn down and the guard towers, the prisoners set fire to them. They broke out all of the windows in the close-by buildings and burned a couple down. The men just went wild.

Four or five thousand of the prisoners took off. They were all over Europe. They took cars, and they took bicycles. They got on Russian tanks. They took off.

In the meantime, within a couple of days, Soviet troops came in. They ran in a bunch of cows and pigs and found some Red Cross parcels in a warehouse. They also found a bunch of shoes in a warehouse. These things were all made available to the prisoners.

I stayed at the camp. I didn't feel that I was healthy enough to get out, and even if I had been, I really didn't see the sense in it. The war wasn't over; it was complete chaos. All I wanted to do was just get out of Germany. I was so sick of the chaos. I just wanted to get out.

At any rate, I stayed in the camp.

The camp was on a little peninsula. The first day, I walked back to the end of the peninsula, where there were some cows. Guys were running them around, trying to catch them and milk them. A few were butchered, and everybody got sick from eating too much.

There were about ten or twelve cartons of brand new GI shoes in a building. I found a box marked with my size, and took my shoes off, threw them down, and put a brand new pair on. I went back about a week later, and there wasn't a new pair of shoes left. There were only old shoes lying around there with one exception. There was one crate of brand new shoes, size 13 D, I think. But many of the guys had new shoes on.

To France

We stayed there for about two weeks. Zemke and the others negotiated with the others to let us fly out. B-17s were flown in, and we were flown out aboard them to France, to Camp Lucky Strike. There were two other camps, one called Old Gold and one called Chesterfield.

The one I was in was Camp Lucky strike. It was tents out in the countryside. There must have been 15,000 people there, or something like that. We were waiting to be shipped home.

There was an airstrip nearby. Eisenhower flew in, and I happened to be in a group of three or four hundred people who were at the airstrip when he came in and got out of the airplane. I have a picture that a friend of mine gave me—somebody took a picture there. The fellow who lives in Tucson is the one who gave it to me the other day. There were two or three dozen of us when Eisenhower got out of the plane. He wanted to know how we were being treated. We said, "Fine." He asked if there was anything he could for us. We said, "Yeah, we want to go home."

Eisenhower said, "The injured go home first, you guys go home second.

We can't get you out of here any faster, because there's a limitation on boats; we're still fighting a war in the Pacific. We have a lot of injured to take home. The only way we could do it would be to double load the boats. You don't want to do that, do you?"

We said, "Yeah, we want to do that."

He said, "Do you know what that means? It means that you put twice as many people on the boat as you have beds, and you get the bed for twelve hours and then you're up on deck for twelve hours."

The guys said, "That's okay, we want to go home."

So the next day, Eisenhower started doing that. He moved people out of there.

We only had one suit, one uniform. We were given a new uniform when we got to Lucky Strike. There were also mess halls. We were on hospital rations. There were huge garbage cans full of chocolate milk. As soon as we finished breakfast, we'd take our canteen cup and get in line to get a cup of chocolate milk. As soon as you got your cup, you'd get at the end of the line again and see if you couldn't get another one. Then we'd eat lunch. There wasn't anything else to do anyway.

But the guys were hungry. They weren't being fed that much, because they didn't want them sick.

There were three tents for showers. The middle tent had showerheads in it. In the first tent you went in, there were big bins. You took off your clothes. If you had a shirt, size 15, you threw it in the bin marked 15. Your socks and shorts, you threw in the proper bin. You took your shoes and your pants and belt, and the stuff in your pants, and walked into the shower tent and took a shower. Then you went into the third tent. Clothes from previous times had been laundered, so you went to the bin and got a pair of socks, a pair of shorts and a shirt and wore them until the next shower.

A lot of people were run through there. You could take a shower whenever you wanted to, and you'd get clean clothes, but they weren't the same ones. Nobody cared. Everybody was very happy to be there.

Stalag Luft I, Barth, Germany

It's on the Baltic. There were four compounds in the camp. The compounds were built as needed. Compound I was for the British. Then Compound II, where I was located, and Compound IV had just been completed in December of '44. Gabreski was the commanding officer of Compound IV.

Each compound held just over 2,000; the camp held 9,000 men. The prison camps were administered by the German military; those people were housed outside the camp.

The compounds were separated by high, double, barbed wire fences. Machine guns were mounted in the guard towers. There was a warning wire about thirty feet inside the camp, inside the tall barbed wire. If you crossed that warning wire, you were shot, and this happened in several cases.

The guys who went over the wire could have done it on purpose, but I knew a couple of them just forgot about it. One of these went over to chase a ball, for example. The guys were playing ball and he went over there chasing it, so I heard.

The people in my compound weren't allowed to go into another compound. When new prisoners came into the camp—this camp really started to build up in '43, the military, the American and British military had an internal camp hierarchy. It was all done by rank. The British Colonel headed up the camp around September, when I got there. It was about that time that Zemke became a POW.

Zemke was now the ranking officer. He'd been a colonel for a long time. The colonel was the highest rank there. So he became the internal camp commander. Other ranking officers who came in, then, were on his staff—like an adjutant. There was a fellow by the name of John Fisher, a lawyer from New York City. I recently found him and corresponded with him. He was, of course, the Judge Advocate, or whatever the law arm of the staff is. That was what he was doing there.

Incidentally, we did set up a ground school in the camp. Fisher taught a course in law. I talked to him a couple of times about law and took a couple of courses about law. That was probably one of the main reasons I went to law school when I got out of prison camp. I was influenced by what they (law teachers) said and did.

Each compound, then, had a commanding officer, usually a Lt. Colonel. In one case it was Lt. Col. Wilson, in another case it was Lt. Col. Gabreski. Another one we had was a full Colonel, Spicer. Each barracks had a commander, usually a captain. There was an adjutant in each barracks.

We went out for roll call twice a day, and counted by the Germans. It was all done in a military fashion. Each barracks had a security officer, for example.

So you had this military hierarchy that was established within the camp. Colonel Spicer, who was the commanding officer of our compound, Compound III, made a speech at one of the counting parades we had, reminding everybody of some of the German atrocities that he and several others had seen when the Germans had fired into a group of civilians up in Belgium as he and his group were being brought in after capture. He reminded everybody that the Germans were the enemy and told them to quit fraternizing with them, to quit being so friendly and trading with them.

It had a lot of effect. The German commandant charged him with inciting a riot, and Spicer was sentenced to solitary confinement. He was in solitary confinement near the camp, what we called the cooler, the solitary confinement building. People who were being punished were put in solitary confinement for a certain number of days.

At any rate, Spicer was in there for a long time. When the Soviets came in, they went over to the camp and said, "Okay, you can leave now. You're free. The camp has been liberated." He said, "I've got one more day to make it an even six months. I think I'll just stay the night." And he did.

This photo of Lyle Shafer (circled) with most of his roommates in Barracks 9, Room 9, was taken with a "liberated" camera by a liberated POW on May 2, 1945.

Printed with permission of Basil Lyle Shafer and The Oral History Archive of The American Airpower Heritage Museum.

The Strafing Kid

Narrated by Joe Peterburs, P-51 Fighter Pilot
8th Air Force, 20th Fighter Group, 55th Fighter Squadron
Edited by Erik Dyreborg

The beginning

I enlisted in the US Army Air Corps on the 30th of November 1942, five days after my 18th birthday. I went to basic military training, college training, and then to classification where I was selected for fighter pilot training.

Pilot training was completed in the southeastern United States. I flew PT-17's in primary, BT-13's in basic, and AT-6's in advanced.

I graduated as a 2nd LT. fighter pilot on 15 April 1944—19 years old. After graduation we were given ten days leave before going on to replacement combat fighter pilot training. Prior to enlisting I had worked the summers at St. Joseph's hospital. It was at St. Joseph's I met Josephine and we became very close. However, some time before I enlisted I broke off our relationship wanting to put all my effort into my training (we were both 17 years old). Needless to say Josephine was very unhappy with me.

Anyway, while on leave I thought I would go over to St. Joseph's hospital to show off my officer uniform and wings to my old co-workers. As I walked by the cafeteria I almost fell over—there was Josephine having lunch with some of her girl friends. I went into the cafeteria filled with young swooning girls, walked up to Jo said "hi how have you been and do you want to go out with me tonight?" She hesitated a bit and then said yes. Of course all of the rest of the girls were green with envy—this handsome young 2nd LT with silver wings, resplendent in his officer's uniform asking their pal Jo to go out on a date!!!! We saw each other every day and night while I was on leave going dancing almost every night at The Roof in Milwaukee.

Pre-combat training

After leave I returned to Napier field where we got some gunnery in the T-6 and then checked out in the P-40N Tomahawk. We read the manual, got some cockpit familiarization time and were turned loose. I remember when I taxied out to the runway I was scarred crapless—that long nose setting out there, hearing and feeling the awesome power of the engine. I lined up on the runway, advanced the throttle, kept it straight with hard rudder to compensate for the tremendous torque, pulled back on the stick, airborne, raised the gear, and was soaring through the sky—what a thrill! I was 19 years old and flying a P-40, even though I had never driven a car. I got ten hours in the P-40 at Napier.

Next I went to Tallahassee, Florida for some overseas indoctrination, no flying. Here they lectured us on, and showed us movies on every type of venereal decease there was in the world and told us how to avoid them (mostly abstinence). Also some lectures on tactics used in the various theaters of operation. From here I went to P-40 combat pilot fighter training at Page Field, Ft Meyers, Florida. Here we got dogfight, strafing, and aerial gunnery dive-bombing etc. training.

One day as I was having a dogfight with another P-40 I was on his tail in a tight turn at about 20,000 feet right over a large cumulus cloud. As I pulled in tighter on my turn the plane snapped and I went into the thundercloud, uncontrolled. One thing I could really do well was recover from a spin so I pulled the stick all the way back with full left rudder, checking the needle ball and airspeed I could see I was definitely in a spin. Then I did normal spin recovery, leveled out using needle ball and airspeed. Came out of the cloud at about 5,000 feet wings level and in about a 10-degree dive.

On one of my flights I hit a large bird on take off and it lodged in the air scoop. I made an uneventful emergency landing.

We all pulled stand by pilot duty, one day when I was on duty I got a call to fly a Sgt. who had an emergency leave to Orlando, Florida. I thought nothing of it thinking I would take him in an A-24 dive-bomber that I was proficient in. When I got to OPS they said I would take him in an L-5 a light observation plane that I had never seen before. They showed me how to start it and cut me loose. With the Sgt. in the back seat I took off and headed for Orlando plowing through several thunderstorms on the way.

The airfield at Orlando was used for B-24 training and there were several in the landing pattern when I arrived, called the tower and they cleared me to land—like a good fighter pilot I landed right at the front end of the runway. The tower started yelling at me to get down the runway B-24's were coming in——I took off again flying a few feet over the runway until I reached the last third, landed, taxied off and dropped my passenger.

The return flight was uneventful.

A buddy (LT. Skroback) and I bought a motorcycle to get around on. Shortly after buying it we were driving down a busy road—Skroback driving and me setting on the back. We had a blowout of the rear tire and I flipped off. The car following us slammed on the breaks and skid to where his front wheel was a couple inches from my head. I gave my share of the bike to Skroback and never rode it again.

In October 1944 I completed training and got my orders to England leaving New York on the 4th of November 1944. In addition to my P-40 time I accumulated over 50 hours in the A-24 and five hours in the L-5. I got a ten-day leave before departure. While on leave Josephine and I saw each other every day and we became engaged.

England

I arrived in Scotland on the 9TH of November 1944 having made an uneventful crossing on the French luxury liner "Isle de France." I was 19 years old and had acquired over 280 hours in the P-40N, and I was ready to go to war.

We had about a week of orientation and then assignments. Six other pilots and myself were assigned to the 20th fighter group and put into a truck, heading for Kings Cliff. I was reassigned to the 55TH fighter squadron.

Of the 145 pilots that rotated through the squadron during the war; 53 (37%) were shot down, 19 were either POWs or evaded, while 33 (23%) were killed. When we arrived, we were told that the average combat life span was 167 combat hours, after that it's borrowed time. The tour was 300 combat hours.

On the day we arrived (18 November) we were entering the airfield, the road passed by the end of the runway. A P-51 was landing, we stopped at the end of the runway watching. The P-51 did a bad bounce. We heard him throw the throttle open and all of us in the truck who were trained in P-40s with high torque, yelled NO!!! Sure enough the P-51 rolled to the left and went in upside down killing the pilot. A gruesome welcome to the unit. We learned later that the group had just recently transitioned from P-38s to P-51s.

I arrived with no time in the P-51 and checked out in a P-51B on 2 December 1944, and flew the B, C and D 51s, through the 11TH of December. I flew my first combat mission in a P-51B on the 12TH of December. The P-51B and C that I started in had a Spitfire canopy i.e. a bubble—I later got a P-51 D and named her "Josephine." You had to have a number of missions in before you got to name your own plane.

Living conditions at Kings Cliff were pretty good for the times. Chow was good and we lived in open bay barracks. We would have a dance every couple of weeks and bus in girls from Peterburough (the closest town).

It was quite disconcerting in the open bay barracks to have some guys humping away after the dance. I remember the group commander had to put out and order that all girls had to be off base within two days after the dance.

Leisure time was spent gambling and playing cards. I became very proficient at bridge and had an RAF Flight Lieutenant as my regular partner. We did very well and won a few bucks.

Drinking would be considered a major problem these days. We did drink a lot—one of my pals almost died from alcohol poisoning after drinking a 5th of Scotch straight down. I guess he had to prove something. I can remember more than one occasion strapping into my P-51 with a big buzz on. A half hour of 100% oxygen would clear the head.

I had a gal that I would take to the dances, we would also go to plays and the opera in Peterburough. There was nothing serious between us, just companionship and definitely no sex. I went to a couple of ballroom dances in London with her and just couldn't get used to how the Brits danced. They would all dance in a circle around the floor—no helter skelter or individuality. For a 19—20 year old kid it was an experience of a lifetime.

11th Mission, January 14th 1945

We were escorting several hundred bombers to a target near Magdeburg when the formation was hit by over 200 hundred ME-109's and FW-190's. The sky was full of fighters dog fighting, B-17 wings, engines, fuselages, and parachuting crewmembers. The falling parts were almost as dangerous as the enemy fighters. I engaged a FW-190 head on. I could see his cannon fire blinking around his nose and responded with my six .50caliber machine guns blazing away. I saw some hits—he kept coming and so did I—we passed each other head on and yards apart. It was truly an exhilarating experience. That day our squadron got credit for shooting down ten and one half German fighters and damaging two others.

I think it is appropriate for me at this time to express my complete admiration and awe of the bravery exhibited by the bomber pilots and their crews. Invariably they would proceed to their targets through flak you could almost walk on and the ferocity of enemy fighters that showed no mercy. Lumbering on at 150 knots they proceeded to their targets with comrades blowing up and spinning out of control to their left and to their right—but always on to the target. In my 49 missions I never saw a bomber waiver or be deterred from its mission. These men were the bravest of the brave, and I only hope that I could have come close to such courage.

12th Mission January 15, 1945

We were to escort a photo reconnaissance aircraft (Spitfire) to Berlin and return. The weather over the target area was marginal, and I don't think he was able to get any good photos. We started back to England, and as we approached the European coast the Spitfire pilot diverged from the course I was on. I called him and asked what the problem was. He said I was on the wrong course and after considerable discussion and arguing he said he was going his way, which was a more southerly direction than mine. I remained on my course and returned to base. I debriefed, and after some checking by our intelligence officer, we found that the Spitfire pilot was missing. By the direction he was going, I believe he ran out of fuel somewhere over the water.

13th Mission January 17, 1945

The bombers' target was Altenbeken, near Paderborn (an area where I have numerous relatives). After the bombers hit their target our flight (black flight—Planchak, Lead, Smith, Keir, and me) hit the deck for targets of opportunity. Together we destroyed a locomotive and damaged a factory. I damaged a high power electric station and destroyed five railroad-switching stations. While strafing the factory, Planchak picked up some hits in his air scoop and started leaking coolant. He made it back to around Duseldorph and had to bail out, he became a POW. This was my second strafing mission. I really loved it and I got the nickname *"The Strafing Kid."*

19th Mission February 14, 1945

We were escorting 1,300 B-17s to their target at Dresden. The bombing raids caused a firestorm that swept through the city destroying it and most of the inhabitants. The escort to and from the target was uneventful except for heavy flak.

With no enemy fighters to worry about, our flight broke off escort. Maj. Gatterdam was flight lead, I was number two and Lt Jack Leon was number three (number four aborted the mission earlier). We came across a truck speeding down a side road and proceeded to attack it. We were at about 10,000 feet and Maj. Gatterdam went into a steep turn and dive. Lt. Jack Leon was in position to take over number two spot so he did. The dive was steep and Jack was tucked in behind lead. I thought he was too close for the angle of attack. I followed at normal interval and from my position I could see Maj. Gatterdam do a hard pull out, Lt. Jack Leon being so close, didn't make it and plowed into the ground, his bird exploding on impact. I gave the truck a blast of 50's and rejoined Maj. Gatterdam. We looked over the area for a while and then returned to base without further incident. We were in the air for six hours and 30 min.

Lt. Leon's death is one of those experiences that is burned into your memory and can be recalled, in vivid detail, as though it just occurred.

Close calls

On the return trip from one of my missions I landed at an airfield in France near where my brother George was stationed hoping to link up with him, but I was unable to contact him so I took off. On take off I forgot to switch from my fuselage gas tank which was empty—it had enough fuel to get me airborne and then my engine quit. I was about 15 feet off the ground and had cleared the end of the runway. I immediately switched tanks, the engine caught and I went merrily on my way—*close call!*

On return from a mission in February the weather was really bad with 0/0 visibility conditions throughout England. My flight leader said we would go down through the soup to 500 feet. If we didn't break out we would climb until we exhausted our fuel (we only had about 15 minutes flying time left) and bail out.

Fortunately we descended below 500 feet (about 200 feet) and broke out over a British field that had its "FIDO" (Fog Intensive Dispersal Operation) working. I saw the runway, so cut my throttle to idle, slowed down to about 200 knots and spiked the plane on the runway threshold and was barely able to stop from running off the end of the runway—*another close call!*

32nd Mission March 17, 1945

I lost my oxygen on the way to the target. We were deep inside enemy territory but I was allowed to return by myself. I was about 2/3 the way out of Germany when I was spotted and chased by four FW-190s. Fortunately it was a cloudy day and I went into the stratus layer and dead reckoned it for about a half hour. I broke out near the French coast and made it to home plate without further incident.

Most of the rest of my harrowing experiences are contained in my combat mission summary in another document. My longest mission was seven hours and five minutes on the 3rd of March. My longest combat hour day was on the 24th of March (nine hours and 45 minutes). That day I flew two fighter sweep missions supporting troops at the Remagen Bridge.

Joe Peterburs in his bird, *"Josephine"* is pictured above. This picture was a
note to his girlfriend, Josephine, home in the States.

49ᵗʰ and final Mission April 10, 1945

On that day, the 20ᵗʰ fighter group was escorting 430 B-17s of the 1ˢᵗ Bomber
Division that were to attack an aircraft assembly factory and an ordinance depot
in the Oranienburg area. I was in "B" group led by Capt. Riemensnider filling the
#4 position in black flight, flying wing to Capt. Dick Tracy.

While over Berlin the bombers were attacked by German ME—262s (twin
engine jets). I observed one ME-262 hit two B-17s, and I proceeded to attack it.

I had about a 5000 foot altitude advantage and with throttle wide open and .50
caliber machine guns blazing, I engaged the jet from the six o'clock position and
was getting some hits and saw smoke.

The jet headed for the deck with me in hot pursuit and Capt. Dick Tracy following close behind me. We chased the jet to an airfield near (Schonwalde) Berlin.
As we approached we could see the airfield was loaded with all types of German
aircraft.

The ME-262 entered a bank of low stratus clouds and we broke off the chase and started to strafe the airfield. Capt. Tracy was hit on his second or third pass, after destroying four enemy aircraft. He had to do a quick bail out at about 300 feet.

He landed in a river near the airfield and was later captured. I continued to attack the airfield by myself and made about five or six passes being hit by intense ground fire on the last three passes. I destroyed at least five aircraft including one FW-190, one JU-88, two ME-109s and one FW-200. I also damaged several others and inflicted heavy damage on several hangers.

Tracy and I were the only ones strafing the airfield. With my bird severely damaged, I knew I had to "bug" out of there quick. As I was deciding which direction to go, I called the group commander, Col. Montgomery; told him of Tracy and my situation and gave him directions to the airfield; said I would head for friendly lines either east or west. After considering the alternatives I decided to head west toward US lines.

The landing

When I was about 15 miles from Magdeberg, I came under rocket attack by a FW-190, fortunately, he missed. However, by this time I had lost a lot of altitude descending below 1,000 feet and was unable to keep my aircraft flying so I bailed out at about 300 feet.

I hit the tail of my aircraft with my right knee, pulled the ripcord, chute opened, I swung once and hit the ground. I got up and saw that I was in the middle of a farm field with nowhere to hide.

In the distance coming toward me I saw about ten people (civilians) and at the same time a flight of four P-51s flew over at about 200 feet, checking out the situation.

My reaction was, get the hell out of here you can't help me but you can make my situation much worse.

POW

As the civilians came closer I took out my .45 cal automatic held it over my head, removed the clip and tossed them in different directions as I did as well with my spare clips.

The civilians were hell bent on doing me in and fortunately at the same time they reached me, a Luftwaffe Sergeant stationed in the area came up on his motorcycle, took out his gun, and held the civilians off.

The sergeant agreed to let the civilians bring me into town where we entered an official looking house. I was placed in a room in the house with five or six older men.

One was the Burgermeister and another had on a Police type uniform and an artificial leather left hand. He pulled out his Luger and wanted to shoot me.

They questioned me and emptied the many pockets of my flight suit. I always carried a rosary with me and that confused them. They asked how could the murderer of women and children (their impression of us) be a catholic?

There was a crowd gathering outside and getting noisy, and it was at this time the Sergeant decided we better take off. He put me behind him on the motorcycle and took off to an airfield.

During the trip he told me that the townspeople were so angry, because a few days before a little girl about three years old had her head blown off by a strafing P-51.

At the airfield I was put in solitary confinement and questioned by the Gestapo for three days. While there, the British bombed the airfield and surrounding area, and I spent the nights in a bomb shelter with the Germans.

Stalag 11 and the forced march

My Luftwaffe guard could speak a little English and I spoke a little German. He gave me a lot of information on the airfield and the types of aircraft and testing they were doing there. His main concern was that I would vouch for him as treating me OK when the Americans came. I think that when I left I gave him a note to that effect. I was moved by rail (boxcar) from the airfield to Stalag 11. While waiting for the train to leave one of the German railroad men gave me a swig of snaps, wow!!

Stalag 11 was in the process of evacuating because of advancing allied forces. After two days I was put with about 100 British soldiers and we started our way on foot toward the east. We were on the forced march for about ten days during which there were constant attacks by allied fighters supporting advancing allied forces.

I remember our German guards were really ticked off about our rations. We were eating from Red Cross packages and they had a loaf of brown bread and water. We would spend the night at German farms sleeping in the barns and once in awhile we were able to scrounge an egg or two.

German army vehicles were almost at a stop, unable to manoeuvre because the roads were completely clogged by civilian refugees. It was complete pandemonium with thousands going east and thousands going west. German army motorcycles were scooting up and down the roads trying to establish some order but were completely helpless.

The escape and the Russians

I ended up at a POW camp at Luckenwalde (Stalag III) where most of the prisoners were Russian and Scandinavian, as well as Capt. Tracy who had been there since he was shot down.

Capt. Tracy told me he was in the river, the entire period of the attack on the airfield. Shortly after the Germans pulled him out of the river Goering himself showed up really mad, and he thought they were going to shoot him. After intense interrogation, he was shipped off to Luckenwalde.

Within about a week Tracy and I along with an Air Force Sergeant (later to find out was Frank E. Lewis) escaped, (security was practically non-existent) and joined a Russian tank unit.

After joining the Russians, we entered the town of Juterbug. It was a nice little town with some fine apartment complexes. We—about 10 Russian soldiers and me went into one of the apartments that were furnished real nice. The Russians were making a real fuss and one of them positioned himself in the center of the living room and sprayed his burp gun as he turned in a circle destroying everything in sight. I thought it weird but said nothing. I could tell at that time there was an underlying distrust of us by the Russians.

As we were moving from Juterbug to Wittenberg on the Elbe, Russian Stromovick fighters were providing close air support for the lead tanks, preceded us. We were passing hundreds of dead German soldiers along the way and had a couple of minor skirmishes ourselves.

As soon as the German civilians found out there were some Americans in the column they sought us out and begged us to stay with their daughters and sleep in their houses so the Russians wouldn't rape them and destroy their homes. We declined staying with the daughters, bit but did stay in their homes for which they were very grateful...

The Germans kept asking us "why are you fighting with the Russians; don't you know you will be fighting them next?" It was sometime during this trek that Capt Tracy, Sergeant Lewis and I got separated. I don't know how or why.

At one point during the journey we stopped at a German farm, the Russians had slaughtered a cow and some poultry and were in the process of preparing a great feast. That evening we sat at a huge table seating over 20 people and ate raw hamburger, steak, duck, potatoes, etc. with lots of wine and vodka. During and after the meal they kept toasting and filling me with alcohol, I don't think I was ever so drunk in my entire life. There were Russian dances and singing and a real roughhouse affair to put it mildly.

The next day one of the Russians officers talked me into "giving him "my wrist watch which he had been admiring for a couple of days.

One time we came across a Russian soldier on a bicycle that was broken. They asked me if I could help fix the bike (this is where the experience of my youth came in handy) the problem was fairly simple for me and I fixed it in about a half hour. After receiving hugs, kisses and thanks we were on our way to Wittenberg on the Elbe. There were a couple days of fighting at Wittenberg before the Germans caved.

Heading west and back to the USA

An American infantry squad crossed the Elbe to make contact with the Russians and I went back with them. They were stationed at Halle and were doing mop up operations. It was during this time that I picked up my sword and other souvenirs including several guns that the army guys swindled me out of playing poker. After a few days with the army I took off on my own.

After a couple hours of hiking across the German countryside I came across a C-47 in an open field picking up political prisoners (dressed in the infamous striped clothing). I talked to the pilot and bummed a ride eventually ending up in Paris where I was summarily deloused and placed under control.

I spent a day or two in Paris then a train trip to Le Havre, Camp Lucky Strike, a POW redistribution center. While there I bumped into Bill McGee who was shot down a couple months before I was. Bill and I decided to go AWOL from camp and return to our unit in England. We went to a nearby airfield and bummed a ride on a B-17 headed for England and we made it back to our unit at Kings Cliff.

Capt. Tracy had already made it back to the group and we had a great reunion. Unfortunately, Bill and I were unable to stay because of our POW status. We were able to hang around for a couple of days before heading back to Lucky Strike by way of a few days in London.

Before I was shot down I had ordered a pair of self designed custom boots from a boot maker in London. When I went by to pick them up he said he had sold them—he understood I was KIA. I was really pissed!

Anyway when we got back to Lucky Strike my contingent had already boarded ship to go back to the USA. They grabbed me, didn't even let me go back to my tent where I had a duffle bag full of souvenirs, i.e. German flying suite, Luftwaffe officer uniform, precious stones, a sketch of me made by a Russian soldier while in prison camp and other things. Fortunately I was carrying a bag with a few souvenirs to show the guys back at the 55TH squadron.

We went to the harbor by jeep, the ship had already pulled out so they put me in a speedboat and took me out to the ship. The ship was in the last convoy to leave Europe and it took seven days to get to New York arriving on the 4TH of June 1945. Bill McGee got home before I did.

From New York I went to Fort Sheridan, Illinois where I was processed and put on 60 days detached service for rest and recuperation. I got back to West Allis, Wisconsin around the 7TH of June and Jo and I made arrangements to get married on the 13TH of June 1945. Since I had not yet turned 21, I had to get the written permission from my mother to get married. Anyway we were married on the 13 of June.

My two brothers

My brother Paul was in the US Navy serving on the USS Plymouth an escort Sub Chaser. They were escorting a convoy of ships off the coast of South Carolina when his ship was torpedoed by a German submarine (U-566) on the 5th of August 1943. Only 85 of the crew of 150 survived. My brother was a motor machinist mate and I am sure was in the engine room where nobody survived. He was 20 years old.

I had another brother, George, who was in the army (a Captain) and participated in the invasion of southern France in 1944 (very little is written about this invasion). He survived WWII.

He was later in Korea with the 8th Cavalry Regiment, 1st Cavalry Division, fighting in the Unsan region of North Korea when the Chinese entered the war and overran their positions on Nov 2, 1950.

In his unit over 600 of the 800 were either killed, captured or missing. His awards included the Silver Star, Bronze Star with 1 OLC, and the Purple Heart with 2 OLC. George was ten years older than me and was 38 years old when he was KIA.

Guilt

As I indicated my first missions were flown in a P-51Cand I had flown some 35 missions in this aircraft.

During the last five or six missions it started to give me a lot of trouble. It would cough and sputter and it took some fine-tuning of the mixture control and throttle to keep it purring. I would right it up and the crew chiefs would do their best to fix it. I had figured out the optimum settings and although alert to the problem I was not overly concerned flying it.

On the 26th of March 1945 one of my best friends, Lt. Ken Pettit was assigned my aircraft for a mission (I was not flying that day). When I found out I immediately briefed Ken on the bird's peculiarities and the settings to use. I told him to be very careful with the bird.

Ken did not return from this mission. The mission after action report read: "We regret to report that Lt. Kenneth L. Pettit of the 55th Squadron, was killed while attempting a crash-landing near Ipswich on his way home. Air Sea Rescue had a fix on his position, as over the city and two minutes later he crashed a few miles north of Ipswich. He had reported that his engine was cutting out and it apparently failed altogether."

I have always felt some guilt about this and think that there should have been something I could have done to prevent this useless and untimely death. Ken was 20 years old.

A couple of days later I was assigned another aircraft and allowed to name her *"JOSEPHINE."*

Post war

54 years later, Werner Dietrich from Burg, Germany contacted me. On 10th April 1945 he was a 13-year-old boy hiding in a ditch and watching the air battles above him. He saw the FW-190 fire it's rockets and miss me, he then saw me bail out and get captured. He knew where my aircraft crashed and in 1996 (after German reunification) he enlisted the aid of a German documentary TV program to help him find and excavate my aircraft. Using the serial number from aircraft parts he began a long and exhaustive search for the pilot. After searching for 19 months he located me.

In May 1998, the TV producer contacted me wanting me to come to Germany for a reunion. My wife had a stroke and I was unwilling to leave her so the TV program producer made arrangements for Werner and their TV crew to visit me in Colorado Springs and make a follow up documentary.

Since then Werner has continued to work on the story finding the pilot of the ME-262 that I engaged. He is Oberleutnant Walter Schuck with 206 victories to his credit. He is still alive and has confirmed to Werner the events of that day. He told Werner he entered a cloudbank at about 3000 feet to escape my pursuit but the damage was already done. His engine blew and he bailed out.

In March 2002 I was surfing the web and came across a German researcher from Oraniengerg who was trying to contact any P-51 pilot that flew on the 10th April 1945 raid on Oranienberg. I contacted him (Mario Shulze) by e-mail and sent him a copy of my experiences on and after the raid.

We were exchanging information by e-mail for about six weeks when Mario asked me if I knew the name of the Sergeant that escaped with Capt. Tracy and me. I did not. Mario said he had correspondence with a Frank E. Lewis in Mobile, Alabama who was a B-17 crew member on the 10th April raid and was shot down over the Berlin—in the Oranienberg area.

Mario said that Lewis' experiences were remarkably similar to mine and he gave me Frank's address. I was able to contact Frank by phone, and indeed he is the Sergeant I mention in my account. He told me that after being captured he was brought to Tempelhoff airfield in Berlin, and it was there he met Tracy.

The two of them were transported by train to Stalag III, Luckenwalde; I arrived a few days later. Tracy and Lewis were already planning the escape when I arrived. Neither Frank nor I know how we got separated, but Lewis and Tracy made it back to England together and each returned to their respective units.

Werner Dietrich and Mario Schulze were both living in East Germany, and consequently they were unable to do any meaningful research until after the reunification of East & West Germany!

Printed with permission of Joseph Peterburs.

Two Little German Girls

Narrated byFrank Lewis, B-17 Bombardier
Written by Mario Schulze, Oranienburg, Germany.
Edited by Erik Dyreborg

"History has lessons for everyone." Thus the now 79-year-old American Frank E. Lewis began his story related to events in WW II when he was shot down during an air raid while over the city of Oranienburg.

Above, Frank E. Lewis pictured in the article of the German newspaper, the "Oranienburg Generalanzeiger."

In the morning of April 10, 1945, 1,315 bombers and 835 fighters of the US Army Air Force stationed in England and western European countries that had been liberated from German occupation took off on a mission to raid airfields of the Luftwaffe located around Berlin and eastern Germany. The main targets were the bases of the German jets, the ME-262s, and the airfield at Oranienburg was one of them!

However, there was another object in the area that ranked high on the target list of the allies, the SS Ordinance Depot, located in the clay-tile works, located near the Concentration Camp in Oranienburg, Sachsenhausen. This became the target for 294 B-17s.

Twenty-one year old Staff Sergeant Frank E. Lewis, who came from Mobile, Alabama, was seated in the nose compartment of a B-17 of the 600th Bomb Squadron, which was part of the lead wing of the 398th Bomb Group. He was the Bombardier and this was his 34th mission. Just one more mission and he'd be on his way home.

20-year old Lt. Joe Peterburs of the 20th Fighter Group escorted the B-17s in his P-51 Mustang. This was his 49th mission.

Within a few days these two men met, (under the most unpleasant conditions, in a German POW camp).

The bomb run began near the town of Wittenberge. "We were 90 seconds away from drop point" Lewis said, "when the German jet fighters attacked. I had my bomb bay doors open, and we got hits by the canons of the ME-262s".

The canon fire killed the Waist Gunner, Tichnor, severed one arm of the Ball Gunner, Boyes, and cut apart the plane at the waist.

"Our B-17 was mortally damaged," Lewis, said, "I immediately dropped the bombs and prepared to exit the plane. I opened the emergency handle on the entrance hatch and fell; head over heals, out of the bomber. All this happened at an altitude of approximately 24,000 feet. Shortly after I jumped the plane blew up. As far as I could tell, three other crew members managed to get out. The rest of the crew went down with the plane and perished upon impact."

"At an altitude of about 1,000 feet, I heard a strange noise. I thought my chute was tearing and looked up but everything was fine. Then, I noticed I was being shot at by some farmers on the ground."

"When I hit the ground, I rolled, got out of the parachute harness and ran as fast as I could, away from the farmers, who were still shooting at me. Luck was on my side, because three German soldiers were coming toward me. I surrendered to them and they protected me from the civilians. They took me to a nearby farmhouse and locked me in a room in the back of the house."

Fighter pilot Joe Peterburs observed the ME-262s attacking the bombers and he immediately started pursuing the German fighters. Together with Capt. Richard Tracy, another member of the fighter squadron, he attacked one of the ME-262s. He scored several hits on the Messerschmitt, but it managed to escape into a cloudbank. When Peterburs and Tracy went below the clouds, they spotted an airfield, where several planes were on the ground and they began ground strafing the planes and after several hits, many of the planes on the ground were burning.

After the third attack, Tracy got hit by ground fire and had to bail out. Peterburs continued attacking, and after his sixth attack, his plane had been hit several times but he managed to continue his flight to the town of Burg where he had to bail out and shortly after his landing, he was also captured.

Meanwhile, Sergeant Lewis, still in the backroom of the house, noticed two young girls standing outside the window of his room. "They were twelve to fourteen years old," Lewis, said, "They were blond, blue eyed, with lovely faces which I shall never forget. One of them acted the lookout. She kept turning her head toward the front of the house, while the other one tried to make me understand that I should open the window while she attempted to climb up to the window. I believe they were trying to give me some cookies. I was very impressed with their courage, but I signalled them that they should disappear, because I was afraid that, if caught, they would be in deep trouble for making contact with the enemy." Frank Lewis has never forgotten the incident and the "two little German girls."

That night he was taken to Berlin-Tempelhof (airport of Berlin) guarded by two soldiers. During the train ride he heard some of the women passengers addressing him with words like "Schwein", "Terror Flieger" and "Chicago Gangster."

In Tempelhof, he was handed over to the Tempelhof Airport Command, and there, to his amazement, he discovered, that the soldiers who had captured him were SS.

"I stayed in Tempelhof for a few days," Lewis said, "I Was treated quite well, and was allowed to eat with the airport personal in their mess hall. After a few days a P-51 pilot was brought in. He was shot down while ground strafing. I was very happy to meet him. His name was Capt. Richard Tracy."

Shortly we took a train to the POW camp at Luckenwalde. Later Joe Peterburs joined them. He had been held for a few days in a POW camp in Altgrabow, before he and other POWs were dispatched eastward on a forced march.

"I stayed in Luckenwalde just long enough to get lice, pneumonia and a pair of shoes." Lewis said, "After that we all sneaked away."

"In Jueterbog we met the advanced units of the Russian tanks. "Joe Peterburs said. "Together with them we fought our way until we reached Wittenberg. On the way there I got separated from the others; finally at the Elbe River I managed to join up with troops of the US Armed Forces."

Joe Peterburs never had any contact with Frank Lewis, until April 2002, when I mailed him a letter and pointed out that there were a number of similarities in his report and the report of Frank Lewis.

Peterburs was able to find Lewis' phone number. "Still, I find it hard to believe what happened." Lewis said, "When I got that call from Joe in Colorado Springs, I almost fell out of my chair." A German thus reunited two American airmen!

Mario Schulze is mentioned in the story: "The Strafing Kid"
Printed with permission of Frank Lewis.

The Swans

The story about Milton Balog, a B-24 pilot
8th Air Force, 445ᵗʰ Bomb Group, 703ʳᵈ Bomb Squadron
Narrated by John Balog
Edited by Erik Dyreborg

The Balog family immigrated to the US from Slovakia around the turn of the century.

The town where they finally settled was New Castle, Pennsylvania, 52 miles north of Pittsburgh. New Castle was a town populated by many immigrants from almost all of the Eastern European countries…Poland, Yugoslavia, Czechoslovakia, Eastern Russia, to name just a few.

The Western Pennsylvania climate and countryside may have reminded them of their former homelands, but more importantly, here there was work in the local factories and steel mills. One of these factories was the locomotive plant where my Grandfather worked as a machinist.

The hours were long, the work was dirty, and the pay modest. However, it was enough to see them through the Great Depression and provided a loving home for his family of four.

It's been about 15 years since I was in New Castle, but when I was last there, the "Slovak Club" remained open at the end of the street that my Grandparents house was on.

All this reminiscing has made me hungry for Kilbasa and holupki, which are polish sausage served with Slovak cabbage rolls stuffed with meat. My Grandma used to make them every Sunday, along with fresh baked bread and cakes!

The story that my Grandfather told me many years ago, was that my dad took flying lessons while he was in High School, because even as a little boy he wanted to fly. My father paid for the lessons by working as an usher at the local theatre, along with doing odd jobs for the neighbours.

By the time he graduated from High School in 1941, he had saved enough money to either buy a car, or pay for half of the price of the plane in the photo (Piper Cub). My father's parents knew how much he loved to fly, had seen how hard he worked, and agreed to pay the other half. Remember that my Grandfather was a machinist.

After his graduation from High School, Milton Balog worked as an Assistant Theatre Manager and continued to fly.

The war

Milton Balog entered active duty February 8, 1944. On September 10, 1944 he was sent to England where he arrived September 19, at the age of 21.

On October 7, 1944, 2nd LT. Milton Balog was on his first mission over Germany. His crew remained on the ground during this mission, unlike the 35 more to come, because today, while flying as the co-pilot with an "old" crew, he was expected to acquire the experience necessary to lead in aerial combat over Germany! His target was the motor transport industries at Kassel where, when attacked by an entire Storm Group of Luftwaffe ME-109 & FW-190 fighters only ten days earlier on September 27, 1944, the 445th had gained the dubious distinction of suffering the highest aircraft loss experienced by a group on a single mission during WWII, loosing 30 of the 35 B-24's that bombed the target.

Fortunately, today's mission went well. Forty of the group's B-24's bombed the target with excellent results and no losses. No doubt, many participants were replacement crews and aircraft that were sent to the 445th because of the earlier "Kassel" losses. Perhaps my father and his crew were one of them?

The back of my father's A-2 Flight Jacket was painted with the head of an American Indian Chief wearing a war bonnet. It's inscription read "Chief FLAK Hack". Perhaps, he chose this name because there was no choice for them, but to "hack-it-out" all the way to the target and back.

During a mission to the oil refinery at Harburg on January 17, 1945, T/Sgt Louis Cohen, did more than hack it. This was to be his 15th and final mission as my dad's radio operator and apparently he was not sitting on his FLAK Jacket that day, because he was wounded severely enough to require that he be permanently removed from flight status.

Jay Ream, my father's navigator on 24 missions, told me that midair collisions were a constant fear. Many bombers collided over Southeast England while hundreds of aircraft were trying to climb through the fog and gather into proper formations. Many other collisions occurred while taking evasive action and some just by virtue of flying tight formations through clouds.

During the early stage of one mission, while still forming the bomber stream over England, the 445th and another unknown group were at the same altitude and laterally transitioned entirely through one another. Perhaps, it was great flying, or maybe just luck, but that day no one died due to a mid-air.

However, their luck would end on December 11, 1944 while bombing the marshalling yards at Hanau, Germany. The group went into heavy clouds while maintaining formation. As they entered, two B-24's were just off the right wing, but when they emerged both had vanished. The two aircraft and their eighteen crewmembers were reported lost.

On another mission their B-24 was badly hit and Milton Balog nursed the crippled ship back to base in England and brought it in. The plane exploded soon after its nine-man crew scrambled to safety. For this Milton Balog was awarded the Distinguished Flying Cross

On March 17, 1945, Milton Balog had flown the 35 missions required to complete his tour. However, when he was told the group was to raid Berlin the following day and as Berlin was one place where he hadn't been, so he volunteered for the Berlin raid on March 18, 1945.

The Balog Crew. Photo taken in the States just prior to departure for England:

Standing L to R: 1Lt. Milton Balog-Pilot, 2Lt. George Young-Co-Pilot, and 2Lt. Milton Altman-Bombardier.

Squatting from left to right is: T/Sgt Edward Porter-Engineer, S/Sgt Joseph Gagnon-Waist Gunner, T/Sgt Louis Cohen-Radio Operator, F/O A. Marciano-Navigator, S/Sgt Donald Newmann-Waist Gunner, S/Sgt Delbert Vaught-Tail Gunner.

Having flown 36 missions, Milton Balog returned to the States where he arrived May 24, 1945. On September 9, 1945, he was relieved from active duty as a Captain at 22 years of age. Apart from the DFC, Milton Balog was awarded the European African Middle Eastern Theatre Ribbon with three Battle Stars, a Air Medal with five Oak Leaf Clusters and the World War II Victory Medal.

The swans

Flying was in Milton's blood and after the war he took a job with Capitol Airlines. He remained with the airlines after its merger with United Airlines in 1961. He flew an average of 80 hours per month.

Friday, November 23, 1962, the day after Thanksgiving, Milton Balog was the command pilot of United Flight 297, a four engine Vickers Viscount turbo prop, en route from Newark N.J., to Atlanta, GA, with a scheduled stop in Washington, D.C. at noon.

During his approach to Washington, D.C., a couple living near Ellicott City, Maryland heard a plane's engines sputtering, a sound very much like a tractor motor choking. Suddenly, there were three thunderous explosions as the plane crashed at the edge of the woods. Flames leaped higher than the treetops through a dense layer of black smoke hovering above the wreckage.

Debris and bodies were strewn over an area of 100 to 150 yards. The largest piece of wreckage was 15 feet long and the tail of the plane was found a quarter of a mile from the main wreckage. Aside from one intact engine, the wreckage looked like scrap.

A team of white-coated state troopers silently searched out, and then tagged, what remained of the thirteen passengers and four crewmembers badly burned bodies.

The discovery of the remains of a large bird at the crash site led investigators to believe that the plane collided with a Whistling Swan weighing perhaps 14 pounds. This initial speculation was later validated in the FAA report, which says:

"Aircraft was handed off to Washington Approach Control on approaching the terminal area after a normal flight from Newark. Pilot responded to vectoring instructions and suddenly went off the radar—scope.

All indications point to in-flight structural failure whereby the aircraft received major damage to the horizontal stabilizer on being struck by two large birds. The aircraft dove from 6,000 feet to approximately 400 feet then became inverted and crashed in that attitude. All occupants were killed immediately by the impact."

At the time of his death, Capt. Balog had accrued 16,230 total hours of flight time. The initial few hours of this were gathered as a teenager, while discovering freedom at the controls of his Piper-Cub. Many more, hard-earned hours were added to his total while fighting for freedom. The remainder and the majority were flown as a professional airline pilot. I am confident that to him ALL were a gift. My father died doing the thing he loved most in life.

Printed with permission of John Balog.

THEN And NOW

Poem by Keith Abbott, B-24 Pilot
15th Air Force, 459th Bomb Group, 756th Bomb Squadron

THEN we wanted to play the game,
even if our efforts would be meager.
When the second great war came,
we must have been too young and eager.

To keep our enthusiasm from waning,
we were swiftly sent overseas for combat,
after only a few months of training
in a thoroughly-planned air corps format.

Exploding shells and bullets came in double time,
we learned fast what an air war encumbers.
Every mission had a reason to sign
a death warrant for those going down in numbers.

We still can't recall why we chose to fly,
and to fight in those far-away skies.
Some of us lucky ones have yet to die.
NOW, who will hear our last goodbyes?

Afterword

By Erik Dyreborg

When the "Memphis Belle," a B-17 from the 91st Bomb Group, and her crew completed their tour of 25 missions on May 19, 1943, they were the first crew and plane to return to the States.

Fortunately, most airmen completed their tours of twenty-five, thirty, and even thirty-five missions, but some were not that lucky and were shot down on their first mission, after a few missions, and even on their last mission.

One airman experienced the following:

"Arriving back to base after our 25th mission, we buzzed the tower, waved, almost blew down the warm-up tents put up for the line crew. Our pilot was highly reprimanded for this. Extra Scotch we had saved from previous flights was brought out and we drank well.

Two days later came the blow—prior to the date we finished our 25th mission, new orders had been issued from the States. The requirement now was thirty missions to be eligible for furlough to the States.

They can't do this, we said—they did it.

All ten of us were back to pull the last five missions. They turned out to be five Berlin area missions in a row."

This airman was shot down on his 30th and last mission. He spent a year as a POW in Stalag Luft IV.

Airmen who crash-landed or bailed out over Germany or German occupied countries and who managed to evade and escape were lucky, but they also had guts. For some of them, their evasion and escape lasted only a few days, for others, it was several months.

One B-17 crew crash-landed on Sealand, Denmark on April 11, 1944. In only four days, the entire crew arrived in Malmoe, Sweden; an escape organized and carried out by the Danish underground and their Swedish helpers. Some airmen were on the run for several months, and some hid for almost a year before being liberated.

The situation for the airmen who became POWs was quite different. They were often wounded when they were captured, and in many cases not treated properly by the Germans. Bailing out of burning planes, forced to leave behind a dead or seriously injured buddy was, undoubtedly, a violent experience for them.

Airmen captured by German soldiers were far more fortunate than the ones caught by angry German civilians. Many American airmen, the so-called "Luft Gangsters" and "Terror Fliegers" did not survive their meetings with German civilians.

Eventually, the downed and captured airmen became POWs and spent the rest of the war in a POW camp. I've often thought about how many valuable young-man years were wasted in those camps—thirty or forty thousand or more.

In Germany, the POWs were very cold during the winter months. Their quarters were little more than large shacks with small stoves and inadequate fuel supplies. Lack of food was a way of life. Many of these youngsters looked like skinny old men by the time they were freed. What could they do to pass the time? They read, played cards, using handmade cards, attended classes, organized orchestras, and put on plays, when possible.

The situation for an American POW in Japan was even worse than the situation in the German Camps. Japanese guards beat one of the airmen in this book almost daily. Conditions in a Japanese POW camp or jail were stark and brutal beyond description.

Many thousands of the POWs in Germany were on the forced marches in the beginning of 1945, the so-called Death Marches. More than one thousand did not survive the marches. They died of hunger and illness and some simply because they lost the will to live.

Straggling marchers (POWs) were sometimes escorted by the German guards into the woods and executed. Often there was a shot, and the German guard would come back to the formation alone.

I've often wondered how one survives the POW experience? How did these men manage to fit back into civilian life in the States? How did they manage to live a normal life with their families? How did they manage to get a job, competing on equal footing with those who didn't have to carry the load of the POW experience? How did they deal with the feelings of having been a POW?

Some people considered the ex POWs cowards for having surrendered. When the POWs were awarded the POW Medal a couple of years after the war, many people considered this way out of line. Why award an ex POW a medal since he had just packed up and quit?

What were the airmen supposed to do when they were shot down in the middle of Nazi Germany? Were they to fight their way through a foreign country with a sidearm, even though they did not know the language, and run some 350 miles to the nearest neutral or friendly country without food? The Americans did not surrender of their own free will; they surrendered because they had no other option.

I know airmen who were awarded various medals during and after the war, including the POW Medal. The POW Medal is the one they treasure.

Unfortunately, many ex POWs were, and some still are, ashamed that they were caught and had to surrender. Many of these men will carry this heavy burden for the rest of their lives, a burden they have never been able to lay aside.

As POWs in Nazi Germany, these young men faced an uncertain future. They were in the country of their enemy. The language was strange as was the attitude of their captors. These airmen did not know when the war would come to an end, and for many of them, the situation became almost unbearable. Most of them "fought" their own daily war to stay alive to be able to return home.

The POWs came back, not just to continue their lives, but also to tell us, you and me, about their experiences, and reluctantly, about their suffering, physically and mentally.

Some people, those who have never experienced being a POW, often say, "I can imagine how it was." It is impossible for one who has not lived through this experience to have the slightest notion of the way it really was.

I have read numerous stories about the experiences of POWs, and I have talked with many of them. During these conversations and readings, I began to think about experiences I'd not previously considered. How does it feel to be so cold for months? How does it feel to be starving all the time? How does it feel to be without medication? How does it feel to march for months (the Death Marches), when you're hungry and sick?

Most of the generations following the war have no idea of what real hardship and privation are. If we're cold, we just turn up the heat. If we are hungry, we go buy something to eat. If we're sick, we stay home in bed and take medicine that is easily and quickly available.

How does it feel to be a Prisoner of War? How does it feel to be imprisoned, unable to do what you want? I really cannot know. I've always been free. I've never known anything else. I guess I take my freedom for granted.

However, I often do think about, how lucky I am, thanks to those many thousands young men, who in the face of the greatest danger found the strength to persevere and thus secure peace and freedom. I admire and respect them.

0-595-28237-7

9 780595 282371